ALSO BY KARL ROVE

Courage and Consequence

The Triumph

of

William McKinley

WHY THE ELECTION OF
1896 STILL MATTERS

—◦—

KARL ROVE

Simon & Schuster

New York   London   Toronto   Sydney   New Delhi

Simon & Schuster
1230 Avenue of the Americas
New York, NY 10020

First Simon & Schuster hardcover edition November 2015

SIMON & SCHUSTER and colophon are registered trademarks of
Simon & Schuster, Inc.

For information about special discounts for bulk purchases,
please contact Simon & Schuster Special Sales at 1-866-506-1949
or business@simonandschuster.com.

The Simon & Schuster Speakers Bureau can bring authors to
your live event. For more information or to book an event contact
the Simon & Schuster Speakers Bureau at 1-866-248-3049 or
visit our website at www.simonspeakers.com.

Interior design by Joy O'Meara

Manufactured in the United States of America

10 9 8 7 6 5 4 3 2 1

Library of Congress Cataloging-in-Publication Data

Rove, Karl, author.
    The triumph of William McKinley : why the election of 1896 still matters
/ Karl Rove.
        pages cm
    Includes index.
    1. Presidents—United States—Election—1896.   2. McKinley, William,
1843–1901.   3. Bryan, William Jennings, 1860–1925.   4. United States—
Politics and government—1893–1897.   I. Title.
    E710.R87   2015
    324.973'88—dc23   2015032290

ISBN 978-1-4767-5295-2 (hardcover)
ISBN 978-1-4767-5296-9 (pbk.)
ISBN 978-1-4767-5297-6 (e-book)
ISBN 978-1-4423-9640-1 (audiobook)
ISBN 978-1-4423-9641-8 (e-audio)

To the Modern McKinley Men:

H. Wayne Morgan
Lewis L. Gould
R. Hal Williams
Charles W. Calhoun

CONTENTS

The Triumph

of

William McKinley

———◦———

CHAPTER I

Sense of Duty

————◁◦▷————

On July 24, 1864, a twenty-one-year-old Union first lieutenant was sent on a suicide mission near Kernstown, Virginia. An officer in General George Crook's Army of the Kanawha, he was ordered to ride across an exposed battlefield swept by Rebel musket and artillery fire and tell the men of the 13th West Virginia to withdraw before they were overrun and cut to pieces by Confederates under General Jubal Early, who were close to splitting the Union left.

If the Rebels succeeded in driving Union forces out of the Shenandoah Valley, they might threaten Washington, D.C., further erode Northern support for the war, undercut Lincoln's reelection, and strengthen the South's chances of ending the conflict through a negotiated settlement with a politically divided North.

The lieutenant probably wasn't concerned about these details as he mounted his horse. He was focused on staying alive. Comrades saw him charge "through the open fields, over fences, over ditches" as cannon fire and bullets sprayed the battleground. His tent mate thought he had been hit by an exploding shell, but a "wiry little brown horse" emerged from the smoke with its rider erect and unhurt. He reached the West Virginians and ordered them to withdraw.[1]

The lieutenant, William McKinley Jr., was to become the twenty-fifth president of the United States. Upon returning from his ride, his commanding officer—Colonel Rutherford B. Hayes, himself a future president from Ohio—said, "I never expected to see you in life again."[2]

· · ·

SOME HISTORIANS WRONGLY CREDIT McKinley's winning the White House in 1896 to Marcus Alonzo "Mark" Hanna, a wealthy iron and coal magnate turned political power broker. Others are content to overlook McKinley, instead spotlighting his second vice president and successor, Theodore Roosevelt.

Yet in 1896 McKinley outmaneuvered the political bosses within his own party to win the Republican nomination and then defeated the Democrats' young, charismatic spokesman for the rising Populist movement—William Jennings Bryan—for the presidency. In the process, McKinley modernized the Republican Party by attracting to it workers, new immigrants, and the growing middle class, allowing the GOP and its policies to dominate politics for the next thirty-six years.

McKinley was the first president in more than two decades to win with a significant popular majority. He took office during a severe, prolonged depression that was quickly replaced by strong growth and prosperity on his watch. He annexed Hawaii and waged a short, successful war with Spain that freed Cuba and gave America control of the Philippines, Puerto Rico, and Guam. He instituted policies that ensured America would be recognized as a global economic and military power. Enormously popular, he was easily reelected, only to die at an assassin's hands six months into his second term.[3]

For much of the nineteenth century, the United States had been a nation divided. The period after the Civil War saw growing discord between the agrarian South and West and the industrialized North and East. There was friction between debtors worried about their mortgages and loans and the merchants, bankers, investors, and depositors who had lent them the money. There was increasing antagonism between labor and management, and profound disagreements over how the economy should be organized and its benefits distributed. All this was reflected in brutal political battles over esoteric issues like tariffs and currency that nonetheless deeply affected the lives of ordinary people.

In many ways, these clashes weren't about economics—they were about competing visions for America. Through the nineteenth century, the United States filled the frontier with settlers and established firm control over the continent. Yet these pioneers were rocked by periodic financial panics and lived on loans from merchants and bankers until their crops came in, leading some to blame Eastern financiers for fleecing them as they carved out lives far from the Eastern seaboard's money centers. Some Americans resented those who appeared to dominate the nation's political institutions, and as the century drew to a close, these critics became increasingly vocal. While an agrarian protest movement was sweeping the South, the Plains, and parts of the Midwest, labor was also organizing across the country, a result of increased industrialization.[4]

In 1896, McKinley emerged as a political leader uniquely suited for the moment. He understood and championed blue-collar voters while drawing support from captains of industry. He was from a small town in rural Ohio, but as president presided over a rapidly modernizing urban industrial power. His economic concerns appeared parochial, but he viewed them through a national lens. The last of the Civil War generation to occupy the White House, he helped unite the country after decades of division.

A SHADOW HAS BEEN cast on McKinley's reputation by a remark he made that he learned more from people than from books. Though he was well read and well educated, biographers still assumed the throwaway line justified a narrative that William McKinley was not particularly thoughtful or intellectually curious. Yet his election is widely seen as one of the most consequential in American history, leading to a dramatic political realignment.[5]

So was McKinley a fortunate man who rose through luck and the guidance of others, as popular commentary suggests? Or was he a leader, very much in control of his own destiny, content to steer quietly but deliberately, focused on reaching goals more than on claiming credit?

In fact, McKinley was a principled man with strong convictions. He was ambitious—most who attain the White House are—but for him, his ambition seems to have been chiefly driven by principles.

Understanding McKinley starts with knowing his forebears, who sprang from Scotland, moved to Ireland, and then came to America, taking up residence in Pennsylvania and, finally, Niles, Ohio, where the future president was born January 29, 1843, the seventh of nine children.[6]

The Scotch-Irish made an impact on America that far outweighs their numbers. Settling on the frontier, many Scotch-Irish families cut farms out of dense forests while suffering hunger and deprivation and repelling Indian attacks. The story of McKinley's ancestors follows this narrative. He had men on both sides of his family who fought in the American Revolution, after which his forebears moved west to Ohio, when the state was still a fertile wilderness. His grandfather and father were ironmongers, digging ore out of hillsides, chopping wood, tending fires, and smelting metal in small furnaces.[7]

Hanna—who had a more mangled yet somewhat similar lineage—once said McKinley received all the Scottish reticence of their shared heritage, while he got all the Irishman's gregariousness. There was something to the remark. Hanna enjoyed politics' jocular side, while McKinley remained personally reserved from childhood to the White House.

Reserved shouldn't imply disengaged. The wife of McKinley's principal Ohio political rival once said he was a man who wore many "masks," making it hard to read his emotions or intentions. McKinley's reserved nature wasn't just artifice. It was the deliberate approach of a disciplined man who went about his business in a systematic way. He didn't let his emotions cloud sound decision making or affect his relations with others.[8]

McKinley's parents were Methodists and held a deep faith common on the frontier. His father was especially religious, writing his then-forty-one-year-old son in 1884 upon hearing of a family medical crisis to ask, "Is your faith strong[?]" Reserved like his son, Father McKinley was a frugal hard worker with a reputation for integrity. While not well educated, the elder McKinley nonetheless read widely and was fond of reciting favorite lines from a prized volume of Shakespeare.[9]

Young William was close to both his parents—especially his mother, as his father was often away on business. Nancy Allison McKinley descended from Puritans who fled Old World religious persecution and helped William Penn found Pennsylvania. In the New World, her ancestors maintained their faith's quiet intensity. Nancy had charge of the Niles Methodist church, keeping it clean and well maintained as if it were her home. A neighbor remembered she "ran the church, all but the preaching." Mother McKinley (as she became known) tended to ailing friends and boarded traveling ministers and teachers in the family's home. She also served as the small town's peacemaker, resolving quarrels and neighborhood disputes.[10]

In Niles, where the family lived until William Jr. was nine years old, the McKinleys occupied a long, narrow wood-framed home with a general store on one side—close quarters where a mother could keep her children constantly engaged in constructive activity. All her children had chores and were expected to rise early and turn in early. As a boy and young man, William would return home from school to help his mother with her work around the house.[11]

The McKinley home was not without education or culture. The family had a Bible and, unusual for the time, a small library that included David Hume's *History of England*, Edward Gibbon's *Decline and Fall of the Roman Empire*, and Charles Dickens's early works. Family members regularly read many of the nation's leading periodicals, including *Atlantic Monthly* (reportedly favored by William) and Horace Greeley's antislavery *Weekly Tribune*.

McKinley developed a lifelong fondness for the poetry of John Greenleaf Whittier, Henry Wadsworth Longfellow, and Lord Byron, reflecting a romantic streak. The sentiments of these writers shaped his character. Whittier was a founding member of the American Anti-Slavery Society. Longfellow was an active abolitionist and used his poetry to draw attention to the cruelty of treating people as property.[12]

Because the senior McKinley was not well educated, he wanted his children to be. So the family left Niles and resettled in Poland, Ohio, which had a better school. McKinley was a serious scholar who spent considerable time on his studies. Yet while working part-time at the post office or at other odd jobs, he still found time to help organize his school's "Debating and Literary Society," where he excelled at speaking and arguing. At seventeen, he graduated from the high school and, because of his grades and maturity, was accepted as a junior at Allegheny College in Meadville, Pennsylvania. Sadly, he fell ill his first semester in 1860 and left after a few weeks.[13]

William's mother long desired for him to enter the ministry and insisted the family regularly attend church, Sunday school, tent revivals, and camp meetings. Young McKinley needed little encouragement. Enrolling in Sunday school even before starting regular school, he was always dedicated and sincere in his faith. "God is the being above all to be loved, and served," he once said. He studied the Bible with the "especial thoroughness" that would characterize his future work in law and politics.

He picked up some Greek, Latin, and Hebrew, and was "eternally asking questions" in Sunday school, going "to the bottom of the subject," as one acquaintance later recalled.[14]

At fifteen, McKinley felt strong enough in his faith to be baptized into the Niles Methodist Church at a camp meeting in 1858. For the rest of his life, through the Civil War's brutal combat, his wife's long illness, and in trying political battles that (on occasion) resulted in his defeat, McKinley's faith informed his character and his relationships with others. It gave him optimism that God's plan was working in his life and in the world. The Christian acceptance of life's tribulations in "Nearer My God to Thee" made it his favorite hymn.[15]

The *Weekly Tribune*'s presence in the McKinley home hints at another force that shaped McKinley's character—an intense opposition to slavery. Ohio was a northern state, but McKinley grew up a short distance from the Ohio River—and on the other bank was a slave state, Virginia, later home to the capital of the Confederacy. The Underground Railroad ran through northeast Ohio near where McKinley lived. Slavery's existence in a neighboring state gave people in Northern border states an intimate personal experience with the cruelty of human bondage that some came to deplore. Northerners like McKinley were incensed when the new federal Fugitive Slave Act required them to capture and return any escaped bondsmen. The senior McKinley was a staunch Free Soil man; he and his wife were passionately against slavery.[16]

As a consequence, so was young McKinley. Mother McKinley later described the family as "very strong abolitionists" and said her son "early imbibed very radical views regarding the enslavement of the colored race." He even argued with pro-slavery Democrats who worked at a local tannery. It is unlikely that the teenager won them over, but he had formed a core principle that would govern his life. Slavery was wrong and must be resisted. Every person—regardless of color—ought to be free.[17]

Slavery wasn't the only social force to shape McKinley's views and character. He came of age as the world around him began to take off. Like in other states in the emerging Midwest, Ohio's population and industries boomed, especially as the opening of canal systems gave its farms, mines, and nascent factories access to global markets in the 1820s and '30s. When made a state in 1803, Ohio had 45,000 citizens. By 1850, there were 1,980,000.[18]

These Ohioans came from Ireland, England, Germany, and elsewhere in America, all drawn by fertile land, opportunity, and the promise of prosperity. Ohio became more politically critical, with an ever-rising number of congressmen as its population grew, and a new reputation as a battleground in which presidential elections were settled. Competition between the parties was fierce in this politically divided state. From the Civil War to the century's end, the five Republicans elected president were born in Ohio.[19]

Agriculture initially drove Ohio's economy. In the 1840s, Ohio was a leading producer of wheat, corn, and, because corn grows animals, livestock and wool as well. But by the Civil War, coal and iron had also become pillars of its economy and Ohio had more miles of railroad track than any other state. This was key to the state's prosperity. With railroads and waterways, farmers and manufacturers could reach and profit from global markets, and in war, the rails could deliver men and matériel to the front quickly.[20]

Ohio continued its rapid expansion after the Confederate surrender at Appomattox and, like other Midwest states, became a center of agricultural and industrial innovation as Ohioans developed "reapers, seed drills, steel plows, cultivators, binders, and steam threshing machines" and created a slew of innovative companies that became household names while transforming commerce, among them Procter & Gamble, founded in Cincinnati when William Procter (a candlemaker) and James Gamble (a soap maker's apprentice) joined forces in 1837; National Cash Register, founded in Dayton in 1884; and Standard Oil Company (which John D. Rockefeller took to national prominence), founded in Cleveland in 1870.[21]

In short, the Ohio into which McKinley was born and to which he returned after combat reflected America's changing condition. As in many rapidly expanding economies, the influx of people and uneven growth created controversies even as they fostered prosperity and created new fortunes.

AS A VERY YOUNG man, McKinley made a life-changing decision. When Southern cannons battered Fort Sumter, Lincoln called for volunteers for three-month enlistments. Recruiters spread across the North to encourage sign-ups. In Poland, Ohio, a young lawyer named Charles E. Glidden stood on the Sparrow House tavern steps to urge the town's young men to enlist. "Our country's flag has been shot at," Glidden declared as women in the balcony above sang and prayed. "Who will be the first to defend it?" McKinley—then eighteen—attended the rally, but didn't rush to join, instead taking time to talk with his cousin William McKinley Osborne.[22]

The two young men decided they must enlist, so McKinley pled their case to his parents that night. Despite his mother's hesitance, they received permission to join the Poland men at Fort Jackson, near Columbus. When they arrived, they learned no three-month enlistments were available—the nation had already met Lincoln's quota. William, his cousin, and the other Poland men could go home, or they could enlist for three years or the duration of the war, whichever was longer. All but two Poland volunteers voted to fight through to the war's end.[23]

William—mustered in as a private—explained three days later to his sister Anna that he enlisted "to serve my country, in this her perilous hour, from a sense of duty." Since, he wrote, Americans were blessed to be citizens "of this highly favored land," it is "our duty to throw ourselves at the altar of our Common Country."[24]

McKinley's faith underpinned that sense of duty. During his early days in training, he joined a regular prayer service for the soldiers and, in the diary he kept during the war's opening months, wrote this passage as he and his comrades prepared for combat in West Virginia's rugged mountains:

> Tomorrow's sun will undoubtedly find me on a march. It may be I will never see the light of another day. Should this be my fate, I fall in a good cause and hope to fall in the arms of my blessed redeemer. This record I want to be left behind, that I not only fell as a soldier for my Country, but also as a Soldier of Jesus.[25]

These beliefs led McKinley to display courage on the battlefield on more than one occasion. Two years earlier, McKinley's regiment was east of Antietam Creek, near Sharpsburg, Maryland, on the Civil War's bloodiest single day—September 17, 1862. McKinley's comrades and other Union troops went into action at 2 a.m. After twelve hours of brutal combat, they captured a key bridge and by early afternoon were over the creek, sheltered from Confederate fire, waiting to attack Sharpsburg.

Worried that his men were hungry, McKinley—then a commissary sergeant—decided to act when the army's supply train finally arrived near the front. He confiscated a pair of wagons, organized stragglers to load them with beef, pork, crackers, beans, and coffee, and recruited a volunteer to handle one wagon while he drove the other to take the food and drink to their famished Ohio comrades.

Making their way along a wooded road, the men were twice ordered to turn around: McKinley's comrades were across an open field, a killing ground raked by Confederate fire. He talked his way past the first officer and simply ignored the second. Rebel cannons opened up when McKinley's wagon burst out of the trees and roared onto the field and toward the bridge. Comrades saw the wagon charge forward "at breakneck speed, through a terrific fire of musketry and artillery" that "threatened annihilation to everything within its range." A cannonball blew away part of his wagon, but McKinley safely reached the cheering men of the 23rd Ohio.

As he moved among the wounded, pouring coffee from a bucket, one badly injured soldier said, "God bless the lad!" McKinley later called that "the highest reward" he could have received. Soon sent home on a recruiting trip, he was awarded a second lieutenant's commission by Ohio governor David Tod. McKinley was nineteen. When comrades lobbied years later for him to receive the Medal of Honor for that day at Antietam, he blocked their effort.[26]

Throughout the war, McKinley was often in the center of action and had at least two horses shot from underneath him. His coolness under fire brought a final promotion after the Battle of Cedar Creek in the upper Shenandoah Valley.

As at Kernstown, the Confederates were attacking with the hope of driving the Federals out of the valley. But unlike at Kernstown, the commanding Union general—Philip Sheridan—was not on the scene. Returning from a conference in Washington, he spent the night in Winchester, about twelve miles away. Waking to artillery fire early on October 19, 1864, Sheridan realized his army was under a major attack. The small, scrappy, bowlegged cavalryman mounted Rienzi, his giant jet-black gelding, gathered his command staff, and galloped south.

Along the way, Sheridan ran into retreating Union troops and urged the men to turn around. Upon reaching the front, one of the first officers he saw was McKinley, deploying a battery to pour grapeshot into the advancing Rebels. McKinley brought Sheridan to Crook. The two generals soon decided on a counterattack. After probing the Southern lines and discovering a weak point, George Armstrong Custer's cavalry division delivered a smashing blow to the Confederates.[27]

For his heroism at Cedar Creek, McKinley was promoted to brevet major, giving him the rank, but not its pay. Still, he was content, preferring "Major" above any other title he was to have in life. "I earned that," he later explained. "I am not so sure of the rest." The comment was revealing—to his life's end, he remained proud of his military service, yet was remarkably modest about his exploits. This willingness to fight for his beliefs would emerge again later, when McKinley's political life was on the line.[28]

Shortly after McKinley joined the army, an old veteran gave him advice: "Do little things not exactly under your supervision. Be conscientious in all your duties, and be faithful, and it will not be long until your superior officer will consider you an indispensable assistant." It was counsel McKinley took to heart, for in 1899 as president, he gave nearly identical advice to a nephew serving in the military in the Philippines. This attitude caught Hayes's attention, McKinley's commanding officer for most of the war's first three years. In a letter home, Hayes called McKinley "one of the bravest and finest officers in the army." Much later, Hayes explained, "I came to know him like a book, and love him like a brother." Having watched his protégé's time in the military, Hayes said, "Young McKinley was a man of rare capacity for a boy of his age."[29]

Oliver Wendell Holmes Jr. once remarked, "The generation that carried on the war has been set apart by its experience." This, too, was true of McKinley. At the war's close, he was a twenty-two-year-old brevet major who had risen through the ranks from private. He had deeply held moral convictions and risked his life defending his country's existence. He was a quiet but determined man with a deep, abiding faith in God, the United States, and the capacity of hard work to change the world around him.

Like many veterans, McKinley had to decide on a peacetime career and where to settle. As he grappled with these questions, he also decided to become politically active. Like many in the generation of warriors who saved the Union, he was unwilling to trust the Democratic Party, which had opposed the conflict. McKinley had always been a Republican, but after the war, his passionate support for the GOP led him to consider running for office in a state filled with ambitious men who would dominate the nation's politics.[30]

POLITICS DURING MCKINLEY'S LIFETIME was practiced with an intensity difficult to comprehend today. After the Civil War and perhaps because of it, Americans had deep emotional attachments to their political parties, which produced astounding turnout. In the twenty years between 1876 and 1896, an average of 79 percent of voters turned out in presidential elections, compared to 54 percent over the past two modern decades. Turnout was even higher in the North; for example, reaching 88 percent in New York State in 1876.[31]

Many people passionately believed the republic's very future depended on which party won and what policies were enacted. Campaigns were national educational efforts with lectures, debates, books, posters, and pamphlets driving home the party's message, itself embodied in carefully drafted platforms that were widely circulated and discussed. Speeches— that era's equivalent to TV ads as a campaign's principal way to share its message—were particularly important, and parties covered target states with hundreds of orators.

The scope of each party's efforts was enormous. When parties "canvassed," workers ascertained the outlook of every single voter in each precinct, producing a precise tabulation of the party's anticipated vote. To sustain these vast armies of workers, parties relied on patronage, boodle, and sometimes corruption.[32]

After Ulysses S. Grant left office in 1877, the nation's political system became a mess for two decades. The Republican and Democratic parties were evenly matched, with the South solidly Democratic and most of the North and East Republican. Presidential elections were decided in a handful of perennial battlegrounds—Ohio, Indiana, New York, New Jersey, and Connecticut. No president was elected with more than 50 percent of the popular vote in the five elections after 1872. Two Republicans— Rutherford B. Hayes and Benjamin Harrison—won the White House with fewer popular votes than their Democratic opponents by carrying the Electoral College. Hayes's election involved a dispute about Florida's results that lasted for months. A third Republican—James A. Garfield—won the popular vote by just 7,368 votes.[33]

In the 1874 midterms, the GOP lost its Reconstruction-era dominance of the House of Representatives. Afterward, there was divided government for two decades, with each party controlling the White House and both houses of Congress for only two of the next twenty-two years. During this era, both parties used parliamentary maneuvers to gridlock Congress and block the resolution of major issues. Democrats in the House even refused to answer roll calls, thereby denying a quorum to consider any legislation. Antics like this caused Henry Adams to decry Washington as "more and more incompetent."[34]

The country's political system grew increasingly preoccupied with two major issues. One pitted farmers and others who carried a lot of debt, and the politicos who represented them, against those who believed in stable and sound money. The issue they fought over was currency, or more precisely, which medium to use for money—paper, gold, or silver, with the last receiving more attention as years went by. As historian Richard Hofstadter asked, "Who today can understand without a strenuous effort of imagination the passions once aroused by the cry for free silver?" Yet the currency issue increasingly dominated the national debate in the Gilded Age, especially during times of economic adversity.[35]

The second issue pitted manufacturers and those who worked in vital industries against consumers forced to pay more for life's necessities, such as sugar, cotton, wool, and cloth, as well as needed manufacturing goods. This issue—tariffs—also saw those who believed in a limited and constrained government fighting those who believed in a more activist national government.

Both issues were proxies for larger debates about how to grow the economy and ensure that every American benefited from it, and about what the proper role of government should be. McKinley's Ohio was a microcosm of the nation on these issues, with an electorate narrowly divided over them, especially currency.

Tariffs were the form of taxes by which the federal government funded itself in the nineteenth century and often the subject of passionate debates. Many people in the Gilded Age saw tariffs as a way to grow the economy by protecting American businesses against foreign competition. They believed high tariffs were necessary to produce a prosperous modern industrial economy and create innovation and competition. Their opponents believed tariffs reduced the spending power of every consumer, hitting farmers and rural communities hardest, and transferred money from the deserving poor to the greedy rich.

Because they are taxes, tariffs have been a contentious issue since 1816, when then–House Speaker Henry Clay made them a core element of his "American System," which sought to strengthen the new republic by promoting economic growth. The American System was pitched as "an act of national resistance" to overseas powers, a scheme that would make the United States economically as well as politically independent from the Old World.

Nonetheless, tariffs sparked bitter political conflicts, including the nation's first secession crisis in 1830, when South Carolina's John Calhoun asserted a state could nullify federal laws it considered unconstitutional. Calhoun had in mind the 1828 "Tariff of Abominations," which slapped steep duties on commodities desperately needed by Southerners. South Carolina responded to the tariff by threatening to block federal revenue collectors at its ports. Congress ended the emergency in 1833 by reducing tariffs to 20 percent while authorizing military force to put down nullification efforts, if necessary.[36]

During the Civil War, tariffs were raised five times to fund the Union war effort, reaching an average of 47 percent on most items. They remained high after the South's defeat, in part to pay off the war debt. Opinion about them remained divided, largely along sectional lines. Many Northern manufacturers—including those in McKinley's Ohio—favored high tariffs for protecting their industries, while Southern (and increasingly Plains and Midwestern) farmers opposed them because they didn't benefit from them, but instead paid higher prices for goods. Tariffs also provided funds to the federal government to pay pensions to Union veterans, which didn't sit well with Southerners since Rebel veterans were ineligible for federal pensions.[37]

Some people strongly believed tariffs benefited the wealthy, enriching well-to-do business owners at the little man's expense with a system so opaque, it was hard to tell who was benefiting and by how much. Decrying protection as "unfair and tyrannical," a Democratic congressman in the 1880s charged tariff schedules were "sired by a lobby of hired agents of monopoly" and written "in a secret conclave," not in the Capitol. A battle over a copper tariff led an observer to complain that Washington was so corrupt that the entire Congress should be in prison.[38]

There was also a fundamental disagreement over protection's role in promoting competition. Its opponents believed protection led to "vicious combinations" of "industrial monopoly" and was responsible for the rise of trusts, industry-wide monopolies that robbed consumers through higher-than-justified prices. Advocates of protection said it promoted more-robust domestic competition, pointing to declining prices for manufacturing goods protected by higher tariffs. In reality, neither trusts nor declining manufacturing goods' prices were caused by protection. They were more likely the result of the nation's rapid industrialization and the introduction of new technologies and production methods that dramatically increased productivity.[39]

The parties could not resolve this issue because there were profound differences in their ideologies. Republicans favored an activist national government that ensured the rights of freed slaves, enabled white and black Republicans in the South to vote, made permanent the political and social gains made in the Civil War, and promoted American industrial expansion. Tariffs provided revenues that made a more energetic government possible, especially when they produced government surpluses, as they frequently did in the postwar period.

On the other hand, Democrats favored states' rights, limited government, and tax cuts. Their leaders like President Grover Cleveland assailed protective tariffs as a "vicious, inequitable, and illogical source of unnecessary taxation." While the party was solidifying white rule in the South by systematically extinguishing black voting rights there, it recognized its weakness in the North. So the Democrats tried restoring their national dominance by standing up for the little man at a time of rapid industrialization.[40]

The battle over tariffs reflected a much larger, anxious debate over how wealth would be distributed in an America still inventing its economy, who deserved protection in this tumultuous new world, and how the federal government should be financed. This contentious issue also added to tensions lingering from the Civil War. Depending on who was talking, tariffs either led to prosperity, good jobs, and high wages, or they eroded prosperity by robbing from the poor and giving to rich manufacturers. It was an issue that McKinley would have to master and make his own if he was to succeed in the politics of a rapidly industrializing, yet farm-rich state.

The other issue dominating post–Civil War politics was the volatile question of currency, specifically the demands of an increasing number of Americans for an expansion of the money supply by minting an unlimited amount of silver coins that would be accepted for debts on the same basis as gold. This issue was similarly fraught with risk for politicians from closely divided battlegrounds like Ohio.

Farmers were especially interested in the money issue, because so many were debtors caught in a vicious system. In the South, many farmers were forced into the crop lien scheme where local "furnishing merchants" supplied them with necessities in return for title to their crops. At "settlin' time," the farmers' debts routinely exceeded the value of their harvest, adding to their outstanding loan balance.[41]

In the Midwest, farmers were squeezed by declining grain prices offered by buyers and mills and exorbitant freight and grain warehouse rates. Those who owned their own land tended to do better, but half of Midwestern farmers in the Gilded Age had mortgages or were tenant farmers and had to get credit each spring from the furnishing merchants or a local or private bank. Mortgages came from far-distant Eastern insurance or mortgage companies that charged high interest rates. While farmers were hammered by declining commodity prices, their creditors benefited from an appreciating currency as tariff duties paid in foreign gold bolstered the U.S. dollar.[42]

The currency debate revolved around explosive questions of what constituted money, how much of it there should be, and who should control its creation. Over the Gilded Age, the country divided between advocates of "sound" or "hard" money based on the gold standard, and those who favored "soft" money through currency inflation.

Initially, many who favored inflating the currency supported paper money, even though America's paper money experiment with "Continentals" during the Revolutionary War failed. Continentals had depreciated rapidly, causing massive inflation and undermining the revolutionary cause's credit. The sentiment "Not worth a Continental" led the new nation to rely on gold and silver coins and banknotes redeemable in specie. After 1836, silver appreciated beyond its statutory ratio with gold and fell out of use as debtors paid in the more abundant and therefore proportionally cheaper gold. Mints stopped coining silver dollars except for trade with countries that had silver currencies, such as China, and America operated on a de facto gold standard.[43]

That changed when the Civil War caused people to hoard any available coins, gold or silver. The nation left the gold standard in December 1861 when the Treasury followed banks in preserving its dwindling gold supplies by refusing to redeem notes in the yellow metal. In February 1862, Congress authorized the use of unsecured paper money, quickly dubbed greenbacks, as legal tender. Additional paper money was authorized in June 1862 and January 1863. The scarcity of metal coins also caused the issuance of fractional paper notes for pocket change. By war's end, $372 million in greenbacks and $18 million in fractional notes were circulating, more than 30 percent of the nation's money supply.[44]

While paper money allowed Lincoln to finance the war effort, greenbacks—like Continentals—depreciated in value, raising costs for goods and services. People held on to the gold and silver coins that they still possessed and resorted to bartering and even using postage stamps encased in small metal frames to pay for purchases. Fiat paper money bred inflation, and by the end of the war, the cost of living had nearly doubled for ordinary people.[45]

The national debt, which stood at $2,808,549,437.55 at war's end, also complicated matters. Roughly $1.6 billion of that debt came in the form of "5-20" gold bonds, which required 6 percent interest paid in gold in five years and the balance paid off in twenty years. Servicing and retiring that debt threatened to significantly decrease the government's gold supply, which led to raucous and bitter political fights.[46]

Two camps emerged. One was composed of Americans—especially farmers in the South and Midwest, mostly debtors—who felt they were being crushed by low prices for what they raised and who wanted more money in circulation, believing that would enable them to earn more for their products and to afford life's necessities. They believed the amount of money in circulation was inadequate and that the federal government must expand the quantity of currency to keep the economy growing.[47]

While united in backing inflation as a concept, there was disagreement on how much was necessary or how the federal government should inflate the currency. Some wanted to issue more greenbacks; others supported maintaining the Civil War level of paper money. Still others favored allowing local banks to issue notes or redeeming only some of the fiat currency. Over the postwar period, many inflationists came to believe the answer was to let all the growing riches of silver being ripped from mines in Nevada, Colorado, Montana, Idaho, and elsewhere be coined into money.

Opposing them were those who favored stopping inflation and strengthening the government's credit with a currency based on gold. These hard-money advocates argued government must retire fiat paper currency and return to gold and paper redeemable in gold. They argued if America retained its wartime unsecured paper currency, it would not attract foreign investment, manufacturers and farmers would be unable to compete with foreign producers, and inflation would erode consumer purchasing power. The greenbacks must be retired quickly to wring inflation out of the system. In other words, shrink the money supply.

Inflationists were dealt a setback in April 1866 when the Republican Congress passed the Contraction Act, permitting the Treasury to withdraw $10 million in greenbacks over six months, then $4 million a month at its discretion. A recession turned public opinion against the contraction of the money supply and led to the act's repeal in February 1868, but only after $44 million of greenbacks had been withdrawn.

For the next several years, hard- and soft-money men kept debating how and how fast to repay the war debt, when Washington could resume redeeming greenbacks in gold, and whether to contract or expand the money supply. Each faction grew more determined to fight it out in Congress and at ballot boxes across America.

At the beginning of his political career, McKinley cut his political teeth on the currency issue and tariffs. He straddled on currency. He believed in sound money, but like many Midwest Republicans, hoped the country could reach a balance allowing for mild inflation that relieved the problem for farmers and debtors of too little money without creating one of too much.

He did not hedge on high tariffs. He favored protection as the way to create good jobs and high wages. For McKinley, the protective tariff was partly an economic issue of how America could cope in an increasingly global world. It was also an issue of nationalism, of protecting American workers and companies from unfair foreign competition. And it was a moral issue: how best to promote general prosperity and reap the benefits of a society where work was valued and safeguarded.

Through the decades that followed the Civil War, McKinley understood economic issues were part of a broader fight over what kind of country the United States would be. The animating principle of McKinley's political career was a concern for creating conditions that would allow ordinary people to rise. His combat experiences provided him with an intimate connection to Americans from all walks of life, and he never insulated himself from them. He understood the larger moral dimensions of these issues and how to explain them in ways people could grasp. This ability would help make him an important actor in the nation's story as the United States moved toward the twentieth century's dawn.

But in April 1865, he was an army major hoping the war was drawing to a close.

CHAPTER 2

Early Beginnings

————◁◦▷————

O n April 9, 1865, when news of Lee's surrender reached Winchester, where McKinley and his comrades were bivouacked, two hundred cannons boomed. Recently named divisional chief of staff, Major McKinley ordered the town's lamps and lanterns lit that night to celebrate the war's end and the Union's salvation.[1]

His regiment was quickly demobilized, leaving McKinley's future uncertain. He considered making the army a career but declined a commission after his father argued that prospects for advancement in the peacetime military would be poor. He was soon home in Poland, a small town eight miles south of Youngstown, wrestling with what to do with his life.[2]

McKinley decided on the law. It was a respectable profession, though Hayes wrote from Washington where he had taken his seat in Congress (to which he had been elected while still in combat) to say it was a bad idea. "A man in any of our western towns with half your wit ought to be independent at forty in business. As a lawyer, a man sacrifices independence to ambition which is a bad bargain at best." McKinley was not swayed. Hayes was a lawyer himself and McKinley had not spent four years away from Ohio to now move farther west.[3]

The twenty-two-year-old McKinley would train for the law as Lincoln had—by finding an attorney who would let him read law books in his office until he mastered the subject matter and could pass the bar. He was soon offered such an apprenticeship.

Charles E. Glidden had stood on Poland's tavern steps in 1861 to urge the town's young men—McKinley among them—to enlist. Now thirty, he had been elected judge in Mahoning County and was in a position to help McKinley. By fall 1865, the Major occupied a desk at Glidden & Wilson, his head buried in law books until late at night. In school, McKinley had a reputation for "studying, studying, studying." That habit resurfaced, but he still found time to serve as president of the Everett Literary Society, a young men's self-improvement group that hosted debates and speech competitions. McKinley often won. He was a convincing speaker with a pleasant manner that engendered trust among listeners.[4]

In September 1866, encouraged by his sister Anna, McKinley entered New York's Albany Law School. His roommate recalled he "worked very hard, often reading until one or two in the morning." He ate ice cream for the first time at a reception after the dean's pretty daughter explained the concept. The Major left Albany in early 1867 after one term and that March was admitted to the Ohio bar. Again prodded by Anna, he moved to Canton, Ohio, where she was a school principal. The town had 5,000 people, was near coal mines and water, sat on three rail lines, and had a promising future as a manufacturing center. It was just the kind of rising place for a twenty-four-year-old lawyer to begin postwar life.[5]

At first there wasn't much legal work for the newcomer, but McKinley's diligence caught the attention of George W. Belden. One evening, the older lawyer came into McKinley's small quarters, complaining he was ill and unable to handle a case on the next day's docket. Would the Major step in? Unsettled by having so little time to prepare, McKinley agreed only when Belden said the case would not get heard if McKinley didn't take it. The Major spent all night prepping for his first appearance. As he opened his argument, saying, "What we contend for in this lawsuit," McKinley glanced toward the rear of the courtroom. There sat Belden with "a slight smile." The Major's well-organized presentation was persuasive and a few days later, Belden dropped by with a $25 fee. McKinley protested it was too much for a day's work, until Belden replied he had received $100. Not only did McKinley win the case and earn a handsome sum, but he demonstrated his ability to prepare and a talent for presentation. Belden invited him to become his partner. McKinley accepted.[6]

An ardent Democrat, Belden was an unusual mentor for McKinley, whose strong Republican views were already known. As U.S. Attorney for

Northeastern Ohio in 1859, Belden prosecuted the "Rescuers." These were townspeople, professors, and college students from Oberlin, Ohio, who helped a fugitive slave flee to Canada. But unlike many Ohio Democrats who opposed the war, Belden was dedicated to a Northern victory. It is unlikely that if he had been a Peace Democrat, he would have been attracted to young McKinley or the Major to him.[7]

Naturally tolerant and easygoing, McKinley joined more than a law firm. He regularly attended the First Methodist Church, teaching in the Sunday school and then becoming its superintendent. McKinley had become a Mason when he and other Northern officers reopened the Winchester Lodge after observing a Union doctor share his cash with Confederate POWs because they were fellow Masons. The Major now joined the Canton Lodge and would remain active in Masonry the rest of his life.[8]

He became involved in the Knights of Pythias, a fraternity devoted to world peace. He joined the YMCA literary society, which hosted debates. He offered a particularly effective defense of women's suffrage in one of them. He soon became the Y's president. Like many comrades, he joined the nation's largest veterans' group, the Grand Army of the Republic (GAR), and the Loyal Legion, a group for Union officers. He regularly attended reunions of the 23rd Ohio.[9]

McKinley joined these groups because it was a common practice of the times and a way for him to improve his community. It also allowed the Major to develop a wide and eclectic circle of friends, even including Democrats and many Irish and German Catholics. This networking could help him land legal work and be an asset if he decided to run for office.[10]

IT WAS NOT ALL community service and law for the handsome young twenty-five-year-old. McKinley also took part in Canton's social scene and in the summer of 1868 found himself at Meyers Lake, west of Canton. The town's young people frequently gathered there at a lakeside inn.

Sitting outside with his sister Anna on a bright day, McKinley was taken with a slim young woman who was sitting at a picnic table. She had chestnut hair piled high and twisted in the Victorian fashion, large blue eyes, and a confident, athletic manner. Rather than daintily picking at her food as women of the time were expected to do, Ida Saxton was tucking into her creamed chicken and waffle with gusto. McKinley later said he fell in love right then. Anna knew Ida and introduced the Major to her. Later, Ida could recall only his title, not his name.[11]

Nothing could come of their meeting. She was involved with another major, Joseph W. Wright, recently of the Confederate army. A Marylander without slaves, he had fought for the South as a matter of principle. After the war, he worked on an Arkansas newspaper before earning a law degree and moving to Canton, where he was a salesman for a farm implement manufacturer. Wright's moonlighting as a lawyer brought him into contact with James A. Saxton, Ida's father.[12]

The Saxtons were one of Canton's oldest, most prominent families. This close-knit clan's patriarch, John Saxton, Ida's Scotch-Irish grandfather, arrived in Canton in 1814, shortly after the town's founding. He wanted to be a publisher. After determining Canton could support a newspaper, he procured a press from his native Pennsylvania and printed the *Repository*'s first issue on March 30, 1815. When the enterprise proved profitable, Saxton married his childhood sweetheart, Margaret Laird, daughter of Scottish immigrants, and brought her to the thriving village, where they raised six sons and a daughter in a brick home on South Market Street.[13]

Their oldest was James A. Saxton. He and his siblings were raised in comfortable prosperity. John's success as a publisher enabled him to build offices and a printing plant, and he and his brothers—James's uncles—created a string of moneymaking businesses, starting with a nail factory. Their commercial spirit was passed on. James opened a hardware store in 1834 at age eighteen and followed with a dry goods business before marrying into another entrepreneurial family, the Dewalts. They were part of the original German Dunkers, an Anabaptist sect who had settled Canton. Since 1809 they had owned the town's Spread Eagle Tavern and brewed beer. George and Christiana Dewalt were contemporaries of John and Margaret Saxton. Their daughter Kate married James Saxton on August 20, 1846, in Canton's First Presbyterian Church. The couple then moved into her parents' family home at Eighth and South Market. Kate was pregnant within two months and on June 8, 1847, gave birth to a daughter, named Ida.[14]

The bright, happy girl spent her first three years in her grandparents' home, growing so close to both her mother and her grandmother Christiana that it was difficult when she and her parents moved out of the Dewalt house into their own home next door. A few years later, James Saxton sold his hardware and dry goods businesses and started the Stark County Bank.[15]

Ida also idolized her grandfather, John Saxton. He was an ardent abolitionist, committed Republican, and, even more unusual for the time, a staunch believer in women's education, beliefs shared by his son James. A committed Christian and an elder of First Presbyterian, John helped found Canton's public schools, served in local government, and tended to the city's poor, unemployed, and sick. His readiness to offer food, money, or a kind word was a powerful example for his children and grandchildren, especially Ida.[16]

She entered the Canton Union School in September 1853. For the next eight years, Ida studied English, math, science, drawing, and vocal music, the last complemented by piano lessons at home. The school's principal was Betsy Cowles, a gifted educator and, like James Saxton, an abolitionist and women's education advocate. The two organized the Canton Anti-Slavery Society before Cowles left town in 1857.[17]

Ida finished middle school in spring 1861, but because of the war, took a gap year to help the Union effort, making bandages while her mother served as the Soldiers Relief treasurer. In the fall of 1862, Ida entered the Delhi Academy, in Delaware County, New York, 160 miles northwest of Manhattan. The academy's principal was a familiar face, the formidable Miss Cowles. While Ida was pleased to be reunited with her mentor, both women found the area too Democratic and hostile to Republicans and abolitionists. Miss Cowles left after the 1863 spring term; Ida returned home, too, and enrolled at Cleveland Female Seminary. She graduated in June 1865 after finishing the school's rigorous curriculum of advanced math, geography, grammar, history, and penmanship, as well as electives including French literature, music, singing, drawing, painting, sculpture, and piano. Ida excelled in languages, picking up French, Italian, and Greek.[18]

Ida's father, a practical man, wanted Ida to receive the best possible education. So Ida went off that fall to Brooke Hall Female Seminary in Media, Pennsylvania, a forerunner of a modern women's college. Brooke emphasized not only academics but also physical fitness. Ida became an enthusiastic walker, leading hikes through nearby woods and hills. The girls also played cards and games weeknights, went to Friday night dances, regularly attended church, and visited nearby Philadelphia for weekend shopping, concerts, opera, and plays. Amid the daughters of some of the

East Coast's great families, Ida flourished, growing into a pert, smart, opinionated, and confident young woman who made friends easily and seemed to be particularly empathetic. Ida graduated in June 1867 and returned to Canton.[19]

Unlike most other affluent young women then, Ida went to work. For two years, she played an increasingly vital role in her father's bank, calculating interest payments and dividends and handling loan applications, mortgages, and complicated financial matters. Her father enjoyed her company, trusted her judgment, and respected her abilities, but he also wanted her to be independent. "I have seen enough girls left stranded by sudden losses of means," he said. For her part, Ida later said she "never ceased to be grateful" for the opportunity to become a "practical woman of experience."[20]

Her life was not all banking and business, though. The attractive twenty-year-old was a bright presence at parties, church socials, and concerts. "Every man in town promised to be a brother to me," she later said. "And oh! I did have such a good time." While James Saxton had taught his daughters that the decisions of if, whom, and when to marry were theirs, he could not help being worried about unworthy suitors. It's not clear what he thought of Wright, but he did make it clear he had had enough of young lawyers swarming around Ida.[21]

Still, sometime in 1868, Ida and Major Wright became an item. She arrived at the Schaefer's Opera House Halloween ball on his arm, costumed as the "Queen of Hearts." Friends considered this as tantamount to an engagement.[22]

Knowing marriage would profoundly change her life, Ida decided to have one last great adventure as a single woman. She and her sister Mary—nicknamed Pina—would take a six-month grand tour of Europe, beginning in June 1869. They would visit England, Scotland, and Ireland, then jump across the English Channel to the Continent before returning to the States. Wright moved temporarily to Louisville for his employer. The two sweethearts pledged to write each other frequently, with Ida promising to buy him a special gift on her travels.[23]

James Saxton engaged Miss Jeanette Alexander to serve as guide and chaperone for his daughters. Alexander found Ida headstrong, confident, and impossible to manage. In turn, Ida didn't trust Alexander. They clashed over Alexander's plan to bring her brother along to manage the group's money. Ida thought it an attempt to rip off her generous father and felt herself fully capable of keeping meticulous track of her own two-thousand-dollar budget.[24]

The trip was more than galleries and museums, cathedrals and monuments, natural wonders and mountains. It was also a liberating experience for the sisters. Ida pierced her ears, drank wine for the first time, walked ten to twenty miles a day, hiked the Alps, and, scandalously in Miss Alexander's eyes, allowed gentlemen friends to take Pina and her to the theater in Paris. In London, she was introduced to Rutherford B. Hayes's brother-in-law. Ida was not impressed with the unattached young doctor, who mentioned an old army comrade now living in Canton, Major McKinley.[25]

Ida and Wright corresponded frequently, their letters warm and hopeful. She would find his missives waiting at the banks from which her father had arranged for her to draw cash. In August, Wright explained he was in Canton recuperating after becoming ill on a business trip. Ida wrote her mother, saying, "Mr. Wright is not so sick I think, but I want you to show him very marked attention and do all you can to make his stay in Canton pleasant."[26]

The sisters and their chaperone arrived in Geneva on Saturday, September 25. Mary went to dinner but Ida went to the bank to get Swiss francs and pick up the latest letters from home. Mary returned to the hotel to find Ida weeping on its terrace. Joseph Wright had died of meningitis on September 2. The next morning, Mary told her parents that the news "was a fearful shock." Ida was understandably deeply depressed, writing, "I know I should not feel so, but I cannot help it."[27]

A few days later, she pressed her parents for details, asking, "How long he was sick? If he suffered? Who took care of him?" "Mr. Wright spoke in his last letter he would be either in Canton or New York to meet me," she wrote. "Only think that now he is dead, and buried. I cannot realize it." Her life had changed irrevocably with the death of the man she expected to marry. "Things will be very different from what I expected when I get home."[28]

Though Ida considered remaining in Paris to study French, the sisters were back in Canton before Christmas. Ida had presents for each child in her Sunday school class and "one ambition" for the New Year, namely to "master the intricacies of finance." She would bury her grief in work. In a way, that was welcome news to her father, who was content to pass more of the bank's operations on to his eldest daughter. Her extensive schooling, intelligence, and judgment gave him confidence she could handle its complex affairs. Ida thought her work in the bank "the most valuable course in her whole education."[29]

THE WORK ALSO BROUGHT her back into contact with Major McKinley. After James Saxton brushed off suggestions from mutual friends that he consider the young lawyer for the bank's legal business, Saxton was added in November 1869 as a defendant to a case on which McKinley was already a member of the defense team. To the surprise of some defendants, McKinley won the case. When the Major personally delivered a substantial check for the banker's share of the award, Saxton was impressed.[30]

Whatever Ida thought of McKinley's legal skills, she was more impressed when, as YMCA president, he introduced famed New York newspaperman Horace Greeley at an appearance. The Major was eloquent and captivating. Soon he was a regular guest at the parties in the third-floor ballroom of the Dewalt home, which, though Christiana Dewalt still lived there, was now full of Saxtons and was more often referred to as the Saxton house. Another frequent guest later remembered how the Major's "affable manner soon gained him admission to the upper crust of Canton society." McKinley "was the most handsome, dignified and graceful human being."[31]

The now-twenty-six-year-old McKinley had gained new stature in 1869 while Ida was abroad when he was elected Stark County prosecutor. It was an electoral upset. Stark County was Democratic and the GOP nomination for local offices was considered of little value. But McKinley's web of relationships and winning manner did the trick for him. The post was not a difficult responsibility and he could handle unrelated legal business on the side. The only significant public issue McKinley took on during his two-year term was illicit liquor sales, especially in the town of Alliance, among the young men attending Mount Union College. McKinley used the confession of a sixteen-year-old student from Pittsburgh named Philander C. Knox to convict some saloon owners, an action that linked McKinley with the temperance movement and won his mother's approval.[32]

His family was also gathering in Canton. First, some siblings relocated there, then his parents, though the senior McKinley was often in Michigan, where he had invested in a pig iron furnace.[33]

The courtship between Ida and McKinley lasted a year. There were long walks. He became a regular caller, sometimes twice in an evening, once for conversation, a second time to say good night. She often visited McKinley's law offices above the First National Bank, the rival to her father's First Canton. They even paid a local boy to carry letters to each other. At a church social where Ida was scooping ice cream, he tried taking away a tray of bowls but succeeded only in dumping the desserts on her. He was horrified, but she laughed.[34]

It was soon clear that Ida was in love again, but Wright's sudden death left a scar. Once when McKinley was late for a party, Ida became anxious, asking, "Have you seen the Major? Do you imagine the Major is sick? Has the Major been called to the city?"[35]

Among their rituals was meeting on a corner near First Presbyterian, where Ida taught Sunday school, and First Methodist, where he was Sunday school superintendent. One Sunday, McKinley told her, "I do not like this separation every Sunday, you going one way and I another. Suppose after this we always go the same way." Ida replied, "I think so too." Soon after on a carriage ride behind a team of bays and at the top of a hill outside town, McKinley proposed. Ida immediately accepted. "My fate was sealed," McKinley fondly recalled, and James Saxton told his soon-to-be son-in-law, "You are the only man I have ever known to whom I would entrust my daughter." The Major wrote Hayes, "It is now settled that Miss Saxton and I will unite our fortunes. I think I am doing the right thing. Miss S. is everything I could hope for."[36]

"Fortunes" might have been a poor choice of words. McKinley made $1,000 a year as prosecutor and some from legal work on the side. He owned a modest house, but with his sisters. Ida came from one of Canton's richest families and her father earned $53,000 in 1869, nearly a million dollars today. Still, McKinley asked his brother David in San Francisco to buy a ring of California gold with small diamonds around a red ruby. A pall was cast over the young couple's preparations for their wedding by the death in October of Ida's grandmother, which hit Ida and her mother Kate hard. The widow Dewalt left her home to Kate.[37]

Ida and William were married January 25, 1871, in the unfinished new building of First Presbyterian, with a thousand guests, three hundred standing around the sanctuary. Ida wore an ivory satin gown with Mary in pink silk and a friend in yellow as maids of honor. McKinley's brother Abner and his cousin William McKinley Osborne were groomsmen. McKinley's father was absent, away in Michigan managing his furnace. (The senior McKinley's finances were precarious: he was supported by gifts from his children, William Jr. and Anna included.) [38]

The newly married couple caught the late-night train east for a honeymoon in New York and Washington. They posed for photographs in Manhattan. In Washington, McKinley apparently shared a secret with his new bride. He hoped to follow his old commander, Hayes, into politics. Ida was thrilled, soon telling family and friends "her husband would someday be president of the United States." [39]

The couple returned home on Valentine's Day and moved into a residential hotel so they could consider their housing options. Ida was then battered by the third loss of someone close to her in less than two years: John Saxton, her grandfather, role model, and the family patriarch, died April 16 at the age of seventy-nine. [40]

A few days later, the young couple settled into a house on North Market Street, a gift from James Saxton. There was talk of moving into the Saxton house, but Kate said, "no young woman does as well as under her own roof." Regardless, Ida was soon under the Saxton roof: pregnant, she spent the late summer and fall under her mother's watchful eye. A baby girl arrived Christmas Day. They named her Katherine, after Ida's mother and grandmother, and called her Katie. [41]

The baby was a Christmas gift that more than compensated for McKinley's narrow defeat that fall for reelection as county prosecutor. That itself was only a small setback for McKinley. His law practice was on solid ground even before James Saxton had begun steering more of his legal and bank business the Major's way. [42]

By late summer 1872, Ida was pregnant again. The good news was paired with bad. Ida's beloved mother, Kate, was dying, probably of cancer, and in terrible pain. At Christmas, Ida and McKinley gave their daughter Katie the small rocking chair Ida's parents had given her. It was Kate Saxton's last Christmas: she died March 14, 1873. Because of the closeness of the relationship with her mother, "the shock was too great" for Ida. "Her nervous system was nearly wrecked." [43]

Two weeks later, Ida gave birth to a second daughter and named her Ida. It was a very difficult end to a troubled pregnancy for mother and daughter. The child was sickly from the first, and as her mother struggled to regain her own health, the baby grew weaker and then died of cholera on August 20, 1873. Having already been devastated by the loss in a very short time of Joseph Wright, grandparents to whom she was very close, and her mother, this unexpected and premature death was a heavy blow. For Ida and William, baby Ida's death marked "the beginning of the great sorrow that was to hover like a cloud over the remainder of their lives."[44]

Ida herself was sick, bedridden for nearly six months. It is likely that her immune system and that of her daughter were compromised during the pregnancy, leaving both vulnerable to infection and disease. Ida may have also suffered some kind of fall that led to a concussion or even more traumatic brain injury, while injuring her spine.[45]

Ida's father, alarmed by her condition and alone in the Saxton house except for his ne'er-do-well twenty-three-year-old son, George, invited the McKinleys to leave their home and live with him. They accepted. A platoon of maids, servants, and cooks would make Ida's life easier.[46]

Overwhelmed, Ida became severely depressed and "hysterically apprehensive" about Katie, holding her in her lap for hours in a darkened room, crying. When Abner McKinley found Katie swinging on the garden gate and invited her for a walk, his niece replied, "No, I mustn't go out of the yard or God'll punish Mama some more."[47]

In addition to depression, Ida suffered severe headaches and an acute sensitivity to light, rapid motion, and sound. Even the hairpins used to hold her coif in place could bring on agony, so she cropped her hair short. On an August 1877 camping trip, some young boys began banging out music on homemade instruments, causing McKinley to fly out of his tent and ask them to stop: Ida was being tormented by a headache. Yet a few weeks later, she hosted a piano recital at her home with no ill effects.[48]

She began suffering epileptic fits, probably the result of brain trauma from a fall. Headaches often signaled one was imminent. Her body would stiffen; she would become oblivious to her surroundings, make a hissing sound, and shake uncontrollably. Often she did not know she had had a seizure and would pick up the conversation in midsentence. She sometimes fell out of her chair or, if walking, slumped to the ground. She had facial tics and contortions. It is difficult to diagnose more than a century later, but doctors now believe Ida suffered a central nervous system injury to her left frontal lobe that resulted in epilepsy and partial paralysis or muscle weakness on her right side. The headaches and seizures lasted the rest of her life.[49]

If a seizure came on in public, her husband would cover her face with a handkerchief until it passed. William Howard Taft was once talking with McKinley with Ida present and as he asked the Major for a pencil, Ida began hissing and suffered a seizure. McKinley reached for his handkerchief with one hand while giving Taft the pencil with his other. It left Taft discombobulated.[50]

Ida's persistent weakness on her right side caused her to hide her right hand in photographs and public appearances. In addition, she had phlebitis, which made it painful to walk or stand, likely aggravated by a spinal injury that caused nerve damage that made her mobility issues worse. Still, after being virtually hospitalized in her own house for six months, these maladies did not keep Ida from traveling and entertaining in the years ahead.[51]

By March 13, 1874, Ida felt well enough to attend her first party. In the meantime, as the McKinleys lived under James Saxton's roof, little Katie grew into an outgoing, animated young girl and McKinley's law practice flourished, in part because of his father-in-law's needs or referrals. Saxton encouraged him and Ida to purchase a large office building across the street from the Saxton home, even lending them the money. McKinley moved his law office there and rented out the remaining space for income.[52]

But then on June 25, 1875, the McKinleys suffered another misfortune. Ida's worst fears were realized. Katie died of scarlet fever. It was almost too much to bear. Friends worried about Ida, buried under her grief and praying for her own death. McKinley would not let her go, even though he too felt keenly the loss of his "favorite Christmas present."[53]

Ida's pregnancies, her illnesses, and the rapid deaths of so many people to whom she was so close transformed her from the spirited, self-confident woman McKinley had married two years earlier into a near invalid. McKinley understood what the death of six of the closest people to her in less than six years must have done to his wife.

Ida became his constant focus. She clung to him fiercely and demanded much of his time, which he gave willingly. McKinley did all he could to assure her of his continuing love. He stopped riding horses and cut back on walking because these activities took him away from Ida, preferring instead to take her on carriage rides. He was quick to attend without complaint to her every whim and need. He would excuse himself from meetings or visitors to periodically check on her and sit in the darkened parlor at night, talking with her. When the two were apart because of business or politics, he would write her frequently.[54]

Ida's illness kept her from his swearing-in as a congressman. When it took place in March 1877, she was in Philadelphia's Infirmary for Nervous Diseases under the care of Silas Weir Mitchell. He was a neurologist whose remedies required forced bed rest and a high-caloric, milk-based diet. His patients were isolated in darkened rooms, prohibited from entertainment or reading. His methods were used on Virginia Woolf and thought to do more harm than good. At least Mitchell viewed epilepsy as a physical, not a mental, disease, unlike most doctors of the time. Ida was in Mitchell's care for perhaps three months and McKinley wrote to her as many as three letters a day.[55]

McKinley offered to sacrifice his political dreams, telling her, "If you would suffer by the circumstances surrounding me in a competition for public station, I will devote my ambition to success in private life." But she strongly supported his career, perhaps even saw in it a way to some of the happiness denied her by the death of her children and the onset of ill health. So she responded, "Your ambitions are mine."[56]

He gave her the support the grieving mother needed. "Ida would have died years ago," one friend later remarked, "but William would just not let her go." The couple would have no more children. For the rest of her life, she kept Katie's photo on her dressing table and hung a larger version on her bedroom wall, the image hand-tinted with yellow hair, pink cheeks, red lips, and blue eyes. Ida took to displaying Katie's rocking chair next to her own childhood chair, often draping them with Katie and little Ida's clothes.[57]

Ida could be challenging. She was—for a period—intensely jealous. In summer 1881, after Ida and McKinley returned from their tenth-anniversary California vacation, she felt neglected when the Major was out of town and accused him of an affair. It ended in "a frantic scene." Soon after, McKinley and two of his brothers were walking when they met an attractive neighbor woman. As they neared the Saxton house, McKinley pleaded, "please don't walk into the yard with me. Ida might see you." Later that fall, after a memorial service in Cleveland for President Garfield following his assassination, McKinley mentioned seeing "a handsome lady" friend of the family's. Ida erupted in a jealous outburst ended only by an epileptic seizure.[58]

Even in calm waters, Ida could be demanding, especially in private around family and friends. Mark Hanna's precocious Boston nephew, David Rhodes, spent the summer of 1896 at his uncle's Cleveland home. When the McKinleys stayed a week there participating in the city's centennial celebration, the teenager reported to his father, Hanna's brother-in-law, the historian James Ford Rhodes, that "Mrs. McK has been somewhat more flighty than usual during the last few days . . . to the great annoyance of Aunt Gussie and Aunt Mary Phelps whose nerves are on the point of entire collapse from their constant effort to fulfill her outrageous whims."[59]

But McKinley accepted Ida's condition and behavior without complaint or bitterness. It was part of God's plan and his faith was deepened rather than shaken. "His first consideration was to soften the blow for Ida as far as he could," a contemporary observed. "His devotion to her grew with her dependence on him." Ida's reliance on him, suggests McKinley's preeminent biographer, "fulfilled his need to be loved, and that mattered most." The Major reacted stoically to his daughters' deaths and his wife's deteriorating health, hardly ever speaking of either and never complaining about the latter. In a rare reflection years later, he wrote a friend about the death of a child, "Only those who have suffered in a similar way can appreciate the keenness of such affliction." He forever enjoyed the company of children.[60]

BY NOW, MCKINLEY'S LEGAL apprenticeship was finished. He was one of Canton's leading lawyers, respected for his preparation and admired for his skills of presentation and persuasion. Because of those talents, he was forced into handling a lawsuit with political ramifications. In March 1876, coal miners in the Tuscarawas Valley struck for higher wages. Management brought in strikebreakers. Violence broke out. A mine operator was severely beaten and several mines burned. By June, twenty-three miners had been arrested and were facing trial. When no one volunteered to defend the miners, McKinley was pressured into the job.[61]

The opposing counsel was familiar. McKinley had beaten William A. Lynch for county prosecutor in 1869, before Lynch returned the favor two years later. A partner in Canton's preeminent firm, Lynch represented the mine owners, who were led by a slender thirty-nine-year-old Cleveland businessman with a long, gray patriarchal beard named Mark Hanna.[62]

Six years older than McKinley, Hanna was born in New Lisbon, Ohio, in 1837 to Scotch-Irish Quaker parents. His father was involved in the family business, started by Hanna's grandfather. It was the leading wholesaler and distributor in what was then a bustling market town on the Ohio River, on the state's eastern edge.[63]

In 1852 the family moved to Cleveland, where the Hanna men started a grocery wholesale business that grew into a distributor for all kinds of commodities. Hanna began working there as a warehouseman in April 1859 after being expelled from Western Reserve College. He had printed up a fake program mocking the school's junior class talent performance, using "racy" language pillorying it as a burlesque show. As the company began running steamboats on the Great Lakes, hauling sugar, molasses, and foodstuffs and returning with cargoes of pig iron, iron ore, and salt fish, Hanna took on other responsibilities. He was variously a clerk, steamboat pursuer, and traveling salesman. He had a natural talent for business.[64]

Hanna assumed the company's leadership in 1862 when his uncle died, his father having withdrawn from the firm for health reasons. At his mother's urging, Hanna hired a substitute to take his place in the Union Army, though he joined a militia that was called up in 1864 when the Ohio National Guard replaced regular army units in forts around Washington. Before his four months of Guard duty service, Hanna married C. Augusta Rhodes, whose father, Daniel, was a wealthy Cleveland iron and coal merchant and ardent Democrat.[65]

After the war, Hanna nearly went broke building an oil refinery before selling it to a high school classmate, John D. Rockefeller, in 1867. The domineering Rhodes then pressured his son-in-law to leave his family's business and devote his talents to a new partnership—Rhodes & Company. Hanna was then just thirty. For the next twenty-seven years he made the partnership a major player in iron and coal, transforming it into a vertically integrated business that owned mines, furnaces, smelters, steamships, and warehouses. Along the way, he purchased the *Cleveland Leader*, picked up the city's Opera House at a sheriff's auction, bought control of Cleveland's west-side streetcar company, and organized one of the city's most profitable banks in 1884. He never reentered the oil business.[66]

Politics slowly interested him. He was elected to the Board of Education in 1869 and though a lifelong Republican given his Quaker forebears' abolitionist views, bolted the local GOP in 1873 when it fielded an unacceptable mayoral candidate. As the thin, young up-and-comer with the wavy beard thickened over the 1870s into a beefy, clean-shaven middle-aged man with thinning hair, Hanna increased his political activity.

He was an unusual businessman. He had a good relationship with employees, keeping his door open to the lowliest deckhand or miner. He paid them fairly, covered expenses of injured workers, and provided reasonable working conditions. He recognized labor's right to organize and endorsed collective bargaining and arbitration. He avoided serious labor disputes, often settling them at the outset by meeting with disgruntled workers. About the only serious strike Rhodes & Company had was at the Massillon mines in 1876.[67]

Despite the high-powered counsel opposing him, McKinley proceeded to get all but one miner off. He then refused the $120 the miners had collected for his fee, adding to his reputation as the workingman's friend.[68]

The trial gave Hanna his first glimpse of McKinley, but he later did not recall meeting the Major. The coal baron was distracted by a terrible attack of hives and "smeared with sulfur ointment" to ease the itching and could walk only with a cane. The friendship between the two men would have to wait eight years, until spring 1884. In the meantime, McKinley's legal apprenticeship was over, but his schooling in a new craft was under way and about to reach a critical test.[69]

CHAPTER 3

Political Apprenticeship

————◦————

One fall evening in 1867, William McKinley stepped onto an empty dry goods box to make his first impression in politics. His audience stood in the front yard of a home in New Berlin, Ohio, or sat on benches in front of a post office next door. As men held torches to illuminate the scene, the event's organizer—George Bitzer—asked the evening's principal speaker—Judge James Underhill—if the "young strip of a boy" was up to the task of promoting the GOP candidate for governor, Rutherford B. Hayes.

McKinley, then just twenty-four years old, quickly dispelled any concerns about his abilities. He spoke for an hour without notes in support of his old commander and left Bitzer stunned. "I just wondered where he got all of those words and ideas," he said later. The old German was also taken by the Major's "kindly manner" and "hearty handshakes." McKinley's political debut had been a success.[1]

Still, while it was an indication that McKinley had a future in politics, he had much to learn. He would spend the next several years being trained the old-fashioned way. Through hard work, he became conversant with the issues, gained a feel for how voters reacted, built important friendships, and turned himself into a powerful orator. He would absorb lessons from failures as well as successes and came to understand he would help himself in the long run by helping others.

While McKinley had a talent for speaking and grew up steeped in the ideals that made the GOP the party that saved the Union, freed the slaves, and stood for the expansion of American commerce, he still had to translate those beliefs into effective arguments. So he studied what other Republicans said in newspapers, speeches, pamphlets, and party platforms. He refined their ideas and converted them into his own words, leavened by the values of his faith and upbringing. His habit of hard, diligent work helped prepare him.

Politics in the latter half of the nineteenth century was a contact sport. The Major himself understood this from the start. That night in New Berlin he offered a blistering attack on Hayes's gubernatorial opponent, Democrat Allen G. Thurman. McKinley's main argument was that Democrats who had opposed the war couldn't be trusted with high office. He questioned Thurman's patriotism. "Every energy of his mind was directed against the war measures of the Union party," McKinley said. "This nation for the present must be confined to none but its preservers, its enemies must be kept out of the council chambers." If this sounds harsh today, it was common at the time. In elections after Appomattox, Republicans turned Clausewitz's dictum that war is "the continuation of politics by other means" on its head, treating politics as a continuation of the Civil War by other means.[2]

Democrats also engaged in scorched-earth tactics. By the time McKinley stepped on that dry goods box, Ohio Democrats had already launched racially charged attacks. They claimed that GOP support of black suffrage would "foment discord and disorder." Democrats argued that Republican efforts to guarantee black voting rights through the Fourteenth Amendment to the U.S. Constitution and a proposed state constitutional amendment would impair the country's "material prosperity." The Ohio Democratic platform declared that allowing blacks to vote would "produce a disastrous conflict of races." Thurman also attacked Hayes for the GOP's treatment of the Civil War paper money. Republicans worried that leaving all the "greenbacks" in circulation would spark a destructive period of inflation, so they withdrew some of them, which reduced the money supply. Democrats took the opposing view, believing that putting more currency in the hands of people was necessary for prosperity. This argument would continue to play out in the nation's politics for decades.[3]

Since the state was narrowly divided between the two parties, Ohio's election results that year were a mixed bag. Hayes won, but by just 2,983 votes out of 484,227 cast. Still, he carried the rest of the state GOP ticket with him and took Stark County (a boost for McKinley). But Republicans lost the argument on the state's voting rights amendment, which failed 45 percent to 55 percent. The election also saw many black voters being kept from casting ballots.[4]

The election results taught McKinley three lessons. The first was that many Ohioans trusted Hayes's character and record and agreed with him on one major issue—currency—which mattered more than their disagreement with him on another issue less important to them—black voting rights. The second was that because Ohio was narrowly divided, its elections would always be hard fought. In the Buckeye State, the quality of candidates and their campaigns mattered a great deal. The third was the importance of perseverance when fundamental questions were involved. The state constitutional amendment failed, but McKinley would never stop fighting to protect black voting rights.

McKinley also learned a few smaller tactical lessons. One was to not let yourself get upstaged. Charles F. Manderson, then Stark County attorney and later U.S. senator from Nebraska, rode with McKinley to a joint speaking appearance and got the Major to tell him what he planned to say. Taking the podium first, Manderson proceeded to deliver McKinley's speech. Manderson even had the gall to ask from the podium if the Major would kindly hand over the statistics he had in his pocket. McKinley was shocked that someone would steal his speech, but he never again shared his remarks in advance.[5]

Another element of McKinley's political education was subtler and illustrated a larger trend. In 1868, McKinley was an early supporter of Ulysses S. Grant for president. The Major organized clubs of young men throughout Stark County to boost the former general for the Republican nomination. McKinley was gratified at the enthusiastic response Grant received as the GOP underwent a generational change. During the Civil War, older Republicans—almost all former Whigs or Democrats—governed, while younger men who had never experienced a time without a Republican Party went to war. Energized by Grant, Hayes, and other wartime commanders, young Republicans like McKinley were now increasingly being drawn into politics.

In a surprise recognition of his talents and possibly because of the generational shift, the Major was elected Stark County Republican chairman, a job that normally went to a longtime workhorse. The political novice drew on his military training and managerial skills to arrange a canvass of every voter in the county, learning in the process the importance of an efficient organization.

That fall, McKinley demonstrated his speaking abilities when he shared a stage with New York's lieutenant governor Stewart L. Woodford. Woodford later praised the Major's oratorical abilities at the GOP state headquarters in Columbus, prompting party leaders to invite McKinley to make more campaign appearances. The Major was one of many speakers in the effort, but Grant handily carried Ohio as well as Stark County—an indication that McKinley was an effective and rising party leader.[6]

That success led to McKinley's first race for office. In July 1869, the now-twenty-six-year-old was given the Republican nomination for Stark County prosecutor, considered an empty honor because Stark leaned decidedly Democratic. But McKinley threw himself into the race. He spoke virtually every day through mid-October, appearing in every hamlet and neighborhood. He also made "raids upon the ranks of the foe" by soliciting support from Democratic friends from church, YMCA, Masons, and other groups he had joined. These relationships paid off. He won the October election while most of the GOP county ticket lost. McKinley's victory taught him that in a closely divided electorate, even a small number of defections could have big consequences because each defection takes one vote away from your opponent while adding one to your column.[7]

Two years later, McKinley learned the consequences of a candidate losing key swing voters. Democrats made the Major's prosecution of saloon owners an issue. German and Irish friends who had voted for McKinley in 1869 turned against him in 1871 because he had strictly enforced liquor laws. The Major lost by 143 votes.

However, the defeat was just a speed bump for McKinley's political career. He now had a reputation as a diligent officeholder and vigorous campaigner, and, it turns out, a desire to aim higher. He had his eye on the 17th Congressional District. So he remained politically active. He campaigned for Grant and the GOP ticket in 1872 by speaking around the state, joining in the celebrations when the president carried Ohio with 53 percent of the vote, and Stark County with 62 percent, and won reelection.[8]

•   •   •

THE FOLLOWING YEAR WOULD profoundly change the Major personally and shape the politics of the nation for years to come. At home, McKinley would watch his family fall apart as Ida suffered through a terrible pregnancy, the troubled birth of baby Ida in April, and the infant's death in August. The Major could do little but watch in anguish as his mother-in-law died, his daughter slipped away, and his wife turned into an invalid.

Across the country, a sudden stock market collapse in September caused millions of Americans to lose their jobs, paychecks, and homes and forced many to face terrible deprivation, even starvation and death, ending the country's postwar prosperity. The Panic of 1873 started when a prominent Wall Street investor committed suicide after learning that one of his holdings, the Warehouse & Security Company, would declare bankruptcy and drag down two large sugar importers with it. A major brokerage failed on September 13. Things spiraled out of control six days later when Jay Cooke's firm collapsed. Cooke had helped finance the war effort but was now ruined by the failure of his firm's Northern Pacific Railroad stock offering, which he was building to tap the Plains' rich farmland. Police dispersed anxious investors who stormed his offices, but couldn't stop a run on banks and brokerages. The New York Stock Exchange soon suspended trading for ten days. Grant had stayed with Cooke the night before his firm went bankrupt, but the financier never mentioned his difficulties.[9]

The Panic of 1873 spread rapidly. Banks closed, companies failed, and commerce seized up. On October 28, ten thousand factory workers were laid off in one day in Dutchess County, New York, alone. A month later, the *New York Times* warned, "financial convulsion will throw multitudes out of employment at the most critical period of the year" and charity "will hardly meet the most pressing necessities." By November 1874, an estimated 25,000 men were unemployed in St. Louis, almost 20 percent of adult males, while 10,000 were out of work in New York and in need of a "crust of bread" and "place to sleep."[10]

By Christmas, hundreds of thousands of people were out of work, leading to mass meetings in Chicago, where agitators demanded starving laborers "combine against capital" and "resort to force." Things were worse in rural areas that lacked soup kitchens and charities. Some Nebraskans "had nothing to eat but baked squash and pumpkin," while others had "one meal a day, for weeks." An estimated 10,000 Cornhuskers faced starvation. In Washington, D.C., there were reports of families living "where no food has been tasted in three or four days." In late 1874, farmers in Piatt County, Illinois, sent four train cars of provisions to north-central Kansas, racked not only by the panic, but also by drought. Even then there was not enough food to last two weeks. "The condition of the people is fearful to contemplate," a relief worker wrote. While the economy gradually improved, the panic did not end until 1879. It was the nation's longest contraction, even longer than the Great Depression.[11]

There were many causes of the Panic of 1873, most of which had been building for years. The economy was highly leveraged. Wall Street experienced a speculative boom. Banks made too many loans to shaky ventures. Manufacturing expanded too fast, outpacing demand and creating a problem of overcapacity. Insurance companies were stretched thin with claims from large fires in Chicago (1871) and Boston (1872). A surge in railroad construction resulted in too many miles of track for too few passengers and too little cargo. World grain prices had been falling since the end of the Franco-Prussian War, for with peace came an increase in European agricultural production that ended export sales for many U.S. farmers.[12]

The Panic of 1873 had political repercussions. Suddenly the value and volume of money became red-hot political issues, and, as they did, new political lines and alliances were formed. Congressmen in both parties blamed the panic on deflation caused by the withdrawal of the greenbacks, which contracted the money supply. They believed more money in circulation was necessary to restore prosperity, even if that meant inflation. So in April 1874, Congress passed the Inflation Act, approving $44 million in new greenbacks. President Grant drafted a message for signing the bill, but then realized he disagreed with all he had written. To his cabinet's surprise, he vetoed the measure. He believed one of government's highest responsibilities was to provide a currency that held its value. That meant one that was gold-backed. The president did acknowledge that a sudden return to using only currency supported by gold "would bring bankruptcy and ruin" to debtors, and therefore he favored a gradual withdrawal of Civil War paper money. Midwest and Plains Republicans warned his veto had damaged the GOP in their increasingly soft-money regions.[13]

Grant's veto also made it difficult for Republicans to avoid blame for the depression. That, along with charges of administration corruption, cost the GOP its House majority in the 1874 midterms. This led to another setback for inflationists. During the lame-duck session after the election,

Republicans passed the Resumption Act, requiring the Treasury to redeem up to $300 million in greenbacks with gold starting in January 1879. This would further shrink the money supply and strengthen the dollar's value. In a sop to inflationists, the measure also replaced the 10¢, 25¢, and 50¢ paper notes with silver coins. Grant signed it in January 1875, before Democrats took control of the House for the first time since 1858. It was now impossible for the new Democratic House to expand the money supply with greenbacks if there was a Republican president or Senate.[14]

In response, soft-money advocates moved away from greenbacks and toward a ready alternative. Western silver production was increasing rapidly, which made it possible to expand the money supply by coining silver dollars. This would also depreciate the currency by putting even more money in circulation, especially if the government paid for the silver by printing paper money.

This was a significant and sudden reversal in the political landscape. Before the panic, silver men had supported the 1873 Coinage Act, which demonetized the white metal. This seemingly uncontroversial reform was approved in the House by 110 to 13 and in the Senate by 36 to 14 in February, after three years of discussion. Among other provisions, it formally ended the Treasury Department's silver purchases and silver dollar production, which had actually ceased years earlier since the white metal was scarcer and worth more than gold. Even members from Western mining states supported the bill's passage, though it put the United States on the de facto gold standard.[15]

With the legislative ground shifting under them, silver advocates now had to explain their past support for the Coinage Act and, in the process, create a useful public enemy for their cause. They took to calling the Coinage Act the "Crime of '73," depicting it as a nefarious plot to hand control of America's economy to British financiers and European financial houses. They argued that repealing the Coinage Act and requiring the Treasury to mint large volumes of silver dollars would expand the money supply, make cheaper money widely available, and break the money power's grip on the economy. The Free Silver men's arguments reflected their constituents' anger. Typical of their rhetorical excess was Texas congressman John H. Reagan's denunciation of the Coinage Act as "the greatest legislative crime and the most stupendous conspiracy against the welfare of the people."[16]

The Major heard these charges, as Ohio quickly became a center of silver agitation. For the moment, he was personally insulated against the panic's worst features. His family had moved into the Saxton home shortly after baby Ida's death and he had steady rents from the office building while his law practice also grew. His father-in-law's bank and friends needed a good lawyer in bad times.[17]

McKinley, now thirty-two, began a new phase of his political education, learning the politics within his own party and stepping onto a statewide stage in the 1875 Ohio governor's race, a campaign with national implications. Democrats seized on the GOP's last-minute passage of the Resumption Act to depict Republicans as tools of a foreign money power, indifferent to the people's suffering. Nowhere was the battle fiercer than in Ohio, where Democrats held the governorship. Republicans were afraid that if the GOP did not win it back, the 1876 presidential race would be lost.

McKinley played a significant role in this fight as Buckeye Republicans wrote their platform and picked their gubernatorial candidate. Stark County Republicans made the Major a delegate to the state convention for the first time, and surprisingly, 17th Congressional District delegates named him their Resolutions Committee representative to help draw up the state platform.

In the Gilded Age, platforms were each party's key election document, a formal summary of policies drafted by senior party leaders. This is what made young Mr. McKinley's selection surprising. He was practically a kid. His presence was a sign of his growing stature in state politics and the generational change under way in the GOP.[18]

The famed Kansas editor and Republican activist William Allen White once observed that Ohio Republican politics "combined the virtues of the serpent, the shark and the cooing dove." It was often fractured, rural versus urban, or between regions, sometimes over philosophical differences. The GOP front-runner for governor, Cincinnati judge Alphonso Taft, found himself with these problems as McKinley and other delegates arrived in Columbus on June 2 for their convention. Rural Republicans distrusted the big-city judge. Other delegates disliked his opposition to a court decision restoring Bible reading in public schools.[19]

These men clamored for Hayes. But after two terms as governor, from 1867 to 1871, Hayes understood it would be tough to win a third term and declined to run against Taft. That did not matter to McKinley and

Hayes's other friends. They were determined to nominate him anyway and did. With McKinley and his fellow Stark County delegates whipping up support, Hayes won by better than 2:1 on the first ballot.[20]

In his first look at statewide politics, McKinley saw how a candidate's natural popularity was critical to victory, how party leaders paid close attention to ordinary voters' concerns as they considered candidates and platform planks, and how, in an era of intense political competition, even state elections were fought over national issues.[21]

McKinley returned to Canton with increased confidence in his political skills, having impressed many new friends across the state with his customary thoroughness in helping draft the platform. It was also good to be a friend of Hayes. Soon after the Major arrived home, however, his beloved Katie developed scarlet fever and died on June 25, deepening Ida's depression and bringing on a round of seizures. For a time, politics was not a top priority for McKinley, even as the state race heated up.[22]

Though governors had nothing to do with the issue, the Resumption Act dominated the campaign nationally and in Ohio. The incumbent Democrat governor, William Allen, was renominated on a platform that devoted four planks to pummeling "forced resumption" as having already "brought disaster to the business of the country," though it would not happen until 1879. Instead of retiring greenbacks, Democrats demanded they be made legal tender for all transactions except where gold was required by contract.

On the stump, Allen blamed Republican tight-money policies for the Panic of 1873 and called for expanding the money supply for farmers, laborers, and merchants. Democratic papers joined the assault, claiming GOP hard-money policies enjoyed the "great satisfaction of the bondholders and the moneyed classes" and denouncing Hayes as a tool of "the money power." Banners reading NO FORCED RESUMPTION appeared at Democratic rallies.[23]

Hayes tackled the issue straight on, making an unapologetic case for sound money, a currency backed by gold that could be redeemed for specie upon demand. He formally opened his campaign July 31 by attacking Democrats for backing "a depreciated currency" and warned that "an inflated and irredeemable paper currency" was "the parent of panics." Only resumption could save America's credit. Given public sentiment and the poor economy, it was a difficult argument to make. So despite McKinley's personal difficulties, party bigwigs pressed him to help sell the GOP's case. The Major agreed to some appearances and spoke locally before attending rallies in battleground counties across Ohio.[24]

Hayes won by 5,544 votes that October, carrying Stark County in the process and teaching the Major the value of directly taking on a campaign's big issue, something that would make the difference in his own battles. The campaign also deepened McKinley's friendship with Hayes, who as Ohio governor was immediately the front-runner for the GOP presidential nomination the following year, which he won.[25]

Because McKinley had impressed party leaders with his Resolutions Committee service, made new friends, and honed his political skills, he improved his chances for the next political step—winning the GOP nomination for Congress. Despite the tragedies at home, 1876 seemed right for him to run, especially with Hayes at the top of the ticket. There was some feeling in the 17th District that the incumbent Republican congressman, Laurin D. Woodworth from Mahoning County, should not seek a third term and that after twenty years without a congressman from Stark, it was Canton's turn.

But it was still an uphill climb for McKinley. The incumbent was a former state senator, Civil War veteran, and lawyer. Three other Canton men were running: Judge Joseph Frease, former state senator H. S. Martin, and, awkwardly, Dr. Josiah Hartzell, until recently the editor of the *Repository*, owned by McKinley's father-in-law. McKinley was the youngest.[26]

Leaving nothing to chance, McKinley stumped in two rural counties that didn't have a hometown favorite in the race—Columbiana and Carroll—and then gently invaded his chief opponent's home turf. The Major demonstrated that sometimes in politics the softer sell is more powerful: he made the case for himself without attacking his fellow Republican directly. The final step to securing the nomination was building support in Stark County, which would pick its delegates to the district's convention by popular vote. It became clear that the race was now down to two men: McKinley and Woodworth. So, as the *Repository* pointed out, if people wanted a "candidate from Stark County they must vote for McKinley." When Stark voters went to the polls on August 13, McKinley carried every township except one.[27]

McKinley was soon nominated by acclamation at the district convention after his opponents—realizing the result was a foregone conclusion—withdrew. Most delegates departed after McKinley was nominated, but the few who remained considered a resolution urging the "restoration of the old silver dollar." Many seemed supportive but uneasy about endorsing it, so the idea was dropped. McKinley would soon find he couldn't ignore the silver issue so easily.[28]

Two weeks later, McKinley kicked off his general election campaign. In the Gilded Age, congressional contests were short, lasting from late summer through mid-October in Ohio, or through the first Tuesday after the first Monday in November for most other states. This made for busy, faster-paced campaigns. McKinley worked nearly every day but Sunday mornings. He covered the district for nearly forty days straight by train, horse, and carriage in all kinds of weather.[29]

His campaign—like others of the time—revolved around speeches by the candidate and surrogates, delivered at outdoor rallies, in auditoriums, or from the steps of houses, saloons, courthouses, and bandstands. Before radio or television, speeches were the main way voters judged candidates. Could they educate, inform, persuade, and even entertain? Brevity was no virtue. McKinley's stump speech lasted an hour at the campaign's start but grew to two hours by the end as he wove in new attacks, rebuttals, and jokes. The Major had to keep the material fresh because he spoke in most of his district's communities several times. If he repeated his speech, voters would know.[30]

Party leaders focused on towns and neighborhoods with more swing voters or where turnout would drop without special attention, giving these areas more rallies and speakers targeted to local groups. German-speaking orators, for example, were a staple for both parties in the 17th District's Dunker and Pennsylvania Dutch communities, especially since McKinley didn't speak German and some German-Americans spoke no English.

Many people from both parties turned out when a candidate came to town, so the Major expected to be interrupted or heckled by Democrats. His response was a test. At McKinley's first Youngstown appearance on September 21, he praised Hayes for over an hour and mauled the Democratic Party for being split over currency. New York governor Samuel J. Tilden, a hard-money man, was the Democratic presidential pick, while Indiana governor William Hendricks, a soft-money inflationist, was his running mate. Their differences had been papered over during their convention but became clear after Hendricks made indiscreet comments to reporters. After highlighting them and trashing Tilden's record, McKinley asked the crowd, "Would you have such a man for President?" When a Democrat yelled back, "yes!" McKinley provoked laughter by genially responding that the heckler "must need reformation."[31]

Campaign rallies were spectacles, a form of political fun that lasted for hours. They included rituals—parades, bands, and picnics, even glee clubs that serenaded the crowds—that involved entire communities and strengthened the link between the party and its partisans. Consider the Major's kickoff rally September 1 in East Liverpool, an Ohio River town known for its potteries. It was in "The Wigwam," a temporary wooden meeting hall whose sole purpose was to host political events that fall. The Hayes Club brass band paraded into the hall and played for the thousand attendees before McKinley spoke.[32]

Rallies often featured clubs of local party activists or supporters of a candidate who marched in homemade uniforms with handsome cloaks, hats, and insignia, carrying colorful banners with slogans or pithy insults. It was quite a sight near the 1876 campaign's end when the two hundred uniformed men of the Salineville Hayes and Wheeler Guard escorted McKinley through town to an evening rally with flaming torches. The enthusiasm of these clubs and the vigor of their activities were important measures of the campaign's strength. When Republican marching clubs traveled miles to hear McKinley speak in Columbiana County, a local paper admitted that "such enthusiasm has not been manifested" since the Civil War.[33]

Sometimes there were debates. That first election, McKinley faced his Democratic rival, Levi L. Lamborn, a physician and amateur horticulturalist. The two were friends: Lamborn would later write the definitive study of carnations. Carnations became McKinley's favorite flower, which he took to wearing in his lapel every day.

In their one and only debate, Lamborn pummeled Republicans over currency while McKinley pled ignorance about the Free Silver resolution at the GOP district convention. The Major disliked discussing currency because he knew that the issue increasingly split his own party. Many Republican farmers with mortgages and bank loans wanted a mildly inflationary currency so they could repay their debts with depreciated dollars. So McKinley tried appeasing them by straddling the issue. This allowed Democrats to charge he was trying to appear pro-silver in front of silver men and an honest-money man when in front of gold standard supporters. They were right.[34]

One of the campaign's most important activities was the canvass. Today's campaigns use sophisticated computer microtargeting to pair the right volunteers with prospective supporters and then find out their preference by phone, online, or knocking on their front door. In 2012, both the Obama and Romney campaigns used these techniques to contact nearly a third of voters. In the Gilded Age, local party activists tallied the candidate preferences of every adult male in their neighborhood and town and reported the information to the county party, which then endeavored to have undecided or doubtful voters talked to by someone they held in confidence. Patronage employees provided some of the labor to do this, but in McKinley's district, most campaign workers were simply volunteers who felt passionately about the GOP's success. Many were wartime comrades from the 23rd who had returned to northeast Ohio.[35]

Still, the candidate's personal character and ability to bond with voters deeply affected the outcome. McKinley's pleasant manner, firm handshake, willingness to look everyone in the eye, respectful bearing, and approachable nature were assets in his one-on-one campaigning. While the Major spoke several times a day, he also stopped by each town's post office and most newspaper offices, visited barbershops, mills, shops, and factories, walked up and down main streets and popped into stores, and once even accompanied a doctor on his house calls. In an election in which just over thirty thousand men voted, McKinley was seen or met by thousands of them.

On Election Day, October 10, the Major's charm and hard work paid off as the political apprentice won the 17th Congressional District seat by a healthy margin of 3,304 votes, 51 percent to 41 percent. But his work was not finished. His reputation as a fine orator and friendship with Hayes had netted him an unusual invitation for a freshman congressman and, at thirty-four, the youngest member of Congress. The GOP's campaign managers wanted him to open for Senator James G. Blaine at a big unity rally in Philadelphia.[36]

WHEN THE NEW 45TH Congress met in October 1877, McKinley was immediately thrown into a bitter two-year-old fight over currency. He would soon learn that straddling an important issue could cost him. In this instance, he let himself get into a position of being disloyal to a close friend who just happened to be the newly elected president of the United States.

Hayes (like Grant before him) faced pressure to abandon the government's policy of using gold to withdraw greenbacks from the money supply. Also like Grant, Hayes was willing to use his veto to block legislation that would force the Treasury to stop redeeming greenbacks. So soft-money Democrats pressed the case for silver to inflate the currency. On behalf of Americans who felt crushed by hard-money policies, the silver men sought to put the United States on a bimetallic standard that used gold but also used silver in the form of new silver dollar coins.

This was a fight over fundamental principles. Both sides saw the struggle over the money supply as a fight over the nature of the country's economy. The silver men believed this was about how to create economic opportunity for ordinary Americans struggling on farms and in factories. The gold men saw it as an existential battle over whether the country would have a strong currency of stable value, which they believed essential to growth and prosperity. The fact that this fight started in earnest during a period of prolonged economic suffering only heightened tempers of many partisans on both sides who were deeply passionate in their beliefs. There would be fire as they grappled with each other.[37]

At the center of this fight was the silver cause's greatest congressional advocate. Orphaned at fourteen, Richard Parks Bland was a country lawyer in Lebanon, Missouri, who farmed and raised apples on the side. He had spent time in California, then Nevada, where he prospected and took up law and politics before returning east. Soon after his election in 1872, he became the leader of the Free Silver forces in Congress. So strong was his identification with the movement that Bland's nickname became "Silver Dick."[38]

As Mines and Mining Committee chairman, Bland introduced assorted bills putting the United States on a bimetallic standard of gold and silver, finally settling on a version providing for a silver dollar legal for all debts and transactions. Recent declines in silver prices meant these dollars would each contain 82¢ of the white metal. For two years, his bill was stalled by filibusters, forcing Bland to agree in August 1876 to a commission to study the currency issue. When the House returned in December for a lame-duck session, Bland introduced his silver dollar bill again. After hours of wrangling, the Speaker allowed a vote and it passed. It was a symbolic victory. The Senate refused to consider it before adjourning. Bland would have to start fresh in the new Congress.[39]

That is where matters stood when McKinley was sworn in on March 4, 1877, days after the currency committee, now dubbed the "Silver Commission," issued its report, arguing silver's low price resulted not from overproduction, but lack of demand from Germany dropping its silver money. Silver's value would rise if the United States minted silver dollars. The report blamed the gold standard for "failing prices of commodities and real estate, diminishing public revenue, starving, poorly-paid, and unemployed laborers, and rapidly multiplying bankruptcies." Prosperity required unrestricted use of silver on the same basis as gold.[40]

After the House reconvened in October 1877, Bland reintroduced his Free Silver bill—much to the dismay of those, such as McKinley, who preferred starting their careers on a less contentious issue. The House passed the bill in weeks by a wide bipartisan margin.[41]

McKinley—who in 1875 had campaigned for Hayes as a hard-money man and defended resumption and then ducked and weaved when Free Silver was raised in his own 1876 campaign—said nothing during congressional debate, then voted for Bland's bill. So did most Ohio Republicans, including Hayes's own congressman.[42]

Two weeks later, the Senate Finance Committee reported its version, amended by Iowa Republican William B. Allison, a distant cousin of the Major's mother. Though a hard-money resumptionist, Allison was eager for a compromise that would appease the silver men without alienating currency moderates like himself.

Allison was concerned that requiring mints to purchase all the silver presented to them as Free Silver advocates demanded would transfer control of the money supply to domestic and foreign silver suppliers. So instead he proposed mints would purchase no less than $2 million and no more than $4 million of silver a month, most of America's silver production, which would then be made into silver dollars. This would mildly inflate the currency through the paper money printed to purchase the silver. After a seventeen-hour, often-drunken debate, the Senate approved Allison's measure on February 16, 1878, by 48 to 21, with both parties split.[43]

Five days later, after debating an hour, the House—including McKinley—voted 204 to 72 to concur with Allison's compromise. Bland reluctantly accepted it but pledged, "This war shall never cease . . . until the rights of the people are fully restored and the silver dollar shall take its place alongside the gold dollar."[44]

Hayes vetoed the newly christened Bland-Allison bill seven days later, arguing that using a 412½ grain silver dollar worth 90¢ to 92¢ as legal tender on the same basis as a gold dollar would damage America's credit and discourage the foreign investment the United States needed to finance its debt and economy.[45]

The House and Senate immediately overrode Hayes's veto. The same day it was vetoed, Bland-Allison was law. The country was on a bimetallic standard. McKinley voted to overturn his former chief's veto, as did nine of ten Ohio Republicans. James A. Garfield—the only one to sustain Hayes—described the situation as "an epoch of madness."[46]

Still, resumption went forward successfully in January 1879, as the New York offices of the U.S. Treasury paid out $135,000 in gold for notes the first day while taking in $400,000 of gold for notes, adding $265,000 to the nation's gold reserve. The Treasury had made bankers and the public confident paper and gold were worth the same by amassing a $142 million gold reserve to buy back greenbacks.[47]

The combination of Bland-Allison's passage, resumption's success, and a recovering economy temporarily put the Free Silver issue on the congressional backburner. Until the next economic downturn, currency moderates could argue silver had been given a role, albeit as the junior partner to gold. Given their leadership on the silver issue, observers speculated that Bland and Allison would both be contenders for higher office in the future.

The same could not be said for McKinley. By voting for Bland-Allison and supporting the override of President Hayes's veto, freshman congressman McKinley had deserted his friend and wartime commander and backed a bimetallic currency he refused to endorse in his campaign. The Major was straddling the currency issue, or worse, demonstrating he had few convictions on the subject. If he were to rise within the GOP and Congress, McKinley would have to find other issues of national importance on which to make a reputation for leadership and consistency.

CHAPTER 4

Rise and Fall

————◄○►————

For the next six years, McKinley's reputation would grow in battles over the era's biggest issue—the protective tariff. He would emerge to take command as the Republican House floor manager on the issue. But having made himself a respected leader, he would be driven abruptly from office by extreme—but routine—partisanship.

He and Ida slipped into Washington with ease, living at Ebbitt House, a white Second Empire building with marble floors and chandeliers. Two blocks from the White House, the Ebbitt was one of Washington's most fashionable hotels. Because of their friendship with the Hayeses, the McKinleys attended private dinners at the White House and were frequent guests at events there. Ida occasionally traveled and, if she felt up to it, had the Major take her to the theater. Otherwise she was content to entertain lady friends or crochet slippers, booties, and other items to donate to needy children or area hospitals.[1]

From the start, McKinley preferred work to socializing. He collected papers and mail from the lobby by 7 a.m. and then spent two hours working before breakfasting with Ida. Only committee chairmen were then provided Capitol offices, so he had an office in the hotel across the hall from his and Ida's fifth-floor suite. There he could work, take meetings, or smoke a cigar with colleagues yet bounce across the hall to check on Ida frequently.[2]

McKinley was popular with colleagues. His pleasant manner, affable nature, willingness to listen, and personal kindness won friends on both sides of the aisle. He enjoyed humor, as long as it was not vulgar, rarely swore, and displayed what one observer called a "quiet irony and a graceful lightness." Slow to take offense, he tried giving none in return. Thomas B. Reed of Maine, who entered the House with McKinley, once complained, "My opponents in Congress go at me tooth and nail but they always apologize to William when they are going to call him names." [3]

Instead of going out on the town, McKinley carefully read bills, consumed reports and newspapers, collected facts, and became an expert on House rules. Unusual in Congress, he did not rush to speak and became known as a man who spoke only when he had something to say. [4]

McKinley could have hardly picked a more critical issue to make his own. In the Gilded Age, protective tariffs (as with currency) enflamed political passions and dealt with important questions of how to create jobs in a rapidly industrializing nation and who should benefit most from the country's economic expansion. Each side in this debate believed its approach would create prosperity and that only its ideas could prevent economic ruin. Those who opposed tariffs—many Southern Democrats—viewed high tariffs as a war tax unjustified in peacetime. They were especially offended when Washington began running large surpluses. They wanted a simple low rate on imports that would yield only enough to pay for government's essential functions, a concept called "tariff-for-revenue."

Supporters of protectionism saw it as an instrument of national unity and themselves as defending the interests of American workers, industries, and agriculture. They believed high tariffs promoted the growth of domestic manufacturing and farm production by ensuring there was a robust local market for items produced in the United States and that American wages were higher than those paid in Europe. Both sides considered their opposition devils. Each party had both reformers and protectionists in its ranks, but the GOP's cadre of tariff reformers was small while the number of Democratic protectionists was much larger. [5]

The tariff issue was a natural fit for McKinley. His father and grandfather were both ironmongers and his district had a growing industrial sector and farmers—especially wool growers—who depended on the protective system. His focus was also timely, as House Democrats decided to try slashing tariffs before the 1878 midterms, as tax cuts were popular with the Democratic base. Rather than impose tariffs to protect American industries, free trade Democrats called for duties based solely on what revenue was needed to run the federal government, "not for protecting one class of citizens by plundering another." This meant a low duty on every import, not higher duties on some items made or grown domestically.[6]

Democratic Ways and Means Committee chairman Fernando Wood of New York responded in January 1878 by cobbling together a bill that sharply cut duties on cotton, glass, hemp, liquor, and iron while keeping tariffs high on coal, chemicals, dyes, and other industrial necessities. Some pro-reform papers criticized its limited cuts and sloppy drafting.[7]

McKinley gave his maiden House speech on April 15 on Wood's bill. Unlike tariff defenders who argued protection was needed by a specific factory or industry, McKinley defended high tariffs as economic nationalism that benefited American workers and consumers by keeping wages up, fostering domestic competition, and spreading prosperity by keeping out goods made by poorly paid foreign labor. The Major supported protection because it meant decent wages for laborers, not because it helped wealthy businessmen.

Because of the lingering depression, his speech brought to the surface anxieties about making significant changes to the tariff policy. "Any material adjustment of the tariff system," McKinley said, was a "delicate and hazardous undertaking" and could further damage manufacturing and mining, deepen the economic panic, and harm job creation.[8]

Wood had produced a letter from Worthington & Company—a Michigan manufacturer—that said it could still compete against European firms if tariffs were cut. McKinley turned Wood's argument against him. Worthington, he revealed, hired convict laborers at 32¢ a day. Of course it would remain competitive, but that meant little to honest laborers who needed good wages to support their families. Striking a populist note, McKinley attacked Wood for raising duties on sugar and other staples that ordinary people bought, while lowering duties on silk, satins, and velvet that only the rich purchased.[9]

Representative William "Pig Iron" Kelley, the ranking Republican on Ways and Means and avid protectionist from iron- and steel-rich Pennsylvania, was impressed by the freshman member's speech, as were other Republicans. Two months later, a coalition of Democratic protectionists and Republicans killed Wood's bill. McKinley had played a big role in its defeat, deftly framing the issue in a bipartisan way by focusing on laborers.

The bill's defeat constituted a formative experience—and lasting political achievement.[10]

Understanding that McKinley was a dangerous foe, congressional Democrats quickly moved to end his career. Speaker Samuel J. Randall of Pennsylvania and his lieutenants demanded the Democratic-controlled Ohio legislature redraw McKinley's district. The existing lines had been set for a decade, but state Democrats obediently shifted McKinley's Republican counties into other congressional districts and paired Stark with neighboring Democratic strongholds, giving Democrats an estimated 2,500-vote edge. Not willing to count solely on the gerrymander to deliver the coup de grace, Democrats then fielded Union general Aquila Wiley, who had lost a leg at Missionary Ridge in 1863, hoping he would erase McKinley's advantage as a veteran.[11]

Republican papers denounced the Democratic gerrymander as a "fraud" that would backfire. It did. McKinley won by 1,234 votes. Hayes wrote to an old comrade about the Major's victory, saying, "He was gerrymandered out and then beat the gerrymander. We enjoyed it as much as he did."[12]

In 1879, as the tariff battles settled down and with Bland-Allison calming the currency issue, McKinley drew national attention by opposing Democratic efforts to gut voting rights protections in federal elections. From the perspective of McKinley and most Republicans, the issue was first a moral concern: Democrats wanted to remove the few remaining tools Washington had to guarantee fair federal elections. If a black man in the South could not vote, then every American's right was at risk.

This was also a question of political survival. By using threats, violence, and fraud to deny Southern Republicans—black and white—the right to vote freely and have their ballots honestly counted, Democrats were wiping out the GOP below the Mason-Dixon Line. This made it hard for Republicans to win the popular vote for the presidency or the U.S. House and could cost them the White House whenever Democrats won a handful of Northern swing states to combine with their Solid South.

Despite the outrage of House Democrats, McKinley would not relent on the issue. He returned to it at the 1879 Ohio GOP convention, drafting a plank attacking Democrats for committing "fraud, violence and corruption in National Elections," and continued to condemn Democrats for stealing elections in the South.[13]

Before McKinley's 1880 reelection campaign, Republicans had recaptured control of the legislature and restored his district to its traditional configuration. His opponent was unknown, but the Major still hit the trail hard with speeches virtually every day. As a result he won in October by 55 percent to 45 percent, a large margin for competitive Ohio.[14]

Garfield and his managers came to believe the White House would be won that year on the protection issue and asked McKinley, the GOP's most effective advocate for it, to stump in the East after his October victory. The Republican emphasis on the waffling of the Democratic nominee, Winfield Scott Hancock, on the tariff question settled the race in manufacturing states above the Mason-Dixon Line. Garfield carried the Northeast, except New Jersey, and enough of the Midwest and West to decisively win the Electoral College, 214 to 155, while winning the popular vote by 7,368. Republicans also took back the House.[15]

In December, McKinley was unexpectedly given President-elect Garfield's spot on the powerful Ways and Means Committee. Speaker Randall picked McKinley—still in his sophomore term—over more senior Republicans. He arrived on the committee just before Garfield triggered the next big tariff battle, in which McKinley again proved his mettle.[16]

With Washington, D.C., running a large surplus, Garfield was worried that Democratic calls for tariff reductions were hurting the GOP and suggested a commission to recommend revisions to the tariff schedules to reduce the surplus. But on July 2, 1881, before he could advance the idea, he was shot by a deranged office-seeker, lingering painfully until mid-September.[17]

When the new Congress met in December, Garfield's successor, President Chester A. Arthur, endorsed the commission, urging "a careful revision" of the schedules. House Ways and Means chairman Pig Iron Kelley began drafting a bill that the Major helped move through the committee and, as Kelley's lieutenant, spoke in favor of on the House floor on April 6, 1882.[18]

Again, McKinley gave a powerful speech, this time to reassure protectionists they could vote for an overhaul of tariff schedules. Business should not fear "an intelligent and businesslike" revision of the tariffs as long as protectionists led the review. As the GOP's most influential voice on tariffs, McKinley's endorsement carried weight.[19]

The House and Senate voted to create a nine-member expert

committee, with their recommendations due in early December. While McKinley and his colleagues waited for the results of the commission's hearings, Democrats won back control of the House in the midterms.[20]

The commission's report in early December was a surprise. It proposed reducing duties an average of 25 percent on consumer items and raw materials needed for manufacturing that were not available in the United States, while keeping high duties on value-added goods produced domestically, like pig iron, scrap, and steel. Sugar went on the free list, but since the GOP's loss of the House meant Pig Iron would soon be out as Ways and Means chair, he ignored the report and pushed a bill reducing tariffs overall by just 1.47 percent, while raising them significantly on many critical items.

McKinley didn't like the measure. He was disappointed that Republicans failed to make reasonable cuts to the tariff schedules and expand the list of items imported free, thereby undercutting Democratic calls for greater reform. Derided as the "Mongrel Tariff" by critics, Kelley's bill was adopted late on March 3, the 47th Congress's final day. McKinley was one of a dozen Republican no votes. Arthur quickly signed the bill.[21]

McKinley was present when the new Democratic Congress met in December 1883. Though the Senate was unlikely to pass tariff reform, the popularity of tax cuts emboldened Democrats to raise the issue again to boost their chances for the 1884 presidential race. For the third time, McKinley would lead the House GOP opposition to another Democratic tariff bill.

Illinois Democrat and Ways and Means Committee chairman William R. Morrison offered a bill reducing duties 20 percent on all manufactured articles and expanding the free list. Speeches on the motion to take up the measure were so dry, it was suggested congressmen conduct debates from their bedrooms by telephone.[22]

Having just turned seventy and in ill health, Pig Iron deferred to McKinley, who gave the opening speech in opposition targeting Democratic protectionists, torn between party loyalty and their principles. McKinley attacked the bill as too complex. It set duties for too many goods, divided into too many categories, each with its own set of calculations. Morrison interrupted. Would the Major support a 20 percent across-the-board cut in all tariffs? McKinley turned the strength of Morrison's approach—simplicity—into a weakness. For some goods, the Major replied, a 20 percent cut would be justified but for many goods it would "destroy some of the great manufacturing industries."

McKinley went after the bill in a way that gave Democrats from working-class districts indigestion. It would "reduce the price of labor in the United States." He then closed by calling the bill a political document with no chance of becoming law. "No interest is pressing it," McKinley said. "No national necessity demands it. No true American wants it." He urged Democratic protectionists to stand firm. "The interests of this great people are higher and greater than the ambitions or interests of any party."[23]

After weeks of debate, McKinley announced that at the debate's end, a motion would be offered to strike the enacting clause, which left the bill in limbo unless another sponsor stepped forward. This clever maneuver gave protectionist Democrats cover to say they could support other versions of the bill with a different sponsor. In reality, it would kill it.[24]

Knowing the bill's fate would be settled by keeping Democratic protectionists, McKinley yielded to former Speaker Randall, who had orchestrated the 1878 gerrymander to defeat the Major. Randall spoke to a hushed chamber, explaining it would be "vindictive" to change the rules after businesses had invested in plants and equipment because of protection. Morrison's bill was "a firm, first step towards free trade." That question was better taken up after the presidential election, which would be decided by laborers, whose wages would be reduced by protection's end.

To emphasize the bill's bipartisan opposition and give Democrats further cover to vote no, McKinley had a Democrat, fellow Ohioan George L. Converse, move to strike the enacting clause. Morrison was named teller for the bill's supporters while Converse was named teller for its opponents. When Converse stood in front of the Democrats, Morrison snarled, "Get over on the other side where you belong." The tellers counted 159 to strike the enacting clause to 155 opposed. Forty-one Democrats and 118 Republicans were ayes, while 151 Democrats and only 4 Republicans were nays. Republicans and protectionist Democrats cheered, applauded, and waved papers. Pointing to the Republican side, Morrison said to Randall, "your friends are cheering you." The man who tried to end McKinley's career four years earlier with a gerrymander had helped him bring a victory for protection.[25]

McKinley did not celebrate long. Eighteen months earlier, he had a squeaker in the 1882 midterms. All Republicans faced stiff national head-winds, but there were bigger problems in Ohio. People complained that a Stark man had held the seat for three terms and that was enough. The Buckeye State GOP's tough anti-liquor stance hurt with German and Irish voters.[26]

When the ballots were tallied, McKinley defeated Democrat Jonathan H. Wallace, a Columbiana lawyer, by eight votes. The Major grumbled to Treasury secretary Charles J. Folger about his narrow victory. Just beaten for New York governor by the biggest margin in history, Folger responded, "Eight votes is a mighty big Republican majority this fall."[27]

But the election was not over. There was no chance Democrats would allow McKinley to remain in the House. It was just routine politics. Since the Civil War, both parties challenged close elections and, if they had a House majority, threw out their opposition and seated their party's man. So while McKinley was provisionally seated, Wallace announced he would ask the House Elections Committee in a new Democratic Congress to throw the Major out.[28]

Even though the House Elections subcommittee, with a Democratic majority, rejected Wallace's claim, on May 14, 1884, the full House Elections Committee overrode the subcommittee and recommended 6-to-5 to oust McKinley and replace him with Wallace. A week later, Elections chairman Henry Turner presented that recommendation to the House. At the day's end, Turner asked McKinley if he would speak. Members crowded around him, but his clear, strong voice could be heard throughout the chamber. A practical man, McKinley kept his remarks short. He knew with a Democratic majority, there would be only one outcome.[29]

"I only ask from this House, the majority of which is opposed to me politically, to administer in this case the law and the precedents which they have always administered," the Major said. No technicalities: if his reten-tion depended upon rejecting ballots where Wallace's name was misspelled, "then I do not want my seat." But even counting those, "I still have an unquestioned majority." He thanked members "on both sides . . . for the attention and courtesy with which they have listened." After applause sub-sided and McKinley finished shaking hands, Turner spent an hour talking while every Democrat was rounded up. Then McKinley was ousted. It was no surprise to him, who accepted expulsion with a fatalism afforded by his faith and by the fact his party had done the same to Democrats.

Seven Democrats voted for McKinley, among them some of his greatest adversaries on the tariff issue. Democrats and Republicans crowded around to express their regrets, while "none approached Wallace to congratulate him." McKinley collected his bags at the Ebbitt, attended an informal reception, and caught the 10 p.m. overnight to Canton. Even Democratic papers acknowledged he had been "one of the ablest and most accomplished members on the Republican side of the House."[30]

The political apprentice had risen in skill, leadership, and reputation, but after seven years in the House, his political career appeared finished. Earlier he had advised a friend not to seek office. "Before I went to Congress I had $10,000 and a practice worth $10,000 a year," McKinley said. "Now I haven't either."[31]

WILLIAM MCKINLEY MAY HAVE been thrown out of the House that May of 1884, but rather than destroy him, it made him a political martyr and helped create a successful political future. McKinley's opening speech against the Morrison tariff had made him a big star. In large part as a reaction to his ouster from the House, he was elected permanent chairman at the 1884 Ohio GOP convention and nominated as a national convention delegate. The latter was a problem. He supported James G. Blaine for president, but Ohio senator John Sherman was running. McKinley did not want to be put in a place of opposing him. He asked his name be withdrawn, but delegates yelled "no! no!" and "you cannot withdraw!" as he was elected by acclamation. When asked his presidential preference, McKinley dissembled, saying, "I absolutely haven't any."[32]

At the GOP national convention, McKinley would further his relationships with two Ohio men who would have a lot to do with his future. The first was another rising young Republican, whom McKinley met when he was Resolutions chairman at Ohio's state GOP convention in 1883.

Joseph Benson Foraker was then a thirty-six-year-old Cincinnati lawyer who had served three years as a Superior Court judge before resigning in 1879 for what he called a "temporary illness" (probably a breakdown). The outgoing governor, "Calico Charlie" Foster (a nickname from his career selling dry goods), supported him as his successor.[33]

Foraker campaigned forcefully, covering Ohio's eighty-eight counties and delivering three or four speeches a day. His oratorical skills earned him the nickname "Fire Alarm Joe," but he lost by 12,529 votes as two contro-versial antiliquor constitutional amendments went down, taking the GOP with them. McKinley stumped extensively, earning Foraker's gratitude. "I have never known any popular orator able to accomplish more than he," Foraker later wrote. McKinley returned Foraker's praise, writing him after the election, "no candidate for Governor has ever made a more brilliant canvass and the friends you made will stick to you through life." The for-mer might have been true, but not the latter.[34]

The second relationship was McKinley's friendship with Mark Hanna. The two men had bonded at the Ohio GOP gathering and were soon trading chatty letters about the upcoming national convention. Hanna told McKinley he was "gratified that we are to be partners in our efforts to name the next President." As it turns out, their alliance did lead to a future president, but not that year.[35]

When they arrived at the 1884 Republican National Convention, McKinley and Hanna shared the broadly held sentiment within the party that the incumbent Republican president, Chester A. Arthur, should not be nominated. But there they parted. Hanna was for Sherman. McKinley was for Arthur's leading challenger—Blaine, Garfield's secretary of state. Blaine was a reluctant candidate. Some of his political ambition died with Garfield. Arthur was reluctant, too, but pride and animus toward Blaine kept him in the race.[36]

The convention was held in Chicago's Exposition Center, its podium draped with Union battle flags, with portraits of Washington, Lincoln, and Garfield over the stage. Delegates were seated in oak chairs with McKinley's Ohio at the front left. Foraker sat in the first row next to a stanchion with a red, white, and blue shield on top from which hung a blue silk banner that read OHIO, with the state's motto and insignia. Each delegation had a similar banner. McKinley sat behind Foraker. Imme-diately at his back was the "Blind Orator," Judge William H. West, like McKinley a Blaine man.[37]

Neither Blaine nor Arthur had enough votes to win on the first ballot, so the balance of power rested with favorite sons such as Sherman, but only if Ohio's delegates were united. They weren't. Foraker unsuccessfully pleaded with the Ohio Blaine men to support Sherman at the delegation's meeting. But McKinley had made his commitment and would keep it. Foraker was not happy with his new friend's refusal.[38]

While the Blaine men lost the test vote over the temporary chairman, the anti-Blaine forces were themselves divided and unable to coalesce around one candidate. Ohio split on the vote, which killed Sherman's chances by showing his home state was not united. The *New-York Tribune* declared, "Sherman is out of the race" and "his friends are charged with treachery," meaning McKinley and the Buckeye Blaine men. Foraker agreed on both points.[39]

The Blaine faction elected the remaining convention officials, including McKinley, who was made Resolutions chairman. It was unusual for a first-time delegate to be given such an important role, but smart to name a Blaine man from a critical state, especially when its favorite son was being slow-rolled out of contention. The Major had also handled the platform duties at his state convention well and his expulsion from the House and leadership on protection gave him stature.

McKinley showed that this confidence was well placed as he wrote a strongly protectionist platform that was well received and adopted unanimously. When the convention chairman lost his voice—and with it, control of a heated fight over reducing Southern representation at future conventions—McKinley replaced him and used his strong, calming voice to restore order and guide the debate to a close.[40]

The convention reconvened that evening for nominations. After two lesser candidates were named, Maine yielded to Ohio. From his seat behind McKinley, Judge West rose and was guided to the stage. The "Blind Orator" whipped the crowd into a frenzy by describing his candidate, then launched a near riot by using Blaine's name. With McKinley and other Blaine men cheering, the demonstration took twenty minutes to burn out, despite the band's best efforts to end it. Arthur's name was then offered, to a much less enthusiastic reception. It was after 11 p.m. when Foraker appeared onstage.[41]

Foraker undermined Senator Sherman with his nomination speech. "Fire Alarm" Joe opened by saying Republicans would carry Ohio, suggesting it did not matter who the nominee was. Later, apropos of nothing he said, "No man's admiration is greater than mine for that brilliant genius from Maine." The gratuitous Blaine tribute had the "effect of a match in a powder magazine," wrote a reporter. The frenzied mass of delegates cheered and the galleries turned into a swaying, yelling mob, screaming for Blaine. When order was finally restored, Foraker described what Republicans desired in their nominee. Blaine supporters took to chanting their candidate's name at the end of each sentence.[42]

When nominations finished, Foraker unwisely moved that the convention vote. It was after midnight. Blaine had momentum and yet as Sherman's manager, Fire Alarm was trying to speed up the process. Wanting the balloting the next day, the Blaine camp moved to adjourn. By now the hall was chaotic. Order had to be restored. McKinley had had enough of the chaos caused by Foraker's foolishness. He collected leaders for all the contenders, convinced them voting after midnight was in no one's interest, got the chair's attention, and announced, "The gentlemen all around us are willing that the motion to adjourn until 11 o'clock this morning shall prevail." McKinley suggested a voice vote, which carried at 1:46 a.m. Delegates went to grab a few hours' sleep.[43]

That night, Foraker established his national reputation as an orator but made two mistakes. He claimed he "innocently precipitated" the Blaine demonstration by praising the Maine candidate, but there were always suspicions it was deliberate. And he also foolishly tried rushing a late-night vote. By contrast, McKinley exhibited rare poise for a novice, stepping in to calm a floor fight and then saving the convention from picking its nominee in the middle of the night. Here, thought many party leaders, was a young man with judgment and leadership.[44]

After three days, the anti-Blaine men still had no strategy. It showed when voting began Friday midday. Interrupted by frequent demands for states to be polled, it took twelve hours to cast three ballots, with Blaine gaining on each one. After the third ballot at 1 a.m., Illinois appeared ready to move to Blaine, which would stampede the convention. Foraker moved to adjourn. Blaine's managers protested and the hall dissolved into chaos, with delegates screaming as the chairman tried organizing a fourth ballot. After nearly half an hour of disarray, McKinley rose, quieted the crowd, and declared, "I hope no friend of James G. Blaine will object to having the roll call of the States made." Call the roll and "vote the proposition down." Again, the Major calmed the waters and the motion to adjourn was defeated.[45]

Unexpectedly, Foraker then rose to nominate Blaine by acclamation. Arthur men screamed "No! No!" while Blaine men cheered this premature surrender. The floor dissolved into a mess, with men screaming motions and making demands. Foraker withdrew his motion. By now guests were stamping their feet and chanting Blaine's name. Then Senator John "Black Eagle" Logan delivered Illinois's 31 votes to Blaine and Ohio's remaining Sherman men abandoned their man. Blaine won with 541, to 207 for Arthur. The hall exploded with delegates and guests cheering and screaming and waving whatever was close at hand. A conga line appeared on the floor, with Coloradoans hoisting a stuffed eagle and Kansans unfurling a large blue state flag displaying sheaves of wheat and bunches of corn. Cannons boomed outside.[46]

While the Major's performance won him admirers across the country, Sherman was unhappy, writing Foraker, "The unexpected defection of McKinley . . . made your task difficult." McKinley had work to do to repair his relationship with his state's powerful senior senator.[47]

BUT FIRST, THE MAJOR would have to get himself back in Congress. Democrats had gerrymandered him again, throwing Stark into the adjoining district centered on Summit County and represented by Democratic Representative David R. Paige. It had a comfortable, though not large, Democratic edge of 900 votes.

Republicans made McKinley's reelection a priority, pouring resources and speakers into it. Hanna, impressed by the Major's national convention performance, was eager to help his new friend, urging associates in Massillon to reelect McKinley. "All our interests demand it," he wrote. McKinley focused on laborers, circulating tributes from the strikers he had defended in 1876 that called him "the working man's friend." He also stumped with "Uncle" Shelby Cullom, an Illinois U.S. senator popular with farmers.[48]

In an extraordinary testament to McKinley's loyalty at the convention and the importance Republicans placed on his return to Congress, Blaine, the GOP presidential nominee, appeared for the Major in late September events in Akron and Stark County. A banner at an Akron parade on one side of the Barber Match Company wagon proclaimed, WE HAVE NO FAITH IN THE DEMOCRATIC PARTY, BECAUSE IT HAS WRONGED THE COUNTRY ONCE AND HAS NOT YET REPENTED THEREFOR. On the other side it promised, WE WILL LIGHT YOU ON TO VICTORY IN OCTOBER.[49]

All these efforts paid off on October 14 as McKinley defeated Paige, 52 percent to 48 percent, with a 2,019-vote margin despite the district's Democratic edge. Jonathan H. Wallace, the Democrat seated when McKinley was ejected from the House, was also beaten.[50]

For the next two years, McKinley enjoyed so much popularity at home that in 1886, Democrats could not recruit a candidate until a month before the election. In what was supposed to be a competitive district, McKinley cruised to a 54 percent to 46 percent victory and became one of the senior Republicans in the House.[51]

During those years, McKinley also had to navigate Ohio politics, as he became a recognized statewide leader and was urged to run for governor in 1885. He declined. Whatever McKinley thought after the 1884 national convention, he wanted to help elect Foraker. Better to have potential rivals beholden than to deny them help easily given and difficult not to reciprocate.[52]

Foraker again forcefully stumped in a campaign that revolved around black voting rights, liquor regulation, and charges Standard Oil money was used to elect Democratic U.S. senator Henry B. Payne. As Foraker's man in northeast Ohio, Hanna served on the campaign's executive committee while McKinley spoke extensively for the ticket. Foraker won by 17,451 votes. McKinley now had a friend in the governor's office, but was the state big enough for two rising Republican stars?[53]

Their difficulties began quickly. The oil inspector was state government's most lucrative post. Paid big fees by Ohio's many refineries, the inspector had an army of patronage jobs. McKinley and Hanna both recommended allies for the job. Hanna complained about McKinley's interest to the governor, saying, "He wants the earth." Foraker reappointed the incumbent, stinging Hanna, who thought he was close to Fire Alarm.[54]

AFTER CLEVELAND CAPTURED THE White House for the Democrats in 1884, Hanna decided he wanted to run a presidential campaign and thereby become "a national political luminary." After settling on Sherman, Hanna set out to make him the nominee in 1888, using business contacts throughout the country and frequently meeting with the Ohio senator in Washington to plot moves. He even attempted to recruit Foraker, asking him to lobby Michigan governor Russell A. Alger to endorse Sherman.

Foraker probably received the request cordially but likely seethed in private. He and Alger both saw themselves as candidates.[55]

As governor, Fire Alarm Joe had begun moving around the country, causing a presidential boomlet he found "gratifying," but admitted later was "the beginning of trouble." The trouble was that Sherman wanted to run again and this time, McKinley and Hanna both supported him. Uneasy about the ambitious governor, the Sherman men decided to seek a formal endorsement of the senator at the 1887 state convention. Knowing that could keep him from running, Foraker opposed the move but failed to stop it. Hanna then invited Foraker to a war council with Sherman and McKinley to plot strategy, but Foraker refused. The governor didn't want to be hot-boxed into closing his options.[56]

At the meeting in late June 1887 in Canton, whatever animosity Sherman had toward McKinley from the last national convention dissipated. The two men had developed a sincere friendship. Hanna wrote Foraker about the meeting in advance, but still the governor complained to Sherman that it was held "without notice to me" and a hostile war council, where "a lot of political Indians were getting ready for the war path."[57]

The Ohio oil inspector's job came up after Foraker won reelection that fall. Ready to cut ties with both men, Foraker appointed George Cox, a Cincinnati machine Republican. If the governor sought higher office, better to have the oil inspector's patronage and money controlled by a close ally. This effectively ended Hanna's once self-described "lively admiration and warm friendship" with Foraker.[58]

The relationship between these two young, ambitious Ohio Republicans—Foraker and McKinley—would become complicated. They would soon be at odds over more important things than the oil inspector's patronage.

CHAPTER 5

Three Steps Closer, One Step Back

———◇———

The economy was one of the most important forces shaping America and therefore its politics in 1888. After the Panic of 1873, the country saw rapid growth in the 1880s, particularly in the North. As the economy industrialized, more laborers saw high tariffs as helping secure their jobs. Southern and Western farmers, hit by drought and dependent upon the success or failure of foreign harvests, did not. They blamed protection for making every imported good they bought—from sugar to dishware to clothes, fabric, and other necessities—more expensive and condemned the gold standard for making credit tight, farm prices too low, and currency less available.[1]

Then there was the Democratic Party's recovery. In 1884, New York governor Grover Cleveland became the first Democratic president since the Civil War. He won because of a complicated confluence of circumstances. The South was made solidly Democratic by the repression of black and white Republicans and the North splintered by three factors. Insurgent Republicans defected, drawn by Cleveland's promise of civil service reforms and repulsed by questions about Blaine's character. The Prohibitionist Party drew just enough GOP voters to cost Republicans key states. And the economy faltered in 1884 when a Republican was in the White House.

Even then, the race was close. It was a party victory for Cleveland and a personal defeat for Blaine. Cleveland's victory depended upon what one historian calls Blaine's "series of accidents, misjudgments and shortfalls," including his famous failure to quickly renounce a supporter's charge in the election's closing days that Cleveland stood for "Rum, Romanism, and Rebellion."

AS PRESIDENT, CLEVELAND MADE two major attempts to reduce tariffs, framing his efforts as responsibly reducing the government's budget surpluses by returning it to working people in tax cuts. Both times, Cleveland's principal opponent in the House was McKinley, who would soon be called the "Napoleon of Protection" for his staunch defense of high tariffs.

Democrats made their first attempt in 1886, believing that cutting tariffs while the government was running a $100 million surplus would help the party in the midterms. Ways and Means chairman William R. Morrison prepared a tariff reduction bill, déjà vu from two years earlier.[2]

Once again, McKinley led the GOP opposition. He needed a new playbook because many of Randall's Democratic protectionists were gone—defeated or retired. Thus he paid special attention to issues affecting wool growers and other farmers adversely affected by Morrison's bill, hoping to peel off rural Democrats. The strategy was tested on June 17 when the House considered whether to take up Morrison's new bill.

Outwardly confident, Morrison was worried, telling Cleveland the night before that though Democrats were the majority, he might not have the votes. He didn't. The motion to consider his bill failed, 140 ayes (4 Republicans and 136 Democrats) to 157 nays (122 Republicans and 35 Democrats). McKinley had outflanked Morrison by winning Northern Democrats from agricultural districts. Morrison threatened to try again. McKinley replied, "We'll be ready to meet you then," before sitting down to applause. The bill was not brought up again.[3]

A year and a half later, Cleveland tried again, sending a blistering annual message to Congress focused on one subject: the need to reduce tariffs, an issue "upon which every element of our prosperity depends." Because tariffs were too high, the federal government's surplus was too large, Cleveland thundered, an "indefensible and a culpable betrayal of fairness and justice." These "inequitable and illegal" taxes must be immediately cut for the benefit of laborers, farmers, and families.[4]

McKinley laid out the GOP case against this newest Democratic tariff reform at a Boston Home Market Club dinner in early February 1888 with a well-prepared speech. As an alternative to gutting protection, he called for ending domestic taxation and picked apart the arguments for free trade, suggesting it would bring down the economy. Guests gave "a round of hearty cheers." It was another impressive performance and excellent preparation for this coming fight.[5]

It took the new Ways and Means chairman, Roger Q. Mills of Texas, until April 2 to present his bill to the House. It dramatically expanded the list of duty-free items and slashed tariffs on pig iron, rails, glass, earthenware, and woolen goods. The House clerk, who moonlighted as a *Louisville Courier-Journal* reporter, leaked the bill in advance, giving McKinley time to write a committee minority report.

McKinley excoriated the majority for writing the legislation in secret, "without the knowledge of the minority and . . . discussion in full committee" or comments from affected industries or workers. McKinley characterized the Mills bill as "a radical reversal of the tariff policy of the country," calling it "disastrous if not entirely ruinous to many American industries." It was also crassly political, meant to be the Democratic platform in the coming presidential election. McKinley's mentor, Pig Iron Kelley, was delighted with "every sentence of the Major's report."[6]

McKinley led the GOP floor debate. Democrats outnumbered Republicans 170 to 154. The platoon of Democratic protectionists had been thinned in recent years and was under intense pressure from the administration, which threatened to withhold patronage.

Still leader of the high-tariff Democratic Party, Randall joined McKinley in mid-May to double-team Mills. Ill and weak, Randall hit the bill for cutting tariffs rather than direct internal taxes and appealed to Democratic protectionists to support Jefferson's tariff principles. His time ran out before he finished and Mills refused to let him continue, drawing the ire of friends and foes alike. McKinley yielded some of the Republicans' time to the former Democratic Speaker before taking the floor himself.[7]

McKinley began by echoing Randall's call for cutting direct internal taxes, then rejected Mills's claim that it was impossible for a workingman to buy a $10 suit, asserting it could be done. Leopold Morse, a Massachusetts Democrat and haberdasher, heckled McKinley, saying, "Not at my store." The Major turned on him, producing a suit bought from Morse's store, waving a bill of sale for $10 and asking, "Come now, will the gentleman from Massachusetts know his own goods?" The House dissolved into laughter. When he finished, McKinley was mobbed by colleagues and received "round after round of applause."[8]

Randall's platoon of Democratic protectionists had shrunk to a squad: four Democrats joined the Republicans in opposition but Democrats were in the majority and approved the Mills bill and sent it to the Senate, where Republican senators mangled it, leaving it to die before the election.[9]

WHEN OHIO REPUBLICANS LEFT for their national convention in Chicago in June 1888, McKinley's pick was Sherman. His loyalty to his candidate would help the Major capture the national spotlight.

Foraker, always driven by his own ambition, was outwardly supportive of the senator, but privately hoped to be on the ticket. Foraker may have dispatched a lieutenant, Asa Bushnell, a Springfield businessman and former state GOP chairman, to parley earlier that spring with New York's "Easy Boss," Thomas Collier Platt, and Pennsylvania's boss, Senator Matthew S. Quay, about Fire Alarm's candidacy. In March 1888, papers reported on Foraker's outreach efforts. Perhaps to distract attention, the governor bitterly complained to Hanna about being left out of Sherman's preparations, despite being the nominal head of the Ohio delegation.[10]

Foraker then got word that Hanna was to be Sherman's convention manager and someone else would nominate Sherman. Apparently the Sherman men did not trust Foraker with reprising either of his roles from the last convention. All this made Foraker petty. He complained to Hanna in May about giving up his hotel rooms next to the delegation headquarters and being moved to a nicer suite one floor up. "I prefer to retain my rooms." His ambitions burned even hotter after Democrats nominated Allen G. Thurman of Ohio for vice president in early June. Shouldn't Republicans turn to a young, rising Ohio man, like its forty-two-year-old governor, for vice president if not the top slot?[11]

But as the convention approached, everyone's attention was on James G. Blaine. As the party's candidate in 1884 and a firm advocate of protection, Blaine had a large, loyal following. But he didn't want the nomination. He dreaded another campaign and, as a hypochondriac, believed it could kill him. Instead, he hoped to have a second turn at secretary of state. Some delegates thought they should nominate him anyway.[12]

The prospect of convention chaos made one group extremely happy—the party's bosses. Blaine's popularity ensured no one else could steamroll the convention. With a murky outcome, the bosses could offer support in exchange for patronage and cabinet posts.

When the national convention opened, the jockeying was well under way. Most of Sherman's managers had been in town plotting for days. Hanna dominated their second-floor headquarters at the Grand Pacific hotel, working in shirtsleeves, fanning himself, and mopping his brow with what looked like an American flag. He told reporters Sherman would have 300 votes on the first ballot, in striking distance of the nomination. McKinley publicly pegged Sherman's support at 360. Both were raising expectations when they should have been lowering them.[13]

Amid the spectacle of the convention's opening day, two developments stood out. The first was the appearance of colorful ribbons with Foraker's face and below his image, the words "No rebel flags shall be surrendered while I am governor," a jab at President Cleveland's call for Ohio to return captured Confederate battle flags. At the top was his slogan, "Vim, Vigor, Victory."[14]

The second development was the quiet and growing trust in an emerging national leader whom many thought worthy of the presidency. Remembering his important role in the 1884 convention, all the factions settled on McKinley as chairman of the Resolutions Committee to draft the party's platform.[15]

On the second day, delegates called on Foraker, still angling to be on the ticket, to speak. He obliged with a punchy address, saying they had to write a platform and choose a candidate. The first was "not difficult," he said. "There is not an intelligent schoolboy in all the land who does not already know what our declarations will be." It was a shot at McKinley, who was in charge of drafting the platform. Foraker then described the right candidate's qualities as good moral character and loyalty to the Union. It was general enough to apply to almost anyone, including himself. The *Chicago Tribune* reported the speech made "Gov. Foraker the favorite of the convention." McKinley and Hanna knew what Foraker was doing.[16]

The third morning, McKinley received a standing ovation when he appeared onstage to read the platform, wearing a red, white, and blue Sherman badge. He attacked Southern violence against black voters, slammed Democratic tariff reform as favoring Europe over the United States, and called for reducing the federal government's surplus by cutting taxes or slashing duties on tobacco and goods made abroad that "cannot be produced at home." Another plank backed "the use of both gold and silver as money" and criticized Cleveland's efforts "to demonetize silver." McKinley did not want to take a position on the politically volatile topic and was back to straddling the currency issue. He was interrupted thirty-two times by applause. The platform was adopted unanimously.[17]

The convention's main event—nominating the party's ticket— followed. Lesser figures were put forward first. The real action started with the nomination of former Indiana senator Benjamin Harrison, a successful lawyer who fought under General William T. Sherman, the Ohio senator's brother. Harrison was severe and unbending, but inexplicably popular in his quintessential swing state.[18]

Iowa offered Senator William B. Allison, a quiet legislator with a talent for compromise. Michigan nominated Russell Alger, the state's governor, who had fought under George Armstrong Custer at Gettysburg. Platt's New Yorkers offered Chauncey Depew, a Yale-educated lawyer who managed the fabulously wealthy Vanderbilt family's interests. He was a placeholder. The Easy Boss, Platt, knew Depew could not win, but his candidacy united New York, which would help Platt when he moved the state's delegates to his eventual pick.[19]

To show that Sherman had substantial support outside his own state, a Pennsylvanian, Daniel H. Hastings, placed Sherman's name in nomination, with Foraker seconding him. But it did little good. Sherman led on the first ballot, but with only 229 votes, far fewer than Hanna and McKinley had predicted. After peaking on the second ballot, Sherman began declining on the third, a sign his candidacy was dead. The anti-machine men moved to adjourn so they could regroup and come up with a new candidate.[20]

There was growing sentiment that if Sherman couldn't win, then the party's most consequential protectionist advocate, McKinley, should be put into play. The idea took root in many states. Texans claimed nearly two dozen delegates from their state would support McKinley as soon as Blaine faltered. A caucus of Connecticut, New York, Pennsylvania, and other delegations agreed to support McKinley "should a favorable moment arrive." Congressional colleagues wired encouragement. Support came from men who admired McKinley's leadership in the tariff fights and his oratorical prowess, as well as from some bosses who were interested in further scrambling the convention.[21]

This troubled the Major, who discussed it with Hanna around a table at Sherman's Grand Pacific headquarters. As the men fanned themselves and smoked cigars, McKinley reached for a blank telegram form and wrote a short statement explaining he would refuse to be drafted. Hanna was impressed by what he read and then later by what he would hear.[22]

When the convention reconvened Saturday, the *Chicago Times* endorsed a Blaine-McKinley ticket, but delegates were realizing Blaine was unavailable, so they were turning to the Major. When he received a vote from Connecticut early in the roll call, he stood on a chair and nervously sought recognition from the stage. Once called on, he waited until delegates fell silent.

McKinley then told them he was bound by his state party to support Sherman, a responsibility "my heart and my judgment approved." Someone yelled "Sit down, we'll make you president," but saying Sherman "trusted me in his cause," McKinley continued. "I cannot with my sense of personal integrity, permit my name to be used in this convention." He asked that delegates not vote for him and stepped down to a thunderous ovation.[23]

Hanna was dumbstruck, later writing, "For the first time, it occurred to me that he was a logical candidate for the presidency in years to come." If McKinley had entered the race, Hanna thought, he would have immediately won many Blaine men and Harrison backers. But personal honor made him refuse. His selflessness convinced Hanna that the Major "was destined to become a great power in national politics."[24]

On the fourth ballot, Sherman kept dropping, ending at 235, only 19 ahead of Harrison. Despite McKinley's plea, he received 11 votes. The fifth ballot ended with Harrison at 212 to Sherman's 224 with Alger and Blaine growing modestly. Things were so unclear that when the convention returned at 4 p.m., it recessed until Monday. The afternoon session had lasted just thirty minutes.[25]

Pressure was mounting for McKinley to run amid rumors Blaine would declare. Foraker chose this moment to tell reporters it was his "duty toward Mr. Sherman as well as the party" to vote for Blaine and bring most of Ohio with him. "I have been faithful and true to Mr. Sherman," he said. "I cannot be accused of unfaithfulness or treachery," just as his words and actions justified charges of both. Foraker's ambition, ego, and his irritation at the attention given McKinley led him to defect.[26]

The bosses pressured McKinley to become a candidate, but the Major refused to abandon Sherman. It was not a reaction the Easy Boss understood. Calico Charlie Foster later told a friend he heard McKinley "use violent profanity only once in his life. It was when he refused to be nominated by the Platt crowd at the convention of 1888."[27]

Hanna wired Sherman to suggest that only McKinley could prevent Blaine's nomination. "Who do you advise? Can Ohio afford to lose this opportunity? I regret the situation but fear I am right." Sherman wired back: "Let my name stand. I prefer defeat to retreat." If McKinley entered the race, it would be "a break of implicit faith."[28]

Delegates tried to make McKinley break that faith. Californians said if not Blaine, then McKinley, who had "an unmistakably good feeling" among their delegates. He would get 25 of the 28 Massachusetts delegation, according to its secretary. Illinois was ready to split, half for Blaine, half for McKinley. Connecticut leaned toward the Major.

Worried his convention plea was not enough, McKinley visited delegations Saturday night to personally ask them to stop. Told that 15 of New Jersey's 18 delegates would vote for him, McKinley said that he would rather lose his "good right arm" than accept a nomination that way. Impressed, the delegation's chairman, Garret A. Hobart, backed off. When McKinley got to sleep early Sunday morning, he was awakened by Ohioans in the next room plotting to nominate him. The Major appeared in his nightgown and demanded they cease.[29]

Sunday morning, Andrew Carnegie, who was hosting Blaine at his Scottish castle, wired a second time that Blaine was not a candidate and favored Harrison. Party leaders sent agents to Indianapolis to meet with Harrison after church and that afternoon Platt took a ride with Stephen B. Elkins, a key Harrison advisor, and returned believing he would be secretary of the Treasury in a Harrison administration, with all the customhouse patronage.[30]

Harrison was nominated Monday after three more ballots. Sherman's star had, as far as the presidency was concerned, winked out. Yet Hanna discovered a new man in whom he could invest his skills, energy, and purse. At forty-five, McKinley was young and energetic, with achievements that attracted many Republicans. The "exasperating days of the Chicago convention" inspired Hanna to devote himself to making McKinley president.[31]

Hayes agreed that his former comrade's reputation had grown, telling McKinley, "You gained gloriously." While ambition was necessary in politics, Hayes believed "the surest path to the White House" was to never allow "ambition to get there to stand in the way of any duty, large or small."[32]

McKinley and Hanna left Chicago, wiser in the ways of convention politics. For the second time, the two men had seen how chaotic and unpredictable a convention could become. They observed the power of machine states like New York and Pennsylvania. From inside Sherman's campaign, they learned more about how to manage men, expectations, message, and momentum, sometimes through the cruel expedient of mistakes. They saw that a candidate needed a united home state to win and realized that was difficult to achieve in factionalized Ohio. They also understood that McKinley had a growing national clout, not simply from his leadership for protection and his impressive stints as Resolutions chairman but also from the impression that he "waved aside the glittering temptations of the Presidency rather than betray a friend."[33]

McKinley and Hanna also picked up lessons from the fall campaign. McKinley easily won reelection but the presidential race was very close. Harrison beat the incumbent, Cleveland, by winning twenty states with 233 electoral votes but lost the popular vote by 90,592, or 0.8 percent, as Cleveland carried eighteen states. Three of them had black majorities— Louisiana, Mississippi, and South Carolina—that might have gone Republican if blacks had not been kept from voting.

Republicans were successful in large part because Pennsylvania senator Quay—who managed the Harrison campaign—concentrated money, speakers, literature, and organization on the four swing states of Indiana, New York, Connecticut, and New Jersey. Harrison carried the first two and with them, the Electoral College, and nearly won the last two. Quay also strengthened the GOP's outreach in the border states and the upper South, leaving Harrison almost taking Maryland, Missouri, North Carolina, Virginia, and West Virginia.[34]

Additionally, Senate Republicans helped the GOP campaign effort by presenting an alternative to the Democrats' tariff-for-revenue. They passed a bill to cut internal taxes to reduce the surplus while GOP orators exploited weaknesses in a Democratic tariff bill. This allowed Republicans to play offense the entire campaign. The party's orators borrowed generously from McKinley in framing the tariff debate around pocketbook issues and nationalism, talking about jobs, wages, and growing markets and pounding British support for free trade. By contrast, Democrats often sounded incoherent. Cleveland did not campaign or even vote, and the DNC effort was disorganized.[35]

McKinley and Hanna were impressed by Quay's disciplined focus and saw the vital role of organization and money targeted at the right places. They learned the power of a broad campaign of persuasion to educate and convert and understood that in a close race, victory depends on using resources wisely and presenting policies like protection in ways that allowed voters to see how their daily lives would be improved.[36]

THE 1888 ELECTION HAD another powerful implication for McKinley. Republicans won the House, which meant they would elect a new Speaker. Some colleagues began promoting him for the post, which would be filled in December 1889 when the 51st Congress would meet.[37]

But first, McKinley had to contend with a political problem at home. Foraker wanted another term as governor, but no one had ever served three consecutive terms. Some Republicans worried Foraker would lose. While McKinley's name was widely discussed as a possible replacement, the Major agreed to nominate a constituent, Asa Jones, for governor. Seven other men ran, including Foraker.[38]

Nonetheless, Foraker won renomination. When the Major moved to smooth over ruffled feathers by calling for the nomination to be made unanimous, Foraker repaid the courtesy by saying McKinley should be elected senator. But the *Plain Dealer* read the situation correctly: the governor "was looking at McKinley but talking for Foraker."[39]

The 1889 general election was brutal and close, like most Ohio contests. On October 4, Murat Halstead's *Cincinnati Commercial Gazette* claimed the newspaper had documents proving James E. Campbell, the Democrat candidate, sponsored a bill in Congress requiring a standardized ballot box after secretly signing a deal with its manufacturer for a share of the profits. Campbell called Halstead "a double liar" and challenged him to produce the documents. Foraker pounced, claiming Campbell's scheme was an attempt to "steal a million dollars" and started carrying one of the ballot boxes onstage with him.[40]

Halstead refused to print the contract, but Democrats found it and made it public. It included signatures from prominent Republican investors in the "Ballot Box Trust," including McKinley, Sherman, and Vice President Levi Morton, and Democratic Speaker John G. Carlisle. It was explosive, but a hoax. The signatures had been traced from official documents and Halstead duped by the box's manufacturer, Richard G. Wood, who fled to Canada.[41]

Foraker had let ambition cloud his judgment and called the state's senior GOP senator (Sherman) and most popular GOP congressman (McKinley) crooks. In November, Fire Alarm Joe lost reelection by 10,872 votes, or just over 1 percent.[42]

McKinley probably regretted losing the governorship, but not Foraker's defeat. Regardless, the Major had little time to ruminate. He was campaigning for Speaker. McKinley was a strong candidate but not the front-runner. That was Maine's Thomas B. Reed, a man of substantial girth whose enormous forehead made him appear larger than he was. He had deep, dark eyes and a walrus mustache, which made him look like a six-foot-three, three-hundred-pound bowling pin with facial hair. He was an intellectual with a library of five thousand books, Maine's largest private collection. Five hundred volumes were in French. His wit was fast and cutting, his humor irreverent and biting. He was feared more often than loved. The election was November 30, 1889, two days before the 51st Congress held its first session.[43]

Five men were running. Since McKinley refused to solicit support, Hanna established a war room at the Ebbitt a week before the election and canvassed for commitments. Other members and friends helped, such as Minnesota governor William R. Merriam, who worked his state's delegation. Freshman Ohio congressman Charles H. Grosvenor kept a tally of commitments.[44]

Massachusetts congressman Henry Cabot Lodge ran Reed's headquarters at the Wormley Hotel. To canvass new members from freshly admitted Western states, Lodge recruited Teddy Roosevelt, along with former South Dakota territorial delegate Richard F. Pettigrew.[45]

It took two ballots. Reed led the first with 78, six short of a majority.

McKinley was in second at 39. A Reed man from Oregon arrived in time for the second ballot. Roosevelt and Pettigrew converted four new Western congressmen to Reed and two non-Westerners moved to Reed, putting him over the top by a single vote. The Major moved to make the vote unanimous. This was not the last time the two men would compete.[46]

Afterward, Roosevelt told McKinley that while he didn't support him for Speaker, he "hoped some time to vote for him as President." That was unlikely if Reed ran. Grosvenor was sour, claiming McKinley had twenty-one more pledges than votes. McKinley viewed the discrepancy as proof of man's moral frailty rather than a comment on Hanna's efforts. One Ohio congressman said of Hanna's work, "I do not know that he was influential but he was certainly active."[47]

Since McKinley's countenance reminded him of the former French emperor, Reed had taken to calling him "Napoleon" behind his back and confided in his diary that he thought McKinley was "a man of little scope." Still, Reed named him Ways and Means Committee chairman. That made sense. Reed was the parliamentarian, McKinley the expert on protection. Reed didn't want to lead the tariff battle. "Last night," the Speaker had written in his diary, "I studied Protection. There is a Sahara." The issue was too dry and arid to interest Reed.[48]

With the House narrowly divided, Democrats signaled they would obstruct Republicans by refusing to answer roll calls on the House floor, thereby denying the House a quorum to conduct business. Reed soon directed the clerk to list as "present" any member on the floor and declared a quorum. When a Democrat claimed Reed had no right to count him present, Reed responded, "The Chair is making a statement of fact that the gentleman from Kentucky is present. Does he deny it?" Congressman William H. "Howdy" Martin of Texas, a six-foot-six veteran of Hood's Confederate Brigade, threatened to forcibly remove Reed from the dais. Reed didn't flinch. Martin took to sharpening his Bowie knife on his boot sole each day while sitting in front of the Speaker. But led by McKinley and Congressman Joe Cannon, the House sustained the Speaker's ruling and Republicans began moving legislation.[49]

McKinley entered Reed's "Sahara" immediately. After Harrison's election as the first Republican president with a GOP House and Senate since 1874, Republicans believed they had a responsibility to reduce the surplus by revising the tariff schedules upon the principle of protection. Harrison raised the issue in his inaugural and in his annual message to Congress.[50]

Fortunately for McKinley, his defeat for Speaker allowed him to tackle the most important issue dividing the parties. Showing he had already given the matter great thought, McKinley quickly offered two bills in early December. One reformed the customs system and was approved in June 1890. Despite Democratic criticism, the law was left unchanged the next time their party controlled Washington.[51]

The other bill was loosely based on legislation Senator Allison had already drafted. McKinley's version made three major changes in the tariff system. For the first time, it levied duties on all foreign agricultural imports. Republicans were worried about growing discontent among farmers, hit hard by drought and dropping prices. Every foreign farm import that was also produced in America, from barley to beans and meat to tobacco, now had a duty or, in the case of wool, a higher one.[52]

The second major change reduced the surplus by adding sugar to the free list and cutting internal taxes on tobacco. Americans had long grumbled at paying $55 million a year in sugar duties. Southern cane growers would receive a bounty for each pound they produced to keep their plantations profitable.

Finally, the bill addressed inequities that had grown or been discovered in recent years, generally by modestly raising tariffs or, in dozens of cases, adding items to the free list. The most prominent change was a new 2.2¢-per-pound duty on tinplate. Tin was on the free list, but the absence of a tinplate tariff meant the country was flooded with finished tin imports while America's nascent tinplate industry floundered.[53]

McKinley often worked past midnight, meeting with interested parties at the committee rooms, accepting callers at his Ebbitt office, and handling mounds of letters and reports. Ida complained to Hayes, "My good husband's time is all occupied so that I see but little of him."[54]

Anyone who wanted to testify did so at the committee's open hearings each morning. McKinley and other members smoked cigars as 1,400 pages of testimony were collected. If the Major thought an industry was being "selfishly demanding," a reporter observed, he would ask questions "as to what the industry required to be prosperous, not what the man required to be rich." After three weeks of floor debate and following the addition of the tinplate tariff by the margin of a single vote, McKinley's bill passed the House by 164 to 142, with no Democratic support and two Republicans opposed. The bill went to the Senate Finance Committee, which reported its version June 18.[55]

Colorado senator Henry M. Teller and Western silver Republicans held the bill hostage, demanding free coinage to pry it loose from the Senate. Senator Sherman proposed replacing Bland-Allison by requiring that the Treasury increase its purchases to 4.5 million ounces a month, virtually all the U.S. domestic production. Paying with Treasury notes redeemable in gold or silver would increase the money supply. Still, Free Silver men were not happy, with Missouri senator Francis M. Cockrell saying there was "not a scintilla" of free coinage in the bill because it limited the government's silver purchases and Alabama senator John Morgan, a former Ku Klux Klan Grand Dragon, denouncing Sherman's "fine Italian hand." But mining state Republicans released the tariff bill. People insisted on redeeming the Treasury notes in gold, not silver, drawing down the nation's gold reserves.[56]

McKinley's tariff bill hit another snag. Blaine—who got another turn as secretary of state—wanted Latin American countries that benefited from sugar's addition to the free list to reduce tariff barriers to American goods or else lose their trading advantage. Blaine felt a reciprocity clause would calm farm belt discontent and undermine the emerging Populist movement. Blaine's reciprocity amendment became one of the bill's major features. The Senate approved the measure September 11 after 496 amendments by Rhode Island senator Nelson Aldrich, the bill's Senate manager, so it went to a conference committee to work out the differences.[57]

By September 26, 1890, House conferees had accepted 272 of the Senate amendments and negotiated compromises on 173 more while the Senate withdrew the rest. McKinley complained to colleagues, "I scarcely know what will be the end of it." Members were eager to go home to campaign, so on October 1, both chambers approved the modified bill with little debate. Harrison came to the Capitol to sign it before Congress adjourned two and a half hours later.[58]

Passing a large piece of legislation in such a short time was an extraordinary achievement, given the GOP's narrow majority and Democratic bitterness over Reed's management. Much of the credit goes to McKinley, who succeeded because of hard work, patience, a readiness to embrace an open process, and cordial personal relations with his ideological—but not personal—Democratic free trade adversaries. The measure was quickly labeled the McKinley tariff.[59]

Democrats howled, claiming it would raise the cost of living, reduce exports, increase the surplus, and lower wages. That didn't happen. In the year following the law's implementation, both imports and exports rose, as McKinley predicted. He forecast a $61 million reduction in duties over the next year: They dropped $52 million and duties were levied on a smaller share of imports. The next year, a bipartisan Senate committee investigated charges that the cost of food, clothing, and other necessities had risen and unanimously concluded prices were lower on 214 common household items. Even tariff critic Ida Tarbell admitted, "Manufacturing goods generally fell in price in 1891." But that was in the future. In the month that followed the tariff's passage, McKinley faced a different reality.[60]

THAT FALL, McKINLEY WAS up for reelection and the Democrats' number-one target. He was running again in a gerrymandered district specifically designed to defeat him that included heavily Democratic Holmes County. Expecting to win by 3,000 votes, Democrats nominated a popular former lieutenant governor, John G. Warwick. He was also from Stark, which Democrats hoped would further undercut McKinley.[61]

The Democratic National Committee (DNC) took control of Warwick's effort, sending in money, organizers, and speakers. Democrats covered Holmes in broken-down wagons, posing as peddlers and offering tin coffeepots at exorbitant prices and 5¢ tin cups and plates for 25¢ so they could blame the McKinley tariff for the increases. Republicans responded with a pamphlet, titled *Better Days for Farmers,* that tried to explain how the McKinley tariffs would increase domestic prices and markets without raising the cost of living. It was difficult reading and unpersuasive.[62]

McKinley officially kicked off his campaign October 8 in Millersburg, seat of Holmes County, but was soon off stumping for others—he had to repay favors to Ways and Means Committee colleagues. When Harrison spoke in Ohio in mid-October, McKinley was campaigning in Michigan for Representative Julius C. Burrows, before heading to Wisconsin to help another committee member, Robert M. La Follette Sr.[63]

Reed appeared in Stark County with the Major. The Speaker hadn't helped when he joked earlier, "Just now the thing which is destroying the world is the McKinley bill." Ida was so nervous about the outcome that McKinley spent election night with her rather than with supporters.[64]

The Major was defeated by 302 votes out of 39,816 cast that November. Ohio Republicans lost 9 seats, and thus were reduced to 7 of the state's 21 congressmen. It was a wipeout nationally: Republicans dropped from 179 House seats to 88 while Democrats picked up 83 seats to end at 235. For the third time in sixteen years, the House changed hands. Marking the era's political turbulence, a new party entered Congress with the election of eight Populists. The GOP managed to keep control of the Senate, but only with unreliable Western silver Republicans.[65]

In retrospect, the McKinley tariff was passed too close to Election Day to be fully explained and Democratic attacks were too fierce and difficult to answer quickly. Sugar did not go onto the free list before the voting, so people didn't feel the drop in its cost until after the election. Before higher duties became effective, manufacturers raised prices to increase their profits. Blaine had tried convincing Harrison to handle the issue in a special session in 1889 so the GOP had time to explain it before the midterms. Hayes had also warned the party faced annihilation if it pushed the bill.[66]

However, it wasn't just the tariff. Led by Lodge, Republicans fought for a controversial law—branded the "Force Act"—providing federal supervision in federal elections to guarantee black voting rights in the South. This enraged small-government advocates and bigots. There were other issues, including an administration scandal over veterans' pensions, dissatisfied Republican farmers defecting to the Populists, and public disenchantment with the first billion-dollar federal budget. When a Democrat complained about this, someone—the remark was erroneously attributed to Reed— callously responded that America was a billion-dollar country.[67]

In defeat, McKinley adopted a confident, forward-looking tone. A despondent George Frease, the *Repository*'s editor, asked the Major how he should explain the election. McKinley scrawled an editorial that began, "Protection was never stronger than it is at this hour. And it will grow in strength and in the hearts of the people." It had been pilloried and its supporters defamed, but "increased prosperity, which is sure to come, will outrun the maligner and vilifier."[68]

He was more sanguine in private. "I agree with you that defeat under the circumstances was for the best," he wrote Hanna. "There is no occasion for alarm. We must take no backward step."[69]

CHAPTER 6

Resurrection

———<o>———

There is no mistaking the implication of McKinley's cryptic note. Sometime between the 1888 national convention and his November 1890 defeat, with Hanna's encouragement, McKinley decided to run for president.

McKinley saw opportunity in his congressional loss. It relieved him from serving in a beleaguered House minority. It bolstered his stature as a political martyr—the Republican protectionist whom Democrats were desperate to defeat. It also freed him to find a better position from which to run for president.

McKinley needed a political post from which to mount a presidential bid, whether that was in 1892 at the end of Harrison's term or in 1896. A fresh electoral victory would raise his standing even further, and a statewide election would demonstrate his appeal. Fortunately, such a perch was available in 1891—the Ohio governorship, the same post that launched Hayes into the White House fifteen years earlier.

The Major could win it. He and Hanna understood Ohio Republicans had actually done well in 1890, winning all three statewide offices on the ballot by comfortable margins. Though Republicans couldn't overcome the Democratic gerrymandering, McKinley's protectionist message helped his fellow Republican House candidates win more votes than Democrats and run ahead of the party's statewide ticket. Besides, a governor's race in a competitive state would provide a good testing ground for a presidential bid.[1]

However, McKinley would need an old foe's help to win. In March 1891, he visited Foraker at his Cincinnati home to ask the former governor to nominate him at the state convention. This request appealed to Foraker's vanity, who took it as evidence McKinley felt he was a friend, not "lacking in any quality of manly fidelity." But McKinley's visit didn't demonstrate friendship. It showed McKinley's political savvy. He knew the untrustworthy Foraker would realize it was in his own interest to agree. Both men wanted party unity: McKinley to guarantee his nomination and Foraker to restart his political career and diminish the hostility of the Major's supporters.[2]

This exposed an essential difference between McKinley and Hanna. McKinley knew there are no permanent enemies in politics. The sometimes-hotheaded Hanna, on the other hand, had told a reporter the previous March that Foraker "allowed his ambition to get the best of him," and had been "a very heavy load for some time." I "am done with him," Hanna had said.[3]

A thousand Republicans met McKinley and paraded him to the Neil House on a blistering June 16 for the state GOP convention in Columbus. The next day Foraker "outdid any of his past performances" and nominated McKinley. The former governor roused the delegates with a stirring recitation of the Major's record and character and closed saying, "Every Republican in Ohio loves him, every Democrat in Ohio knows him and fears him."[4]

Behind the scenes, however, Foraker packed the Resolutions Committee to stop any endorsement of Sherman's renomination to the Senate as he now wanted to replace him when his term was up in 1892.[5]

National issues dominated the general election, with the state Democratic platform devoted primarily to a call for free and unlimited coinage of silver and an attack on protection. McKinley responded in his August 22 kickoff in Niles, Ohio. The Major viewed a giant parade from the second-floor balcony of his boyhood home before speaking from a platform on the Union School lawn. Among the marchers were the young women of the Mineral Ridge Ida McKinley Club, dressed in matching red and white dresses and carrying blue umbrellas.[6]

McKinley quoted Cleveland about the dangers of Free Silver and supported "the double standard" of gold and silver, along with paper notes redeemable in coin. But he also warned that without an international agreement setting the ratio between the metals, silver would depreciate and gold disappear in hoarding. While Campbell, the incumbent governor, said he was willing to take a "chance" on free coinage, McKinley responded he wasn't.[7]

He defended the tariff law that bore his name at a Labor Day rally in Cincinnati, saying there was "not a line of that law that is not American, not a page of it that is not patriotic, there is not a paragraph that is not dedicated to the American home." Campaign badges appeared, featuring a small tin plate inscribed along its rim, "made of Ohio steel and California tin," with the slogan "McKinley and Protection." By Election Day, the Major had made more than 140 speeches and covered 84 of the state's 88 counties, 23 in the last two weeks.[8]

McKinley closed with mammoth rallies in Cincinnati (where Foraker joined him) and on election eve in Canton, where supporters would yell, "What's the matter with McKinley?!" to which others responded, "He's all right!" McKinley was elected governor with a 21,511-vote margin, carrying in a GOP legislature where Republicans outnumbered Democrats more than 2 to 1.[9]

While understanding it was critical to McKinley's presidential ambitions to become governor, Hanna had focused on Sherman's reelection to the Senate, raising money across Ohio and in Chicago and Pittsburgh to flood the state with operatives and funds to help legislative candidates who supported Sherman, not Foraker. He left the management of McKinley's campaign to William M. Hahn, a Richland businessman whom he and the Major had installed as GOP state chairman.[10]

In winning, McKinley took a vital step toward the White House, but learned a lesson that would ill serve him in the future. He had handled Democratic calls for Free Silver by using Campbell's congressional voting record to muddle the picture while offering a nuanced description of his own monetary views: he was against Free Silver unless there was an international agreement. This wouldn't work in a presidential campaign. McKinley had not yet found language to deal with the currency issue, perhaps because his own record was jumbled.

In January Hanna's work for Sherman paid off as Republican legislators renominated him by 53 to 38. The senator wrote Hanna, "Without you I would have been beaten." Foraker would have to look elsewhere to advance his ambitions.[11]

•   •   •

AS 1892 BEGAN, MCKINLEY was no longer a political apprentice, but a national leader who wanted to be president and whom others wanted to be president. He and Hanna had to decide if he should try for the party's nomination that summer. President Benjamin Harrison was personally unpopular with many Republicans angry about his personal treatment of them, especially over patronage. Even McKinley, rarely ruffled, had left the White House after discussing a judicial vacancy, upset with the president's haughty attitude and refusal to listen. The Major never returned while Harrison sat in the White House.[12]

Though he had undertaken suicide missions in the Civil War, McKinley would not do so as a politician. He decided not to challenge the president at the party's national convention in Minneapolis, but would be ready if Harrison did not run. If the president did seek a second term, the convention would be an opportunity to raise the Major's profile, make new friends, and meet potential supporters.

The Major used the spring to prepare. He made several high-profile speeches, among them one to the American College Republican League at the University of Michigan. Responding to a toast "to American Protection," the Major drew the evening banquet's longest and most enthusiastic demonstration and lambasted House Democrats "as weak and vacillating."[13]

Other Republicans began the New Year firmly opposed to the president's renomination and created a "Grievance Committee" to attract other malcontents. Their leaders were ironically the powerful New York and Pennsylvania Republican bosses who had made Harrison the nominee in 1888, Platt and Quay.[14]

Platt seethed at Harrison's failure to make him Treasury secretary. He was called the Easy Boss, but behind his unflappable exterior was a man who settled scores. His ally, Quay, had brilliantly managed the president's 1888 race, running a disciplined and well-funded effort beyond the abilities of Harrison's circle, but had then been ignored on patronage. He had retreated to his library, considered one of the country's finest, to read and bide his time.[15]

The two bosses were being helped to dethrone Harrison by James S. "Ret" Clarkson, the publisher of the *Iowa State Register* and Republican national chairman. Clarkson's nickname came from his habit of writing "Ret[urn] Clarkson" on articles going to the typographers so he could proofread their work to ensure they had correctly deciphered his atrocious handwriting. Although Harrison had named him Republican National Committee (RNC) chairman, Clarkson felt the president would lose the election and hoped Blaine would run.

Foraker was another ally of Platt and Quay. He later claimed Harrison "was entitled" to renomination, but was urging Blaine to run. At the Ohio convention, he got himself and Asa Bushnell elected national convention delegates as Blaine men and forced McKinley's managers to agree that they would not bind the delegation for Harrison with what were called "instructions." While Foraker liked the state platform that did not endorse Harrison's reelection, he was unhappy with its lengthy praise of Governor McKinley's record and his namesake tariff bill.[16]

Would the secretary of state run this time? Platt, Quay, and their allies may have known the pressure being put on Blaine by his wife, Harriet. She hated Harrison. The president had refused to name Blaine's son assistant secretary of state, appointing him to a lesser post. That April, Mrs. Blaine had personally asked the president to jump her son-in-law, an army colonel, over seventy more senior officers and make him a brigadier. Harrison refused and Mrs. Blaine stormed out, saying, "You had a chance to please us once."[17]

Harrison was now a reluctant candidate, disliking his job and hating Congress. He did not commit to run until the spring and then mostly out of pique with his secretary of state. While he and Blaine agreed on most foreign issues, they didn't like each other and Blaine's thirst for the presidency was palpable. Old and in bad health, Blaine wanted one last run and finally made his move with a terse resignation on June 4, just three days before the Republican convention. Within hours, the president replied with a similarly curt acceptance. Telling reporters he merely wanted "personal freedom and peace," Blaine blamed Harrison for viewing him "with suspicion and distrust" and the president's friends for considering him "guilty of duplicity," which of course he was.[18]

Blaine's resignation quickened the pulses of anti-Harrison men in Minneapolis. Foraker said he "should not be surprised" if Blaine won on the first ballot. Hotel lobbies, bars, and hallways were full of rumors about defections from Harrison.[19]

Blaine's entry did not affect McKinley's plans. He would not wage an overt campaign, but remain loyal to the president, while Hanna gently scouted out support for the Major as a fallback candidate. If Harrison faltered, the Major would hold himself aloof while friends organized a draft. Neither McKinley nor Hanna hoped one was necessary. Harrison had made it hard for any Republican to win that fall. The two Ohioans were laying groundwork for the future, not reaching for the prize in 1892.[20]

That is why the day before Blaine's announcement, Hanna reached out to Foraker and personally asked for his help in unifying the Ohio delegation. Foraker was touched that Hanna came to him hat in hand. "This feeling made it easy," Foraker later wrote, "for me to forget Mr. Hanna's past unfriendliness." While still helping Blaine, Foraker promised to support the Major on the first ballot, "notwithstanding a number of McKinley's appointees, and other friends from Ohio," he told Hanna, talking in "a very offensive way" about him. McKinley was better than Harrison, Foraker thought, and a chaotic convention might break for Blaine or even Foraker himself.[21]

Harrison's fortunes stabilized by Monday. Alger withdrew in favor of Blaine, but the anti-Harrison forces splintered with talk about Sherman, Allison, and, increasingly, McKinley. Harrison's managers—called the "Twelve Apostles"—remained focused on Blaine, dispatching Frederick Douglass, the former slave and now reform advocate, to remind black delegates that Blaine had opposed the Force Bill protecting Southern voting rights. At a Saturday strategy session that lasted until Sunday morning, the Apostles had decided on a convention-eve "secret meeting" with every Harrison delegate. Their object was to lock in the Harrison men, and if a majority of the delegates attended, Harrison's victory would be certain. The meeting had the desired effect.[22]

On Monday, June 6, McKinley was picked unanimously as permanent chairman. The anti-Harrison forces wanted to keep him visible in the event of a stampede. Harrison's managers had met with McKinley that morning and were reassured he remained "firm and loyal to the President." Both sides knew from the last convention that McKinley would keep order. Reed arrived and immediately met with Clarkson. Reed hated Harrison for appointing an archenemy as the port collector in Portland, Maine, then pardoning the man's brother. Though he had long disliked Blaine, he was better than the president. Reed, of course, was available if Blaine wasn't.[23]

The buzz about McKinley continued growing as his cousin William McKinley Osborne, now a Boston police commissioner, worked over the Massachusetts delegation. Talk in Pennsylvania and elsewhere led reporters to call the Major "a very dangerous candidate," which was a way of saying he could win if he ran. Despite his pledge to support the Major on the first ballot, Foraker told reporters Ohioans would support Blaine.[24]

Tuesday morning, Clarkson gaveled the meeting to order. The Convention Hall was a giant pine box built inside the Industrial Exposition Building. Delegates and guests entered through the exposition's brick façade under an eagle with a red, white, and blue shield in its claws with stars on a dark blue background above, surrounded by bunting. The building's newly planed pine timbers smelled good but the sweltering heat caused resin to drip from the ceiling. There were many No Smoking signs.

RNC members and dignitaries sat on the back of the stage while hundreds of reporters flanked it. Delegates were in front. Behind them were more guests who sat on uncushioned chairs in galleries. People walked onto the stage via a slanting staircase, creating dramatic entrances. The only banner was at the hall's back, facing the stage, with yellow letters on blue saying, AMERICAN WARES FOR AMERICAN WORKMEN, AMERICAN MARKETS FOR THE AMERICAN PEOPLE, and PROTECTION FOR AMERICAN HOMES.

Delegates unanimously confirmed McKinley as permanent chairman. Dressed in a black Prince Albert coat with high collar, his hair brushed and face pale, he took the stage to cheers and began, "Gentlemen of the convention." Someone yelled, "Three cheers for McKinley!" and the hall roared them out before he could start again. Speaking without notes for roughly seven minutes, McKinley heralded the GOP's record in passing every pledge from its early platforms into law—including freedom for the slave and a transcontinental railroad. He defended protection, saying it "stimulates American industries and gives the widest possibilities to American genius and American effort." Then he slammed new Democratic tariff proposals and closed by insisting on "a free ballot and a fair count" as "the greatest constitutional guaranty." This provoked delegates to call for Frederick Douglass, who stood to acknowledge their cheers. There was less talk in the hallways, hotel suites, and watering holes about Blaine, more about Reed and McKinley, and plenty about Harrison, who appeared to be winning.[25]

A credentials fight over Alabama would tell each camp's strength. When delegates convened Thursday evening, Harrison men had dominated the credentials committee and the anti-administration camp was forced to challenge Alabama's approved slate. For more than four hours the sides went at each other, while McKinley "blandly conducted the proceedings with a palm-leaf fan" to stay cool. He kept the convention from tying itself into parliamentary knots several times so it could finally have a test vote of the two camps' strengths. At midnight the roll call stopped when the lights failed. The band played "We Won't Go Home Till Morning" until they returned. Harrison won the test vote 436 to 432½, close but enough to guarantee his renomination.[26]

The next morning, the *Los Angeles Times* endorsed the Major, while the *New-York Tribune* reported, "McKinley is the dark horse." Both newspapers' publishers were the Major's friends. The anti-Harrison men were so desperate for McKinley's support for Reed, their fallback if Blaine faltered, that they approached Hanna to promise the Major the secretaryship of the Treasury if he would endorse Reed. Hanna refused.

Only Harrison and Blaine were nominated. As he seconded Blaine's nomination, Stephen W. Downey, who served in Congress with McKinley as Wyoming's territorial delegate, turned to the Major on the stage and said, "when four years more roll around, we will make you President."[27]

When the roll call reached Ohio, McKinley challenged its count, thinking his alternate had voted for him rather than Harrison (he was mistaken). Harrison won a first-ballot victory with 535⅙ to 182⅙ for Blaine and 182 for McKinley (a handful of votes went to other candidates). Without mounting an organized campaign or even being nominated, McKinley captured as many votes as the anti-Harrison bosses won for Blaine. As the meeting ended, delegates yelled at the Major, "Your turn will come in 1896!"[28]

McKinley was carried into his hotel on the shoulders of admirers before refusing their demands for a speech, saying, "What voice I have left is for Harrison and my heart goes with my voice." Exhausted by the day's exertions and blistering heat, he and Herman H. Kohlsaat, a Chicago baker who used his profits to buy newspapers, went to their room, ordered ice water, stripped down to their undershorts, flopped on the bed, and fanned themselves. Hanna arrived. After Kohlsaat draped the sofa with the bed's top sheet, Hanna stripped to his skivvies, threw himself on the couch, and croaked, "My God, William, that was a damned close squeak!" [29]

Hanna was right. McKinley had kept his commitment to Harrison and yet could have been nominated by a convention close to stampeding. The Major was grateful it did not. No Republican would have an easy race after Harrison, especially following that convention fight. Instead he and Hanna considered what lessons to take from Minneapolis. They would need a strategy for 1896.

CHAPTER 7

The Major's War Plan

———◦————

H anna was amazed by what he saw at the Minneapolis convention. "The demand from the people for McKinley," he wrote, "was even more outspoken" than four years earlier. It would have hurt McKinley to actively seek the nomination in 1892, but next time, Hanna thought, "[t]he popular demand for his candidacy would override all opposition." [1]

Notwithstanding Hanna's heady thoughts, spontaneous demand is rarely enough in politics. Victory in a race for the presidency generally requires a well-run campaign built on a thoughtful strategy. Fortunately for McKinley and Hanna, they were methodical men. They knew from personal experience how chaotic political conventions could be. Instinctively, both men worked through the challenges of running for president and considered what was necessary to win.

There is no letter from one man to the other, no memo from a consultant or manager, and no record of a single brainstorming session where they hashed it all out. But from what they did, what they said, and how they drew in others in the years that followed the 1892 convention, we can see the contours of McKinley's strategy to win the nomination.

The first, most essential task was to unify Ohio Republicans. A divided Ohio delegation killed Sherman's chances in 1888 so a divided home-state delegation would undercut any candidate's argument that he had the broad appeal necessary to win the presidency. McKinley must have his home state strongly behind him. He and Hanna also knew that in the serpent pit that was the Buckeye State's GOP politics, there was an ambitious rival. While Foraker spent 1893 and 1894 building his law practice, he still thirsted for higher office and could destroy the Major's chances.

Both Hanna and McKinley felt that the nomination and general election would be settled over pocketbook issues. Therefore, the campaign should emphasize protection and ignore currency. Old Civil War animosities no longer rallied Northern Republicans as effectively as they once had. Protectionism united Republicans, split Northern Democrats, and attracted the laborer vote, a swing bloc that neither party dominated. McKinley was the party's undisputed leader on the tariff issue, but protectionism would need to play a bigger role in the GOP's messaging than it had in the past. By contrast, the currency issue pitted Midwestern and Western silver Republicans against Eastern hard-money Republicans, so it risked dividing the party. McKinley wanted to avoid that.

McKinley knew he would not win the nomination as a regional candidate; he must run a national campaign. He had to start with Ohio, then win as many Southern Republican delegates as possible (Southerners represented a quarter of the convention's total delegates). He must pick up support in the Midwest, West, and even Mid-Atlantic and Northeast. Illinois, with the fourth-largest delegation, was key since Ohio (third largest) would presumably be for McKinley, while New York (first) and Pennsylvania (second) would be under the control of party bosses and therefore tougher to win.

By ceding no state or region, McKinley was treading in dangerous territory. To run a national campaign, he would have to challenge the machine bosses by recruiting their intraparty state rivals to his cause. Initially, McKinley was reluctant to go after New York and Pennsylvania delegates, but Hanna pressed him. This too was difficult, but extremely lucrative if carried off.[2]

Favorite-son candidates, on the other hand, did not scare McKinley. He believed GOP activists would see through the charade of candidates who were using home-state friends to get rewards even though they had no chance to win.

McKinley and Hanna understood it would be a mistake to trade promises of patronage, power, or cabinet posts for delegates. Once you start striking political bargains like that, you can't stop. Machine bosses such as Platt and Quay had been burned by verbal understandings and might insist on written pledges, which if revealed could burn any candidate who made them. McKinley wanted to come to the presidency "unmortgaged," to have won the nomination because delegates thought he was the right man and had the right platform, not because he'd cut all the right deals.

The Major didn't set out to be an opponent of "the Combine," as the Republican leaders of well-organized, disciplined party organizations tied together by patronage, power, and money were called. He understood such arrangements were part of the Gilded Age political landscape. However, over the course of the campaign, McKinley came to understand the bosses opposed him because he wasn't willing to mortgage his campaign to them. So McKinley eventually decided to convert the bosses' opposition into an asset by running against them and their methods as a reform Republican.

For both Hanna and McKinley, being extremely well organized was probably encoded into their DNA. They did not establish the haphazard operation typical of most primary campaigns. Instead they worked to create a highly disciplined organization, which led them to deploy agents around the country to do the preliminary work of identifying McKinley supporters in the states. Most were Ohio associates—including Charles W. F. Dick, an Akron lawyer and former GOP state chairman; William M. Hahn; and Joseph P. Smith, the state librarian. William McKinley Osborne was another agent, as was John Hay. Hay, who had been Abraham Lincoln's personal secretary and number two at the State Department under Garfield, had married a Cleveland girl and taken over the family's company when her father committed suicide. Enormously wealthy, he now lived on Washington's Lafayette Square and was wired into the capital's gossip. These men and others helped recruit leaders in each state to work to elect McKinley men as delegates to local, congressional district, and state GOP conventions, then to the national convention. This was the Gilded Age equivalent of the presidential primary season, not elections open to party members or voters, but a multistage series of local, district, and state conventions.[3]

It would be impossible to run every state and territorial effort from Canton, so the men in the states were put in charge and were responsible for devising a plan that met with McKinley and Hanna's approval and then carrying it out, adjusting as necessary.

McKinley and Hanna began organizing early. There was no incumbent Republican president. The field was wide-open. Candidates and the bosses usually waited until the election year itself to throw together an effort, but from McKinley's perspective, waiting that long left too much to chance and unnecessarily ceded territory to those party bosses who already had their machines in place.

McKinley represented a generational change within the party. He was the last of the Civil War generation to be president, so he put special emphasis on appealing to a younger generation and empowering its leaders to rise in the GOP.

The Major was also a different kind of Republican who felt the GOP must broaden its base. It was losing strength because the North was becoming less Anglo-Saxon Protestant and Southern Democrats were extinguishing the voting rights of Republican blacks. The GOP would win national elections only if it gained support from new ethnic immigrant laborers in the North—often Catholic—while finding a way to defend free and fair elections below the Mason-Dixon Line and attract more votes there by emphasizing protection.

In politics, it pays to be lucky. But to win, Hanna and McKinley could leave nothing to chance. They would insist on instruction for national delegates. This meant using their grassroots majorities at district and state conventions to vote to direct their national delegates to support McKinley as long as he was in the race. This would keep rogue delegates from deserting when offered patronage or other enticements. Instructions from the grassroots were a powerful way to keep delegates in line since they did not want to return home from the national convention and explain why they had broken faith with their state's GOP rank and file.

If a front-runner lacked a majority of delegate support before the convention, he often fell prey to a deadlocked convention or the combined animosity of his competitors. The McKinley men would go for an absolute majority of delegates. It was also necessary to have a majority among the members of the Republican National Committee. Control of the RNC would protect any delegate majority.

To gain support, McKinley would also make good use of his many relationships. He made friends while serving in Congress for almost fourteen years, attending three national conventions, and campaigning around the country. These friends could now help deliver delegates at the national convention and their states in the general election, especially because many of these relationships were so deep with McKinley.

He made strong, close friends more easily than most politicians. While self-interest is often the basis of political associations, true friendship is a more powerful bond. Rather than deals and boodle, the Major and Hanna would draw on these friendships to foster grassroots support and build a sense of inevitability for McKinley's candidacy.

Finally, McKinley needed to demonstrate that his campaign was about something larger than himself. Every person who runs for president is necessarily ambitious, but the overly ambitious (Foraker) reeked of self-interest. Grassroots Republicans found it attractive that in public and private, McKinley came across as selflessly committed to the country's greater good through the protective system.

McKinley began executing this plan in the fall of 1892 by spending nearly three months campaigning for Harrison and the GOP ticket. This would strengthen his dominance on the tariff issue, create goodwill among party leaders, and deepen his support among the grassroots.

The Major received an estimated 1,500 invitations. Hanna and RNC chairman and former Montana congressman Thomas H. Carter, one of Harrison's "Twelve Apostles," planned an exhaustive whistle-stop tour to put McKinley before hundreds of thousands of voters. For example, he barnstormed Missouri, Kansas, Illinois, Indiana, and Michigan in late October, traveling 2,000 miles and delivering twenty-six speeches in just five days. His message was well received by Republicans and Democrats alike, especially laborers. Recalling the McKinley Tariff's wool provisions, a Missouri Democrat stockman yelled at one rally, "Three cheers for the man who saved our sheep!" At another stop in Peru, Indiana, 30,000 turned out, many brandishing tin cups from new local factories. In Detroit, young women working at the Standard Pearl Button Company insisted on showing their gratitude for high tariffs. It was unladylike to cheer, so they waved handkerchiefs.[4]

He spoke in every kind of venue, from New York's Carnegie Hall to a Beatrice, Nebraska, Chautauqua. There McKinley delivered a two-hour defense of high tariffs, pummeling Democrats for stripping passages from their platform that mildly defended protectionism. He was as popular in the tent as he was in the hall. McKinley did not neglect his home turf, appearing with Foraker and Whitelaw Reid, the party's vice presidential candidate and *New-York Tribune* publisher, to formally kick off the Ohio campaign at a monster rally in Dayton.[5]

He spent the election's final week in New York before making five stops in Pennsylvania on his way home. His proclamation that "[p]rotection cheapens everything but men" brought applause and gifts everywhere, including a red, white, and blue weaving shuttle from textile workers and a tin ingot from foundry men. A group of laborers appeared on his Philadelphia stage with a tinplate banner painted with the state seal. The crowd went wild when McKinley quipped, "There is another trophy of protection." He rarely mentioned currency, even though many silver Democrats made it their principal issue.[6]

While McKinley helped other Republicans by drawing crowds and praising protection, his 1892 campaign also allowed him to road-test his words, hone his speaking skills, and, most important, make new personal and political friends. Harrison lost to Cleveland (who made history as the only president elected to two nonconsecutive terms), but the Major's future appeared brighter than ever. "He is bound to be the nominee," his secretary wrote.[7]

THAT SOUNDED PLAUSIBLE UNTIL a few months after McKinley's impressive 1892 canvass. Like a sudden clap of thunder, the Major received news that had the potential to destroy his political aspirations, drive him from the governor's office, and leave him penniless.

On February 17, McKinley was on a train to New York to speak to the Ohio Society and then to pick up Ida. She had been undergoing treatment for epilepsy from Joseph N. Bishop, a Manhattan specialist in "nervous diseases and troubles of women." There was a telegram waiting when McKinley reached Dunkirk, near Buffalo. Robert L. Walker of Youngstown, Ohio, was bankrupt.

The two men had been childhood friends. Walker loaned him money for law school and for each of his early congressional campaigns, which the Major promptly repaid. McKinley had returned the favor in recent years by cosigning notes for Walker's tin stamping business. The Major thought the notes totaled $10,000. Walker's business was now insolvent and the notes had been called. McKinley would have to pay. It would take most of his life's savings. Distressed, he canceled his speech, arranged for his brother Abner to escort Ida home, and caught the first train to Youngstown.[8]

By the time McKinley reached Youngstown, the magnitude of the disaster had grown. Walker had the Major sign blank notes because, he said, he did not know if his bank would renew part or all of a single loan. In reality, Walker was using McKinley's blank notes to borrow additional money from banks all over northeast Ohio. Friday morning, the notes were thought to total $20,000. By day's end, the figure was $70,000, three times McKinley's net worth. When the Major saw Walker, bedridden and crying in anguish, McKinley comforted him, saying, "Have courage, Robert, have courage! Everything will come out all right." He then issued a statement: "I will pay every note of Mr. Walker's on which I am an indorser, and not one shall lose a dollar through me." McKinley was facing not only his political career's end. He could be bankrupt, too.[9]

McKinley traveled to Cleveland the next day and met with Myron T. Herrick, a banker serving on his gubernatorial staff. To pay off a note, a local industrialist had already given Herrick a $5,000 gift. Another friend, Herman H. Kohlsaat, learned of the mess from the morning papers in New York. "Have just read of your misfortune," he wired, "My purse is open to you" and offered to come to Ohio.[10]

The Major and Herrick met Kohlsaat when he arrived in Cleveland Sunday morning. "McKinley was pale and wan, with black rings under his eye," the Chicago publisher recalled, and "could not speak for his emotion. Tears rolled down his cheeks." The men met with other friends to discuss what to do. They estimated McKinley owed $90,000. "I wish Mark were here," McKinley said in a rare display of dependency. Hanna was out of town dealing with business difficulties of his own.[11]

When Ida arrived from New York, she insisted on using her inheritance to pay her husband's debts. The men who were gathered in Herrick's study discouraged her: that $75,000 would be her only support if McKinley was impoverished or died. "My husband has done everything for me all my life," Mrs. McKinley replied. "Do you mean to deny me the privilege of doing as I please with my own property to help him now?" John Tod, the wealthy and irascible son of Ohio's wartime governor, snapped, "Because McKinley has made a fool of himself, why should Mrs. McKinley be a pauper?" Kohlsaat explained if McKinley was to stay in politics, his wife's assets must be pledged or else critics would say the Major was hiding assets by putting them in her name.[12]

By late Tuesday, the total debt was now estimated at $110,000, more than William and Ida's combined net worth. Their friends settled on creating a trust that would buy the Walker notes, using the McKinleys' assets as collateral, thus keeping their property from being liquidated at auction. Herrick, Kohlsaat, and Judge William R. Day would be the trustees. Kohlsaat unhelpfully told the press McKinley's "affairs are a complete wreck" and that he would resign and resume his law practice. The governor immediately denied he was resigning. McKinley's impulsive friend had done him a disservice. It would not be the last time.[13]

McKinley executed a "deed of assignment," turning all he and Ida had over to the trustees. Over the next few weeks, $40,000 was raised in Chicago. Hanna and Herrick dragged their money sack through Cleveland. Many others stepped in to help the Major. From Cincinnati, Representative Bellamy Storer sent $5,000 and Charles Taft $1,000. Hanna solicited funds in Pittsburgh with the help of Philander C. Knox, now a wealthy attorney but once the Mount Union student who was McKinley's star witness in his prosecution of saloon owners. John Hay sent $3,000. McKinley later asked for the list of donors, but the trustees refused. Strangers sent money, including coins from children. "I admire you as an honest man. I admire your integrity and manliness," wrote a Zanesville, Ohio, railroad engineer. "Draw on me at sight for $500." McKinley thought such donations made him appear a beggar, so he returned them with his thanks, but many were anonymous.[14]

Hanna and the trustees raised over $130,000. Herrick negotiated a 10 percent reduction in the Walker notes held by banks, and by June, they had all been paid. McKinley thanked Hanna, Cincinnati lawyer and friend Thomas McDougal, and the trustees for their "noble generosity," but insisted he would pay the trust back. He sent Herrick regular payments, but rather than pass them on to the fund's contributors, the Cleveland banker invested the money, leaving McKinley's estate $200,000 at his death.[15]

Ironically, the Walker notes actually enhanced McKinley's White House prospects. Since his first impulse (and that of his wife) was to do anything necessary to pay the debts, the incident strengthened his reputation for integrity. Republican papers praised him, with one saying, "Everybody must feel profound sympathy for a [sic] honest and honorable man who gets into trouble through doing a kindness to a friend." Even Democratic papers generously applauded his conduct, saying the affair "will raise him in the public estimation as a man." The *Plain Dealer*, normally vituperative, editorialized, "The entire country will sympathize with Governor McKinley . . . and it is hoped matters can be arranged without loss to him."[16]

THE MAJOR WAS RENOMINATED for a second term in June. With his own financial difficulties on his mind, the Major alluded in his acceptance speech to the country's economic distress. The economy was sputtering, he told the delegates. Businesses were collapsing, factories closing, blast furnaces going cold, and men losing their jobs. Cleveland had said that for the economy's health the Treasury's gold reserves must not fall below $100 million, yet they had. Cleveland blamed it on the Silver Purchase Act and called for its repeal, but the economy had been good under Harrison when the silver law was in operation.

Instead McKinley blamed the faltering economy on the lack of business and consumer confidence caused by Democratic threats to undo the protective system. The Democratic platform's demand for a tariff-for-revenue only pushed business and financial leaders to hunker down, he argued, rather than expand their enterprises.[17]

The country descended rapidly into a deep depression that would last almost four years and was more severe than the Panic of 1873. There were many causes for the latest economic calamity. Some were international. London's Barings Bank failed in 1890 because of bad foreign investments, prompting a global financial crisis. Capital was withdrawn from the developing world, including America. The European grain crop failed in 1891, giving U.S. farmers a lucrative year in 1892, but that disappeared the next year when Europe enjoyed a bumper crop. Some causes were secular. Disruptive new technologies led to bankruptcies and closings of companies that could not adjust to them. Then there was the railroad boom's end, as there were few places left without tracks.

Even then, the United States might have avoided the worst of the panic had it not been for two laws McKinley voted for and, in one instance, wrote. The Sherman Silver Purchase Act had eroded confidence in the dollar as it caused European financiers to worry the United States would abandon the gold standard and adopt an inflationary silver currency. They withdrew gold, reducing both the Treasury's reserves and much-needed foreign investment in the United States. Then there was the McKinley

Tariff, which by reducing imports also reduced the flow into the Treasury of gold to pay for duties. Sugar's addition to the free list was also responsible for shrinking gold payments for import duties. This, coupled with big increases in spending under Harrison on veteran pensions and on harbor and river improvements, erased the surplus and threatened to plunge the government into deficits, further eroding confidence in the dollar domestically and abroad.[18]

Walker's bankruptcy was an omen. The Reading Railroad went under that same month, unnerving investors. By April 22, the Treasury's gold reserves fell below $100 million for the first time since the Panic of 1873 as people frantically exchanged paper money for gold and hoarded it. In early May, the stock market abruptly declined sharply, led by railroad and industrial stocks. By May's end, between loans being called, dropping sales, and plummeting stock prices, two dozen companies were failing a day.[19]

India ended its use of the silver standard June 26, dropping white metal prices from 81¢ an ounce to 62¢ in less than a week. Western mines were shuttered and the Union Pacific and other railroads that transported silver were slammed. Within a month, out-of-work miners were threatening to loot Denver banks. The militia was called out, federal troops were put on alert, and business owners slept in their shops with guns in their hands. Tent camps were set up to house thousands of unemployed men until they could be shipped out of town.[20]

This continued through the summer, with the Erie & Western Railroad going under in July. Hundreds of banks failed, wiping out their depositors' savings. New York Stock Exchange officials considered closing, at least temporarily. At the Missouri state line, police met trains from the West, declared the unemployed paupers, and turned them away. Some miners headed to the farm region for work while many went to Chicago.[21]

By August, 25,000 men were out of work in Cleveland. Chicago's mayor warned that his city's 200,000 destitute men needed help or "we will have riots that will shake the country." In October, the Northern Pacific was put into receivership. As winter arrived, there were reports of starvation in mining and lumber camps. Chicago City Hall, police stations, and churches were opened to give the unemployed a warm place to sleep.[22]

Against this developing backdrop, McKinley opened the GOP's fall campaign in Akron, nationalizing his reelection campaign by blaming the poor economy on Cleveland's effort to reduce tariffs and open the country to a flood of foreign goods. The Democratic platform denounced protection as an "unconstitutional fraud" and promised to rapidly end protection, hurting Ohio factory workers and farmers. West Virginia congressman William L. Wilson, the new Ways and Means chairman, and his committee were already working on a tariff reform measure.

It did not help Ohio Democrats, some of whom harbored mildly protectionist sentiments, that McKinley's Democratic opponent, Lawrence T. Neal, played a critical role at the Democrats' 1892 convention in scrubbing from the Resolutions report any positive references to protection.[23]

While McKinley devoted most of his speeches to tariffs, he also exploited a growing division between Cleveland administration gold men and Free Silver Democrats. He reminded voters the state GOP platform favored "honest money, composed of gold, silver and paper, maintained at equal value," suggesting McKinley was more open to silver than Neal, a hard-money man, was.[24]

But McKinley unexpectedly created a problem inside his own party when he picked a fight with the country's largest, most politically powerful interest group, the American Protective Association. Despite its name, it had nothing to do with tariffs. It was a virulently anti-immigrant and anti-Catholic pressure group. Founded in 1887, the APA represented a strain of extreme Protestantism that wanted to keep "the institutions of our Government" from "the direction and heavy hand of a foreign ecclesiastical potentate," by which they meant the pope. This group of nativists and religious bigots was a reaction to the Catholic Church's promotion of parochial schools and to growing Catholic immigration.[25]

Fed by fear of popish power and drawing on paranoia about bloc Catholic voting, the APA grew quickly and while nominally nonpartisan, it tilted toward the heavily Protestant, Anglo-Saxon Republican Party. It used secret rituals and titles for its leaders loosely based on Masonry, opposed Catholics holding public office, and wanted to restrict immigration. The group became a significant force as its endorsement—or opposition— could make the difference in close elections, especially in the volatile Midwest, where APA membership was large. In 1893, the group was at the height of its power.[26]

So it was worrisome when that fall, Ohio APA leaders telephoned McKinley to demand he fire two Catholic prison guards. They warned, "This is a test case." McKinley knew crossing the organization could hurt.

He had won in 1891 by 21,000 votes, a margin equal to one-third the APA's Ohio membership. Still, he told the APA the Constitution protected religious liberty and the Catholic prison guards would keep their jobs. He also pointedly did not answer an APA questionnaire, leading the Ohio chapter to omit the gubernatorial race from the voter guide it circulated to its members.

After hearing what McKinley had done, Hanna arranged for a priest to tour parishes telling Catholics of the governor's actions. Within days, the Catholic bishops of Cincinnati and Cleveland praised McKinley for wise leadership, which was tantamount to an endorsement. A few weeks later, McKinley won reelection by nearly 81,000 votes, with 54.5 percent. For Ohio, that was a big victory.[27]

Part of the reason for it was McKinley's success in attracting the labor vote again by touting his record on their issues. At his urging, Ohio now had arbitration for labor disputes and penalties for keeping workers from joining unions. The Major had also proposed safety protections for factory, construction, streetcar, and railroad workers.[28]

But McKinley won mainly because voters blamed Cleveland for the deepening depression and because of the sharp divisions between the Major and Neal over protective tariffs. Once thought to be the depression's cause, the McKinley Tariff was increasingly viewed as the means to salvation. As men were laid off and despair grew in homes across the country, tariff reform was thought a mistake.

A November 18 *Cleveland Leader* cartoon illustrated this changing view. Uncle Sam stood on a hill with factories, smelters, and smokestacks behind him. He was gesturing toward a rising sun labeled "McKinley 1896," while a band of tiny men labeled "Dem. Ways and Means Committee" tugged on a rope tied around Uncle Sam. "You can't pull me down now, boys," he said. "Don't you see that prosperity is dawning?"[29]

MCKINLEY WAS OVERWHELMED WITH Republican invitations to stump in their states and districts for the 1894 election. McKinley campaigned even more than he had in 1892, with the longest and most extensive barnstorming trip in the history of American politics. In two months, the Major traveled more than 13,000 miles by rail, visited 19 states and more than 300 communities, delivered roughly 375 speeches, and was heard by an estimated 2 million people. McKinley's message was that protectionism would restore prosperity and Democrats could not govern. It was time for a change.[30]

McKinley opened with a New England tour before the early September elections there, then picked it up again in late September with ten speeches in Indiana before moving west to Missouri and the Plains, then striking northeast to Minnesota, Wisconsin, and Michigan. He spent most of mid-October canvassing Ohio before heading south to New Orleans.[31]

The New Orleans trip was largely self-interest. Yes, Republicans hoped to pick up Southern congressional seats, but the GOP's realistic targets were not in Louisiana, where Democrats had violently suppressed black voting. Instead, McKinley wanted to project a message throughout the Southland that its growing manufacturing sector would benefit from protection, remind Louisiana planters he was the author of the bounty provision that rewarded them for tolerating cheap sugar on the free list, and, perhaps most important, gratify the Louisiana Republican Party leaders who had begged him to come. They would send sixteen delegates to the national convention. He spoke at the Auditorium Athletic Club to an enthusiastic 12,000 people, the largest political meeting ever held in the city. McKinley made his way north, mobbed in West Virginia, Pennsylvania, New York, and Illinois before returning to Ohio.[32]

The exhaustive schedule was possible because the Major had a private railroad car and, sometimes, his own engine. Party officials knew that was the only way he could cover the necessary ground. Having his own train also made it practical for reporters to accompany him, guaranteeing national coverage. Reporters were amazed at the speed of his entourage, sometimes running all day at more than 60 miles an hour.[33]

There were always enthusiastic, capacity-only crowds at McKinley's stops. Reporters were taken aback with the mobs that strained to get into halls already jammed to the rafters. It was often difficult for McKinley to leave events, and police were frequently called to clear a path to his carriage. While large crowds in big cities were understandable, it was harder to explain why 30,000—mostly farmers—camped out for up to two days in bad weather near Olney in southern Illinois to hear the Major speak at eight thirty on a wet Monday morning. Or how 30,000 people arrived in Hutchison, Kansas, some on trains from Oklahoma, Nebraska, and Texas. McKinley obliged the huge throng there by speaking twice.[34]

As he did in 1892, his 1894 speeches hit on simple but tough points. The choice was between two great economic theories. One was that America would be prosperous if we "give a part of our market to foreigners at the expense of our own production and labor" through free trade. The other theory held people would prosper with protection of "the home product represented by home labor." Protection would create jobs, raise farm prices, and restart the nation's mines, smelters, and factories. He admitted that while "the people thought they had too much tariff under the Republican administration they are now thinking they have too little under the Democratic administration." In keeping with his strategy, McKinley rarely spoke of currency and when he did, it was to call it "a dead issue."[35]

At times, the Major traveled with Civil War veterans who rallied their former Union comrades. President Grant's son, Fred, campaigned with McKinley across Iowa and was mobbed by crying veterans saying, "I was with your father." Entire communities were decorated with patriotic bunting, flags, posters, and lithographs of the Major. The men of Baker & Shattuck's packinghouse in Springfield, Illinois, concocted a display out of tin cans and flags. There were even casualties: in late October, a cannon used to announce McKinley's arrival at Arcola, Illinois, exploded, blinding one man and blowing off another's hand.[36]

He attacked the president at every stop—"Cleveland has been president nineteen months, and they're the longest nineteen months since the war." In Wisconsin, he responded to Democratic claims that the country was prosperous in Cleveland's first term by saying it was because Cleveland was "operating and administrating laws which were passed by Republicans."[37]

All along the trail, there was talk of a future presidential bid. In Springfield, Illinois, as McKinley prepared to take the podium after an enthusiastic welcome, someone yelled, "Three cheers for McKinley, our next president," setting off another demonstration. In St. Paul, as McKinley started to speak, a man shouted, "Our next president!," causing three cheers and more applause. The University of Michigan Republicans met him at the Ann Arbor depot shouting, "McKinley in '96!" The mayor of Kansas City, Missouri, introduced him by saying, "If the signs are propitious two years from now, the slogan will be, 'He comes from Ohio and his name is William McKinley.' "[38]

Everywhere he went, party leaders traveled with him, gossiping in between stops and catching up with their old friend or getting to know this rising national leader. Men later recalled their time with McKinley in 1894 as the moment they committed themselves to his cause, even if they didn't realize it then. Still, some people were unhappy. Missouri APA leaders were miffed over being seated in the back of the hall in Kansas City and whined about it. But still, McKinley had made many new friends and impressed many party sachems.[39]

The most important acquaintance McKinley made that year was present at his stop in Lincoln, Nebraska, in early October. Just twenty-nine years old, Charles G. Dawes was tall and slender with a red droopy mustache, hair parted in the middle, and big ears. He had visited McKinley in Columbus earlier in the year and joined him when he came to Nebraska. After Hanna later met him, he said, "He doesn't look much."[40]

Born in Ohio, Dawes had worked as a railroad surveyor at seventeen, graduated from Marietta College at nineteen, and went to Cincinnati Law School before heading west in 1887. His law office was in the same building as another young lawyer, five years his senior, named William Jennings Bryan. The two were members of a book and debate club, the "Round Table." After Bryan bested him in a debate over Free Silver, Dawes researched and wrote a volume on the banking system. Some days, Dawes and Bryan ate at Cameron's fifteen-cent diner with the University of Nebraska ROTC instructor, Lieutenant John J. Pershing.[41]

Dawes had made a name taking on the railroads over exorbitant freight rates and monopoly actions, and made some money with shrewd investments in real estate, banking, and a packinghouse. He was also intensely interested in politics and an avid reform-minded Republican. Neither McKinley nor Dawes understood how big a role he was to play in the Major's future, but by year's end, the energetic, gawky young man was feeling out GOP leaders in Nebraska, the Dakotas, and Wyoming on the Major's behalf.[42]

McKinley closed the 1894 campaign with an election-eve rally at Canton's Tabernacle. When he appeared, the audience "was on its feet as one man. Hats were tossed, handkerchiefs were waved and the tumultuous applause drowned out all efforts to speak." The Major was moved. It's unlikely he foresaw this reception as he signed over his life's assets and Ida's to pay the Walker notes the previous year. He told his neighbors that the next day was the twenty-fifth anniversary of his election as county prosecutor, his first office. Pushing back his emotions, he returned to his stump speech on protection and prosperity. He spent the night at his mother's, cast his ballot the next morning, and headed back to Columbus to await the returns.[43]

It was a Republican triumph. Ending the Democrats' two years of controlling the White House and both chambers of Congress since 1858, the GOP spectacularly picked up 130 seats in the House, with a lopsided 254-to-103 majority, and narrowly took the Senate. Politicians being politicians, party leaders immediately turned their eyes to 1896.

THOUGH MCKINLEY HAD WEATHERED a near-catastrophic personal crisis, won reelection amid the Panic of 1893, and seen his efforts benefit Republicans in the 1894 election, the GOP presidential nomination remained a distant goal.

Realistically, he was not the front-runner. That title belonged to New England's Thomas B. Reed, the Combine's preferred candidate. Reed would be elected Speaker again in 1895, and with so many Republican congressmen dependent on his goodwill, he had a ready-made national organization.

And while McKinley's role as the "Apostle of Protection" won him support among laborers that was unusual for a Republican, many party leaders still blamed him and his namesake tariff bill for the party's 1890 defeat and worried he would lose and drag the party down with him. Then there was his refusal to placate the APA and the distrust of the bosses. McKinley had a rough path ahead. To overcome such powerful opposition, he needed some early success.

CHAPTER 8

Audacious First Strike

———◄◦►———

McKinley ran the first modern presidential primary campaign. Before him, candidates left themselves in the "hands of friends" and maintained a low-profile, hands-off posture. They rarely spoke except as an officeholder or party leader and avoided appearing to seek the office. The office sought the man, or at least was led to him by string-pullers and bigwigs who began working for the candidate shortly before state conventions were held in spring of the election year itself.

The field was typically flooded with favorite-son candidates, generally governors or senators. Most had little chance to win and drew modest support outside their state. Some were encouraged to run by supporters at home. Others were prompted by party bosses to run to freeze their state's delegation until it could be traded at the convention for rewards of cabinet posts, prestigious appointments, or control of Treasury or post office patronage jobs.

Since 1872, no one in an open race for the presidency (when an incumbent was not running for reelection) had had a delegate majority when the convention began. A majority was obtained by deals made generally at or near the convention itself. It was almost more important to be the most popular second choice, in a position to collect delegates as other candidates fell. This made sense, considering that in the five GOP national conventions after 1872, only 1892 went a single ballot, and that year featured an incumbent running for reelection. There were 7 ballots in 1876, 36 in 1880, 3 in 1884, and 8 in 1888.[1]

Much time and energy was spent on the composition of the state delegation, with factions driven by local issues or personalities jockeying to be delegates. Before McKinley, state conventions often focused more on who would go to the national convention than on whom they would support when they got there.

Delegates in the South—the GOP's "rotten borough," a region that produced no Republican electoral votes but had a quarter of the seats at the national convention—were generally obtained by money and political promises in deals arranged with state leaders who were generally (but not always) white. Black Republican voters who made up the vast bulk of the GOP's Southern base were handled through their leaders and always at a distance. No Republican stumped for the nomination by appearing before a black GOP audience. That would have cost him support among white leaders of Southern party organizations.

McKinley would also have to deal with the Combine, who played an inordinate role in Republican conventions. The Combine was led by Thomas Collier Platt of New York and Matthew S. Quay of Pennsylvania. The two men's large delegations to the national conventions gave them inordinate power, especially since they influenced nearby states, like Connecticut and New Jersey. The Combine leaders were pragmatic, interested more in winning than in any particular issue, as long as the outcome included things that would cement their position and power.

There were also bosses who stood atop urban machines, as in Philadelphia, Pittsburgh, Cincinnati, and Chicago's Cook County. There were even Southern bosses, such as Powell Clayton, whose "Minstrel" faction ran Arkansas, though it was never easy in the region, especially after a Democrat won the White House in 1885 and took away the postmaster, revenue collector, port collector, and other patronage jobs on which Southern Republicans depended.

This was the age-old system McKinley faced. No one had successfully challenged it before him, but McKinley would systematically upend it, changing the nature of how future Republican candidates would run. He began with an early, in-depth organization, structured, deliberate, and intense, run by men who were loyal to him, and built around the idea that McKinley would restore prosperity by returning the country to a policy of protective tariffs.

The candidate was an active presence in that organization, regularly consulting with and guiding its leadership. He actually campaigned for the presidency, first behind the scenes and then in public—not nonstop like modern candidates do, but in a more sustained way than any Republican candidate before him.

With the audacity he had demonstrated on the battlefield, the thoroughness in preparation he had shown in every endeavor in life, and the charm and integrity displayed in his public and private character, McKinley would try winning the nomination in a different way than any candidate before him. He would aim for early success by taking a vacation.

THE LAST TIME A GOP presidential candidate won electoral votes in the South was 1876. But the region's 222 national convention delegates were nearly half of what was needed to nominate. The Southern bloc was so large that if it united behind one man, he would probably win. McKinley wanted those votes. If Southern delegates split among several candidates, it would take multiple ballots to nominate someone.

Cultivating Southern Republican leaders could be tricky and expensive. Most were political outcasts at home, with little chance of winning local or state elections because of the Democrats' overwhelming strength in the region, especially as it extinguished black voting rights. Many Southern Republicans were also poor; a substantial number were black and poor. It was customary for campaigns angling for delegates to offer cash, convention expense accounts, and promises of jobs from a new GOP administration. Additionally, Southern Republicans were notorious for switching allegiances when promised larger envelopes of cash, bigger expense accounts, or more patronage.

McKinley wanted to do it differently, without a battle over boodle. He and Hanna believed a better way to recruit Southern GOP leaders was to have them spend time with the candidate. Yes, there would be necessary expenses to organize and get delegates to the state and national conventions. But there would be no endless money tap. If Southern men came to have a personal relationship with the Major, agree with him, and believe that he was likely to win the nomination and the presidency, then they were more likely to stay loyal. And while he consciously did not set out to do this, McKinley would do the heretofore unthinkable. The "very radical views" on race he imbibed from his abolitionist parents would lead him to openly appear before black audiences to solicit their support.

McKinley could conveniently make inroads in many states at one time by inviting the region's GOP leadership to southern Georgia, where Hanna had a winter home. Thomasville, Georgia, was the Palm Beach of its time. The fashionable winter resort was a picturesque small town in gently rolling pine hills near the state's southern border. From October to March, wealthy Northeasterners and Midwesterners escaped the cold back home by taking cottages or houses for several pleasant months of dances, horse races, bird shooting, tennis, and carriage rides.

For McKinley's purposes, it helped that Thomasville was located on north-south and east-west rail lines that provided easy connections throughout the South. Several weeks in mid-March were blocked off, inquiries made, and invitations sent to Republican leaders, some with offers of help with transportation for those who could not afford to get there without it. When his travel was announced, McKinley said it was "for a little rest and outing." This fooled no one. His trip was obviously about politics.[2]

McKinley was familiar with the region. He had campaigned there in four elections and served with forty-three Southern Republicans in the House, many with whom he kept in touch.[3]

The Major's wartime experience had taught him that the most powerful bonds among men came from shared beliefs and camaraderie. So he wooed Southern GOP power brokers. He invited some to travel with him, starting with H. Clay Evans, a former Chattanooga, Tennessee, mayor who had served in Congress with McKinley. His nickname was the "Southern Cyclone." Evans had been elected Tennessee's governor in 1894 by a razor-thin 748 votes but was denied office by the Democratic-controlled legislature, which invalidated 20,000 GOP ballots. Clay Evans rode with McKinley to Atlanta, giving the two men plenty of time to talk, especially when a train wreck blocked the tracks, delaying them several hours. When a reporter asked if their trip together "carried any political sensation," they laughed.[4]

McKinley also accepted invitations to visit the homes of GOP leaders. For example, Georgia Republican chairman Alfred E. Buck was a Maine man who moved south after fighting there in the Civil War, serving in

Congress from Alabama and as U.S. marshal for north Georgia. He hosted McKinley at his Atlanta home with GOP bigwigs from Georgia, Tennessee, Alabama, and South Carolina before the Major spent the next day meeting with them one-on-one and in small groups.[5]

McKinley included his political visitors in social events held during his stay in Thomasville. Hanna hosted a gathering at his home for out-of-town Republicans, along with influential "winter Georgians" whose presence would impress the Southern party leaders. About a dozen GOP grandees also participated in a fancy party held a few days later by town fathers at the Mitchell House, Thomasville's finest hotel, and then went to a private meeting upstairs.[6]

But mostly, McKinley sat in a sunlit parlor in Hanna's rented Renaissance Revival mansion in Thomasville with a guest or two or a small group, talking about the future and hoping to convince his visitors they were friends with the man who ought to be the next president. We do not know the names of all the men who sat in those comfortable chairs, their cigar smoke curling upward. Given McKinley's and Hanna's meticulous nature, the list was likely extensive, but only some names show up in the local paper, hotel registers, and subsequent letters.[7]

This personal approach paid political dividends almost immediately. North Carolina's newly elected U.S. senator, Jeter C. Pritchard, the only Southern Republican in the upper chamber, left Thomasville a committed supporter. By April, former U.S. senator Powell Clayton—a tall, blond-haired, blue-eyed, one-armed veteran and boss of the Arkansas GOP—led a parade of "Toothpick State" Republicans in endorsing the Major. P. D. Barker of Mobile, Alabama, and a group of Yellowhammer Republicans he had brought to Georgia signed up. Barker was aligned with William Youngblood, the state's GOP national committeeman, who had been thought to be a friend of the New York boss Platt.[8]

Dozens of other Republican leaders were converted into McKinley men during the Southern swing. Among them were Florida GOP chairman Dennis Eagan and an ally, John G. Long, and even perhaps Robert Smalls, a former slave who served with McKinley in the House after winning fame in the Civil War by loading a coastal steamer, *The Planter,* with other slaves and sailing it under the guns of Confederate batteries protecting Charleston, South Carolina, to safety with the blockading Union fleet. By fall 1895, "the Captain of *The Planter*" was canvassing the South, making speeches to black Republicans on McKinley's behalf.[9]

THREE OF THE MORE interesting men recruited in Thomasville were R. R. Wright, S. B. Morse, and John H. Deveaux, black Republican activists from Savannah. Wright was president of Georgia State Industrial College for Colored Youth and Professor Morse taught there. Deveaux was editor of the *Savannah Tribune,* a black Republican newspaper. Seen on the streets in Thomasville, he told reporters "no conference had been held on the subject of delivering votes to McKinley in the convention." That was a lie.[10]

From what happened next, it's likely the men impressed upon McKinley the role of black voters in the Southern Republican cause and the challenges they faced from the Democrats' relentless efforts to deny them access to the ballot box and a fair count.

By Monday, March 28, McKinley left for Jacksonville, Florida, where Eagan and Long had arranged a reception at the St. James Hotel. The Major was well received, but some local Republicans threatened to send a competing whites-only delegation to the national convention if McKinley "should tie to the black end of the party."[11]

This conundrum confronted every Republican candidate seeking Southern delegates. The party's White House hopefuls rarely ventured south and none had campaigned among black Republicans. In some states, two GOP organizations vied for national recognition: the regular Republicans, which included both races, and the "Lily Whites," whose name explained it all. There were many white Southern Republicans like those in Jacksonville who took offense if black Republicans received too much attention. In an age of widespread bigotry, and in a region where a black might be lynched on a whim, no presidential hopeful had ever addressed a public gathering of black Republicans during the primaries. Black support was typically arranged by aides and done so at a distance.

By morning, the grumbling about "the black end of the party" had produced a counterreaction. Jacksonville's black Republicans, who provided the bulk of the local party's votes, wanted to meet McKinley. Osborne was dispatched with Eagan and Long to visit Rev. Joseph E. Lee, a black

Republican and the state party secretary. The four men "decided it would be bad politics to turn the colored man down in Florida," and told McKinley. He agreed. So after the Major met privately with Lee, twenty black Republicans, led by a timber company manager, trooped into the St. James for an hour-long private session. McKinley was impressed with the business and professional men and everyone left charmed.

Eagan and Long had encouraged McKinley's outreach, telling reporters that they supported allowing blacks "to participate in the public courtesies extended to Gov. McKinley." That was also McKinley's instinct. Weeks earlier, he had written Hanna, "We can never give our consent to a practice that disenfranchises any of our fellow citizens. I believe the time is coming when that injustice will be corrected, largely by the people of the South themselves, but in the meantime, we cannot abate our insistence upon the exercise of constitutional rights." As citizens, black Americans deserved the vote and black Republicans deserved McKinley's respect. The Jacksonville reception was a first for a presidential hopeful of either major party.[12]

Three days later, in Savannah, McKinley again did something no candidate for either major party's nomination had done. He campaigned before black voters, speaking in a church at a public meeting arranged by Deveaux and President Wright. According to one organizer, McKinley was "gladly received by our people."[13]

The following day, McKinley left for Washington and then home in Canton. Knowing the Southern swing was only just a step, McKinley, Hanna, and their agents, such as Osborne and Joseph Smith, kept in touch with the new supporters. They began building an in-depth organization south of the Mason-Dixon Line aimed at winning delegates instructed for McKinley.

Amazingly, the opposition had not yet stirred and would not do so for months. The Major had stolen the march on them. Platt would later write, "He had the South practically solid before some of us awakened."[14]

BUT McKINLEY WAS NOT on the move just in the South. While in Florida, the Major bumped into Hamilton Disston, a prominent Philadelphia businessman, land speculator, and Matthew S. Quay's friend. McKinley quizzed Disston about Quay's views on the contest. Disston said Quay spoke "very highly" of the Major but was uncommitted. McKinley shared that he was confident of Minnesota (its former governor William R. Merriam had been with him in Georgia), as well as Nebraska, Wisconsin, Missouri, Indiana (if Harrison did not run), Ohio, and West Virginia, and was reasonably confident of California and Oregon. Disston dutifully reported all of it to Quay. McKinley's behavior may have shown he had forgotten the lesson of Manderson stealing his speech in 1867. More likely it was a sign of McKinley's confidence: he wanted Quay to know his developing strength.[15]

Yet McKinley's strategy of competing everywhere meant little unless he actually did so, so the Major and his lieutenants looked northeast to find more opportunities. They knew that as the front-runner, Tom Reed could ill afford defections in New England and that the Speaker's acerbic personality and the region's strong protectionist bent might provide openings for the McKinley campaign.

Then John Addison Porter, a wealthy young philanthropist and president of the Hartford McKinley Club, invited the Ohio governor to appear before the group's impressive membership at an April 9 dinner. It was a busy day, with McKinley first visiting the Connecticut State Capitol where he was welcomed by Governor Owen V. Coffin and presented to the legislature by Speaker Samuel Fessenden, a Reed man. Afterward, the Major spoke before five hundred guests at the Foot Guard Armory, an imposing gray stone fortress, joined by Coffin, Fessenden, and Connecticut's two U.S. senators, Joseph R. Hawley and Oliver H. Platt, at the head table. The Major demonstrated his proficiency in the tariff by spending two hours explaining how Cleveland's reform had reduced revenue and created debt, and why protection would restore prosperity and bring higher wages.[16]

News reports said the event proved two things—"(1) that the McKinley presidential boom has a distinct stature in New England, and (2) that the field is to be diligently cultivated. The Buckeye favorite was hailed at the banquet table as the next President." [17]

MCKINLEY EVEN LOOKED TO Illinois, where the odds were stacked against him. The state already had a favorite son who coveted the presidency and was backed by two ruthless men who controlled the state's GOP machinery. McKinley would need a strong leader for his Illinois campaign if he hoped to win. He strangely picked a man who had lived in the state a matter of weeks.

In January, Charles G. Dawes, his wife, and their two children had left Lincoln and moved to Illinois. The intense young lawyer who had spent time with McKinley that fall in Nebraska had decided to become an entrepreneur and make bustling Chicago his home.

Dawes took his profits from real estate, banking, and meatpacking investments to buy gas utilities. The twenty-nine-year-old had started down this path the previous July when he investigated buying a Peoria, Illinois, gas company on behalf of an investor group. He was unimpressed with the Peoria deal, so he bought a more promising prospect in La Crosse, Wisconsin. His investors may have been surprised when the brainy entrepreneur showed up with the deed to a different gas company, but the venture was very profitable.[18]

Now Dawes stalked the Northwestern Gas Light & Coke Company in Evanston, Illinois. In a coup, he bought it in a competition with Chicago National Bank's John R. Walsh. Dawes then audaciously presented Walsh with a business plan so solid that the bank president loaned the younger man money to modernize and expand the company.[19]

Dawes had continued helping McKinley's nascent presidential bid after they had seen each other in October, reaching out to the North Dakota GOP chairman, W. H. Robinson, and Wyoming congressman F. W. Mondell, among others, on the Major's behalf. He was also active in shaping up McKinley's Nebraska organization, recruiting friends and his brother Beman Gates Dawes (nicknamed "BG"). Impressed, McKinley had Hanna meet with Charles Dawes in January to take his measure.[20]

McKinley had bigger things in mind for young Mr. Dawes than mining his address book. With his keen eye for talent, the Major had decided Dawes would command his campaign in what was already thought to be an important—if not the most critical—contest of the GOP presidential primaries. So before the Southern swing in March, Hanna asked Dawes "to look after matters in Illinois."[21]

It was a stunning choice. Dawes had never managed a campaign. He was a newcomer to Illinois. He was very young. And he would face two of the most formidable foes of McKinley's aspirations for the GOP nomination.

One was John R. Tanner. He enlisted in the Civil War, fought under Sherman, and lost his father and two of three brothers in combat and POW prisons. As a downstate state legislator, he threw his support behind

Governor Shelby Cullom's 1883 bid for U.S. senator. Cullom rewarded him by having President Arthur appoint him U.S. marshal for Illinois's Southern District. Tanner thereafter became the senator's trusted advisor. He angled for Cullom to run for president in 1888 and then tried making him the state's favorite son for the 1892 convention. Tanner was state Republican chairman during the GOP's tremendous 1894 sweep before engineering Cullom's reelection in 1895. In the process, Tanner cemented an alliance with the Cook County Republican machine that he hoped would make him the GOP candidate for governor in 1896.[22]

McKinley's other foe was William Lorimer, a thirty-four-year-old freshman congressman and head of the Cook County Republican machine. He was called the "Blond Boss" because of his light hair and complexion. Born in England to a Scotch Presbyterian minister, his family immigrated to America when he was five and moved to Chicago in 1870 when he was nine. His father died three years later, leaving his family penniless. To support them, Lorimer sold papers, shined shoes, hauled coal, collected laundry, painted signs, drove a wagon in the stockyards, and became a streetcar conductor and union organizer.[23]

At age twenty-two, he first voted in the 1884 presidential election. Parties—not election officials—then printed ballots. When Lorimer arrived at the polls, there were no Republican "ticket peddlers" distributing ballots. So he walked to a nearby polling place, scrounged up ballots, and returned to his precinct to vote and give out the rest to other Blaine men.[24]

Lorimer's disgust with the party's poor organization led him to organize a Republican club in his ward, turning it from a Democratic stronghold into a GOP one. He was rewarded for that with a seat on the Cook County Republican Central Committee. Two years later, he was given a county water department job. At the age of twenty-eight, he was appointed the department's chief, overseeing 1,300 patronage workers. Within two years he had used that army to make himself the boss of the Cook County GOP and was elected to Congress in 1894. He had a real talent for organizing men. The quiet Blond Boss was no orator, yet people paid attention when he spoke. He once said, "I think there is a time and a place to talk; that has been my policy all my life."[25]

Tanner and Lorimer were allies for mutual convenience. Cook County could provide Tanner half the convention votes for his gubernatorial nomination. The Blond Boss wanted the additional patronage that a friendly governor could provide and an advocate who could swing downstate Republicans behind a Chicago man for the U.S. Senate—namely him—if an opportunity arose.

Neither was inclined to support McKinley. Both men sensed it was in their interest to stick to the usual course, keeping Illinois up for grabs by running a favorite son and then cutting the best deal possible with the Combine at the national convention, delivering the fourth-largest delegation for a candidate who would offer them certain useful considerations. Tanner and Lorimer also probably wondered about McKinley's smarts in having a Nebraska hick run his Illinois campaign, a man with no connections to the state's political structure. They routinely made mincemeat of well-meaning novices like Dawes.

They did not yet understand that despite his youth and ignorance of Illinois politics and players, Dawes was meticulous, well organized, and energetic. He was a natural leader who quickly commanded the respect of his colleagues. Dawes began systematically ferreting out the best McKinley men to thoroughly organize their county, congressional district, and state conventions.

The campaign's pace quickly grew so intense that Dawes split the state into three areas and brought on allies to head the campaign in each of them. General John C. McNulta worked the Chicago area, General C. W. Pavey handled the state's southern counties, and William G. Edens covered the northern ones.[26]

Nearly thirty years Dawes's senior, McNulta was a Bloomington lawyer and cigar manufacturer who had been active in Illinois GOP politics since returning from the Civil War. He had been involved in virtually every GOP presidential contest since then, was elected in 1872 to a term in Congress, and failed in a bid for the GOP gubernatorial nomination. He knew everyone and everyone knew him.

Pavey, like Tanner, was from the state's far southern region, known as "Little Egypt." He, too, was nearly thirty years older than Dawes, and a longtime Republican operative who had been appointed internal revenue collector by Garfield.

Edens was only thirty-one, a railroad conductor, and an official in the Brotherhood of Railroad Trainmen. Like Dawes, the trim young man parted his hair in the middle and had a talent for organization. Edens was also active in the National League of Republican Clubs that had an extensive national network of young friends.[27]

Dawes started a card file of supporters in each of the state's 102 counties. Over the next year, this would become an elaborate system that tracked which county, congressional district, and state delegates were for McKinley and which were not and which local conventions had instructed and which had not. Dawes updated his tally regularly and used it to help McNulta, Pavey, and Edens target where they needed to cultivate more support for McKinley.

Hanna initially tried managing the Illinois campaign long-distance by letters and occasional visits, but by May, Dawes was in full command and Hanna began pulling back. However, before doing so he met with Dawes and Herman H. Kohlsaat to discuss Tanner. The next day, Hanna and Dawes spent the afternoon with Tanner and William Penn Nixon, publisher of the Chicago *Inter Ocean*. Dawes thought he heard Tanner pledge himself to McKinley.[28]

Hanna and Dawes might have believed Tanner said that, but it was naïve for Dawes or Hanna to think Tanner would back the Major. Unlike Lorimer, there was little they could do to help Tanner win the governorship. This May 11 meeting was not the last time Dawes would take Tanner at his word.

Uncle Shelby Cullom's favorite-son candidacy had been an object of conversation since January, though the *Chicago Tribune* called it "a great joke." But Tanner and Lorimer liked the favorite-son candidacy's potential. Uncle Shelby was popular downstate and Lorimer's machine could deliver Chicago, where Cullom was not as respected. Together the combination could help lock up the state. Then the two party bosses could deal with their Eastern counterparts for rewards that might include funds for the Illinois gubernatorial campaign and patronage.[29]

Meanwhile, Dawes's card file grew in size and importance as McNulta, Pavey, and Edens covered the state and their young commander tracked their efforts. By the summer, Dawes was trying to gain the support of the new Chicago mayor, George B. Swift, on the theory that the enemy of one's enemy can be your friend. Swift had been elected in April and almost immediately went to war with Lorimer.

The mayor fired thousands of city employees and replaced them with supporters, but some of those he fired were Lorimer's men. The Blond Boss retaliated, having the Republican-controlled Cook County Board fire Swift supporters from county jobs and replace them with Lorimer's men. Swift and Lorimer then fought for control of the county Republican organization. The Blond Boss prevailed, taking over the executive committee and most of the city ward organizations and even electing himself Cook County GOP chairman. Still, Swift's endorsement would give McKinley a foothold in Cook County and a ready army of supporters.[30]

There was one problem: Kohlsaat. The publisher was a childhood friend of the mayor and one of his most important supporters. Kohlsaat discouraged Swift from helping McKinley. While Kohlsaat and the Major were close, Kohlsaat didn't want Swift to endanger his political future by endorsing a presidential candidate. Once again, the publisher had different priorities than McKinley.[31]

MEANWHILE, SINCE AT LEAST January, McKinley and Hanna had men covering the entire country, organizing everywhere. McKinley believed in aligning authority with responsibility, so agents were told to find the right men to build an organization in each county and congressional district that could deliver a McKinley majority in their local and state conventions, preferably instructed to support the Major. They were to report to Hanna and he was available for advice and reasonable expenses for their work, if need be. McKinley would follow up by letter, meet with important prospective supporters, or otherwise reinforce the men they recruited.

One of Hanna's agents was John Hay, who reported tidbits he heard from Senators Henry Cabot Lodge and Don Cameron, both close friends and neighbors. Lodge was the brains behind the Reed campaign and Cameron fancied himself the leading silver Republican presidential prospect. Hay's link to Cameron also gave the McKinley operation a back channel to Senator Quay, Cameron's Senate colleague and the Pennsylvania GOP boss.

Hanna was impressed with Hay's gossip from Cameron, Quay, and Lodge. "I think you are as good at the game as either of the Penn[sylvania] Senators," Hanna wrote Hay, "and I am perfectly willing to leave them in your hands." Hanna probably didn't know that Hay had had an affair with Cameron's wife, Lizzie, whose uncle was Senator John Sherman, and was now pursuing Lodge's wife, Nannie.[32]

Men like Hay were critical to McKinley's early organizational efforts in early 1895. Osborne focused on the Northeast and a few Southern states. Joseph P. Smith handled most of the South, while William Hahn split the Midwest with Charles Dick, another former Ohio GOP state chairman, and covered some Western states. Myron T. Herrick even played a role on his four-month vacation to California, meeting with state party leaders and reporting back.[33]

McKinley put more agents into the field earlier and in a more systematic and highly structured way than any other candidate or the Combine. And even then, the Combine did not have as many men circulating nor an emphasis on instruction. It was not in their interest to instruct delegates: that made it more difficult to trade them at convention time.

THEN MCKINLEY WAS DEALT a blow that could have derailed his campaign by making it impossible to unite Ohio. McKinley's second term as governor was up in November and he would not seek a third one, nor attempt to name his successor at the state Republican convention in Zanesville on May 29. That didn't keep Hanna from having his own aspirations to be the Ohio kingmaker: he backed former state attorney general George K. Nash to succeed the Major.

What neither anticipated was that Joseph B. Foraker would reappear after a two-year hiatus and attempt to grab control of the Ohio Republican Party. After failing to unseat Senator Sherman in January 1892 or advance himself at that year's GOP national convention, and still tarnished by his disastrous bid for a third term as governor in 1889, Foraker had gone underground, rebuilding his law practice and waiting for a chance to re-emerge on the political stage.

Fire Alarm Joe Foraker said he returned only because Republican "enemies" complained he had chosen to "neglect" the party's "interests for his own." And while McKinley might have thought the rocky relationship and earlier disagreements were behind them, Foraker's perspective was different, writing later with customary flair that "a battle royal was to be fought between two great factions" at the convention because "nothing short of a genuine trial of strength would satisfy either."[34]

One man—Foraker—was coming to the state convention looking for a fight while his target—McKinley—was hoping to have everyone happy and unified behind him. Regardless of the outcome, unity was at risk now. This was not going to be pretty.

Fire Alarm Joe coaxed a reluctant Asa S. Bushnell to run. Foraker and his ally George Cox, boss of the Cincinnati Republican machine, kept their forces in reserve, bleeding enough votes to Bushnell on each ballot to keep his total growing. Then, when delegates turned toward Bushnell after midnight on the sixth ballot, Cox's Hamilton County men moved as a bloc behind him, putting him over the top and forever in their debt.

Foraker then dictated the rest of the ticket, stacked the state central committee, named the state chairman and national committeeman, and won an unprecedented endorsement of himself for the U.S. Senate seat held by Democrat Calvin S. Brice, which was up in January 1896. "The Hanna men were not allowed to surrender," a contemporary later wrote. "They were captured, and even their side arms were taken."[35]

The results were widely seen as a serious defeat for McKinley. "The McKinleyites got nothing, not even civil treatment," said one paper. They were beaten by "revolutionists, bent on the overthrow of the McKinley power in Ohio." The *Cincinnati Enquirer* said, "McKinley Presidential stock has taken a great fall," while the subhead in the *New York Times* banner read, "The Governor may not have his state's solid backing at the national convention." The Major's nomination depended on a united Ohio delegation. That appeared to be in jeopardy. Even McKinley's men admitted "his archenemy was in complete control."[36]

The Combine exulted in the Zanesville results, hoping it provided an opportunity to put their Ohio friends to use. Clarkson reached out to Foraker and reported to his superiors that there was a chance to split Ohio and kill McKinley's chances.[37]

One bit of good news for McKinley was that the Zanesville platform endorsed him for president and said the state's Republicans "pledge him the absolute and unswerving support of Ohio at the next national convention." Platforms could be broken or ignored, but this was a strong endorsement, difficult to disregard, even harder to abandon. Foraker would have killed this plank if he could, but McKinley's home-state support was too strong. Occasionally a realist, Foraker also came to understand he needed a united effort to elect Bushnell and carry a Republican legislature if he was to go to the Senate. If Foraker broke with the platform's endorsement of

McKinley, the Major's men could well break with the platform's endorsement of Foraker.[38]

Fire Alarm Joe was also canny enough to know June 1895 was not the time to fracture the Ohio GOP. The national convention was a year off. If McKinley displayed weakness, there would be time to undermine him. For now Foraker was content with his return to power and stayed quiet when Hanna claimed, "Ohio will send a solid and loyal McKinley delegation."[39]

The Ohio platform contained another problem for McKinley. A plank that McKinley helped write endorsed bimetallism, the use of gold and silver as "standard money" with "parity of values of the two metals." The impossibility of achieving parity drew abuse from gold advocates such as the *Nation,* which characterized the Ohio plan as "a throwaway to silverites." The Ohio GOP's tilt to the white metal added to suspicions that McKinley preferred silver or a straddle. For now, the Major was content being murky. In perhaps the biggest mistake of his emerging campaign, he still considered the issue inconsequential. He would be proven wrong.[40]

CHAPTER 9

The People Against the Bosses

————◄◦►————

The two most powerful Republican Party bosses were of the same mind on the presidential race. Their states—New York and Pennsylvania—had the convention's largest delegations and were the largest sources of Republican campaign contributions. They believed they controlled the RNC and had a coast-to-coast network of similarly minded party leaders that the press took to calling the Combine.

The Combine's strategy for 1896 had worked many times before: put as many favorite sons into the field as possible to keep the situation fluid and their options open. A candidate like Reed would be acceptable—he was New England's favorite son—but better that New York and Pennsylvania (and states they influenced, such as Connecticut and New Jersey, and party leaders throughout the South) withhold support until the eventual nominee felt indebted and therefore more compliant on cabinet posts and patronage.

The more heavy-handed of the two, Thomas Collier Platt, was then sixty-two years old. Tall, slim, slightly stooped, with thinning hair, sad eyes, and a close-cropped gray mustache and beard, Platt had risen rapidly in U.S. senator Roscoe Conkling's "Stalwart" machine after the war. He was elected to the Senate in 1881, only to resign in tandem with Conkling a few months later to protest Garfield's appointment of a nonmachine man as New York port collector. The two senators thought they would immediately be reelected in a rebuke to Garfield that would force him to put their ally in this important patronage post. But neither man was returned. Conkling's career ended and Platt went into exile until he resumed his climb to domination of the Empire State GOP in 1887. By 1895, he was called "the Easy Boss" for his soft manner, but because of his long exile and slow return to power, he had a hard edge and a wariness of possible adversaries.[1]

Platt's pragmatic compatriot was Pennsylvania senator Matthew S. Quay, also sixty-two, a small, trim man with bushy eyebrows and a walrus mustache. He had received the Congressional Medal of Honor for heroism at Fredericksburg. He had taken control of the Keystone State GOP away from the state's senior senator, J. Donald Cameron, then was dethroned when reform elements split from the party in 1882 and the GOP lost control of Pennsylvania. He recovered and was elected U.S. senator in 1887 before brilliantly managing Harrison's campaign. Unlike Platt, he lacked a nickname and a penchant for grudges.[2]

The two men's holds on their states seemed solid, but Quay knew how tentative his position could be, having overthrown Cameron to take control of Pennsylvania and then been thrown out himself temporarily. So when he was challenged again at home, he knew he would have to act fast and audaciously. In spring 1895, Quay's pick for the GOP's Philadelphia mayoral nomination had been knifed at the last minute by David S. Martin, a McKinley man and local power broker. Led by Martin, anti-Quay elements then challenged Quay's position as boss. In response, Quay made a bold move: he would personally contest the reelection of the state GOP chairman, B. F. Gilkeson, who had unwisely joined Quay's rivals.[3]

Running for state chairman was dangerous. If Quay lost, he would lose all power, have no role in the 1896 convention, and not be reelected to the Senate. But if Quay won, he would rule Pennsylvania stronger than ever.

Already without federal patronage since a Democrat was in the White House, Quay would not have state patronage to help grease his path. The Republican governor, Daniel H. Hastings, was friendly with Quay, but also with Quay's adversaries. The Pittsburgh machine and most of the railroad magnates joined Martin's Philadelphia men in opposing Quay. Steel and coal companies, while grateful for Quay's past help, were leery of getting involved in an intraparty fight.[4]

So Quay knitted a coalition of rural Republicans antagonistic to corrupt big-city machines, Civil War veterans eager to support one of their own, and urban reformers who were suspicious of bosses but eager for a leader to oppose corrupt machine practices.[5]

Tensions were high as the August 1895 state convention loomed. Each side's careful count showed that Quay had slightly more delegates. Emboldened, Quay insinuated that six new Hastings-appointed appellate judges might be denied the party's nomination, and confronted one opposition leader with documents alleging he had stolen government monies. Quay threatened to give them to the authorities unless he caved. Quay went to court to compel Gilkeson to cough up the party's ledgers, which showed he had dipped into its war chest for personal expenses. Quay men swarmed the convention hotels wearing large badges reading, "What Did He Do With It?" After an all-night negotiation, the anti-Quay forces surrendered. Credentials challenges were amicably settled, Hastings's judges were slated, and Gilkeson withdrew and nominated Quay. Quay now had more power over the Pennsylvania GOP, and his longtime critics—the Republican reform wing—had an unexpected champion.[6]

By cementing his control of the Pennsylvania GOP, Quay also put himself in a stronger position to influence the 1896 race, in part by damaging two presidential hopefuls as he saved his own political life. Senator Don Cameron had stayed out of the chairman's fight and now, as a Free Silver man, found himself at odds with the state party's support of a sound-money plank. Quay had engineered the provision, knowing it would damage Cameron's presidential ambitions as the Eastern champion of Western silver interests. Benjamin Harrison—believing Quay's defeat "would be a good thing for the party"—was also hurt. The bad blood between the two men after the 1888 campaign meant the former president would get little Pennsylvania support if he ran.[7]

Still, the close call revealed anti-Quay sentiment in Pittsburgh and Philadelphia that McKinley and Hanna could exploit for delegates.

THERE WERE TWO POTENTIAL GOP presidential candidates who had independent bases of support, and whom the bosses could not easily manipulate—Harrison and House Speaker Thomas B. Reed. They had the most strength outside their home state and region. Both were in a position to take advantage of McKinley's Zanesville defeat, but neither actively pro-moted himself as a possible Republican contender in 1895. Instead, in the timeworn parlance of Gilded Age politics, they put their fate "in the hands of their friends." The presence of both men as possible candidates helped the Combine as Harrison locked up Indiana and froze allies around the country while Reed was naturally expected to hold all of New England. This freed the Combine to focus its attention on promoting favorite sons in other states.

"Apathetic" would be an understatement of Harrison's attitude about the 1896 contest. While boosters talked up his chances, Harrison was disinterested. He wrote a former appointee, "I am in sympathy with those who think they are entitled to have a new name." [8]

Louis T. Michener, his former political advisor and now a Washington lawyer and lobbyist, peppered Harrison with letters full of political gossip designed to spur his former boss into action, warning against trusting John K. Gowdy, the Indiana GOP chairman, or reporting on efforts to get West Virginia and Indiana to instruct for the former president. Michener addressed his letter to Harrison's private secretary, E. Frank Tibbott, and clumsily used "H.-" or "Hart" instead of Harrison's last name to give his former chief plausible deniability if a letter leaked.

Reed, the Combine's preferred choice, was in a better position than Harrison, in part because he actually wanted to run. After crushing the Democratic filibusters as House Speaker from 1889 to 1891 and ably lead-ing the Republican minority since then, he was also the GOP's most popu-lar figure. He was set to become Speaker again in late 1895, when the new Congress was seated. "The Democratic mortality will be so great," Reed had predicted before the 1894 midterms, "that their dead will be buried in trenches and marked 'unknown.' " He was right. [9]

But, like Harrison, Reed was strangely passive. North Carolina Re-publicans endorsed him in August 1894, but Reed did not seek any other states' endorsements in 1895, even as McKinley used his new friendship with Senator Pritchard to keep Tar Heel Republicans from renewing their support of the Speaker. [10]

Instead, Reed endured the last two months of the lame-duck Dem-ocratic Congress that ended March 3, spent the summer at the beach in Maine, and returned to Washington in November to be elected Speaker, only without his famous walrus mustache. After supposedly falling asleep in the House barber's chair, he awoke to find the barber had waxed his treasured mustache. Shocked, Reed ordered him to shave it off, saying, "You've made me look like a darned catfish."[11]

Reed was now content to leave his aspirations "in the hands of friends" and wait until the convention neared, but no one "friend" was in command of the Reed campaign. Instead, there were three.

Joseph H. Manley was Republican national secretary, Maine's committeeman, and Reed's manager. He was a longtime operative who had helped in each of Blaine's presidential bids. Though Reed and Blaine were antagonists, Reed welcomed Manley's help since Manley knew national Republican leaders. But Manley was neither well organized nor steady. He was more of a busybody, as events would show.[12]

The second chief was the brainy Massachusetts senator Henry Cabot Lodge, who had served with Reed in the House. He canvassed fellow senators and organized the Bay State. Reed later decided Lodge would lead his efforts at the national convention, raising the possibility of friction with Manley, who had worked the RNC and state party leaders for months.

Reed further confused the situation by making Illinois representative James F. Aldrich his official campaign chairman. Aldrich was energetic and personally committed to Reed, but as a sophomore congressman, he was not influential. He didn't begin work in earnest until 1896 and was then focused on recruiting House members, which left Reed with nothing like McKinley's systematic outreach or extensive grassroots organization.[13]

Reed did have the advantage of the polished pen of Theodore Roosevelt, who was having the time of his life as a newly appointed New York City police commissioner. In a sign of his enthusiasm for his appointment in 1895, Teddy had written his sister that he was spending nights "tramping the street, finding out by personal inspection how the police were doing their duty."[14]

Still, TR had higher ambitions. After a crushing third-place finish in the 1886 New York mayor's race and on the outs with Platt, he knew doors were closed to him in the state. The only way to resurrect his political career was to secure an appointment in a Republican administration in Washington. So while the New York City Police Department absorbed most of his energy, Roosevelt wrote articles in influential journals, praising Reed's leadership in ending the Democratic filibuster and advancing sound-money principles.[15]

TR took it upon himself to defend Reed on currency because he believed the election would be dominated by the issue and, as he told Lodge, there was a "very widespread feeling among good solid Republicans here that Tom Reed has straddled the financial issue." He warned Reed must forcefully oppose Free Silver. "He can not keep the Silver fanatics with him, and . . . the sound money men at present feel that he is luke-warm in the matter."[16]

Roosevelt had seen this coming, having told Lodge earlier that he regretted "Reed did not make a strong anti–free silver coinage speech" early in 1895. "Had he done so . . . there would not now be the slightest opposition to him in New York." But Reed had neither the interest nor the campaign leaders who would have sensed and dealt with this weakness.[17]

The *Nation* slapped Reed around the day after TR's warning to Lodge, saying the notion that the former Speaker was safe on currency meant "it must have been some other Reed whom the Populists chased into the cloakrooms in the last Congress" when he flirted with a silver bill to bedevil Cleveland. The magazine warned that "his honest-money friends in the East have in vain besought to pull his Sino-Shaksperian [sic] head out of the sand" on the money issue. McKinley apparently wasn't the only candidate with problems on currency.[18]

SINCE REED AND HARRISON had "friends" to manage preparations, the Combine leaders and their agents focused on favorite-son candidates who could lock up their own states and be manipulated. These men were less well known outside their states and had little chance of winning. But they would be indebted to the Combine for its help; lightning might strike, and if it didn't, they could strengthen their right to patronage and other considerations by delivering their supporters to the convention's ultimate winner.

The machine men sent each other coded letters to report progress, organized the favorite sons, and requested assistance, especially money, from Platt's financial backers. Quay suggested they begin in April 1895 by dispatching J. Sloat Fassett, an Elmira, New York, lawyer and newspaper editor, for a nearly three-month tour of the Midwest and West to sample opinions about the race. A Platt lieutenant, Fassett had friends across the country from serving as RNC committee secretary before Manley and as

temporary chairman of the 1892 convention. McKinley men had been collecting such information for months.[19]

Iowa's U.S. senator William B. Allison was near the top of the Combine's list of favorite sons. Allison left politics to his longtime handler, Ret
Clarkson. Clarkson's biggest concerns were preparing an Allison campaign
biography and ingratiating himself with Platt and Quay. His most important link to the Combine was Grenville M. Dodge, a fabulously wealthy
railroad engineer who now lived in New York but had represented Iowa for
a term in the House. Dodge was Platt's paymaster and Republican fund-
raiser extraordinaire. Ret also had many friends who owed him: he had
been first assistant postmaster general under Harrison, handing out lucrative post office jobs across the country. This was especially important in the
South. For his part, Allison was focused on helping Iowa legislative candidates in the 1895 state elections. They would decide if he was reelected
senator in January 1896.[20]

While Dodge and Ret worked Iowa for Allison, Lorimer and Tanner
were talking up Illinois's favorite son, Uncle Shelby Cullom. They had had
no difficulty in coaxing him into the race. A fringe player twice before, the
senator wanted the nomination "more than he had wanted nearly anything
in his career." This blinded him: Cullom apparently didn't understand that
the alliance between Tanner, his longtime handler, and Lorimer, whose
Cook County machine had opposed his reelection in 1895, was for mutual
benefit, not out of loyalty to the senator. He was their tool. Cullom and the
machine men thought their cooperation made it unlikely anyone would
challenge him for Illinois's convention voters. They were mistaken.[21]

Platt had his own favorite son ready for New York, Governor Levi
P. Morton. He had an impressive resume: congressman, ambassador to
France, and Harrison's vice president. After Harrison's defeat, he had
remained in Washington until the Easy Boss brought him home to best
Senator David B. Hill in the 1894 gubernatorial race. But the tall, clean-
shaven, round-faced Morton had drawbacks: he was a multimillionaire
New York banker and he was seventy-one. If elected, he would be the old-
est president in history.

West Virginia senator Stephen B. Elkins also began angling for
favorite-son status in 1895. He had served as Harrison's war secretary and
had deep connections throughout the West, where he had made his fortune as a young man. While he managed his coal and rail business interests

from New York, he lived in West Virginia and had helped steer the GOP's rise to power there. He was interested in being vice president and figured offering himself for president would help secure the number-two spot. He purchased the *Cincinnati Commercial Gazette,* southwest Ohio's most important paper, and whose editorials could cause problems for McKinley at home.[22]

Elkins made a Western swing in May 1895, accompanied by Richard C. Kerens, his business partner and a McKinley man. The two stopped in New Mexico and Colorado for a mix of business and politics, followed by political events in Montana and Oregon. Elkins made speeches along the way in which he favored the use of silver money, but he avoided endorsing Free Silver. Otherwise, Elkins was content to spend 1895 watching and waiting.[23]

Minnesota senator Cushman K. Davis became a favorite-son candidate when Minnesota representative James M. Tawney said in spring 1895 that his state would send "a solid delegation" for Davis to the national convention. Davis was a leading Republican voice on foreign affairs but had grabbed headlines by supporting Cleveland's tough actions against the Pullman strikers in 1894, wiring union officials that "you are rapidly approaching the overt act of levying war against the United States." Realistically, Davis had no chance, but the Combine hoped he would hold Minnesota's eighteen delegates against former governor Merriam's efforts in the state for McKinley.[24]

There was also talk of Kentucky governor William O. Bradley and Tennessee's Clay Evans, but just with Morton, Allison, Cullom, Elkins, and Davis in the race as favorite sons, along with Reed and Harrison, the Combine had roughly 304 of the 463 votes needed to nominate. That was even before they influenced neighboring states or reminded Southern brethren of past and future favors.

MORTON WAS THE FIRST of the Combine's proxy candidates to be tested against McKinley when they both attended the Southern Exposition in Atlanta in September 1895. The men had lunch the afternoon of their joint appearance and visited for an hour before the elderly New York governor went for a nap, while McKinley stood under the trees on the exposition's grounds and greeted fairgoers.[25]

They spoke later in the auditorium packed with 25,000 Civil War veterans from the North and South. McKinley and Morton were seated onstage with Confederate lieutenant general James Longstreet, an active Republican, between them. Saying, "Americans never surrendered except to Americans," the Major called for a "fresh baptism of patriotism," saying "the best way to get it is by immersion." McKinley told the crowd, "The war has been over for 31 years. The bitterness and resentment belong to the past and its glories are the common heritage of us all." He ended by proclaiming, "If we ever fight again, and I pray God that we may never have to . . . we will fight on the same side and we will fight under the same flag." [26]

Georgia governor William Y. Atkinson then hosted dinner for Morton and McKinley. Morton refused requests to speak, so the audience then called for McKinley. He gave a short, patriotic talk, saying, "We take no orders from any other nation; we accept no governmental standards but our own, and we acknowledge no flag but the stars and stripes we love." The *Atlanta Constitution* took notice, writing, "McKinley, unlike Morton, knows how to arouse the enthusiasm of a crowd. Besides being a broad man he is a great orator, a quality which Governor Morton lacks." [27]

The *World* later stirred up trouble by reporting that McKinley told the New Yorker he "would make a magnificent President" and hoped if he couldn't win, Morton would be nominated. The Democratic paper alleged McKinley promised if he could not be nominated, Ohio would support Morton, expecting a similar pledge in return. But "Morton, with a little smile, thanked Gov. McKinley for his contingent promise of help but said 'it was too early to speak.'" Georgia's Reconstruction Republican governor, Rufus Bullock, and Morton's private secretary supposedly witnessed the exchange during a carriage ride. This did not sound like McKinley. The Major knew that if Morton withdrew, Platt would decide where New York went, not the governor. The newspaper was exaggerating. [28]

STILL, THE COMBINE WONDERED: was McKinley pliable or another wooly-headed reformer surrounded by amateurs best left to flounder on his own?

In May 1895, former Michigan governor Russell A. Alger was sent by the Combine to visit Hanna. Alger reported to Quay he had posed two inquiries on behalf of "our committee." The first concerned patronage and cabinet positions. That made Hanna uncomfortable. McKinley's intention was that he "should stand without a single fetter, before the people, if he receives the nomination." That kind of talk was mystifying and naïve to the machine men. Alger's second question concerned collusion with anti-Platt forces in New York. Alger was assured "no pledges, understandings, or encouragements" had been or would be given to Platt's rivals. That was perhaps untrue: there was an active New York McKinley League, led by Platt's enemies and encouraged by the Major.[29]

At the end of May, McKinley attended an unusual dinner at Chauncey M. Depew's Manhattan mansion. When Depew, Cornelius Vanderbilt's money manager and Platt's stalking-horse candidate at the 1892 convention, sent an invitation, it was wise to accept. Twenty-four men enjoyed an excellent meal and then rose for cigars, after-dinner drinks, and conversation until midnight.[30]

At the table were three presidential hopefuls (McKinley, Harrison, and Morton), one vice presidential aspirant (Elkins), one boss (Platt), several of Platt's critics, and other officeholders, plutocrats, and politicians. Two city police commissioners were present: Frederick D. Grant, son of the former president, and Theodore Roosevelt. Although Montana senator Thomas Carter's Free Silver pronouncements upset Harrison, little of substance was said that evening. The host explained he wanted to bring everyone together "to smooth out the political acerbities of the hour." It also gave Platt an opportunity to see McKinley up close.[31]

There was also talk of a Combine-McKinley sit-down, though nothing came of it. Quay rebuffed Hanna's attempts to get him to visit McKinley in Ohio. Instead, Hanna went to New York to confer with the bosses, including Platt, Quay, Manley, and Senator Nelson Aldrich of Rhode Island. According to Myron T. Herrick, "Hanna succeeded in convincing them that McKinley was the strongest candidate." Considering how they acted in the months ahead, that was certainly false.[32]

Hanna returned to Cleveland, where the McKinleys were staying at his home. Reports of what transpired next vary in detail, but not substance: it was a telling moment that would set the direction and theme of McKinley's campaign for the GOP nomination.

Herrick and Kohlsaat were present when Hanna reported on his Combine meeting. Herrick recalled that McKinley, Hanna, and others were with him in Hanna's library on a Sunday morning. Hanna passed around cigars. McKinley listened while Hanna said to him, "Now, Major, it's all over but the shouting. Quay wants the patronage of Pennsylvania, Aldrich of New England, and Manley of Maine. Platt wants that of New York, but he wants it in writing: you remember he was fooled on Harrison. I think they are willing to leave this region to me." The last line was jarring. It does not sound like something Hanna would say, especially in McKinley's presence.[33]

While Kohlsaat thought the group met in Hanna's den after Sunday dinner, he had similar recollections. Hanna told McKinley, " 'You can get both New York and Pennsylvania, Governor, but there are certain conditions.' McKinley: 'What are they?' Hanna: 'They want a promise that you will appoint Tom Platt Secretary of the Treasury, and they want it in writing. Platt says he has had an experience with one President (Harrison) born in Ohio, and he wants no more verbal promises.' "[34]

Herrick later wrote that "McKinley's face grew serious—in fact, hard" and he "remained silent for quite a little while" before finally saying, "Mark, some things come too high. If I were to accept the nomination on those terms, the place would be worth nothing to me and less to the people. If those are the terms, I am out of it." Hanna responded, "Oh no, not so fast. I mean that in these terms the nomination would be settled immediately, but that does not mean that their terms have got to be accepted. There is a strong sentiment for you all over the country and while it would be hard to lick those fellows if they oppose you, damned hard, I believe we can do it."[35]

Again, Kohlsaat's memories were similar. "McKinley was smoking a cigar. He threw his head back and let the smoke curl up . . . then got up and paced the little room. . . . 'There are some things in this world that come too high. If I cannot be President without promising to make Tom Platt Secretary of the Treasury, I will never be President.' Hanna: 'New York and Pennsylvania will clinch the nomination—with the votes already in sight.' McKinley: 'I can't do it, Mark.' 'Well,' Hanna replied, 'we have got to work harder to make up that big block of voters, but we will get them!' "[36]

Herrick and Kohlsaat may have exaggerated some of the details, but in the summer of 1895, McKinley decided he would not accommodate the machine men. This was either out of principle—he wanted to become president unbound—or perhaps caution, since he knew the Combine would repudiate him instantly if they found someone more pliant.

Herrick recounted that at the meeting, McKinley asked, "How would this do for a slogan? The Bosses Against the People?" There was some discussion, generally favorable. Ultimately someone reversed the phrases and it became "The People Against the Bosses." The Major would use the opposition of Platt, Quay, and other machine men to appeal to reform-minded Republicans sick of their party's Gilded Age excesses. He would run to win the race on his terms.[37]

BUT FIRST, HE HAD to do all he could to keep Ohio in his column, difficult at any time, trickier when Foraker was involved. Fortunately, McKinley was enormously popular. Bushnell needed his backing to win the governorship and Foraker was counting on a Republican legislative majority in the Senate. McKinley set out to make himself useful to both men, campaigning whenever and wherever they wanted and calculating that Foraker's loyalty depended on how much he credited the Major for helping the ticket.

He was the headliner when the Ohio GOP kicked off its fall campaign in Springfield on September 10, speaking before a crowd of 30,000 to 40,000 and firing up the Republican faithful with both Bushnell and Foraker watching the crowd's excited response.

For the rest of the election, except for his Atlanta trip, McKinley was "inconspicuous on the national stage . . . indefatigable at home," putting his popularity to work for Bushnell directly and Foraker indirectly. He campaigned as if he were on the ballot. In a way, he was. "Huge crowds greeted McKinley everywhere with roaring approval" and GOP concerns about the labor vote faded as miners and mill and factory workers turned out to cheer the "Napoleon of Protection."[38]

As the election drew to a close, McKinley appeared at a Cleveland rally that even the hostile *Plain Dealer* admitted was large and enthusiastic. When McKinley's name was mentioned, "the crowd broke loose and for four or five minutes it yelled so loud that the band, which began playing 'America,' was almost drowned out."[39]

In November, the entire Ohio GOP ticket was swept in. Bushnell was elected by 92,622 votes (a bigger margin than McKinley's 1893 win) and the GOP won a huge legislative majority that guaranteed Foraker his Senate seat.[40]

On the day in January when the legislature elected Foraker to replace Democratic senator Calvin Brice, McKinley visited Foraker at his hotel. Fire Alarm Joe later recalled that the Major came "to congratulate me . . . and to talk over with me his prospects for the Presidency." McKinley wanted Foraker to go as an at-large delegate and help his campaign. While Foraker claimed he "hoped and believed" McKinley would be nominated, he feared "a repetition of the charges of treachery and bad faith" he had suffered after previous national conventions. The Major persisted, pledging that Hanna would "have frequent consultations" with him and saying, "I shall be pleased to see and confer with you at any time." It must have pleased Foraker to know he could have Hanna grovel at his leisure, but it probably mattered more that the Major thought enough of him to raise the issue personally and offer an open door to him. Fire Alarm agreed to be a delegate and help make McKinley the Republican nominee.[41]

Part of Foraker's willingness may have come from recognition that he was a freshman senator, 1896 was not likely to be his year, but he was young enough (forty-nine) to have more chances at the White House. Foraker had to have known how much affection Ohio Republicans had for McKinley. All this made it more likely Foraker would keep his pledge to back the Major for the White House.[42]

On a clear, cold January 13, the largest crowd in Ohio history gathered in Columbus to see one governor leave and another take office. McKinley and Bushnell entered the ceremony arm in arm and were greeted with loud applause. When McKinley stepped forward, it was to "tremendous cheers." As his last official act, he presented Bushnell with his commission, saying, "No act in my four years' incumbency has given me more genuine pleasure than this. I know it will not be out of place to say, for it is in my heart to say it, that you have my warm and sincere personal good wishes, both in your public and private life."[43]

McKinley and Ida returned to Canton that night. Their old home on North Market had become available and McKinley had quickly bought it.

He told Whitelaw Reid's *New-York Tribune* that he and Ida were delighted to be back "in the house which twenty five years ago we took up our house keeping as newly married people." As the McKinleys prepared to celebrate their silver wedding anniversary, his presidential campaign had been under way in earnest for more than a year.[44]

CHAPTER 10

Democrats Fall Apart

———◄◦►———

In the years running up to the 1896 election, the Democratic Party was pulled apart by economic and sectional forces. Republicans rejoiced as Cleveland's hold over his party disintegrated and new radical leaders rose within it, and the GOP regained its strength in Congress. Surely the White House would fall to the Republicans next time. But politics rarely moves in a simple, sure line. What Republican leaders did not yet grasp was that the new movement growing inside the Democratic Party could splinter old allegiances and remake the political system, and not to the GOP's advantage.

The high point of Democratic unity came on March 4, 1893, when Cleveland was sworn in for his second, nonconsecutive term. For the first time since James Buchanan, the Democratic Party controlled the presidency and both houses of Congress.[1]

But political power doesn't equate to political equanimity, let alone unity. In the waning days of the Harrison administration, the Panic of 1893 erupted, plunging the country into severe economic hardship. Cleveland returned to the White House facing an immediate economic crisis. He and many in his circle saw a strict adherence to the gold standard as the best way to shore up the economy. Others, including many Democratic leaders in the West and South as well as farmers and workers, believed prosperity would return only by increasing the money supply through expanded use of silver. This group came to strongly disagree—even hate—how the president addressed the growing depression.

Cleveland, who was not adept at forging unity within his party, began his second term by calling for sound money—meaning gold—and then spent the next several months further infuriating silverites. The approach ignited a political civil war within the ranks of the Democrats. How that war unfolded, how it ended, and who emerged on top would have serious repercussions for the nation's politics for decades to come.

THE WAR WITHIN THE Democratic Party was sparked by a sharp decline in the Treasury Department's gold reserves. If those reserves fell too low, it was possible that the Treasury might not have enough of the yellow metal if people wanted to exchange too much of the country's $524 million in greenbacks or silver notes for gold. If that happened, the value of the dollar would collapse, exports and imports disappear, the economy crater, and people reduced to barter.[2]

At the time, it was generally accepted that the Treasury needed to maintain at least $100 million in gold reserves to ensure the currency was not in danger. By April, they dipped below the $100 million mark. Cleveland blamed the dropping gold reserves for all the bad economic news that followed that year—the stock market's collapse in May, a wave of bank failures across the South and West, a meltdown in Western silver mining states when India abandoned the silver standard, and growing unemployment as thousands lost their jobs daily. But instead of worrying about declining gold reserves, many Americans blamed the president's inaction for the economy. Soup kitchens were soon called "Cleveland Cafes."[3]

The president and Treasury Secretary John G. Carlisle believed the culprit was the 1890 Sherman Silver Purchase Act. They knew silver notes issued under the Sherman Act to purchase bullion were recycled for gold coin, which held greater value. By undermining confidence in the dollar, the law also led European investors to sell American investments, thus drawing down U.S. gold reserves as foreigners took their profits home.[4]

So the president called on Congress to repeal the Sherman Silver Act, arguing the panic resulted from "unwise laws." Prosperity would not return until the Treasury stopped trading valuable gold for less precious silver. Bad money was driving out good. The president committed political capital to repeal the Sherman Act to halt the panic—and thereby pushed off his planned tariff reforms, an issue he campaigned on in 1892.[5]

He was savaged by Free Silver supporters. Their leader, Missouri representative Richard P. Bland, denounced Cleveland's call for repeal as part of "a conspiracy" between English banks and Wall Street. America's reliance on the gold standard, Bland claimed, led to the depression by shrinking the money supply, causing prices to drop and money to become too dear.

Some silver leaders threatened violence. Colorado Populist governor David H. Waite told a rally in July that "it is better infinitely that blood should flow to the horses' bridles than our national liberties be destroyed," earning him a nickname—"Bloody Bridles Waite." [6]

As Congress argued over the Sherman Act for the next three months, the country's economic situation deteriorated. Drought and falling prices devastated farmers, while factory and rail workers, miners, and store clerks lost their jobs. In August, *Bradstreet* reported on the "enforced idleness of nearly 1,000,000 wage-earners." Economists estimated two million were unemployed, one of every six workers. [7]

Williams Jennings Bryan, a young sophomore Democrat in the House from Nebraska, was one of Cleveland's most vocal critics, arguing the gold standard meant lower prices for U.S. goods and would make the nation "an English colony." The people wanted more silver, he argued, because it would restore prosperity. Cleveland stood with "the moneyed interests, aggravated wealth and capital, imperious, arrogant and compassionless." Democrats must decide between the "work-worn and dust-begrimed" people and the plutocrats. [8]

Despite silver rhetoric like that of Bryan, the House repealed the Sherman Act, with Democrats split 138 in favor to 78. For now most Democrats stood with the president, though he had to threaten some with assorted political punishments. [9]

Senate rules allowing unlimited debate and the bipartisan opposition organized by Tennessee Democrat Isham Harris and Colorado Republican Henry Teller made the upper chamber rougher sailing. By late October, most Senate Democrats wanted a compromise that would placate the silver faction and released a letter outlining one, believing Carlisle supported it. Cleveland was livid, telling the press the law "should be unconditionally repealed" and threatening uncooperative Democratic senators. [10]

On October 30, the Senate capitulated and repealed the Sherman Silver Act by 48 to 37. Democrats were split, 26 to 18, with all but three of the negative votes from Southerners. The House concurred, but only after

Bland accused Cleveland of encouraging the panic in order to force the country under the gold standard and Bryan condemned his own party for ignoring the people. Half the grand bargain of 1890—the silver purchase law that enabled passage of the McKinley tariff—was gone and Democrats were bitterly divided.[11]

Repeal temporarily stopped the gold reserves' decline at $84 million, but it raised the political stakes for Cleveland. Now that he had signed the remedy he said would relieve the nation's distress, the economy was his and the Democratic Party's responsibility.

The grim economic news kept coming. Joblessness, hunger, and homelessness grew and the confidence of consumers and businesses remained low and political tensions increased. By year's end, 600 banks and 15,000 companies had closed, major railroads entered bankruptcy, and the American Federation of Labor pegged unemployment at 3 million. These were not the results Cleveland promised.[12]

In January 1894, the gold reserves dipped to a new low—$62 million— and Cleveland responded by using debatable legal authority to issue $50 million in bonds, paying a hefty 4 percent interest rate in gold. Financiers, foreign banks, and Wall Street snapped them up. Silver advocates were enraged. Kansas Populist senator William A. Peffer accused the president of selling "the people's credit to appease . . . these misers of Wall Street." Silver men in Congress retaliated, passing a bill increasing the money supply by requiring all the silver bullion in the mints—$55 million worth—to be turned into coins. Cleveland vetoed it, saying, "Sound finance does not commend a further infusion of silver." Gold Democrats sustained his veto.[13]

The veto further alienated silver Democrats. Bland predicted "people will elect a President in sympathy with them—someone not so tender of the interests of the bulls and bears of Wall Street." A South Carolina Democratic congressman said Cleveland was "worshipping at the shrine of the golden calf of Wall street." Bryan warned, "The South and West will get together and rid themselves of Eastern domination."[14]

THE ECONOMY DID NOT improve in 1894, especially on the Plains, which were suffering from drought and lousy farm prices. That summer, a Kansas farm wife wrote her governor, begging for help.

I take my Pen In hand to let you know that we are Starving to death. Hail destroyed our crops. My Husband went away to find work and came home last night and told me that we would have to Starve. He has bin in ten countys and did Get no work. . . . I haven't had nothing to Eat today and It is three oclock.[15]

There was growing civil unrest, including a protest march of thousands of unemployed men on Washington who demanded $500 million in new greenbacks to put the jobless to work on construction projects. The protest collapsed in May when its organizer, Jacob "General" Coxey, was arrested for trespassing on the Capitol grounds. But even if Coxey came off as a crank, the administration appeared coldhearted for its handling of the affair.[16]

Cleveland gained a particularly vicious enemy who would turn the party against its sitting president over his sending 12,000 federal troops and 3,600 federal deputies to restore order in Chicago and protect railroad traffic throughout the Midwest. This was ostensibly to guarantee the U.S. mail's delivery, but it was actually to stop violence and break a sympathy strike of railroad workers called to support Pullman Car Company employees who had walked off the job in a wage dispute.[17]

Cleveland's actions made Illinois Democratic governor John Peter Altgeld furious. The wiry, slight man with a closely cropped beard was a politician who called officeholders a "cowardly hang-on class." He boasted of spending "his whole life in the enforcement of the laws," but gained notoriety by pardoning anarchists found guilty of the Haymarket bombing in Chicago. A wealthy real estate developer, he was an economic radical who hated the money power and was thoroughly silver in his views. German-born, Altgeld was intense, angry, and tough, and he hated Cleveland's interference in his state.

The day after the army arrived in Chicago, Altgeld sent Cleveland a blistering letter calling the action "unjustifiable," prompted by "men who had political and selfish motives," namely railroad magnates whose trains were not running. Cleveland had violated "a fundamental principle of our Constitution." Altgeld argued "the exercise of the police power and the preservation of law and order" was a state, not a federal, prerogative, and demanded "the immediate withdrawal of these troops."[18]

Cleveland's reply was just 128 words. "Federal troops," he telegraphed

the governor, "were sent to Chicago in strict accordance with the Constitution and laws" to end the "obstruction of the mails." This was "not only
proper, but necessary."[19]

This angered Altgeld more. He accused the president of violating "the
principle of local self-government," imposing "military government," and
acting like the Russian czar. Altgeld again demanded a withdrawal. Cleveland's response was even more terse. He had the authority and the situation
demanded "active efforts." The president's new foe would soon attack him
with more than words.[20]

THAT SUMMER, CLEVELAND GAINED another enemy and the silver movement
a powerful education tool with the publication of a thin, twenty-five-cent
book titled *Coin's Financial School,* the fictional account of lectures delivered by a mysterious teenage financial genius who demolished the arguments of the nation's leading gold advocates.

Essentially a graphic comic book, the book was the work of William
Harvey, a lawyer turned silver prospector turned pitchman for the "Elixir
of Life" turned silver lobbyist with a Chicago publishing business on the
side devoted to Free Silver. Americans purchased a million copies, leading
a Democratic gold congressman to complain about the "little free silver
book . . . being sold on every railroad train by the newsboys and at every
cigar store" and "read by almost everyone."[21]

CLEVELAND'S SUPPORT FROM CONGRESSIONAL Democrats declined with
the economy. He had an opportunity with tariff reform to find common
ground with silver Democrats and boost his party before the midterm
elections, but failed when Congress passed the Wilson-Gorman Tariff in
August 1894. When Ways and Means Committee chairman William L.
Wilson drafted the bill the previous December, he had put raw materials,
such as coal, copper, iron ore, lumber, and wool, on the free list and reduced duties on manufactured items by roughly 15 percent. On the floor,
rural Democrats, many strong silver men, amended the bill to put sugar on
the free list and create a federal income tax.

But over the next five months, Maryland Democratic senator Arthur P.
Gorman added 634 amendments restoring many duties to their levels in

the McKinley bill. Cleveland protested, calling this "party perfidy and party dishonor." However, the Senate ignored him and the House concurred with Gorman's revisions. A cartoon titled "A Humiliating Spectacle" depicted the president in chains being dragged behind a chariot driven by a triumphant Gorman, crushing a tiny figure under his wheels— Wilson in a professor's cap. Cleveland was disgusted by the bill and let it become law without his signature. He wanted tariff reform, and if he had vetoed Wilson-Gorman, the McKinley Tariff would have remained on the books.[22]

The attempt at reform turned into a political fiasco. It kept Cleveland from placating Democratic silver senators and congressmen who supported cutting tariffs and it robbed Democrats of an achievement to run on in the fall elections.[23]

But not even good tariff reform could have saved Democrats in 1894 unless it sparked an immediate economic turnaround. Democrats controlled Washington, and Cleveland had promised that repeal of the Sherman Silver Act would restore prosperity. With unemployment still high, wages stagnant, business and consumer confidence shattered, and America racked by hunger, homelessness, and deprivation, Democrats were demolished in the midterms. In twenty-four states, no Democrat won national office.[24]

Ironically, while the Democrats lost many of their congressional seats in the North, the party's silver wing was left largely intact because it was centered in the South and West. So the defeat strengthened the silverites within the party. Bryan, however, would not be among the Democrats returning to Washington. He had barely won reelection in his previous election, and knowing the year would be tough on his party, declined to run for another term. He would depart the House in March 1895, harboring bigger ambitions.[25]

When a second round of gold bonds failed to stabilize the gold reserves, Cleveland asked Congress to authorize the issue of fifty-year gold bonds by public sale, to require customs duties to be paid in gold and to retire greenbacks and silver notes when they came to the Treasury. This last provision would prevent paper currency from being recycled to purchase gold bonds but would also reduce the money supply. Democrats who had earlier stood with Cleveland were no longer in office or were too frustrated with his economic failure to aid him. Most senators opposed his proposal, but

House Democrats beat them to the punch, defeating the bill, 125 ayes to 243 nays.[26]

Carlisle then opened direct negotiations with J. P. Morgan and August Belmont, a New York financier who represented the Rothschilds and European financial houses—the kind of moneymen Bland, Bryan, and Free Silver Democrats had lambasted. Carlisle planned to issue bonds using his existing authority, but asked the bankers if they would guarantee that gold would come from abroad and financiers' storehouses, rather than from exchanging silver notes for Treasury gold or withdrawing gold the bankers had on deposit at the Treasury. Cleveland himself met with Morgan and Belmont to discuss the issue. He could not afford another bond issue that drained the reserves.[27]

The financiers agreed. The Morgan-Belmont syndicate kept its word, importing gold and drawing on its stockpiles to prevent any further drain on the Treasury's reserves, which soon rose to $107 million, above the $100 million floor. The infusion of gold came just in time. At one point, the New York subtreasury was down to $9 million in gold and was about to receive a check to withdraw $12 million. Had that check arrived before the new gold reserves, the government could not have paid it.[28]

On February 20, the Morgan-Belmont syndicate sold on the open market the bonds it had purchased for a profit of $7 million or more. Wall Street didn't begrudge Morgan and Belmont their profits for averting calamity and shoring up confidence in the government's finances. But to many in the South and West, the deal proved Cleveland was in thrall to the money power. Democratic Free Silver men raged at this latest evidence of America's subservience to foreign financial powers. Bryan assailed "insidious bankers" and "foreign financiers" before arguing that Democrats owned "no great debt of gratitude" to the president. "What has he done for the party? He has attempted to inoculate it with Republican virus, and blood poisoning has set in."[29]

EACH OF CLEVELAND'S ACTIONS on currency had angered silver Democrats. Now they decided to end gold's domination and restore "the Dollar of the Daddies," as Bland and others called a silver currency. That required winning the presidency in 1896, which in turn required beating the incumbent Democrat for the party's nomination.

In early March, American Bimetallic League president Adoniram Judson "A. J." Warner tried providing a way to do that. The former Ohio Democratic congressman and Union general organized the Silver Party, which he hoped would attract white metal Republicans and Democrats. The new party called currency "the dominant issue," lashed both parties for "subservience to the gold power," and recommended Joseph C. Sibley for president in 1896. He was a one-term Pennsylvania congressman beaten for reelection in 1894 and, unusual for an Eastern Democrat, was for Free Silver. He now raised horses, after selling his oil refinery to John D. Rockefeller.

The Nevada congressional delegation of two Republican senators and a Democratic congressman immediately signed up for the new Silver Party, but there were few other high-profile recruits. Democratic silver men were particularly unimpressed. These insurgent Democrats were more confident about taking over their own party than they were about winning with a fledgling party bankrolled by Western Republican mine owners.[30]

Not wanting to desert the Democratic Party, Bryan tried summoning congressional Democrats to discuss reorganizing it along Free Silver lines. Texas silver representative Joseph W. Bailey not only disliked Bryan, but considered his focus too narrow, saying, "Man cannot live by bread alone. A party cannot succeed with naught but silver." Others agreed. Bryan had to settle for a letter signed by thirty-one Democratic representatives, mostly those retiring from the House like Bryan or defeated like Silver Dick Bland. The manifesto asserted, "The money question will be the paramount issue in 1896" and urged the Free Silver Democratic majority "to take charge of the party organizations" and make them "an effective instrument in the accomplishment of needed reforms." Less than what Bryan wanted, it was nonetheless the first public declaration that silver men would try seizing control of the Democratic Party.[31]

ONE OF CLEVELAND'S TOUGHEST enemies agreed silver Democrats must mount a coup, and he had an idea how to do it. After refusing an invitation to honor Cleveland on Jefferson's birthday by saying, "To laud Clevelandism on Jefferson's birthday is to sing a Te Deum in honor of Judas Iscariot on a Christmas morning," Altgeld started a national drive to reorganize the party on a strictly Free Silver basis by ordering the Illinois

Democratic Party to call a special state convention to decide its position on the money issue.[32]

Democratic state chairman and Illinois secretary of state William H. "Buck" Hinrichsen and Altgeld knew that Illinois Democrats, especially outside Chicago, were strongly pro-silver. They wanted to attack the sitting Democratic president by rejecting his currency policies. They hoped this would spark other state conventions across the country to rebuke Cleveland and commit to sending delegates to the national convention who would support a Free Silver platform. Altgeld and Hinrichsen knew the Democrats' national convention rules gave them a better shot at pushing a pro-silver plank through than at nominating a pro-silver candidate. The platform required a simple majority of delegates while the nomination required a two-thirds supermajority. They believed that a silver platform would bind the eventual nominee and attract the million Populist voters who showed up in 1892. Hinrichsen also believed a pro-silver plank would also be attractive to 30 percent of Republican voters, thus guaranteeing a Democratic victory.[33]

Cleveland responded to Altgeld by issuing a public letter to the Chicago Honest Money League dinner calling for gold Democrats to attend the convention in force, but Bland blasted the gold standard as "a stench in the nostrils of the plain people" and Altgeld criticized the letter, saying, "Its weakness almost excites pity." A week later the Honest Money League threw in the towel and urged its members not to attend the special convention, knowing they would lose badly.[34]

Still, the special convention was seen nationally as a showdown, not only between gold and silver, but also between Cleveland and his enemies. The *Illinois State Register* welcomed delegates to Springfield with an editorial bashing the president for breaking the 1892 Democratic platform's pledge to use gold and silver as money with equal purchasing power.[35]

At the convention in the state Capitol, a parade of silver leaders abused Cleveland for his manifold sins. Among them was William Jennings Bryan, whom Hinrichsen had invited. They knew each other from Bryan's college days. Wearing a light-colored cashmere suit and tan shoes, the Nebraskan was greeted by a demonstration as men cheered and women in the galleries waved handkerchiefs. In an hour-long speech, he described the gold conspiracy as "international in extent and destined . . . to produce more misery than war, pestilence, and famine." He called Cleveland an "instrument in the hands of concentrated wealth," saying the president was "not the Democratic party—Democracy is greater than any man." [36]

Delegates called for Altgeld, who was not scheduled to speak. Thunderous applause and cheering shook the chamber when he appeared. The governor offered an impromptu defense of Free Silver, arguing the gold standard had reduced wages for workers, prices for farmers, and sales for merchants while keeping taxes, interest, and fixed costs high. Republicans would not solve the nation's economic woes. "They believe in the doctrine that it is the business of the government to help enrich people and let those few rich people throw a few bones to the poor." He called for "the uprising of an indignant and a wronged people," saying, "The Democratic party must again stand for Democracy, and no longer for plutocracy!" [37]

The convention approved a platform that demanded "the free and unlimited coinage" of gold and silver "at the ratio of 16 to 1 without waiting for the action of any other nation," and pledged to reorganize the Illinois party on a Free Silver basis. Illinois's example led seven more state parties to similarly reorganize themselves. Several were expected—Colorado and Utah were both silver mining centers. But Mississippi and Louisiana were surprises.[38]

The most important special state convention besides Illinois was in Missouri in early August, a result of a letter of encouragement Altgeld had sent to Governor William J. Stone. Missouri was significant because it was home to the leader of the silver movement in Congress, Richard P. Bland, who was the presumed front-runner for the Democratic nomination.

The convention opened at noon, a giant arch hanging over the stage, inscribed "16 to 1" and featuring a bimetallic keystone, half silver, half gold, its columns covered in large silver-and-gold-painted dollars. Bland declared, "Missouri and Illinois in 1896 should fire the first gun" in the battle to control the national Democratic Party. More speakers denounced Cleveland and his policies before the convention adopted a platform that warned of a secret conspiracy that fastened the gold standard upon America without the people's approval. There was a move to endorse Silver Dick for president, but Bland had the old-fashioned view that the office should seek the man more than the man the office. Silver Democrats solidified control by voting to double the state committee and then named silver men to the new slots. From their regular convention in Fort Worth, Texas,

Democrats wired a message of solidarity "for true bimetallic coinage and against a single gold coinage" as they, too, endorsed Free Silver.[39]

The special state conventions, as important as they were in consolidating and energizing Free Silver support in states that held them, did not constitute a national movement. They were isolated events, without much coordination or follow-up. So the Central Bimetallic League tried creating a national movement when 2,200 Free Silver men met in Memphis in mid-June. Twenty states—every Southern one, most of the West and Midwest, some territories, and Pennsylvania—were represented.[40]

The case for reorganizing the Democratic Party along Free Silver lines was made in a diatribe by newly elected U.S. senator from South Carolina Benjamin "Pitchfork Ben" Tillman. Never a man for subtlety and a vicious racist, Tillman eviscerated Cleveland as "first cousin to Benedict Arnold," described the president's congressional allies as "cuckoos," and predicted the Midwest, Plains, and West would join the Solid South in 1896 in electing a Free Silver Democrat as president. Tillman had received his nickname after calling Cleveland "an old bag of beef" and threatening to go "to Washington with a pitchfork and prod him in his old fat ribs."[41]

The meeting considered a draft platform that declared "a conspiracy of selfish interests" had caused "widespread depression and suffering" by imposing the gold standard. It called for a coordinating committee of a man from each state to "devise measures to advance the cause of bimetallism." Delegates enthusiastically approved the document, but it was meaningless. The crowd was divided between advocates of silver men in each party seizing power, backers of the new Silver Party, proponents of fusion between the Democratic and Populist parties, and silver Democrats intent on taking over their party. There was no chance a coordinating committee could resolve the fundamental disagreement over the best way to advance the silver cause.[42]

After adjournment, three Democratic senators—Arkansas's James K. Jones, Indiana's David Turpie, and Tennessee's Isham Harris—met at the Gayoso Hotel to discuss how they could gain control of the Democratic Party. The Democratic National Committee had been elected at the 1892 convention and was narrowly controlled by Cleveland. A parallel structure was needed to counter it, not the new Silver Party or a nonpartisan group. The senators agreed to create a Bimetallic Democratic National

Committee of one man from each state. Its goal would be "a thorough organization" of the party on a Free Silver basis as "a necessary and proper means of controlling" the 1896 national convention. Harris suggested this group coordinate with silver Democrats in every state so "none but pronounced advocates of the white metal will be in the national convention." The three urged interested states to send representatives to Washington in two months to perfect the new Bimetallic DNC.[43]

On August 14, 1895, silver men from thirty-seven states and territories assembled in Washington's Metropolitan Hall with Jones in the chair and Hinrichsen as secretary. Speakers drummed home the message that silver Democrats must organize to defeat the administration and gold Democrats, then passed a resolution to undertake "a thorough and systematic organization of the Democratic masses," and formed a national committee of one man per state, each charged with organizing his state, every county, and every precinct.

Reporters and some pro-Cleveland Democrats did not take the new organization seriously because few participants had national reputations. But leaders of most insurgencies are fresh, and while many involved in this one were not known nationally, they were young rising stars within their states.[44]

This movement was focused on an idea, not personalities. The men involved were intent on grabbing control of the local, state, and, eventually, national Democratic Party machinery to elect a national convention to write a platform endorsing free coinage of silver at 16-to-1. Then they would worry about who should stand on that platform.

This Free Silver principle was their primary concern, the man who would be their nominee a distant second. Principle first, candidate second. Cleveland and sound-money Democrats may not have yet realized it, but they had a major problem. A band of Rebels was coming and all hell was about to break loose.

1

At eighteen, William McKinley enlisted in the 23rd Ohio and fought through the entire Civil War.

2

McKinley received a battlefield commission as second lieutenant for heroism at age nineteen, then went on to become a brevet major, a title he preferred to any other for the rest of his life.

After the Civil War, McKinley began practicing law in Canton, Ohio, where he met and married Ida Saxton, a young, spirited woman from one of the town's most prominent families.

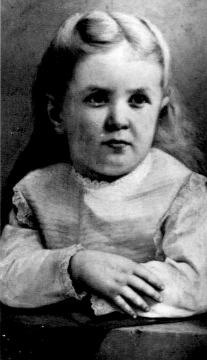

McKinley called his first daughter, Katie, his "favorite Christmas present." His second daughter, Ida, was born a year later.

Ida doted on Katie, but after Baby Ida and Katie both tragically died— Baby Ida of cholera and Katie of scarlet fever— Ida suffered from seizures and depression, becoming a virtual invalid.

7

Ida and William's Canton, Ohio, home would eventually become the site of the Front-Porch Campaign.

8

After winning his first congressional race in 1876, McKinley rose to become the GOP's preeminent spokesman on protective tariffs, an issue that deeply divided the parties and the country.

After being gerrymandered out of Congress in 1890, McKinley resurrected his political career by becoming governor of Ohio.

11

Marcus Alonzo Hanna and McKinley met in 1876, but their consequential friendship would not blossom for a dozen years.

12

Political novice Charles G. Dawes would work on the Major's behalf in the Midwest soon after meeting him in 1894. He would go on to manage his Illinois primary campaign and then his Chicago headquarters in 1896.

13

McKinley's loyalty to fellow Ohioan John Sherman at the 1888 GOP national convention convinced many—especially Hanna—that the Major should be president.

14

To win the Republican nomination, McKinley needed Ohio governor "Fire Alarm" Joseph B. Foraker in his corner to help unite the state. That was a huge challenge, given Foraker's own large ambition.

15

Republican bosses like New York senator Thomas Collier Platt—the "Easy Boss"—were accustomed to controlling national conventions, where they would trade their support for favors, patronage, and power.

16

Along with Platt, Pennsylvania senator Matthew S. Quay led "the Combine," an alliance of state party bosses. McKinley would have to beat them to win the Republican nomination on his terms.

CHAPTER 11

Maneuvering

———◦———

At first, the Combine's bosses were unimpressed with McKinley's "traveling salesmen," but by fall 1895, some machine men were realizing Hanna's agents were part of a much larger organization. While the bosses had sat back, counting on favorite sons to muddle the contest so they could then select the nominee, McKinley had been growing stronger.

Manley may have recognized the Major's strength on a trip he took in October and November through the Midwest, South, and West to find out where Republican leaders stood on Reed. He came back reluctant to talk to reporters, though he did say he favored "an aggressive campaign" and an early convention in San Francisco. This was a little odd—he had reserved thirty rooms in Chicago, the convention's expected site—but it was also a sign that the bosses were focused on controlling where the convention would be held as a way of bolstering their position. They could curry favor with the Republicans of a prospective host state by lending their support to its bid. The right city could boost its favorite son, make it easier to turn out supportive crowds, and save the Combine from having to raise money for the convention.[1]

McKinley's men had a different goal. They were happy to concede the selection of the convention's site and instead focus on key decisions that would be made shortly before the convention: which delegates would be seated and who would run the show.

So while the RNC met December 10 to decide on which of six cities would host the convention and when it would be, the McKinley

151

men—while numerous and visible at the meeting—could not have cared less about these decisions. Instead, the McKinley managers were focused on making certain they had a majority on the RNC, which would set the convention's roll by provisionally deciding any credentials challenges and recommending the convention's officers, both subject to delegate approval.

At a Canton meeting a few weeks before the RNC met, Joseph P. Smith presented a tally based on reports from McKinley's agents of which RNC members were supporters. The campaign's best guess was that 21 members were for McKinley, 13 uncommitted, and 17 Combine men. If that was accurate, McKinley was five votes shy of a majority on the committee. If McKinley won firm control of the RNC, it would be virtually impossible for the Combine to take over the convention. What's more, if he won this control quietly—and did not reveal it by trying to influence the convention's location—then the Combine might not understand his strength until it was too late.[2]

So four days before the RNC meeting, a big group of the Major's friends set up a headquarters at Washington's Arlington Hotel, where the gathering was to be held, so they could buttonhole individual committee members. Hanna led the group, which included Osborne, Hahn, Smith, Ohio representatives A. L. Conger and Charles H. Grosvenor, and former Ohio chairman Charles Dick. For the next several days, the McKinley group worked at strengthening relationships with the RNC members, not pressing for any convention site. After two days of deliberation on December 9 and 10, the RNC settled on St. Louis on the fifth ballot.[3]

THE VICTORY WAS LARGELY the work of the "Old Man," Chauncey I. Filley, who led the Gateway City's host committee. He was a fixture in national GOP circles, having been a delegate to every convention since 1864 and Missouri's committeeman from 1876 to 1892. Appearing in his trademark large, old-fashioned black hat, the sixty-six-year-old gray-bearded and mustached politico argued Missouri was neutral ground (no presidential candidate hailed from the state) and Republicans had won 10 of the state's 15 congressional seats in 1894. St. Louis also had a Republican mayor and its financial guarantee was solid. The RNC set the convention for June 16 to 18.[4]

Holding the convention in St. Louis did add to McKinley's problems in Missouri, already the site of a bitter intraparty battle. Richard C. Ker-ens, the state's national committeeman, had beaten Filley for the post in 1892 and the two men were still fighting over control of the state GOP. Kerens supported McKinley. Filley said he supported the Major, too, but was slippery and more concerned with controlling Missouri than helping McKinley. Kerens wrote McKinley to reaffirm his support after hearing rumors that people were questioning his commitment. On the other hand, the "Old Man," as Filley was called, sent a go-between to whine. McKin-ley had to reassure the intermediary that he considered Filley a "sincere friend." If the controversy continued, McKinley would be hurt if either man cut a deal with the Combine. It could also harm the GOP's chances to carry the state in the general election.[5]

The machine men became unsettled by Hanna and his team swarming the RNC meeting and by hearing from Manley that McKinley's agents were organizing states and undermining the Combine's favorite-son strat-egy. But how to slow him down or stop him? Here, the bosses' pragmatism was a weakness. They felt it was too early to settle on one candidate to oppose the Major. But it is harder to win by being against someone than it is being for someone.[6]

TO SLOW MCKINLEY, PLATT put his favorite son officially in the race. After a late New Year's Eve dinner in Manhattan with Platt, Depew, and other Empire State Republican dignitaries, Morton declared for president with a press statement shortly before midnight that emphasized his "distinguished career . . . and his ability and conservative judgment." To announce with a news release right at midnight on New Year's Eve reeked of panic.[7]

There was speculation that Morton's strange, late-night announcement was Platt's attempt to blunt McKinley's growing strength in the state, es-pecially in western New York. Though Morton was unlikely to get much national support, his candidacy largely unified the Empire State delegation under Platt's control.[8]

But Morton had to demonstrate strength outside New York to be viable. So Republicans across the country began receiving a leaflet titled "Some Important Political Facts," circulated by an unnamed "NEW YORK REPUBLICAN" and datelined Springfield, Illinois. The piece argued that Morton was an experienced, well-prepared leader who would win New York, causing "a long period of Republican supremacy." A lengthy statement from Platt on the flyer's reverse emphasized his state's electoral importance and urged the GOP to name its first New York presidential candidate. The leaflet bungled the issue of Morton's advanced age, saying, "His health, for the past year, has been excellent."[9]

Morton wrote allies from his vice presidential days, but found many were less than encouraging. Alabama RNC committeeman William Youngblood responded with a three-page letter grumbling about "the conduct of the Reed-Morton combine" and warned that despite "the large amount of money being sent into this state by your managers and the managers of Mr. Reed . . . McKinley will get a large majority of this delegation."[10]

Hanna saw Morton's entry as the start of a more contentious phase of the campaign. "The enemy have begun an assault on our lines," he wrote Hay, "so that we are obliged to put on our men in the field at all points to hold our position."[11]

Morton's entry didn't dispel doubts among the Combine. On January 7, Platt, Manley, Clarkson, and William M. Crane, the Massachusetts RNC committeeman who was locking up New England for Reed, met in New York to discuss the situation. Platt believed Quay must "order some sort of demonstration in Pennsylvania" for Morton to "repress the growing belief" that he was not a serious candidate. Quay was unenthusiastic.[12]

Quay, Filley, and Platt then met and conferred on Morton's chances at Quay's Washington, D.C., home. Quay and Platt were skeptical about reports of McKinley's strength, believing they were "fake business." But Quay was coy about backing Morton, telling reporters only "that he is against McKinley, as well as Harrison, on any and all occasions."[13]

Filley said he supported the Major, but if he was a solid McKinley man, he would not have been allowed to attend a private confab of McKinley's biggest foes. Filley also later reported to Clarkson on possible Allison delegates in Missouri. Until the national convention, Filley would play a dangerous game—professing loyalty to McKinley while privately helping the Combine.[14]

Platt spun reporters about the D.C. meeting, suggesting that former Wisconsin senator John C. Spooner would help Morton, that Alger was a possible running mate and would deliver Michigan, and that Morton was doing well in Kentucky and Missouri. He also said Morton would be endorsed by the *Inter Ocean* and win Illinois after its favorite son, Cullom, faded. Platt wanted to leave the impression Morton was rising and McKinley fading.[15]

Platt returned to New York "elated" with what he heard at the meeting about Morton's support, especially that Quay was "impressed with the increasing proportions of the Morton boom." He said Quay expected Pennsylvania would be "carried away by the popular enthusiasm for Morton." In a slap at the Major, Platt announced that S. J. Sanford, who had hosted McKinley in Knoxville, Tennessee, the previous September, was for Morton. Sanford believed what was needed "was not so much a high tariff," but a strict adherence to the gold standard.[16]

While Platt worked to dampen McKinley's sense of inevitability, reporters weren't buying that Morton was the Easy Boss's real choice. They thought "Platt is as much for Reed as ever, with Allison as second choice" and the show was all about stopping Harrison and McKinley. Osborne read the situation similarly, warning his cousin, "This combination of Quay-Platt-Clarkson and others is for Reed and this Morton candidacy is to throw us off our ground."[17]

HIS TERM AS GOVERNOR over, the Major returned to Canton, transforming his home into a campaign headquarters. A telephone on his library wall was connected to Hanna's Cleveland office. Smith shuttled between Canton and Cleveland with updates or instructions. James Boyle and Captain H. O. S. Heistand, a West Point graduate and Ohio National Guard instructor, handled correspondence and telegrams in Canton, assisted by Mrs. McKinley's cousin Sam Saxton and a typist. The table was routinely set for twelve so McKinley's team could talk over lunch. Reporters dropped by and prowled Canton's streets for gossip.[18]

As McKinley was ramping up his campaign, former president Benjamin Harrison shook the contest by announcing February 3 that he would not run. His statement read, "To everyone who has proposed to promote my nomination, I have said: 'No.' There has never been an hour since I left the White House that I have felt a wish to return to it." Harrison explained to Elkins why he had acted, saying, "I do not like to appear to be in the attitude of the little boy that followed the apple-cart up the hill, hoping the tail-board might fall out!"[19]

This was a setback for the Combine. Despite Platt and Quay's hatred of the former president, they wanted him in the race to tie up Indiana and delegates around the country who supported him out of loyalty. Harrison's withdrawal put Indiana's thirty delegates up for grabs and removed the most potent favorite son who could hinder McKinley.

Illinois Republicans thought Cullom benefited from the withdrawal because he was from a neighboring state and friends of Allison were "popping up all over" Indiana, but as a journalist observed, Hanna "cannot but regard the withdrawal . . . in the most favorable light because of the well known strength of Gov. McKinley in Indiana."[20]

At the Major's direction, Charles Dick quickly tracked down Indiana chairman John K. Gowdy, vacationing at the French Lick Resort, and the state's GOP hierarchy was soon in the McKinley camp. A week after Harrison's exit, an Indiana Morton man reported to the Combine that the Major's forces "have jumped right into our State and have been working it day and night since Gen. Harrison's withdrawel [*sic*]. These McKinley fellows have almost taken our breath away by the enthusiasm they manifest for their candidate."[21]

In March, Morton sent a team to Indiana, believing that as Harrison's vice president he had cordial relationships with many Hoosier Republicans. His agents left disappointed, convinced the state was lost. McKinley was simply too strong. McKinley's success in Indiana further soured Harrison. By April he was privately for Allison, but he remained aloof from the contest, as hostile to Platt and Quay as they were to him.[22]

AS THE LAST GOP president exited the 1896 race, another candidate entered it. The McKinley men had an unusual idea on how he should declare. The Chicago Marquette Club's annual dinner in honor of Lincoln's birthday was the Midwest's preeminent Republican gathering. Tickets were only five dollars but difficult to get because every big dog Republican in the region and their pals from across the country attended the evening of fine food, wine, cigars, and speeches. The keynote address was a big deal and McKinley had been invited to give it. It would be the only speech he would give outside Ohio all year and the perfect place to make waves.[23]

To take advantage of the Major's appearance, Hanna and Dawes invited McKinley men and influential Republicans from around the country. In his ornate handwriting, Dawes kept a roster of the invitees, alphabetical by state. Many were Southern Republicans, like Alabama's William Youngblood; Florida's John Long, Joe Lee, and Dennis Eagan; and Georgia's Alfred Buck and Professor R. R. Wright. All the Southerners but Youngblood had visited McKinley the previous March in Thomasville.

Some were Republican state chairmen and RNC members supporting McKinley or leaning his way. To ensure there was widespread coverage of the Major's remarks and reception, Dawes also invited editors from across the country. Hanna and Dawes even included adversaries on the guest list, among them Manley.[24]

But most invitees were McKinley boosters such as North Carolina senator Jeter C. Pritchard, who was flattered to be in the campaign's inner circle. Many met with the Major, Hanna, or other campaign officials at a special reception before the Marquette Club dinner, mingling with the Major and other supporters at what Dawes called "private interviews."[25]

The dinner was held in the largest room available in Chicago, the Auditorium Hotel's ninth-floor banquet room, which could seat 718 people. There was an overflow room on the sixth floor that accommodated another 350. After dinner, the tables were removed as the men enjoyed cigars so the crowd of more than 1,000 could gather on the ninth floor to hear the speakers. As guest of honor, McKinley would deliver the principal address, a birthday tribute to Lincoln.[26]

His introduction provoked what the hostile *Chicago Tribune* admitted was "a hearty roar of greeting" as "every man in the uncomfortable crowded room was on his feet in an instant." The yells "grew into earsplitting shrieks of delight and spontaneously from every pocket came a handkerchief which was frantically waved," giving McKinley a moment to let the adrenaline stop. Dawes reported, "The Governor seemed a little nervous . . . but when he rose to respond to his toast he was as calm and collected as possible," leaving a "magnificent impression."[27]

McKinley praised Lincoln as a humble man who began without privilege or position yet "whose achievements have heightened human aspirations and broadened the field of opportunity to the races of men, a leader who transcended mere politics." Because of Lincoln, "No man need be in any doubt about what the Republican Party stands for. It stands now, as ever, for honest money and a chance to earn it by honest toil." The reception at the end of his remarks mirrored his beginning.[28]

Then came the surprise. Nebraska senator John M. Thurston, speaking on "The Impending Contest," declared that McKinley would be a presidential candidate and encouraged the crowd to back "that man whose name would be recognized as an American platform in itself." The banquet hall rang with even more enthusiastic cheers than those that had greeted McKinley. "The Republican masses have one name enshrined in their hearts," Thurston said, "one name ready to burst forth hallelujahs from their lips." The dinner's final orator, Senator Pritchard, seconded the endorsement.[29]

McKinley had, in effect, declared his candidacy. It was a risky way to do so. Most candidates generally announced (if they did at all) by a short interview with a friendly paper, a brief letter to supporters, or even short remarks in their hometown. McKinley had gone to Illinois, a vital state in the nomination process, and made a spectacle. What if the crowd hadn't responded so wildly? Dawes and others on the Marquette Club board had made certain it was a McKinley audience with friendly press coverage, but the Major had raised the importance of Illinois. A defeat there now would be a serious, perhaps fatal, political blow.

Even though a few editorials threw darts at his remarks, it was a good night for McKinley. He had given a speech to wide acclaim in a critical battleground on a topic that minimized the Combine's opportunities for criticism. His formal entry into the race drew national attention, with papers reprinting all or large parts of his remarks.[30]

The Combine responded with more proxy candidates. The next day, former Nebraska senator Charles F. Manderson, who had taught McKinley an early political lesson by stealing his speech in Canton in 1867, joined Allison, Bradley, Cullom, Davis, and Morton as Combine favorite sons. The response at the Cornhusker state central committee meeting the following day, however, was mixed. Even local Allison and Reed men were lukewarm about Manderson. The wealthy railroad baron was the lawyer for the Burlington & Missouri.[31]

McKinley's organization quickly showed its value. Five days later, the Nebraska McKinley Club hosted an evening of speakers led by Senator Thurston at Lincoln's New Funke Opera House, advertised as "for Protection and Protection's Champion. Aye, For the People!" There was music by the McKinley Glee Club and out-of-towners received a special excursion refund of two-thirds of their fare.[32]

A *Chicago Tribune* survey of Iowa, Kansas, and Nebraska editors also hurt Manderson's launch. While Iowa publishers were strongly for Allison, "a great majority" in Kansas and Nebraska were for McKinley, with Allison "a general second choice." Of the 88 Cornhusker editors, 71 were for McKinley, 6 for Manderson, 5 for Allison, and the rest scattered. Dawes visited Lincoln a few days later and was delighted to find that Manderson was "whipped in Nebraska, despite Burlington & Missouri Railroad political machine."[33]

The Combine's agents were hearing the same things. One grumbled that "Thurston is making a very disagreeable fight" in Nebraska. The Combine men still thought McKinley could be beaten in the state, but that was wishful thinking. The machine men moved to strengthen some of their struggling favorite sons. Clarkson told Allison supporters in Kentucky to be for their governor, William O. Bradley, but this undermined the Combine strategy, as some Republican activists recognized these favorite sons were merely placeholders who would be rapidly discarded when Platt, Quay, and the other bosses had settled on their real candidate.[34]

The next candidate the Combine put into the contest was more troublesome for McKinley. In late February, twenty-five Pennsylvania congressmen petitioned Quay to become a presidential candidate. "In deference to friends whose wishes could not be disregarded," the senator instantly agreed. County conventions began instructing their delegations to the April 23 Pennsylvania state convention to support Quay.[35]

His entry meant McKinley had little chance of winning more than a handful of Pennsylvania delegates and also denied him the support of James M. Swank, president of the powerful Iron and Steel Association in Philadelphia. Swank now rebuffed Hanna's request for help, saying his group must stay neutral as it was "under heavy obligations" to Reed, Allison, Quay, and, of course, McKinley. "My hands are tied," Swank wrote. "I have no choice but to look on while others are stirring up the political elements." He then chastised McKinley for not having taken his advice in the past and dismissed talk of "a 'combine,' " saying it did not exist "except in the sense that McKinley, having the lead, is naturally antagonized by the field." Actually, Swank was working closely with Quay.[36]

Still, McKinley benefited from Quay's entry. In response, Philander C. Knox, Pittsburgh's GOP boss Chris Magee, and other western Pennsylvanians gave $6,000 to McKinley, including $1,000 from Magee himself.

Hanna was no longer McKinley's only campaign donor. The flood of favorite sons did not panic McKinley, who told Whitelaw Reid, "Every new entry in the field, it seems to me, has a tendency to weaken our Eastern friends."[37]

One of those "Eastern friends" came in for criticism. "The Reed of former days has disappeared and in his stead there comes a man whom none recognizes," editorialized the *Washington Post*. There were no jokes, sarcasm, or wit, just a "smooth-faced, smooth-talking politician who is looking for votes." Reed had decided to act presidential and thereby lost the hard partisan edge that had attracted some Republicans to him. And he had little to say about what he would do as president.[38]

It wasn't just Democratic papers that were critical. Some of Reed's supporters were concerned that he was faltering, with Roosevelt continuing to grouse. While sympathetic to his friend's concerns, Lodge warned Teddy, "It would be a great misfortune to have McKinley nominated. . . . If I could tell you all I have learned since his campaign has progressed, you would be as completely alarmed over the prospect of his presidential nomination as I am."[39]

AT THIS POINT, EVEN the Combine men knew their effort was floundering and that they needed a new plan. In late February, Clarkson hatched the idea of a three-week trip through the Midwest and West to ensure that the RNC members there would help guarantee Combine control of credentials and convention organization. He would also sew up delegates along the way. His proposed itinerary was Illinois, Missouri (where he would also meet with Kansas and Oklahoma leaders), Arkansas, Texas, New Mexico, and Arizona en route to California before heading to Oregon, Washington, Idaho, Wyoming, Colorado (where he could also meet Nevadans), and then Nebraska before returning to Des Moines. It was a good plan, but too late. McKinley had been covering the region by agent or letter for more than a year. Regardless, with Platt and Quay's approval and eight thousand dollars provided by Dodge, Clarkson began his twenty-state Midwest and Western tour. He told the press "his trip has no connection with politics," but Platt and Quay minions accompanied him.[40]

A few days later, New Hampshire's senior U.S. senator and Reed's New

Hampshire manager, William E. Chandler, attacked McKinley in a widely carried interview. The move was likely to have been blessed or even instigated by the Combine, not because McKinley was the front-runner, but because he was the most visible. A blow from Chandler would get attention, given his stature as a founder of the Republican Party and secretary of its first national convention. Chandler accused McKinley of "fat frying" large donations out of "millionaire manufacturers" and using "similar corrupt methods" in a campaign that was "a boodle canvass from start to finish." McKinley, Chandler charged, "has placed himself in the hands of managers who are seeking to nominate him by the lavish use of money," raising questions of "Who will own him and make merchandize of him if he is elected?"

While "all Republicans sympathized with McKinley in his business misfortunes" involving Walker's notes, there were concerns about the "corrupting" of the nomination process by those who paid off McKinley's debts in 1893. How large were those gifts and what was "Mr. McKinley's present financial condition?" Chandler called on him to make "a plain and explicit statement" about his finances and to "repudiate any such canvass" bankrolled by cash extorted from businessmen, which he suggested totaled $250,000.[41]

Representative Charles H. Grosvenor, McKinley's leader in the House, hit back, saying raising campaign donations was normal and legal, that Chandler "assumes the truth of mere rumor" and had provided no proof for his smears. He suggested the senator was a "hypocrite" in complaining about campaign funds. This was a reference to the contested 1876 presidential race, during which Chandler, a Hayes man, carried $10,000 in cash in a carpetbag to the Florida recount. The money was used to grease palms and ease local officials' consciences. When the recount ended, Hayes carried Florida by 862 votes.[42]

Newspapers, especially Democratic papers, also mocked Chandler as an unlikely agent for campaign finance reform. Several Republican congressmen (including supporters of Chandler's candidate, Reed) repudiated the attack, a sign it may have not been authorized by Reed or that McKinley's friendships with former colleagues remained firm.[43]

Chandler fired back that "Republicans would be defensive rather than on offensive" if McKinley were nominated because the GOP "shall have to meet the charge" that it was shaking down corporate beneficiaries of protection for campaign money. An Alabama Democrat then read Chandler's interview into the *Congressional Record* so Democratic representatives could mail the attack postage-free using their congressional frank.

Though Pennsylvania papers had raised the issue earlier, Chandler's decision to push it was a mistake. He was over-the-top, unsupported by witnesses or evidence, and, as one paper described, came across as "thoroughly, wrongly sincerely—and indiscreetly—angry." His comments were ignored by many and labeled as hypocritical by those familiar with his record. Chandler's reputation was as someone who "likes nothing so much as a fight," observed one paper. "When he can find no one in the opposition to direct his batteries upon he selects someone in his own party." [44]

The charge did more harm to Chandler than to McKinley. The Major's public image as a man of impeccable personal integrity and the anti-boss candidate was too strong. Even Democratic papers came to McKinley's defense, with one saying "[t]here was nothing" in the Walker notes episode that showed McKinley was anything but "a high minded, honest and honorable man." Chandler himself recognized the backlash, telling a reporter nearly a week later, "I said nothing unkind of McKinley personally." [45]

CHAPTER 12

The Battles Begin

————◄◦►————

In the Republican nomination fight in 1896, the attacks that really mattered were not the ones like Chandler's in the papers, but in the state conventions that determined who would attend the Republican National Convention in St. Louis.

These state conventions saw bitter political combat (in the case of Texas, with pistols, knives, and broken furniture) and the raw exercise of power. Sometimes the majority prevailed, and, on occasion, control of the process and underhanded maneuvering gave a determined minority the day. In too many instances, competing slates of delegates emerged, each claiming to be the state's true representatives—claims that would have to be settled in credentials fights at the national convention.

McKinley won more of the fifteen state conventions where he and the Combine forces went toe-to-toe from late January to late March, but the Combine emerged with a narrow lead in delegates. However, beneath the surface, trends were emerging that gave the Major's men reason to be hopeful and the Combine cause for concern.

THE ONE STATE WHERE McKinley could not afford defeat—where even a divided delegation would be seen as a loss—was Ohio. If the Major did not have unity at home, his nomination would be impossible. By rights, there never should have been doubt about Ohio. But the Buckeye State was also home to Fire Alarm Foraker, a man with outsize ambitions and a history of undercutting those he promised to support if doing so advanced his goals. Hanna and others with experience with Foraker were "distrustful and could not but show it."[1]

They should not have worried. McKinley's long and patient cultivation of Fire Alarm—likely coupled with Foraker's realization that he couldn't afford to oppose a man so popular with Ohioans—led Foraker to give McKinley his unwavering support. That support included giving a stem-winder of a speech at the state's convention. Foraker's keynote, editorialized the *Plain Dealer*, "was far beyond the expectations of the McKinley backers. No higher praise has ever been given the Ohio candidate. No more glowing eloquence has been heard in his behalf. The compact sentences, the well chosen words, had the ring of sincerity."

Frequently interrupted by applause, Foraker called McKinley "the ideal man, statesman, the typical American leader and the veritable American idol." When he said, "We owe it to ourselves as well as to him to do it with spirit, to do it with earnestness, to do it with unanimity, to do it in such a manner, in short, as will signify to the whole nation that he has now, and will have at the St. Louis Convention, the united, hearty, cordial, enthusiastic, unqualified support of Ohio," delegates and guests roared their agreement. By unanimous vote, the convention instructed for McKinley, adopted a platform, elected Bushnell, Foraker, Grosvenor, and Hanna as at-large delegates, and adjourned after just three hours.

McKinley immediately wrote Foraker to say the speech "was perfect—it could not have been better." The Major's understanding that there are no permanent enemies in politics—along with his all-out effort for the GOP state ticket in the 1895 campaign—had brought about the necessary outcome. Unlike Hanna, McKinley had never let himself develop a personal antipathy to Foraker but rather had aimed to keep a cordial relationship with his rival, even when they disagreed and even after Foraker had done a drive-by on him in the Campbell Ballot Box Hoax. Still, it wouldn't be Foraker without a problem. Before agreeing to go to St. Louis, Foraker demanded McKinley support an ally of Fire Alarm for RNC committeeman.[2]

Things also went smoothly for McKinley in Arkansas, Kansas, Wisconsin, and South Dakota, with their combined 68 delegates. Allison had hopes for some of the states, but Arkansas's Powell Clayton and the national committeemen in Kansas and Wisconsin, Cyrus Leland and Henry Payne, made certain their states were solid for the Major.[3]

McKinley's two other victories made the Combine realize it had a problem. The Combine expected to win the first convention—Louisiana in New Orleans in late January. For decades the state's RNC committeeman and Combine ally, former governor and senator William Pitt Kellogg, had dominated the Pelican State GOP long-distance from his Washington, D.C., mansion. He supported Reed, but six weeks earlier he and his candidate were victims of a quirky alliance between the state's McKinley men and former governor Henry Clay Warmoth.

Warmoth initially backed Harrison out of gratitude for past patronage, but since the former president appeared disinterested, Warmoth covered his bets by shifting to Reed while cooperating with McKinley. At a December state central committee meeting, Warmoth worked with state chairman T. A. Cage, a McKinley man, and Osborne to overthrow the machine by adding thirty members to the central committee, many of them for McKinley. When they were finished, Kellogg no longer controlled the state party apparatus. The Reed camp claimed bribes were involved, including "railroad tickets [and] stimulating beverages in abundance." Afterward Warmoth wrote McKinley to reaffirm his loyalty to Harrison; McKinley replied he understood and flattered Warmoth for holding a position of "manliness." Words were a small price for winning control of Louisiana.[4]

At the state convention in late January, Kellogg led Reed supporters in a failed attempt to oust Cage as chairman and then had to accept a slate of two Reed and two McKinley at-large delegates. This was called a "moderate victory" for Reed, but it was a face-saving gesture by Hanna to placate Kellogg. McKinley had ten of sixteen Louisiana delegates, having already won most district conventions. Allison was shut out, despite his support for domestic sugar subsidies, a popular position in Louisiana.[5]

The other loss was more damaging for the Combine. As the Minnesota GOP convention opened on March 24, a party leader rose and read a telegram from Senator Cushman Davis that said, "I am bound to, always did, and do most loyally respect the wishes of Minnesota. For that reason I request that my name be not considered." Davis ended his favorite-son candidacy because McKinley men had dominated the congressional district meetings the day before and three of five districts refused to endorse Davis. The convention instructed Minnesota's eighteen delegates for McKinley. In private, Davis blamed his defeat on Merriam and his "stupid harloting" on behalf of the Major.[6]

The Combine's failure in Minnesota unsettled Reed, who summoned Platt. It is unclear if they met, but the Speaker then wrote the Easy Boss to ask "if we could concentrate a little more" on Wisconsin, Minnesota, and Indiana. Reed was too late. Minnesota and Wisconsin were already gone and Indiana appeared to be in McKinley's hands as well.[7]

THE COMBINE FOUGHT BACK in Iowa and New York. The Iowa Republican State Convention on March 11 was the formal launch of Allison's campaign and his last real success. It was called "without a doubt the most enthusiastic" political event ever held in Iowa, and "from beginning to end, an Allison convention." He would stay in the race, but the Combine knew his utility was holding Iowa's thirty delegates until the bosses settled on a candidate. Hanna unintentionally made that easier by sending agents to work county conventions in a vain attempt to instruct them for McKinley. Clarkson wrote Platt that left "Iowa people very angry" with the Major's methods. There was a downside to competing everywhere.[8]

On March 24, Platt turned the New York convention into a display of home-state strength for Morton and, while he was at it, his leadership. As delegates prepared to consider the platform, Platt unexpectedly entered the Manhattan hall, "the signal for a hearty greeting, the delegates and spectators cheering wildly and the band playing 'Hail to the Chief.'" Some observers were surprised at Platt's appearance. He had spent two days in bed after his wife, "a heavy woman," fainted and fell on him, throwing him into a piece of furniture and leaving him battered.[9]

New York's four delegates-at-large were instructed for Morton. McKinley supporters failed miserably at trying to kick Platt and his ally, state GOP chairman Edward Lauterbach, off the slate. The machine men dominated most of the state's thirty congressional districts and the state's seventy-two-member delegation, but there was still some hand-to-hand combat in New York City districts with its mayor, William L. Strong, leading the McKinley forces and in western New York districts around

Buffalo. This gave McKinley a minority of the delegation, with many of them subject to credentials challenges.[10]

The Combine enjoyed small victories when they won three territories and another state in late March. New Mexico Republicans met in Albuquerque the same day as the New York convention and, led by William Henry Harrison Llewellyn, a lawyer in Las Cruces and member of the New Mexico Territorial House, picked an uninstructed slate of five Combine men and one McKinley man. However, uninstructed delegates needed more attention than instructed ones. Free agents, they could forget past pledges and were ripe for someone to convert.[11]

Three days later, after what one paper called "undoubtedly the rawest case of machine politics ever sprang in the territory," Oklahoma Republicans defeated instruction for McKinley and elected six Reed supporters. This meant the Combine also got the Indian Territory's six delegates, its delegation generally dictated by the more-organized Oklahoma GOP. That same day, Massachusetts Republicans gathered in Boston's Music Hall "to give their earnest and active support" to Reed, as well as all thirty delegates. The next day, the *Baltimore American* endorsed Reed, saying, "When the time comes the South will rise spontaneously to his name." The *American* was unaware of McKinley's early success in the region.[12]

The Combine's modest delegate lead at the end of March didn't change the fact that overall, the early contests were bad news for the machine men. McKinley's organization had taken states Platt and Quay expected to win, such as Louisiana and Minnesota. This caused the bosses to lash out. Platt penned a tough letter to Alger, demanding he discredit rumors he was for McKinley by delivering Michigan for the Combine. Alger denied supporting the Major, claiming he had simply said, "That my State is for him; and this is from me no seed that I have sown." He argued the GOP would be fine with any of the major contenders. Alger clearly worried about his relationship with Platt, asking wistfully, "Can we not be friends even if we represent different candidates?" The question proved Alger was dissembling when he said he wasn't for McKinley.[13]

THE MAJOR, HOWEVER, HAD a long way to go, and the Combine was now resorting to a tactic that would allow the RNC to decide at the convention whose delegates were seated. In three March state conventions—all in the South—the Combine waged brutal campaigns that ripped each state apart and resulted in competing delegations, each demanding recognition in St. Louis as the state's official representatives.

Mississippi and Florida both met March 5. A former slave led each side in Mississippi: James Hill, a former Mississippi secretary of state, for McKinley, and John R. Lynch, a former state house Speaker who also served three terms in Congress and was temporary chairman at the 1884 national convention, for the Combine. The state convention of roughly 250 men split, leaving both Hill and Lynch to claim theirs was the official delegation. Lynch was bankrolled by Clarkson, who soon bragged that Dodge's cash had put half of Hill's men and all of Lynch's in the Combine's pocket. Lynch journeyed to Canton to convince McKinley to seat him but Hill had been working the South for more than a year for the Major, and McKinley was loyal. The RNC would decide who cast Mississippi's eighteen votes. Florida Republicans split after battling until 4:15 a.m., producing two slates, one instructed for Morton and another of eight "pronounced McKinley men." [14]

Those two states were nothing compared to the disaster in Texas. Its earlier congressional district conventions had produced a mixed result. Of the 26 delegates elected at them, everyone agreed that McKinley had 6, Reed 3, and Allison 1. The other 16 were contested after Allison and Reed challenged delegates McKinley won and Reed challenged the few that Allison took. Texas was already a credentials problem. It was about to get worse. [15]

Delegates began arriving in Austin on Sunday, March 22. By Monday morning it was clear to reporters "the McKinley band wagon was leading the procession" with most of the delegates supporting him. The Allison and Reed forces were scrambling to stop McKinley by talking up an uninstructed delegation. Texas was so important because each side had sent an agent to help: Myron T. Herrick for McKinley and former New York assemblyman Isaac L. Hunt for the Combine. [16]

The Combine men couldn't agree on a united anti-McKinley strategy. While Norris Wright Cuney was Allison's leader, two men—R. B. Hawley, a wealthy white Galveston merchant, and William M. "Gooseneck Bill" McDonald, a black teacher and fraternal leader from Forney—claimed to speak for Reed. This left the Combine split, despite news reports that Reed and Allison forces were working in concert. [17]

This was frustrating to Cuney, the state's leading black Republican. For nearly thirty years, the attractive, wealthy, and well-spoken Cuney had been a major power in the state and national GOP. He kept the Texas GOP a biracial party, having not only the backing of the state's black Republicans but also the support of many white Republicans. Named customs inspector by Grant and Galveston port collector by Harrison, he had attended every national convention since 1872 and been the state's RNC committeeman since 1884. He and Clarkson had been close friends for decades; because of Clarkson's support for his port collectorship, Cuney had ignored Hanna's invitation to Thomasville in 1895 and made excuses when Hanna sent representatives to his home in Galveston to discuss him leading the Major's Texas effort.[18]

After a strategy session that broke up at 1 a.m. Monday, the wily Cuney decided to force unity among the Combine men by running for temporary chairman and playing the race card. Most Southern GOP convention delegates were black. The Texas gathering was no exception. Cuney would endeavor to get McKinley's black supporters to back him for temporary chairman by saying "white men [are] trying to crush the negro." Then as chairman, he would stack Credentials and replace McKinley delegates with men friendly to the Combine. This possibility so unnerved the McKinley men that they tried engineering an alliance with Reed against Cuney by offering to split the statewide delegates. Nothing came of it.[19]

The convention started Tuesday with McKinley's Texas leader, state GOP chairman John Grant, presiding over the temporary chairman's election. Cuney was so successful in rallying black delegates that they refused to let his white challenger withdraw when the roll call showed him losing decisively, with Cuney backers yelling, "We don't want him to withdraw, we want to beat him." Cuney won by better than 2 to 1.[20]

He quickly used his power to make Gooseneck Bill the Credentials chairman and stacked the committee. By Wednesday, McKinley delegations from nine of the biggest counties were replaced with supporters of Cuney and the Combine. In seven other counties, Gooseneck proposed seating the existing McKinley delegations with an equal number of Combine men, giving every man half a vote. In thirteen smaller counties, each represented by a single delegate, a Combine man would replace the McKinley delegate. Friendly railroads provided free passes to bring replacement delegates to Austin overnight. By these means, roughly two hundred votes were taken from McKinley and given to the Combine. Even then, Cuney had not stolen enough. The Major still had a solid majority.[21]

The convention was scheduled to begin at 10 a.m. Wednesday, so McKinleyites showed up early, grabbed seats in the front and center of the hall, and waited. Food and drink had to be found; many poorer black delegates had expected things to wrap up Tuesday and were now without room or board. To occupy time, the Major's supporters sang "Rally Round the Flag" and "John Brown's Body" and paraded a large flag with McKinley's picture on it. Impromptu speeches were offered, delivered by men standing on chairs.[22]

It was 1:15 p.m. before Cuney gaveled in the convention. First order of business was the Credentials report. McKinley floor managers moved for a substitute, but Cuney refused to recognize their motion. The McKinley forces demanded a roll call. Cuney ordered a voice vote. "The noes outnumbered the ayes two to one," a local paper reported, "but without twitching a muscle or moving a hair, Cuney said decisively, 'The ayes have it and the report is adopted.' " The air was rent with angry screams as McKinley delegates moved toward the stage, menacing Cuney and his lieutenants. When a black delegate threatened to bolt, Cuney dismissed him, saying, "Well then, go bolt and be damned." Undeterred, Cuney steamrolled through the election of the permanent chairman, who unsurprisingly was himself. With "the complacency of a child," a local reporter wrote, Cuney ruled "the McKinley crowd out on every shuffle."[23]

When it was time to pick four at-large delegates and four alternates, the hall "had resolved itself into a troop of shouting, surging dervishes." Cuney ignored demands for a roll call. Instead he shouted for a voice vote and immediately declared the Combine's slate the winners, though the McKinley men still outnumbered Cuney's followers.

The hall exploded. The McKinley men stormed the stage, aiming to push Cuney aside and install Web Flanagan, the GOP's 1890 gubernatorial candidate, in his place. "One burley negro came plowing through the jam," an Associated Press reporter wrote, "pushing men in front of him as if they were so much chaff." Behind him was a determined, fast-moving, angry mob of five hundred McKinley men. Cuney expected the assault: his people were prepared to defend the podium and him. "The first negro to reach the stand made a lunge at Cuney's head with a fist," an eyewitness wrote, but little Bill Ellis, Cuney's longtime right-hand man, moved faster, pulling his revolver and shoving it in the assailant's face. "The two men eyed each other for ten seconds," then grappled and went down with "the howling crowd swaying around and about them." A large table on the stage collapsed under the combatants. Delegates grabbed broken pieces as weapons. Chairs and other tables were smashed over heads or against bodies. Fists, bludgeons, bottles, knives, and razors appeared. Other pistols were drawn, but luckily not used. The fight went on for twenty minutes before the city marshal and a squad of officers arrived and began indiscriminately clubbing delegates.[24]

When the fracas had ended, Cuney spoke briefly but passionately. "I love my friends and do not hate my enemies," he said. "I care not what men say of Wright Cuney so long as Wright Cuney's conscience doesn't accuse." He had come to Austin "seeking harmony." Talk of that was "farcical now." On voice votes, he gaveled through the statewide electors, adjourned the convention, and marched out, taking some Combine men with him.[25]

It was 5:45 p.m. As party chairman, Grant called the remaining delegates to order, elected a slate instructed for McKinley, and adjourned by 7:15. Grant was pleased 626 of the convention's 790 delegates had remained. The Major's Texas supporters took affidavits from delegates emphasizing Cuney's arbitrary rulings. But still, at the end of the day, every delegate was up for grabs. No one controlled Texas.[26]

The Lily White Republicans complicated matters on April 20 in Houston by selecting a third delegation to vie for recognition in St. Louis, but no matter. The Combine was certain that Cuney, a longtime RNC member, had enough friends on the committee that it would select his delegation among the three competing for recognition.[27]

The Austin Furniture Company ran an ad suggesting "that Republican split" could be put "back together with a Standard Co. automatic sewing machine." But the Texas outcome was bad for McKinley. The question of who would cast the state's thirty votes would be in doubt until St. Louis. McKinley was shown to be vulnerable in a Southern state. The Major's Texas chief, John Grant, had been "no match for Cuney as a political general," with observers writing that the veteran black Republican leader "through political finesse" deprived Grant of the "advantage he had in mere numbers." Grant's failure to win a clean, uncontested victory and his constant pestering for money eventually made Hanna hostile to him. Worse, there were already at least fifty-six delegate slots being contested and the primary season was just getting into full swing. The McKinley men needed an upset.[28]

CHAPTER 13

McKinley Gains Traction

———◇►———

While his campaign battled the Combine in state and district conventions around the country, there was something larger going on. McKinley was emerging as a leader who had the temperament, principles, authenticity, and fortitude in the face of adversity to be president. There is no magic combination of personal traits that leads voters to conclude that a candidate is up to the presidency's demands. There are usually moments when Americans feel they gain a sense of a candidate. Presidential timber isn't enough to win the White House, but it is a prerequisite for people to believe in the candidate and see his election as a worthy cause.

The moments that give supporters this confidence could happen when adversity allows the candidate to display his true character. Or they could emerge when a candidate takes on a tough challenge, such as pushing back against a pressure group's objectionable policies. When those moments materialize, a candidate's response can make or break his candidacy.

Long before April 1896, McKinley had had a run-in with the American Protective Association. He was about to have another that would allow him to rise above tactical considerations and display the principles and character of a broad, national leader. But first, there was a convention coming up in the neighborhood of the front-runner. Its outcome would show, in an unmistakable way, that McKinley was the candidate who could beat the Combine and become the GOP presidential nominee.

•   •   •

NEW HAMPSHIRE WAS THE only state convention left in March and was believed solid for Reed. But that was before it was gaveled into session in Concord's Phenix Hall on March 31. The convention chairman, Senator Chandler, endorsed Reed as "our energetic, strong, positive and magnificent New England leader." He then introduced the Resolutions chairman, Manchester *Mirror and American* publisher Henry M. Putney, as "that veteran editor" and joked, "May I call you a veteran?" Putney replied, "Call me anything you like," drawing laughter from the hall. Chandler didn't laugh at what came next. Putney, a McKinley man, took control.[1]

Putney's drafted platform declared for Reed and McKinley equally. "We recognize as most conspicuous among such candidates New England's noble and illustrious son, the Hon. Thomas B. Reed of Maine," it said, "and that pure and able statesman and champion of protection, the Hon. William McKinley of Ohio." Delegates applauded enthusiastically.[2]

Chandler decided not to contest Putney's joint endorsement, assuming a Reed slate would be elected. It was a decision he "bitterly regretted" when the convention picked an uninstructed delegation "likely to go for McKinley." There was no sugarcoating the defeat. The *New York Times* screamed, "Mr. Reed Loses a State," blaming it on Chandler's attacks on McKinley. These had not only angered the Major's friends, but also given Chandler's intraparty rivals back home an excuse to settle old scores over similar treatment at the senator's hands.[3]

The Reed camp pushed back, arguing the joint endorsement was not damaging. Chandler dismissed "the anomalous platform," while Senator Lodge repeated Chandler's spin, saying, "There really was nothing in the resolutions to cause comment unfavorable to Reed." But both men knew this was a blow to Reed, a sign of the front-runner's weakness.[4]

Chandler made excuses, claiming that he was blindsided by Putney and that the dual endorsement did not represent the state's Republicans. In an open letter, Putney said the opposite was true. The convention was not for Reed, "not a bit of it," Putney argued. "It was a McKinley convention. You should be thankful that it was satisfied with accommodating the anti-McKinley combine." He also accused Reed of being controlled by "the Platts, the Quays and Clarksons." The New Hampshire upset boosted the confidence of the Major's managers. After reviewing the recent results and preparations for the upcoming conventions, Hanna wrote McKinley, "Nothing can stop us now."[5]

HOWEVER, SOME THOUGHT THEY could. What followed was a critical moment as the APA set out to destroy the Major. The attack was brutal and could have deeply damaged the McKinley campaign. Even though the APA had declined in recent years as internal disputes and financial difficulties sapped its effectiveness and some Midwestern Democrats used the group's controversial statements to sway immigrant voters, it remained large, influential, and dangerous. It was the rare Republican who publicly bucked the group.[6]

APA leaders wanted to restore the group's reputation as a kingmaker. After screening the Republican field, National Advisory Board chairman J. H. D. Stevens declared that all GOP presidential candidates were acceptable except McKinley and gave a litany of the Major's offenses. He and his advisors were pro-Catholic and anti-APA. As governor, McKinley had appointed Catholics to posts he had promised to APA members. He refused to meet with APA leaders. The Major belonged to a secret Catholic men's organization.[7]

Some McKinley advisors, notably James Boyle and Joseph Smith, believed the Combine was behind the attacks. McKinley himself couldn't care less who was responsible. The attack was an opportunity. The APA had overreached. McKinley rose above it publicly, but allowed Hanna to hit back, knowing that in politics, the counterpunch is often more powerful than the punch.[8]

Hanna told reporters the APA had not asked for a meeting. He was McKinley's manager, so he would have known. Then he undermined the APA's credibility by denying some of the more explosive charges. He and Boyle were not Catholic, but Episcopalian. McKinley did not belong to the Ancient Order of the Hibernians or the Young Men's Institute, but was a trustee of Canton's First Methodist Church. The campaign issued a list of "secret societies" to which McKinley belonged. He was "a Freemason, a comrade of the Grand Army of the Republic, a member of the Union Veteran Union, of the Sons of the American Revolution, of the Loyal Legion, and of a college fraternity." The McKinley camp was mocking the APA, belittling its attack by showing how normal the Major's associations were. Hanna then set out to pressure the group into line by urging McKinley supporters who were APA members to lobby its Supreme Council, which met in May.[9]

McKinley wanted to ensure his team had the right tone when pushing back. He wrote Osborne, saying, "The [APA's] course is extraordinary in American politics and I can not but think that it will react upon its authors and others related to it. Think for a moment—the leaders of a secret order seeking through its organization to dictate a presidential nomination. A committee sitting in secret judgment on a public man and whose report and judgment are to be binding upon all its membership. It may hurt locally here and there, but in the broad sense it cannot hurt. But whether it does or not, we can not afford for any stake to narrow our platform, or consent to countenance any abridgement of the constitutional guarantees of religious freedom." He also let Dawes know his views.[10]

The APA Advisory Board reaffirmed its indictment of McKinley and sent agents and materials to county and congressional district conventions in Illinois. This unnerved some McKinleyites but most felt the APA's attack "died a bornin'," as the Major's Winnebago County, Illinois, chairman reported. While APA men "are doing some harm," wrote a Springfield, Illinois, Republican to Dawes, "I do not see how we can fail." Within a week, even Smith, ever the worrywart, was "satisfied that the APA explosion has turned out to be a boomarang [*sic*]."[11]

The APA had been manhandled, not deeply wounded—that would happen only if the organization was forced to reverse itself in May, when the Supreme Council met—but the dispute was evidence that the Major lived by his convictions, even if that meant engaging in a tough fight and potentially alienating some supporters. The decision to push back against the APA signaled that rather than accept the offensive demands of a radical organization, McKinley would stand for the religious freedom of all Americans. It was, in some ways, to be expected from a campaign whose slogan was "The People Against the Bosses." Sometimes the bosses were interest groups like the APA—bullies with agendas that needed to be confronted.

WHILE THE COMBINE BATTLED McKinley in March, its chief operative was missing from the action. Ret Clarkson was on the Western swing that Platt and Quay had approved, leaving just days before Kansas Republicans met on March 9 and returning two days before the New Hampshire debacle. Approving Clarkson's absence during such a critical time is evidence of how clumsily the bosses ran things outside their states.

Clarkson saw many people and returned with plenty of news. Unfortunately for the Combine, much of it was inaccurate, happy talk from men who depended on Clarkson to channel money to them from Platt's New York donors. For example, Tanner told Clarkson he was confident he and Lorimer would take most of Illinois's 48 delegates. And while the machine men's Kansas allies admitted they would not beat instruction for McKinley, they believed they could take 18 of the state's 20 delegates on the second or third ballot. That, of course, assumed the St. Louis convention went three ballots.[12]

Clarkson reported in New Mexico and would select five Combine men and one McKinley supporter as delegates, but much of the intelligence he picked up out West was wrong. For example, he thought the RNC members for Arizona, Idaho, and Nevada were safe; that most of California would be anti-McKinley; that Arizona and Nevada would be solid for the Combine; that Idaho had been flipped from leaning McKinley; and that Utah and Washington State were likely for the Combine. He was wrong about all of them. None of these Western states would play out the way Ret thought, except New Mexico.[13]

Clarkson also made mistakes. His biggest resulted in Wyoming instructing for McKinley. He summoned Willis Van Devanter, an associate of Wyoming senator Francis Warren, to meet on his private train car near Denver in late March. Clarkson wanted Warren's help on arranging Wyoming to send an unpledged or favorite-son delegation to St. Louis.

Clarkson erred by also inviting former senator Joseph M. Carey, whom Warren had ousted. Van Devanter was upset when he learned his boss's rival was coming. Even an offer of money in return for an unpledged delegation couldn't smooth things over.

Out of pique with Carey, once Warren learned of the confab, he gave the go-ahead to instruct for McKinley and then wrote Hanna, "I am now of the opinion that when the time comes there will be a harmonious [sic] solid vote from Wyoming." By the next month, the senator told Hanna to "put Wyoming down for six votes on your private tab and kindly inform Maj. McKinley what he can depend upon, absolutely from Wyoming." If

Clarkson hadn't invited Carey, Wyoming might have been uninstructed. Personal rivalries can make a big difference.[14]

Clarkson later credited his Western tour with blunting the McKinley boom in the region, without which "our friends would have been stampeded." But the Combine got few votes in the region and his frequent references for the need to "equip our friends" probably annoyed Platt. The Easy Boss was finding it costly to fund the campaigns of several candidates at the same time.[15]

Clarkson was back in New York by early April, writing Allison about encouraging news on the Mississippi credentials dispute and reporting positive developments in Georgia. He congratulated himself for having "had to resist nearly everybody's opinion" that the Texas campaign should not be put in Cuney's hands and lamented that unless more newspaper support for Tanner's efforts could be lined up, "we will lose Illinois, I am afraid, and that would be fatal." His report showcased his shortcoming. He could identify and diagnose problems, but rarely could he prioritize them or come up with solutions. In a campaign manager, that is a deadly combination.[16]

THE PACE OF STATE conventions quickened in April, with seventeen before the Illinois showdown on the twenty-ninth. The Combine took three, including one of the most important, Pennsylvania, Quay's home front. The Keystone State would have the second-largest delegation in St. Louis (64 delegates), but its convention in Harrisburg was small—289 men. Quay was in control, winning the test vote on credentials, 200 to 72. After that, delegates endorsed him for president and defeated by 178 to 65 a motion to name McKinley as the state's second choice. There was almost a fistfight when a Quay man attacked the motion by saying it would "belittle and make ridiculous the grand compliment the convention had paid to Quay."[17]

Soon after the convention, Quay's rivals in Philadelphia circulated rumors that more than a third of the state's 64 delegates would vote against him. Quay responded by sending a telegram to each delegate, asking where he stood. Fifty-eight of the 61 replies Quay received affirmed they would vote for him and three were noncommittal. Three delegates were not heard from. Quay was on the defensive, his status as a favorite son tarnished as he headed to the national convention.[18]

Reed carried both Rhode Island with 8 delegates and his home state of Maine with 12. The latter was a splendid show, but the speaker was dead in the water. That same day, the *New York Times* pronounced his campaign over, declaring, "Mr. Reed says nothing. Perhaps he thinks there are some greenback or cooper or wampum States yet to select delegates, and he is waiting to hear from them before settling the dispute as to his true sentiments." The *Times* was a Democratic paper, but even a Reed man like Teddy Roosevelt felt the observation was correct.[19]

MCKINLEY HAD A BETTER April than the machine men, taking seven of the seventeen states, with 112 delegates, giving him the lead. The Major's romp started in Oregon, which instructed for him unanimously, his victory engineered by wool growers. The Major then easily won instruction in North Dakota, Tennessee, and Virginia, where "McKinley badges were in evidence everywhere" and black delegates hissed at the mention of Stonewall Jackson, the famed Confederate war hero. Among the Tennessee delegates was Knoxville banker S. J. Sanford, whom Platt had been quick to call a Morton man in January. Now Sanford was bound by instruction to support McKinley "in letter and spirit," which must have caused chuckles in Canton.[20]

The Major did so well in his next two unambiguous victories—Nebraska and Georgia—that his supporters there focused on different priorities and turned on each other. More than a thousand Republicans gathered in Omaha. Senator Thurston moved that the delegation be instructed to support Manderson as a favorite son if McKinley could not win. This was a compromise dreamed up by Thurston to further party unity that was approved by the McKinley high command in Canton. But even Charles Dawes's brother B.G., a Nebraska businessman and McKinley leader, did not like the idea, having earlier written Dawes that "I am afraid things have gone too far for that." Grassroots McKinley supporters wouldn't stand for it. Instead, B.G. grimly informed his brother, "we will give iron-clad instructions and every thing will be lovely." That was exactly what the convention did, supporting a straight-out endorsement of McKinley by 488 to 410.[21]

The Georgia state convention opened on the twenty-ninth in Atlanta with a fierce but lopsided battle between the Major's forces and the

Combine, with a Quay man telling an Atlanta paper, "We are anything to down McKinley." That would be difficult to do: John H. Deveaux, the state party's secretary, whom the Major met in Thomasville the previous year, and Chairman Alfred E. Buck prepared the delegate roll in the back room of Buck's law office. The Reed forces then tried rushing the doors when Buck demanded to inspect tickets before allowing anyone to enter. Tempers boiled and by the time police were called, delegates were allowed to enter, and the convention was gaveled in, they were high. Though a distinct minority, the anti-McKinley faction threatened a bolt.[22]

As compromises, there were no instructions and a Reed man was added to three of the four at-large delegates pledged to McKinley. The Major's forces caved after Reed's leaders argued white McKinley men wanted to deny black Republicans their fair share. Since blacks made up two-thirds of the convention, former Democrat J. F. Hanson of Macon was swapped out for a black Republican, H. L. Johnson, the law partner of Reed's state manager, W. A. Pledger. Pledger had said earlier that his goal was to keep Hanson, a white, from going to St. Louis.[23]

The convention deteriorated into near chaos again when the McKinley men turned on each other. Professor R. R. Wright attempted to take Johnson's place and was kept from objecting to the arrangement only by being pulled back into his chair by his coattails by another McKinley man. Wright's supporters seemed likely to walk out. But the drama caused minimal damage, as the convention quickly adopted a platform endorsing McKinley's policies and adjourned. Despite the hubbub, McKinley was pleased, writing he was "grateful" for Buck's "splendid work." The Combine immediately reached out to Wright to encourage a credentials challenge, but Wright and his allies remained loyal to McKinley. Wright was later rewarded by being named a McKinley alternate.[24]

FOUR APRIL CONVENTIONS HAD more complicated outcomes. Some picked split delegations with both McKinley and Combine men; others selected uninstructed delegations whose preferences were hard to see. These results meant more work for the candidates and their managers as they tried to sway these delegates.

At the Kentucky state convention, the McKinley forces were led by the *Lexington Leader* publisher, Sam J. Roberts, who used to live in Canton.

He played a smart but dangerous game. The state's twenty-six delegates were instructed to back its governor, William O. Bradley, as long as his name remained before the convention, then vote for McKinley. The McKinley camp won one of the four at-large slots and wisely did not take umbrage at Bradley's ambitions. Instead, they kept pressure on the freshman governor so Kentucky would swing over when it became apparent he was out. That required tact and patience from the McKinley men.[25]

The next day, New Jersey delivered an enigmatic outcome. Generally a Combine ally, the state's twenty delegates had been delivered to the bosses' candidate in previous national conventions. This time, Garden State Republicans selected an uninstructed delegation, hinting they were against Morton and Platt by expressing the hope that former state house Speaker and state senate president Garret A. Hobart would be considered for the ticket.[26]

Six days later, Connecticut also picked an uninstructed delegation, though McKinley's name "met with an outburst of enthusiasm that astonished the Reed men." Leading the cheers for the Major was John Addison Porter, his host in Hartford in 1895. The Major's partisans claimed that two-thirds of the delegates were McKinley men, but there was no way to prove that since delegates refused to make a public declaration. It was a similar outcome for Maryland Republicans in Baltimore. Although "seven-tenths of the delegates . . . wore McKinley badges" and the draft platform strongly recommending his nomination was "loudly cheered," a motion to instruct was voted down and an uncommitted slate picked.[27]

These four states with uncertain outcomes had 74 delegates who would draw a lot of attention from all the candidates in the weeks before the St. Louis convention.

FOR HIS PART, MCKINLEY was not just gaining delegates in unexpected places. By manhandling the APA, he was also preparing for the general election by continuing to show himself to be a different kind of Republican. And his strategy and organization were demonstrating his prowess as a competitor. He had won New Hampshire, a state long thought to be the convention possession of Reed from neighboring Maine, and had a shot to win support in New Jersey—a state that had long served as New York's little brother.

Elections in a large, diverse country like the United States rarely offer uncomplicated story lines. The Major's campaign had not been one of unbroken success, but the narrative of this race was becoming one of his audacity, organization, and relentless focus. Now McKinley was about to make a run at a high-profile prize. Everyone was set for Illinois, but few were prepared for the outcome.

CHAPTER 14

High Stakes in Springfield

————◦————

Most observers agreed that as Abraham Lincoln's adopted home and final resting place, Illinois and its 48-member delegation—third-largest behind New York and Pennsylvania—could settle the GOP presidential contest. McKinley's advisor Charles Dick called the Illinois convention the "Gettysburg of the fight."[1]

Dawes had been building his card file for more than a year and he and McNulta, Pavey, and Edens had worked hard to dominate as many downstate counties as possible to offset the machine's strength in Lorimer's Cook County. The goal was to get each county to instruct its delegates to support McKinley at the district and state conventions.

Each congressional district convention selected two national delegates. The McKinley camp didn't care who those men were as long as they were instructed for the Major. It was a hard fight in many districts: Lorimer and Tanner were helped by some of Cullom's Republican House colleagues, who sought uninstructed delegates the Combine could control.

Each county also sent delegates to the April 29 state convention in Springfield. While it would pick only four at-large delegates, district delegates who were instructed for anyone but McKinley could claim the state convention trumped any guidance they had been given at their district meeting.

The Blond Boss—Lorimer—and Tanner were confident they could handle McKinley's amateurs. They had dealt with bumblers in the past, but the machine men were about to suffer a few surprises.

• • •

CHARLES G. DAWES HAD pulled his opening trick on January 27 at the state GOP's annual dinner in Springfield, colloquially known as the "Love Feast." Typically, the evening featured praise for all the party's statewide elected officials. Uncle Shelby Cullom was looking forward to basking in flowery speeches about his achievements, character, and future.

Dawes arranged for a spirited display when McKinley's name was mentioned. He was pleased at the "thunderous applause" and cheers that erupted when the Major was hailed for his advocacy of protective tariffs. The demonstration eclipsed any other display and left Cullom sputtering. Angry at McKinley's "invasion," he complained to reporters, saying, "I have attended these Republican love feasts for twenty-five years, and I have never yet known one turned into a mere scrabble of candidates."[2]

The demonstration also rattled the Blond Boss, who wired Hanna the next day to request "an important interview" in Chicago. Hanna and Osborne joined Dawes for the meeting, but unexpectedly, Lorimer was a no-show. Instead, he, Tanner, and RNC committeeman Thomas N. "Doc" Jamieson sent word they were "taking care of Illinois politics and are not friendly to outside interference."

It was a turning point for Dawes, who had thought Tanner and Lorimer could be persuaded into joining the movement for the Major. "That settles it," he wrote in his diary. "No alliance can be made with the regular party organization. It is now McKinley and the people against the 'County' machine and its state branches."[3]

A new test for the young manager came a few days later when Kohlsaat told Dawes his *Times-Herald* would support two men for the 6th Congressional District national delegate slots who were not McKinley men. To Dawes this was a betrayal: Kohlsaat was close to McKinley and his *Herald* was the only pro-McKinley Chicago paper, yet Kohlsaat now undermined McKinley because of personal local political concerns. Irritated, Dawes immediately went to Cleveland to see Hanna, seeking permission to field a McKinley slate in the 6th. It was a good meeting, with Dawes writing in his diary that Hanna said "he would stand by me in any fight I decided it best to make. Is disappointed at Kohlsaat's decision." McKinley phoned Kohlsaat and then wrote a personal letter for Dawes to give him. "The Governor agrees we must fight. He gives me full authority."[4]

Dawes returned to Chicago to be confronted with a Combine surprise. Lorimer called an emergency meeting of the Cook County central committee on February 3 that voted to hold ward, city, and town conventions on February 14 and the county convention to select state delegates February 15. This was highly unusual. Typically, Cook County held these conventions just weeks before the state confab, but Lorimer was determined to deny the McKinley camp time to organize. He wanted his county's delegation, a quarter of the state convention's total and half the votes needed for control, to be solidly anti-McKinley. Tanner paid for the snap conventions by getting $10,000 from Clarkson. Ret got the money from Grenville Dodge. Tanner acknowledged the largesse by asking Clarkson for more money. Privately, Dawes fumed, saying, "This is not fighting fair. But we will make the machine sick before we get through with them."[5]

Back in Chicago, Dawes met with Health Commissioner William R. Kerr, a powerful force in city politics because of his department's many patronage jobs. He told Dawes that if Kohlsaat "would give the command," Mayor George B. Swift was "anxious to make the fight for McKinley." Even after the Major's phone call and letter, Kohlsaat wouldn't budge on the 6th District delegates nor allow Swift to endorse McKinley. Dawes called Kohlsaat's stubbornness a "bitter disappointment," but he couldn't afford to circumvent him by reaching out to Swift.[6]

Dawes felt he must respond to Lorimer's show of strength, so he rallied the McKinley forces by holding a protest against the snap conventions. The "Indignation Meeting" on February 10 attracted "the most prominent men of the city." They passed a resolution condemning the machine's "hasty and ill-advised action," arguing that it gave Republicans too little time to properly select delegates and nominate candidates for Congress, state legislature, and local office. Attendance was less than Dawes hoped, but the quality of attendees showed McKinley's campaign had oomph in the city. Short, pudgy, and ever-quotable former congressman William E. Mason drew applause when he said, "One of my Irish friends told me today nobody is for McKinley except the people."[7]

BY EARLY MARCH, THE results of Dawes's work were visible. Sangamon County, home to Springfield, instructed its state delegates to back Cullom, but it was only the second county to do so while thirteen had instructed for McKinley. The 7th District convention then instructed for McKinley, giving him two delegates at the national convention, and the Major was just five votes shy of a majority in the 14th District with four counties yet to select delegates and some uninstructed delegates quietly supporting McKinley, despite Uncle Shelby's strong-arming.[8]

Cullom complained, "The McKinley forces are organized all over my state." He also objected to the "large amount of money spent in Illinois by McKinley workers." Two days later he told reporters he wouldn't spend any money to advance his candidacy. Of course, he didn't need to; Tanner and Lorimer were doing that for him. But admitting to being outorganized and outspent wasn't smart. Some Illinois Republicans didn't take his bid seriously and he wasn't giving them any reasons to do so.[9]

Dawes kept plugging away in his walk-up office at the Auditorium, updating his card file. The night of March 14, he described the "past week a busy week . . . marked by the 'unconditional surrender' of the machine politicians who find it useless to combat further the sentiment among the people for McKinley." But there had been no surrender. His diary notation was bravado or delusion. Dawes then decided to go for instruction in Logan, Cullom's hometown. If the senator was beaten there, he might give up the fight.[10]

Dawes pulled it off as Cullom's home district—the 17th—fell to McKinley, as did two other downstate congressional districts with two others teetering in the Major's direction. Despite these victories, the *Chicago Tribune* suggested the "tide appears to be turning against McKinley." But it wasn't, and Cullom was looking for a way out.[11]

On March 29, Dawes conferred with McKinley, Hanna, and Smith about a potential bombshell. Through federal district judge Peter S. Grosscup, Cullom had offered to withdraw in return for certain considerations. But McKinley "would not make these concessions," Dawes wrote in his diary. "He proposed to take the place . . . unmortgaged." The next day, the two districts that had been teetering fell into the Major's column. Another district went for McKinley within days. Dawes was running a juggernaut.[12]

With the convention less than a month away, Dawes was in constant touch with Canton. On April 3, he received encouragement from Smith, who observed, "Illinois has some of the most adroit and cunning political schemers on this continent. Next to those fellows in Louisiana and Texas I have never seen their equals in duplicity and scoundrelism."[13]

Meanwhile, Dawes and McNulta continued negotiating with Cullom through Grosscup. On April 12, Dawes noted in his diary that he and McNulta were in Ohio, meeting with McKinley, Hanna, and Smith "over Cullom matter with satisfactory conclusion." McNulta wired Grosscup to come to Canton, suggesting he be "prepared to go further East" to carry the McKinley's camp's latest position to Cullom in Washington. But nothing came of it. Grosscup didn't come.[14]

Two days later, the McKinley forces locked down the 12th District of Joe Cannon, a close Cullom ally. Several congressmen were meeting with Hanna when he received the report. Smith wrote Dawes, "You should have heard their shouts of gratification."[15]

On April 17, Dawes finally had a breakthrough with Swift, who had reached out to him. But the mayor, operating independently of Kohlsaat, wanted to be a statewide at-large delegate. That was a problem. Dawes now faced a choice: fight for a slate of men to be sent to the national convention and get involved in local fights and personality conflicts, or keep pushing for instructions and leave it up to the district or state conventions to settle on the men bound to carry out the order. The McKinley men were pursuing the second approach and couldn't make Swift a delegate without risking their entire strategy.[16]

Two days later, Dawes and McNulta were summoned to Grosscup's apartment and told, "Cullom will withdraw if Tanner does not object." Dawes didn't think Tanner would object, but after Dawes and McNulta conferred with the GOP state chairman for an hour, Cullom was still in the race. "Tanner promises fair treatment in convention," according to Dawes, who thought that settled the issue. In reality, Tanner had offered a meaningless promise. He and Dawes had different interpretations of "fair treatment."[17]

With the state convention looming and pressure building, some McKinley men began sniping and looking for someone to blame should McKinley come up short. Kohlsaat took a shot at Dawes, saying, "Our people have been entirely too magnanimous or gullible in this matter." Odd words from someone who refused to allow Swift to declare war on the Cook County machine. One Springfield Republican complained to the Major, "We have the delegates, but no organization." But with Dawes, the one thing McKinley was sure he had in Illinois was organization. He shared the letter with Dawes without comment.[18]

The next day, a victory in the last congressional district convention before the state meeting gave the Major at least 34 of the 48 Illinois delegates. Both sides realized the Illinois state convention could be the Combine's last chance to break McKinley's momentum and allow the bosses to do their horse-trading at the national convention that they did so well.[19]

THE CONVENTION DID NOT start until Wednesday, but some of the 1,335 Illinois GOP delegates began arriving in Springfield on Saturday, April 25. Dawes summoned the state McKinley leadership for a final caucus in his Leland Hotel suite Sunday night.[20]

Dawes outlined the plan: the campaign would not offer candidates for convention chairman or delegates-at-large, but focus solely on the question of instruction, insisting it be voted on before the state ticket was nominated. This would allow the Major's opponents to name the convention officials and exercise a lot of influence over the names of the delegates, while focusing all the McKinley forces' energy on locking in the delegates.

Swift "made a direct attack upon my plans," Dawes later wrote, "claiming that I was inexperienced and unacquainted with the general situation." Seeking to replace Dawes as leader, Swift argued for delaying any decisions, hinting they should fight over a McKinley slate, not instruction. Dawes replied with a fifteen-minute speech, understanding "[i]t was a question of my life or death as a political manager. When I finished nearly every man in the room was on his feet, and my point was won. . . . Had this not happened, we could have had no organization the balance of the week." If the thirty-year-old had not weathered this crisis, it is likely that much of the preceding months' hard work would have been for naught.[21]

Still seeking to sideline Dawes, Swift's allies complained to the press that the McKinley camp had a "multiplicity of officers and paucity of privates." What Swift didn't accept was that he was one of the privates. After his Sunday night speech, Dawes was in charge and the mayor could only sputter and intrigue.[22]

To lead the floor fight and speak for McKinley during the convention, Dawes settled on Frank L. Calhoun. The forty-eight-year-old Calhoun, with a high forehead and a long, droopy mustache, had grown up in Ohio and was a childhood friend of McKinley. Ironically, when Cullom was first elected senator, questions were raised as to whether as a sitting governor he was eligible. To argue his case, Uncle Shelby picked a young state representative and brilliant lawyer—Calhoun.[23]

Cullom arrived Monday afternoon. Attending the convention was dangerous. If he lost, being present could further undermine his prestige. The enthusiasm for McKinley was so obvious, Cullom had to reaffirm he had not withdrawn, telling a reporter, "All such talk is nonsense," and predicted he would take 30 to 32 of the state's 48 delegates.[24]

Tanner and RNC committeeman "Doc" Jamieson had settled on Chicago alderman Martin B. Madden as temporary convention chairman and Orville F. Berry, a prominent downstate state senator, as permanent chairman. Madden, a handsome and clean-shaven forty-one-year-old, was chairman of the city council's Finance Committee and, being "the shrewdest" of the Chicago machine's managers, a frequent target of reformers.[25]

Dawes and Tanner finally settled on when the instruction vote would occur. Tanner offered to hold it after the entire state ticket had been named but before the selection of university trustee candidates and national convention delegates-at-large. Dawes agreed. The *Chicago Tribune* characterized this as a McKinley defeat, but Dawes got what he wanted: Tanner couldn't move to adjourn until after voting on instruction.[26]

There was continued maneuvering over the four statewide delegates. Lorimer had picked his slate, but Swift wanted one of those slots and was still pressing the McKinley campaign to back him. A Dawes lieutenant— probably McNulta—let reporters know the campaign's position, saying, "What the thunder do we care who the delegates are? What we want is the instructions."[27]

Wednesday morning, Illinois Republicans convened at "The Dome," a wooden hemisphere about 222 feet high, resting on four square, two-story brick boxes. It had been built for the World's Columbian Exposition, held in 1893 in Chicago. After the world's fair it was taken down, put on railcars, and reassembled at the State Fair Grounds two miles outside Springfield. The Dome had room for 13,000. Half a dozen gigantic flags hung from its big oval ceiling along with 102 streamers, each bearing an Illinois county's name. Large portraits of Lincoln, Douglas, and Grant decorated the upper gallery while pictures of other famous Republicans hung from its railing. Cullom was among them; McKinley wasn't.[28]

After the convention came to order at 12:15 p.m., Calhoun offered a motion to vote on instruction after the attorney general nomination, as agreed upon. Cullom's manager, former congressman David Littler, tried breaking the agreement by objecting. He was quickly slapped down—even the Blond Boss kept promises made so publicly.[29]

AROUND 3 P.M., IN the middle of a roll call, a telegram was delivered to Jamieson on the floor. The small, dark-haired party boss realized the message the telegram carried would destroy the morale of Cullom's supporters and deliver a debilitating blow to the Combine. Vermont had just rejected Reed, all but guaranteeing its delegates for McKinley.

Around the time the Illinois proceedings were heating up, Vermont Republicans had gathered in Montpelier's "Golden Fleece" community hall expecting a Reed victory. But in the Green Mountain State, the Combine didn't get a warm reception. At a unity rally the previous evening featuring Vermont senator Redfield Proctor and his Nebraska colleague and Green Mountain native John M. Thurston, every mention of McKinley was met by a rousing cheer. It turned out McKinley's supporters outnumbered the opposition by two-to-one. Alarmed, Proctor, a Reed man, hastily wired a warning to Manley.[30]

The next morning, as Illinois began its deliberations, McKinley benefited in Vermont from old friends and early preparations. Led by Resolutions chairman John W. Stuart, a former congressional colleague of the Major's and a Middlebury banker, the convention went overwhelmingly for McKinley. For party unity they agreed not to instruct, but all the delegates—including Proctor—felt morally bound to McKinley. The convention's strong result for the Major had its start in an 1892 vacation the McKinleys took at Osborne's summer house that was coupled with several days of campaign speeches at huge rallies across the state. Vermont was the second brutal loss in New England for Reed.[31]

As other telegrams arrived in Springfield trumpeting McKinley's upset victory, the Blond Boss and his agents were reduced to arguing that the Major had failed to gain an official instruction in Vermont. It didn't matter. The news electrified the Major's followers who smelled an even bigger upset in the making in Illinois. Dawes issued a statement: "The McKinley forces are increasing every hour."[32]

The Illinois convention ground forward, with Tanner winning the gubernatorial nomination followed by a bruising, multi-ballot battle for lieutenant governor. When Tanner's running mate was finally selected, Berry recessed the convention. The machine men needed time to calm its delegations and "bargain further." Dawes and his crew wanted to work the opposition's weak spots overnight.[33]

THURSDAY MORNING, SWIFT CONTINUED pressuring Dawes to cave on instruction, probably because of machine hints that the mayor would be made a delegate if that happened. Dawes refused. The convention was gaveled to order at 9 a.m. for nominations for secretary of state, treasurer, auditor, and attorney general. Each roll call took nearly an hour or more, and there were seven of them for the four races before Charles E. Fuller, a Combine man, moved to instruct for Cullom late that afternoon. This kicked off a floor demonstration of delegates from Cook County and Springfield. The McKinley men waited for the demonstration to end before moving to amend the resolution.[34]

As the machine's floor show petered out, Calhoun tried to be recognized, but Chairman Berry called on Sol H. Betha, a young Chicago lawyer waving from the other side of the hall. Betha did Calhoun's work, moving to substitute "McKinley" for "Cullom" in Fuller's resolution. The hall exploded as "the convention resolved itself into a gathering of shouting, yelling, stamping, enthusiastic frantic men and women" that shook the Dome in support of the Major. The Peoria police chief tied a big McKinley portrait to his umbrella and waved it in a frenzy.

During the six and a half minutes before order could be restored, Calhoun made his way to the stage to second the motion, saying, "The common people of this country, who neither hold office or seek office, the plain, common people, who patiently bear the burdens of this country . . . with one voice proclaim that protection is the measure and that William McKinley is the man of the hour." Another storm swept the hall. When the Dome finally quieted, the crowd could hear Union war veterans standing with Champaign's "One-Armed" McCullough singing, "Marching Through Georgia."

The Blond Boss had one curveball left. Madden moved to add language saying that if McKinley failed to win the nomination, Illinois Republicans could accept Reed or Allison. In one brutal movement, Cullom was thrown overboard and the Combine's true goal was revealed:

ABM—Anybody but McKinley. Calhoun called on the Major's men to vote no on the Madden amendment. If the Madden amendment failed, the convention would then turn to the question of instruction for McKinley and McKinley only.[35]

The roll call of 102 counties took nearly an hour. After the first 15 counties, it was 41 aye and 78 no on Madden's ABM motion. Cook County voted 267 aye to 78 nay, giving the machine men a two-to-one majority, their high point. The remaining counties were strongly pro-McKinley, voting three-to-one no, leaving the final tally 503 aye to 832 no. McKinley had taken Illinois with 62 percent. As the roll call ground to an end, Jamieson made his way to the podium to tell Berry to end it. The Combine was beaten.[36]

The machine men withdrew the Madden amendment and moved that the at-large delegates be instructed for McKinley by acclamation. With a huge shouted "Aye!" the convention agreed. Berry didn't bother calling for nays.[37]

Dawes was quickly pressured to select the delegates, but having them instructed was enough for the thirty-year-old manager. Swift then lost his bid for an at-large delegate seat. Littler withdrew from the at-large contest in favor of former governor Richard Oglesby, a McKinley man. Littler and Oglesby were brothers-in-law, but disliked each other intensely. The platform was adopted unanimously and the convention sputtered to a close after 7 p.m. in semidarkness: the Dome was not designed for night gatherings.[38]

CULLOM GRACIOUSLY CONCEDED, SAYING Republicans "have shown that they want the delegates-at-large to support Maj. McKinley for president." The Blond Boss was generous, too, calling Calhoun "shrewd, smart and practical." Lorimer had reason to be content. He lost the national delegate battle, but Swift was made weaker by failing to dislodge Dawes and losing his own bid for at-large delegate. And Lorimer had his man as the party's gubernatorial nominee.[39]

There was little solace in the defeat for the Combine. They knew they'd been whipped, with the Massachusetts GOP chairman warning, "McKinley has out-generaled us all to pieces." All the papers proclaimed the nomination contest effectively over. Kohlsaat's *Chicago Times-Herald* said the next morning, "The people rose and fell upon the machine. They smashed it . . . and trampled the fragments into dust." The *Chicago Tribune* reported that among Washington power brokers, "there is but one sentiment of 'that settles it,' " while the *New York Times* wrote that the Major won by "a majority as unexpected to the supporters of McKinley as it was staggering to Senator Cullom and his friends." It may have been unexpected for Cullom, the Blond Boss, and the Combine. It was not for Dawes. His meticulous card catalog had forecast the McKinley sweep. The only way for the Combine to win the national convention now was for a majority on the RNC to rule out McKinley men in credentials fights to make a first-ballot victory impossible.[40]

One historian argues that Dawes's role in Illinois was overstated and his leadership flawed. The demonstration at the GOP Love Feast was "apparently a failure" because it didn't diminish the Combine's opposition. The "indignation meeting . . . was also unsuccessful" since the Cook County snap conventions went forward. Dawes was "easily defeated in the bargaining" that went on for months before the convention and was "one small part of McKinley's largely undisciplined strength in the state." McNulta, an old practiced political hand, was more important to McKinley's success.[41]

This is wrong. The "Love Feast" outburst gave McKinleyites hope and unsettled Cullom. The "indignation meeting" stiffened the resolve of McKinley men to fight the Blond Boss on his Cook County turf and pick up delegates there for the Major. Dawes, while naïve and prone to think he'd bested the machine when he had not, succeeded in making the instruction vote invulnerable to a snap adjournment. Though young, he stood his ground when Swift attempted a coup and knew the best man for floor leader was Calhoun. A less effective leader might have lost the debate with Swift or insisted on the spotlight himself. McNulta offered perhaps the second-best tribute to Dawes's leadership. He wired McKinley that night, "After the hottest contest known in this state, your friends under the able leadership of Dawes have performed what was promised."[42]

Smith wired Dawes to say, "Thank God we can all retire in peace you have proven yourself a hero and a general." Still, in the flush of victory Dawes was not ready to forgive everyone. When Kohlsaat soon asked him to personally invest in the *Herald*, Dawes told the wearisome publisher, "It [is] out of the question."[43]

After receiving the news of the Illinois victory, McKinley sat down to write Dawes. "I can not close the day without sending you a message of appreciation and congratulations," he told the young man in whom he had placed all his trust. "There is nothing in all of this long campaign so signal and significant as the triumph at Springfield. I cannot find words to express my admiration for your high qualities of leadership. You have won exceptional honor. You had long ago won my heart."[44]

CHAPTER 15

Last-Minute Attacks Before St. Louis

A fter Illinois, the Combine had two chances in May to blunt McKinley's momentum. The machine first tried enlisting Harrison. He disliked McKinley, thinking, among other things, that he was evasive on currency. So the day after Illinois, Benjamin F. Tracy, one of Platt's closest confidants, reached out to him. "There is only one person who can stop McKinley & that person is yourself," Harrison's secretary of the navy wrote his former chief. "If you can prevent your state from instructing for Mck I thing [sic] you can be nominated." [1]

But the former president knew it would not be that easy and dismissed the idea. "The favorite son business has been sadly overworked," Harrison observed. "The bringing into the field of some persons whose candidacy was not regarded as sincere and the apparent attempt to take large blocks of delegates to the convention for the purpose of transferring to somebody else very naturally excited popular resentment and the benefit has accrued to Mr. McKinley." He was right. Nor did Harrison trust the Combine. He knew what Platt thought of him. [2]

On the eve of the state convention, the Combine sent a coded telegram through Senator John H. Gear of Iowa to Louis T. Michener, pledging to unite behind Harrison "if Indiana would not instruct for McKinley." Michener refused to convey the message. He understood Platt hated the former president, knew Quay was no longer for Harrison, and doubted "Allison would agree to anything of the sort" because the Iowa senator still believed he could win. [3]

The Combine's scheming proved useless. In Indianapolis on May 7, the eighty-eight-year-old former navy secretary under Hayes, Richard W. Thompson, brought thousands of delegates and guests to their feet screaming, "I know McKinley, I honor McKinley, I am for McKinley." Indiana's thirty delegates were instructed for McKinley by almost five to one.[4]

The machine men's second chance to slow the Major was in West Virginia nine days later. An uninstructed delegation would boost Senator Elkins's chances to be VP, but he faced enormous pressure at home, where Albert B. White, a powerful GOP figure and future governor, was leading the Major's effort. McKinley also lobbied Elkins, writing in April that "I know a simple hint from you would make it easy for the people to do what is in their hearts to do" and instruct. After Illinois, Elkins realized he could not buck the Major, so he grudgingly watched the state convention become a McKinley lovefest. Six other state conventions with 134 delegates fell to McKinley, starting in California on May 5, and including Michigan, Wyoming, and North Carolina.[5]

STILL, THE COMBINE MEN were given more opportunities when five more Southern and Western conventions produced sets of contesting delegations, each claiming to be the official Republicans of their states. This further scrambled the delegate picture and promised more credentials battles at the national convention.

The largely black South Carolina Republicans instructed for McKinley at their convention in April. On the delegate slate for St. Louis were former representative Robert Smalls and three black Republicans who had run for Congress, all McKinley men. However, dissatisfied Combine men bolted and organized a competing delegation falsely claiming to be McKinleyites. The South Carolina situation got more complicated a week later when the Lily White Republicans overwhelmingly defeated instruction for McKinley but adopted a resolution saying, "Either McKinley, Allison, Morton, Reed or Quay would be acceptable." By the end, the Palmetto State had three competing delegations. Both Alabama and Arizona emerged from their conventions with two delegations apiece, and a third slate popped up in Louisiana.[6]

None of these was as acrimonious as the Missouri convention in mid-May, where forces loyal to Richard C. Kerens and Chauncey I. Filley battled for two days. Kerens was an early McKinley supporter and the more reasonable of the two. Filley pretended to favor McKinley even as he conspired with Platt, Quay, and Clarkson. His antics led one Combine operative to complain, "His methods are past my understanding." McKinley worked at keeping on friendly terms with Filley while Hanna took a dislike to Old Man Filley, which grew into intense hostility.[7]

Delegates were locked out of St. Joseph's Opera House for three hours as the factions wrangled behind closed doors over credentials. There was a riot when Filley men smashed their way into the hall with a battering ram. Police were required to restore order. It took until 11 p.m. for the Credentials Committee to finish. Floor fights over the platform and delegates continued until five thirty the next morning. The convention instructed for McKinley, reelected Filley state chairman, and endorsed replacing Kerens as committeeman with the Old Man. Afterward, the McKinley managers had to soothe hurt feelings on both sides, while worrying that Filley's men on the delegation might drop McKinley and that the split could linger and hurt chances for winning Missouri in the fall.[8]

The Delaware convention split between a group led by former senator Anthony C. Higgins and a faction led by his archrival and former mentor, J. Edward Addicks. The two men and their followers had hated each other since Addicks conspired in 1895 with the Democratic governor to keep Higgins from winning a second U.S. Senate term. The Addicks faction elected an uninstructed delegation, while the Higgins men picked a McKinley delegation. Unsettled state delegations like Delaware's played right into the Combine's preference for chaos.[9]

McKinley also lost four conventions outright in May, but the Combine—nearly all of whom were gold standard backers—didn't profit as these losses came in states dominated by silver supporters. Colorado, Idaho, Montana, and Nevada all sent Free Silver delegations to St. Louis, threatening a bolt if they didn't get an acceptable silver platform or candidate. Idaho senator Fred DuBois warned, "The republicans of Idaho will not vote for any man unless he is a friend of silver," and Colorado's senator Henry M. Teller said, "I do not intend to support a candidate on a gold standard platform or on a platform of doubtful construction."[10]

Currency was shaping up as a big problem, both for St. Louis and, ominously, the general election. The Western conventions raised the possibility that a dangerous rift was opening within the party over the money issue, which could lead to a bolt of silver Republicans in St. Louis and a broken, divided GOP heading into a tough fall election.

NOW THE FRONT-RUNNER AFTER Illinois, McKinley began taking fire. In early May, the leading Free Silver magazine, the *National Bimetallist,* hit him on currency for trying to "straddle the issue." The magazine charged he told "western Republicans that he is their friend on the silver question" while allied with Senator John Sherman, who supported "gold as the standard and silver as small change." This was a slap at the campaign's release of a letter from Sherman to the Brooklyn Young Republicans on April 27 that said, "There can be no doubt as to the attitude of Major McKinley on the money question. He is committed in every form . . . to the republican policy of maintaining the present gold coin of the United States." Silver coinage should be reserved "for the minor transactions of life." [11]

Silver Republicans in Congress had been feisty all year, threatening to amend the party's major tariff bill with a Free Silver provision, stalling Cleveland's measure authorizing the issuance of gold bonds, and keeping GOP Senate leadership from passing a tariff bill designed to set up protection as the issue in the presidential campaign. Teller took responsibility for the effort, saying, "As this is a political play, we will play politics on our side." Silver Republicans would oppose any protective tariff bill unless free coinage was included. [12]

By denying Republicans an election-year legislative package, Teller exposed a serious rift. Free Silver had deprived the GOP of its Senate majority. Teller had already told friends, "The demand is that we shall repudiate our financial views or go out. I will not abandon my views on finance and so I must go out not because I want to go out but because I am to be driven out." [13]

The silver men turned their attention from the party at large to McKinley. In March, Senator John P. Jones of Nevada accused him of being "neither flesh, fish, nor fowl" on currency but rather "a straddler, pure and simple." Silver Republicans, he asserted, wanted a true "gold bug" like Morton so the issue would be resolved. [14]

The attacks on McKinley's integrity were so persistent that the Major responded with an open letter in the *New-York Tribune* on March 14. He referred to his past currency statements in the *Congressional Record* and said, "My official career is an open book." This did not stop critics. The *Baltimore Sun* said it is "impossible to discover exactly where Ohio's 'favorite son' stands in regard to the money issue." GOP honest-money papers like the *Chicago Tribune* ridiculed his tangled record. So did Democratic papers like the *Austin Statesman,* which said, "McKinley's heart is too big for any one currency. He loves them all, gold, silver and money."[15]

In early April, Jones's Nevada colleague, Senator William Stewart, released a curt letter to McKinley. "Are you for the gold standard . . . or are you for the restoration of the bimetallic laws as they existed in this country previous to 1873?" The senator demanded a response, saying, "Neither silence nor an evasive answer will exonerate you from an attempt to deceive somebody." The Major did not reply, but the issue was not going away. Later that month, Stewart reiterated his demand and pointed to Sherman's recent comments that McKinley supported "the present gold coin" while McKinley's Western supporters "claim that you are in favor of the free and unlimited coinage of silver at the ratio of 16 to 1." "Will you define your position or will you continue to hold out hopes to both sides one or the other of which you must disappoint after the election?" Again, McKinley ignored him.[16]

Despite the Major's silence, the silver issue drew attention at GOP state conventions, and not just the ones held in Western mining states. Free Silver had been raised in Indiana, Michigan, and Washington State, where all three GOP conventions backed a bimetallic currency. Tar Heel Republicans went further, calling for more greenbacks as well. The McKinley managers dropped an honest-money plank in West Virginia so as not to offend the Major's many local silver supporters. A substantial silver minority in Minnesota led by a popular young Republican, former representative John Lind, had nearly won a platform fight. The Kansas convention had almost split, with a silver man urging delegates to "make a platform of its own, without the aid or consent of the East. . . . We know what we want. Let us say so."[17]

Once the state conventions concluded, McKinley's campaign mailed circulars to anyone who wrote him about currency. It said he was running on his record and making no promises about policy or appointments. A sheet of quotes from speeches and editorials accompanied the letter and declared "McKinley for sound money. His Congressional record and success prove this. The Republican party stands opposed to the unlimited coinage of silver under existing conditions." It said McKinley believed, "Whatever dollars we have . . . must be good dollars—worth one hundred cents, whether it be gold, silver, or paper." The circular included endorsements affirming McKinley was for sound money. Doubts lingered among honest-money men, but more troubling, the document's release hardened silver Republicans' opposition to McKinley. Silver would soon cause trouble for the GOP.[18]

DAWES TRAVELED TO CLEVELAND for lunch with Hanna in May. While they were savoring their Illinois win, the papers were filled with a full-scale attack by Platt, who thought he could salvage a victory in St. Louis if he raised enough doubts about McKinley. Platt told the press McKinley "will get the Republican party into turmoil and trouble." He was not "well-balanced" like Morton; not "great" like Reed; not "trained and educated" like Allison; and not "an astute political leader" like Quay. He was "too amiable and much too impressionable to be safely entrusted with great executive office," Platt sniffed.[19]

He belittled McKinley's signature achievement. McKinley was not responsible for the tariff law that bore his name; Representative Nelson Dingley Jr. and Senator Nelson Aldrich had done the hard work. While Republicans wanted higher tariffs, they didn't want McKinley's "radical and extreme view." Then Platt focused on the currency issue. "If Major McKinley has any real convictions on the subject, they are not revealed in his votes or his speeches." Platt charged that the Ohio platform plank on currency—which it was rumored McKinley had drafted—showed the Major was unreliable on the financial question for it proposed "another experiment in silver coinage." Platt was no dummy. As long as the convention was about McKinley versus the field of Reed, Allison, and the remaining favorite sons, the Major was likely to prevail.[20]

To win, Platt knew he must reframe the debate from one about personalities to one about an idea, in this instance, the gold standard. While McKinley was a straddler who wanted to avoid the issue so as to not offend the silverites, Platt knew that most national convention delegates were gold men. He wanted them to consider who would advance their views. It was a long shot, but Platt would now do everything he could to depict McKinley as untrustworthy on gold and, as a result, unworthy of the loyalty so many delegates felt toward him. Like the Bimetallic DNC men, Platt sought to stress principle first, candidate a distant second.

Three days later, Platt hit hard again at McKinley's currency views. McKinley was unreliable on gold, the Easy Boss asserted, and prone to "crazy schemes to make money out of all sorts of paper resting on all sorts of security." He accused the Major's handlers of using bribes of money and patronage promises to win delegates, ridiculing McKinley's anti-boss reform stance as "one of the most contemptible humbugs that has characterized his canvass."

Platt also assaulted McKinley's character, but tied it to his new strategy, saying the Major handled the financial issue "not from settled principles and convictions, but in accordance with what he considered at the time to be popular." Platt's attacks would continue until the convention, and they had the potential to resonate. Many business-oriented Republicans in the East were concerned about the Major's currency views already.[21]

Friday, the *Sun* published a lengthy analysis of McKinley's congressional record on the money question, accompanied by a front-page poem titled "The Straddle Bug."

> *My words have been for silver,*
> *My silence stood for gold,*
> *And Thus I show the teaching*
> *Of some great sage of old.*
> *And if there is a question*
> *As to just what I meant,*
> *I'll answer that quite fully—*
> *When I am President!*[22]

The *Nation* feared McKinley's platform would endorse bimetallism. "No one doubts that McKinley would stand on any kind of a platform offered him," its editors charged, urging that a gold platform be forced on him in St. Louis. Without it, the Republicans would lose the Northeast. That assumed, however, there would be a gold Democrat nominee.[23]

Other opponents of McKinley sensed Platt's attacks were hurting McKinley and could be an opportunity to galvanize opposition to him.

Michener reported to Harrison that there was a growing sentiment "that McKinley cannot be trusted on the financial question."[24]

Finally engaged, Reed joined the assault, saying that one of McKinley's slogans, "Advance Agent of Prosperity," reminded him of circus performers from his childhood. "It never came up to the show-bills," Reed said, "but there was always at least one first-class acrobat who rode two horses at once." If that wasn't clear enough, the *Nation*'s editors thundered, "The McKinley canvass has been a country-circus advertising dodge from the start." Reed had a sharper dig, saying, "McKinley isn't a gold bug, McKinley isn't a silver-bug. McKinley's a straddle-bug."[25]

PLATT'S ONSLAUGHT, HOWEVER, DID not cause a fellow Combine leader to fight harder. Instead, Matthew S. Quay decided to throw in the towel. McKinley was likely to win and it was time to begin unifying the party. Quay now undercut his Combine partners. He suggested Platt tone down his anti-McKinley rhetoric, and then invited him to Washington so he could tell him in person that he would go at McKinley's invitation to Canton. There, Quay would make peace.

On May 20, McKinley's confidant and his campaign's resident troublemaker, Ohio representative Charles H. Grosvenor, spilled the beans about the meeting, and the press descended on Quay. He was restrained, explained he was going because he had received "a polite invitation," and refused further comment.[26]

Though Quay had informed the Combine about McKinley's invitation, still Clarkson met with Quay and reported to Platt. Hanna was not consulted. Quay thought McKinley would win and saw the invitation as McKinley's "desire for conference on a friendly line" to the Combine. Clarkson had advised Quay to demand McKinley respect the "interests and rights" of Platt "before anyone's [*sic*] else" in New York. Quay agreed and wanted Platt to "understand that he would protect him . . . as he would protect himself."[27]

McKinley was waiting on the platform when Quay arrived at 10:26 a.m. on May 22, and personally drove him to his home, where they met for several hours. Then he and Quay returned to the depot in McKinley's carriage, shook hands, and exchanged good-byes before Quay boarded the 1:21 p.m. eastbound. Reporters groused that neither man would "give an inkling of what was said." Quay was only slightly less guarded on the ride home, saying, "We have had a very pleasant and satisfactory interview." To discourage further conversation, he discussed potato prices and refused more questions, saying, "I am corked up tighter than sealing wax."[28]

While "details of their meeting were left to speculation," the *Washington Star* suggested Quay had visited McKinley to acknowledge "the supremacy of the Ohio man." Quay had allegedly told party leaders before going to Canton that "I fear we shall have to accept McKinley, not because we want him, but because the people do." If true, it would make sense that he wanted to make peace with the likely nominee.

One historian says it is reasonable to infer that Quay promised not to make any last-ditch effort against McKinley in return for a promise by the latter not to meddle further in Pennsylvania. Quay's biographer suggests another goal "was to repair the McKinley-Platt relationship," but speculates he was unsuccessful, as McKinley parried his advice to summon Platt to Canton, "saying Platt was welcome at any time, but that he would not ask him to come."[29]

Reluctant to quit, Platt sent a lieutenant, J. Sloat Fassett, to get the full story from Quay. Fassett reported the senator was satisfied McKinley had at least 470 delegates, more than enough to win, and "was unwilling to divulge what had taken place between himself and McKinley," Fassett wrote in a letter to the Easy Boss. "He said that no agreement had been entered into which would militate against the agreements which have heretofore been made between you and him."

Quay's estimate was conservative: his state-by-state summary shows he underestimated McKinley's strength in the South (especially Alabama, Florida, Georgia, Tennessee, and Virginia), overestimated the staying power of favorite sons in New York and Kentucky, and assumed the Combine would still control credentials through the RNC.

Fassett reported that Quay preferred Pennsylvania governor Daniel Hastings to be vice president (which would remove a political rival), but thought McKinley's team appeared to be leaning to Reed, who Quay believed "would not consent." Quay had also sought more to place Platt "in touch and in communications with Hanna and McKinley than to accomplish any definite or particular point," Fassett wrote. Quay's judgment was "the second place would go pretty nearly wherever the New York delegation wanted it to go." It was also the Pennsylvanian's impression that "the attitude of McKinley's mind toward you was not imbittered [*sic*] nor hostile; that he appreciated that you were carrying on a game of politics for the nomination of a man closer to you."[30]

Fassett's secondhand account was not enough for Platt. He made a quick trip to Washington on May 30 to visit with Quay personally, and returned to New York the next morning after trying to convince Quay to remain Pennsylvania's favorite son. Quay agreed but saw no way to beat McKinley. By June 1, he was telling reporters that McKinley had 479 votes, 19 more than needed for the nomination.[31]

HANNA AND HIS TEAM were already in St. Louis, holding late-night sessions in smoke-filled back rooms dealing with critical issues that would shape the convention's outcome and, whether they knew it or not, deeply affect the general election. One of those issues was currency. As they did, Roosevelt wrote to Lodge on June 10, hoping the convention would approve a "most vigorous" currency plank that opposed Free Silver and endorsed the gold standard. Teddy believed this was good policy and good politics, writing, "A straddle will gain absolutely nothing . . . If we assume a timid, halting, negative position I fear we shall get whipped."[32]

Roosevelt was more candid with his sister. "McKinley, whose firmness I utterly distrust, will undoubtedly be nominated, and this in itself I much regret," he wrote, "but what I now fear is some effort to straddle the finance issue. Such a move would be bad politically, not to speak of its being disastrous to the nation." An "open fight should be made against" Free Silver, both for "party expediency and from the standpoint of public morality."[33]

CHAPTER 16

Battle for an Idea

———◁◦▷———

A s 1896 began, the nation was in the fourth year of the deepest depression in its history, and Cleveland's ineffective actions had caused
many Americans to tune him out. A run on the gold reserves forced him
in January to announce a fourth bond issue, this one for $65 million. After
he rejected an unsolicited offer from J. P. Morgan, the bonds were sold by
public auction, drawing in paper currency that could be retired without
further draining gold. The reserves never again fell near the red line at
$100 million.[1]

However, since winning the White House a second time, Cleveland
had issued $262 million in gold bonds, a staggering sum that infuriated
many Democrats. The president they elected had broken faith with them.
He was lining the pockets of Wall Street and foreign financiers by piling
debt on farmers, workers, and shopkeepers. He was incapable of restoring
prosperity and indifferent to the starving families, foreclosed homes, abandoned farms, and shuttered factories his hard-currency policies created.

Saying, "The high office of President has never been so prostituted,"
Senator Pitchfork Ben Tillman labeled Cleveland's bond issues as an
"endless chain with thieves at one end and dishonest officials at the other."
With the British ambassador in the gallery, Missouri senator Francis Cockrell said on the Senate floor, "Let us haul down Old Glory, hoist the gold
standard, and cry out 'long live the Queen of England.' "[2]

Determined to fight back, silver senators passed a free-coinage bill in
February. Some Republicans supported it out of convenience—a Cleveland

veto was certain, so they could diminish silver antagonism back home by backing it. Two weeks later, the House defeated the bill with most Democrats supporting it. The episode added to the Democratic grass roots' hatred for their president as they began the process to pick their 1896 nominee.[3]

AS THE NOMINATION PROCESS began in mid-January, the DNC picked Chicago for the national convention. Chicago wasn't a "victory for sound money," as the *New York Times* claimed. The Midwest was a hotbed of silver sentiment and Governor Altgeld would make certain Chicago provided a silver-friendly welcome, with galleries and streets filled with white metal Democrats.[4]

The next day, the Populist Party National Committee set its convention. Its leaders were split over tactics. The "middle-of-the-road" or "midroad" faction were hard-liners who wanted Populists to keep their distance from both major parties ("stay-in-the-middle-of-the-road") and opposed narrowing the platform to just Free Silver. They argued for an early convention to kill the Silver Party, undercut Democratic silverites, and smoke out squishy Populists who wanted to advocate silver at the expense of the rest of the People's Party's agenda.[5]

The other faction, the "fusionists," was led by party chairman Herman E. Taubeneck and James B. Weaver, the 1892 Populist presidential candidate. They expected Democrats and Republicans to nominate gold advocates or straddlers and wanted Populists to meet after both major parties did so they could gather silver bolters from both parties and sweep the established political system aside while downplaying their party's broad reform agenda.[6]

Fusionists dominated the Populist leadership and set the convention for St. Louis on July 22, after Republicans and Democrats met. Middle-of-the-roaders were furious, believing the party would be undermined if Democrats went for Free Silver. If it did, Senator Peffer asked, "Then what of the People's Party?"[7]

CLEVELAND AND HIS CABINET appeared largely clueless about Free Silver's strength and the work being done by the Bimetallic Democrats.

Cleveland's new postmaster general, William L. Wilson, the former Ways and Means Committee chairman who had carried the president's tariff bill, recorded in his diary that he and the president agreed that it was vital to keep the Chicago convention from endorsing Free Silver. Both felt that "defeat seems inevitable" in the 1896 general election, but that Democrats who defected to the Populists over currency or to Republicans because of the economy would eventually return if Democrats remained an honest-money party. "Keep the platform right, and the National party sound," Wilson wrote, and "the future need not greatly worry us."[8]

Still, the president was concerned that the flood of Free Silver orators—including Bland, Tillman, and Bryan—covering the country was effective at promoting the Free Silver doctrine. So Cleveland encouraged Carlisle, Wilson, Secretary of Agriculture J. Sterling Morton, Secretary of War Daniel S. Lamont, and Secretary of the Interior Hoke Smith to defend the administration's financial policies, particularly in the South and West, where silver sentiment was strongest. Smith, an ambitious young Atlanta publisher, was especially willing. He felt it would help him run for office later, but was bested in a month-long series of debates with Georgia congressman and former House Speaker Charles F. Crisp. Even Smith's private secretary admitted, "All hell couldn't stop" the silverites. The interior secretary's reception ranged between "icy coldness and almost mob-like hostility."[9]

By contrast, Treasury secretary John G. Carlisle fared better. In what a congressional Democrat called "the best single gold-standard speech ever delivered since the world began," Carlisle argued that labor prospered only if workers were paid in sound money. When the dollar's value fluctuated, it was felt first by laborers through rising unemployment and "uncertain purchasing power and less value" for their wages. The Treasury secretary pointed to the joblessness and declining wages suffered by workers in Mexico, Japan, Chile, and other "free coinage silver monometallic countries." He offered some populism of his own, saying Free Silver would grant life insurance companies, banks, and corporations "the privilege of discharging their debts to the people by paying 51 or 52 cents on the dollar."[10]

Silver agitators (one thought to be William "Coin" Harvey) interrupted Carlisle with shouted questions until police removed them. Messenger boys flooded the aisles, handing out envelopes marked "official proclamation from the chief officers of the labor unions of the United States," containing a circular detailing Carlisle's earlier support of silver and alleging he changed his views "to secure a seat in Cleveland's cabinet." While the secretary was well received by the four thousand trade unionists in the hall and acclaimed by sound-money papers around the country, his appearance was ineffective in stemming the silver tide in Illinois. It was not enough to have cabinet secretaries defending the administration's policies.[11]

Cleveland compounded his mistakes by preventing another strong, pro-gold candidate from running. Cleveland had decided he wasn't running again, but did not announce that so another gold Democrat could develop a broad national appeal. This left hard-money Democrats with no strategy, no new leader, no national effort to encourage the election of like-minded delegates to the Chicago convention. There was nothing except a narrow majority on the DNC worried about their political skins back home.[12]

IN APRIL, THE BIMETALLIC DNC's preparations paid off when silver won the Oregon, Washington, Colorado, and Mississippi Democratic conventions, all by larger-than-expected margins. These were contests over an idea, not over candidates, and the rhetoric was often apocalyptic, with the Oregonians declaring, "If the Democratic party would survive, it must declare for free and unlimited coinage of silver." Colorado ordered its delegates "to bolt the national convention unless it should declare for free silver" after Tillman excoriated Cleveland's policies as "unknown to any man who has a scintilla of Democracy."[13]

Cleveland had hoped to win some Missouri delegates. A substantial gold faction in St. Louis argued that "harmony and fair play" should dictate a delegation with both gold and silver men. Rejecting this as an offer from "representatives of corporate interests," the Free Silver forces dominated the Sedalia convention. Nicholas M. Bell, a silver leader, threw a glass of water in the face of state chairman Charles C. Maffit, a gold man, after Maffit called Bell a turncoat and threatened to trash him, saying, "I'll warm your jacket in a little while." Maffit was then defeated for delegate as the convention instructed for favorite-son Silver Dick Bland and adopted the unit rule.[14]

Cleveland expected allies would carry Alabama, but they lost everything as Free Silver men bound the delegation by unit rule. The president took Alabama's loss as a serious setback.[15]

There was no battle at the Nebraska convention in Omaha, since every gold Democrat in the state stayed away. The meeting picked a solidly silver delegation of sixteen with Bryan an at-large delegate. In a prearranged move, Bryan's close friend James Dahlman moved that the convention instruct for Bryan for president; Bryan then asked the motion to be withdrawn, saying, "I do not believe in contending for honors until the contention for principles is settled. When we have framed out principles, there is time to put up candidates." The savvy Bryan was unwilling to be an official "favorite son" but wanted people talking about him. A week later, six hundred Nebraska sound-money Democrats met in Lincoln to select delegates. Republicans were not the only ones with credentials challenges: Nebraska would not be the last, nor the most important. That itself would be a surprise.[16]

It was not all bad news for Cleveland. The final April convention, Michigan, was believed to be in silver hands. Democrats instead endorsed Cleveland, adopted a platform that reaffirmed the 1892 platform, and defeated a Free Silver plank. It was a brutal battle. The test vote came on election of an at-large delegate. A gold man won. The honest-money faction then won the rest of the contests and the platform by healthy margins. The silver forces were not appeased when they were offered a mostly silver list of alternates. "That's right," shouted one white metal leader. "Give us anything you have left." The victory was not total—silver had 11 of the state's delegates and gold 17—but since the state invoked the unit rule, the delegation's majority would decide how Michigan would cast their votes.[17]

The victory was an unexpected tonic for the Cleveland administration. Wilson excitedly wrote in his diary, "Just as I was about retiring, [Henry T.] Thurber [Cleveland's private secretary] called me up on the telephone to read a dispatch announcing that the Michigan Democratic Convention had elected a sound-money delegation and endorsed the Administration. Light out of darkness." Some administration supporters saw it as a turning point. Kentucky representative James B. McCreary predicted that now "the sound money sentiment will control in the Chicago convention."[18]

This unexpected victory came about after Cleveland had begged his former postmaster general, Don M. Dickinson, to make a fight in

Michigan because of "the extreme importance to the country and to our party of a clean, distinct, and unequivocal declaration on the money question." Reluctantly, Dickinson had replied, "I will face about and do my best," and did so, smashing the silver forces decisively.[19]

Still, as April ended, the first month of Democratic primary battles had produced four gold victories and six silver. Gold had 127 delegates, silver had 101, and Nebraska's 16 votes were undecided with a credentials challenge. Silver didn't have the majority it needed to write the platform, let alone the two-thirds to dictate the nominee. Cleveland's allies had just pulled off a big upset. Could they do it elsewhere?

"THE SILVER MEN SEEM dazed by the victory . . . in Michigan," Wilson wrote. "Sound money Democrats are filled with hope, and now believe that they will control the Chicago Convention and save the party organization from the fatal plunge and the indelible stain of declaring for dishonest money." The president wished Illinois would be a similar upset.

But before the gold men could win Illinois, there would be 27 more Democratic state conventions with 348 delegates up for grabs and the Bimetallic DNC dominated 17 victories over the next six weeks in every region except the Northeast, while gold Democrats carried 10 states, only two of them outside the Middle Atlantic and New England.

Cleveland had hoped state pride for Carlisle might put Kentucky in the gold column. The editor of the *Owen News,* a sound-money man, had a better take on the landscape, writing that "[p]olitics down here has gone mad. Every crank in the country is loose and nothing less than a stone wall will stop them." Unfortunately for Cleveland, the editor was right. When the convention opened, jeers and insults drowned out the state chairman as he praised Cleveland and Carlisle. The silver man elected temporary chairman by more than three-to-one proceeded to stack Credentials and Resolutions. Credentials tossed out a Louisville district's sound-money delegation composed of Carlisle's friends. The platform declared for silver and offered a "severe denunciation of so-called 'sound money' Democrats." The convention then elected silverites as 24 of 26 delegates, bound them by unit rule, and then instructed them for Senator Joseph C. S. Blackburn for president. Blackburn accepted the endorsement, telling the four thousand delegates that "the gold standard has dominated for over twenty years until the masses are impoverished."[20]

Kentucky was a huge blow for the administration. If Carlisle could not defeat silver forces led by a neophyte like Blackburn in his home state, what chance was there for gold in Chicago? Two weeks later, Wilson's West Virginia went for silver easily.[21]

THE OUTCOME OF THE six weeks of conventions between May Day and mid-June made clear the Bimetallic DNC leadership had done its job in taking control. Gold men were outnumbered by big margins in almost every state silver carried. North Carolina Democrats adopted a silver platform by a vote of 826 to 31. Iowa voted almost three-to-one to adopt its silver plank, and Tillman counted twenty gold men in attendance in South Carolina.[22]

Virginia may have been the best example of the Bimetallic DNC's superior organization. Its silver Democrats held a rally the night before the state convention with most of the delegates in attendance. Representative Peter J. Otey, the Bimetallic DNC member charged with organizing the commonwealth, explained, "We did not propose to have the Virginia Convention Michiganized." The Free Silver platform was approved by nearly four-to-one.[23]

The silver men gave no quarter. When a gold man or straddler made it onto the delegation by accident or at a district convention as in California, Kentucky, and Virginia, the Free Silver majority bound their delegations under the unit rule so any gold voices would be silenced by their state's silver majority in any roll call.

Honest-money Democrats were more accommodating. For example, though they controlled the convention, Florida's gold men split the delegation with silver five-to-three for the sake of party unity and fairness. Delaware, which endorsed the gold standard unanimously, let a silver man sneak onto the delegation. Neither of these gold states invoked the unit rule. The silver men were ruthless and uncompromising, while the gold men would take what they could get and put party unity over the money issue.

The silver camp was also solely focused on state platforms and downplayed any discussion of candidates. They were energized about an idea, not personalities. Only four of the seventeen silver states in this period instructed for a candidate, and three were favorite sons.

The acrimony grew as silver forces dominated state conventions and the gold men could not match the Bimetallic DNC's organization. In Tennessee, Cleveland supporters were forcibly expelled from the state convention. In South Carolina, Pitchfork Tillman savagely attacked Cleveland as "the most damnable traitor ever known."[24]

Though outmaneuvered and with the contest moving against them, gold Democrats refused to go down without a fight. Their defiance paid off with more surprise victories in South Dakota and Maryland. A bigger bombshell exploded June 10 as Minnesota Democrats gathered in St. Paul for an expected prairie silver gathering. The white metal men were about to learn an old warhorse still had some fight in him. For decades, National Committeeman Michael Doran had been a political power. Though burned in effigy during Cleveland's first term for obtaining insufficient patronage from the White House, the aged warrior made a last battle for his leader, targeting German and Scandinavian Democrat farmers in small towns and rural counties leading up to the convention.[25]

The result of his labors became evident when in a test vote on the election of the convention's temporary chairman, the gold candidate won by nearly two-to-one. Doran reacted by proclaiming, "The old man's here yet!" After spirited fights, the convention supported a gold plank and sent an uninstructed delegation to Chicago with 11 or 12 gold men among the 18 delegates.[26]

Doran wired Cleveland's private secretary, "We carried Minnesota for gold after the most desperate fight on record." But after his extraordinary upset, Doran turned down requests to lead the delegation. He soon left for Europe, not to return until after Chicago.[27]

Wilson and others in the cabinet were finding it difficult to understand how "so many who ought to be right are wrong, and others who are right are afraid to jeopardize their popularity by confronting a craze." Earlier, Wilson had scribbled, "I cannot help hoping that the wild political storm now passing over the country will spend its force . . . wrecking a few reputations, but leaving our general welfare unscathed."[28]

Some sound-money Democrats still believed the battle could be won if the gold forces caught some breaks in late June's remaining state conventions and if powerful voices could be deployed to Chicago to persuade delegates not to take Democrats over the cliff. One of these optimists was Michigan's Dickinson, who urged Cleveland to send advocates for their cause to Chicago to lobby delegates. By June 10, Cleveland agreed and said he had begun "to agitate the subject in question where I thought it would effect the best results."[29]

FORMER NAVY SECRETARY WILLIAM C. WHITNEY was the first to take action, cancelling plans for a long European vacation, though his trunks were already stowed aboard the White Star Line's *Teutonic*. Encouraged by Cleveland, the New York financier and thoroughbred breeder had decided to organize a gold presence at the national convention.

Cleveland and other honest-money Democrats now knew silver would have a majority at the convention and that they must deploy a new strategy. Whitney would attempt to lead a disciplined gold minority of more than one-third of the delegates, enough votes to decide the outcome of the nomination. He would use that bloc's power to plead with the silver camp for a platform compromise to keep the party from breaking apart over the money question. "If unlimited silver coinage is made the Democratic rallying cry at Chicago," he told reporters, "the party may be disrupted."[30]

Whitney assumed he would find partners among the silver men who feared a split over currency and wanted a compromise, but Wilson confided to his diary that Whitney "does not comprehend the madness of the free silverites or the hopelessness of trying to accomplish anything by reason, appeal or entreaty." Whitney also thought gold standard supporters would agree to be led by someone who favored international bimetallism and had recently fancied himself a presidential possibility.[31]

Still, the president was happy the financier was involved, but admitted he didn't know "how Whitney will be 'hitched up' and with whom if he goes." Neither did Whitney, who was making it up as he went along. Sound-money Democrats finally had an energetic champion willing to fight. Whether he could be effective and organized was still unknown.[32]

WHITNEY WAS NOT THE only honest-money Democrat to sound a call to action. At the urging of the New York Chamber of Commerce, Cleveland released a public appeal. Published in the *New York Herald* the same day as Whitney's announcement, the letter had a tone of incredulity. "I refuse to believe," the president wrote, "that when the time arrives for deliberative action there will be engrafted upon our Democratic creed a demand for the free, unlimited, and independent coinage of silver." "The Democratic party is neither unpatriotic nor foolish" and "such a course will inflict a very great injury upon every interest of our country which it has been the mission of Democracy to advance, and will result in the lasting disaster to our party."[33]

Reaction from silver was swift and ugly. The *World-Herald* called the appeal "pathetic." Cleveland had no influence with Democrats "he has ignored and whose cherished principles he has spat upon," and his letter was "a formal call for looters" to steal the Democratic convention. Saying it would "have little or no effect," the *Atlanta Constitution* called it "a queer letter." Even a gold organ, the *Minneapolis Journal,* admitted that "Unless a surprising and preternatural change takes place," the Chicago convention would "declare squarely and with a 'rebel yell' for free silver."[34]

By June 17, silver Democrats had won 349 delegates and carried 23 state conventions, while gold Democrats had won 230 delegates and 14 conventions, with Nebraska's 16 delegates challenged in credentials. The silver men were just 117 votes from the majority needed to write the platform. Fortunately, gold Democrats needed only about 77 votes to get the one-third of the convention needed to block a nominee. There were 306 delegates yet to be elected at state conventions, 72 of whom would come from New York and likely to be gold.[35]

So despite how well the Bimetallic DNC had done, even if it nearly ran the table on all the other state conventions except New York and then won the Nebraska credentials fight, it would be short of the two-thirds needed to pick the nominee and thereby forced to deal with the increasingly obstinate honest-money Democrats.

That assumed Free Silver won Illinois, which was coming up fast and for which the president still had some hope of poaching a few delegates. But first, the Republican National Convention was about to meet and pick the man the Democrats would face, and write the platform on which he would stand.

The front-runner for 1896, U.S. House Speaker Thomas B. Reed of Maine, was content with leaving his efforts in the hands of others, while McKinley broke with tradition and aggressively organized as early as 1894.

Massachusetts senator Henry Cabot Lodge was one of Reed's chief supporters and helped lead the fight at the GOP convention for a plank supporting the gold standard.

Long before Theodore Roosevelt was McKinley's second vice president, he worked against the Major. As New York police commissioner, Roosevelt saw Reed as his ticket to a job in Washington and worried that McKinley was weak.

4

Platt and Quay relied on favorite-son candidates to tie up delegates and keep the race fluid until the national convention. Iowa senator William B. Allison was a leading proxy candidate because of his ties throughout the Midwest.

5

Illinois was the most important Republican primary contest. McKinley's victory over Illinois senator "Uncle" Shelby Cullom, the Combine's favorite-son candidate in the race, was a sign the bosses were beat.

Illinois representative William Lorimer (the "Blond Boss") (TOP LEFT), Illinois GOP chairman John R. Tanner (TOP RIGHT), and Texas Republican powerhouse Norris Wright Cuney (BOTTOM RIGHT), all worked on behalf of the Combine, causing problems for McKinley at their state conventions. Lorimer and Tanner later maneuvered their way to the U.S. Senate and Illinois governor's mansion, respectively.

9

At the 1896 Democratic convention, incumbent president Grover Cleveland was repudiated by his party's Free Silver wing.

Colorado senator Henry Teller bolted the 1896 Republican convention over the silver issue and attempted to run as the silver presidential candidate, but could not get enough Republican or Democrat support.

11

The Irish-born Bourke Cockran would use his oratorical powers to urge fellow Democrats to break with their party and support Republican William McKinley.

13

The Democratic front-runner for 1896, Missouri congressman Richard "Silver Dick" Bland, had led the fight for three decades for the free and unlimited coinage of silver, believing an inflationary currency would create prosperity.

Republicans seized on the radical and often bigoted attacks of South Carolina's "Pitchfork" Ben Tillman to tarnish Bryan and the entire Democratic ticket in 1896.

Though few Americans had heard of William Jennings Bryan before the 1896 Democratic National Convention, his fiery Cross of Gold speech galvanized the delegates and won him his party's presidential nomination.

At his first major appearance after the national convention at Madison Square Garden, Bryan flopped. He was exhausted and ill-prepared.

16

Both McKinley and Bryan chose Easterners for running mates: New Jersey's Garret Hobart for the Republicans and Maine's Arthur Sewall for the Democrats.

17

18

Political buttons have long been part of the campaign process. Samples of those pushing McKinley, Bryan, and Free Silver are shown here.

Mark Hanna served as RNC chairman in 1896, the GOP's chief fund-raiser and the man responsible for reconciling with the Combine bosses after their defeat by McKinley.

McKinley's character was so respected that William Randolph Hearst's *New York Journal* instead vilified Hanna, depicting McKinley as his puppet.

21

By Election Day, Bryan had covered enough miles to travel three quarters of the way around the world. The frantic pace did not always serve Bryan well.

22

Hanna and others pushed McKinley to hit the trail, but he refused and instead campaigned from his front porch, delivering tailored remarks to delegations that traveled to Canton, Ohio, to meet him. Though Bryan clocked more miles, McKinley's messages were better prepared and more helpful to his cause.

CHAPTER 17

Credentials and Currency Fights

————◁○▷————

As Republican delegates gathered in St. Louis, there was still a chance the nomination could slip out of McKinley's grasp. He had won a series of victories against the Combine—some in unexpected places—and delegates instructed to vote for him outnumbered the delegates of any other candidate. But there were at least two battles left. One was over the many challenges between competing delegations.

To be seated, delegates needed the Republican National Committee to accept their credentials. This year, the RNC faced the largest number of credentials challenges in the party's history, with at least 141 of the 924 delegates contested. If these challenges were won by the Combine and the delegates added to Platt's New York and Quay's Pennsylvania totals, the Combine would have two-thirds of the votes it needed to pick the party's nominee—even before turning to the bosses' friends in a dozen other states. Each challenge would be decided by the fifty-one-member RNC. Both sides were eager to find out who really had a majority there.

MCKINLEY'S MANAGERS LEFT LITTLE to chance. Even as Hanna met with key lieutenants in Cleveland and then in Canton with the Major before heading to the convention, former Ohio congressman and Judge Albert C. Thompson and Grosvenor arrived in St. Louis to take the lead on credentials with testimony and affidavits for each challenge.[1]

The Combine's credentials defense, however, suddenly became a disaster. Clarkson had been preparing briefs for each contest but became critically ill on the train from New York to St. Louis. Bedridden in a Philadelphia hotel, he would not make the convention on which he had worked more than a year. A ragtag group hastily replaced him, but they were ill-prepared.[2]

The rest of the McKinley high command arrived in St. Louis on Wednesday, June 10, after working through the night in Hanna's special train car, reviewing notebooks on each delegate and alternate, whom they were for and whether they were instructed, along with summaries for each credentials contest. Hanna checked into St. Louis's Southern Hotel and plunged into meetings. The campaign's suite was decorated with a mural of four reclining female figures with a fifth woman standing, brandishing a drawn sword and a shield labeled "protection." The painting was an odd choice for a political headquarters.[3]

GOP national chairman Thomas Carter of Montana presided as the RNC began credentials hearings in the Southern Hotel's Ladies Parlor. A Catholic bookseller-turned-lawyer, Senator Carter had an impressive long, gray patriarchal beard.[4]

The first vote, a Combine challenge to the at-large Alabama delegates, was a test vote. After lengthy arguments, Arkansas's Powell Clayton moved to seat McKinley's four delegates and Senator John H. Gear, Clarkson's proxy, offered a substitute to seat the Combine delegation. Idaho senator George Shoup then moved that all eight contestants be given half a vote each. When the vote was tallied, Shoup's motion lost 38 to 7, a crushing blow to the Combine. The machine men were dumbfounded: McKinley's men had complete control of the RNC. By the time the meeting adjourned at 10:30 p.m., McKinley's men had won 14 contests in Alabama and Georgia and Reed, 2.[5]

The first day's hearing left Reed's manager Joseph Manley and Connecticut committeeman and House Speaker Samuel C. Fessenden, both Combine men, bewildered. They had not expected the Major's men to be so numerous and well prepared. The McKinley men's control was so complete that they even gave the Combine men the occasional seat, if the merits justified it. After the RNC meeting, a reporter overheard Manley say to Fessenden, "Well, I'll be jammed if I ever saw anything like this," to which the Connecticut House Speaker replied, "There never was anything like it."[6]

Cornered by the press, Manley blurted out, "The convention will nominate Gov. McKinley on the first ballot for the Presidency. It is useless to attempt to deny this will be the result." McKinley controlled the RNC and hence credentials and the convention. That was "settled conclusively" by "the overwhelming vote" on Alabama. Reed would decline to run for vice president.[7]

Word that Reed's manager had ended his bid without even talking to the candidate spread quickly. When Manley later walked past Fessenden at dinner, the Connecticut Speaker spat at him, "Joe, the Almighty God hates a quitter. I have been a soldier in actual war, and am a faithful soldier of Reed now, but my general has deserted." After receiving the news of the betrayal, Reed wired Lodge that "Manley's conduct is too disgusting to characterize." Others labeled Manley a traitor. He apologized to Reed, saying, "It was a great mistake and I shall regret it the rest of my life," but the damage was done.[8]

THE COMBINE COULD STILL make gains, depending on how the rest of the credentials challenges played out. If McKinley's men were seen as too unfair, the majority of the convention could vote to overrule the RNC. What's more, most of those vying to win their credentials fights were loyal soldiers in someone's political army, and many were politically powerful themselves. Ignoring that or callously discarding a bloc of delegates could create problems for McKinley, now or later. So the Combine knew what it was doing Thursday when it accused the Major's forces of "fraud and bribery" after the RNC decided for McKinley in credentials challenges in Alabama and Kentucky and all but two of nine seats up in Florida and Georgia.[9]

And the McKinley men knew what they were doing, too, when they let the Combine's men make their case for being seated. Sometimes no one could undermine the Combine's credibility better than the machine's own men. For example, Mississippi's battle pitted James Hill and John R. Lynch, two veteran black Republican leaders, against each other over four at-large delegate seats. Hill was the state's committeeman and a McKinley loyalist. With small oval glasses, long flowing hair, and bushy muttonchops, and brandishing a cane, he made a passionate case for his delegation. Things became so heated with shouted slurs and violent threats that Carter threw Hill, Lynch, and state chairman L. B. Moseley out of the room. This was followed by a unanimous vote for Hill and the McKinley men. The Combine was so embarrassed, they did not support the men they had bankrolled.[10]

The McKinley camp then overreached by trying to reconsider a Florida seat already awarded to Reed. The New York committeeman, William A. Sutherland, protested and Ohio's Hahn insulted him about "methods employed in New York that were not open and above suspicion." Cooler heads prevailed and reconsideration was defeated. It was a foolish move that could have jeopardized the Major's gains.

In many cases, the outcome of a credentials fight depended upon personal considerations. For example, a few days before the convention, Missouri's Filley forced the McKinley camp into damage control by saying the Major would not win on the first ballot. The remark raised questions about the undependable Old Man. So when a Missouri credentials challenged reached the RNC on Thursday, the committee replaced two Filley men in Missouri's 12th District with Kerens men. All four contestants were pledged to McKinley, but this gave Kerens a clear majority in the delegation, guaranteeing his reelection as committeeman. Filley was furious.[11]

By the end of its second day, the RNC had seated twenty-two additional McKinley men and two more Combine delegates. Platt arrived in the city in a bad humor as the committee broke. The Combine leader was painfully aware he had been outorganized, outprepared, and outflanked on credentials. Platt denounced the RNC's actions as "arbitrary and unfair," complaining, "The only question which appears to have had weight in the proceedings . . . was whether the contestants were for or against McKinley." Combine leaders were used to being in charge, not being soundly whipped. Platt threatened that the remaining sixty Empire State delegates would bolt the convention if challenges to twelve New York delegates went against him. Afterward, someone described as "very close to McKinley" dismissed New York's threats to bolt, saying, "Let them." It sounded like Hanna, who now intensely disliked Platt. Wyoming's Carey urged caution. As the biggest battleground state, New York was critical to victory.[12]

Platt's angry talk encouraged some of the Combine's men, but still the machine's headquarters felt like "a funeral." The tall, thin, stooped, "sallow-faced" Platt "seemed tired and worn," and his problems were just beginning. The McKinley camp undercut Morton's presidential candidacy by floating him as a running mate, leaving Platt sounding rattled when he said he did not regard Morton's case "as hopeless by any means." [13]

Friday, Platt softened his tone after meeting with Quay, saying he was asking only that the New York challenges be decided "upon their merits." A Platt lieutenant was not as restrained, saying of Hanna, "No iron man from Cleveland can run the Republican party of New York State." [14]

By Friday, June 12, with 106 challenges still left to consider, the RNC finally tackled one of the most dramatic, Delaware. The two warring camps, bitter and angry, spilled into the parlor several hours later and sat in a semicircle of chairs facing the committee and went at each other. The group led by former senator Anthony Higgins was for McKinley; the other faction, led by J. Edward Addicks, a wealthy owner of gas utilities and aspiring senator-to-be, was for Quay. Higgins denounced Addicks as the leader of a criminal conspiracy "against law and honor," and called him "a political bandit" who had used bribery to control the state convention. An ally, Washington Hastings, shook his finger at Addicks while denouncing him as "governed by a base and selfish ambition." [15]

Caleb B. Taylor delivered the Combine's response, insulting Higgins by calling him an ingrate. Addicks also spoke, claiming he had been victimized because he'd busted up the worst criminal ring the GOP had ever seen. "I made Higgins Senator," he said, "then I whipped him because he was a wart on the Republican body politic." Neither Taylor nor Addicks denied a bribery charge leveled by the Higgins side.

In his reply, Higgins refused to say Addicks's name, calling him "that creature" and saying he showed himself to be "the moral idiot that everyone in Delaware knew he was." Vermont senator Redfield Proctor then accused Addicks of conspiring in 1895 with Delaware's Democratic governor to stop the Republican legislature from electing a U.S. senator when the GOP was one shy of the majority in the Senate. The seat was still vacant. Neither side looked good, so after two hours, the RNC washed its hands by referring the controversy to the convention by 41 to 9. [16]

Saturday morning, the committee rapidly seated McKinley men in Tennessee and South Carolina, then took up the three-cornered affair in Texas, immediately ruling out the Lily Whites, leaving their decision between the Reed/Allison group, led by Norris Wright Cuney, and John Grant's McKinleyites. Cuney's side argued he was lawfully elected temporary chairman. Grant's side responded that Cuney won only "by circulating the report that Dr. Grant had said no colored man should be made chairman" and attacked Cuney for refusing to take roll call votes and pointed out that of 901 delegates, 641 had remained amid the debris of the riotous Austin convention after Cuney departed.[17]

Despite Cuney's many long-standing friendships on the committee, his claim went down 17 to 23. Fessenden then moved to refer Texas's statewide delegates to the convention. In a victory for the Combine, he prevailed by 27 to 20, probably because some of Cuney's longtime friends on the committee felt guilty. Still, all McKinley's district delegates were seated, in part because Cuney made threats against the committee that weren't well received.[18]

With the New York contests coming and tensions rising between Platt and Hanna, Foraker urged the McKinley camp not to confront Platt but to "let him down as easily as possible and not attempt to break up his State." Hanna refused the good advice, saying, "As Mr. Platt has gone in for a fight, he must take his chances." Grosvenor called conciliating the Easy Boss "nonsensical." Since Platt was "honestly defeated," he should "take the same medicine that he has himself administered to those who opposed him in New York." Such statements were shortsighted. The McKinley men would need the Easy Boss's help in the fall.[19]

The RNC took up the long-anticipated Empire State contests late Saturday night. So many New Yorkers crowded into the parlor that some had to be thrown out. Platt won the first three contests when the anti-Platt men withdrew their challenges or didn't show up. Hanna was "thunderstruck," but he shouldn't have been. The would-be McKinley delegates had to deal with the Easy Boss back home and he could threaten rebelling New Yorkers in ways Hanna might not comprehend. The RNC battled over seven other contests until late into the evening.

It was after midnight by the time New York's 12th District was taken up. John S. Wise, a brilliant lawyer who had been elected to the U.S. House in his native Virginia in 1884 and served with McKinley, represented the Major's men, former RNC treasurer Cornelius N. Bliss and New York City park commissioner S. V. R. Cruger. Congressman Lemuel E. Quigg made the case for Platt's side. He and Wise went at it, with New York's Sutherland, Senator Thurston, and other RNC members lobbing questions. Pointing at Bliss, Edward Lauterbach warned the GOP must "be on guard against these rich men." Wise then introduced affidavits from a majority of the district's delegates affirming they had voted for Bliss and Cruger. Sutherland's motion to seat the Platt men was defeated. Hahn's motion to seat all four men with half a vote each—a conciliatory gesture—was adopted 27 to 23. It was now the middle of the night and in between votes RNC committeemen were dozing in corners or sprawled on a table behind Carter.[20]

After McKinley men were—surprisingly—seated by unanimous vote in New York's 13th, a Manhattan silk stocking district, the RNC took up a contentious dispute in New York's 15th District. It was 2:35 a.m. and the McKinley men were seated by 28 to 16 despite Quigg's best efforts and energetic remarks by Lauterbach. Platt's cause was not helped by Lauterbach's comments earlier in the day that the RNC was bent on "grand larceny."[21]

After all the personal attacks and vitriol, Platt won six out of the ten New York challenges. Still, he dismissed the national committee's action as "an outrage on decency." An ally warned that if McKinley was nominated, "the gentlemen who are now so loud in their declaration that they can do without New-York will be on their knees to Mr. Platt."[22]

Well-prepared and with surprising strength on the RNC, the McKinley forces had prevailed in credentials challenges on 120 of their delegates while their opponents won 21. To win now, the Combine would have to overturn the decisions favorable to McKinley on the convention floor or find an issue that would persuade enough of the Major's men to defect. The former seemed unlikely given the fairness of the credentials process, but the latter was nearer at hand for the Combine than the McKinley men understood.

EVEN AS CREDENTIALS GROUND to a finish, there was a fight brewing over the party's currency plank that could split the GOP and put at risk the Major's general election chances. The dispute was not easy to resolve. Both silver and gold men were firing at McKinley, enraged at his desire to focus on protection and ignore the money question. When pressed, McKinley offered platitudes. He was for gold, silver, and paper, all "as sound as the government and as untarnished as its honor," as he had written in the Ohio platform. He opposed free coinage but backed an international bimetallic agreement—which was unlikely—to set the ratio between gold and silver. In the meantime, he supported "the present standard," which meant gold. With so many evasions and buzzwords, McKinley looked like a straddler.[23]

Herrick believed that until the convention, McKinley felt his position was "vague enough to please the Eastern men without offending those from the West." There was reason for such a strategy. McKinley wanted the votes of states like Michigan and Kansas where silver was popular. As Charles Dick explained, the McKinley managers sensed "a strong silver sentiment" among many Republicans that the Major's men "did not care to antagonize." Hanna believed supporting the gold standard could lose McKinley the nomination, and if McKinley didn't straddle, silver men could revolt. But McKinley wasn't going to get off that easy, as he had seen while under the attacks of newspapers and Platt following his Illinois win. His gold adversaries in the Combine would no longer let him straddle.[24]

Platt was correct in thinking there was strong support for gold among the delegates. The *St. Louis Post-Dispatch* reported that as many as 651 delegates were pro-gold, 87 pro-silver, and 180 with unknown views. Though not many state conventions had endorsed gold, there was a clear gold majority in St. Louis.[25]

McKinley's press chief, Perry Heath, downplayed the issue when he arrived in St. Louis, saying that only four states would insist on gold. He was wrong. And Grosvenor was half right when he suggested gold bugs had no place to go, while silver bimetallists might defect if the GOP endorsed gold monometallism.[26]

Senator Teller weighed in Saturday night, telling reporters that only a clear declaration for silver was acceptable. He would not support a gold candidate on a gold platform or "a platform of doubtful import." If McKinley were nominated on a straddle, "all the tariff in the world won't help . . . without free and unlimited coinage of silver."[27]

Teller didn't know that before Hanna left for St. Louis, McKinley had given Hanna a draft currency plank that was a complete straddle. It called for "maintaining all the money of the United States whether gold, silver or paper at par with the best money in the world and up to the standard of the most enlightened governments." Further, the proposed plank said that while Republicans welcomed "bimetallism based upon an international ratio," until that treaty could be negotiated, it was the country's "plain duty" to "maintain our present standard." Also, the plank opposed "the free and unlimited coinage of silver at sixteen to one."[28]

Debate about the currency plank grew heated as more delegates arrived. Silver men preferred using the Ohio or Indiana GOP platform "as a beginning," then bending its language toward the white metal. But the gold men were beyond compromise. Platt told reporters, "I am for a gold standard platform and opposed to the Ohio idea," which "may be interpreted one way in the East and another way in the West. It is not satisfactory in the East." Platt received help on the currency issue as the *New York Times* called McKinley guilty of "contemptible evasions and cowardly paltering." Quay also chimed in: "I hope the money plank will be gold in good, strong, cold terms."[29]

Although Senator Lodge had been an international bimetallist until a visit to Europe the previous year, when he saw how unlikely a global agreement was, he now strongly favored the gold standard and threw the Reed forces into the fight, telling the Massachusetts RNC committeeman to go to war for a gold plank.[30]

Yellow metal supporters pressed the McKinley managers all week until Hanna finally admitted "this platform business is the most embarrassing question" he faced. He had fifteen draft currency planks "from free silver to gold monometallism," prepared by "all kinds of people, from cranks to newspaper editors." It was now clear to Hanna that a straddle would not do.[31]

Late Friday, he, Herrick, Merriam, Wisconsin RNC committeeman Henry Payne, Senator Proctor, and Associated Press general manager Melville E. Stone met to discuss language at the McKinley suite at the Southern. Party leaders and supporters of the Major were shuttled in and out all evening. Kohlsaat showed up at ten, uninvited, direct from the depot.[32]

The McKinley men argued about the word *gold* until 3 a.m., when they finally agreed to use it. Herrick showed Clay Evans a penciled rough draft with the word in it and Kohlsaat later claimed Hanna said to him, "Are you satisfied now, you damned crank?" Stone then used the long-distance line to McKinley's home to read the proposed plank to the Major, who asked if his team was in agreement. Told yes, McKinley "reluctantly . . . acquiesced" and requested a phrase pledging the party to work for the international agreement.[33]

The next morning, Hanna told visitors it would be a clear-cut gold plank. Robert Patterson, manager of the *Chicago Tribune* and Illinois's Resolutions Committee member, emerged from a meeting with Hanna and pronounced himself "content." "I can at least say that the money plank of our platform will declare for the gold standard."[34]

Yet all weekend the McKinley leaders continued straddling. Hanna gave Foraker a draft to show Resolutions Committee members who supported "the present standard" and Alger told reporters the platform should "convey to the friends of sound money the conviction that the party is opposed to the free coinage of silver" yet at the same time "not antagonize those who have silver leanings." But silver men were irreconcilable. On Sunday, Senator Henry M. Teller told the press the mountain West would bolt unless the convention endorsed Free Silver.[35]

In the face of the McKinley managers' attempt to straddle and Foraker's insipid draft, Platt held a meeting Sunday night in his suite with party leaders including Lodge, Manley, Fessenden, and Quay. They agreed on a counterproposal: "We favor the maintenance of the existing gold standard, and are opposed to the free coinage of silver except by international agreement for bimetallism with the leading commercial nations of the world."[36]

Lodge and former Massachusetts governor Eben S. Draper then called on Hanna, who was "not prepared to surrender." He had drafts that had a similar sentiment without using the word *gold,* but the Combine and its allies insisted on the word. Only silver Republicans would be put off by it and they were lost already. Hanna appeared unconvinced.[37]

Platt, Lodge, and the Combine prepared for a fight by lining up sound-money delegates from the Northeast plus others from Illinois, Minnesota, Tennessee, Washington State, and Wisconsin. Agents were sent to states that had declared for gold. Filley, for example, worked Maryland, making his dislike of Hanna known there. Within twenty-four hours, Platt had a list of more than 500 delegates supporting gold, a majority of the convention.[38]

Lodge and Hanna ran into each other Monday morning. "How is the most unreasonable man in St. Louis?" inquired Hanna. "I am not unreasonable," Lodge replied. "So long as the engine is painted red I do not care what color you paint it." Lodge took Hanna's genial tone to mean he understood the gold bugs had the votes on the currency plank. Sometime that day, Representative Lemuel E. Quigg told Grosvenor, Herrick, and Merriam of the coming floor fight and learned "there was a disposition to meet the views" of the gold forces. Monday afternoon, after a majority of delegations declared for a gold plank in their state meetings, Lodge issued a statement: "We have won the fight. Gold is the victor. The Committee on Resolutions will declare for the gold standard, and that declaration will be adopted by the convention."[39]

Foraker had named a subcommittee on the currency plank of seven gold and one silver man—Teller. This would not have happened were the McKinley camp still against using the word *gold*. As the subcommittee began work that night, the McKinley managers publicly capitulated. Merriam called on Platt, and Kohlsaat visited Lodge to officially concede to inserting the word *gold* into the platform.[40]

The currency plank subcommittee heard from Teller, who offered several silver planks, all rejected 8 to 1. Then in an empty upstairs hallway of the Planter's Hotel, away from crowds and prying ears, the subcommittee members tinkered with the McKinley camp's draft and settled on the language, saying the GOP was "opposed to the free coinage of silver except of international agreement with the leading commercial nations of the world, and until such agreement can be obtained the existing gold standard must be preserved." Lodge later said it "was not written by any one man," a view Foraker shared, describing it as "a mere expression of a common sentiment." Almost as an afterthought, Lodge suggested inserting "which we pledge ourselves to promote" after "international agreement," unintentionally echoing McKinley's comment to Stone in the middle of the night Friday. The Resolutions Committee adopted the plank 41 to 10.[41]

MCKINLEY HAD RUN BY offering a straddle on the money question, but endorsed gold at the convention. If he had done so early in the primary season, it might have cost him delegates, but to endorse gold on the convention's eve reconciled the Combine's gold bugs and helped energize the party. Some allies tried to give him the credit, with the *New-York Tribune* writing, "The platform will be just what everybody who has not been blinded by malignant hate of McKinley has known all along it would be." But that was not true. McKinley had preferred a straddle and even now he wanted to ignore currency to focus on protection.[42]

But why did the McKinley men keep pressing for a straddle until Monday night when they had decided on Friday to cave? Perhaps it was Hanna's pique with Platt. More likely, the McKinley managers knew there would be a fight on something. They would rather spar with the Combine over currency than fight over a running mate or a plank McKinley really cared about, such as protection.

The man who successfully pressured McKinley to accept a gold plank was Platt, who called it "the greatest achievement of my political career." He was deluged by praise. One businessman wrote that the Easy Boss had won "more glory and honor . . . than if you had named a President." Even the *New York Times,* normally critical of Platt, praised "the full great and good work he has done." Platt was probably pleased when the *Times* dismissed McKinley as "nerveless" and "timid and weak-kneed."[43]

CHAPTER 18

GOP Convention

———◄○►———

B y Monday, June 15, the day before the GOP convention opened, a car-
nival atmosphere reigned in St. Louis. South Carolina delegates sold
a bourbon, lemon juice, and sugar concoction they called "the McKinley." For twenty-five cents, peddlers sold canes topped with a tin blob that
resembled McKinley's head. Button and badge salesmen were impossible
to avoid. Dark blue handkerchiefs dotted with white stars around a stern
portrait of the Major were hawked. They could be waved during demonstrations or used to wipe off sweat in the un-air-conditioned hall.[1]

The festivities drew attention away from forces in the convention that
would hurt or help the party's general election chances. Still to come were
a fight over gold and silver that threatened to drive silverites from the party
and the final resolution of credentials battles that needed to be deftly handled lest there be permanent damage.

Much of this was known to delegates as they entered the convention
auditorium, five stories tall and made of heavy pine covered by white
stucco. Eight interior trusses, wrapped in red, white, and blue bunting
and separated by large panels covered by eagles with twelve-foot wings
extended, held up the ceiling. Large windows on the hall's east and west
walls were separated by forty-five posts, each capped with a shield bearing
a state's name above its coat-of-arms. There were three levels of galleries
on each wall. A giant president's flag—deep blue with an eagle bearing a
gold-bordered shield of red and white stripes with white stars underneath

a semicircle of thirteen stars—was hung from the ceiling in the middle of the hall.[2]

A huge George Washington portrait hung above the stage, framed in flags and a giant eagle with outstretched wings underneath. Lincoln looked down on the podium, flanked by white screens, one displaying the slogan "Republicanism Is Prosperity" and the other "To the Polls, Ye Sons of Freedom." To soften the glare, the halls' arc lights were covered with red, white, and blue silk Japanese lanterns, hung amid dozens of state and foreign flags draped from the ceiling. It was a grand setting for the GOP to pick its nominee.[3]

Ushers and assistant sergeants-at-arms manned the twenty-four main doors and sixteen gallery entrances. Handsome engraved tickets were required, a different color for each session. Their face bore images of the Eads Bridge and the Missouri log home Grant built in 1856 after leaving the army and being reduced to selling firewood. The reverse was an engraving of the convention hall.[4]

The eleventh Republican National Convention opened at 12:20 p.m. Tuesday with Rabbi Samuel Sale delivering the opening prayer. This avoided criticism the APA would have leveled at a Catholic invocator, while not bowing to the APA by having a Protestant. The APA was not in charge. A different kind of Republican was, someone open to different faiths within the GOP.[5]

All of the pieces were falling into place for McKinley Wednesday as delegates handled housekeeping matters and Senator John Thurston, who had been elected permanent chairman, took the podium. The tall, thin, bespectacled Nebraskan with a receding hairline and trim handlebar mustache had announced McKinley's bid for president at the Marquette dinner in February. Now dressed in a black Prince Albert coat with a boutonnière in his lapel, Thurston waited for silence, then explained what a Republican administration would mean for America. Thurston's "voice, strong and ringing, commanded silence right from the start" and he exuded natural enthusiasm with big gestures and obvious energy. His speech was short— about three minutes, if read straight through—but took much longer to deliver because Thurston milked each line, pausing so delegates could vent their emotions. He ended by pledging "a deathless loyalty to all that is truly American, and patriotism as eternal as the stars." Delegates cheered as he was presented with a giant floral shield of red, white, and blue roses.[6]

When the convention met that afternoon, Credentials chairman J. Franklin Fort of New Jersey, a McKinley ally, presented his report. After a day and a half rehashing Texas and Delaware, the committee recommended seating the Higgins men in Delaware and the Grant men in Texas, and adopting the RNC's temporary roll for all other states, a complete win for McKinley. But the Combine didn't surrender that easily. Iowa representative William P. Hepburn offered a minority substitute to seat Addicks in Delaware and Cuney in Texas and force the committee to reconsider all other contests, arguing none of the challenges had been examined on "the merits" by "any competent tribunal" and calling the RNC's setting of the temporary roll "a most dangerous precedent."[7]

Of course, the RNC had set the temporary roll in all past conventions. What Hepburn really objected to was McKinley's control. This set up the convention's first test vote. Delegates cheered as their states were called, New Yorkers yelling particularly loud when Platt announced their vote. When the roll call concluded, 14,000 men and women grew quiet as clerks checked their tallies. When Thurston announced the minority report was rejected 551½ to 350½, "the McKinleyites howled themselves hoarse." Despite a few defections (mostly because of Filley in Missouri), the Major won the test vote with 61 percent, giving him a 200-delegate margin. The full Credentials report was then adopted on a voice vote.[8]

As delegates went to dinner, Platt responded to the Combine's loss on credentials by announcing New York would nominate Morton for vice president and had 387 votes from twenty states already. Realistically, Morton was going nowhere, but his candidacy helped Platt keep his forces united, angry with Hanna and full of resentment. He wanted influence. One way to get it was to have Morton as vice president again, with control over New York patronage and influence on policy. But Platt was just barely holding together his scheme. Morton had decided Sunday not to accept the vice presidential spot. Platt had to change Morton's mind or else the Easy Boss would be embarrassed and see his hold over New York weakened and his ability to make deals undermined.[9]

So Platt deployed his boyhood friend and Harrison's former navy secretary, Benjamin F. Tracy, to persuade Morton. Tracy wired Platt on Monday that he had phoned the governor, who said "he don't want it. I said: You must take it. He said: Why should I. I said: Party has been kind to you and you must be kind to party; It is absolutely necessary to prevent disaster." The two men met later that afternoon. Early the next day, Tracy reported Morton was reluctant but "if drafted will serve," and the Easy Boss quickly announced he would offer Morton's name before Morton changed his mind.[10]

WHILE PLATT TRIED SALVAGING Morton's candidacy, the Resolutions Committee was working hard on the platform. By now, everyone knew currency would be the platform's flash point. The *New York Times* marked Tuesday, June 16—the convention's first formal day—with a front-page poem:

> *The silver bugs, with all their force*
> *Are shouting silver 'till they're hoarse,*
> *The gold bugs cry, "Now you go slow,*
> *We'll have it gold or bust the show";*
> *The straddle bugs all show a streak*
> *Of office seeking as they speak;*
> *The bed bugs, (simply out of fun,*
> *Aware that they're 16 to 1)*
> *Abstain from shouting, ignore fame,*
> *But they will get there just the same.*

Teller was already angry, telling reporters, "The game was all fixed" as the committee's gold bugs "work together like a machine." He cautioned reporters, "Wait and see" what else he had up his sleeve.[11]

The Resolutions Committee considered the gold plank one last time Wednesday evening. The vote was 40 to 11. The white metal men representing Idaho, Montana, Nevada, and Utah joined Teller in saying they would leave the GOP if the convention endorsed gold. The silver men from Arizona, California, New Mexico, North Carolina, Oklahoma, and Wyoming did not. The scene was set for a spectacle on the convention floor if Teller did not get his way.[12]

After Thurston opened the next morning's session, Foraker read the platform to the convention, his strong, clear voice adding force to key words and phrases. He drew cheers during the protection plank's four long paragraphs. But when he turned to the currency plank and read, "the existing gold-standard must be maintained," the convention's minutes noted "the proceeding was here interrupted by a demonstration of approval on the part of a large majority of the delegates which lasted several minutes." A reporter put it more colorfully: "the whole audience rose to its feet and millions of butterflies seemed to be flying over the heads of the people as flags and fans and handkerchiefs burst into sudden life." [13]

After Foraker moved for adoption of the platform, Teller presented the silver Republican substitute and was "vigorously cheered" by the silver state delegations as he appeared onstage. Tall, white-haired, with a beard and high forehead, he had helped found the Colorado Territorial Republican Party and was President Chester A. Arthur's interior secretary. [14]

With a trembling hand, Teller drank a glass of water while the clerk read his substitute. Delegates politely heard the courtly senator say he advocated Free Silver doctrines "because I believe the progress of my country is dependent upon it." He pointed to GOP victories on bimetallic platforms and called an international agreement a declaration of "the inability of the American people to control their own affairs." Eyes filling with tears, he told delegates "the Almighty created these twin metals . . . that the world should use them." He denounced the gold plank, threatening, "I cannot subscribe to it, and if it is adopted I must, as an honest man, sever my connection" with the party. The convention then rejected his silver substitute 818½ to 105½ and adopted the platform on "an almost unanimous vote, amid great applause." Platt was still trying to slow the convention up and so dispatched Depew to ask Hanna for a recess, but was turned down flat. "The business of the convention must be finished today," the Clevelander replied. [15]

Teller was recognized and introduced Utah senator Frank Cannon. Only recently selected to represent the newest state and attending his first national convention, Cannon did not command the respect Teller did. The Kansas editor William Allen White had given a black North Carolina delegate a dollar for his seat in front of Hanna so he could observe McKinley's man. As Cannon began speaking, White heard Hanna ask Grosvenor who he was. When told, Hanna replied, "Looks like a cigar drummer!" As the Utah senator droned on, Hanna sarcastically said, "They ought to admit a lot more of those little sand patches and coyote ranges out West as states." Cannon went too long, provoking calls of "Time! Time!"

Then Cannon's remarks turned bitterly personal. "The Convention has seceded from the truth." Its actions would lead to "the eventual destruction of our freedom and our civilization." When he said that "the Republican party, once the redeemer of the people" is "now about to become their oppressor," delegates began hissing and heckling. Hanna joined in the abuse, yelling "Go! Go!" and "Goodbye!" as others shouted, "Good-by, my lover, good-by! Put him out! Let him print it! And to hell with him!" Banging his gavel, Thurston admonished Cannon, who shook his hand and Foraker's and left the podium.[16]

During the Utahan's speech, the silver men had begun gathering near the stage. When Cannon finished, Teller led twenty-three silver delegates down the center aisle and out of the hall. One McKinley silver man, North Carolina's Senator Pritchard, was so moved by Cannon's remarks that other Tar Heel delegates had to restrain him from departing. Hanna stood on his chair, shouting, "Go! Go! Go!" as delegates yelled, "Go to Chicago!" and the band played loudly.[17]

Teller was weeping as he led his ragged detachment out, causing the *Nation* to later mock him, calling silver "the first raw metal that has ever been wept over." Alerted by wire, Colorado governor Albert W. McIntyre ordered the state guard to fire a cannon salute to their senator, which one Centennial State delegate said "meant war."[18]

Teller's silver Republican men caucused. As they entered the Southern Hotel, DuBois ran into Proctor, who begged him, "Oh, Fred, don't leave; go back, go back and stay where you belong." DuBois replied, "I hated to do it but as an honest man, true to my people and my convictions, I must go." The walkout stirred strong emotions, but it was not yet apparent just how complicated the silver Republicans' bolt would make the Major's general election chances.[19]

IT WAS A BRIGHT, sunny afternoon in Canton, with a gentle breeze blowing. Sitting in his library beneath portraits of Lincoln and Grant, McKinley listened to the convention on a long-distance line. Ida and his mother were across the hallway in the parlor with friends. As nominations were called for, McKinley peeked in to ask, "Are you young ladies getting anxious?" The women were amused by reports Grosvenor was fanning Hanna's head.[20]

The secretary called the roll. No state offered a candidate until Iowa nominated Allison with a dreadful speech by a railroad lawyer no one knew. Massachusetts's Lodge nominated Reed, saying, "We want a president who will protect at all hazard the gold reserve of the Treasury," and "By what he has done and what he is, we know what he can do." Reed's admirers exploded with cheers.[21]

New York put forward Morton. Chauncey Depew came from the back of the hall to applause from his home state. A practiced orator, he used every trick in his repertoire, making delegates laugh when he asked how silver bolters would feel when they saw heaven's golden streets, getting Ohioans on their feet by praising Garfield and Indianans on theirs by lauding Harrison. Depew closed by saying Morton would "place the Empire State solidly in the Republican column."[22]

When Ohio was called, Foraker's appearance kicked off a wild demonstration. McKinley supporters waved thousands of flags while delegates brandished ten-foot poles with plumes of pampas grass dyed red, white, and blue. Dressed in a black frock coat, standing collar, and blue polka-dot tie, Fire Alarm Joe stood at the podium while "the multitude rose sea-like" and "a vast whirlpool of color" swirled around the hall.[23]

His text was short, but powerful. He started slow and deliberate. "It would be extremely difficult . . . to exaggerate the disagreeable experiences of the last four years." The Democratic administration had been "one stupendous disaster." The Chicago Democratic convention was "an approaching national nightmare." It remained for Republicans to meet the American people's expectations. "What do the people want? You all do know."[24]

Without mentioning his name, Foraker described the Major. After five minutes of praise, Foraker finally used the words "William McKinley" and the convention went "raving mad." Pandemonium broke out, with delegates cheering, horns blaring, grass plumes swaying madly, and a giant McKinley portrait parading around the floor. The mob sang and shouted for thirty minutes, the band playing song after song. Hanna waved a handkerchief as the mass of screaming delegates marched around isolated islands of Combine men sitting with arms folded in the New York, Pennsylvania, Iowa, and Massachusetts delegations. Kerens jumped on a chair and waved his grass plume vigorously, inspiring the mob to yell louder. When the band swung into "Marching Through Georgia," he used his plume as a baton and sang along. The crowd joined him, ending the celebration with "The Star-Spangled Banner."[25]

All McKinley could hear on his phone was a loud hum. The wild shouts, cheers, music, chants, and horns overwhelmed his primitive connection. He remarked, "This grows interesting. I wonder what Foraker is about." When order was restored, Foraker drily observed, "You seem to have heard the name of my candidate before." The Major, a connoisseur of oratory, liked Foraker's touch, telling those around him, "Ah, that is like him. He knows what he is doing and is all right." [26]

At 4:10 p.m., the convention started its first and only ballot. McKinley sat in his study, listening as each delegation cast its votes, "calmly ticking off states on a pad." Illinois was particularly sweet. McKinley won all but two votes: the holdouts were the Blond Boss—Lorimer—and John M. Smyth, the other 2nd District delegate. Both voted for Reed. [27]

McKinley was taken aback when New Hampshire voted for Reed, saying, "There must be a mistake." He apparently didn't know the delegation had decided for unity's sake back home to vote Reed on the first ballot and McKinley on all others. [28]

When New York cast its votes, a young lady sitting with Ida realized victory was at hand and congratulated her. Mrs. McKinley gently whispered, "Hadn't you better wait until my husband tells me?" When the roll call came to Ohio, McKinley was 20 away from victory. Then Foraker announced all 46 Ohioans were for McKinley, putting him over the top. The Major went across the hallway to say, "Ida, Ohio's vote has given me the nomination." She and his mother wept. [29]

At 6:15 p.m., Thurston announced the tally—McKinley 661½ votes; Reed 84½; Quay 61½; Morton 58; Allison 35½—prompting "one great outbreak" of singing and cheering. The giant McKinley portrait was again paraded through the hall. A pretty girl in the gallery drew attention by dancing and waving a flag as delegates played leapfrog, yelled, threw hats in the air, and waved grass plumes, handkerchiefs, flags, and even umbrellas. A cannon boomed twice outside as the band played. [30]

Lodge moved to make it unanimous, seconded by Hastings, then Platt, and on behalf of Allison, Iowa congressman David B. Henderson, who said the Republican "rank-and-file," not Hanna, would run the fall campaign. Meant as a compliment to the grassroots, it came off as a slight to McKinley's managers and Hanna knew it. He rose to say, "I am now ready to take my position in the ranks alongside of my friend, General Henderson, and all other good Republicans from every state, and do the duty of a soldier until next November." [31]

The convention turned then to McKinley's running mate. The Major had preferred Reed but knew the Speaker would never agree. Platt wanted Morton, but the governor reversed course and pulled out Thursday morning. Even if Morton wanted it, McKinley was unlikely to reward the Easy Boss, who had fought him until the end.[32]

In fact, McKinley had settled on New Jersey's Garret A. Hobart before the convention. It made sense. An Eastern running mate provided geographical balance. A successful attorney and popular former state house Speaker and former state senate president, Hobart could carry New Jersey, a traditional battleground. He was also well liked in the New York business community and on a cordial basis with Quay and Platt. Hobart had stopped in Canton en route to St. Louis and then wrote his wife that McKinley offered him the second spot. Hanna ordered Dawes to line up Illinois for Hobart, well before the voting.[33]

McKinley's selection of Hobart didn't keep other names from being offered. There was much enthusiasm for Clay Evans, and not just among Southerners. Wisconsin's Representative Robert La Follette seconded his nomination, bringing delegates to their feet cheering the prospect of resurgent Republicanism below the Mason-Dixon Line. Former governors of Rhode Island and Connecticut were offered by Combine die-hards and a Virginian demanded that the divide between North and South "be forever obliterated" by nominating Confederate general James A. Walker, who led the Stonewall Brigade at Gettysburg. The convention duly selected Hobart, 533½ to Evans's 280½, with 79 votes for seven other candidates. Delegates made the nomination unanimous at 7:40 p.m. and then adjourned for the last time.[34]

Hobart got the news while biting into a tenderloin in the Planters Hotel dining room, when a well-wisher rushed in to address him as "Mr. Vice President." Famished, he polished off his steak before retiring to receive supporters.[35]

As delegates spilled out of the convention, celebrating their new ticket, Hanna went to phone McKinley and then greet a steady stream of fans until early in the morning. Herrick saw another man outside the hall "standing quite alone with his hands clasped behind him under his coat tails, looking at the setting sun." It was Platt.[36]

•   •   •

NO FAN OF MCKINLEY in the past, the *Chicago Tribune* had to admit none-theless, "The people have won at St. Louis." The Major's victory was "a hard blow to bossism" and a victory of the "rank and file of the party over its self-centered and presumptuous leaders," namely the Combine. McKinley's victory presaged a major change in future nomination battles in which the power of the bosses would be diminished and the power of voters and candidates elevated.[37]

McKinley won because he had executed his strategy and waged a well-organized effort. Ohio was totally unified, in large part because the Major's personal diplomacy kept the mercurial Foraker in line. The currency issue was marginalized until the convention and the campaign delivered a clear, effective message centered on protection, arguing that McKinley would restore prosperity. He did not allow pressure groups, such as the APA, to dictate to him. That would have been convenient in the primary but dangerous for the general election.

Then there was the Major's decision in mid-1895 to turn the Combine's opposition into an asset by openly running against the bosses. As the re-form candidate, he drew into his campaign a new generation of the GOP's rising stars, most spectacularly in Illinois with Charles G. Dawes.

As he had planned, McKinley started early and was a national candidate who competed everywhere. His early groundwork helped sweep the South—196½ to 26½—while his forays into New England wounded the front-runner, Reed. His energetic outreach crippled the Combine's favorite-son strategy in Illinois, Indiana, Kentucky, Michigan, Minnesota, Nebraska, Tennessee, and West Virginia and helped keep Platt and Quay worried about insurgencies in their home states.

McKinley drew on his many personal relationships, never got embroiled in making deals involving cabinet posts and patronage, and kept his campaign out of needless local fights by focusing on instruction rather than naming delegates.

Much of the credit for success goes to his having a strong organization, something no other candidate had and which in politics "counts for more than anything else," as one observer put it. That organization was made possible by Hanna's leadership, and $100,000 from the Cleveland man's pocket and tens of thousands from other supporters.[38]

The Major also benefited from a belated, lackluster effort mounted by his opponents. The Combine had treated this contest as they had every other one since 1872, but McKinley had changed the rules. Reed in particular had made a mistake by not becoming the clear champion of the gold standard as Roosevelt had wanted. The votes on the Free Silver substitute showed the sentiment for gold was even larger than for McKinley.

AS WORD OF MCKINLEY'S nomination spread, Canton went wild. His old tent mate, General Russell Hastings, was sitting next to the new nominee and said, "Major, I congratulate you. . . . Now you have just a quarter of a minute before you are mobbed." A telegram announcing his nomination triggered a blast from cannon on a bluff overlooking Canton. Ninety-nine other rounds followed. Factory whistles, clock chimes, horns, and "brass mouthed calliopes" shrieked and made noise.

Before the roll call was complete, cheering neighbors had surrounded McKinley's home. They were soon joined by delegations from surrounding communities who raced to get to Canton first. Alliance won. Militia companies with bands, drums, and bugles led 15,000 people from the courthouse. McKinley's birthplace, Niles, sent a trainload of supporters armed with tin banners, tin buckets, tin canes, and tin whistles. One of Niles's largest employers was a tin factory protected by the McKinley Tariff. Between 5 p.m. and midnight, McKinley addressed an estimated 50,000 people.[39]

McKinley laid out the campaign's broad themes. "What we want in this country is a policy that will give to every American workingman full work at American wages. A policy that will put enough money into the Treasury of the United States to run the Government. A policy that will bring us to such a period of prosperity and of plenty as that we enjoyed for more than thirty years prior to 1893." For McKinley, the election hinged on the protective tariff and the money question could be largely ignored.[40]

Some observers knew differently. Postmaster General Wilson learned of McKinley's nomination at a North Carolina train station as he returned to Washington and confided to his diary that there was "a craze in the Republican party, an attempt . . . to dodge the financial issue."[41]

THE MORNING AFTER THE convention, New York police commissioner Theodore Roosevelt "attracted the attention of the whole room" when he showed up at Police Headquarters "with an ivory-colored button, as large as a silver dollar," bearing portraits of McKinley and Hobart. Roosevelt boasted his button was "the first of its kind in New York."[42]

That same morning, the Republican National Committee met in St. Louis. One of the Major's allies was missing: California committeeman Michael de Young had been defeated that week for reelection by Adolph B. Spreckels, who ran his family's Hawaiian sugar company. In 1884, angered when de Young's *San Francisco Chronicle* alleged he defrauded shareholders, Spreckels confronted the publisher in an alley and shot him twice. He won acquittal for attempted murder by reason of temporary insanity. Still, the committee was populated with plenty of new McKinleyite committeemen, so it was no surprise Hanna was unanimously elected RNC chairman, formally placing him in charge of the fall campaign. He was also empowered to appoint an Executive Committee that would serve as the campaign's directors.[43]

Talking with reporters afterward, Hanna dismissed the silver bolt and said he did not know where the campaign headquarters would be, other than acknowledging the "strong sentiment" for New York. It did not build confidence among Republican leaders when their new chairman said, "I am wholly unfamiliar with the routine methods of conducting a national campaign; for that reason I am not prepared to say yet what the program will be." Hanna then boarded a train for home.[44]

Tired, Hanna parried questions from reporters on the train, saying, "One thing is certain. I am going to try and take it easy until about the 1st of August." He had told his brother-in-law that he planned to sail from Maine up into the Canadian Maritimes, a trip that would take most of July.[45]

But McKinley's campaign was already in deep trouble and the fallout from the silver Republican bolt and the looming Democratic convention would dramatically damage the Major's political outlook. Hanna did not know it yet, but if he stuck to his plans for the cruise McKinley would lose the general election.

CHAPTER 19

Republicans' Shaky Start

———◦———

McKinley and Hanna were in a dangerous place. Hanna ended the Republican National Convention wanting to take a vacation, and McKinley, too, wanted to recharge and think about his acceptance speech. So both men were slow to move and plan the fall campaign. They dithered and thus squandered a chance to prepare for a battle in which a charismatic opponent would almost overwhelm them before the general election began.

There were nearly three weeks between the Republican and Democratic conventions. A lot can happen in that span of time. And a lot was happening. The Democrats were freeing themselves from much of the blame for the depression by arguing that Free Silver would raise prices for farmers, make money more available, and reduce the burden of debtors, thereby restoring the nation's prosperity. If they succeeded in selling this, the Democrats could unite disaffected voters from every party, perhaps setting in motion a realignment that would make the political landscape problematic for McKinley. The election was in danger of slipping away, and McKinley and his men did not realize it.

MCKINLEY FACED SEVERAL IMPORTANT questions, starting with where to locate his headquarters. This was critical because it would show if the McKinley men understood where the election would be decided.

Historically, it had been in New York, the country's political center and the GOP's traditional source of funds.

There were other decisions. Who would sit on the RNC Executive Committee and help set strategy, develop the message, raise money, and execute the election plan? This group helped unite the party by giving major factions a seat at the table. Would McKinley speak in key battleground states? If so, where and how often should he be on the road? As a congressman, he had campaigned for many other candidates, so there was an expectation that he would campaign for himself by traveling through critical states.

And when should the campaign's first two big events be scheduled—the formal notification of the candidate and then his official acceptance, at which the candidate issued the most important statement of the campaign? These were rituals from a time when a candidate did not hear of his selection until a slow-moving letter or newspaper arrived. While the telegraph had erased that delay, having a committee officially notify the candidate was a convenient excuse to showcase him and drive home his message.

One question the McKinley high command thought was settled was the campaign's principal message. Of course, it would be protection. That issue united the GOP, while currency unsettled some Western and Midwestern Republicans. McKinley's desire was to put the tariff issue to the front and bury the currency issue. But in this he was almost fatally wrong.

The McKinley men began grappling with these questions the Monday after the Republican convention, when McKinley picked up Hanna at the Canton station. The new RNC chairman was accompanied by Clay Evans, William McKinley Osborne, and NYPD commissioner Frederick D. Grant. The discussions with Hanna and these informal advisors over a three-hour lunch were centered on the Executive Committee. For party unity, it needed to include Combine men. Platt was a nonstarter to some, especially Hanna. The Easy Boss had been an implacable foe to the end and his addition would be a terrible affront to the New York McKinley League men. But the Combine could not be shut out of the campaign's leadership. Everyone was on the same side now.[1]

At the lunch and in the days that followed, the committee began to take form. As Speaker, Reed would not serve on the Executive Committee, but Manley could represent his interests. Quay had a keen political mind and Pennsylvania was a critical state. He was also close to Platt. If Quay was on the Executive Committee, then the Easy Boss did not need to be.[2]

But McKinley and Hanna found Quay difficult to recruit. He initially declined, so Hanna pressed him. Quay continued balking, citing his health. Hanna tried shaming him, writing July 6 that "not having your name announced on the Ex. Comm. will embarrass me very much and wish you would reconsider." He reminded Quay that he had made Hanna "serve on the Advisory Coun[cil] in '88 against my will." Jokingly, he offered to put Quay and his family on one of his company's steamers for a Lake Superior vacation, "only do not go back on me." McKinley then wrote Quay to say his service "would inspire a confidence that with you on the committee the pathway to victory in November would be made clear." The candidate's personal appeal cinched the deal: the Pennsylvanian said yes.[3]

The Major wanted Dawes and Osborne on the committee, Dawes to represent the critical battleground of Illinois and Osborne to be his eyes and ears in the East. McKinley summoned Dawes on Friday, June 26, to tell him. Interestingly, Hanna did not confirm Dawes's selection until ten days later, possibly a sign Hanna was not as impressed with or was jealous of the Major's favorite.[4]

The Major and his luncheon guests also discussed when McKinley should be formally notified and then officially accept. They settled on late June for the notification, but delayed setting a date for the acceptance. Hanna didn't see the campaign beginning until at least August and felt it wise to wait "until we know what our opponents do at Chicago." After McKinley took the group back to the station, a florist showed up at the Major's house with sod and flowers to pretty up the lawn for the week's expected—and more numerous unexpected—visitors.[5]

Hanna talked with reporters at the station before catching the 4:15 home. He told them there had been progress on the Executive Committee, but more work to do. When asked about McKinley's message, Hanna quickly replied, "Oh, it will be strongly tariff, you may be sure of that." He brushed off silver, saying, "[t]he people—I mean the masses—are most deeply concerned about the tariff. Give us a chance to earn some money . . . they are not grumbling about the kind of money." A few days later, he was more emphatic: "The tariff is the only issue, of course."[6]

The candidate was probably the source of Hanna's insistence that protection be the primary issue. Speaking to 250 Ohioans from Zanesville who visited that evening, McKinley spoke almost exclusively about tariffs, with only one sentence on currency. The Major felt protection would bring victory, so his strategy was to "talk tariff, think tariff, dream tariff" and downplay currency even if Democrats split over silver. "You don't get customers through the mint," he later told visitors, "you get them through the factory." Protection would give the GOP a decisive edge on the issue of restoring prosperity.[7]

Some Republicans were not so confident. When McKinley said, "This money matter is unduly prominent. In thirty days you won't hear anything about it," his friend Judge William R. Day disagreed, replying, "In my opinion, in thirty days you won't hear of anything else."[8]

But after the final gavel fell in St. Louis, Democratic politicians and newspapers immediately opened fire on the new nominee, with many focusing on currency. Illinois governor Altgeld called the GOP a "plutocratic association" and said McKinley's platform could be summed up with "two capital Gs—Gold and Greed." William Jennings Bryan called the Major "the weakest man" Republicans could have chosen. The GOP's gold plank set up "a clear cut issue" for the race "between the money changers and . . . the struggling masses, who produce the wealth and pay the taxes." Bryan predicted McKinley would "try to avoid the silver question and force the fighting upon the tariff, but he will fail."[9]

REPUBLICANS WERE ALREADY SUFFERING desertions in the West because of Free Silver. Inundated with telegrams of support from around the country, Colorado's silver Republican senator Henry M. Teller and the other delegates who bolted the GOP convention talked late into the night. Some favored a silver Republican ticket, others a fusion with the Populists, and a few even supported a silver Democrat, if one could be nominated. After much discussion, the silver Republican bolters issued a startling statement. Teller would run for president on either the Democratic or Populist line or both. Political parties are "the means, not the end . . . the voice, not the sense," the silver Republican manifesto declared. "Monetary reform stands as the first requisite" for a return to prosperity. America "cannot much longer exist free and independent . . . nor can its people much longer be free" unless Free Silver is adopted. The question was whether "the remaining conventions will have the courage and the generosity to unite" in support of Free Silver by picking Teller.[10]

Silver Republicans would go to the Democratic National Convention to talk up Teller as the Democratic nominee; or, if it nominated a gold man or a straddler, he would run as a Populist or Silver Party man. Teller was quickly supported by Colorado's Democratic national committeeman and the leading Texas Free Silver paper, which endorsed former Texas U.S. senator and Confederate postmaster general John H. Reagan as Teller's running mate.[11]

Teller also caucused with Populist Party chairman Herman E. Taubeneck. The two announced they had reached "a perfect agreement . . . and henceforth we will work along the same lines." This was imprecise but pointed to a united front of Populists, silver Republicans, and silver Democrats. Taubeneck endorsed Teller for president as a man "upon which all Populists may consistently unite."[12]

Some Republicans were rattled, especially those from the West. California's de Young told reporters the silver Republican bolt would have "a deleterious effect" on McKinley's chances for the White House. If Democrats endorsed Free Silver, "[they] would take California" and "a number of heretofore reliably strong Republican Western states." Republicans could lose every state west of the Mississippi. Pairing those eighty Electoral College votes with the Solid South and Democrats could win the White House without a single state east of the Mississippi and north of the Mason-Dixon. Free Silver was all the rage in Western and Midwestern farm country, yet McKinley believed that the issue would go away.[13]

THE NIGHT BEFORE MCKINLEY'S formal notice of his nomination, the nearly fifty members of the RNC Notification Committee gathered in Cleveland with Hanna and prepared to descend on Canton, many of them increasingly concerned about Republican defections over the silver issue. There was discussion of a speaking tour for the Major through Indiana, Illinois, Michigan, Missouri, Kansas, and Nebraska. McKinley would not like that idea.[14]

On Monday, June 29, Hanna and the dignitaries arrived in Canton on the midday Cleveland Valley train. The GAR band, host committee members with large red badges, and a fleet of decorated carriages were waiting to take them to McKinley's home. Its lawn had been spruced up with flowers and covered with chairs for the official visitors with standing room for thousands behind them. At 12:10, the Major emerged onto his vine-clad porch, prompting "cheer after cheer." Mother McKinley and Ida joined him. In a short speech, Thurston officially informed him of his nomination, crediting it to "a popular demand" for "protection and reciprocity." The Democratic administration's abandonment of these policies had led to "sufferings and losses and disasters to the American people" and their restoration would mean the return of "American prosperity." Spectators applauded enthusiastically.[15]

McKinley had carefully considered his response, reviewing it with Dawes and others. Looking rested, he spoke from a manuscript in his right hand, with his left in his pocket. "Great are the issues involved in the coming election, and eager and earnest the people for their right determination," he said. Americans must be put back to work, the nation's home market restored, and trade reopened on a fair basis. This would require "protection and reciprocity, twin measures of a true American policy." Higher tariffs would provide the needed revenues for government's operations. These policies were proven, having provided "unexampled prosperity for more than thirty years."

McKinley spent half as much time talking about currency. The maintenance of the country's "spotless credit" required that every kind of American money, "whether of paper, silver or gold, must be as good as the best in the world." He believed "the dollar paid to the farmer, the wage-earner and the pensioner must continue forever equal in purchasing and debt-paying power to the dollar paid to any government creditor." When the Major talked currency, his was still the language of the straddle and waffle.[16]

The Major's failure to focus on currency immediately drew criticism from both Free Silver and gold editorialists, but McKinley was not concerned. His main worry was how to handle the supporters who kept showing up at his home. That Wednesday, Hobart came for a quick visit, their meeting broken up by an unexpected delegation from Medina County, Ohio. McKinley introduced his running mate, who gave his first campaign talk. McKinley then obliged five hundred glassworkers carrying glass canes and wearing glass badges and three thousand Christian Endeavorers, an evangelical fellowship of mostly young women, with speeches. Kerens then stopped by to discuss Missouri's situation and a petition from prominent Catholic Republicans concerned about alleged promises made to the APA. The Major's days were busy, but were they productive? Until McKinley's time was better planned, he was going to be constantly interrupted by visitors demanding his time and words.[17]

McKinley complained he needed more structure imposed on his days. Swamped by unannounced visitors, he couldn't write his acceptance or answer correspondence. He also wanted a vacation. Osborne urged that he and Ida visit his Massachusetts summer home. But the Major felt he must wait until the Democratic convention before making vacation plans and thought journeying east "would be jumping out of the frying pan into the fire."[18]

THE FIRE CAME ANYWAY as the GOP was jolted by major defections in Minnesota. Representative Charles A. Towne, former representative John Lind, the sitting Republican lieutenant governor, and several state senators announced they were bolting the GOP because the convention endorsed the gold standard. "We cannot accept the new faith," they said. "On matters of National principle no man can reasonably be asked to submit to party dictation." They also raised the specter of fusion of silver Republicans, Democrats, and Populists on a state ticket.[19]

Even Illinois was vulnerable to silver defections. RNC committeeman "Doc" Jamieson told McKinley and Hanna that Illinois was "debatable ground" and that the state GOP needed lots of literature on the financial question, because "the free silver movement amounts to a craze."[20]

It was worse in the Plains states. Republican leaders were worried that McKinley had "a very small chance of carrying" Kansas if silver Democrats joined with the state's Populists, as they were attempting to do. As long as wheat sold at thirty-five cents a bushel, "no Kansas farmer can get either a gold or a silver dollar" to pay his mortgage, buy machinery, or plant next year's crop, one Sunflower State Republican complained. The Plains states were a problem for McKinley because, as the journalist William Allen White put it, the whole region "was built on borrowed money." Farmers were struggling under the triple whammy of recession, decades of falling commodity prices, and seemingly unending debts owed to furnishing merchants and Eastern bankers. Free Silver, with promises of instant price increases and cheaper debts, sounded good.[21]

Yet McKinley continued avoiding the money issue. The day after the Minnesota bolt, a thousand millworkers from Tuscarawas County, Ohio, visited him. Half the men were protectionist Democrats. As close as the Major got to currency was to say "all of us want good times, good wages, good prices, good markets; and then we want good money always." The *New York Times* criticized him: "not a word of denunciation of the silver craze has come from his lips; not a word in favor of maintaining the gold standard."[22]

Perceptive Republicans knew this issue was being mishandled. In early July, Hanna begged President Harrison to make a major address in New York City the following month to kick off the campaign in the East so the "issue not be switched off to silver." It would be the first important surrogate speech after McKinley issued his acceptance. Harrison quickly responded he was open to it, but gave Hanna solid advice: "We cannot make the issues—they make themselves." Right now, "[s]ilver is the leading issue that most agitates and interests the people" and McKinley should turn it to his advantage. Hanna demurred but was resigned to a hard summer, writing his brother-in-law, "I would have been glad to have escaped the responsibility of managing the campaign, but there was no way out of it." It would be several weeks before he could vacation: "I must get the work of education started before I can take my necessary recreation."[23]

The next day, Hanna announced that the RNC Executive Committee would meet July 14 in Cleveland. The group's membership was starting to leak, though reporters got some of the names wrong. The papers were right there would be no New Yorker. McKinley couldn't appoint Platt without alienating key supporters and couldn't appoint a McKinley Leaguer without offending the Easy Boss. But McKinley and Hanna needed to find a way to make peace with Platt; otherwise New York could be lost and GOP fund-raising in the city crippled.[24]

Republican activity ground to a halt as party leaders awaited the Democratic show in Chicago, believing that the convention would only improve the GOP's chances for victory. Hanna's brother Howard told the press the Democrats' convention would be ugly. He predicted the economy's "stagnation" would continue until the election. "The silver question is somewhat of a craze," but would die. There would be "the greatest Republican victory this fall since the founding of the party." He expected McKinley, Hanna, and Abner and their families to join him on his yacht sometime in August.[25]

CHAPTER 20

The Silver Edge

———◇———

As its final Democratic state conventions approached, the Democratic Party was being systematically remade from within. The party that had nominated Grover Cleveland for president three times in twelve years was now abandoning him in dramatic fashion, repudiating his policies, his record, and him personally.

Disgruntled Democrats were grabbing control of their party across the country, driven by a powerful idea that promised to end a severe and prolonged economic depression—Free Silver. Many men wanted to be silver's champion as the Democratic presidential nominee—front-runner Silver Dick Bland and his principal challenger, Horace Boies, a former governor of Iowa, among them. But in the weeks leading to the Chicago national convention, the first test of strength was whether the silver men could fight off gold's desperate attempt to force compromise. These days were capped by an ugly surprise that could only add to the party's bitter divide, especially if its creators pulled it off.

THE FINAL SILVER STATE conventions were filled with vitriol aimed at the president. An Ohio delegate demanded the removal of a portrait of Cleveland, calling him "that arch traitor, that Benedict Arnold of the Democratic party." Indiana silver men heckled a preacher when he asked for "divine protection for the President" in his invocation.[1]

Silver leaders accused each other of being insufficiently radical and

248

excoriated each other in platform debates or delegate contests. "In the atmosphere of the hour," Josephus Daniels later wrote, "a man had to be militant for 16 to 1."[2]

There were even dirty tricks. Arkansas easily approved a silver platform and delegation, but argued late into the night over instructing for Bland. After midnight, a delegate read a wire from Teller announcing he had bolted the GOP and urging Arkansas Democrats to back the leader who could unite the silver men from all parties—Bland. The endorsement stampeded the convention over the objections of the governor and both U.S. senators. Arkansas instructed for Bland. The next morning, the wire was revealed as a forgery.[3]

By now, silver had its majority to write the platform but was short of the two-thirds needed to nominate their candidate outright. New York, a gold stronghold, had yet to hold its convention. The Empire State would put gold over the threshold of having a third of the convention's votes, giving the yellow metal camp leverage. If the convention could not nominate a candidate without some gold votes, the honest-money Democrats could use that power to gain concessions on the platform or even the candidate himself.[4]

WITH TENSIONS RISING, WHITNEY unveiled his strategy to forge a compromise between the silver and gold camps in an open letter in the June 21 Sunday papers. The former navy secretary argued Free Silver at a 16:1 ratio to gold would commit the United States to buying the world's white metal at twice market prices, leading to "the worst panic and distress we have ever seen."

He suggested Democrats instead unite behind a platform calling for an international agreement setting the ratio between gold and silver. He announced he would lead prominent Democrats to Chicago to press for this international bimetallism policy and agreement on a candidate acceptable to both wings of the party. His choice was former Massachusetts governor William E. Russell. Without concessions, "disruption of the Democratic Party might occur." Russell soon agreed to accompany Whitney, but declined to be a candidate.[5]

Though there were gold Democrats who would rather bolt than straddle, the financier's open letter was widely reprinted and praised by some sound-money papers. The *Chicago Tribune,* for instance, commended "its irrefutable soundness" but warned, "A large mass of Democrats . . . are not intelligent enough to comprehend it" and would rely on "dishonest dema-gogues" like Governor Altgeld of Illinois.[6]

Silver leaders slammed the statement. An Arkansas congressman said, "The idea that Mr. Whitney can go to Chicago and do like the wise men of the East who went to St. Louis—buy up enough delegates to make a gold platform—is ridiculously humorous." The *Washington Post* doubted "the utterance will change anyone's opinion."[7]

At a late-night strategy session the day before the New York Demo-cratic convention in Saratoga Springs, New York, on June 24, Whitney, Senator David Hill, former governor Roswell P. Flower, and other Empire State leaders agreed the state party would endorse Whitney's international bimetallism rather than a straight-out gold plank, thereby providing lever-age to influence the national platform and nominee.

Whitney also thought a New York endorsement of international bimet-allism would also help recruit powerful Democrats who could persuade silver delegates to accept compromise in Chicago. The plank was approved unanimously, yet the New York Democrats' platform and Whitney's com-promises were panned as "weak and colorless."[8]

The day after the New York convention, one silver leader gave his un-compromising reaction. Senator Tillman told his audience at Manhattan's Cooper Union, "You are the most ignorant and benighted community in the United States." The "wealth gatherer" in New York, he said, "sits on a velvet cushion waiting for dividends to ripen" from fruits "stolen from . . . the toilers here as well as in South Carolina and Illinois." Retribution was coming. "We expect," Tillman warned, "to elect a president, a house and a senate without men like you." They would do something about "the money of this country" that was "congested in the coffers of Wall Street."[9]

Altgeld also trashed Whitney's outreach. Welcomed by thousands at the Illinois convention in Peoria who "shouted like a thousand devils," the fiery governor rejected Whitney's call for conciliation. "Too long have we listened to the counsel of men who have not a drop of Democratic blood in their bodies," he said. Offstage, he blasted Whitney and "the loud-mouthed goldbugs of his class" for having "never led the party to anything but humiliation and defeat." There would be no compromise.[10]

Whitney spent the next week recruiting his "persuaders" to go to

Chicago before he and several dozen allies left Grand Central Terminal the afternoon of July 1 on three parlor cars stocked with fine food and wine. It was quickly dubbed "the Gold Train." Whitney told reporters his mission was to convince Southern and Western delegates "of the fallacy of their position." That was hard to do when people were tentative in their opinions. It was impossible when they had an unshakable belief in their cause. "We will do the best we can," the former navy secretary said.[11]

SINCE THE BATTLE WAS joined in August 1895 with the formation of the Bimetallic DNC, silver Democrats had focused on capturing control of their party, not on advancing a specific candidate. White metal Democrats had agreed to prioritize principles first, candidate second.

Now that all the state conventions had finished, it was appropriate that candidates began stirring. There was a front-runner, a competitor, some conventional favorite sons, an unconventional possibility, and a really dark horse.

The front-runner was Missouri's Richard P. Bland, the party's leader in the free coinage fight for more than two decades. Silver Dick had won instruction in Missouri, the New Mexico Territory, and Texas, and in Arkansas by fraud, while a *New York Times* survey found him the top choice in Colorado, Kansas, and South Carolina, with support in Illinois and Mississippi.

Despite this, the sixty-year-old Bland was perhaps too old and too often in ill health. Moreover, his campaign was criticized for having violated the understanding that the silver movement would focus on getting control of the platform and worry about the candidate only after that had been achieved. Bland and his managers had been too open and active. Several states had turned down instruction for Bland because his allies had worked too hard to win them. He had also fumbled attempts to hit the Free Silver speaking circuit in 1895, falling ill on a swing through Colorado and scrapping a lecture tour through the South planned by his brother-in-law when the first events in Georgia were poorly attended.[12]

As tradition dictated, Bland would not be at the convention, but remain at his farm in Lebanon while managers did the wheeling-and-dealing. But Bland made sure delegates heard from him by giving regular interviews to reporters. The *World*'s James Creelman met Silver Dick in his apple orchard, resting from cutting hay behind a horse-drawn mower. The two men moved to the parlor of Bland's modest, two-story brick farmhouse, interrupting his four-year-old daughter's piano lesson. Bland downplayed the idea of a sectional divide, saying it was not the West and South against the East, but "the productive masses" in all regions against "the fund-owning classes." Creelman asked Bland how the country would avoid a depression since free coinage would debase the currency. Bland dismissed the notion, saying free coinage would push silver's price up to $1.29 an ounce, making it more valuable than gold. Interview over, Bland returned to his hayfield, his daughter following him. The next day, Bland hosted another reporter, gaining more coverage in papers that picked up the articles.[13]

Trailing Bland was former Iowa governor Horace Boies. Though only the Hawkeye State instructed for him, the *Times* said "Uncle Horace," as he was called, had support in Alabama, the Dakotas, Georgia, Idaho, Illinois, Oregon, Texas, and Utah. The only Democrat to be Iowa's governor since 1855, Boies was a former Republican who left the GOP over high tariffs and prohibition. He won a two-year term with support from beer-drinking Germans and Central Europeans in 1889 when Republicans were punished at the polls for overreaching on the liquor question in Iowa. Like Bland, sixty-seven-year-old Uncle Horace faced questions about his energy and health. More important, there were concerns he was anti-labor and retained Republican views on financial and business issues.[14]

The Democratic favorite sons were less numerous than the Republican field, but like their GOP counterparts, they were large egos who saw themselves as the party's nominee or ambitious men who felt there was little to be lost by running, and indeed maybe the vice presidency, a cabinet post, or greater prestige to be gained. However, they had no string pullers to manage them like the Republicans had with Platt or Quay.

Unlike most favorite sons, South Carolina's Pitchfork Tillman had traveled outside his state, appearing at a dozen state conventions promoting his interests. But his violent language and exotic appearance—he had one eye and was often unkempt—made him a nonstarter. En route to Chicago, Tillman warned, "If the Democratic party doesn't adopt free silver, it ought to die, and I have a knife with which I'll cut its throat."[15]

Other candidates had little support. Senator Joseph C. S. Blackburn of Kentucky had votes in California, Virginia, and West Virginia. John R. McLean, owner of the *Cincinnati Enquirer,* had the backing of Ohio, though he hadn't lived there for more than a decade. Former Oregon governor Sylvester Pennoyer was hoping a Westerner would be picked for vice president—namely, him.[16]

There was some talk of Adlai Stevenson, but his four years as Cleveland's vice president tainted him, despite Stevenson's quiet opposition to his chief's policies. Coming from a battleground state, Indiana governor Claude Matthews had appeal, but had refused to hold one of Altgeld's special conventions in 1895 and was thought to be insufficiently radical. The sole gold Democrat was former two-term Pennsylvania governor Robert E. Pattison, who served as a protest vote for sound-money delegates.[17]

There was an unconventional contender for the Democratic nomination. Colorado Republican senator Henry M. Teller was interested in both the Democratic and People's Party nominations, but Missouri governor Stone spoke for many in his party when he rejected the Colorado silver senator, saying, "The Moses of the American people will be a Democrat tried and true." Hinrichsen was more blunt. Asked if Teller was acceptable, the Illinoisan snapped, "Not in a thousand years." Populist fusionists were furious at this response, with Taubeneck threatening, "If the democrats cannot meet us half way on a man like Senator Teller," then they would be "responsible for a division of the silver forces." Teller's candidacy quickly died and he went home to Denver July 1 to be met by 100,000 cheering people.[18]

Then there was the dark horse William Jennings Bryan, who had long ago decided he should be president, though he may have been the only one to think so. While most observers were unaware the thirty-six-year-old former two-term Nebraska congressman was running, no Democratic contender had prepared harder or more meticulously over the past year and a half than he.

He had made an abortive run for the U.S. Senate in early 1894, then retired from Congress to avoid getting beaten in the fall midterms. Even before leaving Congress, Bryan had become a *World-Herald* editor, writing opinion pieces. Writing was better than lawyering, but it didn't pay much.[19]

To make a living, Bryan went on the speaking circuit in March 1895. Then, like today, former politicians could make good money if they could talk, create controversy, and didn't mind travel. At first, Bryan received $50 a speech plus expenses, then $100 an event, then as much as $200 a speech. It was good money. There was a real demand for speeches on currency and the young Nebraskan dominated the market. In the year and a half before the convention, Bryan gave hundreds of speeches in every region. He honed his message, found arguments that hit a chord, and developed phrases that elicited applause or laughter, all while filling the family exchequer.[20]

The brash young Nebraskan welcomed controversy, telling Southern audiences in summer 1895 that "nothing in heaven above, on the earth, not in hell beneath" could make him vote for a gold Democrat on a gold platform. Honest-money Democrats thought that ended his political career, but it increased his appeal among silver men. Everywhere he went, Bryan encouraged silver Democrats to capture the local and state party machinery and kept careful records of those he met, making his list of silver men better than any other candidate's. He carried on a voluminous correspondence with them, soliciting news, sharing editorials, and promoting efforts to take over the Democratic Party.[21]

One of Bryan's more consequential relationships began when he visited Texas in June 1895 and met thirty-two-year-old Charles M. Rosser, the new superintendent of the North Texas Hospital for the Insane. An active Democrat, the trim, tall Texas doctor was impressed with the young Nebraskan, writing later that Bryan's speech before an overflow crowd at Dallas City Hall was the best that he ever delivered.[22]

Besides gaining a lifetime friend in Rosser, the visit also earned Bryan an invitation to the large and influential Texas State Fair to keynote "Silver Democratic Day." There Bryan made what the state's leading silver paper called an "eloquent" address packed with "powerful arguments." Eastern financiers opposed Free Silver not because bimetallism would mean 50¢ dollars as they claimed, Bryan said, but because they "desired to collect their debts by a 150 cent dollar or a 200 cent dollar" in gold. Afterward, Rosser introduced him to Governor Charles Culberson, former governor James S. Hogg, and other luminaries. Bryan told them Bland should be the nominee but confided in Rosser that he actually wanted and expected to be the standard-bearer.[23]

By November 1895, Bryan had concluded it would be so. He felt the "logic of the situation" left no other outcome. His extensive speaking had put him in touch with many silver leaders who he thought would control the Democratic convention. He felt comfortable he could sway them to his side at the right moment. So Bryan stepped up his efforts, traveling more in the first half of 1896 than he had the previous year. He was away so often, he missed his birthday in March. His wife sent a telegram: "The family sends loving birthday greetings to its head. Mary."[24]

He mailed friendly state chairmen and Bimetallic DNC members copies of the 1895 Nebraska silver plank he had drafted, encouraging its use as a template for their platforms. He asked them for the names and addresses of every likely national delegate and then quickly wrote to each of them when they were elected. His letter extolled the silver movement's "Principles First" approach, promoted a silver platform and candidate in Chicago, and included a collection of his speeches and opinion pieces. One was his February 24 *World-Herald* editorial about Democratic gold bugs' demands that silverites pledge to support the party's nominee no matter who and what his platform. Bryan disagreed. "The party is a means, not an end." Silver men should demand a silver ticket and platform in Chicago or bolt. By affirming every Democrat's "right to abandon the party whenever the party abandons the cause of people," Bryan was keeping his focus on the financial issue, not any specific candidate. Principles first. It just so happened he aligned perfectly with those principles. The piece was a hit.[25]

If Bryan received a letter encouraging him to run, he typically replied, "I don't think it wise to encourage a contest for the nomination until platform adopted." But there were exceptions. In late April, Josephus Daniels offered the support of his Raleigh *News & Observer* editorial page, saying, "I think you are right in saying we ought not to go to Chicago thinking about men, but of the platform, but you will have many friends who want you on the ticket." The young, ambitious Daniels had served as Secretary of the Interior Hoke Smith's chief of staff but broke with Cleveland over his financial policies.[26]

Colorado's DNC committeeman liked Bryan's plank, too. This emboldened Bryan to confide that if the convention went for silver, Nebraska would nominate him. Looking back years later, Charles S. Thomas, by then a U.S. senator, wrote, "Here was a young man barely thirty-six, living in a comparatively unimportant Republican state west of the Mississippi River, audaciously announcing his probably [*sic*] candidacy for the presidential nomination. The very seriousness of the suggestion emphasized its absurdity."[27]

·   ·   ·

THE WEEK BEFORE THE national convention, Democrats began piling into Chicago and candidates ramped up their efforts. Bland's men opened a headquarters in the Auditorium Annex and began offering "Cornfield Handshakes," grasping a delegate's right hand while putting a glass of whiskey into his left. Still, there was little energy for his candidacy.[28]

Managers for Uncle Horace papered his headquarters in the Palmer House with pictures of him in farm clothes. Unlike Bland, Boies slipped into Chicago to meet delegates early one morning the week before the convention but left by day's end. Bland men complained he had put on airs by wearing his muddy farm boots. There were dustups as the two camps defaced each other's posters.[29]

Governor Matthews established his operation in the Palmer House, but lacked the signage of the Bland and Boies efforts, let alone Bland's hundred-proof beverages. The Hoosiers began cultivating Southerners, emphasizing Matthews's Kentucky birthplace and farm background.[30]

Bryan had no headquarters and denied he was running, telling reporters, "You can announce me as being out of the Presidential race. In fact, I never was in it, save by the kind mention of a few enthusiastic friends." His disavowal was about the only newspaper mention of his possible candidacy so far that week. Still, his presence in Chicago upset Altgeld because the governor thought he had already discouraged Bryan from the race, having told him in early June, "You are young yet. Let Bland have the nomination this time. Your time will come."[31]

Even after these attempts to dissuade him, Bryan kept making contacts in Illinois. His persistence annoyed Altgeld so much that in late June, the governor finally asked a mutual friend, *New York Journal* editor Willis J. Abbot, to "tell Bryan that he's young enough to wait a few years. Dick Bland has earned this nomination and shall have it, if I can influence this convention." Altgeld was more blunt with Hinrichsen, saying, "Buck, tell Bryan to go home—he stands no more chances of being nominated than I, and I was born in Germany." He even threatened to block Bryan from speaking at the convention if he continued flirting with a run. All these efforts were to no avail. Bryan kept pressing his case.[32]

BEFORE THE CONVENTION OPENED, both gold and silver men wanted to know how to handle key battles over temporary chairmen and potential delegate challenges. The former would name the platform chairman and run the convention, while the latter could affect the ability of a candidate to get the necessary two-thirds supermajority.

Just after noon on Monday, June 29, the Bimetallic DNC leaders— Bryan among them—declared the Chicago convention's first battle would be over control of the convention machinery. The silver leaders were deeply concerned that the DNC, dominated by Cleveland allies, would make a gold man temporary chairman. He would then appoint the Resolutions and Credentials Committees, making a silver platform difficult and a silver candidate impossible. The bimetallic men chose Senators Jones of Arkansas, Turpie of Tennessee, and Daniels of Virginia, and Governors Stone of Missouri and Altgeld of Illinois, to demand the DNC put forward a silver man. If a gold man was offered, the Free Silver forces would be fighting a long tradition. Democrats had always ratified the temporary chairman the national committee proposed.

DNC chairman William F. Harrity turned the bimetallic men down in a heated private meeting. Altgeld threatened the gold men and Hinrichsen angrily declared that if Harrity tried seating a gold man on a voice vote, there would be violence. If it came, he would bet on "the boys in soft hats from the South and West," meaning ex-Confederates and cowboys.[33]

The bimetallic leadership met Wednesday night to prepare for the DNC fight over temporary chairman and, if a gold man was offered, for a floor battle as well. Altgeld pushed the group to support killing the two-thirds supermajority rule for nominations and then offered an even more incendiary idea. There should be a silver delegate caucus "for the purpose of discovering our candidate." Let the bimetallic men settle on a candidate before the convention began. The winner would have the backing of all the white metal forces. Deciding on the ticket in advance would allow the convention to finish its business in a day, he argued. It would also give Altgeld enormous influence over the decision.

Border state leaders supported this, but Southerners opposed it. Tillman declared it "unwise for the silver men . . . to split up into factions in favor of any candidate" before the convention began. "The platform should be first made and then place the candidate on it," he said. Fortunately for Bryan, silver Democrats would side with Tillman, defeating Altgeld's idea to name a ticket before the convention even began.[34]

· · ·

WHITNEY'S GOLD TRAIN ARRIVED at 4:40 that afternoon. He checked into the Auditorium Annex and met Harrity, who warned him about silver's plan to dominate the convention. Whitney still hoped he could produce compromise, but Harrity had seen the opposition up close. The silver men didn't have compromise in them and they had the numbers.

Senator Hill, who traveled with Whitney, deliberately checked into another hotel and kept his distance. If he had any chance to be temporary chairman, he could not be seen as Whitney's man. When reporters called at his hotel, he returned their cards with the note: "Just arrived; nothing to say at the moment." [35]

Whitney's traveling party dispersed to scout the sentiment of the delegates. They soon reported back that the silver men were often "bitter with a sense of injustice and burning with a desire for redress." One of Whitney's deputies marveled, "These men are mad." [36]

The New York financier called a strategy session that evening in the Auditorium Annex's big corner parlor. After taking off their coats and calling for palm fans to cool off, the gold men discussed their options. The general sense was the Silver men could be defeated if they went for 16-to-1, but some suggested the situation was so dire that sound-money men should bolt before the convention began. Whitney urged fighting until the end, which is where things stood when the session broke up after midnight without a battle plan. [37]

One silver leader had left town. Bryan had a paid speaking engagement—a debate on currency in Crete, Nebraska. He'd be back in Chicago Sunday.

SATURDAY, JULY 4, BEGAN with a bang. Altgeld returned from a few days in Springfield and closeted himself with Hinrichsen, who told him 33 Illinois delegates were for Bland, 14 for Boies, and 1 each for Stevenson and Teller. Delegates were bound by unit rule, so Bland was the candidate. Altgeld let Hinrichsen make the endorsement. It was a huge boost for Silver Dick. [38]

The silver forces were angered by Cleveland using a national holiday to insult his intraparty adversaries in a July Fourth public letter. The president warned that America's progress "is the result of a wise observance of the monetary laws that control national health and vigor." Free coinage was "a radical departure" and "mistaken policy." Even Whitney's crew understood Cleveland was toxic. His portrait in the New York suite disappeared by Saturday.[39]

The only chance Hill had to be temporary chairman was for silver men to lose their nerve or offer someone who fractured the silver camp. The yellow metal men had no influence on the platform. They could have some say over the nominee if they kept their gold bloc united since there were thought to be around 360 gold delegates, about 50 more than the third needed to block. But gold could not suffer any credentials defeats or defections.[40]

Whitney conducted an early Saturday morning strategy session in his suite and then called on Hill and other gold leaders at the Palmer House. They agreed to formally make Hill the DNC's candidate for temporary chairman and discussed preparations for credentials fights in Florida, Nebraska, South Dakota, and Texas.[41]

At about 1 a.m., the Bimetallic DNC's five-member steering committee settled on Senator John W. Daniel of Virginia to run for temporary chairman. The battle had been joined.[42]

The gold men put on a display of enthusiasm Saturday as five to six thousand sound-money Democrats crowded into the Auditorium for an evening of speeches. The platform was jammed with Cleveland allies—past and current senators, congressmen, governors, and party heavyweights. Every seat was filled except in the uppermost galleries, while the standing room and aisles were packed tight. Former Massachusetts governor William E. Russell was the evening's star, attacking silver men for opening the door to "division, defeat, dishonor." Free Silver's "radical departure" would lead to economic calamity. Asserting fifty cents of silver was worth a dollar would hurt savers who would be paid "in depreciated currency," people with insurance policies would receive "money of less value than they parted with," and "every wage earner" would "suffer a reduction of his wages." "Whitney for President" buttons started circulating, but a financier was not going to win this convention.[43]

After spending five days dealing with the 51-member DNC, Harrity was working to make certain still gold had its majority. There were at least 19 silver DNC members. There might be others: Silver said they had 25 votes and were working on the 26th. If Harrity lost his majority—or if the convention rejected the DNC's temporary chairman choice—control of credentials was in jeopardy and with it, the gold men of Florida, Michigan, Nebraska, South Dakota, and Texas. Harrity couldn't let that happen.[44]

That night, the honest-money Democrats discovered a battle over the temporary chairman wasn't the only one they would face or even the most dangerous to their cause. They discovered the bimetallic men planned to toss out four Michigan gold delegates and replace them with Free Silver men, tipping the majority within the Wolverine State delegation and under the unit rule, giving silver all 26 votes and, perhaps with that, two-thirds of the convention. The silver Michiganders making the challenge claimed gold won only because of "the villainy and fraud practiced by the hench-man of Cleveland." However, 25 delegates were chosen by unanimous votes at the state or district conventions; the 26th won with a 173-vote majority. Gold Democrats would have to stop this latest assault from the white metal fanatics on the convention floor. But would they have the numbers to do so?[45]

Bryan returned to Chicago the next day with his wife, Mary, after his Independence Day debate on the silver question hosted by the Crete Chau-tauqua. Bryan had been thinking about what to say if given an opportu-nity to address the convention and tested lines for audience reaction in Crete. He liked a phrase he had used in a congressional speech a year and a half earlier and closed with it, saying, "You shall not press down upon the brow of labor this crown of thorns. You shall not crucify mankind upon a cross of gold." The crowd's enthusiastic reaction made him recognize "its fitness for the conclusion." He probably was unaware of how consequential his choice would be.[46]

CHAPTER 21

The Logic of the Situation

————◄○►————

Ha! Ha! Ha!
Who are we?
We are the Bland Club of K.C.
We're hot stuff;
That's no bluff.
Vote for silver
And we'll all have stuff.

That was what the Kansas City Bland marching band chanted as it arrived in Chicago and was good-naturedly pelted with paper missiles by supporters of other candidates. People shouted, "Measures, not men," "No political bum," and "Sixteen to one" in hotel lobbies and on street corners. Free Silver advocates were not yet in charge, but they were running uninhibited through the city.[1]

There were discordant notes as slurs of "Down with the hook-nosed Shylocks of Wall Street" and "Down with the Christ-killing goldbugs" were chanted by bigots. The failure of silver leaders to denounce these anti-Semitic cries as they were repeated over the coming months would unsettle Jewish voters.[2]

Gold advocates appeared to have a majority on the DNC and could control the temporary roll and propose the convention's officers, giving gold influence over the Resolutions and Credentials. Silverites would then need to overcome the gold men on the floor, where a majority would elect the officers, settle credentials, and appoint a platform, but two-thirds was required to nominate the presidential candidate. No candidate was near a majority, let alone a supermajority. For while the silver movement was powerful, it had not coalesced behind a strong front-runner. The situation was ripe for a dark horse to emerge, but it would take quite a few lucky breaks to arrive at an inspiring and surprising moment for him to do so.

THE FIRST TEST VOTE that mattered came when the DNC met at noon in the Palmer House's large parlor with Chairman William Harrity of Pennsylvania presiding. He wanted to see if gold still had the majority on the DNC before taking up the issue of the convention's temporary chairman. A safe place to do this was in settling the few credentials challenges.

One of the most important credentials challenges featured Michigan, a state the gold bugs fairly won but whose delegation the silverites were now trying to claim by swapping out four gold delegates for silver men, thereby giving silver a majority in the delegation and, since the state was under the unit rule, all of Michigan's 26 votes. If the bimetallic men succeeded, they would have a two-thirds convention supermajority. But the state's silver committeeman had not filed the challenge's required paperwork, so the DNC voted unanimously to seat the gold-dominated Michigan delegation provisionally. Silver men promised to file the forms and fight again.[3]

Next came Nebraska's credential challenge. Lawyers for the gold slate charged the silver men had bolted the convention, a charge the silver faction called ludicrous. "Fully confident" that they would be recognized on the merits, the silver men were shocked when the DNC voted 27 to 23 to seat the gold delegation instead. The vote shut Bryan out of the convention for now since he had only a guest pass, not a delegate's floor badge.[4]

Satisfied now that gold men still had a majority on the DNC, Harrity turned to the selection of the temporary chairman. Gold men offered Hill; silver put forward Daniel. The vote for Hill was 27 to 23. The Gold men hoped the silver men would respect tradition and vote for the DNC-backed temporary chairman on the floor.[5]

Dickinson rushed to Hill's room to tell him the result. Hill was indifferent to the news, which was his usual demeanor, but he may have also been aware he could lose. When reporters asked how the drafting of his keynote was coming, Hill replied, "What's the use of preparing a speech I may not have a chance to deliver?"

However, there was already dissention among the silver men over the temporary chairmanship. The solidly silver West Virginians would vote for Hill out of respect for tradition. Others were considering defecting. How many was unclear. Maybe tradition had enough power to swing it for Hill, who was personally popular in the South. The bimetallic leadership decided to get a firm whip count for the floor fight on the temporary chairmanship.[6]

At the same time, there was still no consensus on a nominee. Kansas came out for Silver Dick and a *New York Times* survey said Bland remained the front-runner with 264 delegates, followed by Boies. Gold's Pattison was third at 98, then everyone else trailed far behind. The *Times* survey found 313 undecideds. No one was close to the 620 needed. Delegates were "groping," said the *Courier-Journal*.[7]

Prodded by Josephus Daniels, North Carolina delegates offered to endorse Bryan. Bryan suggested they wait until Nebraska's credentials challenge was resolved. Still, Daniels told reporters from the *Washington Post* and *Baltimore Sun* that Bryan would be nominated. A *Post* reporter reacted by saying, "He is the only man who thinks so."[8]

The nomination contest was up in the air in part because the silver forces were focused on preliminary skirmishes—credentials and the platform—and were without leaders capable of creating a consensus around a candidate. Senator James K. Jones, perhaps the most respected bimetallic leader, might have led such an effort, but he was hobbled because Arkansas's delegates were instructed for Bland. The void meant gold backers might be able to influence events by trading their votes for concessions from the least objectionable silver candidate. That required gold to maintain control of a third of the convention delegates.[9]

DEMOCRATS MET TUESDAY, JULY 7, at the Coliseum, then one of the world's most prominent convention halls. The arena could easily accommodate 15,000 people, comfortably seated in chairs so new they "still smelled of the forest," as a reporter put it. The space was open, featuring a lofty ceiling with no interior columns blocking the view. Large, open arched windows filled the room with light and let in a steady breeze off Lake Michigan just to the east. Above the stage were large portraits of the Democratic presidents from Jefferson to Cleveland beneath a giant eagle with a U.S. shield in its talons. Most important, for an age before sound systems, the acoustics were excellent—nearly every speaker could be heard in every corner, unless hoarse or weak of voice.

The hall was tense as an Episcopal priest offered the invocation. One reporter wrote, "The prayer is about the only part of the preliminary proceedings which is likely to pass unchallenged." He was right. As soon as Harrity said, "For temporary chairman—Hon. David B. Hill of New York," Alabama's silver national committeeman, Henry D. Clayton, moved to substitute Senator John W. Daniel of Virginia as temporary chairman. The silver men cheered and shrieked, throwing hats and canes skyward. An Arkansan stood on his chair, flapping his arms and screaming like a bird. Tillman threw himself into the fury, yelling and waving his hat. It took time for the crowd to settle.[10]

Each side made its case. A big man in a white waistcoat, New Jersey's former state chairman Allen L. McDermott, begged the silver majority, "Don't begin your Convention by violating a tradition," namely that the DNC selected the temporary chairman, and appealed for unity by reminding delegates of the constancy of Northern Democrats.

There were more speeches—almost a dozen, many interrupted by heckling from the opposing side. Louisiana's B. W. Martson—a silver man with a "prize-fighter's face," big mouth, and pompadour hair—got so unsettled from the constant uproar that he took to crossing the stage to a table with a water pitcher, pouring a glass, and drinking it. When he said, "We will make this glorious country blossom like a rose," there was such a reaction that he went to leave the platform, but then turned and emptied the pitcher into his ninth glass of water, held it up, and downed it. Someone yelled, "What! A Louisianan drinking water!" provoking laughter and cheers as the sugar planter walked off.[11]

Marston's feeble silver arguments didn't hurt the silver cause. The roll was called on the motion to substitute Daniel for Hill. Though about two dozen silver delegates voted for Hill, gold hopes for tradition were dashed when Harrity announced the results: "The tellers agree in their tally and report the vote as follows, Yeas, 556; nays, 349; not voting, 1." Hill had abstained, Daniel was temporary chairman. Silver had won the round.[12]

Galvanized by a Virginian's rebel yell, the floor erupted in a twenty-minute demonstration. Men stood on chairs, waving flags, banners, canes, and handkerchiefs. The band rolled through a series of patriotic marches with the crowd chanting, stamping, and singing. The gold men's worst fears were confirmed: silver men were still short of the two-thirds mark needed to nominate a thoroughgoing white metal candidate, but in control and determined to kill any leverage sound-money Democrats had.[13]

Daniel delivered his keynote, laboriously reading from a text. He urged unity, reminding Eastern delegates that the South and West had "supported the men you named for president" and "submitted cheerfully to your compromise platforms" and "patiently borne repeated disappointments as to their fulfillment." The only hope for Democrats was to adopt "the views of the majority." If it was meant to be conciliatory, it was not taken as such.[14]

There were calls for Hill to speak, including cries from silver men. He ignored them, casually eating a sandwich in his seat in the New York delegation. With a shout, the convention adjourned, kicking off another joyous silver demonstration as the Coliseum emptied.[15]

The Resolutions Committee went to work to finish the platform for Wednesday's convention session. Senator Jones was selected chairman and appointed a subcommittee of six silver and three gold men who prepared a draft. Bryan was pleased with their product, claiming, "The money plank was there as I had written it two weeks before." But everyone knew a floor fight was coming over currency and that the nomination itself was up for grabs. Asked by a reporter who would be nominated, Senator Harris replied, "Ask me how many miles to the moon; I could tell you about as well." Tillman echoed his colleague, saying, "The Lord in heaven only knows." Even Altgeld, a Bland man, admitted he didn't know. "That is one of the secrets the good Lord has not confided to me."[16]

ON WEDNESDAY, JULY 8, tensions were already rising, with a Missouri man confronting some New York delegates, saying, "We don't give a ——— whether New-York likes it or not, or whether the State votes the Democratic ticket or not."

The podium was draped with a flag, there were fresh roses on the stage, and the day was cool as Senator Daniel, tall, wearing pince-nez glasses and a double-breasted frock coat, called for committee reports. Since none of the committees were ready, delegates called on party leaders to speak, hoping for red meat or entertainment.

The first speaker was the largest delegate in Chicago, three-hundred-pound former Texas governor Jim Hogg, who removed his wad of chewing tobacco so he could, with clear voice, pummel Republicans over protection. Then Senator Blackburn of Kentucky blamed the depression on the gold men who had run the nation's economy the last two decades. "Christ with a lash drove from the temple," he told delegates, "a better set of men than those who for twenty years have shaped the financial policy of this country." One of those men was a fellow Kentuckian, Treasury secretary Carlisle. That attack thrilled the silver faction, but caused gold men to heckle, boo, and hiss. After each speaker, the gold men chanted "Hill! Hill! Hill!" [17]

By now, Daniel's voice was completely gone and California senator Stephen M. White was presiding. He was to be named permanent chairman, so no one objected to him taking the gavel now. Bryan had been floated for the permanent chairmanship, but supporters of other candidates shot him down. Then R. H. Henry, owner of the Jackson, Mississippi, *Clarion*-Ledger, moved "that Hon. W. J. Bryan, of Nebraska, be invited to address the Convention," but Bryan was still stuck in the Credentials Committee meeting, trying to get his silver Nebraska delegation recognized. These would be two of many lucky breaks that would put Bryan in the spotlight at just the right moment by keeping him out of it now.

Again, gold men cried, "Hill! Hill! Hill!" White caused laughter by asking, "What is the use of calling for a man who is not present?" Instead, the convention voted to hear from Altgeld; but he stood on his chair and demanded Hill speak. The Illinois governor was causing trouble, knowing Hill was caucusing with the gold members of the Resolutions Committee. Someone convinced Altgeld to take the stage and he appeared in a wine-colored coat and black pants, sparking a wild reception, complete with a wall of noise, flying hats, and waving handkerchiefs. [18]

The short, wiry governor's hand trembled when he held it up to still the crowd. He began in a soft, slow voice that rose and sped up as he delivered a fiery attack on the money power, drawing from his Peoria state convention speech from two weeks earlier. He blamed the depression—"the streets of our cities filled with idle men, with hungry women and with ragged children"—on a vicious conspiracy. Between 1873 and 1890, "the

large security-holding classes" connived "to make money dear and property and labor cheap." Demonetizing silver reduced the money supply
and raised gold's value, thereby increasing the burdens for debtors and the
wealth of bondholders.[19]

He offered a cure for the depression. The government's debts and the
people's debts had been incurred when money was both gold and silver.
Let them be repaid with money of both metals. Altgeld was explicit:
through Free Silver, devalue the currency, reduce the value of all debts, and
thereby repudiate a portion of them. He also rejected calls for compromise
in the convention. Who were behind these calls? "The large banks in the
East" that "control the whole banking system," as well as the papers, he
answered, all guilty of "money terrorism." He finished to cheers and a
boisterous demonstration.[20]

THE CREDENTIALS COMMITTEE WAS ready to give a partial report. Chairman John H. Atwood of Kansas said he needed more time to settle the
Michigan dispute, but asked the convention to replace the Nebraska gold
men with Bryan's silver delegation. The partial report was approved. There
were wild cheers as the gold Nebraskans left and the white metal Nebraskans entered the hall bearing a large blue banner with silver letters that
read 16 TO 1, while a fat young man carried another blue banner embla-
zoned W. J. BRYAN CLUB.[21]

The Resolutions Committee finally finished drafting the platform,
a full-throated repudiation of the sitting Democratic president. Besides
backing Free Silver at 16 to 1, it endorsed a national income tax, an end
to lifetime tenure for judges, a tariff for revenue only, expanded antitrust
regulation, stricter railroad regulation, restrictions on immigration, and
arbitration of labor disputes. It opposed Cleveland's injunctions, federal
interference in local affairs, and third terms for presidents.[22]

To help sell the document to the delegates, Jones asked Bryan to "take
charge" of the currency debate. Jones felt Bryan was the only prominent
silver leader who had not spoken to the convention and believed Bryan was
due a speaking role for his work. The Boy Orator of the Platte was now "in
the very position for which I had at first longed," he later recalled, in part
because Jones may not have taken Bryan's candidacy seriously.[23]

Hill and Bryan discussed arrangements and agreed to an hour and twenty minutes for each side. Tillman and Bryan would speak for silver. Pitchfork told Bryan he wanted to close and required fifty minutes. Hill objected, saying if Tillman wanted to make a long speech, he should open. The New Yorker did not want Tillman to follow him, knowing the South Carolinian would spend his time abusing him. Tillman accepted the opening slot for silver, making Bryan the closing speaker, which the Nebraskan preferred. Then came news that the platform debate would be held over until the next day, giving Bryan more time to prepare.[24]

Sometime after 3 p.m., Atwood sent word his Credentials Committee was ready to report. The Leavenworth lawyer then asked the convention to give the silver men the two-thirds supermajority they sought. The committee had voted to replace four Michigan gold delegates with silver men, giving silver a majority of the delegation and, because it was bound by unit rule, control of all of Michigan's 26 votes. Gold men were enraged at the theft.[25]

Combined with recognizing Bryan's silver Nebraskans, giving each territory six, rather than two, delegates, and now taking over Michigan would mean a total shift of 50 votes away from gold toward silver, giving the white metal men two-thirds of the convention delegates.[26]

A fierce debate ensued. Gold men argued there had been no protests or challenges at the Michigan convention itself and the national delegates had been elected by big margins. The state Credentials Committee of seven gold and five silver men had unanimously approved its roll.[27]

Even some silver men saw this as a raw power grab to steal the gold men's legitimate Michigan victory. Delaware's John F. Saulsbury, a Free Silver man, called it "an injustice." One of the seated Michigan silver delegates warned, "We have got enough votes in this Convention to nominate a free silver candidate by two-thirds majority without committing highway robbery."[28]

Their pleas didn't matter. Though 42 silver delegates backed seating the Michigan gold men, the convention voted 558 to 368 to throw them out and end the hopes of honest-money Democrats for even the smallest measure of influence in the proceedings. Gold Democrats felt betrayed and abused and they had been. For many of them, this justified bolting.[29]

The evening's biggest demonstration erupted. Southern rebel yells mixed with Western Indian war whoops as silver delegates waved hats and flags and hurled insults at their gold neighbors on the floor. Three bands swung into action. One played "Dixie," further energizing the Southern silver men. A Bland banner was raised, turning up the volume of cheers as Free Silver celebrated its two-thirds majority—the 620 delegates needed to nominate a candidate. It had also created a substantial bloc of Eastern Democrats who were thinking now of abandoning the party.[30]

The clock was approaching ten, so Jones preferred to adjourn rather than present the platform. The debate on the platform was going to take hours and was better done when everyone was fresh. The convention adjourned.[31]

THE DAY HAD SET the landscape upon which the presidential candidates would now compete. Bland was still the front-runner, with Boies in second. Other candidates—Blackburn, Matthews, McLean, Pattison, Pennoyer, Sibley, Stevenson, Teller, and Tillman—were "lagging far in the rear," as the *Chicago Tribune* put it. Bryan wasn't mentioned.[32]

Still, Bryan had renewed confidence in his prospects. That night, *Rocky Mountain News* publisher Thomas M. Patterson lobbied him on behalf of Teller. Bryan responded that "it would be easier to bring disappointed Republicans over to the Democratic party than to carry the victorious Democrats" to a Republican candidate. Patterson then asked Bryan who the nominee would be and was taken aback when Bryan said he "had as good a chance . . . as anyone." Bryan had Nebraska, half the Indian Territory, on the second ballot and was sure there would be others. Patterson left amused at someone so brash.[33]

When Bryan and his wife were at dinner with Dr. Charles M. Rosser, their meal was disturbed by Bland and Boies men chanting their candidate's names on the Dearborn Street sidewalk outside the Saratoga Restaurant. "These people don't know it, but they will be cheering for me just this way tomorrow night," Bryan told his wife and his friend. "I will make the greatest speech of my life tomorrow in reply to Senator Hill."

Skeptical, Mary turned to Rosser and asked, "Don't you think that Mr. Bryan has a good chance to be nominated?" Before the Texas doctor could answer, Bryan said, "So that you may both sleep well tonight, I am going to tell you something. I am the only man who can be nominated. I am what they call 'the logic of the situation.'"[34]

CHAPTER 22

Cross of Gold

———◦———

The silver men "were looking for a Moses," and William Jennings Bryan might be him. That was how the *New York Evening Post's* Francis E. Leupp explained to two veteran political observers sitting next to him the story he was preparing to file that said Bryan was "looming up as a candidate." The two men were dumbfounded. Like most people at the convention, they didn't even know what Bryan looked like. Leupp had to point him out—the "youngish man with a smooth face, high forehead, and pronounced jaw . . . sucking on a lemon," preparing to close for the silver side in the platform debate. "If Bryan gets before them while they're in this condition, they're gone," he told them.[1]

As Senator Jones droned through the platform, provoking a reaction only when he said "The free and unlimited coinage of both silver and gold," Bryan sensed "weakness at the pit of my stomach." That sometimes happened before a big speech. Normally, he would lie down, but that was impossible. So he ventured to a concession stand for a sandwich and coffee. A *Kansas City Star* reporter whispered, "Who will be nominated?" Bryan told him, "Strictly confidential, not to be quoted for publication, I will be." The reporter laughed.[2]

One of the most erratic and divisive men in Chicago, Senator Tillman, opened the defense of the silver plank. Short and round with one good eye fiercely gleaming and a sunken cavity where his left one should have been, he gave a violent and angry fifty-minute speech. "I come from the South—from the home of secession." Hisses filled the room, and when

270

they faded, Pitchfork Ben responded, "There are only three things in the world that hiss—a goose, a serpent, and a man." Unrepentant, he said that in 1860 South Carolina "led the fight in the Democratic party which resulted in its disruption." "That disruption of that party brought about the war. That war emancipated the black slaves. We are now leading a fight to emancipate the white slaves." Tillman was comfortable forcing another "disruption" to end Northeastern dominance of the Democratic Party. The South and West were now united: the currency question had become "a sectional issue." As he uttered these words, much of the hall hissed loudly. Cupping his hands to better scream his insults, Tillman assailed Cleveland as "undemocratic and tyrannical" and guilty of "usurpations of authority deserving of impeachment." He closed by calling for Democrats to "unite the disjointed and contending or jealous elements in the ranks of the silver people."[3]

Nothing in his speech made unity seem likely. Tillman, however, did set the stage for Bryan to make silver a national cause. The *Atlanta Constitution*'s editor Clark Howell, a Georgia delegate, scrawled a note to Bryan on an envelope. "You have now the opportunity of your life in concluding the argument for the majority report. Make a big, broad, patriotic speech that will leave no taste of sectionalism in the mouth and which will give a sentiment that will touch a responsive chord in the heart of the whole country. You can make the hit of your life." Bryan scribbled back, "You will not be disappointed. . . . I will speak the sentiment of my heart."[4]

Jones unexpectedly returned to the stage to disavow Tillman. "I am a Southern man," he said. "I and those who feel as I do know that it is not sectional—it is confined neither to section, country, or clime—it is the cause of mankind." For a few minutes, the hall was united, as even gold men cheered.[5]

Senator Hill offered the minority case, batting away Tillman's insults, saying, "I am a Democrat: but I am not a revolutionist." New York received "our Democracy from our fathers, and not from South Carolina." Every delegate favored using gold and silver, he said. The question was "between international bimetallism and local bimetallism." America could not attain bimetallism alone.[6]

Hill broadened his attack, asking why the income tax was now a test of "Democratic loyalty." Why assail the Supreme Court? Why support term limits for judges when "our Democratic fathers" wrote lifetime tenure into the Constitution? The silver men howled abuse. "If we keep in the good old paths of the party, we can win. If we depart from them we shall lose the great contest which awaits us." Reporters called it "the ablest and most logical speech" of Hill's life and said, "If reason could have swayed the convention Mr. Hill would have compelled by his speech a merciless revision of the platform." But it lacked an audience interested in compromise.[7]

Wisconsin senator William F. Vilas followed as sound money's second advocate, with an incoherent speech that chewed up time, causing Governor Russell to fear that his remarks, the final minority address, would be cut short. Bryan heard Russell complain and suggested each side get ten minutes more. Hill agreed. "I cannot say that it was entirely unselfish on my side," Bryan later admitted. "I needed it for the speech I was to make." What seemed to have been a minor change Bryan later called an "unexpected bit of good fortune." It was.[8]

As Russell appeared onstage, the clean-shaven former Massachusetts governor knew the fight was lost. "There is but one thing left to us," he said, "and that is the voice of protest." Great principles were being discarded and "new and radical leadership" was insisting on "a new and a radical policy." Ahead was "the darkness of defeat and disaster" in the fall, which would bring renewal based on principles the minority advocated. Josephus Daniels later wrote that it was the "the great speech of the convention," except for the one that followed. Russell would die a week later of heart failure while fishing in Canada. He was thirty-nine.[9]

Bryan was the final speaker on the platform debate and in a position to stampede the convention, but only because of an improbable chain of seven accidents. The first occurred on Monday when the DNC voted to provisionally seat the gold Nebraska men. That kept Bryan from being selected temporary chairman: he was not a delegate at the time of the election, and therefore he was ineligible. If he had been chosen, he wouldn't have closed the currency debate.

The second was when other presidential candidates blocked him for the permanent chairmanship. They didn't want him to have the exposure, no matter how unlikely a candidate he was. If he had been permanent chairman, he would not have been the platform's floor manager.

Bryan had four more lucky breaks Wednesday. The convention asked him to speak, but he was in Credentials. Jones asked Bryan to be silver's manager on the currency fight because the Nebraskan hadn't yet spoken.

Tillman insisted on opening the debate, leaving Bryan to close. And because the Resolutions report was held overnight, Bryan had time to prepare his pitch-perfect summary. The final accident that made possible Bryan's success was Russell's complaint that resulted in increasing Bryan's time. It is hard to see how Bryan could have had the same impact if he had been forced to cut his remarks by a third.

If any of the seven breaks had played out another way, it is unlikely Bryan would have stepped on the stage to move a party with a thirty-minute speech that no one who heard it would ever forget.

The chair called for "Honorable William J. Bryan, of Nebraska." The poet Edgar Lee Masters said Bryan "sprang" from his seat and moved vigorously toward the stage, taking stairs two at a time and striding quickly to the podium. As the crowd cheered and Nebraskans waved red bandanas, Bryan stood erect, wavy hair brushed back, left hand on the lectern, right hand up with palm open, jaw forward, head back, a tall, clean-shaven young man in a short black coat, trousers that bagged at the knees, low-cut vest, white shirt, and string tie. Frenzied delegates chanted "Bryan, Bryan, Bryan! What's the matter with Bryan?" The chairman reminded him of the time limits; Bryan put his pocket watch on the podium. He had no notes, having memorized his speech or at least its outline.[10]

In a slow, conversational tone that caused his audience to lean forward and listen intently, Bryan began on a note of humility. "It would be presumptuous, indeed, to present myself against the distinguished gentlemen to whom you have listened if this were but a measuring of ability; but this is not a contest among persons." Bryan argued Free Silver was more important than any person. "The individual is but an atom; he is born, he acts, he dies but principles are eternal." He called the issue "the cause of humanity," its outcome dependent on "a contest of principles" greater than any that voters had decided.[11]

Bryan's voice was powerful, clear, and resonant. Daniels felt "the man on the farthest seat in the great auditorium could hear his every word" even though Bryan "did not seem to raise his voice at all." Bryan spotted Governor Hogg to his left and Ollie James, a Kentucky delegate, on his right, both big men with clean-shaven, open faces, watching him intently and smiling. Focusing on them made him feel he was speaking to two friends. "My nervousness left me instantly," Bryan wrote later.[12]

This battle, he explained, had been joined with his 1895 congressional

Free Silver manifesto, followed by the formation of the Bimetallic DNC that sought "to take charge of and control the policy of the Democratic party." This had been achieved "with a zeal approaching the zeal which inspired the crusaders." This had been disruptive. "Old leaders had been cast aside" and "new leaders have sprung up to give direction to this cause of freedom." "A question of principle" had sparked conflict. Silver had won. Bryan was not attempting to convert anyone: that contest was over.[13]

He dismissed fears of sound-money men that Free Silver "shall disturb your business interests," saying their definition of a businessman was "too limited." They should think more broadly. "The man who is employed for wages is as much a business man as is his employer. The attorney in a country town is as much a business man as the corporation counsel in a great metropolis. The merchant of the crossroads store is as much a business man as the merchant of New York. The farmer who goes forth in the morning and toils all day . . . is as much a business man as the man who goes upon the Board of Trade and bets upon the price of grain." Each sentence brought shouts as Bryan milked it for applause. Rosser was in the gallery next to a skeptical farmer who had been leaving when Bryan took the stage but was caught by the Nebraskan's words and stayed. After Bryan declared, "The miners who go a thousand feet into the earth . . . are as much business men as the few financial magnates who in a back room corner the money of the world," the farmer threw his hat in the air, yelling, "My God! My God! My God!" as cheers rang through the hall and the galleries looked like a snowstorm because of the waving handkerchiefs. Someone screamed, "Go after them, Willie," driving the Coliseum into a deeper frenzy.[14]

Free Silver was the cause of this broad class of working Americans, Bryan declared. These Western and Southern "hardy pioneers" were in no mood to bargain with Easterners in big cities, home to a money power that "scorned" and "disregarded" and "mocked" ordinary people. "We beg no longer, we entreat no more; we petition no more. We defy them!" All but the gold men stood and screamed their agreement. Then Bryan dismissed Vilas's fears of revolution and defended the income tax by saying Free Silver men stood with Jackson "against the encroachments of aggregated wealth." The income tax was not unconstitutional ("read the dissenting opinions," he snapped), but "a just law." He suggested Hill's international bimetallic agreement would never be signed because other major powers "don't want it at all," causing laughter and cheers. After he opposed national banks issuing their own notes, he paused as if he were finished. Cries of "Go on! Go on!" rang out.[15]

Bryan did. Why was currency more important than protection? Because while "protection has slain its thousands the gold standard has slain its tens of thousands." The Republicans picked "the man who used to boast he looked like Napoleon." It was a cheap shot: admirers, not McKinley, came up with the "Napoleon of Protection," but when Bryan said the Major "was nominated on the anniversary of the battle of Waterloo" and faced similar imminent defeat, the crowd hurled abuse at the GOP standard-bearer. Rather than attack McKinley more, Bryan said "no private character, however pure, no personal popularity, however great, can protect from the avenging wrath of an indignant people the man who will either declare that he is in favor of fastening the gold standard upon the people, or who is willing to surrender the right of self-government and place legislative power in the hands of foreign potentates and powers." At that, men screamed at the top of their lungs, waving wildly whatever they could. It was so loud Bryan could not continue. He raised his hand and begged for quiet, saying, "I have only ten minutes left." Had he not had those extra minutes, he might never have delivered his most effective lines.[16]

While Republicans say they believe "the gold standard is a good thing," he said, "their platform pledges . . . to get rid of the gold standard, and substitute bimetallism" by international agreement, a contradiction he ridiculed. Bryan proclaimed this "a struggle between the holders of idle capital and the struggling masses who produce the wealth and pay the taxes."[17]

Bryan argued, "There are two ideas of government." Republicans believed "if you just legislate to make the well-to-do prosperous," then "their prosperity will leak through on those below." Democrats believed "if you legislate to make the masses prosperous their prosperity will find its way up and through every class that rests upon it." He identified Free Silver with rural and small town America, saying the populated East favored gold, but "those great cities rest upon these broad and fertile prairies. Burn down your cities and leave our farms, and your cities will spring up again as if by magic. But destroy our farms and the grass will grow in the streets of every city in the country." The farmers, stock raisers, small town lawyers, planters, and provincial shopkeepers of the West and South cheered, but this appeal to a rural America that was giving way to a great industrial power in bright, big cities would not help in the general election. Already, about a quarter of Americans lived in those cities Bryan just disparaged.[18]

"It is the issue of 1776 over again," he said as he came to his close. America will not wait for permission from other nations to have Free Silver. "We shall restore bimetallism, and then let England have bimetallism because the United States have." "If they"—the money power—"dare to come out and in the open defend the gold standard as a good thing, we shall fight to the uttermost." It was time for the line he had used on the House floor and found so effective at the Crete Chautauqua. As he said, "You shall not press down upon the brow of labor this crown of thorns"— he moved his hands down the sides of his head, his fingers slowly drawing invisible spikes about his temples, blood dripping from the scratches. He then proclaimed, "You shall not crucify mankind on a cross of gold," arms thrust out at right angles, chest forward, and head back, the crucified man personified. He held this pose for a few moments, then his arms fell to his sides, he stepped back, and his chin dropped. A second or so later, he straightened, turned, and walked off the stage, the hall in what the *Atlanta Constitution* called "fearful silence."[19]

The Coliseum was quiet a moment more and then exploded. Men and women jumped on their chairs screaming, arms and fists striking at the air. Hats sailed skyward or were waved along with handkerchiefs, flags, canes, fans, umbrellas, newspapers, and coats, anything that could be grabbed and flourished. "I had never dreamed that a mortal man could so grip and fill with enthusiasm thousands of men," Daniels later wrote. The floor and galleries were a mass of "frenzied throngs" of "shouters . . . besides themselves."[20]

A Texas delegate—W. W. Gatewood—took his state's standard and made his way to the Nebraska delegation, where he waved it frantically next to the Cornhusker State's. Tennessee's standard quickly joined them. Other delegates carried their standards toward Nebraska in solidarity. Altgeld forbade the removal of his state's marker, but when Bland's Missouri standard appeared next to Nebraska's, he allowed the Prairie State's to be grabbed from Hinrichsen and rushed toward the others. A roar went up. Soon all but the eleven gold states' standards were massed around Nebraska's, a clutch of purple sticks pumped wildly up and down. Altgeld "looked savage" as Illinois delegates took part in the Bryan demonstration.[21]

One journalist described the screaming in the Coliseum as louder than a "volley of siege cannons." A dozen men—among them a twenty-one-year-old Georgian named James T. Hill, the convention's youngest delegate—rushed the Nebraska delegation, hoisted Bryan on their shoulders, and paraded him through aisles jammed with frenzied delegates violently grasping at the young orator. His bearers eventually tired, leaving him to stand on a chair where everyone in the hall could see him. The standards formed a conga line behind South Carolina's and wove their way round the floor as delegates and guests, frantic and wild, responded to what they had just heard. Two bands played different tunes, making it impossible to hear either. Men and women screamed, wept, and bellowed, with roar after maniacal roar crashing into the air until eventually, everyone was emotionally spent and order was restored with difficulty. When exhausted delegates and guests took their chairs, Saulsbury of Delaware stood on his and gave three cheers for Bryan, to which someone in the gallery yelled, "What's the matter with Bryan for president?" [22]

Clarence Darrow, later Bryan's adversary at the Scopes Trial in 1925, had never seen an audience so moved. "Mr. Bryan told the Democratic convention what he believed," the Chicago lawyer later wrote. "They listened with desires and hopes, and genuinely with absolute confidence and trust. Here was a political Messiah who was to lift the burdens that the oppressed had borne so long." Even Altgeld was impressed, admitting, "That is the greatest speech I have ever listened to." Then he asked Darrow, "What did he say, anyhow?" [23]

Bryan later recalled Daniel Webster's maxim that the "essentials for a successful speech are eloquence, the subject, and the occasion." Bryan felt he had the last two: Free Silver was an issue of "transcendent importance" and the moment the climax of "a revolt in the Democratic Party—a fight won by the rank and file against all the power of the Administration, and of the power of the big corporations and the metropolitan press." Modesty kept him from crediting his own eloquence, yet his success was the result of skill, practice, and a keen sense for what his audience wanted to hear, as well as seven lucky accidents. [24]

This speech aimed to rally the silver base, not to persuade ("We beg no longer, we entreat no more; we petition no more. We defy them!"). Bryan was speaking to true believers. He treated political opponents as enemies ("In this campaign there is not a spot of ground upon which the enemy will dare to challenge battle"); deployed the language of civil war ("In this contest brother has been arrayed against brother"); used military metaphors ("We are fighting in the defense of our homes"); compared silver Democrats to Christian crusaders (They "began the conflict with a zeal approaching the zeal which inspired the crusaders who followed Peter the Hermit"); and pitted class against class ("Upon the side of the idle holders of idle capital, or upon the side of the struggling masses?"). From the start, he was defiant. It was masterful, memorable, and effective.[25]

Other campaigns knew Bryan had upended their calculations. "Boys, we are lost," said a Missouri delegate. "It looks that way," replied Senator George G. Vest, who was to nominate Bland. Defections began. Georgia, which Bland had counted on, caucused after adjournment and decided to go for Bryan. Alabama appeared moving toward Bryan, and Bland's managers in Lebanon, Missouri, received wires that they were bleeding support elsewhere. A reporter was probably correct: "Had the vote been taken immediately at the conclusion of his speech," Bryan "would have been undoubtedly nominated by acclamation."[26]

Delegates approached Bryan and Nebraska allies to pledge their support or ask questions that worried them. One asked, "Did he drink to excess?" and was relieved to learn he abstained. Had Bryan declared he would not support a gold candidate? Yes, he had, an answer that pleased the questioner. Later, as Bryan left the Coliseum, someone gave him a rabbit foot, saying "Keep it, Mr. Bryan. It will bring you good luck."[27]

The votes on the platform and its rejection of Cleveland went fast. Gold took all the votes of 11 states and most in 4 others. Silver took all the votes in 33 states and territories and most in 3 more. It was the first convention vote since Michigan had been stolen: silver men now had more than two-thirds of the delegates, giving them control over the nomination if they could unite on a candidate.[28]

When delegates returned that evening, the arc lights made the hall stifling hot. There was a crush at the entrances. It was tough to create the semblance of order, despite the police detail being doubled. The galleries were disorderly and gold men appeared to be overrepresented. Every chair was taken and hundreds clamored outside for tickets.[29]

The roll call for presidential nominations began. Arkansas yielded to Missouri to place Bland in nomination. Senator Vest stressed Bland's decades as "the living, breathing embodiment of the silver cause," but he could not be "heard ten feet away" because of his weak voice and the unruly crowd. Delegates chanted "Bryan, Bryan, W. J. Bryan." Vest's remarks fell flat until he closed by rhyming that "Give us Silver Dick / and silver quick / And we will make McKinley sick / In the ides of next November."[30]

Hal T. Lewis, a lawyer and soon-to-be Georgia supreme court justice, took the stage when Georgia was called. He had only five minutes to prepare, but he was ready. "I did not intend to make a speech," he said, but simply nominate "a distinguished citizen, whose very name is an earnest of success." He has stood "among the leaders of the Democratic hosts like Saul among the Israelites, head and shoulders above the rest." This man "needs no speech to introduce him . . . no encomium to commend him," the young lawyer said. "I refer, fellow citizens, to William J. Bryan, of Nebraska." "Like a geyser," a *New York Times* reporter observed, "the enthusiasm spouted boiling hot" in a huge demonstration, almost the equal of the one following Bryan's speech that morning. The Nebraskan's supporters screamed, cheered, paraded, and waved anything they could as two bands played simultaneously. Someone let loose with blasts from a foghorn they'd smuggled into the hall. Lewis waited ten minutes but with no sign of the spectacle abating, he left the stage. No more words were needed. The hall was awash with Bryan's name as delegates and guests shouted, cheered, and applauded. Bryan, however, was not in the hall. He was lying on his bed at the Clifton, exhausted from the past days' exertions and his morning speech.[31]

Senator Turpie then nominated Indiana governor Claude Matthews, in the evening's longest speech. The near octogenarian, shaking from age, barely glanced up from his text when he read. As he droned on, a joker yelled, "I nominate Cleveland!," causing three cheers for the president. Iowa was next and former representative Frederick White took the podium, emphasizing Horace Boies's record as governor and trying to make a virtue of the Iowan's lack of pizzazz. "There would be "no rockets sent up . . . no sensational performances" with Uncle Horace as president. The lengthy, dry, and defensive address led to a perfunctory demonstration that was sputtering out until a piercing scream came from the gallery.[32]

Dressed in white from hat to shoes, twenty-two-year-old Minnie Murray, publisher of the Nashua, Iowa, *Free Silver Reporter* and a Boies supporter, was "swaying, jumping, clapping her hands" and standing on a chair and shrieking "Boies! Boies! Boies!" Her antics soon attracted the hall's attention. Someone thrust a small flag into her hands. She swung it vigorously until the shaft broke. The yells increased. A larger flag was handed to her. An Iowa delegate carrying a giant Boies banner made his way from the floor to her side, jumping over press tables and the rail dividing the floor from the gallery and pushing against people jammed in the aisles. His approach led the woman in white to more frantic exertions. When the Boies flag reached her, she waved it but it was too heavy. The flag bearer convinced her and her fiancé to go to the convention floor, where she ran around, cheered by the crowd, until she dropped from exhaustion. The "Lady in White" was the evening's sensation, not her candidate.[33]

Bryan fell asleep just before 11 p.m. There was a stack of telegrams when he awoke half an hour later, leading him to remark, "Well, I see they are still at it. They are certainly the most remarkable set of people."[34]

All that was left were favorite sons and a gold standard-bearer. Kentucky nominated its U.S. senator Joseph C. S. Blackburn. Ohio offered publisher John McLean, whose attraction was his personal wealth that could pay for the campaign.[35]

Alienated, gold Democrats did not offer a candidate. Massachusetts wanted to name Russell, but he declined "because of the platform." New Jersey "does not desire to nominate any man upon the platform of this Convention." New York had no candidate. Neither did Pennsylvania, but it would have something to say when it came time to voting. The convention adjourned after midnight. It would be a short night for delegates.[36]

Bland had spent the day at his farm, overseeing the painting of a side porch and ruminating with a reporter over a wild rabbit infestation. He summoned a doctor, saying he was "feeling very nervous and wanted something to 'brace him up.'" Dr. McCombs asked, "Do you think you will be nominated?" Bland laconically answered, "Yes, I am sure of it. I do not want it but it seems to be coming my way."[37]

Hogg and Jones pressured Bryan to let the balloting start that night. Bryan demurred, saying, "If the people want me nominated and that feeling could not endure overnight, it would perish before the campaign was a week old." He told reporters "the convention is in the control of sincere friends of free silver and I am willing to trust their judgment whether they vote now or next week."[38]

· · ·

RISING TEMPERATURES REPLACED COOL breezes overnight. Delegates and guests, "tired and weary" from their late Thursday night, cooled themselves with fans, waving them more frantically as the Coliseum grew hotter. The hall was also more crowded as scalpers had been selling an "unlimited supply" of passes.[39]

Senator White gaveled the convention to order at 11 a.m., introduced the invocator, accepted the nominations of former governors Robert E. Pattison of Pennsylvania and Sylvester Pennoyer of Oregon, and ordered the first ballot. It took five, but it was still over in a relatively short time.[40]

With 620 needed for the nomination, Bland led on the first ballot but with only 235 votes. Bryan followed at 137. The news was telegraphed to Lincoln, Nebraska. A crowd had gathered around the Democratic headquarters before 10 a.m., jamming the storefront and spilling onto the streets. Someone lit a match in the office, not knowing there was a gas leak. The blast shattered windows, knocked people down, and singed one man, but didn't discourage Bryan's neighbors from clamoring for the latest news.[41]

Many gold men were abstaining. Whitney sat in the New York delegation, looking at the ceiling and fanning himself vigorously as former governor Flower announced "in view of the platform adopted by this convention and of its actions and proceedings . . . we decline to further participate." Silver men chanted, "Put 'em out!" When Bryan gained more than Bland did on the second ballot and closed the gap, Whitney told reporters, "I am going home."[42]

Silver Dick ran out of steam on the third ballot and the fourth ballot sealed his fate. Surrounded by angry, agitated delegates pointing and gesticulating, Alabama's chairman paused ten seconds—an eternity in this setting—before announcing his state was moving from Bland to Bryan. Pandemonium broke out. A new banner popped up: BRYAN, BRYAN: NO CROWN OF THORNS, NO CROSS OF GOLD. After the chairman refused their request for time to consult, Illinois delegates had voted for Bland before leaving the hall to confer while the fourth ballot was being tabulated. Hinrichsen and others were pushing hard for a switch to Bryan. The conference was acrimonious.[43]

When the clerks finished their tally, Bryan had moved into first place while Bland's total dropped. A huge demonstration erupted when delegates figured out Bryan was the front-runner. "The hall was a howling mob," wrote a *Chicago Tribune* reporter, "and not a living soul could hear a word." Virginia's Carter Glass wrestled with another Bryan man for the state's standard, before realizing they backed the same man. Governor Hogg got in a fistfight with Representative George B. McClellan Jr. over New York's standard. Bryan supporters were soon parading standards from twenty-five states around the floor.

Bryan quietly told reporters the contest was over. An Illinois delegate emerged from the conference room, grabbed the state emblem, and joined the Bryan conga parade on the floor. Bryan men cheered, believing it signaled Illinois was theirs. By now Bland knew his numbers were falling. When a front-runner drops, it's impossible to resume upward movement.[44]

Before moving to the next ballot, White announced he was "about to enforce" that "two-thirds of the vote given" will nominate the candidate for president. That meant if 160 gold men abstained, then 512 votes were needed for the nomination. Illinois, Ohio, and West Virginia all passed on the fifth ballot, leaving Bryan a hundred votes short. The secretary returned to states that had passed and called for Illinois. Waving his gray hat over his head, Hinrichsen said, "Illinois's 48-votes for William J. Bryan" as Altgeld sat glowering. That broke the dam. McLean stood on his chair and frantically waved his hickory cane. Recognized by White, he cast Ohio's 46 votes for Bryan. The Nebraskan was now at 497, just shy of a two-thirds majority.[45]

Governor Stone signaled White. Knowing what was coming, delegates and guests were "in an uproar" as the Missourian appeared onstage. The hall quieted as everyone strained to hear Stone read a letter Bland had given him days earlier and had just telegraphed Stone to deliver. If his candidacy would obstruct the nomination of a free coinage man then "I wish my name at once unconditionally withdrawn from further consideration," Bland had written. "The cause must be put above the man."[46]

The hall was drenched in noise as excited delegates and guests screamed, stamped their feet, and waved anything they could while the band played "Dixie." As delegates yelled "Let Georgia lead!" the Peach Tree standard led a parade of other guidons around the hall as bands played "Marching Through Georgia" and "15,000 men, all on their feet, cheered and waved and kicked like howling dervishes." [47]

Bryan received the news in his Clifton Hotel room and then went to the barbershop for a shave. A reporter found him tilted back in the chair, face covered in lather. Once he'd been shaved, Bryan shook the reporter's hand and said, "In order that I may have no ambition but to discharge faithfully the duties of the office, I desire to announce that if elected I shall under no circumstances be a candidate for re-election." When he returned to his suite, he pulled from his pocket the good-luck charm he had been given the day before and told reporters, "That's what comes from having a rabbit's foot." [48]

CHAPTER 23

Change Course or Fail

————◦►————

T he McKinley men gloated over Bryan's nomination. They could not
believe that anyone so young, inexperienced, and extreme had won
the Democratic nomination. Bryan's Chicago platform was a direct assault
on the sitting president of his party, alienating Cleveland's supporters and
splitting the Democratic Party.

McKinley and the Republican managers did not grasp how Bryan
and Free Silver were already roiling the GOP in Midwestern and Western
states, and were slow to meet the threat.

JULY 10 FOUND HANNA visiting McKinley in Canton when the telegraph
in an upstairs room clattered with news from Chicago. Grinning broadly,
Hanna spoke to reporters on the porch, saying, "Bryan's nomination is the
best that could have been made for Republican success." This was more
than campaign bravado. Hanna believed that Bryan lacked the maturity
and stature of Democrats like Bland, and that his platform would "bring
disaster" as a document more in line with the views of the Populists than
the conservative, small-government agenda Democrats had run on before.
McKinley stood silently at his side, smiling.[1]

The next afternoon, McKinley framed the election in prepared remarks
to a visiting Cleveland group. It was the most important contest since the
Civil War, "a struggle to preserve the financial honor of the Government."

Democrats would "debase" the currency, making impossible investments "in productive enterprises which furnish employment to American labor." The Major offered "a sound policy . . . which will give encouragement and confidence to all," namely protection. McKinley believed it was the campaign's most important economic issue and that voters would be drawn to his tariff policies because they would raise wages, create jobs, and furnish "adequate revenues" for the federal government.[2]

The McKinley men were ignoring the political reality. Bryan's selection created a new dynamic. He carried little of the baggage that better-known Democrats were saddled with because of the depression. By explicitly repudiating Cleveland's hard-money policies, Bryan separated Democrats from the depression and the unpopular Democrat in the White House on whose watch it happened, undermining Republican arguments that the country needed to change the party that controlled the presidency in order to restore prosperity. Bryan was also identified with a policy that many Americans buried in debt felt would help them—expanding the money supply by coining all available silver at a ratio of 16-to-1. Inflating the currency would effectively reduce the value of the debts Americans owed. Farmers especially understood that Free Silver would let them pay off merchant or bank loans and mortgages with cheaper dollars. This was in sharp contrast to what McKinley was offering: higher tariffs that would furnish the government, not farmers, with needed revenues and thereby increase business confidence. Bryan was making an appeal directly to millions of people who felt aggrieved in a tough economy. McKinley was appealing to businessmen, a smaller group that Bryan's voters often resented, instead of the broader mass of voters.

Hanna could tell reporters, "With a tariff sufficient to fill the public treasury we shall hear the last of free silver talk," but that did not convince many voters who felt that Bryan's plan promised real relief for them. Laborers liked protection, but Free Silver was popular in farm country and cities devastated by depression. Both parties were calling for change, but for the moment, the Democratic plan had the edge.[3]

TO BEAT BRYAN'S MESSAGE and develop a winning general election strategy, McKinley needed a strong GOP Executive Committee. But it took a month of deliberation before Hanna announced the committee on July 13. There were six Midwesterners (counting Hanna), three Easterners, a border state man, and a Southerner.[4]

Executive Committee members had been euphoric over Bryan's nomination, but their enthusiasm had dissipated when they met in July 15 in Cleveland. They now realized they faced a tough fight. The men loosened ties, shed coats, and sat in shirtsleeves, fanning themselves against the heat as they discussed the situation. The Electoral College looked bad. Bryan would carry the South, and probably the border states that had voted Democratic since 1872. Republican defections jeopardized virtually all the West and Plains states. If Bryan carried those, he needed to carry only Illinois or any two other Midwestern states up for grabs—Indiana, Iowa, Michigan, Minnesota, or Wisconsin—and he would have the White House.[5]

If the GOP took Ohio and every state north and east of it, McKinley would have 139 electoral votes, well short of the 224 needed for victory. And that total included three battlegrounds Democrats won in 1892—Connecticut, New Jersey, and New York. Ohio was also always close. It was a sobering moment for the McKinley men.

The committee's first big decision was where to place the campaign's headquarters. Rather than have one, the committee settled on headquarters in both Chicago and New York. Hanna said the two offices would be of "equal power, importance and scope," but that was unrealistic. Chicago would be the principal headquarters. The Midwest was the battleground and Illinois its epicenter. It made little sense to direct the fight there from over seven hundred miles away in Manhattan. It was from Chicago that most speakers were dispatched and boxcars of literature printed. The Executive Committee agreed pamphlets and other material were needed, but felt little urgency about everything else. Speakers, rallies, and the rest of the campaign could wait until September.

When asked who was in charge, Hanna replied he would "be in the saddle, so to speak, and be found in both places." "There is no person in charge in either New York or Chicago except myself," he told reporters in a display of ego. "I am responsible for every detail of this campaign." In reality, it was impossible for Hanna to be "responsible for every detail." In the 118 days left until the election, he would spend 70 of them away from Chicago, mostly in New York and Cleveland. Hanna would function as the campaign's chairman, spending most of his time raising money and tamping down intraparty fights.[6]

The campaign's manager was Charles G. Dawes, McKinley's choice to lead the Chicago headquarters. The thirty-year-old would run the campaign's operations, supervise the staff, build its organization, direct its flood of materials, and target key voter groups.[7]

Dawes took seriously the directive McKinley gave him after the Executive Committee meeting that he was "responsible for *all* funds spent in the campaign." This effectively put Dawes in charge of the campaign, subject to McKinley and Hanna's direction and the Executive Committee's formal decisions. By his fourth day on the job, Dawes was "beginning to realize the great responsibilities and burden of my position."[8]

With his customary meticulous attention to detail, Dawes applied business practices to politics, perfecting a system to track the campaign's cash, pledges, payments, and obligations. He hired bookkeepers to run the system and updated McKinley and Hanna with reports. He also required competitive bids, telling Osborne "everybody seemed, at first, to have the idea that they could rob the Committee on the matter of contracts, but we have gotten them over that feeling."[9]

Within days, Dawes was organizing groups for veterans, black voters, Germans, first-time voters, insurance agents, and women (who could vote in Colorado, Utah, and Wyoming). The National League of Republican Clubs, a businessman's group, and the American College Republican League were both drawn into close coordination. The College League was especially well organized in the Midwest. Dawes even had a group for the latest craze—bicycles. A McKinley "Wheelmen" organization recruited young men who had taken up riding bikes. Each department had a director and staff with an action plan and budget, both monitored by Dawes.[10]

He put a priority on organizing traveling salesmen, who came in contact with many small business owners as they zigzagged around the country selling their wares. They were effective communicators and knew from personal experience sound money's importance and the absence of business confidence.

Since McKinley's team expected to run a campaign of persuasion, William M. Hahn and Perry S. Heath were key players. Hahn had run Harrison's speakers bureau in 1892 and now managed a growing horde of McKinley orators, some paid for their appearances. These included foreign-language speakers and experts in farm and labor outreach.

Heath, a forty-one-year-old editor who wore old-fashioned high collars, had handled Harrison's public relations in 1888. This time the Indianan was responsible for every printed piece the campaign distributed, as well as a news bureau that churned out statements and, once a week, ready-to-use printing plates with articles, photos, and drawings. These went to small town newspapers with a combined readership estimated at three million but that lacked the money and technology to prepare these items themselves. Heath had big responsibilities: within weeks, the pressure was so intense he nearly had a breakdown.[11]

The committee did not deal with the question of whether McKinley would stay in Canton for the election's duration or take to the trail. It had been customary for presidential candidates to stay largely out of sight while surrogates waged the campaign, but Hanna told McKinley, "You've got to stump or we'll be defeated." The Major replied, "I cannot take the stump against that man." He knew he would be unable to match Bryan's flashy show or pace. So Hanna sent Herrick to lobby McKinley, who told the Cleveland banker it would be an "acknowledgement of weakness" to stump since he had already announced he wouldn't. Besides, it was unpresidential and counterproductive. "I might just as well put up a trapeze on my front lawn and compete with some professional athlete as go out speaking with Bryan. I have to *think* when I speak."[12]

McKinley also refused Dawes, explaining, "If I took a whole train, Bryan would take a sleeper. If I took a chair car, he would ride a freight train. I can't outdo him, and I am not going to try." By late July, the Major had had enough, telling the press that "during the heat of the campaign, I will pass the time quietly with my wife at our home."[13]

Despite McKinley's desire to be a traditional candidate who waited in silence for the nation's decision, people kept showing up in Canton, some invited, some with advance notice, and some without warning. One day it was several hundred Republican women, accompanied by a women's brass band. The next day, more than a thousand Union Civil War vets, accompanied by squads of uniformed horsemen and a military band, marched from the train station to the Major's lawn.[14]

One week, McKinley had hundreds of glassworkers arrive in Canton, followed by the University of Chicago GOP Club, led by its president,

Harold L. Ickes (later FDR's interior secretary), bearing a marble bust of the Major.[15]

After these were more glassworkers, this time from Pittsburgh, their union president saying, "We believe in bimetallism . . . the use of both gold and silver as money," and proclaiming their allegiance to protection. The day after that, four hundred veterans and tinplate workers braved a flooded rail line to travel to Canton.[16]

Crowds even followed McKinley. After a long-planned talk to Mount Union College students, the Major went to catch a train at the Alliance depot and found more than a thousand workmen waiting. He talked briefly about currency, channeling the speeches he had given labor men in his congressional campaigns, saying, "We want good prices and good wages, and when we have them we want them paid on good dollars."[17]

By July's end, McKinley felt he must reaffirm he would remain in Canton and not campaign despite Hanna's concerns and those of worried Republican leaders. But he and Ida were unlikely to have a quiet fall if people kept coming to Canton, disrupting his days and trampling his lawn. No one seemed to know what to do about it.[18]

What to do about currency was an even bigger unresolved issue for the Executive Committee. At their final mid-July planning session, the McKinley man met with Wisconsin representative Joseph W. Babcock, chairman of the GOP Congressional Committee, about coordinating efforts. While the Major's men wanted to focus on protection, congressional Republicans knew the country was on fire about Free Silver. Maine's senator Eugene Hale thought Bryan upended the campaign, writing, "The political situation was entirely changed by the Chicago performance. . . . We could have beaten an old-fashioned Democratic nomination and ticket without trying but the new movement has stolen our thunder."[19]

From Republicans on the election's front lines, Dawes and Heath learned well before McKinley and Hanna that the campaign's principal issue was the one the Major and his RNC chairman wished to avoid—silver. The headquarters was flooded with requests for literature and speakers on currency, not protection as McKinley and Hanna expected. Out of necessity, Heath's first pamphlet was on the money issue—a four-page appeal to miners, showing they were paid less in Free Silver countries.[20]

Hanna, too, was finally alarmed, canceling his vacation and writing to his brother-in-law, "The Chicago convention has changed everything."[21]

• • •

WHILE DAWES TOOK COMMAND in Chicago, Hanna headed to New York to open the headquarters there, organize the campaign in the East, and begin tapping the GOP's big donors in the city. There he would be forced to deal with two large problems. First, Hanna would have to decide who would lead New York—Platt's regular Republican organization or the state's McKinley League. The latter were well-meaning supporters of the Major whom the Easy Boss had generally whipped during the primary. Then Hanna would be forced to respond to Easterners who thought the campaign's most pressing issue was sound money, not protection.[22]

Wearing a light gray suit, a white vest with soft blue stripes, tan shoes, and a straw hat, Hanna pulled into Grand Central Terminal the morning of July 21 and caught a hack to the Waldorf. He then went with Osborne and Frederick Grant to the Metropolitan Life Insurance building at Twenty-Third Street and Madison Avenue. By twelve thirty, Hanna had settled on a suite of ten offices on the fourth floor of the Renaissance Revival marble office tower and returned to the Waldorf for lunch, where a Platt man grabbed him by his lapels and gabbed about a "proposition."[23]

When asked by reporters if currency would be the campaign's focus, he demurred and indicated protection would be more important. "The kind of money people are to have is an issue, but so is the need that money enough shall be raised by revenue to pay the expenses of the government," meaning the tariff.[24]

When asked by reporters whether he would visit the Easy Boss, he left the impression it was not a priority, saying, "I may see Mr. Platt." He then suggested he could talk with Platt about who would run New York "without getting in a fight" and mentioned some of Platt's archenemies in the GOP. Not a very auspicious start, especially when the state GOP chairman, Platt's man Charles Hackett, told reporters the party organization "is greased and in running order. It is at Mr. Hanna's disposal." All Hanna had to do was tell Platt he was in charge.[25]

That night, Hanna dined with Osborne, Senator Elkins, and Roosevelt. Though not a fan of Platt, Roosevelt knew the Easy Boss was necessary to carry New York, so he pressed Hanna to talk to Platt. Teddy was apparently persuasive, for Roosevelt wrote Platt that evening, "I do hope that you can arrange to see Mr. Hanna while he is in New York. I think

we have a big fight on our hands . . . we need to strain every nerve if we
want to win the struggle." Roosevelt may have written to Platt instead of
Hanna himself because Hanna could not let go of all his animosity toward
the Easy Boss. Roosevelt all but said as much when he wrote to Lodge the
same night that Hanna "feels rather sore with Platt, and not inclined to
call on Platt first; while Platt foolishly stands on a point of punctilio in
refusing to make the first advance."[26]

The big news came on Friday when Hanna sent a hand-carried letter
to Platt. Could they meet? The senator instantly accepted: he would come
when and wherever it was convenient. Platt's speed was likely prompted
by Hanna's press comment that the state and local party committees
would run the New York campaign, meaning Platt would be in charge.
Platt wanted to act before Hanna changed his mind, since the anti-Platt
faction would be angry at the RNC chairman's surrender. They met that
afternoon at Hanna's headquarters. Distrustful, Platt brought Hackett and
Edward Lauterbach along as witnesses.[27]

The Easy Boss liked what he heard: sound money would be the priority issue in New York and his regular party would run the Empire State
campaign. Platt declared the outcome "very satisfactory." When a reporter
jokingly asked if he had "been regenerated," Platt replied, "Yes, I have been
washed in the blood of the lamb." Hanna had taken Roosevelt's advice to
not let his distaste for Platt stand in the way of carrying New York. The
deal done, Platt told Hanna that the preliminary returns of a door-to-door
canvass suggested a 5 percent swing toward McKinley. Republicans had
lost the state in 1892 by 46 percent to 49 percent. If the canvass held up,
the GOP would carry it comfortably this time.[28]

Platt was happy, telling Governor Morton the arrangement "was em-
inently satisfactory" and chortling that Hanna's decision "has created
consternation in the rank of the 'Anti's' and yet . . . there was nothing
else for Mr. Hanna to do except to recognize the regular Organization." It
was a victory for the New York boss and McKinley's hopes for the White
House.[29]

Hanna spent four days in meetings before departing New York. He
settled on Cornelius N. Bliss as RNC treasurer, an opponent of Platt
whose appointment as chief fund-raiser placated the New York McKinley
League men. Party leaders in the East were desperate for money and urged
an aggressive education campaign of literature and speakers to combat

the free coinage sentiment immediately. With Quay in attendance, the Executive Committee discussed "the respective merits" of the protection and sound money but remained undecided about which to emphasize. The men did agree the campaign must focus on working-class voters, as McKinley himself had insisted in conversations with his inner circle. "It is the unanimous opinion of all of us here that our whole attention must be paid to the masses—to the laboring classes," Osborne reported to his cousin. "The people who have got property are all right and can take care of themselves."[30]

A chance meeting on Hanna's first night in New York with John Wanamaker, Harrison's postmaster general and a prodigious GOP fundraiser, paid off. The department store magnate invited Hanna to meet with Philadelphia's money elite on his way back to Ohio, first at the Stratford Hotel with several dozen major donors (including prominent sound-money Democrats) and a two-hour dinner with forty Republican big givers at the Union League before Hanna caught the overnight train home. A letter from Dawes was waiting, warning that the Illinois GOP was trying to "get off" with part of a large pledge from a railroad company. Only Hanna's intercession would keep Lorimer from snaking the money.[31]

Upon his return to Cleveland, Hanna told reporters that he thought "the outlook for McKinley" in the East was "very flattering." "Differences have been settled, misunderstandings explained and long-standing wounds healed." He had resolved the New York leadership question, begun raising money and established a working relationship with Quay, the most experienced Executive Committee member and Platt's man inside the McKinley apparatus. All that was important progress, but Hanna was still falling short in one critical area: the money he had raised was far less than what the campaign needed. He would have to return to New York soon, begging bowl in hand, and raise much more money.[32]

WHILE THE CAMPAIGN IN the East was going better with New York settled, McKinley's position out west continued deteriorating. The Monday after the Democratic convention, Teller and six silver Republican congressional colleagues emerged from five days of discussions in Colorado to formally endorse Bryan and the Democratic ticket and urge Republicans who felt "gold monometallism would be of lasting injury to the country" to join them, since McKinley had now endorsed "the same financial system . . . of Mr. Cleveland." The loss of such prominent elected leaders gave license for grassroots silver Republicans to follow them.[33]

There were troubling signs throughout the Midwest, too, with Republican defections in many states, particularly west of the Mississippi. Senator Gear reported to Harrison's confidant, Louis T. Michener, that "[w]e shall lose rafts of Republicans in Iowa." Former governor Merriam admitted that in Minnesota, "Free-silver talk is at flood tide now" and one of the state's congressmen warned the bolt of silver Republicans and the prospect of a fusion ticket there among silver men of all parties were real threats.[34]

It was not clear how much McKinley would benefit from the Democratic Party's divisions, either. There was neither a gold Democratic ticket nor a strong, high-profile Democratic voice that would call on sound-money Democrats to vote for McKinley. But if he won the Populist endorsement, Bryan was very likely to carry Midwestern states where Populism was strong, such as Kansas and Nebraska.[35]

Many Republicans continued pushing McKinley to confront the silver issue directly, knowing how dangerous it was to ignore or straddle. Roosevelt was one of them, writing his sister in late July that the only way McKinley could win was to make "the main fight . . . for sound finance." Senator Sherman was of a similar mind, urging McKinley to take "active measures" against Free Silver by deploying speakers on the currency question into battleground states. Still, the Major remained wedded to protection as his dominant issue, reminding Senator Elkins in late July that "we should not forget the overwhelming importance of the tariff issue" and telling a GOP congressional leader, "from this time out, there will be less agitation upon the silver question and more talk on the cardinal Republican doctrine of Protection."[36]

The Major was not yet ready to abandon his belief that the race was about protection, reminding Kohlsaat in early August that "thousands of men who are somewhat tinctured with Free Silver ideas keep within the Republican party and will support the Republican nominee, because of the fact that they are protectionists." Stress gold, and those Republicans—and perhaps the election—would be lost, McKinley felt.

McKinley responded to the American Protective Tariff League's Wilbur F. Wakeman, who was upset at the attention some Republicans—especially the Congressional Campaign Committee—were paying to silver. Patience, McKinley counseled, patience. "I am confident that the height of the silver agitation has been reached and that public sentiment is already traveling down the opposition of the hill," McKinley wrote. "Get your tariff army all ready for battle. There will be work for them to do." [37]

The McKinley men had laughed when they learned Bryan would be their opponent. They were now misjudging the appeal of Free Silver. If they did not realize their error and change course soon, McKinley could lose.

CHAPTER 24

Three Revolts

———◁◦▷———

To win the White House, the Democrats had to draw in Silver men from other parties, including the Republicans and Populists. Creating a unified white metal front would bust up the existing party system and vastly improve Bryan's chances for victory in November.

But the young Nebraskan's task was to be made difficult by three revolts. The first was among Democratic newspaper publishers. This emboldened Democratic gold men to revolt by backing McKinley, running a gold Democratic ticket, or staying home. The final revolt was among Populist allies willing to make him their presidential candidate, but on their terms. Handling all this wasn't going to be easy.

NOW THAT BRYAN WAS their candidate, Democrats faced two critical decisions—picking his running mate and winning the Populist Party's endorsement. To kick-start discussions on vice presidential possibilities, Senator Jones summoned a silver leader from each state. Bland was their favorite, but he did not want to be considered, nor did Boies. Senator Blackburn pushed for McLean, whose fortune could underwrite the campaign. He was surprised when the Buckeye State's Bimetallic DNC committeeman, Allen W. Thurman, declared his fellow Ohioan unreliable. Someone mentioned Arthur Sewall, a millionaire Maine shipbuilder with a ruddy face, thick gray mustache, thinning gray hair, and deep-set eyes. He owned banks and railroads and was reliably Free Silver, unusual for a businessman. An Easterner would help make Free Silver a national, not sectional, issue and his wealth could "supply the deficiency" in funding the campaign.

Bryan listened, saying little. Finally, Jones asked Bryan if as "the chosen leader," he had a preference. Rather than offer a name, Bryan dropped a bomb. He would decline the nomination if saddled with McLean. Calling him "an immoral man," Bryan said he would not sell "the party's birthright for his campaign money." The threat was received in silence. Bryan later observed it would be useful to have an Eastern running mate. Bryan participated in, but did not lead, the discussions about his vice president. The new presidential candidate would have to be stronger to bend the campaign to his desires.[1]

Senator White banged his gavel at 11 a.m. the next day. Half the Coliseum's 15,000 seats were empty and more than 250 delegates had departed, mostly gold men. Ten vice presidential nominations were offered. Only four mattered—Bland, McLean, former representative Joseph C. Sibley of Pennsylvania, and Sewall, whom Bryan now quietly supported. The rest were favorite sons or vanity nominations. Delegates swung wildly around for four ballots, with Sewall dropping to a handful of votes on the third ballot before the convention named him unanimously on the fifth.[2]

Sewall received word while boarding a train at the Sixty-Third Street Station for his hotel. After the third ballot, he thought he had lost. Dazed, he said the nomination was "wholly unexpected." While he had not met his running mate before the convention, Sewall thought Bryan "a very fine man." Astonished at the news, Sewall's neighbors in Bath, Maine, rang church bells, set tar barrels on fire, shot off cannons, and paraded around town led by a drum corps whose tunes were drowned out by fireworks and tin horns.[3]

THAT DAY, SENATOR JONES was elected DNC chairman, but only after Tillman demanded to know if he was "the choice of some secret caucus." There was a caucus of one—Bryan wanted the Arkansas senator to run his campaign. At Bryan's suggestion, the DNC voted to hold a notification rally in Madison Square Garden on July 21. Chicago was discussed as the headquarters and while the DNC didn't vote, the idea was well received. Jones disagreed, wanting Washington for the headquarters and a later date for the notification rally. He would eventually get the second, but not the first.[4]

Bryan spent two days arguing with the Notification Committee on when he would be formally notified in New York. The committee wanted more time to build a crowd. Rumors were the Madison Square Garden might slide into August, suggesting indecision when the party needed to be surging.

Bryan and Mary left Chicago at 2 p.m. on the Illinois Central. Declining the offer of a private car and special train, they took seats in an ordinary Pullman, headed for his birthplace of Salem, in southern Illinois. They had planned to stay a week, but as the nominee, it would now be three nights before he returned to Lincoln.[5]

This trip to his childhood home was poignant for Bryan. A few days earlier, few Americans had ever heard of him. Now he was the Democratic presidential nominee, greeted by crowds at every stop. He was overcome with emotion when he arrived in Salem, where he had been two weeks earlier to bury his mother. Standing on his sister's porch, he said, "There is no spot that can ever become so dear to a man as the spot about which clusters sacred memories of early childhood." He shook hands until the long line of neighbors dwindled away.[6]

After resting three days, Bryan was in a good mood, making jokes as he and his family made their way home to Lincoln. At East St. Louis, Illinois, hundreds of railroad workers demanded he speak. "I can understand your curiosity to see a Presidential candidate," he said. "I've been there myself," he added, drawing laughter. At another stop, he asked the crowd if they were going to vote. In response to their cheers, he exclaimed, "All doubt has passed away!" When at a later stop, hundreds crowded close to his car, hoping to shake his hand, Bryan shouted, "Everyone throw up your hands," as he held his in the air. When they followed suit, he said, "Now then shake," and wiggled his hands as the crowd laughed and the train pulled out of the station.[7]

As Bryan grew more confident, his rhetoric gained an edge. He told a crowd in Sedalia, Missouri, that "Parties are but the instruments by which we carry out those policies which we believe in." Later, to thousands waiting at the St. Joseph, Missouri, depot, Bryan defended "agitation" as "the only means" to change "the vicious system of finance" that "allowed a few to gain an unjust advantage over the many."[8]

• • •

BRYAN WAS RECEIVED AS a hero on his journey home, but many Democratic newspapers now openly revolted against him and his platform. Their owners and editors tended to be gold Democrats and businessmen, which didn't dispose them to be enthusiastic about Bryan, and many saw his Free Silver platform as heresy. Because of past experiences with inflationary currencies in Europe, German Democratic editors were particularly antagonistic to silver. Even before Bryan was selected, the Chicago *Staat-Zeitung,* the Midwest's leading German paper, declared German-Americans "have no sympathy with such a platform" of "repudiation of the rankest kind" and "revolutionary," written by an "abominable gang."[9]

More Democratic newspapers bolted after Bryan's nomination. A *New York Times* editorial, reflecting dozens of other papers, condemned "the stealing of the representation of Michigan" and called the platform "a declaration in favor of anarchy and communism." The *Sun* assailed "populism's destructive flame" and condemned Free Silver as a "national dishonor and a monumental anachronism." "From now until the night of election day," the paper editorialized, "the Presidential candidate of every Democrat who favors honest money and who still hopes to crush the enemies of the fundamental principles he was bred in, should be, without hesitation, evasion, or sop to prejudice, William McKinley."[10]

The *Atlanta Constitution* was a rare defender, dismissing the Democratic newspapers' revolt as "considerable sputtering." But two days after the convention, 56 Democratic papers had bolted, either for McKinley or an honest-money Democratic ticket, and two days after that, at least 31 more joined them. The number continued growing for the rest of the campaign. Many Democrats picked up their usual paper to find articles criticizing the Democratic candidate and advocating McKinley or a sound-money Democratic ticket. There was little Bryan could do, but it would hurt in critical battleground states.[11]

SOUND-MONEY DEMOCRATS WERE ALSO bolting the Democratic Party, with some endorsing McKinley. These Democrats believed the Chicago platform was a radical break with their party's orthodoxy, especially on currency. Many were administration supporters while others were businessmen for whom business came first, party loyalty second. While they disagreed with McKinley's protectionism, these Democrats thought tariff policy was a much smaller concern than whether the country's money was debased, its credit and commerce and economy all ruined. McKinley was trustworthy on the money question and with the narrow GOP Senate majority dependent upon Western Republicans who would not support protection without free coinage, they thought the Major wouldn't be able to enact high tariffs.

Some gold Democrats preferred to oppose the Chicago ticket and platform without explaining what they would do, finding it hard to endorse a Republican for president. Their reason for objecting to Bryan was the currency plank. It was "contrary to all my belief," said Delaware's senator George Gray. "Convictions cannot be compromised." Some gold Democrats would vote for McKinley and then their local Democratic ticket, but wondered if there should be a sound-money Democratic ticket to turn out gold Democrats to save like-minded Democrats in Congress and help retake control of the party after its inevitable defeat.[12]

The White House signaled its support for the idea with an administration official "known to enjoy the President's confidence" blessing the creation of a gold Democratic ticket. Whitney added his support in mid-July by repudiating the Chicago ticket and platform. Sound-money Democrats began holding meetings to name delegates to a national gold Democratic convention.[13]

BRYAN HAD NOT ANTICIPATED a competing gold Democratic Party, but this did not divert his attention from achieving his long-standing goal of winning the endorsement of the country's existing third party, the People's Party, or Populists as they were commonly called. Founded in 1890 as an expression of agrarian discontent, Populists were strong in many Midwest states.

There were a million reasons why Bryan wanted the Populist Party convention endorsement when it met in St. Louis on July 22. Actually, 1,041,028 reasons. That was how many votes the People's Party presidential nominee, General James B. Weaver, received in 1892. Bryan felt those

Populist votes were essential to his election. If Populists supported him—particularly in the Midwest—then the country's center paired with a Solid South and the silver West would crush the Northeast.

However, a Populist endorsement had downsides. The party had taken radical stands and its leaders were often outcasts, extremist in their views, rhetoric, and actions. Under no circumstances could Bryan run on the Populist platform. That would be lethal. He had to stand on the planks of Democrats' Chicago platform, which was thought to be radical enough.

Populists had scheduled their convention after the major parties' gatherings, believing both would reject silver. Now they were faced with endorsing Bryan or going their own way. To win the nomination, Bryan had allies among the People's Party fusionists who wanted to bring silver Democrats and Republicans into an alliance with their party. Fusionists like Herman E. Taubeneck, the party's chairman, were numerous among West and Plains state Populists, who had disproportionately more convention delegates because of party rules.

Their opponents in the party were the middle-of-the-road men, mostly Southerners who feared that nominating Bryan would kill the Populist Party. "I appeal to you in the name of good and suffering humanity," one middle-of-the-roader said, "not to allow the Democratic serpent to swallow me up." Texans were among the more radical of the mid-roaders, led by James H. "Cyclone" Davis, a spellbinding forty-two-year-old publisher and lawyer.[14]

After Chicago, Bryan received a "talisman of great potency" from Montana telegraph operators—another rabbit's foot. Not just any rabbit's foot, but one "killed at midnight, in a grave yard with the moon over the slayer's left shoulder." "May your voice never grow weak nor your zeal the less in sounding the slogan of 16 to 1, and may the fight be taken into the enemy's country," the men wrote. "When the battle rages hottest, don't forget the rabbit foot." Bryan would need the extra luck in St. Louis.[15]

POPULIST DELEGATES BEGAN ARRIVING the weekend before the convention, a ragtag group of true believers, cranks, radicals, and eccentrics. They did not embrace parliamentary procedure, decorum, or tradition. Unlike the major parties, Populists did not have private train cars, luxury hotel suites, fine booze, or bands in tailored uniforms. People's Party members were often poor and as low on patience as they were on cash. It was chaos from the moment they started checking into boardinghouses and cheap hotels.

The middle-of-the-roaders had demands. They would endorse Bryan if he dropped Sewall and let the Populists name his running mate. Three presidents had died or been killed in office, "by which the government has passed into the hands of vice presidents," one hard-liner said. If that happened to Bryan, America "will have a national banker for president." Bryan must also endorse the Populist platform or the mid-road men would fight him on the convention floor.[16]

Bryan's representatives—Senator Jones, Governor Stone, and John W. Tomlinson, a close friend of Bryan's and the Bimetallic DNC committeeman from Alabama—were given the demands Monday morning when the party's Executive Committee met. Backed by General Weaver, the Populist standard-bearer in 1892 and chairman of Bryan's endorsement effort, the Bimetallic Democrats rejected the ultimatum. It was the Populists' "patriotic duty to accept the Democratic ticket." The Chicago platform had adopted "many of the Populist principles and nominated candidates so friendly to those principles."[17]

It was hard to decipher whether the fusionists or the mid-road radicals had the upper hand in the convention. A test vote was expected Wednesday on a temporary chairman, but only North Carolina senator Marion Butler ran. He was a mild fusionist. The mid-road crowd then won a vote on a credentials dispute Thursday, but the Bryan men followed that night by electing Nebraska senator William V. Allen permanent chairman by a wider margin, leading the fusionists to believe they were in charge.[18]

ANY ILLUSION THAT THE Bryan men controlled the convention was shattered Friday when the mid-road men moved to change the Rules Committee report to make the vice presidential nomination before the president's. A mid-road man urged fusionists to support the minority report, then nominate a mid-road vice presidential candidate and "we will be in a position to treat with you." After a wild debate featuring speeches by Cyclone Davis and "Sockless" Jerry Simpson, a former Kansas congressman and fusionist, the minority report passed, 785 to 616.[19]

Jones wired Bryan in Lincoln. Would he accept the nomination if the Populists picked someone other than Sewall? Bryan immediately replied he would not accept the endorsement unless Sewall was chosen. Jones showed Bryan's wire around but no one seemed to care.[20]

When the convention met Friday night, the floor was a heaving, restless mass. Tensions were high as the Bryan men tried to salvage Sewall and the mid-roaders prepared to saddle the Democratic contender with a Populist true believer. Sewall and five other Populists were nominated for vice president. The leading Populist was Tom Watson, a thin, severe, forty-year-old, rough-talking lawyer and editor from Thomson, Georgia, a small town southeast of Atlanta. He grew up poor during the Civil War and saw his family lose their small plantation during Reconstruction. An agrarian who opposed industrialization, he was a hater, especially of Southern Democrats. He was seconded by a Georgia delegate who, in response to a shouted question if Watson would stand by the platform, yelled back, "Yes, sir, until hell freezes over, sir."[21]

Sewall was lashed continually in speeches that ended near midnight. The balloting took thirty minutes. Cyclone's 103 Texans put Watson over the top. While states were changing their votes to make it unanimous, the lights went out. They came back on at sixteen minutes before 1 a.m. As Watson was declared the nominee, delegates screamed, "Sixteen to one! Sixteen to one!"[22]

Stone and Jones told reporters they could not see how Bryan could accept the People's Party nomination after Sewall had been rejected. The two men met with Populist allies at 2:45 a.m. and wired Bryan afterward, asking him to reconsider his decision to refuse the Populist nomination. His emissaries heard nothing more from him until the convention was over.[23]

The exchange of telegrams between Jones and Bryan where he said he would not accept the Populist endorsement without Sewall appeared in the Saturday morning papers, but Bryan's threat didn't seem to matter. Sockless Simpson dismissed Watson's nomination as a problem, saying, "We will nominate Bryan anyhow. There is more than one way to whip the devil around the stump."[24]

Presidential nominations were opened. General Weaver offered Bryan by saying Populism had converted the Democratic Party and delegates would violate sacred principles if they failed to endorse Bryan. The young Nebraskan—"a gallant champion"—was "leading a revolt against the plutocracy," and "if we allow the present happy juncture to pass, all the heroic work of twenty years will be thrown to the winds."[25]

Delegates cheered, waving anything they could, including umbrellas, hats, and papers. A giant yellow wooden cross, topped by a paper crown bearing Bryan's closing words from Chicago, was paraded into the hall. But among the enthusiasts, there were islands of silent, brooding mid-roaders in the Missouri, Rhode Island, Texas, and Wisconsin delegations. When Bryan supporters tried grabbing the Lone Star State's standard, a dozen Texans reached for their guns before thinking better of drilling their fellow Populists.[26]

Virginia's James G. Field, Weaver's running mate, rose to second Bryan, then moved to suspend the rules and nominate Bryan unanimously. With his the only name before the convention, this would keep mid-roaders from nominating anyone. Allen, the permanent chairman, called for a voice vote and declared the motion carried. All hell broke loose. Texas hard-liners rushed the stage, kept at bay by a cordon of fusionists. Fights started on the floor before Allen said states could vote for Bryan or anyone else. This only escalated the protests. Field pulled the convention from the brink by withdrawing his motion. Allen ruled other nominations were in order. S. F. Norton, a Chicago greenback publisher and socialist favorite of the middle-of-the-road faction, was nominated, seconded by Cyclone. It was clear to all that the middle-of-the-road men lacked a serious figure to contest Bryan.[27]

Fusionists began spreading the rumor that Democrats would withdraw Sewall if Bryan received the Populist nomination. It was a lie. Late in the roll call, Governor Stone and *Rocky Mountain News* publisher Thomas M. Patterson appeared on the platform. They had seen Bryan's telegram and, concerned about personal honor, wanted Allen to admit the exchange from the podium. Allen refused to allow Stone and Patterson to speak and told them Bryan had sent nothing to him. Harrison Sterling "Stump" Ashby of Texas rose to ask about Bryan's wire. As clerks finished checking their numbers, Allen lied, denying its existence, and then announced Bryan had 1,047 votes to Norton's 331.[28]

Delegates broke loose with wild cheers and marching. The giant cross was again paraded, state standards brought together and used to menace the guidons of mid-road delegations. A large portrait of Bryan was hung off a gallery railing, immediately drawing the standards and giant cross, which were waved back and forth underneath the picture as the crowd cheered. Middle-of-the-road men from Texas massed on the hall's left side.

When the demonstration petered out, the radicals let loose yells of defiance and pushed against the fusionists, looking for fights. As the convention ended, Bryan had the Populist nomination, but his Democratic running mate, Sewall, did not.[29]

That night, the party's national committee replaced Taubeneck as chairman with Senator Butler. Josephus Daniels, who attended the Populist convention at Jones's request, distrusted his fellow North Carolinian, who was not a popular choice among both hard-liners and fusionists. One Populist editor complained, "Butler is a trimmer and a trickster."[30]

Butler's plan was for Democrats and Populists to divide electors in states where the People's Party was strong. In the South, where the Democratic vote was larger, Populists would receive a minority of electors. In the Midwest and West, where the Populist vote was larger, Democrats would receive the minority. Both party's electors would support Bryan, but Populists would run their own vice president. If neither party's VP won a majority, then the Senate would decide, with a coalition of Democrats, Populists, and silver Republicans selecting the man.[31]

In Maine, Sewall said the Populist convention's action "does not change my attitude or plans the least particle." He would not withdraw. In Lincoln, Bryan dug in, ordering a BRYAN AND SEWALL banner hung over his headquarters. In Georgia, Watson told reporters Bryan should embrace the People's Party agenda, which "goes further" than the Chicago platform. He framed the election as a sectional contest: "the north and east" had been built "at the expense of the south and west." He commended Bryan's "unblemished character and brilliant ability" and claimed they "were personal friends" when they served in the House together. But in Congress, Watson had mocked Bryan as "the 'darling' of the Democratic side of the House, the prettiest man in all the bunch" and said Bryan reminded him of "an old fish trap, with one mouth down stream and the other up. It catches 'em a-comin' and a-gwine."[32]

Watson soon vowed he would stay in the race. Sewall should put "the success of the cause . . . above personal interests or aspirations" and withdraw. Sewall wrote privately to Bryan, telling him that what mattered was "the success of the head of our ticket" and that he would step aside if Bryan wanted, a selfless gesture that endeared the Maine businessman to Bryan.[33]

Watson again demanded that Democrats retire "the millionaire candidate from the East" and accept "the Populist nominee of the South" as

Bryan's running mate, but backed by Bryan, Sewall told reporters, "Any man who for a moment entertains such an idea is not worthy of an answer."[34]

Watson's nomination raised the question of whether Bryan should formally accept the Populist nomination. Senator Jones urged Bryan to be cautious and low-key. Bryan told reporters he was certain "a solution of all difficulties will be found in due time." For now, he planned to muddle through.[35]

That might work. Some Populists thought their party and Bryan were better off not formally notifying him, so he would not have to accept or reject its nomination. The notification chairman, Senator Allen, had pushed this idea in St. Louis. One of his committee members had told reporters there would be no official notice because Bryan already knew he was nominated.[36]

By remaining on the People's Party ticket, Watson complicated Bryan's plans to capture the million Populist votes. To put those votes in his column, each state's Democratic party would have to get their state's Populists to agree to endorse Bryan-Sewall in return for Democrats backing Populist candidates for state office or electors.

These negotiations to "fuse" the two parties' tickets began. Both sides were stubborn: Nebraska mid-road men stalled until Democrats threatened to end negotiations, and Kansas Democrats refused to split electors if Populists insisted on Watson. In both instances, agreements were finally reached, but other negotiations would take months, and much effort, to resolve.[37]

BRYAN'S MANAGERS HOPED HIS Madison Square Garden acceptance would show that Free Silver was breaking through in the East, but his journey to New York began on a sour note. Boarding a train on Friday, August 7, he told well-wishers in Lincoln that he would accept the nomination "in the heart of what seems to be the enemy's country, but which we hope to be our country before this campaign is over." Easterners believed this showed Bryan's animosity toward them. His defenders believed it was taken out of context. It's true that more attention was paid to his first phrase—"the enemy's country"—than the second—his "hope" to make it "our country" during the election, but this would have profound implications.[38]

Bryan delivered thirty-eight speeches in five days en route to New York, draining energy and wearing him down. There were tens of thousands of people at his overnight stops, but even in small towns, hundreds or thousands would turn out, expecting a show.[39]

He went on the offense, attacking the gold standard, the money power, and monopoly. In Chicago, he lashed the city's papers and described his opponents as "the great trusts and combinations." In Pittsburgh, Bryan again referred to "the enemy's country," compounding the mistake by saying "not a single private in the ranks will stand closer to the enemy's lines than he in whose hand is the standard." Press coverage was enormous, with Bryan's every word printed on the next day's front page. The country had never seen anything like this tour.[40]

At the Garden, the crowd screamed for ten minutes as he appeared onstage, hands raised, palms out, motioning for silence as a giant American flag dropped down from the rafters behind him. A fat man sitting onstage called for three cheers. The crowd prepared for a humdinger, not knowing the evening had reached its high point.[41]

Bryan pulled out a large manuscript and began to read aloud. He was flat, uninspiring, and without energy. Within fifteen minutes, people began leaving. Bryan leaned against the podium as he read from the thick stack of paper, further draining energy from the hall, which was ovenlike as the city suffered through a record heat wave. Around the thirty-minute mark, someone yelled, "Good night, Billy!" and left. Later, another man screamed, "Put away the paper, Bill, and talk!" By the time Bryan finished his one-hour, fifty-minute recitation, a third of the audience had walked out.[42]

Historian James Ford Rhodes, Hanna's brother-in-law, captured the fundamental flaw: "Bryan, though a orator, was a poor reader." Even Mary Bryan found fault, telling a reporter, "An audience cannot be made enthusiastic by reading to them." As important, Bryan was exhausted and his voice depleted from his many speeches en route.[43]

To sound serious, Bryan also deliberately delivered the speech in a flat tone, failing to give the audience the fighting speech they expected, and devoted too much time to silver and not enough to the income tax, trusts, monopolies, and Cleveland's injunctions, all more important issues to Eastern working-class Democrats.[44]

Roosevelt was brutal, telling his sister, "Bryan fell with a bang." The speech so unnerved Democratic managers that the next day, they canceled the rest of Bryan's planned Eastern trip and sent him on a nine-day vacation.[45]

IN THE MEANTIME, BRYAN gained a formidable opponent when Bourke Cockran returned from Europe. At first glance, the Irish-born lawyer was unimpressive: five feet eleven, plain, gray eyes, mustached, and, though endowed with long dark brown hair, not particularly handsome. But when the stocky former New York Democratic congressman spoke, he exuded charisma, power, and personality. He had just ended an affair with the American-born widow of a British peer. Jennie Churchill had been the wife of now-deceased Lord Randolph Churchill and was mother of a young officer in the 4th Queen's Hussars named Winston. The suitor and the son had become friends. Cockran's talent as a speaker dazzled Churchill, who later wrote he "inspired me when I was 19 & taught me how to use every note of the human voice like an organ. He was my model."[46]

Met dockside by reporters, Cockran described the situation "as the gravest in the history of the country" except 1860. A Bryan presidency would "paralyze industry by using all the powers of Government to take property from the hands of those who created it and place it in the hands of those who covet it." The election was "a contest for the existence of civilization" in which "no man can remain neutral."

Though a lifelong Democrat, he placed Bryan's defeat "above the interests of any organization or party." Cockran would travel the country under the auspices of the nonpartisan Honest Money League without compensation or expenses to encourage Democrats to vote for McKinley or, if one was organized, a gold Democratic ticket, though he believed "support of McKinley is the best method to defeat the socialistic and anarchistic programme adopted at Chicago."[47]

Cockran responded to Bryan in Madison Square Garden a week after Bryan's event, deploying his Irish baritone for a frontal assault on silver. The campaign, he charged, was "a question of whether the powers of this government shall be used to protect honest industry or to tempt the citizen to dishonesty. On this question honest men cannot differ. It is one of morals and of justice." He summoned sound-money Democrats to crush "the seed of Populist Socialism." In contrast to Bryan, Cockran's hour-and-a-quarter speech was delivered without notes and frequently interrupted by applause.[48]

After reading the London papers, Churchill wired his mentor that his speech was "a great moral victory." Platt was ecstatic: "It was the greatest speech I ever listened to. McKinley's election is now assured." But the Easy Boss was making too much of one speech against Bryan and too little of the Boy Orator's talents, which just might be reinvigorated with a vacation.[49]

CHAPTER 25

The Front-Porch Campaign

————◦————

The McKinley men thought they had caught a break when Bryan was unable to unite his increasingly fractured Democratic Party and appeared to have lost his rhetorical edge at Madison Square Garden. But any expectations in the McKinley camp that Bryan was sunk were premature as the Nebraskan, reenergized from his vacation, recaptured his voice and the uncompromising tone of the "Cross of Gold" speech as he barnstormed through the "enemy's country" in upstate New York in late August.

McKinley was realizing he would beat Bryan only if he dealt with the issue that voters wanted him to address—Free Silver—and not just the one he wanted to discuss—protection—and found an effective way to put his message on both these issues before the American people. The election eleven weeks away would not go the Major's way without smart decisions, solid execution, unprecedented organization, and a message that resonated with voters.

BRYAN'S REINVIGORATED AND TOUGHER tone was evident from his first day back from vacation, when he acknowledged his views "would offend some people," especially Wall Streeters. "We want to destroy the business in which they are engaged," he said to cheers.[1]

In Cleveland's hometown of Buffalo, Bryan said he knew some Democrats disagreed with the platform, but they "must either stand upon it or get out of the party." On the gold standard, "there is no middle ground.

Those who are not with us are against us." The crowd of four thousand in the Music Hall roared its approval.[2]

Bryan's more aggressive language helped him again draw big crowds—10,000 in Albany, 20,000 in Knowlesville on the Erie Canal east of Buffalo, 20,000 at Rochester, where he lost his voice, and 15,000 at a Farmers' Alliance picnic near Niagara Falls.[3]

One of his last New York rallies was in Lake Chautauqua's Celeron, a large auditorium flanked by two tall towers topped with onion domes. The crowd was so unruly it took the band playing "The Star-Spangled Banner" to settle them. Men clambered through open windows, packing the aisles and every inch of open space. Supporters stood on chairs cheering when Bryan took the podium, refusing pleas to sit down. Someone cried out that it was too crowded. It took police thirty-five minutes to clear the center aisle before Bryan could say, "Gold is a coward. It has ever been a coward and the reasons the advocates of the gold standard are cowards is because their consciences bring them to the realization that it brings ruin to the human race."[4]

But was it smart for Bryan to have spent numerous days in New York? His party's leadership there had yet to endorse him and so many of the state's gold Democrats abstaining, defecting to McKinley, or hoping for a sound-money Democratic ticket.[5]

IN MID-AUGUST, BEFORE HANNA went east to New York, he again pushed the Major to take to the campaign trail, but McKinley again refused, leaving Hanna to tell reporters, "To settle the matter once for all, McKinley will not take the stump."[6]

Instead, shortly before or after the two men met, the Front-Porch Campaign was born. Supporters were showing up on their own, so why not make a virtue out of it? The campaign could invite groups to come to Canton, emphasizing critical battleground states and key voting blocs such as laborers, farmers, and German-Americans. McKinley would then have ready-made crowds to whom he could deliver targeted and prepared remarks from his front porch that would be reprinted in local papers back home and picked up across America. He would control the message; his visitors would provide the backdrop.

Voters were already reading Bryan's attacks as he barnstormed from one whistle-stop to another, wearing himself out with travel and a dozen or more speeches a day. So why not play to McKinley's strengths of discipline, preparation, and personable courtesy? Canton was on several major rail lines, with easy connections throughout the Midwest, Mid-Atlantic, and border states. Even with excursion fares, it was lucrative business for the railroads, not to mention Canton's restaurants, shops, and hotels.

The idea was not new—Harrison had done a limited version in 1888, speaking in Indianapolis between July 7 and October 25 roughly eighty to ninety times and visiting groups totaling 300,000 people. Like McKinley, Harrison hadn't wanted to travel, saying, "There is a great risk of meeting a fool at home, but the candidate who travels cannot escape him." As his manager, Quay had initially opposed the idea, but after the first events said, "If Harrison has the strength to keep talking, we could safely close these headquarters and he would elect himself." Still, it was grueling. Harrison would often be found at the end of a day, "stretched out on a lounge while a family member massaged his head."[7]

McKinley's approach would be different, as different as a modern factory was from a medieval workshop. In addition to the groups that volunteered themselves, the campaign would invite handpicked groups. Suggested introductions would be supplied to each group's spokesman or their drafts reviewed beforehand. Local color and economic facts would be researched and remarks prepared for McKinley for each occasion. He was not big on impromptu speeches.

Each group would be met at one of Canton's rail depots by the McKinley Home Guards, a mounted troop of volunteers, and often a local band, and escorted under a plaster arch topped with McKinley's portrait in a staging area while the previous group finished visiting the candidate. Then they marched to McKinley's home, arriving at a prearranged time, preceded by a messenger confirming their identity to an aide. Townspeople turned out to cheer along the route, which was decorated with bunting, flags, and campaign posters.

The group would assemble on the lawn and McKinley would emerge onto his porch to be greeted with excited applause. The group's spokesman would deliver his remarks and the Major would respond, reading from a script, his every word captured by the press. Joseph P. Smith transcribed McKinley's remarks and distributed them. There were often flowers for Ida and gifts for the Major. Among those were a beat-up gamecock in a cage

bearing the sign FREE TRADE HAS SPOILED MY FEATHERS / I WANT PROTEC-
TION and a miniature White House with a raccoon tied on top. For bad
weather, there were several indoor venues, with the Tabernacle the most
popular.[8]

At the program's conclusion, there would sometimes be music by a glee
club or band and occasionally a chance to file across the porch and shake
McKinley's hand and share a word. Visitors would offer three cheers for
McKinley before trooping off to get a bite prepared by the ladies of Canton. There were beers discreetly available for the "wets" and sandwiches
and coffee for the "drys." Not only were McKinley's lawn and flower beds
regularly trampled, but pieces of his fence and porch, even his grass and
greenery, were taken as keepsakes. Then McKinley enthusiasts would
board their trains home, excited after seeing the Great Man, up close and
personal.[9]

The Front-Porch Campaign was almost industrial in scale. It took until
August 22 for the effort to ramp up and until nearly mid-September to
hit its stride, but by Election Day there had been hundreds of delegations
totaling 750,000 people that made their way to McKinley's front porch.
Many visitors were part of organizations Dawes had constructed, including
traveling salesmen—the "McKinley Commercial Club"—and even the
wheelmen, who performed intricate bicycle ballet routines to entertain the
Major and his guests.[10]

It's unclear whose idea the Front-Porch Campaign was, but it was probably not Hanna's. He would have claimed credit. Neither was it Dawes's:
he makes no mention of it in his diary. It was most likely McKinley's, with
perhaps advice from Joseph Smith, James Boyle, and other Canton aides.
The whole concept mirrors how McKinley had operated as a commissary
sergeant, staff officer, congressman, and governor: well prepared, thoughtful, meticulous, and planned to the *n*th degree.

FORMULATING THE FRONT-PORCH CAMPAIGN was an important step, but
more consequential was McKinley's decision to change course and tackle
an issue he preferred to ignore—currency. By mid-August, the Major had
concluded that protection must be put aside, at least temporarily, and the
campaign focused on sound money. To win, McKinley had to stop avoiding Free Silver and talk about it. Harrison had been right: voters chose an

election's issues, not the politicians. Judge Day had been right: the free coinage question was not going away. And Reed had been right: Republicans must confront the arguments for Free Silver and beat them head-on or they could be defeated by them.

Emblematic of these growing sentiments among Republicans was a rhetorical bomb set off in eastern Kansas in mid-August. William Allen White, editor of the *Emporia Gazette,* was returning from the post office when a group of Populists surrounded him, "hooting, jeering, nagging me about some editorial utterances." This so irritated the twenty-eight-year-old small-town newspaperman that he "stalked," he said, "as well as a fat man who toddles can stalk," to his office and wrote a broadside blasting the Populist views many Republicans believed animated Bryan's campaign. "What we are after is the money power," White wrote sarcastically. "Give the prosperous man the dickens! Legislate the thriftless man into ease, whack the stuffing out of the creditors, and tell the debtors who borrowed the money . . . that the contradiction of currency gives him a right to repudiate."

White's editorial—"What's the Matter With Kansas?"—swept across the country as fast as the telegraph could carry it and was reprinted in hundreds of papers, adding to the feeling among Republicans that McKinley must take on Bryan's extreme views, especially Free Silver. Reed wrote White, "I haven't seen as much sense in one column in a dozen years."[11]

Much of the reason behind McKinley's conversion to making the money question his principal issue was all the bad news from across the country he had been receiving since Bryan's nomination, especially in the Midwest. In Minnesota, Democrats were peeling away Republicans by running a popular former silver GOP congressman, John Lind, for governor. Iowa Republican chairman H. G. McMillan reported his state's canvass of voters "really looked threatening" because "a large percent of our republican farmers were inclined to adopt free silver as a remedy for the present hard times." In many counties, "the free silver craze has taken the form of an epidemic." A quarter of Republicans were defecting to Bryan over currency, which would easily swing Iowa to the Democrats. The Plains states were in bad shape and the West was even worse. Call it Teller's Revenge, but all the mountain states except perhaps Wyoming were gone, the GOP's chances killed by silver Republicans defecting to Bryan.[12]

Almost by instinct, the Republican campaign responded to these challenges by starting its own door-to-door canvasses earlier than normal. Dawes also dispatched speakers, material, and money long before the September 1 start date Hanna had contemplated after the GOP convention, with Republican orators swarming Kansas in July. Stopping in Chicago on his way to a Dakota hunting trip in late August, Roosevelt watched men load a boxcar with literature being shipped to a state headquarters. Dawes had distributed 15.5 million pieces of material before Labor Day, most of it devoted to sound money, not protection. TR was impressed, writing his sister that "[t]he educational work done about finance by the distribution of pamphlets has been enormous, and it is telling." [13]

This increased pressure on Hanna to raise more money. Many pocketbooks had been shut to the burly Clevelander on his first New York visit, but Hanna's development of a good relationship with Platt, personal introductions by the Great Northern's James J. Hill, a Democrat, to big donors, and favorable reaction to McKinley's new attacks on Free Silver helped open Republican checkbooks. So did Bryan's increasingly harsh tone. John Hay jabbed a Democratic friend, writing him that "[Bryan] has succeeded in scaring the goldbugs out of their five wits." Sometimes fear is better motivation to write a check than complacency. [14]

During his two weeks on the East Coast in late August, Hanna dragged a money sack through New York and Boston and recruited finance committee members and bundlers. Hill or Bliss accompanied him when he called on some donors. Hanna met with J. P. Morgan on the banker's yacht, *Corsair II,* to ask for support and recruited Lodge's son-in-law, A. P. Gardner, for the Bay State committee. The banks, businesses, and corporations (then allowed to make political contributions), and wealthy Republicans gave Hanna more promises to consider his request than checks, but it was a start. Dawes, however, was concerned. With his usual precision, he reported at the end of August that the campaign had raised $115,112.92 and spent $84,268.28 but needed $100,000 more just to meet the campaign's existing contracts and expenses. He wrote Hanna that "[u]pon your efforts in the next few weeks very much depends." [15]

THE GOP CAMPAIGN PREPARED a one-two punch to blunt Bryan's momentum and pump energy into its effort. McKinley released his formal acceptances of the Republican nomination Wednesday, August 26, his letter reflecting the decision to put the currency issue to the front. It was the first issue discussed in his letter. Almost half of his message was devoted to the currency question and less than a third to protection. Free Silver was "a menace to our financial and industrial interests and has already created universal alarm," the Major wrote. It "would not make labor easier, the hours of labor shorter, or the pay better." It would chiefly benefit the mine owner, who could exchange 53¢ worth of silver for a dollar that "belongs to him and nobody else."

"The debasement of our currency" would "reduce property values, entail untold financial loss, destroy confidence, impair the obligations of existing contracts, further impoverish the laborers and producers of the country, create a panic of unparalleled severity and inflict upon trade and commerce a deadly blow." While he wrote, "No one suffers so much from cheap money as the farmers and laborers," the language was that of businessmen. McKinley had a start on a currency message that resonated with working-class voters, but he was not there yet.

Protectionism took a backseat, but the Major prosecuted the issue effectively. "Our men at home are idle," while "men from abroad are occupied in supplying us with goods." The answer was to open mills, not mints. That required "an increase in the volume of business," which depended upon "an increase in confidence," which was impossible without protective tariffs and ensuring "our currency is on a gold basis. Good money never made times hard."

McKinley closed by calling for national unity. "The era of reconciliation" between North and South "has happily come." He quoted George Washington, "There should be no North, no South, no East, no West—but a common country." He promised to work for "prosperity and happiness" for the entire nation. After the bitterness of the Democratic fight and with the harsh words coming from Bryan, McKinley's call for unity was a positive and optimistic message for people experiencing a deep, seemingly endless depression and a political system that appeared broken. The acceptance was reprinted in many newspapers. Its gold emphasis was welcomed by the Eastern sound-money advocates, while its attention to tariffs gave solace to Republicans worried about the labor vote. Dawes ordered a million copies in English and another million in foreign languages from German and Hebrew to Spanish and Swedish.[16]

President Harrison left his Adirondacks vacation to open the New York campaign the day after McKinley's acceptance, giving Republicans two days of good press. He insisted on speaking in Carnegie Hall, with its fine acoustics and reasonable size. There were more than 15,000 requests for the auditorium's 3,200 seats and 500 standing-room spots, all taken six days before. Bunting and patriotic shields covered the balconies. State flags hung over the stage with a giant banner blaring MCKINLEY AND HOBART suspended over the podium. The band played "Hail to the Chief" as the short and stout former president came onstage. The crowd rose, cheered, and waved handkerchiefs and flags. Harrison bowed, sat down, stood again to acknowledge the cheers, and took off his overcoat.[17]

Having written his own speech, Harrison's remarks showed he still had his "power as a phrase maker," wrote a reporter. He walked up and down the stage, glancing at notes and talking for extended periods extemporaneously. Harrison joked he was "on the Republican retired list," but his "interests in my country did not cease when my last salary check was cashed." The Democratic Party divided because its candidate departed from "its traditional principles" and embraced "doctrines that threaten the integrity of the Government, the social order of our communities and the security and soundness of our finances." Gold Democrats were right to bolt.

Harrison said Bryan's attacks on the Supreme Court and Cleveland's injunctions struck at an independent judiciary and "the President's power and duty to enforce all of the laws." "When it becomes the rule that violence carries its end we have anarchy." He charged the Chicago convention was "surcharged with the spirit of revolution." In contrast to McKinley's dispassion and calm, Harrison was emotional and combative, belittling Bryan's radicalism.

Harrison wasted no time on tariffs—"That debate has been won"—but stayed on currency. He was "opposed to cheapening the American workingman and workingwoman" by "cheapening our dollars," saying, "It is not more dollars, but cheaper dollars" that Bryan wanted. This would lead to "disaster and disturbance and disruption." "The first dirty errand that a dirty dollar does is to cheat the workingman." The country would not stand for "the infamous proposition" that America would "become a nation and a people of repudiators." Cheers filled the hall as he left the stage.[18]

•   •   •

THE SEPTEMBER 1 ELECTIONS in Vermont were the first test of whether Republicans were persuading voters that McKinley's sound-money and protection message was better than Bryan's Free Silver one. Republicans were expected to win the governorship, two congressional seats, and the legislature, but the GOP's victory margin mattered. Democrats wanted to keep it below 20,000; it had been 18,000 when Cleveland won the presidency in 1892. Republicans hoped for 23,000, close to what Grant received in 1872 when he annihilated Greeley nationally.[19]

Election Day was cool and fair, so turnout was heavy, but few expected the GOP's record-breaking 39,000-vote margin, an 80 percent landslide. Democrats received only 16 percent. Democratic officials dismissed Vermont as inconsequential, but an astonishing 40 percent of Vermont Democrats voted Republican. The stock market rose, as did Republican claims of states they would carry. But while Vermont was an indicator of what might happen in New England, it was not the Midwest, Plains, or West, where the Free Silver sentiment was so much stronger and was attracting enormous support from nominally Republican voters.[20]

Emboldened by Vermont, Quay argued the campaign should spend more money in Florida, North Carolina, Tennessee, and West Virginia. It was not above Quay to consider the friends he would make there for the next presidential primary election since he was running the South. But the committee was still concerned about fund-raising, so it deferred increasing its spending in the South for now.[21]

Still, the RNC was active in the border states and Upper South. Among its efforts was a widely circulated pamphlet from John Singleton Mosby, the famous Confederate cavalry commander. He had lived in China and visited Mexico frequently. Both had free coinage and "I never saw a piece of gold in circulation" in either, he wrote. "By a natural law, as universal as that of gravitation, the cheaper always drives out the dearer currency." He played on Southern animosity toward the People's Party by chiding silver Democrats for endorsing "the lawless spirit that animates the Populist party."[22]

IN EARLY SEPTEMBER, MORE than eight hundred gold Democrats from forty-four states and territories met in Indianapolis for the "National

Democratic" Convention. The meeting had been spurred by Midwestern gold men concerned that without a sound-money Democratic ticket, gold Democratic congressional and local candidates were doomed.[23]

Delegates met in Tomlinson Hall, decorated heavily in gold—gold wreaths, gold bunting, and gold rosettes. Delegates even wore goldenrod in their lapels. Above the stage were portraits of Cleveland and Jefferson under a gold eagle. The convention's speakers had harsh words for Bryan. Former New York governor Roswell P. Flower called him "ambitious, unsteady and unsafe . . . a demagogue, a word juggler" with "a revolutionary horde behind him." Unlike Chicago, delegates cheered at any mention of Cleveland.[24]

The convention settled quickly on a ticket of Illinois senator John M. Palmer and former Kentucky governor Simon Bolivar Buckner, and adopted a platform that declared for the gold standard with language, supposedly drafted by Carlisle, that disparaged the Chicago platform's Free Silver plank and its attacks on the judiciary and presidential injunctions.[25]

The dignified, bearded Palmer had been elected state senator as a Douglas Democrat in 1852 and reelected as an anti-Nebraska, antislavery candidate in 1854. By 1856 he was a Republican and a Lincoln elector in 1860. When the Civil War broke out, he organized the 14th Illinois, fought in Tennessee, and commanded the 14th Corps under Sherman at Atlanta. After the war, he was elected governor as a Republican in 1868, but left the GOP over Grant's renomination and returned to the Democratic Party, winning his Senate seat in 1890 after three other unsuccessful bids for office.[26]

Buckner was a West Pointer who served in the Mexican War before practicing law in Kentucky. At Fort Donelson in February 1862, his force of 12,000 Confederates was surrounded by Brigadier General Ulysses S. Grant. Asked for terms, Grant replied, "No terms except an unconditional and immediate surrender," winning the victory and a nickname— "Unconditional Surrender." Buckner was later exchanged for a captured Union general and fought until the war's end. Elected Kentucky's governor in 1887, his term was marked by a stunning embezzlement by the longtime state treasurer. When the government teetered on bankruptcy, Buckner advanced it funds from his own pocket.[27]

Cleveland privately applauded the ticket, calling it "a delicious infusion of fresh air." But it was anything but fresh: Palmer was seventy-nine,

Buckner, seventy-three. Palmer was history's oldest presidential candidate, Bryan the youngest. Few gold Democrats thought Palmer-Buckner could win, but they would divert Democratic votes from Bryan in battleground states, help save local and congressional gold Democratic candidates, and provide a vehicle for gold Democrats to regain control of their party after Bryan lost. The reaction from silver Democrats was acidic: Virginia's senator Daniels called the delegates "yellow bellies."[28]

On his way to Chicago for an Executive Committee meeting, Hanna praised the convention, saying Palmer and Buckner would receive "a big vote," especially in Illinois and Kentucky. The RNC leadership realized the gold Democrat ticket could affect the outcome in battleground states, or at least hoped it would.[29]

BRYAN TOOK LITTLE PUBLIC notice of McKinley's acceptance and the gold Democrats' convention. He even ignored Vermont's bad omen for November. Instead, he finally left New York to campaign for labor voters—factory, mine, and millworkers—with forty-seven speeches over five days in four battleground Midwestern states, arguing that blue-collar families would benefit from the Chicago platform's financial planks. He opened his pre–Labor Day offensive in Cleveland.[30]

Every seat and every inch of standing room in the city's Armory was filled as 16,000 Bryan supporters jammed a space meant for half that number. Behind the stage was a backdrop featuring a giant arm holding a hammer above the legend THE FRIEND OF LABOR, and on it was a large white floral arrangement with yellow flowers and purple blooms, forming the words SIXTEEN TO ONE.

When Bryan appeared, people applauded, stamped, and roared their approval for twenty minutes. As the event's chairman tried to introduce Bryan, they went at it again. The chairman gave up and wordlessly motioned him to the podium. The Nebraskan said he stood for "the struggling masses who produce the wealth and pay the taxes . . . rather than with the idle holders of idle capital." Any gold advocate "carries the mask of the burglar and the knife of the assassin." He closed by bashing management for coercing railroad employees to vote for McKinley, and by belittling workers for going along, a charge he repeated the rest of his swing.[31]

Bryan's crowds on the rest of the pre–Labor Day tour were large and his speeches fiery and energetic, and helped memories of the Madison Square Garden speech fade. But the pace was brutal, causing Bryan to lose his voice in Springfield, Ohio, where he said he could talk only briefly because "my voice has been left along the line of travel, where it is still calling sinners to repentance."[32]

Bryan soon made plans to stump in Missouri on September 12, then move south through Kentucky, Tennessee, North Carolina, and Virginia before heading to the Northeast on the twenty-first for an additional week. Most of this was a waste of time. Missouri and Kentucky were true battlegrounds, but the other Southern states were at risk only if fusion with the Populists went really wrong. It was hard to see what Mid-Atlantic states were competitive, other than Delaware. Vermont's results suggested New England was a wasteland for Democrats.

At the same time, Bryan's managers did not have the money to keep up with the volume of speakers and materials Dawes was pouring out of Chicago. Democrats hoped the Silver Party would be a conduit for money from the Western mine owners who created it, but its chairman said it was collecting gifts of ten cents to ten dollars. William Randolph Hearst used the pages of his *Journal* to solicit funds for the DNC and Jones also issued a desperate, public plea that money was slow coming. This made it even more critical to use Bryan's time wisely.

Bryan made time during a stop in Chicago on his tour to visit his old friend Charles G. Dawes. The Democrat was ignorant about the McKinley men's growing confidence and the GOP's growing war chest. All Bryan knew was the size of his crowds and the encouraging reports from Democratic door-to-door canvasses. "Bryan, somehow, imagines he has a chance to be elected President," Dawes wrote in his diary. "He referred to our old silver debates and gave me a conditional invitation to visit at the White House." The next day, Bliss sent Dawes $50,000 in contributions. Senator Jones saw only one check for that amount in the entire campaign. Dawes was about to see those sums routinely. McKinley's front porch appeared to have the better view.[33]

CHAPTER 26

Message for the Workingman

————◦————

A key bloc of voters were laborers, working-class Americans whose lives had been jolted by depression and technological change. In the Gilded Age, neither party had this group locked up. The party that carried this crucial group generally won the election.

From his very first election to Congress—just months after having defended striking coal miners—William McKinley had a special relationship with laborers. He had succeeded in politics because, like many successful politicians, he had the ability to connect with voters personally and understood the issues that affect their lives. This came more easily to him than to other politicians because he truly cared about working people. He ran for Congress in districts that were often gerrymandered to defeat him and always competitive, so he was used to appealing to voters not naturally inclined to support him. Then he was twice governor of Ohio, a state whose elections were always close and tough. And as the foremost Republican advocate of protection, he had framed the issue as one of protecting workers' jobs and wages, not industries or businessmen. To win the presidency, McKinley had to explain why sound money and protection would benefit all Americans.

McKinley faced competition for the laborer vote as Bryan attempted to grow his support beyond its agrarian base by appealing to industrial workers, especially in the Midwest. The charismatic Democrat was arguing Free Silver was as good for factory workers in the cities as it was for farmers in the South and Midwest, depicting Republicans and the Major as tools of Eastern financiers, European bankers, and the wealthy who opposed the workingman's interests. If left unchallenged, his portrayal of McKinley as the status quo candidate who would leave working Americans stranded in bleak economic times could cost the Major the election.

Both candidates knew the labor vote would deeply influence the election's outcome, even decide key states. As September opened, whose message would sway the "toiling masses," as Bryan called them? That of the Boy Orator of the Platte or that of the Napoleon of Protection?

LABOR DAY WAS AN opportunity to appeal directly to these voters, and three candidates offered their best pitches. McKinley struck an inclusive tone, telling a thousand Pittsburgh factory workers and their families visiting Canton on September 5, "We are all equal citizens, equal in privilege and opportunity," with an "equal voice in controlling and shaping the destiny of our great republic." McKinley rejected attempts to "array class against class," and while making a pitch for tariffs, he broadened his message by arguing sound money was better for laborers. They wanted to be paid in dollars "as good as anybody's dollars," he said, and Free Silver would "neither furnish the workingman a job, restore his exhausted savings, nor give him credit." McKinley was still finding his way on currency, but moving in the right direction and giving it top priority.[1]

Bryan's tone was divisive. In a speech in Sharpshooters Park on Chicago's northwest side, he told 10,000 union members and their families, "The common people are the only people that have ever received gladly the doctrines of humanity and justice." He dismissed charges he was a demagogue, saying Jesus had been called one, too. Saying government had a responsibility to restrain greed by putting "rings in the noses of hogs," he endorsed binding arbitration of labor disputes. When he finished, the crowd rushed the platform, nearly toppling it.[2]

Bryan returned to Nebraska right after his speech. In a sharp contrast with McKinley's inclusive tone, at a welcome-home rally Bryan decried the "terrorism and coercion" of company leaders who wished "to compel their employees to support the gold standard," and attacked business combinations, saying, "Do you know what word rhymes with 'syndicate?' It is 'hate.' "[3]

The third candidate to make a Labor Day case was a foe of both McKinley and Bryan. At the Texas State Fairgrounds in Dallas, Thomas E. Watson lambasted Bryan's running mate, Arthur Sewall, as the "representative of monopolies and the money power" and alleged Western Democratic silver men and Southern Populists had agreed "that they would act together and vote together." Sewall's presence on the ticket violated that agreement.[4]

Watson continued his attacks in Texas and then stumped in Kansas, Nebraska, and Colorado over the next several weeks, begging for support from Plains and Western Populists but without much success. Populists in Lincoln kept him from dropping by their headquarters until they removed pictures of Sewall and all Bryan-Sewall materials. When Watson arrived in Colorado on September 18, he was tired and dispirited. Realizing the futility of his efforts, he canceled his appearances and returned to Georgia. Still, the public spectacle of conflict over two running mates for Bryan gave the "appearance of farce to the whole business," observed President Harrison.[5]

UNION LEADERS SOON BEGAN taking sides. Eugene V. Debs and his American Railway Union endorsed Bryan, rejoicing that Free Silver "has unloosed and enraged this railroad moloch" and warning McKinley's election "would mean the perpetuation of a government by injunction, the supremacy of the corporations and the helpless subjection of employees." After the Pullman strike, Debs was a hero to Populists and the Democratic left and a dangerous radical to business leaders, Cleveland Democrats, and most Republicans.[6]

That same night, Terence V. Powderly, the bearded, bespectacled former Grand Master Workman of the Knights of Labor, the nation's largest union, spoke for McKinley at a workingman's mass meeting in Manhattan's Cooper Union sponsored by the New York McKinley League. There were heated arguments between McKinley and Bryan men, resulting in raised voices, shaken fists, and even a few blows before police ejected a dozen men. That didn't stop the sides from heckling each other, causing one small, agitated McKinley man to scream "Snakes!" and "Put the snakes out!" whenever Bryan men hissed.[7]

Powderly bashed the claim that "the silver dollar is the poor man's dollar" as "pure gush." "The dollar of the poor is the dollar which he earns, whether it be gold or silver. The workingman is entitled to the best." A silver dollar would "buy only half what it will now, and the man working for a dollar a day will have to work two days in order to purchase as much for two silver dollars as he now obtains for one dollar of gold or of silver or of paper based on gold." One sign that Powderly's language was effective was that similar phrases began appearing in McKinley's front-porch remarks.[8]

Theodore Roosevelt also offered effective language on currency when he spoke to the New York Commercial Travelers' Sound Money League. His talk, titled "Cash and Credit," framed the currency dispute on a moral basis. Free Silver would not give a workingman "any more money than he has now." He would "have the same number of dollars as he does now, and worth half as much." The election was "a fight for honest money . . . against the debasement of the currency and the impairment of credit." Silver men were demagogues "with a venomous hatred of the well-to-do because they are well-to-do, the thrifty because they are thrifty." The traveling salesmen cheered.[9]

Sunburned and rested, Roosevelt was upbeat after visiting the GOP's Chicago headquarters while returning from a North Dakota hunt in early September. Hanna and other campaign officials told him Illinois, Ohio, and Wisconsin were winnable, though Michigan was "demoralized." Republican defectors in Iowa were now coming back. Much of the West was lost, but some Plains and Pacific Coast states could be won. "The wage-earners are drifting our way and the revolt among the farmers is shrinking rather than spreading," Roosevelt wrote Lodge. "When I was going to my ranch the people there were all nervous . . . coming back it was evident the tide had begun to set our way."[10]

The day Roosevelt mailed his letter to Senator Lodge, Maine elected its governor and state legislature. Reed had been confident that Republicans would "beat the life out of the wild ideas" of Bryan's Democratic-Populist ticket, but even he was astonished at the Republican majority of 48,000, the largest in history. Bryan was scheduled to be with Sewall in Maine in eight days, horrible timing for a candidate whose party had just suffered such a dramatic loss. Together, the results in Maine and Vermont pointed to a wipeout for Democrats in the Northeast.[11]

· · · ·

BY MID-SEPTEMBER, THE FRONT-PORCH machine was cranking as groups arrived in large numbers. The campaign especially encouraged Republican leaders to get working people to Canton. And they came—factory, mine and smelter workers, men from the coke camps, glassworkers, roughnecks from Pennsylvania and Ohio oil fields, mechanics, line workers in tin factories, tool and die makers, men from railroad shops, conductors and firemen, as well as real estate agents, insurance salesmen, salesclerks, bank tellers, and hordes of traveling salesmen.

McKinley finally found his voice on sound money, focusing it as "a great moral principle," saying, "We want no debased dollars any more than we want debased labor." To New York factory workers who told him of the depression's terrible effects, McKinley explained that the economy would not be improved by "dishonest dollars." American workers, he declared, deserved to be paid in dollars "worth one hundred cents each every day and everywhere." Free Silver, he warned a group of real estate agents, would "destroy confidence" and "invite ruin to every enterprise in the land." If America were "to enter upon the experiment of the free coinage of silver," he told Pittsburgh salesclerks, it "would give us at the present price of silver, 52¢ dollars."[12]

He did not drop protection, but now raised it as a subordinate issue, saying he was concerned about "idle mills [and] idle men." He argued that for thirty years, high tariffs had "protected and encouraged American enterprise and American industry" and made it "the greatest nation in the world in manufacturing, in mining and in agriculture." Tariff reform was responsible for the depression. If protection were renewed, prosperity would return.[13]

McKinley pushed sound money and protection to factory workers and farmers alike. He told 3,000 cheering workers at Carnegie Steel's Homestead mill, led by their superintendent, Charles Schwab, that "I am opposed to free trade because it degrades American labor; I am opposed to free silver because it degrades American money." He reminded wool growers hit hard by the Wilson-Gorman law that Democrats' promised tariff reform would "be a cure for all our ills, the panacea for all our troubles. Well, we have now for four years enjoyed partial free trade . . . more especially in wool." His audience laughed. Holmes County wool growers showed up with a banner featuring a plump shiny sheep labeled PROTECTION and a scrawny, bedraggled one labeled FREE TRADE.[14]

The range of groups was astonishing. Stirred by members of their shared war experience and concerned about the value of their pensions, Civil War veterans came to Canton. The campaign changed the normal Anglo-Saxon complexion of Republican rallies, reaching out to ethnic groups such as Germans, Hungarians, Italians, Bohemians, Scandinavians, Poles, and a dozen other varieties of hyphenated Americans. Many paraded up Market Street proudly waving the flag of their adopted land.[15]

The campaign organized "First Time Voter" clubs and had an active presence on campuses through the American College Republican League, so groups of young men showed up frequently in Canton. Among them was the Wood County, Ohio, First Time Voters, dressed in white uniforms. The Major recalled his first vote—Abraham Lincoln in 1864—and reminded the young men of Lincoln's advice in the 1848 campaign for Zachary Taylor. "You young men get together," Lincoln, then a Whig, had written, "form a 'Rough and Ready Club,' and have regular meetings and speeches. Take in everybody you can get. As you go along, gather all the shrewd, wild boys about town, whether just of age or a little under age. Let every one play the part he can play best. Some speak; some sing; and all 'holler.' "

Many delegations included women. The Ladies McKinley Club of Bowling Green wore matching outfits and tam-o'-shanter caps with gold bands. Forty-five young women from Oil City arrived in sailor hats with red, white, and blue ribbons, each holding a rose basket labeled with the name of a state. The baskets fit together to make a large floral pyramid on the McKinleys' porch. Ida was thrilled and invited them inside to thank them personally. Flowers weren't the only gifts. Mechanics presented McKinley with a terra-cotta bust of him made in their factory. Indiana bakers, tin factory men, and millers gave the Major a loaf of bread baked in a tin pan with raised profiles of him and Hobart pressed in it.[16]

There was always music, either from groups' bands or Canton bands that escorted visitors from the stations. There were glee clubs, solo singers who belted out patriotic songs, and even a double barbershop quartet that came with the Vermont Republicans to celebrate their state election victory. Each Vermonter sported a gold necktie, a sprig of Vermont cedar in his hatband, and a handsome badge that read, "Vermont for McKinley, 39,000," the GOP margin in their contest. The barbershop vocalists sang five excruciating verses of their composition, "We Want Yer, McKinley, Yes We Do." [17]

Visitors got a dose of bipartisanship. McKinley told clerks from Marshall Field, Carson Pirie Scott, and other Chicago stores that "party lines . . . are not strong enough to prevail against the country's highest and best interests." To Somerset County, Pennsylvania, families, McKinley described the Democratic Party as "torn and divided," and claimed the GOP was "more closely united" than ever. Only the first was true. There were many Republicans in the Midwest and West who had defected. [18]

By the mid-September, thousands visited Canton every day, especially on Fridays and Saturdays. More than 150,000 people came to Canton in just one weekend, starting September 18, when visitors from Ohio, Illinois, and West Virginia joined Canton residents for a parade, speeches, and concerts to launch the Stark County GOP campaign. McKinley gave eleven talks. He was so tired by day's end, he asked Senator Thurston to give the evening's address after they reviewed a parade from a stand in his front yard. [19]

The next day was the biggest day in McKinley's Front-Porch Campaign as an estimated 100,000 visitors descended on Canton in waves, including factory workers, steelworkers, railroad laborers, traveling salesmen, hardware men, and mill, mine, and factory workers. The hardware men wore white caps and carried flags over their shoulders and tin cups. Each group heard the Major hold forth on sound money, telling railroad laborers Free Silver would mean "a decrease of the purchasing power of the money in which you are paid of fully one-half" and that when business was poor, all "employees suffer both in time and pay." [20]

Reed watched the Front-Porch Campaign from a distance and developed a smidgen of sympathy for his former colleague. "What poor McKinley has to endure moves my compassion," he wrote Platt. "I hope he doesn't hate brass bands." Bookmakers in New York now put the Major's chance of winning at 2½ to 1. [21]

AFTER A THREE-DAY BREAK, Bryan left Nebraska on September 11 for his third tour. He would not return home until Election Day, seven weeks and four days later. He was escorted to the night train by a thousand mounted men, a band, and Lincoln's silver clubs, clad in white duck uniforms with silver capes and carrying flaming torches. Bryan told them that while "a little more than a month ago I went into what I then called the enemy's country," today "there is no enemy's country." He was trying to walk back his original comment, but the mistake was too damaging and could not be erased or transformed.[22]

The Boy Orator made almost a dozen speeches as his train moved across Missouri before entering Illinois and Indiana. He was exhausted by the time he reached Louisville, Kentucky, three days after leaving home, and his tone had turned tough. He was introduced by a former Republican who jokingly called him the greatest anarchist that ever lived. The campaign was between "Plutocracy and Democracy," Bryan said, with the "syndicates, the trusts, and the 'combinations of money grabbers'" on one side and the "'struggling masses' on the other."[23]

After two days in Kentucky, he wasted the next four days in Tennessee, North Carolina, Virginia, and Washington, D.C. Those states appeared safe for Democrats and D.C. residents couldn't vote. The only utility from those stops was Bryan's speeches, reprinted across the country, but he may have hurt himself with his remarks and noticeably unforgiving tone. In Charlotte, he condemned gold Democrats who had bolted, saying they could return only "in sack cloth and ashes." He had been given thirty rabbits' feet by the time he left the state.[24]

Bryan finally took his message to a battleground state with a speech Saturday at Baltimore's Music Hall. Even when he denied being an anarchist, he framed his argument in combative terms. He said he loved law and order so much "that I want the law enforced against the greatest enemies" of it, "those who think that they are greater than the Government itself."[25]

AS THE FRONT-PORCH CAMPAIGN roared through September, there were signs the election was turning in McKinley's direction. The Illinois GOP canvass now suggested he would carry the state by 70,000 votes. Dawes reported that Wisconsin appeared on track to produce "the largest majority ever given." The Nebraska and South Dakota canvasses indicated both states were moving into the GOP column, though Michigan remained shaky. One hundred million pieces of campaign literature had already been shipped, which was undoubtedly having an effect in a country of less than 75 million people. One of the more effective pamphlets was a long letter from a farmer to his brother titled "Dear John" that made the Republican case on gold as better for agriculture.[26]

The campaign armed Republicans for debates with their neighbors with a pamphlet titled "Silver Arguments Simple Answered" that contained rebuttals to the nineteen most common Free Silver claims. The campaign also targeted farmers on protection with a leaflet titled "American Farmers Were Protected by the McKinley Tariff Law," reminding farm voters, many of whom may have favored silver over gold, that the Major's bill set tariffs on foreign agricultural products.[27]

Not leaving anything to chance, McKinley's managers launched another major effort at the end of September, this one to encourage veterans to vote for what was likely to be the last of their Civil War comrades to be president. Since the Civil War, Republicans had "waved the bloody flag" during elections, asking veterans to "vote like you shot." This outreach generally involved speakers, parades, and veterans' auxiliaries, the last drawing on the Grand Army of the Republic, the nation's largest organization of those who fought for the North.[28]

As the Civil War receded in time, appeals to the "Bloody Shirt" fell into disuse. Immigrants and those born after the war had no firsthand experience of the conflict. Team McKinley would now make a bipartisan appeal to veterans based on unity and sound money, drawing on concerns about Free Silver eroding the value of their pensions through inflation and about Democratic attempts to shrink spending on pensions. It was called the Patriotic Heroes' Battalion.[29]

"The Generals' Tour," as the press dubbed it, was launched Monday, September 21, at a rally of veterans and GOP partisans at the Chicago Auditorium. Former Michigan governor Russell A. Alger, who rode under George Armstrong Custer and was a former GAR national commander, opened the program pledging, "We are in the field until the battle is won." Another veteran, General David E. Sickles, paid tribute to Lincoln's leadership, then said, "As I was unable to stand with Jeff Davis on his platform . . . I am unable to stand today on the platform of the Chicago convention." Generally regarded as incompetent, Sickles lost a leg at Gettysburg, ending his combat career. A fellow officer remarked, "The loss of his leg is a great gain to us, whatever it may be to him." A lifelong

Democrat, Sickles was tainted by scandal, having won acquittal in 1858 for killing his wife's lover, the U.S. Attorney for the District of Columbia, with perhaps America's first successful claim of temporary insanity.[30]

The tour needed enlisted men, so McKinley's team recruited James M. Tanner. After losing both legs below the knees at Second Bull Run, Corporal Tanner had become a War Department stenographer. He went to Ford's Theatre when Lincoln was shot and, at Secretary of War Stanton's direction, kept a shorthand record of the night's events. Harrison made him pensions commissioner, in which post he vowed to get the maximum benefit for "every old comrade that needs it." He was fired seven months later for incompetence but remained a popular fixture in GOP campaigns.[31]

The Generals' Tour visited Wisconsin and Minnesota before heading to Iowa, Nebraska, Kansas, and Missouri in early October. These states had a large number of Union veterans and because of the depression, the vets were deeply concerned about any threat to their pensions, whether from silver's inflation or Democratic budget cuts. Alger and his crew covered Midwest and border states for the rest of the campaign, traveling in relative comfort—eventually two private cars and two sleeping coaches, which bore a banner that read 1896 IS AS VITALLY IMPORTANT AS 1861—and lobbing political grenades as they stalked Bryan. By Election Day they had traveled nearly 8,500 miles and held 276 events, often starting at 7 a.m. and not finishing until nearly midnight, the blast of a small cannon announcing their train's arrival.[32]

WHILE MCKINLEY'S CAMPAIGN WAS organized and meticulous, Bryan's was uncoordinated and meandering. Bryan often had to personally look up train schedules to plan his travel, buy his own tickets, and carry his own bags. Rather than riding in a private sleeper car that was put on a siding and hooked on to the connecting train while he slept in the middle of the night, Bryan traveled mostly in coach cars, forced to sit in stations at odd hours waiting for connections. This all put Bryan's voice and health at risk. Senator Butler was appalled by the situation and wrote Senator Jones, warning Bryan would collapse before November if the DNC did not provide him with a travel aide and private train car.[33]

Butler had witnessed the disorganization firsthand when Bryan was forced to leave Washington very late and spend the night in the Baltimore station, waiting for a 6 a.m. local for Middletown, Delaware.[34]

While Delaware had only three electoral votes, it was a battleground state, so Bryan was right to invest his time there with rallies in Dover and Wilmington. After his last event, Bryan collapsed at a friend's home where he was staying. It was a "beastly hot night," according to Josephus Daniels, who was traveling with Bryan. Daniels was alarmed as nurses gave Bryan alcohol rubs until daybreak and a doctor stood by. "The host and I feared for his life. Next morning, however, he was fresh as a daisy." He had to be: Bryan was about to enter the "enemy's country" again.[35]

ONE OF THE MORE difficult things to understand about Bryan's campaign is why he spent so much time in places where he had little chance, like the Northeast. On Tuesday, September 22, Bryan again entered the region by fighting through a screaming, clawing mob to his carriage at Philadelphia's Broad Street Station. He would spend the next eight days in states where Republicans were very strong.[36]

Nonetheless, Bryan campaigned hard, making more than fifty speeches in eight states using his harshest language yet. At the Brooklyn Academy of Music, he declared, "We are fighting an enemy that has never been honest in its dealing." He called Treasury secretary Carlisle a criminal whose "sympathies are with the idle holder of idle capital rather than the struggling masses." In New Haven, Connecticut, Bryan claimed people "have been terrorized by financial institutions" until "it is more dangerous to raise your voice" against them than it was in "an absolute monarchy" such as Russia. In Hartford, home to the insurance industry, he attacked its leaders as "more concerned about their own salaries than they are in protecting the policy holders from the effects of free coinage."[37]

The Nebraskan even punched down, picking fights with McKinley supporters. When Bryan said in New Haven, "If syndicates and corporations rule this country, then no young man has a fair shot unless he is the favorite of a corporation," Yale students started heckling. He ramped up his rhetoric, saying, "I am not speaking now to the sons who are sent to college on the proceeds of ill-gotten gains. I will wait until these sons have exhausted what their fathers have left and I will appeal to their children." The students howled. Bryan insulted them again. "I hardly know what language to use . . . to those who desire to be known not as creators of wealth but as distributors." After a student band starting playing, he attacked the college men again before abruptly leaving the stage.[38]

There were large crowds everywhere. Whether people agreed with what he said or not, they wanted to see the magnetic Boy Orator. Bryan arrived at the Boston Common to find an estimated 50,000 to 75,000 people, the largest gathering in city history and Bryan's biggest crowd. Daniels later wrote, "It seemed to me that the whole creation had gathered that night." No matter what Bryan said, "every sentence . . . was punctured by the sort of enthusiastic applause which one gets from an emotional and sympathetic audience."[39]

Bryan considered his final Northeastern stop—Tammany Hall's headquarters called the Wigwam—"one of the most important events of the campaign." Four thousand machine Democrats greeted him with a wild demonstration of cheers, foot stamping, and shrill whistling. He spoke for an hour, interrupted by frequent applause and egged on with shouts to "hit him again, old man!" But Bryan was exhausted, having reached his breaking point. Reporters saw he "trembled and his face was deathly pale." Those around him could see "he was at the point of collapse" and had to be helped to his carriage in a driving rain.[40]

Bryan shouldn't have bothered stopping in New York. Just two weeks earlier, the silver men who dominated the New York Democratic convention picked a sound-money man, Albany mayor John Boyd Thacher, as their gubernatorial candidate after being assured he supported the Chicago ticket and platform.[41]

While Bryan was en route to Delaware, Thacher had written his state Democratic chairman to say he backed Bryan but not Free Silver. Bryan issued an ultimatum: Thacher must leave the ticket and be replaced with a silver man or Bryan would publicly abandon New York. The brouhaha was resolved when Thacher withdrew from the governor's race, but Bryan had been humiliated in the press. All this transpired before Bryan arrived at the Wigwam, raising questions about why he considered his Tammany stop so important. Every machine man in that hall knew New York Democrats were badly divided and incapable of carrying the nation's largest battleground state. Just after midnight on September 30, Bryan caught a train heading southwest, having wasted much of two weeks, either in the Solid South or the hostile Northeast.[42]

• • •

THACHER WASN'T BRYAN'S ONLY New York headache. Critics bracketed him during his Eastern swing. The gold Democratic ticket of Palmer and Buckner had been well received by sound-money Democrats at Madison Square Garden. Cockran was also in the East attacking Bryan in Baltimore's Music Hall. The Irish baritone had drawn large crowds in seven cities since his Garden speech and was effective because he remained a Democrat while supporting McKinley, even turning down an offer of a congressional nomination from New York Republicans. Cockran served as a solvent, dissolving ties that bound sound-money Democrats to their party in an age of intense, sustained partisan loyalty. He would persuade some Democrats to stay home and others to support Palmer and Buckner's National Democratic ticket. Most, however, would follow Cockran and vote for McKinley.[43]

BY EARLY OCTOBER, MCKINLEY'S front-porch success, the early victories in Vermont and Maine, and the increasing amount of campaign activity had yielded better results in the state door-to-door canvasses and created a sense that Republicans had blunted Bryan's momentum. John Hay wrote a friend, "I think we have got The Boy on the run."[44]

At the end of September, Dawes reported to Hanna that the campaign had received a total of $570,000 in contributions, nearly $455,000 in September alone. The campaign collected four times as much that month as it had raised in the two previous months combined.

Hanna's late August meetings in New York and Boston were paying off. J. P. Morgan and his associates were chipping in, as were others whom the RNC chairman had called upon (including Standard Oil's John D. Rockefeller), and bundlers were tapping friends and business acquaintances. Even Lodge reported to Roosevelt that his son-in-law had gotten into the swing of things and "wrung something like ten thousand dollars from members of the Somerset Club who never gave a dime to any public object before."[45]

CHAPTER 27

Closing Arguments

————◁◦▷————

I n the campaign's closing weeks, neither Bryan nor McKinley chose to be
calculating. Each made his case by stressing his fundamental worldview.
Bryan's was bleak and gloomy. He saw America as a country divided between the many poor and the wealthy few, between good and evil. He cast
himself as the change agent who would end the people's oppression and
overturn the policies that had left many Americans struggling.

McKinley's beliefs came from a more optimistic place. He saw
America—as he believed the Founders intended—as one nation, indivisi-
ble, with all equal before the law, a country on the edge of prosperity and
greatness if the right leaders and policies were in place. And he, too, cast
himself as someone who would bring about change—the restoration of
prosperity and national unity.

In October's first three weeks, the McKinley campaign's strength
would become apparent as its candidate delivered his message and his disciplined organization widened its lead in money, speakers, and material.
The Major needed it all to withstand the assault Bryan was about to launch
on him, on gold Democrats, and on the money power that Bryan believed
was behind them all. If McKinley survived the attack and pushed back
with a message that gave voters hope and a positive reason to support him,
he could be the next president.

• • •

TO CLOSE HIS CAMPAIGN, McKinley argued that confidence in the strength of the dollar and confidence in the nation's system of finance were essential to bringing prosperity back. The Major drew on many voters' concern that a Free Silver victory would deepen the depression by allowing buyers to pay in silver while suppliers insisted on gold. This fear was already causing interest rates to rise, credit to dry up, and European financiers to contemplate cashing out their American investments. "The mere advocacy of free silver," McKinley told a Pennsylvania delegation, has already made "it harder to enter into legitimate public and private enterprises. There is a waiting. There is a distress on every hand. Men do not know what the future has in store."[1]

This argument that gold could stabilize the country's confidence was convincing, but the Major paired it with another message. McKinley frequently discussed his belief in a "common country," but as he saw Americans repelled by Bryan's divisive rhetoric and class appeals, he saw an opportunity to broaden this theme to attract voters with a call for national unity.

As the Boy Orator decried oppression of the poor by the rich, the Major preached, "We are all equal citizens . . . equal citizens in privilege and opportunity." He reminded some West Virginians that their state's interests in mining, manufacturing, and agriculture "are identical and are not different from the interests of every other section." The country would enjoy progress and prosperity when class and regional divisions were set aside and America worked "for the good of all."[2]

McKinley didn't stop appealing to laborers or discussing protection but added these new themes of confidence and unity. Workingmen rewarded him for it. M. M. Garland, president of the Iron and Steel Workers union, endorsed him in October, while laborers from every industry, walk of life, and battleground state kept plowing into Canton to hear the Major's message personally. In politics, optimism is often the ingredient that can crystallize support for a candidate, giving voters reasons to believe their lives will be better.[3]

ON OCTOBER 9, THE McKinley campaign powerfully showcased its appeal for national unity in two cities. The first was Canton. That afternoon, two large trainloads bearing thousands of men, many in gray or butternut uniforms, arrived in town. These were ex-Confederate veterans, mostly from Virginia's Shenandoah Valley, where McKinley had fought. Met at the depot by a mounted escort, uniformed wheelmen on their bikes, a GAR band, and several hundred Union vets, the two thousand Southerners marched to the Tabernacle, where Canton women served lunch to the men and their families. Each ex-Confederate was given a knife from the Novelty Cutlery Company engraved with the American flag, McKinley's portrait, and the words "No East, No West, No North, No South, the Union Forever." There were matching badges, with ribbons half blue and half gray, bearing a similar sentiment.

At 4:30 p.m., the Southern men gathered behind a banner that read UNITED WE STAND. The reverse displayed an American eagle resting on a shield with the words PRESENTED TO THE EX–CONFEDERATE VETERANS OF THE SHENANDOAH VALLEY, VIRGINIA, BY THE EX–UNION VETERANS OF CANTON, OHIO. The men marched up streets lined with cheering spectators and billowing flags, Northern and Southern units mingled together. The march ended at a stage on McKinley's lawn, with the crowd jamming the intersection and nearby streets to witness the historic moment.[4]

McKinley was moved by the presence of men he may have faced on the battlefield. "Patriotism is not bound by State, or class, or sectional lines," he told them, "we are a reunited country. We have but one flag. . . . Sectionalism was surrendered at Appomattox." His campaign stood for "Country first, Country last and Country with stainless honor." McKinley noted this was the first time a Republican presidential candidate had met with ex-Confederates and urged veterans North and South to support "the enthronement of justice and the supremacy of law." The ex-Rebels filed across the porch to shake his hand and returned to the Tabernacle for dinner. The Southerners' bands offered a concert in the Courthouse Square before their trains left for Virginia at midnight.[5]

This show of the unity of former enemies resonated at a time when Bryan was encouraging animosity between regions and classes. To further underscore this theme of unity, the McKinley team created a similarly inspiring scene in Chicago that day, the twenty-fifth anniversary of its Great Fire. The city's Sound Money Association asked gold men to spend their day off marching for McKinley. Promptly at 10 a.m., a cannon in Lake Front Park boomed and the parade began moving through downtown streets.

For the next seven hours, tens of thousands of men marched through Chicago, organized by industry, profession, company, ethnic origin, ward, or shared belief. The *London Daily Mail*'s cynical George Warrington Steevens had expected "to see a big thing—perhaps a matter of two or three hours—but not a thing whose bigness would transcend my powers of estimate and comparison," he wrote later. He counted a hundred thousand men. "The mind was stunned and deadened by the vastness of it."[6]

Noise from bands, drum and bugle corps, glee clubs, and marchers echoed through the streets and bounced off skyscrapers. There were flags, including a giant American one made of umbrellas, "some blue with white stars, others red and white," Steevens wrote, "cunningly marshaled so that from above they presented a giant counterfeit of the stars and stripes."

The procession was a walking encyclopedia of occupations, professions, and trades. One float featured a Mexican cart and a man in Chinese garb flanked by flags and giant silver coins of the two countries with a sign, WORTH 51 CENTS. On another, Uncle Sam stood with a safe and the slogan GUARD THE NATION'S HONOR behind gold battlements with soldiers at each corner. The paper trade put attractive women on its float, holding large rolls of paper. Special phone devices captured the spectacle's sounds so McKinley and Hobart could listen from their homes. Hanna was astounded, saying, "It beats anything of the kind ever seen in the country."

Hanna had just arrived in Chicago after being in New York three weeks, mostly raising money, but also reevaluating the electoral map with the Executive Committee. Quay again pushed for more work in the South. Hanna's first reaction was negative, but by October 4, he agreed to more resources for some Southern states. When more literature and speakers appeared in Georgia, an *Atlanta Constitution* cartoon showed Hanna emptying moneybags to buy the state.[7]

GOP leaders knew this was a long shot, but they could afford it and maybe make Democrats spread their limited resources thinner. Still, the McKinley men knew the race would be settled in the Midwest and were worried especially about Illinois. Hahn was told to put more speakers into the Midwest as well as the border states of Kentucky, Missouri, and West Virginia. Resources and speakers were also sent to Wyoming and the Pacific Coast states. Hanna then departed New York, telling reporters he was ready to meet "our opponents in the open field of battle which they have chosen for the final contest." He would remain in the Midwest through Election Day.[8]

Dawes also began reducing the amount of currency literature while distributing more protection material to state parties. The campaign was almost a reverse image of what it had been in the summer, when Bryan talked currency and McKinley did not. Protection remained the Major's second most important issue, but Bryan rarely mentioned tariff reform, allowing Republicans to have an unchallenged conversation with laborers, miners, steelworkers, sheep raisers, and workers in other once-protected industries.[9]

AFTER LEAVING NEW YORK with his hopes for its electoral votes wrecked, Bryan refocused his campaign on the border and Midwestern states. He had grasped that the election would be decided there, especially in Illinois, Indiana, Iowa, Michigan, and Wisconsin. With the exception of two wasted days in Tennessee helping a silver friend run against one of Cleveland's staunchest Democratic allies in the House, Bryan would spend the last month in Midwestern and border state battlegrounds. He moved to strengthen his message as well.[10]

He first attacked McKinley by name, aggressively and often. In West Virginia, he quoted the Major during the Sherman Act debate as favoring "the largest use of silver" and griped "that when a man changes his mind he ought to have reason for it that he is willing to give." He also charged McKinley was trying to buy the state by spending $300,000. The Nebraskan also took to routinely assaulting gold Democratic bolters. At one stop, he dared them to "summon enough courage" to "declare themselves Republicans" and at another, accused them of wanting to make the Democratic Party an "instrument of plutocracy to overthrow a government like ours."[11]

In Indianapolis, site of the gold ticket's nomination, Bryan was amused to find the Palmer-Buckner headquarters flanked by a pawnshop and a funeral parlor. "This city," he told a state capitol rally, "enjoys the unique distinction of being the birthplace and the deathbed of a so-called party . . . organized for the expressed purpose of electing a Republican candidate for president." Such attacks did Bryan little good, except make it easier for sound-money Democrats to vote Republican with a clear conscience.[12]

Bryan also let Cockran get under his skin as the Irishman trailed him around the country. Bryan punched back, questioning Cockran's character, saying he was paid by sound-money Democrats to vote Republican. In reality, Cockran refused payment for his speaking and believed endorsing McKinley ended his political career.[13]

While Bryan was toughening his rhetoric, he also offered a new theme. Democrats could escape responsibility for the panic and divorce themselves from Cleveland's policies only if voters saw Bryan as the candidate who would take America in a new direction with his Free Silver platform. So Bryan began saying, "We propose something; our opponents propose nothing," and arguing, "the Republican party proposes to continue the present financial condition." This refrain that McKinley was the status quo candidate was constant for the rest of the election. But Republicans replied that McKinley's change was protection, opposed by both Bryan and Cleveland. Bryan was now often on the defensive and lashing out at his opponents with sometimes extreme language. Maybe this was a deliberate decision or perhaps a product of his grueling schedule and lack of sleep and rest. If the latter was the case, Bryan was about to get some relief.[14]

Bryan had traveled like a vagabond for thousands of miles, often riding in any available coach seat, grabbing meals at depots when possible, buying tickets each day for the next leg, and hoping local organizers had arranged a hotel. No more. Senator Butler's letter warning Chairman Jones that Bryan would not last without help on the road had produced results.

Courtesy of the DNC, there was a Wagner palace car waiting when Bryan arrived in Chicago late on October 7. It had a private compartment, sitting area, a comfortable bed, and separate space for press and campaign aides. There was also a kitchen where a cook could prepare meals. Bryan could eat when he wanted, nap between stops, and no longer be awakened in the middle of the night for connections. His car would now be put on a siding and hooked to his next train while he slept. It was named *The Idler*, which Bryan thought "a most inappropriate name," given his frantic pace, but the car was his new home for all but one day of the campaign's final month.[15]

Bryan planned to spend October in the Ohio and upper Mississippi valleys, but where to spend the last week? DNC officials held a late-night strategy session aboard his new car to discuss the decision. Ohio and Indiana were possibilities, but party leaders agreed Bryan should spend the final week in Illinois. Senator Jones and Hinrichsen would set his schedule. Bryan's train left Chicago after midnight, his private car, *The Idler,* at the tail end.[16]

Bryan arrived in Burlington, Iowa, at 5:55 a.m. on October 9 for the first of eight speeches that day to find the morning papers reporting that his law partner was voting for McKinley. This was no surprise for those who knew A. R. Talbot. He was a staunch Republican running for the state senate but still, the press wondered why Bryan could not convert someone so close to him.[17]

Bryan chugged through the Dakotas and Minnesota, then northern Wisconsin and the Upper Peninsula before heading south into "The Mitten" of lower Michigan. It was a colorful swing. He shared the stage in Fargo, North Dakota, with a stuffed eagle that had been carried by a Democratic candidate who canvassed the state on a white horse, wrapped in a flag with the dead bird on his shoulder. In St. Paul, a labor group gave Bryan a gold pen and silver holder with which to sign a Free Silver law. Not to be outdone, Minneapolis unionists fashioned an inkwell from a mixture of sixteen parts silver to one part gold. As thanks, he attacked trusts, syndicates, and corporations, saying they threatened the principles embodied in the Declaration of Independence.[18]

In Minnesota and Michigan, Bryan played off McKinley's new theme of "confidence," calling the Republicans' promises part of "a confidence game" cooked up by Wall Street and other Free Silver opponents. Now rested thanks to his new private car and its comforts, Bryan was even tougher, describing his opponents as "every man who would make a slave of his neighbor." He suggested a new design for the gold dollar. "On the one side should be a blood-sucking leech and beneath the three words, 'Give, give, give.' "[19]

Michael Doran, the former Minnesota committeeman who had orchestrated the gold victory at the state convention, arrived at Bryan's Minneapolis hotel to visit an out-of-town friend and asked what the hubbub was about. When told Bryan was coming for a Democratic rally, Doran replied, "Democratic not by a damned sight." Doran's comment was evidence of Minnesota's badly splintered political scene. Many of its Democratic sound-money men were not reconciled to the Chicago platform or its author. But the GOP was badly split, too. Silver Republicans in Minnesota had bolted, including Representative Charles A. Towne, running for reelection as a silver fusionist, and John Lind, the former Republican turned Democratic-Populist fusion gubernatorial candidate. The Swedish Lind was now a threat to become the first non-Republican governor since 1860. The divisions in both parties scrambled allegiance and made it difficult to count on old voting patterns holding up in this election.[20]

INCREASINGLY, BRYAN HAD TO contend with Republicans and gold Democrats bracketing his events in cities where Bryan spoke, appearing before and after him. The Generals' Tour, for example, criticized him over a *World-Herald* editorial unsympathetic toward veterans' pensions. The editorial was turned into a flyer and was handed out by Republicans at Bryan rallies. Bryan replied that it had occurred long before he joined the paper and didn't reflect his views.[21]

Not so easily handled was the controversy created in Iowa by the author of *Coin's Financial School*. In Clinton, William "Coin" Harvey attacked the Generals' Tour as "old wrecks of the rebellion who have lost all their honor and patriotism and are tools of political shylocks." The audience "yelled, hooted and jeered," forcing Harvey off the stage, and veterans had to be restrained from roughing him up. Members of the tour showed up the next day to offer "scathing rebukes" to Harvey's slur. Bryan tried to ignore the fracas. But while McKinley was shaking hands with former Confederates to celebrate the country's reconciliation from the war, Bryan staying quiet did little to show he could unite the country or cared to.[22]

One of the most effective Republicans bracketing Bryan on the trail was the ambitious young New Yorker Theodore Roosevelt. Teddy earned an invitation to make a series of major addresses for the McKinley campaign after creating an impression on a five-day western New York tour he made with Senator Henry Cabot Lodge at the beginning of October. Lodge had earlier invited Roosevelt to join him, saying, "Now don't say you can't or talk Police. This is more important than Police." Little did he know that Roosevelt was looking for just this kind of opportunity to show the McKinley managers how valuable he could be.[23]

To resurrect his political career, Roosevelt wanted to be in McKinley's good graces to get an appointment if the Major won. Though he thought little of McKinley before the convention, he had been helpful to the campaign since, offering Hanna solid advice about Platt and the currency, and facilitating the rapprochement between the strong-willed Clevelander and the equally stubborn Easy Boss.

Roosevelt was also trying to get to McKinley another way. Back in August, he and his wife, Edith, invited former Ohio representative Bellamy Storer and his wife, Maria, to Sagamore Hill, their Oyster Bay, New York, home. The couples had known each other for eight years and Bellamy was the godfather of Archibald, Roosevelt's youngest. Roosevelt took Maria out in a rowboat on Oyster Bay, which made her nervous, since Teddy rowed, she later wrote, "spasmodically and sometimes absent-mindedly." He confessed he was done with being police commissioner. He was in endless lawsuits with fellow commissioners and now hated the job he had gloried in just a year earlier. He worried he had no political future. "There is one thing I would like to have," he told Maria, "but McKinley would never give it to me. I should like to be Assistant-Secretary of the Navy." Knowing the Major was not enamored with Roosevelt, Maria nonetheless promised she and Bellamy would ask McKinley to appoint him.

Teddy made a show of saying he did not want to interfere with Bellamy's chances to go into the cabinet and would serve under him if Bellamy were navy secretary, but Maria knew that even though they had helped bail McKinley out in the Walker notes fiasco, it was unlikely an Ohio president would give one of eight cabinet posts to another Ohioan. Bellamy had a better shot at an ambassadorship.[24]

Teddy wrote both Storers after they returned to Cincinnati. He both flattered Bellamy and presumptuously pressed his claim, writing, "As I want work, I suppose it would be well for me to accept the Assistant Secretaryship of the Navy, in the very improbable event of my being offered it. But I do not want you to concern yourself about the matter; first, because it is too early; and second, because the really important thing is to get you in the Cabinet or at Paris." But of course Roosevelt wanted Storer to concern himself about the matter. Otherwise, TR might not snag his prize appointment. To Maria, the more politically astute of the two, he reported, "The day after I left you I saw Mark Hanna, and after I thought we had grown intimate enough, the chance arriving, I spoke of Bellamy as the man for the Cabinet, either for War or Navy, or else to go to France" but Hanna was focused on "how to elect McKinley." I can help you and you can help me was Roosevelt's subtle message.[25]

To have the support of McKinley's close friend was valuable. But if

Roosevelt wanted to rescue his political career, he still needed to weasel his way into the McKinley campaign and make his own mark. The speaking tour with Lodge appeared to be an ideal opportunity. Though Lodge was better known, Teddy won their tour's headlines by delivering hotter, more memorable phrases. At one rally, he accused Bryan of holding "principles sufficiently silly and wicked to make them fit well in the mouth of an anarchist leader" and assailed Bryan's call for class warfare as "a borrowed cry . . . heard in Paris and [which] resulted in the horrors of the commune." [26]

At Lake Chautauqua's Celeron, where Bryan spoke in August, Roosevelt called the election a fight "against a government of the mob and for the demagogue." He told of a recent ferry ride where he overheard a drunken Democrat tell passengers, "if Bryan was successful there would not be any more yachts." What would be the next object of Bryan's class hatred? TR warned Bryan's victory "would work much more evil than the success of the rebellion" Lincoln had ended. It was over-the-top, but the crowd cheered its approval. [27]

Lodge and Roosevelt were invited at the end of the tour to visit McKinley. Hay was amused about the visit, writing Henry Adams that the two had been to Canton "to offer their heads to the axe, and their tummies to the harikari knife." McKinley had asked Hay to attend the meeting with Lodge and Roosevelt, but "I had thought I would not struggle with the millions on his trampled lawn." [28]

Teddy wrote his sister that while he was not "among his [McKinley's] favorites," it was a pleasant visit. He must have impressed someone, for Roosevelt was asked to make a major speech in Chicago in mid-October and then trail Bryan through Michigan as part of the GOP's bracketing. TR now had a chance to demonstrate his usefulness and the McKinley campaign had an attack dog to go after Bryan. [29]

In Chicago, the American College Republican League filled the Coliseum with 13,000 screaming students. TR's opening set the tone for his two-hour speech. "It is not merely schoolgirls that have hysterics. Very vicious mob-leaders have them at times and so do well-meaning demagogues," he charged. "Instead of a government of the people, for the people, and by the people . . . Bryan would substitute a government of the mob, by the demagogue, for the shiftless and disorderly and the criminal."

Roosevelt savaged Bryan's theory that prosperity depended on easy inflated money. The quality of money mattered more than its quantity. Roosevelt held up two Mexican dollars, a French five-franc piece, and an American silver dollar, and explained why the French equal of the dollar was worth more because it was backed with gold. Then he used the two bread loaves—a large one purchased with gold and one half its size bought with silver—to illustrate the point: "If the working man can only earn a lean dollar"—a silver one—"he can only buy a lean loaf." He had tested the references in a New York speech earlier and drawn an enthusiastic response. Free Silver "would entail more misery and suffering on the poor man than all the oppression of the most evil-minded capitalist could inflict on him in a century." Bryan "and the men who stand at his right and left hands"—Altgeld and Tillman—"rally to their banners all the forces that make for social disorder and national destruction." They were "demagogues."

Roosevelt closed by denouncing Bryan's "attempt to stir up . . . class hatred," which would "insure the degradation of every class in the community." He "would substitute for the government of Washington and Lincoln . . . a red welter of lawlessness and dishonesty. . . . The laws of right and justice bid you oppose them." The audience stood and roared its approval.[30]

The next day, Roosevelt boarded a train to Jackson, Michigan, arriving shortly after Bryan made a whistle-stop there. Teddy spoke in a giant shed decorated with pictures of McKinley and Hobart and a large flag. He road-tested a new introduction, his text from *Henry VI, Part II* in which the demagogue Jack Cade promises that when he is king, "Seven half penny loaves shall sell for one penny in England. A pint pot of beer shall hold a quart. I shall make it a felony to drink small beers. All shall eat and drink at my score, and all shall wear the same livery." Like Cade, TR argued, Bryan was a demagogue making promises he could not keep and preaching class hatred in equality's name. Roosevelt received a standing ovation for what the local paper called a "brilliant" speech. He was ready for his confrontation with Bryan.[31]

The Majestic in Detroit was packed Saturday morning when Roosevelt opened by saying that while he was normally too busy working, "for I belong to the labor class," the election was so critical he "did not feel at liberty to refuse the invitation" to speak. He mentioned he had been in Jackson and could "have heard an address by the boy orator of the Platte," but didn't because he was reading it that same afternoon "in the words of the greatest master of the English language" that showed "the demagogue is no new feature." Roosevelt then quoted Shakespeare. The crowd roared.

From audience reaction in Chicago and Jackson, he knew what to drop and what to sharpen and was tighter and funnier than in the two previous cities. When a dog barked, Roosevelt ad-libbed, "Another vote for Bryan." He savaged Bryan with his Chicago text, which had been tuned up in Jackson and trimmed by half an hour. The *Detroit Free Press* called it "a masterly address listened to [by] a big crowd."[32]

Bryan apparently felt the pressure of his attack dog. In a long Detroit speech that night (his thirteenth of the day), Bryan spent most of his time replying to attacks—leveled by Roosevelt, Cockran, and others—that the Chicago platform was "lawless." Nothing in that platform, he argued, "suggests lawlessness or threatens the peace and safety of society." Bryan also defended the plank opposing federal injunctions against Republican accusations of "the Democratic party of being in league with lawlessness." Bryan pledged to "enforce every law of the United States."[33]

Like the skilled boxer he had been at Harvard, the ambitious Roosevelt had pummeled Bryan with language much harsher than McKinley's and questioned Bryan's charade by calling him an extremist and a demagogue. Stung perhaps by Roosevelt's speech and other recent attacks, Bryan had been thrown off message and put on the defensive.[34]

IN MID-OCTOBER, MCKINLEY WAS rewarded for his decision years before to reject the American Protective Association and reach out to Catholic voters. Archbishop John Ireland of St. Paul responded to an invitation from prominent laymen to explain his views on the Chicago platform. Ireland's bombshell reply broke nationally on Monday, October 12. While recognizing some would object to a "teacher of religion" opining on politics, the archbishop said he was a citizen, too, and that remaining silent "would be cowardice." Ireland was blunt: America faced its worst crisis since the Civil War. The Chicago platform encouraged "rebellion," using "the old secession doctrine" to oppose presidential injunctions by saying the national government had no power outside Washington, D.C. The platform "threatens the country," Ireland wrote, "with lawlessness and anarchy."

Free Silver would bring upon America "a financial depression far beyond anything which we are now experiencing." "The laboring classes will suffer the most of all from free silver coinage" as their wages' purchasing power was cut in half and commerce damaged, leaving "no work for the people." Ireland then endorsed McKinley, the first time a major figure in the Catholic hierarchy endorsed a Republican presidential candidate.[35]

While Democrats dismissed the letter, RNC officials characterized it "a political scorcher," saying it "would have a powerful influence." Ireland was a prominent Catholic in a battleground state with many Catholics. Any of them with doubts about Bryan and the Chicago platform now had forceful reasons to bolt to McKinley. Ireland's letter was reprinted and widely circulated in other states and Republicans echoed his charge about Democratic "lawlessness." McKinley's willingness to openly ask for Catholic votes was also a historic step for the GOP. The APA would no longer enforce tests of Protestant purity on Republican presidential candidates as McKinley broadened the GOP's coalition.[36]

ALSO IN MID-OCTOBER, RNC dignitaries and McKinley supporters flocked to New York's Olympia Hall ballroom to see a primitive silent film of the Major. In it, McKinley came out of his home, took a document from an aide, doffed his hat, and walked across his lawn to greet a delegation. The McKinley supporters who saw the first GOP moving picture were also treated to performances by a strong man, a flying ballet, and an equilibrist, along with music and dancing by Dutch Daly, the Poluski Brothers, and Miss Kitty Mitchell.[37]

McKinley had no time for vaudeville. By now, his weeks—especially Fridays and Saturdays—were a blur of delegations as the Front-Porch Campaign reached its maximum. October 12 was the biggest front-porch day yet, with a score of delegations arriving on more than forty special excursion trains, as well as the regular traffic, requiring a dozen speeches. People came from at least twenty-two states, filling Canton's streets and squares with swirls of people, bands, spectators, and banners. One read, I AM FROM ROCK ISLAND COUNTY, ILLINOIS, WHERE THERE ARE SIXTEEN M'KINLEY VOTERS TO ONE BRYAN VOTER. WHERE ARE YOU FROM? The day ended with a giant torchlight parade.[38]

The following Saturday was even bigger. Almost forty delegations from seven states showed up, starting at 5:30 a.m. An estimated fifty-nine excursion trains carried over 500 carloads of visitors. McKinley made eighteen front-porch speeches, his most so far. A large presence of Pennsylvanians meant there was more talk of protection, but currency still dominated his speeches as he emphasized confidence and unity.[39]

He also pressed his case against Bryan without using his name. To 3,000 Pittsburgh factory, mill, and mine workers: "The man who would array the poor against the rich, labor against capital, classes against classes or section against section, is not a friend of the country," he said. "[He is] an enemy of the very best interests of every citizen."[40]

ON SUNDAY, OCTOBER 18, Bryan and Mary attended Detroit's Westminster Presbyterian. McKinley attended church in Canton with leaders of the Generals' Tour and walked home in a snowstorm with Alger and General Oliver O. Howard, sharing one umbrella. "The Major got the benefit of it," wrote a reporter, "for he walked between the two Generals, one hanging on each of his arms." Howard, having only his left arm after the battle of Fair Oaks in 1862, was on the right.[41]

The two candidates heard apolitical sermons, but Bryan was the target of tough talk in New York as some of the city's most prominent pastors went after him. At the Church of All Souls, Rev. R. Haber Newton argued "the money question . . . is at heart largely moral." Free Silver would destroy contracts and trust and was denounced at the Brick Presbyterian Church as "immoral . . . compulsory gambling for the whole Nation." At the Church of the Eternal Hope, the pastor declared, "the appeal of a demagogue to class feeling is an offense against the Gospel."

At Second Collegiate Reformed, the text was Genesis 2: "The gold of that land is good." In his sermon at the Academy of Music, Rev. Thomas Dixon called Bryan "a mouthing, slobbering demagogue." While there were different clerical voices, especially in the Plains, many Eastern pastors were especially pro-gold and anti-Bryan. There was just over two weeks before Election Day, and if the clergy rattled public sentiment, things were looking good for McKinley.[42]

CHAPTER 28

Coercion and Farm Prices

———◁◦▷———

"O ctober surprises" are always possible in an election's final days. Sometimes they are launched by opposing campaigns or instigated by other political actors. Sometimes, they emerge because of the economy or an international event. Often they have little effect, but occasionally they scramble the race.

As the election came to a close, Democrats would launch a surprise appeal to working-class voters, but the McKinley campaign would have surprises of its own, and a change in the economy would threaten to rip part of Bryan's rural base away. Farmers had fueled the rise of the silver movement, especially in the Midwest, and Bryan could not afford to lose their votes now.

MCKINLEY REFRESHED HIS CALL for unity during the final two weeks, adding notes of bipartisanship and patriotism. He told a delegation in Canton, "This is a year when patriotic men of all parties have banded together for the common weal."[1]

Wanting to drive this message of patriotism home, Hanna called on McKinley supporters to display the American flag outside their homes and in their communities on Saturday, October 31. The campaign would also organize Flag Day parades and rallies stressing national unity—political and geographic—to create a contrast with Bryan's divisive tone.

The next morning, Bryan said he agreed with Hanna's sentiment and encouraged Democrats to fly the flag on the thirty-first, too, but then foolishly suggested they do so to avoid retaliation from their employers. "I do not want the flags to mark the advocates for free silver for slaughter on that day," he said. "I do not want the employers to go over your town and . . . find who does not say he going to vote the Republican ticket." A simple plea for unity would have been more powerful, but Democrats knew Hanna's call for rallying around the flag would help the Republicans. An unnamed DNC official admitted, "Our people have been kicking themselves because they did not think of something in that line."[2]

This idea that employers would penalize workers who didn't fly the flag at McKinley's suggestion was part of a bigger Democratic strategy. Since Labor Day, Democrats had charged businesses were "using every effort to intimidate its men and compel them by whatever they see fit to endorse McKinley," as one Democratic newspaper put it. The accusations were groundless until a St. Louis department store fired a dozen employees for campaigning for Bryan on company time in mid-October. Democrats threatened a lawsuit and the Republican merchant backed down, rehired the men, and apologized, but the damage was done.[3]

Senator Jones pounced on the opportunity, charging that "[t]he great corporations with scarcely an exception and many of the large employers . . . are engaged in a concerted effort to coerce their employees into voting" for McKinley. Though the Democratic chairman didn't offer examples, it was a charge that, left unanswered, could undermine McKinley's appeal to workers. Hanna immediately responded that workingmen "are not fools, they are not slaves, they are not hypocrites, and they will resent any such accusations being put upon them." He offered a $500 reward for evidence of any coercion. The $500 was never claimed.[4]

McKinley himself addressed it with visiting Illinois railroad workers, saying, "The only coercion . . . today is that of reason, conscience, and experience." This was met with what the Canton paper called "[i]mmense applause and cries of 'That's right.'"[5]

In response, the DNC urged workers "to ask their employers for contracts insuring them against a reduction in wages in the event of McKinley's election." This clever tactic to frighten workers brought a sharp rebuttal from Hanna, who said it was "intended to foment trouble between capital and labor" and perhaps even force "a general strike before the election." Workingmen, he said, should "vote according to their conscientious opinions."[6]

Democrats felt they were on to something with the coercion issue and believed it would help stoke anger toward big corporations and the wealthy. But unless the charge resonated with the personal experiences of laborers, it was just chewing up time Democrats could devote to other issues—such as the income tax, federal interference in labor disputes, or arbitration—that had appeal among workingmen. After a week, the McKinley men pivoted away from the coercion debate by highlighting the endorsement of leaders of the largest railway unions, the Brotherhood of Locomotive Firemen and Brotherhood of Locomotive Engineers. Their leaders said they did not believe that "this country can stand an additional four years of misery and distress" that Free Silver would produce.[7]

BRYAN CONTINUED TO BE bracketed by both Republicans and gold Democrats and kept being thrown off stride. When the Generals' Tour attacked the Democratic Party's calls for slashing and limiting veterans' pensions (in part because only Union vets received them), the Boy Orator replied, "he was a better friend to the soldier than those who wished to submit the financial policy of this Nation to the dictation of foreign powers." Harrison also jumped on a Bryan comment about people who "have been for thirty years saving the country every year," an allusion to the Grand Army of the Republic and the Generals' Tour. "What has he done," Harrison asked, "that makes a slur by him any better than a slur spoken by the old copperheads?" Bryan was making it easy for Republicans to wave the Bloody Flag.[8]

Republicans also deployed a new voice for the final stretch, former Missouri senator and Hayes's interior secretary, Carl Schurz. The decorated Civil War general had left the GOP to support Cleveland, but now returned over the currency question. Schurz went after Bryan over Free Silver, arguing that depreciation of the currency would hurt the poor, workers, small savers, and veterans by cutting in half the value of wages, savings, insurance, and pensions. Schurz was a powerful speaker and well received, especially among his fellow German-Americans.[9]

• • •

THE OCTOBER SURPRISE IN 1896 turned out to be a rise in farm prices, which undermined Bryan's appeal to this crucial part of the electorate. The depression had hit farmers hard, curtailing the domestic market just as new sources of grain and cattle in Argentina, Australian, Russia, and elsewhere came on line and reduced world prices. This had made farmers prime targets for Bryan's currency message. Free Silver advocates blamed the gold standard for low farm prices. Gold-backed currency made each dollar more valuable, they argued, reducing prices paid to the producer. Silver prices and farm prices were inexorably linked. As silver prices had declined, so had farm prices. Prices would not rise without an inflationary bimetallic currency. Only free coinage would—by raising silver prices—increase farm prices. This linkage between white metal and rising farm prices was a critical argument for Free Silver, but it fell apart in mid-October.

As farmers brought in the fall harvest, farm prices rose even as silver prices fell. Wheat reached 70¢ a bushel on October 19, up a third or more since the campaign began. Prices for wheat deliveries in December hit a record 86½¢ a bushel. Corn prices were also higher for both the traditional December and March deliveries. Local prices were good, too, and for a wide range of farm products, from butter to eggs to produce. It was the best year for farmers in decades. Bryan had said such a turnabout was possible only under Free Silver, so the largely unexpected rise in farm prices had profound consequences for Democrats. Bryan's message was now completely at odds with the reality for farmers around the country, especially those in the Midwest states he needed to carry in order to win the election.[10]

With the title "Liars May Figure but Figures Won't Lie," a New York Press cartoon showed a distraught Bryan looking at two thermometers showing low silver and high wheat prices with the caption "Bryan tells the farmers that the price of wheat keeps pace with the price of silver; that the gold standard forced down the price of wheat, and that wheat could not rise till silver rose; but the cold facts are that silver has been sinking and wheat rising." A Midwest agricultural paper quoted a farmer who put it more bluntly: "Too busy down here following the rise in prices to bother with the silver theory."[11]

Republicans seized on the news. The GOP Congressional Committee chairman, Wisconsin representative Joseph W. Babcock, told reporters, "The present market conditions are complete denials of the claims and arguments of Mr. Bryan." The RNC distributed a special supplement to local papers in farm country that contrasted rising wheat prices with silver's fall. Plated and ready-to-print articles were provided to rural papers.

Democrats spun as best they could. Senator Jones claimed rising prices would only increase Bryan's vote. The Democratic Congressional Campaign chairman also dismissed the price rise, saying, "Farmers . . . are not ignoramuses." These were temporary increases and farmers would vote for Bryan "to make the prices permanent." Other Democrats asserted it was a plot by the administration, foreign business interests, or "Northwestern capitalists . . . to force up the price of wheat for campaign purposes," as well as to make "a few dollars."[12]

In reality, the crop in India had failed, Australia's production wasn't enough for its own people, and the Russian harvest was smaller than expected. The result was increased international demand for American wheat and a spike in wheat prices during September and October.[13]

These rising farm prices helped McKinley. Half the nation's farmers didn't have mortgages and weren't part of the debtor class to which Bryan was pitching Free Silver: the price increase had a very positive impact on them. Rising prices also made it easier for traditionally GOP farmers to vote McKinley and gave German, Scandinavian, and other ethnic farmers who leaned Democratic but favored gold another reason to break with Bryan.[14]

FOR BRYAN, VICTORY DEPENDED on Illinois and its 24 electoral votes. In 1888, Harrison won Cook County by 804 votes, carried the state by 3 percent, and won the presidency. In 1892, Cleveland won Cook by 33,350, carried the state by 3 percent, and recovered the White House. So Bryan would devote much of the final week to Illinois. A lot was riding on this time in Chicago.[15]

Bryan poured all his energy into the state, campaigning downstate for two days, then reaching Chicago Tuesday afternoon. "For over a mile outside the Alton and Chicago Railroad station a horde of yelling men pursued the train," wrote a reporter traveling with Bryan. "The noise they made drowned the roar of the cars, and we could scarce hear one another speak. . . . We rolled into the station amid a thunderous acclaim. The sight that met us was unforgettable, and cannot be accurately described. Earth, buildings, almost the sky, seemed to be made of frenzied men, waving their hats, swinging their arms, yelling open-mouthed in fierce excitement."[16]

More than 20,000 people crowded the depot and nearby streets. A wooden sidewalk in front of the station collapsed, dumping a hundred people into a cellar and injuring five. Bryan was nearly crushed by an over-enthusiastic mob that broke through police lines. He had to be rescued by club-wielding officers. His carriage, escorted by thousands of Democratic marching club members, took forty-five minutes to make the mile and a half to his hotel through jammed streets.[17]

Jones and Altgeld overscheduled Bryan in Chicago, filling his three days with twenty-nine speeches in the city and thirteen more in northern Illinois. He began early each morning and went until after midnight, rushing from venue to venue and causing crowds to wait for hours. But every event was packed with thousands, some with tens of thousands, with big crowds milling outside. People were frantic, welcoming him with wild demonstrations and interrupting his speeches with applause, cheers, and shouting.

It was difficult to move him around the city. He had to be lifted through a second-floor window at the stockyards to speak to 20,000 pack-inghouse employees. Police frequently had to carry him through mobs that were "crowding, pushing, surging after him in an uncontrollable throng" and force his carriage through streets packed with enthusiastic supporters.[18]

He often sounded defensive, and his words became more harsh and desperate. At a community college, he warned there were "a lot of men who pose as philanthropists, when the fact is they are trying, because of their greed and avarice, to enslave mankind to make themselves rich." He told the Women's Silver League, "We are seeking to drive out those who have entered the temple and are defiling it."[19]

While his silver message had been weakened in farm country, he continued pushing it and coercion to win the laborer vote, saying, "When a man pays you wages he simply pays you for your work and not for your vote." At most stops, the theme was 16-to-1, with a greeting party at St. Paul's German School of sixteen girls in silver dresses, each bearing a letter to spell out HON. WILLIAM J. BRYAN, and one girl in gold holding a gold exclamation point. There was a similar welcome at Lincoln Turner Hall and at St. Stanislaus, where little girls gave him sixteen white chrysanthemums and a yellow one.[20]

One of his more important addresses was to businessmen at Battery D, a brick armory on Lake Michigan. He adapted the coercion argument by saying he knew silver businessmen had been "summoned before the bankers and told if they insisted upon talking for free silver their notes would not be extended." "When I preach deliverance of the common people from the money-changers," he told the crowd at Battery D, "I preach deliverance to the business men from the tyranny of the banks."[21]

He also called explicitly for repudiation of the nation's debt, saying, "We shall say to our foreign creditors that we intend to pay our coin obligations in either gold or silver. I propose that we shall say to them: 'Gentlemen, if you conspire to make that silver dollar worth less than the gold dollar, we shall pay you in that silver dollar.' You say that is repudiation? I deny it." Those who purchased the government's bond were "charging for the risk they took, and now let them have the risk they were paid for."[22]

Bryan used an early event in the city to rebut charges of anti-Semitism provoked by the incendiary language used by some Free Silver supporters. When presented a silver Star of David by Jewish Democrats, Bryan said, "Our opponents have sometimes tried to make it appear that we were attacking a race when we denounced the financial policy advocated by the Rothschilds. But we are not; we are as much opposed to the financial policy of J. Pierpont Morgan as we are to the financial policy of the Rothschilds. We are not attacking a race; we are attacking greed and avarice, which know neither race nor religion." It was too little, too late. The repeated use of anti-Semitic slurs by some silver men over the course of the campaign and Bryan's silence had turned most Jewish voters against the Democrats.[23]

By the end of his Chicago trip, Bryan was exhausted. Jones and others were concerned he could not sleep and "appears nervous and easily agitated." It had been a remarkable performance for a candidate running on adrenaline, nerves, and little else. Even critics were impressed, with the *Tribune* admitting, "Mr. Bryan's triumphal march through Chicago was like the return of a conqueror." "I am satisfied to leave it with them," Bryan said as he climbed aboard his train car, *The Idler,* to leave the city and Illinois before the campaign's final weekend. "The people must decide and

I feel that the issue is understood and the vital importance of the question appreciated." He soon fell asleep fully clothed on a yellow and red striped blanket in his sleeper, a roll of newspapers for a pillow, his shirt soaked with sweat, and a large bouquet of yellow roses on the floor.[24]

WHILE BRYAN WAS STUMPING in Illinois, delegations kept going to Canton. The week's high point was a parade Wednesday by local residents that reached McKinley's house while its final elements were still being organized at the Courthouse Square. "Canton was divided into two parts this evening—those who marched to Major McKinley's, and those who viewed and cheered the marching throngs," wrote one reporter. McKinley mounted a makeshift stage, illuminated by red, white, and blue lights. He was visibly moved by the outpouring of affection, saying, "It would be a hard heart indeed that would be unmoved by this magnificent demonstration of my neighbors and fellow townsmen, who have assembled here to-night, without regard to party, nationality, or creed, to give expression to their good will for the great cause for which I have been designated to stand."[25]

Betting odds that week in New York ranged from 3:1 to 10:1 for the Republican ticket. Winfield Scott Stratton of Colorado Springs put $100,000 on Bryan to match $300,000 raised by an Eastern syndicate of bettors backing McKinley. The wealthy mine owner said he'd build a public library with his winnings.[26]

TO ENERGIZE THE GOP vote, Hanna and Dawes had as many as 1,400 GOP surrogates in the field. One of the most effective was Reed. The *Washington Post* suggested listeners "rejoice in the clean-cut satire, the strenuous logic and the breezy good-humored argument of a man like Reed. People feel better and more wholesome after an hour with Reed." After stumping the Midwest, the Speaker was dispatched to California for the final seven days. It seemed an odd choice, but Reed had worked on a California ranch thirty-five years before, then taught school in Stockton. He covered the state from south to north, drawing huge crowds and doing the Republican ticket a great deal of good. He made his last appearance on election eve before 15,000 at the Oakland racetrack. By now his stump speech was thoroughly polished, but while the crowd constantly broke out in cheers and applause, Reed was probably bored. After all, he had said, "I regret the tendency in our elections toward blare and display. I object to being exhibited from the tail end of a train like a criminal on his way to jail."[27]

The Generals' Tour ended the Friday before Election Day with a patriotic program at Carnegie Hall featuring forty Civil War heroes and a eulogy for President Grant dramatically punctuated by the appearance of a large backdrop of him in a general's uniform. That weekend also featured the GOP's Flag Day, the largest political spectacle America had ever seen. Boston "was clothed in bunting" for its parade and special McKinley-Hobart Flag Day posters covered windows everywhere. A house on Summer Street featured a large sign, WE ARE DEMOCRATS, BUT WE VOTE FOR MCKINLEY. Ten thousand paraded in Worcester, Massachusetts, and another 10,000 in New Bedford. Twenty thousand took to Hartford's streets; their grand marshal a lifelong Democrat and a Civil War veteran.[28]

Philadelphia "looked as though a dozen Fourth of July displays of flags and bunting had been combined as one," and 23,000 marched in support of sound money in Buffalo, New York, the city's largest parade ever. Twenty-five thousand McKinley supporters trooped through Pittsburgh. The Major listened to them on a special long-distance line that tapped into huge transmitters hung along the route. An estimated 15,000 gold advocates tramped through Detroit. There were Flag Day activities throughout the South, including a large rally in Atlanta.[29]

Cincinnati's three-and-a-half-hour Flag Day parade was marred by the death of a prominent industrialist who died while marching with his employees. Parades weren't limited to big cities. Logansport, Indiana, was decorated not just in red, white, and blue, but also gold and yellow. Two hundred seventy riders accompanied a thousand marchers, "not including . . . the bands and drum corps." The parade route was marked by thousands of sparklers and the evening concluded with "roman candles, skyrockets and such pyrotechnical effects."[30]

Chicago was awash in red, white, and blue. The GOP headquarters at the Auditorium was decorated with twenty new seven-by-twelve-foot American flags hung from windows on Wabash Avenue. The Monadnock Block on West Jackson featured seven hundred flags. There was an afternoon program at the Auditorium featuring patriotic music and speeches, including addresses by Hanna and Dawes and an evening concert of classic music that ended with "The Star-Spangled Banner."[31]

Nothing on Flag Day, however, came close to New York City, whose activities were organized by the Business Men's Sound Money Association. The parade's marshal was General Horace Porter, who led off the procession from Broadway and Worth precisely at 10 a.m., astride a "graceful bay" and wearing a "broad blue sash." Behind him was a mounted escort of one hundred men and the parade's only carriage, containing Mayor William L. Strong, a Republican, and former mayor Abram Hewitt, a past DNC chairman, followed by the association's executive committee walking behind.[32]

Then came the main body of the parade, with the 25,000 members of the Wholesale Dry Goods Republican Club in front, wearing yellow chrysanthemums and accompanied by the West Point Band and McQuade's Drum Corps. Marching sixteen abreast, the division was over 1,500 rows deep. Next came the wool men, under a blue banner featuring a plump, well-fed sheep with 1892 beneath and a starving lamb labeled 1896, and below both PROTECTION, GOLD AND PROSPERITY.[33]

More groups followed, including bankers, stockbrokers, lawyers, students, men from the drug, chemical, paint, and oil trades, railway and steamship workers, insurance men, saddle and harness makers, men in millinery and the flower trade, hide and leather workers, the clothiers league, produce dealers, men from publishing and advertising, the McKinley-Hobart jewelers club, Realtors, men of the Shirt, Collar, Neckwear and Haberdashers League, wholesale fish dealers, cotton brokers, and the Pottery, Glass, and Lamp Association representatives.

One of the best-drilled marching units was Aitken, Son & Company, which sold military uniforms. Onlookers yelled, "Give us a cigar!" to the leaf-tobacco men. Paper workers were followed by two platoons of coal miners in working clothes, carrying torches and picks and covered in coal dust and grime.

At 10:57, Porter and the lead elements came abreast of the reviewing stand at Madison Square on the east side of Fifth Avenue between Twenty-Fourth and Twenty-Fifth Streets, where Hobart, Governor Morton, and members of the RNC, including Platt, Manley, Bliss, and Powell Clayton, congregated. The dignitaries watched the immense display of sound-money strength under a partly cloudy sky. It took eight and a half hours—until 6:30 p.m.—for the last of the estimated 101,000–136,000 marchers to tramp past the reviewing stand, which was illuminated by bright calcium light beams at dusk.

Each division bore signs and banners. WE KNOW NO 'ENEMY'S COUNTRY' IN THIS FAIR LAND OF OURS. Window shade manufacturers carried large fans inscribed, WE'RE HOT FOR MCKINLEY. Lithographers wore gilded breastplates with a gold eagle and McKinley's profile in bas-relief. The publishers and booksellers had a double-sided banner with Bryan on its face, using a sword labeled WILD-EYED FINANCE to halve a silver dollar. The legend read TAKING BIG CHANCES. The reverse featured a silver dollar with a tag, MARKED DOWN TO 40 CENTS. The hide and leather men featured sixteen marchers carrying large silver dollars with big chunks cut out to show the silver coins were debased and one man with an unclipped gold dollar.

And to symbolize gold, there was the color yellow. Yellow in thousands of chrysanthemums on lapels, yellow in slouch hats and military-style shakos, yellow in armbands and sashes and coats and plumes and devices like the gold bugs of all shapes, sizes, and designs that different marching units wore on their chests or shoulders.

As each division or regiment or brigade passed the reviewing stand, the wind came strong from the west, sweeping each flag dramatically out full to the east. "The flag was everywhere," the *New-York Tribune* reported. "It flaunted from every window; it waved from every portico; it flew from every roof; it floated over almost every street; and many times in every block." There were flags hanging from lampposts, flags draped from cornices and roofs, flags hung off telephone lines over the avenue, flags on steeples and town house balconies and hotel entrances, flags waved by tens of thousands of spectators.

Festooned with large flags, the Union League Club, on the east side of Fifth Avenue, was also decorated with hanging strands of red, white, and blue lights and the words MCKINLEY and HOBART spelled out in lights along its top floor. The office tower on the northwest corner of Fifth and Seventeenth Streets had SOUND MONEY spelled out in lights on its façade. Four kites were launched from the Mutual Reserve Building, each carrying a camera that captured the massive flood of men making their way through Manhattan.

Watching from his office in the Metropolitan Life Insurance building, Osborne dialed up Hanna and held the phone out the window so he could hear the din. New York's parade was bigger than Chicago's the previous month. Osborne called his cousin in Canton and again held the phone out the window. The Major proclaimed himself "highly pleased." An estimated 750,000 to two million jammed the sidewalks, jostling each other to get a better view, standing on steps and boxes, leaning out of windows and over balconies, some on temporary stages hastily thrown up. Spectators took to yelling, "What's the matter with McKinley?" to which marchers lustily responded, "He's all right!" Hanna's cultivation of Platt and McKinley's conciliatory attitude toward his former party rivals in New York had paid off. The Major's new friends in the city pulled out all the stops.

Even the cynical and world-weary *Daily Mail* reporter Steevens was impressed. "There were more men tramping the streets of New York in Saturday's parade than there are voters in the States of Colorado, Idaho, and Nevada put together," he wrote. "There was every manner of man in the procession: millionaires in shining silk hats, and working men in corduroy trousers. Fifth Avenue was dark for miles . . . The whole thing was prodigious, crushing, final."

In Canton, forty bands played stirring marches and patriotic music on a day when the delegations started with tin workers at 8:30 a.m. The enthusiasm of a huge delegation from Ohio's Mahoning Valley caused McKinley to discard his prepared remarks and speak off-the-cuff, which he had rarely done. "There is just one class under our flag and we all belong to it," McKinley said. "Glorious old banner it is. So long as we carry it in our hands and have what it typifies in our hearts, the Republic and our splendid free institutions will be forever secure."[34]

MCKINLEY SPENT THE SUNDAY before Election Day attending First Methodist, then taking a walk and going for a carriage ride. An unexpected delegation of first-time voters from Detroit attended church with McKinley, then called on the Major. He shook hands with each before they departed for Michigan.[35]

Bryan and Mary caught a train from Council Bluffs, Iowa, for Lincoln, Nebraska, early the same morning. When he boarded, he sat down to a plate of buckwheat pancakes, though he'd already eaten breakfast. Despite frequent large meals, he had lost fifteen pounds and was thin and pale. Bryan was upbeat, telling a reporter he would take the South and every state west of Pennsylvania, losing only if Republicans farmers deserted him. Even then, "defeat would only inspire him to greater efforts for free-silver," since GOP tariff and currency policies "would stir the nation to its depth and insure" victory next time. When he got home, he noticed McKinley's picture in neighbors' windows. After a few visitors, Bryan limped off to bed, giving orders not to be disturbed.[36]

Dawes was in a reflective mood as Election Day approached, writing that night, "I am so confident of victory . . . that I cannot even contemplate defeat as a possibility. It has been a great privilege. . . . I have kept my hands clean and finish the campaign with a clear conscience." Dawes had good reason to feel that way. He had done his utmost to keep to a minimum the theft and misappropriation that characterized Gilded Age campaigns.[37]

Neither candidate was finished. On Monday, November 2, Bryan spent eighteen hours in a last-minute blitz of Nebraska. While its purpose was said to be to help Democratic congressional candidates, it is never a good sign when a presidential candidate spends his final day speeding through his home state. In September, Democrats said he would carry it by 30,000; now Republicans maintained that rising farm prices and falling silver sentiment meant McKinley would carry it by from 8,000 to 15,000. Someone was wrong.[38]

Bryan summoned what remained of his energy to make twenty-seven speeches, most from the back of *The Idler*. On the return, his talks were often delivered into a cold north wind that rubbed his throat raw. Whenever he saw gold ribbons or McKinley buttons, he chastised their wearers. After the final speech, he had traveled enough miles to equal about three-quarters of the way around the world. He had made six hundred formal speeches, delivered hundreds more talks at whistle stops and to crowds around his hotels and venues, and been seen by two to three million people.[39]

On Monday, McKinley ended with a hometown rally as he had done in every previous campaign, this time at the Tabernacle. Afterward, GOP marching clubs trooped up Market to McKinley's home, where he stepped out into his yard, thanked his neighbors, and said, "The hour for discussion has passed by; the argument is closed. The vast interests of the American people are now in the hands of the people themselves." He then greeted visitors until after ten, while Ida recovered from the grippe upstairs.[40]

ON ELECTION DAY, BRYAN was met at the Lincoln depot by a campaign honor guard and a band that played "Home, Sweet Home" while escorting him to the city clerk's office to complete an affidavit so he could vote, having failed to register beforehand. He told friends, "It's all over but the shouting."

He walked to the fire station's stable on F Street near Fourteenth Street, a black muffler around his throat. The room was dark and lit by lanterns. While horses occupied some stalls, others were used as makeshift polling booths. It took eight minutes for Bryan to mark his ballot, during which a row broke out between the Republican poll watchers and a Free Silver man. One of the Republicans ended the confrontation and provoked laughter by asking, "Why don't you try to be quiet while Mr. Bryan exes his vote for McKinley?" An election judge joked with Bryan, "Sure you've got the right electors?" "I'll take chances on that," he replied, and dropped his ballot in the box. As Bryan prepared to deposit his ballot, a Republican election official suggested all present take off their hats as a mark of respect. All but one spectator did. It was 11:02.[41]

Hundreds of neighbors were standing in front of Bryan's house on D Street when he arrived. When he reached his door, well-wishers yelled for a speech. Bryan obliged for the final time, saying, "I have now done all I can to share in the success of this campaign, and for me there is nothing left but to await the returns."[42]

As was his practice, McKinley voted early. The horse troop that had accompanied delegations to his house sent word they would escort him the four blocks to the polls, but that seemed too much. Instead, he sent word they should come by so he could thank the riders. As he did, a band and a swarm of excited neighbors swept up Market Street. He would have an escort to the polls, like it or not. With his brother Abner and Samuel Saxton, Ida's cousin, McKinley walked to the polls around 8:55.

He entered a local shop about fifteen feet wide, with a big table and four judges, several registrars, and two clerks, and stood in line behind a mechanic in work clothes. Once checked in, he took the fifth polling booth, curtained off by cheap calico. Inside was an unpainted wooden plank, a pencil fixed by cord to the booth's frame, and directions. It took him one minute and eighteen seconds to mark his ballot, emerge from behind the curtain, and formally bow to the crowd jammed into the polling place. He was the 230th voter, out of 378 registered in the precinct. He told a friend, "This is a solemn occasion for me. I am deeply impressed by it." He was home shortly after nine.[43]

More than 13 million voters were beginning to show up at 68,194 polling places in forty-five states, from New England churches to Midwestern stables to Southern courthouses to Western mining camp saloons. It was now up to the American people.[44]

CHAPTER 29

McKinley's Triumph

———◁◦▷———

Gilded Age election nights were chaotic. There were no state election boards collecting and compiling returns. It was left to newspapers and party leaders to make sense of the blizzard of precinct, ward, town, and county results. Newspapers drew huge crowds by projecting updates on giant canvas screens or painting them on billboards. Each party's managers had telegraph lines strung to their headquarters so they could get the most up-to-date numbers and track them on blackboards. Much like we do today, observers compared the returns to past elections and looked for persistent movement toward one candidate or another.

From the start of the evening, the news was good for Republicans. McKinley took every state east of the Mississippi River and north of the Confederacy. West of the Mississippi, he carried Minnesota, Iowa, and North Dakota and then California and Oregon on the Pacific Coast. This amounted to 271 Electoral College votes, 47 more than necessary. With 7.1 million votes, the Major won 51 percent, the highest percentage since Grant's reelection, with nearly 2 million more votes than Harrison had gotten four years earlier—and almost 1.7 million more than any other Republican presidential candidate in history.

McKinley carried every traditional battleground state and every state in the central Midwest that both sides knew would decide the race. He won the Mid-Atlantic region by a huge margin and New England by 2-to-1. The Major flipped ten states Democrats had won in 1892 and two states Populists had carried then.

With 6.5 million votes, Bryan took the South and four states—Colorado, Idaho, Kansas, and Nevada—that Populists won in 1892. He carried three Western states—Montana, Washington, and Wyoming—and two Plains states—Nebraska and South Dakota—that had gone for the GOP four years earlier, as well as the traditionally Democratic border state of Missouri. But all this yielded only 176 electoral votes—less than the 224 needed. In the popular vote, Bryan ran 952,134 ahead of Cleveland's 1892 results, but 88,884 behind the combined Democratic and Populist vote in that election. This meant the 1896 Democratic-Populist combined total dropped just over a point from the previous contest, while the Republican total increased by an astonishing jump of more than a third.[1]

BRYAN RECEIVED THE RETURNS at his Lincoln home, sitting first with reporters and telegraph operators in his study, then having his wife, Mary, bring him telegrams as he lay on his bed, "her face betraying their purport before I received them from her hand," he later wrote. By eleven, Bryan knew he had lost but could not bring himself to admit it, telling a reporter, "The returns are coming in yet, and the fight is not over. Whatever I have to say about the future of our cause I will say in a general address to the country." Then he went back to bed and fell asleep. Believing the election had been stolen, Senator Jones kept Bryan from conceding until Wednesday afternoon, but America knew the winner Tuesday night.[2]

McKinley received the returns at home in Canton, relaxing in an armchair in the dining room as aides read wires with the latest numbers from telegraph operators in the study next door. The Major chuckled at the fulsome tone of a message from Max Pracht, a friend and western fruit grower, and with a smile, read his telegram aloud: "Oregon is ours and the fullness thereof."[3]

Only near midnight did McKinley admit that he had won. At twelve, bells began ringing across Canton, drawing an immense crowd to the Courthouse Square, where people cheered, blew horns, waved flags, shook wooden rattles, shot pistols, and otherwise celebrated. Then they marched the now-familiar route up Market and past the McKinley home. The Major saluted his neighbors from his porch as they rejoiced. He stayed awake until 4 a.m., when the Tippecanoe Club arrived on a special train from Cleveland to congratulate him. Bands and fireworks accompanied the thousand-man club of prominent Republicans. After lingering for ten minutes on the roof of his porch to wave to the excited marchers, the man now selected as the nation's twenty-fifth president said good night, climbed through a window, and stepped out of view.[4]

IT IS IMPORTANT TO remember that Democrats entered the 1896 contest with an advantage in getting to the 224 votes needed in the Electoral College. Their systematic destruction of black voting rights gave them a Solid South with 111 electoral votes. To this base could be added the five border states that had been carried by the Democrats in at least the last five elections with their 47 electoral votes. Silver Republican defections in the Plains and West were likely to produce another 29 electoral votes. This meant Democrats started the 1896 general election with 187 electoral votes to the 138 the GOP had carried in the previous five contests. Despite the depression, McKinley faced an uphill climb following the Democratic and Populist conventions.

There are eight reasons for McKinley's victory. The first is that he conducted a campaign based on big issues, namely, sound money and protection. Voters were deeply interested in both questions. While McKinley initially resisted tackling the first and wanted to campaign exclusively on the second, he came to understand that many Americans wanted to hear where he stood on both.

He and Bryan talked about these consequential issues in ways that drew sharp distinctions. There were no ambiguities in either man's position. Both men saw the issues as bigger than any one person. Both believed, as Bryan said in opening his "Cross of Gold" speech, that "The individual is but an atom; he is born, he acts, he dies but principles are eternal." Their principles, however, were fundamentally different—and those differences helped McKinley win.

The contest over these ideas did allow Bryan to nearly reach his goal of uniting the Democratic and Populist vote from 1892, but it also meant McKinley increased the Republican vote by 37 percent from four years earlier. Rarely have both parties grown their total vote in the same election, and rarely has the increase been the size of McKinley's in 1896.

The way the Major's campaign framed the money and tariff questions was aimed at persuading key voter blocs—laborers, farmers who owned their own land, commercial and professional people, small business owners, and Union veterans—that McKinley was right and Bryan was wrong. The Republicans freshened their appeal to these groups in the election's final weeks by emphasizing national unity and the rule of law. The result was the creation of a new coalition that helped break the political deadlock that had defined American politics for a quarter century.

The second reason McKinley prevailed was that, after hemming and hawing, he took on his opponent's supposed strength—Bryan's advocacy of Free Silver. Initially, the charismatic Nebraskan's call for an inflationary currency made him the candidate of change and divorced him and his fellow Democrats from responsibility for the depression that had occurred on a Democratic president's watch. At the same time, McKinley had muted his views on currency to win the Republican nomination, and at first he preferred to avoid the issue altogether in the general election, feeling his principal interest—protection—gave him a better shot at keeping Republicans unified. If McKinley had stuck to this strategy, it's unlikely he would have won.

Fortunately for the Major, he realized the old political truth that what a candidate thinks is his strong point is often an Achilles' heel. Attack it, and his campaign is crippled. It took McKinley six weeks to decide to tackle Bryan's strength and show that Free Silver would harm Americans, especially laborers. When the Major finally did so, he stopped Bryan's momentum, reversed the flight from the GOP in Midwestern battlegrounds, and drew into his column wavering honest-money Democrats looking for a champion.

It took time for the Major to find the right words to make his case: he began discussing the money issue using the language of economic efficiency and business, but then made it a moral question. He closed the sale with voters when he argued that an inflationary currency would deprive laborers of fair wages, keep farmers from being paid in dollars with the same value as they paid for supplies and necessities, and deprive people of the value of their savings, insurance policies, pensions, and investments. It was morally wrong to repudiate debt and morally wrong to debase the currency. This was a powerful contrast with Bryan, who blamed Wall Street, foreign financiers, and a shadowy, corrupt money power for saddling the country with a gold-backed currency that was responsible for the depression's calamity and the wretched financial circumstances of millions of Americans.

The third reason McKinley won was because he was a different kind of Republican who recognized his party must broaden and modernize its appeal or it would lose. It could not win simply by reenergizing those who had elected Harrison or Garfield or Hayes or Grant. The McKinley managers did not delude themselves that there were millions of stay-at-home Republicans.

Some of the voters who had elected those Republican presidents were now sidelined by violence and intimidation. Grant and Hayes had both won Southern states. But this was not going to happen in 1896 as black and white Republicans in the South found it increasingly difficult to have their ballots honestly counted.

The country was also changing demographically, becoming less Anglo-Saxon and less Protestant. Over the past several decades, there had been relatively less immigration from England, Scotland, Wales, Ireland, and Germany and more from Central and Southern Europe. These new Central and Southern European immigrants had no real allegiance to either party and were up for grabs. If these mostly Catholic and often industrial workers voted Democrat, they would give Democrats a lock on the Electoral College.

To prevent Democrats from achieving a durable advantage in battle-ground states, McKinley would have to expand the GOP coalition by recruiting new allies, including industrial laborers, Catholics, and immigrants. For the general election, he needed to show these Americans that they had a place in the GOP's vision of the nation's future. His was first and foremost a campaign of persuasion aimed at bringing into the GOP people who had not been reliable Republican voters. This was necessary for the party's survival: the GOP had nearly run out of Western states—those places Hanna called "little sand patches and coyote ranges"—to which it could grant statehood to offset Democratic gains elsewhere.

McKinley made a special effort for the laborer vote, the ultimate swing bloc in the Gilded Age. He had credibility with laborers because of his reputation as a friend of workingmen and his leadership on protective tariffs that many blue-collar workers considered crucial to their jobs. Because the Major grew up and made his political career in Ohio—a region with miners, factory workers, and laborers—he was better acquainted with America's modern industrial economy than was Bryan, who had grown up in rural southern Illinois and entered politics on Nebraska's prairies.

McKinley benefited from Bryan's missteps in appealing to urban laborers. The Nebraskan based his silver appeal on arguments more attractive to farmers than urban laborers and failed to stress his support for arbitration of labor disputes, an eight-hour workday, the income tax, and other labor-friendly issues, or highlight his opposition to Cleveland's use of federal court orders to end the Pullman strike.[5]

Propelled by the labor vote, McKinley ran particularly strong in the industrial Midwest. For example, in working-class wards in Chicago, the Major ran well ahead of Harrison's performance, while Bryan couldn't match Cleveland's pace in 1892. The labor vote helped the GOP carry nine of the nation's ten most populous cities.

McKinley's approach as a different kind of Republican also allowed him to offset losses among rural Republicans drawn to Bryan by Free Silver. Republicans had adopted a softer line in the Midwest on liquor issues. McKinley echoed that line, and also made his case with these voters by embracing the gold standard, rejecting the APA's anti-Catholic and anti-immigrant rhetoric, and dropping the GOP platform plank calling for a ban on public aid to parochial schools. This all allowed the Major to pick up Democratic Catholic and Lutheran farmers, especially Germans, Swedes, and Dutch, and beat the past performances of Republicans in many rural Midwestern counties.[6]

McKinley also brought into the GOP ranks recent immigrants from Central and Southern Europe, many of them urban laborers, who were attracted by the Major's practical agenda for jobs, good wages, and rising prosperity. He welcomed all these new allies into his campaign. He invited them to come to Canton, blanketed their homes with materials in their native languages, and covered their communities with speakers. These new voters carried Republicans to victory in many traditionally Democratic areas, from Brooklyn neighborhoods to Chicago's ethnic communities, from Baltimore's factory districts to West Virginia's mining towns. Only the Irish and, to a lesser extent, the Poles and Bohemians remained loyal to the Democratic Party.[7]

The fourth reason McKinley won was that he broadened the electoral battlefield. Because the money question and protection were tearing

Americans away from their traditional allegiances, McKinley and his managers understood the election would be fought in more states and among more voters than in past elections, requiring a bigger, better-organized effort. As one of the RNC Executive Committee members later observed, "the field for action" and "the number of people to be reached, educated and convinced was much larger than in any national campaign in the history of the country."[8]

There is a natural inclination for a campaign to focus first on defense and so it was with the McKinley men. Worried about defections in the Midwest, Plains, and Pacific Coast, the campaign spent much of its resources in these regions winning back wayward Republicans.

But the 1896 Republican campaign also played offense, going after border states and some Southern ones. They sought first and foremost to win these states, second to help boost Republican congressional candidates there, and finally to stretch the DNC's meager resources further. The Republican effort achieved success in its first two goals and may have panicked Bryan into spending valuable September days in states that should have been safely Democratic, like North Carolina, Tennessee, and Virginia.

McKinley took four of the five border states, three of which—Kentucky, West Virginia, and Delaware—had last voted Republican in 1872, and one—Maryland—that had not voted Republican since 1864. The only border state Bryan won was Missouri: Chauncey I. Filley, still angry over his treatment at the national convention, undercut the Republican campaign there. The Old Man decided he would rather feud with Richard Kerens than mount a unified effort.

The Republican effort also allowed the party to pick up two U.S. Senate seats in the border and Upper South regions and hang on to most of the House seats it gained there in the 1894 congressional midterm landslide. The big exceptions were Missouri and Delaware, where infighting caused Republican losses in Congress. Otherwise, the McKinley men's efforts to broaden the playing field paid off handsomely with electoral votes and grateful Republican members of Congress.

The fifth reason McKinley won was that he ran for the nomination as an outsider, undercutting the traditional role played by party bosses in settling the nomination by deals at the convention itself. Yes, McKinley was a longtime member of Congress and a respected national Republican leader familiar with the ways of Washington. But he was an outsider in the sense that he refused to be bound by practices that elevated party bosses over party activists and discouraged candidates from seeking the nomination openly and energetically.

Instead, the McKinley men ran the first modern presidential primary campaign, presaging the twentieth-century emphasis on candidates, not party machines. McKinley drew on the desire of grassroots Republicans to dominate the process rather than to be herded by those atop the party apparatus. He had an in-depth organization in place more than a year and a half in advance of the convention, a clear message that he was the "Advance Agent of Prosperity" and the "Napoleon of Protection," and an emphasis on binding delegates to him personally through his campaign's activities and legally through instruction.

McKinley's convictions and principles led him to three vital actions in the primary that had consequences for both the general election and the country's entire political system in the years that followed. He opposed his party's bosses, thereby making his path to the nomination more difficult, but by running on the slogan "The People Against the Bosses," he thrilled a rising generation of Republicans eager to change politics and change America. He rejected the American Protective Association's anti-Catholic, anti-immigrant appeals. He became the first Republican presidential candidate to actively seek the support of members of the Catholic hierarchy and to mount a robust effort to court immigrant voters. He also reached out to black voters and championed their rights. This last effort probably yielded little in the general election, but it helped solidify Southern black Republicans for their state conventions. All three moves were risky or at least controversial but helped propel McKinley to victory in 1896, first in the primaries and then in November.

The sixth reason for McKinley's victory is that he was seen as a candidate of change. The desire of voters for a change in the country's direction and leadership should have been a strong advantage for Republicans from the beginning, given the deep depression that had made Democratic president Grover Cleveland so unpopular. But Bryan turned the tables by leading his own party to repudiate Cleveland. Then Bryan distanced himself from the president's economic agenda with a reform platform of his own and argued that Republicans were for the status quo, because they, like the president, supported the gold standard.

Still, McKinley found a way to blunt Bryan's strategy. He first used his record as the foremost advocate of protectionism to argue that America had been prosperous until tariffs were reduced and would be prosperous again once they were raised. Rather than shy away from the McKinley Tariff, he embraced it, knowing the voters now looked back on the years around its passage as a better time.

McKinley also went on the offense against Free Silver, devoting more time to attacking its ill effects than defending the gold standard. He was quiet on Cleveland's gold bonds, except to blame them and the president's repeal of the McKinley Tariff for the drop in the government's revenues. Instead, the Major pounded away at what free coinage would mean to each American and to the economy at large.

Bryan dismissed these views as spin from Wall Street and the money power, but McKinley had confidence that voters would ignore the name-calling and focus on how Free Silver would affect them. The Major was correct in this judgment. McKinley's one-two combination allowed him to portray himself as the leader who would change the country's direction and heal the economy.

This leads to the seventh reason McKinley was victorious. He ran as a unifier, adopting the language of national reconciliation. He understood that the country had endured a long period of division. Some of that division was self-perpetuating: because the nation's politics had been broken for decades, Washington could not find a way to respond to the nation's ills, and its failure compounded those problems. Some of the division was an echo of the Civil War's North-South split over slavery, now reinforced by fresh economic resentments that were sectional in nature. Then there was the discontent caused by the long Panic of 1893.

The depression had led many people to question the future of the American experiment. Was its prosperity meant only for the wealthy? Was politics destined to always be contentious and mean-spirited? Could political differences ever be resolved with some modicum of civility and common spirit?

In moments like this, there is a tendency for some people and politicians to adopt a negative, dark tone of opposition to the political system as it exists and the country's direction as they perceive it. McKinley understood that Americans thirsted for someone who could replace discord and rancor with optimism and unity. Bryan, on the other hand, pitted

East against South and West, class against class, and farmer against urban worker. Calling the East "the enemy's country" not only signaled that he was opposed to the region's interests, but viewed its people as adversaries and its growing industrial economy as alien. Bryan's attacks on anyone who disagreed with him became harsher as the campaign progressed, narrowing the pool of people who would vote for him.[9]

Politics is a game of addition, but Bryan played subtraction, and McKinley took advantage of it. The Major's tone was one of unity and reconciliation. The ideas that Americans have a common country with a common destiny and that we can succeed only if we are all in this together were heard repeatedly from the Major's campaign, especially in October.

It was not only McKinley's words, but also his actions, reported daily in newspapers around the country, that made this message convincing to voters. The diversity of groups invited by the campaign to Canton demonstrated McKinley's openness and inclusiveness. The dramatic visit of the ex-Confederates was a deeply emotional moment of national reconciliation. The Chicago sound-money parade and then Flag Day with its massive spectacles drove home the Republicans' positive, optimistic, and inclusive message. These events also gave McKinley's supporters a way to express their views and feel they were involved in something bigger than themselves. This was key to mobilizing the Major's vote.

The Democratic Party was divided between a silver majority and honest-money minority while the Republican Party was split between a gold majority and silver minority. Though both parties were bitterly divided, McKinley's emphasis on unity made his appeal to disaffected members of the opposition party more powerful than Bryan's. The gold Democratic ticket and honest-money Democratic surrogates, most notably Bourke Cochran, contributed to McKinley's success in this.

A CAMPAIGN ORGANIZATION MUST complete three tasks: maximize turnout among the party's traditional followers, target and persuade swing or non-voters, and push its message in the face of an opponent's attacks. McKinley won by accomplishing these tasks, creating the first modern primary and general election presidential campaigns. This was the eighth and most important reason for McKinley's victory: the quality of a candidate's campaign makes a critical difference, and the size and scope of past efforts to win the White House paled in comparison to that of the McKinley men.

McKinley benefited from a work ethic that informed his campaign's methods and influenced the men he collected to run it. It was the Major's nature to prepare, to study and think. In the military, law, and public office, he did his homework, thought ahead, and planned his actions. He extended this habit into his presidential contest by leading his team to develop a disciplined strategy and then execute it. The campaign's larger strategic vision—and its confidence in that vision—sometimes made Team McKinley slow to adapt to changing circumstances, but their preparations generally put the Major ahead of events and his competition.

McKinley and his men met regularly to discuss important strategic questions and then constantly reviewed their progress. The Hanna-led RNC Executive Committee was a critical part of this, but so was the kitchen cabinet from which McKinley sought advice. Given the Major's predisposition to plan and Hanna's similar instincts, the McKinley managers were constantly thinking ahead, a sharp contrast with the Bryan campaign's haphazard decision-making and general disorganization.

It is important to remember that McKinley was at the top of this process, not Hanna. Hanna once told a group of Republican politicos, "Now don't you fellows fool yourselves by thinking that we will be able to give McKinley instructions on how to run the campaign. After you have talked with him, you will find that he knows more about politics than all of us." Or as John Hay put it more colorfully after visiting Canton during the election, "I spent the day with the Majah. . . . And there are idiots who think Mark Hanna will run him!" [10]

McKinley also recognized his own strengths and weaknesses, especially when it came to getting his message heard. It would have been easier to agree to Hanna's demand that McKinley take to the road for a dozen or more days of speeches in critical battlegrounds. The Major would have excelled at the Ohio GOP kickoff, the veterans encampment in Kansas, and a state fair in the upper Midwest. But he knew going on the road could have led to the same kind of frenetic campaigning Bryan was involved in and that the Major himself had undertaken during the 1894 midterms.

Instead, by conducting the Front-Porch Campaign, McKinley put the spotlight on the remarks he tailored to each group that came to Canton— a total of about 750,000 Americans, nearly one out of every twenty of the election's voters. Those messages filled the nation's papers each day, reaching voters hundreds of miles from the Major's front stoop. At the same time, the vast numbers of people willing to trek to Canton demonstrated the deep backing the Republican enjoyed. Bryan drew spectators while McKinley drew supporters.[11]

McKinley and his managers placed a premium on organization, applying business methods to politics, particularly to the tasks of persuasion and mobilization. Republicans methodically organized much of the country, undertaking their traditional door-to-door canvasses earlier and repeating the process later in the fall, checking the attitudes of every voter in key battlegrounds again when opinions were shifting.

Republicans followed their canvasses with an extraordinary amount of literature, the largest deployment of speakers in the party's history, and a wide range of auxiliary groups that targeted key blocs in the electorate. Perry Heath and his people produced more than 250 million pieces of literature, 18 pieces for every voter. Some five million targeted households received an envelope of material each week during the fall. These packets were prepared, addressed, and stamped by a hundred people in a giant workroom in the Chicago headquarters. From the Generals' Tour and the Wheelmen to First Voters and Commercial Travelers clubs for traveling salesmen, no presidential campaign had undertaken the same range and scope of organization as the McKinley effort.[12]

The McKinley managers had three waves of focus in the general election. First, they solidified the Northeast early by having the regular party organization run New York, building a constructive relationship with the Combine bosses, and making currency the principal issue in the region. Second, they made an all-out effort starting in September to convert voters in the Midwest's heartland—essentially every state around Illinois—and in the border and Plains states by confronting Bryan's strong point of Free Silver. And third, they used their superior resources to broaden the map by competing in the South, West, and Pacific Coast, hoping to win upsets in places where the Democrats did not have the funds to compete.

A campaign of this scope required money, which the McKinley campaign had in abundance. Dawes's final report to Hanna shows that the Chicago headquarters' expenditures totaled $1,962,326 and that the New York office spent another $1.6 million, mostly in grants to state party organizations for their activities. Both figures are substantially less than the $12 to $15 million that some historians and critics of McKinley claim the Republicans spent. The Democratic effort, by comparison, raised $300,000. Nearly $41,000 came from a fund-raising drive conducted by Hearst's *New York Journal,* with $15,000 from the publisher himself. One of the Montana Copper Kings, Marcus Daly, contributed $50,000, the DNC's largest gift. Bryan's advocates, both then and today, claim that money was the deciding advantage for McKinley, but history is full of examples of better-funded candidates being bested by those with less money.[13]

IT'S UNLIKELY THAT THESE eight reasons for McKinley's victory would have been enough if the Major had not been an attractive and compelling candidate. McKinley's personal character meant he was widely viewed as an honest man who cared deeply for his invalid wife and had served the country bravely in the Civil War. He had defended striking miners when no other lawyer would (and when he might have paid a price for doing so) and had centered his advocacy of protection on the interests of workers, not their employers. His integrity, empathy, courage, and loyalty gave many voters ample reason to believe he cared deeply about them.

These values all combined to create a public persona so positive even adversaries knew that attacking McKinley directly would likely hurt them more than it would him. Bryan rarely attacked the Major by name and the cartoonists for Hearst's *Journal* focused on Hanna, not the Major. The Clevelander was routinely depicted as an overweight political boss dressed in a suit of dollar bills, pulling the strings of a small puppet labeled McKinley. The cartoons hurt Hanna's feelings, but did McKinley little harm. People thought better of the candidate than to believe the comics.[14]

McKinley was also naturally optimistic or, at minimum, fatalistic. This meant he was not easily panicked. Steady under actual fire in the Civil War, he was similarly levelheaded in political combat. This trait allowed him and those working for him to remain focused even at the height of political battles.

The moments when he was personally shaky or visibly angry were rare and instructive. He nearly fell to pieces when the Walker notes threatened his ability to provide for his wife and was upset during the 1888 national convention when well-meaning delegates jeopardized his personal honor by advancing him for president against Senator Sherman, to whom he had pledged his loyalty. Being able to face success or adversity with calm is a useful habit for a candidate to have in the swirl of a presidential campaign.

Then there was McKinley's capacity for friendship. He was a man who gained the respect and affection of others and maintained it. Hanna is the most obvious example. The Major provided Hanna the chance to achieve his life's dream by making him the leader of his drive for the presidency. Hanna was the subordinate in the relationship: he would himself repeat Herman H. Kohlsaat's line that the Clevelander's posture toward the Major was "always that of a big, bashful boy toward the girl he loves." [15]

Look anywhere in McKinley's presidential campaign and there is likely to be a neighbor, comrade, or colleague who threw themselves with enthusiasm into his campaign. In some cases, these were people who had known McKinley for decades and would do anything he asked. As it turned out, they also tended to be very talented. That was another one of McKinley's gifts: he could spot ability in the most unlikely places. He picked the unknown and very young Charles G. Dawes, who ended up not only running a disciplined national campaign but also outorganized the impregnable Chicago Republican machine.

McKinley saw talent both in people he liked, like Dawes, and in people he wasn't so keen on, such as Theodore Roosevelt. It says something about the Major that both young men played important roles in his campaign and his administration and that both won the Nobel Peace Prize, Roosevelt in 1906 for negotiating an end to the Russo-Japanese War and Dawes in 1925 for his work on German war reparations.

McKinley treated Dawes like the son he never had. After managing the campaign, Dawes remained personally very close to the president, serving as comptroller of the currency at age thirty-one before becoming a successful Chicago banker. He later was a brigadier general in France in World War I, first director of the Bureau of the Budget, Coolidge's vice president, ambassador to Great Britain, and first head of the Reconstruction Finance Corporation.

After the election, McKinley confessed about Roosevelt, "I am afraid he is too pugnacious." But he did resuscitate Teddy's political career by naming him assistant secretary of the navy. Without this appointment, Roosevelt's future would have been impossible. He could not have wired Admiral Dewey to make for Manila and destroy the Spanish fleet. He could not have resigned in a blaze of glory to organize the 1st U.S.

Volunteer Cavalry, better known as "the Rough Riders," and charge up San Juan Hill and Kettle Hill. He could not have been mustered out on September 13, 1898, and then elected governor of New York eight weeks later. Nor would he have been selected as McKinley's running mate in 1900 after the death of Vice President Garret Hobart the previous year from heart disease. The Major's championing of Dawes and of Roosevelt was evidence of his desire to help advance a generation of young Republican leaders.[16]

McKinley not only picked talented people, but he also led them. He knew what people to place in what posts and how to gain the greatest advantage from their talents. He also had the self-assurance of a leader who does not need to be the smartest person in the room. Those who worked with him often wrote of how the Major listened and then decided, expressing his opinion in a way that gave people confidence in his judgment and knowledge that they had been heard. They also knew that while they were trusted with the work, they could trust him with its underlying principles. For instance, while he put Hanna in charge of his nomination fight, McKinley set the rules and tone, including, above all, the decision not to negotiate with the bosses but to oppose them.

McKinley also proved to be a resilient candidate because he didn't take offense easily or give it. Politics was not personal for him. He neither picked unnecessary fights nor participated in ones others started. He had learned somewhere—or perhaps it was a natural inclination—that in politics, today's adversary may be tomorrow's necessary ally.

That was certainly true in how he handled Joseph B. Foraker, who might have derailed his career when McKinley ran for governor in 1891, or four years later when Foraker took control of the Ohio GOP in 1895, or a year after that when the Major needed a united Ohio delegation at the 1896 national convention. In each instance, it was McKinley himself who managed the relationship with the prickly and easily offended Foraker. Yet all these actions occurred after Foraker had publicly smeared McKinley with the 1889 Campbell Ballot Box Hoax.

Nor did McKinley take personal offense from the Combine trying to stop him from becoming the nominee. He personally assured Matthew S. Quay of his respect and friendship, and then supported Hanna's putting Platt in charge of the Empire State campaign, writing the adversaries of the Easy Boss in the New York McKinley League that if they wanted the

Major elected, they, too, should accept the reality that the regular party machinery would take the lead in the fall campaign. This showed a deft political hand and a willingness to let bygones be bygones—something not all political leaders are capable of doing and further evidence that William McKinley won not just because he had the more effective campaign and more convincing message, but because he was the better candidate.

IN WINNING, MCKINLEY ALSO created a new political system. The bigger, stronger electoral coalition that he built for his party in his 1896 campaign endured for nearly four decades, making the period between 1896 and 1932 a time of GOP dominance. The Republican Party was no longer a shrinking and beleaguered political organization composed of white Anglo-Saxon Protestants in the North and Southern blacks being systematically stripped of their right to vote. Instead, it was a frothy, diverse coalition of owners and workers, longtime Americans and new citizens, lifetime Republicans and fresh converts drawn together by common beliefs and allegiances.

During those 36 years, Republicans held the White House for 28, the Senate for 30, and the House for 26. The GOP fell out of power during that period only when the party split apart, as it did when the pugnacious Teddy ran as a third-party candidate in 1912. Outside the South, the GOP was dominant at the state level during this period as well, electing legislators, statewide officials, and governors in numbers that it would not see for another 90 years. Many big cities during this era had Republican mayors and it was not until 1932 that Democrats won a majority in New York State or carried Illinois.[17]

Historians and political scientists mark other electoral realignments with the names of the presidents who brought them about—Jefferson, Jackson, Lincoln, and FDR—yet have often overlooked the man who brought about a new party system in 1896. They have tended to focus on the candidate who was defeated rather than the one who was victorious. Yet had McKinley not run the skillful nomination fight he did or so deftly handled the exciting general election that Bryan's nomination created, the arc of history would have been bent in a different direction. McKinley's campaign matters more than a century later because it provides lessons either party could use today to end an era of a 50-50 nation and gain the edge for a durable period.

The election of William McKinley in 1896 and the subsequent political realignment his victory and presidency brought about were not foreordained. They occurred because McKinley tackled big issues as matters of principle. He drew sharp distinctions while treating his opponents and voters with respect. And he aimed to unite a divided country, reignite the economy, and reinvigorate his party.

In one of the most remarkable and consequential elections in the nation's history, William McKinley succeeded in forging an impressive victory that made him the president of the United States as one century neared its end and a new one—the American century—was about to begin.

ACKNOWLEDGMENTS

Led by H. Wayne Morgan, four historians—the Modern McKinley Men—have done much in recent years to improve public understanding of the remarkable twenty-fifth president of the United States and the era in which he lived. It is to these great scholars that this book is dedicated.

I was introduced to McKinley by one of them, Professor Lewis L. Gould, when he took me on in 1998 for a seminar in researching original source material. I was interested in how Theodore Roosevelt rescued his career in 1896 despite having backed the losing candidate for the GOP nomination. Dr. Gould generously agreed to the topic, but insisted I research the McKinley papers because history got him and the 1896 election wrong. How right he was.

As I began drafting this book, Dr. H. Wayne Morgan could not have been more enthusiastic about the project. His early advice steered me true. I am only sorry that he passed in February 2014 and could not see the final product.

The work of R. Hal Williams and Charles W. Calhoun has not only been important to explaining the consequential years of the Gilded Age, but also essential to informing my thinking, especially Dr. Williams's excellent volume of the 1896 election that is part of the University of Kansas series on American presidential contests.

As much as I have drawn on the scholarship of these four fine historians, any mistakes of fact or errors of judgment in this book are wholly mine.

Many thanks to my agent, the ubiquitous Bob Barnett, for his guidance and his confidence that the story of McKinley and the election of 1896 was one I should tell.

Without the "Ughs," "No!" and "Pull the lens back here" injunctions from my editor at Simon & Schuster, Priscilla Painton, this book would have been a shapeless unpublished blob. Priscilla was indispensable on my first book, *Courage and Consequence,* and her sharp focus was critical in fashioning *The Triumph of William McKinley.*

I am also indebted to the comments, guidance, and recommendations of those who read the manuscript in its raw form: H. W. Brands, Richard Brookhiser, William Horner, Charles Krauthammer, Jon Meacham, Steven Schier, Daron Shaw, and Evan Smith. Their insights helped make this a better narrative. And again, any mistakes are not theirs. Also thanks to Peter Wehner, who read parts of the manuscript and whose friendship and talent I treasure.

This book would not have happened were it not for my extraordinarily talented chief of staff, Kristin Davison. She not only led the research and editing teams, but I came to depend mightily upon her sound judgment, critical eye, and dry sense of humor. Kristin and the ever-talented Brendan Miniter (whom I met when he was my *Wall Street Journal* editor) provided crucial input as the story of McKinley's 1896 campaign unfolded.

I am also grateful for the terrific intern researchers who helped on this book these past three years—Alex Bednarek, Ryan Bullard, Christopher Gaarder, Andrew Georgeson, Nicolas Jaber, and Juliana Lyons. They spent hours in the Library of Congress, historical societies, old books, and Internet archives, sifting through faded manuscripts and discontinued newspapers to find the color and facts needed to bring this story to life.

My scheduler, now Cara Paulan and before her Kaitlyn Shimmin, were also helpful in navigating 1896 while juggling the present-day demands of speeches, column writing, and television appearances.

I am also indebted to the numerous historians, curators, librarians, and archivists at universities, libraries, and historical associations across the country who helped find old records, newspapers, photographs, and other artifacts. They include the staff at the Library of Congress Manuscript Reading Room and Newspaper Reading Room; Mark Holland, Christopher Kenney, Kim Kenney, Beth Odell, and Joyce Yut at the William McKinley Presidential Library and Museum; Lily Birkhimer, Laura Russell, and Lisa Wood at the Ohio History Connection; and Becki Plunkett at the State Historical Society of Iowa.

Thanks also to Joe Rubinfine, American Historical Autographs; Janna

Heuer, Champaign County Historical Archives; Anastasia Pratt, Clinton County Historical Association; Tim Duerden, Delaware County Historical Society; Thomas Lannon, Susan Malsbury, and Brandon Westerheim, New York Public Library; Peggy Dillard, Rosenberg Library; the State Historical Society of Missouri; Marty Miller, Nebraska State Historical Society; Vicki Catozza, Kim Andersen, and Bill Brown, State Archives of North Carolina; Sigrid Perry, Northwestern University Library; Melissa VanOtterloo, Stephen H. Hart Library & Research Center; Margaret Tufts Tenny, University of Texas at Austin; Laura Leeman, Western Reserve Historical Society; and Larry Martins, Yale University Library. I apologize if anyone was unintentionally overlooked and am also grateful to many unnamed professionals who responded to phone calls, emails, and letters. These are unsung heroes, keeping our history alive.

Thanks to Jonathan Karp, as well as all the copy editors and staff of Simon & Schuster, for their confidence in this project and encouragement. I appreciate Don Walker and the superb professionals at the Harry Walker Agency and my fantastic colleagues at Fox News. I will also be forever grateful to Paul Gigot and Mark Lasswell at the *Wall Street Journal* for the privilege of writing for the world's greatest paper each week.

Finally, I am blessed by the love and support of my wife, Karen, who put up with my disappearing into what she called "the way-back machine" to read and write, and for the encouragement of my son, Andrew, who was my first research assistant on this project when I encountered William McKinley in the Perry-Castañeda Library at the University of Texas at Austin in 1998. And finally, thanks to the recently departed Nan, the world's greatest border collie, who knew when I needed a break from the Gilded Age for a walk and tossing the squeaky ball.

NOTES

CHAPTER 1: SENSE OF DUTY

1   Charles Olcott, *The Life of William McKinley*, Vol. 1 (Boston and New York: Houghton Mifflin, 1916), 44–46; Robert P. Porter, *Life of William McKinley: Soldier, Lawyer, Statesman* (Cleveland: N. G. Hamilton, 1906), 93–97; Samuel Fallows, ed., *Life of William McKinley* (Chicago: Regan Printing House, 1901), 88–90, and William H. Armstrong, *Major McKinley: William McKinley & the Civil War* (Kent, OH: Kent State University Press, 2000), 72–75.

2   Olcott, *McKinley*, I, 46, and Porter, *Life*, 97. Besides two presidents, the 23rd Ohio also had within its ranks a future U.S. senator and the forty-sixth associate justice of the Supreme Court, Stanley Matthews.

3   An excellent summary of McKinley's administration is Lewis L. Gould, *The Presidency of McKinley* (New Haven, CT: Yale University Press, 1968). Gould rightly calls McKinley "the first modern president."

4   Robert Wiebe, *The Search for Order, 1877–1920* (New York: Hill & Wang, 1966), 11–27.

5   Margaret Leech, *In the Days of McKinley* (New York: Harper & Brothers, 1959), 24; Walter D. Burnham, *Critical Elections and the Mainsprings of American Politics* (New York: Norton, 1971), 71–90; James L. Sundquist, *Dynamics of the Party System: Alignment and Realignment of Political Parties in the United States* (Washington, D.C.: Brookings Institution Press, 1983), 154–69; and James A. Reichley, *The Life of the Parties: A History of American Political Parties* (Lanham, MD: Rowman & Littlefield, 2000), 184–85.

6   Henry B. Russell, *The Lives of William McKinley and Garret A. Hobart, Republican Presidential Candidates of 1896* (Hartford, CT: A. D. Worthington, 1896), 46 and 48–49; Porter, *Life*, 29–36; and Olcott, *McKinley*, I, 7.

7   Russell, *Lives*, 35–40 and 41–42, and Porter, *Life*, 36.

8   Julia B. Foraker, *I Would Live It Again* (New York and London: Harper & Brothers, 1932), 263.

9   Porter, *Life*, 43, and William McKinley Sr. to McKinley, April 25, 1884, in McKinley papers, Library of Congress.

10 Russell, *Lives*, 41–42; Porter, *Life*, 24–31; Olcott, *McKinley*, I, 5–6; and Richard L. McElroy, *William McKinley and Our America: A Pictorial History* (Canton, OH: Stark County Historical Society, 1996), 6.

11 Russell, *Lives*, 51

12 "Longfellow, Slavery, and Abolition." Longfellow House—Washington's Headquarters National Historic Site, http://www.nps.gov/long/historyculture/longfellow-slavery-and-abolition.htm; Russell, *Lives*, 49–50; Porter, *Life*, 53–54; and Olcott, *McKinley*, I, 13–17.

13 Russell, *Lives*, 53–54, 56 and 58; Porter, *Life*, 53–54 and 57; and Olcott, *McKinley*, I, 6–7, 11 and 20–21. Russell says McKinley attended an unnamed school in Poland for a year before entering the seminary.

14 Russell, *Lives*, 52 and 55–56, and Porter, *Life*, 53–54.

15 Russell, *Lives*, 55–56; Porter, *Life*, 53; and Olcott, *McKinley*, I, 18–19. Russell and Porter put McKinley's baptism in 1858 while Olcott has it in 1853. Porter cites the Niles church records.

16 Russell, *Lives*, 50.

17 Murat Halstead, *The Illustrious Life of William McKinley, Our Martyred President* (N.p.: n.p., 1901), 114.

18 Kevin Phillips, *William McKinley: The American Presidents Series: The 25th President, 1897–1901* (New York: Times Books, 2003), 11, and U.S. Bureau of the Census, "Historical Statistics of the United States: Colonial Times to 1970, Bicentennial Edition, Part 2" (Washington, D.C.: U.S. Government Printing Office, 1975), https://www.census.gov/history/pdf/histstats-colonial-1970.pdf, accessed 3/11/15.

19 H. W. Morgan, *William McKinley and His America* (Kent, OH: Kent State University Press, 2003), 73; and Phillips, *McKinley*, 10–11.

20 Phillips, *McKinley*, 12–15.

21 Charles E. Herdendorf, "Ohio Science and Technology: A 200-Year Heritage of Discovery and Innovation," *Ohio Journal of Science* 96, Nos. 4–5 (September–December, 1996), 68, http://hdl.handle.net/1811/23713.

22 Russell, *Lives*, 61–62; Porter, *Life*, 50–52; Olcott, *McKinley*, I, 22 and 56; and Armstrong, *Major McKinley*, 3.

23 Russell, *Lives*, 62; Porter, *Life*, 49–50; Olcott, *McKinley*, I, 22–24 and 25–26; and Armstrong, *Major McKinley*, 2–4.

24 McKinley to Anna McKinley, June 16, 1861, in the Karpeles Manuscript Library.

25 Aug. 20, 1861 entry in McKinley Civil War Diary, Ohio Historical Society.

26 Nelson A. Miles to Daniel S. Lamont, Feb. 2, 1897; William T. Crump to Cleveland, Jan. 15, 1897; William H. Zimmerman to Cleveland, Dec. 14, 1896; Russell Hastings to Cleveland, Dec. 23, 1896; John A. Harvey to C. B. Lower, Jan. 18, 1897, and "Statement of the Military Service of Brevet Major William McKinley Jr., late Private and Captain, 23d Ohio Infantry," F. C. Ainsworth, War Department Record and Pension Office, Dec. 8, 1896, in M 670 CB 65 (with 1680 Volunteer Service File 83); Letters Received by the Adjutant General of the Commission Branch 1863–1870; Record Group 94; National Archives Building, Washington, D.C.; Rutherford B. Hayes introduction of William McKinley, July 30, 1891, in Hayes Papers, Hayes Library; Olcott, *McKinley*, I, 37–38; Porter, *Life*, 62–64 and 103–4; Armstrong, *Major McKinley*, 1–4, 36–41, and 44–45; and Shelby Foote, *Civil War: A Narrative: Volume One: Fort Sumter to Perryville* (New York: Vintage Books, 1986), 688–704. Several accounts suggest two wagons, but Russell (*Lives*, 81) says one wagon was disabled. In addition, Harvey joined McKinley's other comrades in recommending him to the Congressional Medal of Honor with none of the letters saying Harvey made the dangerous transit of the battlefront with his own wagon.

27 Russell, *Lives*, 116–21; H. W. Brands, *Man Who Saved the Union: Ulysses Grant in War and Peace* (New York: Anchor, 2013), 329; Shelby Foote, *Civil War: A Narrative: Volume Three: Red River to Appomattox* (New York: Random House, 1974), 567–72; and Armstrong, *Major McKinley*, 103.

28 Olcott, *McKinley*, I, 51–53; Armstrong, *Major McKinley*, 87–90, 103; and Rutherford B. Hayes introduction of William McKinley, July 30, 1891, in Hayes Papers, Hayes Library.

29 Samuel G. McClure, "In His Office," *Cleveland Leader*, June 17, 1894; Armstrong, *Major McKinley*, 130; and Rutherford B. Hayes introduction of William McKinley, July 30, 1891, in Hayes Papers.

30 Marshall Everett, *Complete Life of William McKinley and Story of His Assassination: An Authentic and Official Memorial Edition Containing Every Incident in the Career of the Immortal Statesman Soldier Orator and Patriot*, Memorial Edition (N.p.: n.p., 1901), 126.

31 Charles W. Calhoun, *From Bloody Shirt to Full Dinner Pail: The Transformation of Politics and Governance in the Gilded Age* (New York: Hill & Wang, 2010), 8–9; Paul Kleppner, *Third Electoral System, 1853–1892: Parties, Voters, and Political Cultures* (Chapel Hill: University of North Carolina Press, 1979), 44–46; and University of South Carolina Beaufort (American Presidency Project), "Voter Turnout in Presidential Elections," accessed March 23, 2015, http://www.presidency.ucsb.edu/data/turnout.php; and *New York Evening Express Almanac, 1879*, 111.

32 Charles W. Calhoun, "The Political Culture," in *The Gilded Age: Perspectives on the Origins of Modern America*, ed. Charles W. Calhoun (Lanham, MD: Rowman & Littlefield, 2006), 195–200 and 202–7.

33 Calhoun, *Bloody Shirt*, 6–7; Gould, "Party Conflict" in *The Gilded Age*, 218–19, and Michael F. Holt, *By One Vote: The Disputed Presidential Election of 1876* (Lawrence: University Press of Kansas, 2011), 204–43.

34 Calhoun, "The Political Culture," 188–89, and Henry Adams, "The Session," *North American Review*, July 1870, 60.

35 Richard Hofstadter, *The Paranoid Style in American Politics* (New York: Vintage Books, 2008), 138.

36 *Annals of Congress*, 14th Congress, 1st Session, 776–78; Robert V. Remini, *Henry Clay: Statesman for the Union* (New York: Norton, 1993), 137–39; Maurice Baxter, *Henry Clay and the American System* (Lexington: University Press of Kentucky, 2004), 17–33; Merrill D. Peterson, *Olive Branch and Sword: The Compromise of 1833* (Baton Rouge: Louisiana State University Press, 1982), 49–84; and Lence, *Union and Liberty*, especially Calhoun's speeches "Exposition and Protest" (313–65), "Fort Hill Address" (369–400), and "Speech on the Force Bill" (403–60).

37 Tariffs were raised in March 1861, August 1861, December 1861, July 1862, June 1864, and March 1865. Senator Justin S. Morrill (R-VT) led the efforts for the first two tariff increases in 1861 and was the Senate sponsor of the Morrill-Stevens Act in 1861. Congressman Thaddeus Stevens (R-PA) was the House sponsor. Heather Cox Richardson, *The Greatest Nation of the Earth: Republican Economic Policies During the Civil War* (Cambridge, MA: Harvard University Press, 1997), 104–15, 122–26, 133–35; Ida M. Tarbell, *The Tariff In Our Times* (New York: Macmillan, 1911), 6–27; and F. W. Taussig, *The Tariff History of the United States* (New York: G. P. Putnam's Sons, 1910), 158–70.

38 Cong. Richard W. Townsend (D-IL), quoted in "The Debates of Congress," *New York Times*, Feb. 14, 1883, and "The Copper John," *Chicago Tribune*, Feb. 21, 1869.

39 Tarbell, *Tariff in Our Time*, 351–-53.

40 "The Message," *Los Angeles Times*, Dec. 7, 1887.

41 Lawrence Goodwyn, *The Populist Moment: A Short History of the Agrarian Revolt in America* (Oxford: Oxford University Press, 1978), 20–22.

42 Ostler, Jeffrey, *Prairie Populism: The Fate of Agrarian Radicalism in Kansas, Nebraska, and Iowa, 1880–1892* (Lawrence: University of Kansas, 1992), 12–14; Goodwyn, *Populist Movement*, 69–72; and Worth Robert Miller, "Farmers and Third-Party Politics," in *The Gilded Age*, 238–40.

43 The first $25 million issue of Continentals paid for $23 million of supplies. By 1781, $125 million in Continentals could purchase only $6 million of goods. Forrest McDonald, *E Pluribus Unum: The Formation of the American Republic 1776–1790* (Indianapolis, IN: Liberty Fund, 1979), 44–48, and Milton Friedman and Anna Jacobson Schwartz, *A Monetary History of the United States 1867–1960* (Princeton, NJ: Princeton University Press, 1971), 113–14.

44 Don C. Barrett, *The Greenbacks and Resumption of Specie Payments, 1862–1879* (Cambridge, MA: Harvard University Press, 1931), 12–14, 15–24, and 58–78; Irwin Unger, *The Greenback Era: A Social and Political History of American Finance, 1865–1879* (Princeton, NJ: Princeton University Press, 1964), 13–16; and Friedman and Schwartz, *Monetary History*, 16–24, esp. 17. The currency also consisted of gold and silver coins and state and national bank notes while the money supply also included commercial bank deposits.

45 Unger, *Greenback Era*, 15–16, and Barrett, *Greenbacks and Resumption*, 105.

46 Unger, *Greenback Era*, 16–17, and Tarbell, *Tariff in Our Times*, 27.

47 Unger, *Greenback Era*, 36.

CHAPTER 2: EARLY BEGINNINGS

1 Armstrong, *Major McKinley*, 98–99.

2 Armstrong, *Major McKinley*, 101–05, and Colonel G.W. Townsend, *Our Martyred President: Memorial Life of William McKinley* (Philadelphia and Chicago: Memorial, 1901), 38–39.

3 Hayes to McKinley, Nov. 6, 1866, in Hayes, *Diary*, 5:149–50.

4 Russell, *Lives*, 128–29; Porter, *Life of McKinley*, 109–13; Olcott, *McKinley*, I, 22 and 56; Armstrong, *Major McKinley*, 3 and Morgan, *McKinley and His America*, 30–31.

5 Olcott, *McKinley*, I, 56–58; Porter, *Life of McKinley*, 113; Leech, *Days of McKinley*, 10; and Morgan, *McKinley and His America*, 29–30.

6 Russell, *Lives*, 128–31; Leech, *Days of McKinley*, 10–12; Morgan, *McKinley and His America*, 31–32; Olcott, *McKinley*, I, 59–61; Fallows, *Life of William McKinley*, 214–15; and Murat Halstead, *Life and Distinguished Services of William McKinley, Our Martyred President* (N.p.: n.p., 1901), 110–14. Leech says McKinley sought out Belden as a partner. Morgan, Porter, and Olcott say the judge tested McKinley before inviting him to become his partner.

7 For Belden's prosecution of the Oberlin Rescuers, see Brandt, *The Town That Started the Civil War*.

8   Armstrong, *Major McKinley*, 100–101.

9   Leech, *Days of McKinley*, 11 and 15, and Carl Sferrazza Anthony, *Ida McKinley: The Turn-of-the-Century First Lady Through War, Assassination, and Secret Disability* (Kent, OH: Kent State University Press, 2013), 19.

10   Leech, *Days of McKinley*, 12.

11   Mary K. Hawley (Willa Cather), "Two Women the World Is Watching," *Home Monthly*, September 1896; S. F. Call, "A Love Story," *Boston Sunday Journal*, June 2, 1901; and "Mrs. McKinley Has a Sad Birthday," *Philadelphia Times*, June 9, 1901.

12   Anthony, *Ida McKinley*, 7 and 10–11.

13   Russell, *Lives*, 136–133; Olcott, McKinley, I, 65–67; Josiah Hartzell, *Sketch of the Life of Mrs. William McKinley* (Washington, D.C.: Home Magazine Press, 1896), 6–7; and Anthony, *Ida McKinley*, 1–2.

14   Olcott, *McKinley*, I, 66–67; Hartzell, *Sketch*, 8–9; and Anthony, *Ida McKinley*, 3.

15   Anthony, *Ida McKinley*, 4.

16   Ibid., 2–4.

17   Ibid., 4–5.

18   "Life Sketch of the Late Mrs. Ida McKinley," *Stark County Democrat*, (Canton, OH), May 28, 1907; Hartzell, *Sketch*, 11; Russell, *Lives*, 137–38; and Anthony, *Ida McKinley*, 5–7. Anthony mistakenly places the Delhi Academy in Clinton County on Lake Champlain

19   "Was Famous in Its Day," *Evening Star* (Washington, D.C.), Jan. 22, 1898, and Anthony, *Ida McKinley*, 6–7.

20   Russell, *Lives*, 138, and Anthony, *Ida McKinley*, 9.

21   Hartzell, *Sketch*, 11; Olcott, McKinley, 65 and 68; and Anthony, *Ida McKinley*, 7 and 10–11.

22   Anthony, *Ida McKinley*, 10–11.

23   Ibid., 11. Henry S. Belden III, *Grand Tour of Ida Saxton McKinley and Sister Mary Saxton Barber 1869* (Canton, OH: Reserve, 1985), 5.

24   Anthony, *Ida McKinley*, 11–12; Belden, *Ida Saxton McKinley*, 38–39.

25   Leech, *In Days of McKinley*, 15; Anthony, *Ida McKinley*, 12 and 14–16; and Belden, *Ida Saxton McKinley*, 190–91.

26   Anthony, *Ida McKinley*, 12–13, and Belden, *Ida Saxton McKinley*, 181.

27   Anthony, *Ida McKinley*, 14, and Belden, *Ida Saxton McKinley*, 313.

28   Anthony, *Ida McKinley*, 15, and Belden, *Ida Saxton McKinley*, 325–26.

29   "President M'Kinley At Home," *San Francisco Sunday Call*, Nov. 4, 1900; Anthony, *Ida McKinley*, 15–16; Belden, *Ida Saxton McKinley*, 400; and Olcott, *McKinley*, I, 68.

30   Olcott, *McKinley*, I, 67, and Anthony, *Ida McKinley*, 17.

31   Anthony, *Ida McKinley*, 17 and 19, and Hartzell, *Sketch*, 8.

32   Olcott, *McKinley*, Vol. 1, 76; Porter, *Life of McKinley*, 115–16; Morgan, *McKinley and His America*, 34–35; and Leech, *Days of McKinley*, 13–14. Leech mistakenly puts McKinley's election as county prosecutor in 1868. President McKinley appointed Knox U.S. attorney general.

33   Leech, *Days of McKinley*, 13.

34   Olcott, *McKinley*, I, 68–69; "President McKinley at Home," *San Francisco Sunday Call*, November 4, 1900; Morgan, *McKinley and His America*, 36; and Anthony, *Ida McKinley*, 17 and 20–21.

35   Leech, *Days of McKinley*, 13.

36   Russell, *Lives*, 141; Olcott, *McKinley*, I, 125; Hartzell, *Sketch*, 15; "Mrs. McKinley Has A Sad Birthday," *Philadelphia Times*, June 8, 1901; and William McKinley to Rutherford B. and Lucy Hayes, Dec. 13, 1870 in Hayes papers.

37   Russell, *Lives*, 141–42; Leech, *Days of McKinley*, 16; "Mrs. McKinley Has A Sad Birthday," *Philadelphia Times*, June 8, 1901, and Anthony, *Ida McKinley*, 21–22.

38   Hartzell, *Sketch*, 16–17; "Mrs. McKinley Has A Sad Birthday," *Philadelphia Times*, June 8, 1901; and Anthony, *Ida McKinley*, 21–22.

39   Anthony, *Ida McKinley*, 22.

40   Olcott, *McKinley*, I, 70, and Anthony, *Ida McKinley*, 23.

41   Russell, *Lives*, 142; Olcott, *McKinley*, I, 115–16; and Anthony, *Ida McKinley*, 23.

42   Olcott, *McKinley*, I, 76.

43   Russell, *Lives* 142; Porter, *Life of McKinley*, 126; Olcott, *McKinley*, I, 70–71; Hartzell, *Sketch*, 22–23; and Anthony, *Ida McKinley*, 4.

44   Olcott, *McKinley*, I, 70.

45   Anthony, *Ida McKinley*, 25 and 28.
46   "Life Sketch of the Late Mrs. Ida McKinley," *Stark County Democrat* (Canton, OH), May 28,1907.
47   Russell, *Lives*, 136–42, and Porter, *Life of McKinley*, 126–27.
48   Olcott, *McKinley*, I, 70–72, and Anthony, *Ida McKinley*, 25–26 and 36.
49   John C. DeToledo, M.D., Bruno DeToledo, and Merredith Lowe, M.D., "The Epilepsy of First Lady Ida Saxton McKinley," *Southern Medical Journal*, Vol. 93, No. 3 (March 2000), 267–71; Anthony, *Ida McKinley*, 25–26.
50   Olcott, *McKinley*, 2, 263, and Leech, *Days of McKinley*, 19–20.
51   Hartzell, *Sketch*, 26, and Anthony, *Ida McKinley*, 25–26.
52   Anthony, *Ida McKinley*, 28, and "Life Sketch of the Late Mrs. Ida McKinley," *Stark County Democrat* (Canton, OH), May 28, 1907.
53   Morgan, *McKinley and His America*, 39; Olcott, *McKinley*, I, 71; Leech, *Days*, 17; Russell, *Lives*, 142; Porter, *Life of McKinley*, 126; and Anthony, *Ida McKinley*, 33. Olcott and Leech say Katie died in 1876 while Porter and Russell are imprecise but point toward 1875. Morgan is the most reliable on this point with the death on June 25, 1875. It is also hard to believe that if Katie's death was in June 1876, it would not have materially affected McKinley's run for Congress that year with country conventions in July 1876, the Stark County primary in early August, and the district convention mid-August.
54   Olcott, *McKinley*, I, 70–72; Leech, *Days*, 19; and Morgan, *McKinley and His America*, 39.
55   Anthony, Ida McKinley, 35–36, and "A Brief Tour of Bedlam," Joanna Bourke, *Wall Street Journal*, April 12, 2015.
56   "Mrs. McKinley's Lover," *New England Home Magazine*, June 1901; Russell, *Lives*, 143; and Anthony, *Ida McKinley*, 33.
57   Anthony, *Ida McKinley*, 33.
58   Anthony, *Ida McKinley*, 41, and Beer, *Hanna*, 102–4.
59   David P. Rhodes to James Ford Rhodes, July 26, 1896, in Rhodes papers, Massachusetts Historical Society.
60   Heald manuscript, 2:23–24; McKinley to Thomas W. Bradley, Jan. 13, 1900, in McKinley papers; Leech, *Days of McKinley*, 16–17; Morgan, *McKinley and His America*, 39; and Anthony, *Ida McKinley*, 32 and 44.
61   Russell, *Lives*, 132–33; "The Strikers Struck," *Cincinnati Gazette*, May 2, 1876; "Murderous Miners," *Cincinnati Gazette*, May 3, 1876; "Tuscarawas Valley War," *Cincinnati Gazette*, May 6, 1876; and "The Striking Miners," *Cincinnati Times*, May 10, 1876.
62   Olcott, *McKinley*, I, 79–80.
63   Herbert D. Croly, *Marcus Alonzo Hanna: His Life and Work* (New York: Macmillan, 1912), 2–10, 13–16, and 41, and Thomas Beer, *Hanna* (New York: A.A. Knopf, 1929), 21.
64   Croly, *Hanna*, 32, 38, and 40–41, and Beer, *Hanna*, 21–22.
65   Croly, *Hanna*, 32, 38, and 40–41, and Beer, *Hanna*, 22–24.
66   Croly, *Hanna*, 47–53, 57–67, and 70–79, and Beer, *Hanna*, 55.
67   Croly, *Hanna*, 84–89 and 91–95.
68   Leech, *Days of McKinley*, 12, and Morgan, *McKinley and His America*, 40–41.
69   Mark Hanna, "Wm. McKinley As I Knew Him," *National Magazine*, Vol. 15, Jan. 1902, 405; Croly, *Hanna*, 91–95; and Beer, *Hanna*, 78–81.

CHAPTER 3: POLITICAL APPRENTICESHIP

1   Alexander K. McClure and Charles Morris, *The Authentic Life of William McKinley, Our Third Martyr President* (Toronto: W. E. Skull, 1901), 102–4; Russell, *Lives*, 132; and Olcott, *McKinley*, I, 73–74. Russell says McKinley's speech was from Bitzer's porch while Olcott says it was from a tavern's steps. In reaction to anti-German feelings in World War I, New Berlin changed its name to North Canton.
2   Armstrong, *Major McKinley*, 109.
3   Joseph P. Smith, *History of the Republican Party in Ohio*, Vol. 1 (Gale, Sabin Americana, 2012), 232–33.
4   "Negro Voting In Ohio," *Plain Dealer* (Cleveland, OH), Oct. 14, 1867, and Smith, *History of the Republican Party I*, 238–39.
5   Olcott, *McKinley*, I, 74–76, and Morgan, *McKinley and His America*, 33–34. Manderson served as Stark County attorney from 1865 to 1867.

6   Russell, *Lives*, 135; "Large Republican Meeting In Indianapolis," *Jackson Citizen* (Jackson, MI), Sept. 8, 1868; and Smith, *History of the Republican Party I*, 259.

7   "The Result In Stark," *Stark County Democrat* (Canton, OH), October 13, 1869, and McClure and Morris, *Authentic Life*, 105.

8   Leech, *Days of McKinley*, 35–37; Olcott, *McKinley*, I, 64–72; Russell, *Lives*, 136–42; "Abstract of Votes Polled," *Repository* (Canton, OH), Oct. 20, 1871; Porter, *Life*, 115–16 and 122–26; McClure and Morris, *Authentic Life*, 105–6; Smith, *History of the Republican Party I*, 307; and "Stark County!," *Repository* (Canton, OH), Nov. 8, 1872.

9   "A Wall-St. Crisis," *New-York Tribune*, Sept. 9, 1873; "Trouble in Wall Street," *New York Times*, Sept. 9, 1873; "Wall-St. Flurries," *New-York Tribune*, Sept. 10, 1873; "Wall Street Affairs," *New York Times*, Sept. 10, 1873; "New York," *Chicago Tribune*, Sept. 14, 1873; "Failure In Wall Street," *New York Times*, Sept. 14, 1873; "A Wall-St. Flitter," *New-York Tribune*, Sept. 15, 1873; "The Failure of Kenyon Cox," *New York Times*, Sept. 15, 1873; "Jay Cooke & Co." and "The Jay Cooke Failure," *Chicago Tribune*, Sept. 19, 1873; "The Bears Have Their Way," "Failure of Jay Cooke & Co.," and "A Financial Thunderbolt," *New-York Tribune*, Sept. 19, 1873; "The Panic," *New York Times*, Sept. 19, 1873; Geoffrey Perret, *Ulysses S. Grant: Soldier and President* (New York: Modern Library, 1998), 420; Jean Edward Smith, *Grant* (New York: Simon & Schuster, 2001), 575; and William S. McFeely, *Grant: A Biography* (New York: W. W. Norton, 1982), 392–94.

10   "Along The Hudson," *New York Times*, Oct. 28, 1873; "The Homeless Poor," *New York Times*, Nov. 19, 1873; and "The Unemployed in St. Louis," *New York Times*, Nov. 28, 1874.

11   "Mass-Meeting of the Unemployed in Chicago," *New York Times*, Dec. 22, 1873; "The Unemployed," *Chicago Tribune*, Nov. 13, 1874; "Destitution In Nebraska," *New York Times*, Oct. 28, 1874; "The City's Poor," *New York Times*, February 11, 1874; "Alarming Destitution," *Critic-Record* (Washington, D.C.), Feb. 16, 1874; Allen Weinstein, *Prelude to Populism: Origins of the Silver Issue, 1867–1878* (New Haven, CT: Yale University Press, 1970), 57; and Friedman and Schwartz, *Monetary History*, 31.

12   Weinstein, *Prelude*, 56–57; Barrett, *Greenbacks and Resumption*, 173–74; H. W. Brands, *American Colossus: The Triumph of Capitalism 1865–1900* (New York: Doubleday, 2010), 81; Unger, *Greenback Era*, 213–19; Smith, *Grant*, 575–76; and Friedman and Schwartz, *Monetary History*, 42–44.

13   United States Senate, Report No. 703, *Report of the Monetary Commission*, 44th Congress, 2nd session, Vol. I, 121; "The End Of Inflation," "The Effect In Washington," and "Excitement In The House," *New-York Tribune*, April 23, 1874; "The President's Veto," *New-York Tribune*, April 25, 1874; Barrett, *Greenbacks and Resumption*, 177–79; Unger, *Greenback Era*, 233–45; Perrett, *Ulysses S. Grant*, 421–23; Smith, *Grant*, 577–82; and Friedman and Schwartz, *Monetary History*, 47.

14   "Washington," *Chicago Tribune*, Jan. 15. 1875; Barrett, *Greenbacks and Resumption*, 181–93; Unger, *Greenback Era*, 249–63; Smith, *Grant*, 581; McFeely, *Grant*, 395–98; and Smith, *History of the Republican Party I*, 806.

15   Weinstein, *Prelude*, 10, 21–28, and Friedman and Schwartz, *Monetary History*, 113–19.

16   William Graham Sumner, "The Crime of 1873," *Leslie's Weekly*, Sept. 24, 1896, 173; Milton Friedman, "The Crime of 1873," *Journal of Political Economy*, Vol. 98, No. 6 (Dec. 1990), 1159; and Weinstein, *Prelude*, 22.

17   Carl Sferrazza Anthony, *Ida Saxton: The Early Life of Mrs. McKinley* (Canton, OH: National First Ladies Library, 2007), 28, and Croly, *Hanna*, 65.

18   Smith, *History of the Republican Party I*, 336.

19   William Allen White, *The Autobiography of William Allen White* (Lawrence, KS: University Press of Kansas, 1990), 251. Taft's second oldest son, William, was then at Yale.

20   "Political," *Chicago Tribune*, June 2, 1875; [Untitled], *Chicago Tribune*, June 3, 1875, and "The Ohio Republicans in Convention at Columbus," *Chicago Tribune*, June 3, 1875.

21   "The Ohio Republicans in Convention at Columbus," *Chicago Tribune*, June 3, 1875; "Ohio Republicanism," *Cincinnati Enquirer*, June 3, 1875; "Republican State Convention," *Cincinnati Commercial Tribune*, June 3, 1875; "Ohio Republicans," *New York Times*, June 3, 1875; "The State Convention," *Cleveland Leader*, June 3, 1875; and Smith, *History of the Republican Party I*, 338–41.

22   Anthony, *Ida McKinley*, 30–31.

23   "The Ohio Democrats," *New-York Tribune*, June 18, 1875; "The Financial Question," *Indianapolis Sentinel*, July 21, 1875; "Governor Hayes to the Fore," *Cincinnati Enquirer*, Aug. 2, 1875;

"The Ohio Campaign," *Cincinnati Gazette*, Sept. 13, 1875; and "The Ohio Canvass," *Cincinnati Enquirer*, Sept. 18, 1875.

24 "Ex Governor Hayes," *Cincinnati Enquirer*, Aug. 2, 1875.

25 "Splendid Meeting At Lawrence," *Repository* (Canton, OH), Sept. 17, 1875; [Untitled], *Cincinnati Gazette*, Sept. 23, 1875; [Untitled], *Repository* (Canton, OH), Sept. 24, 1875; Morgan, *McKinley and His America*, 40; and Olcott, *McKinley*, I, 77–78;

26 "Announcements," *Repository* (Canton, OH), July 14, 1876, and William Alexander Taylor, *Hundred-year Book and Official Register of the State of Ohio* (Ohio: Westbote, 1891), 102–3, 105–6, and 126. Several sources mistakenly identify Woodworth as a Democrat.

27 "Appeal To Stark Co. Republicans," *Repository* (Canton, OH), Aug. 4, 1876; Russell, *Lives*, 147; Olcott, *McKinley*, I, 80–81; and Porter, *Life*, 119.

28 "The Seventeenth Ohio District," *Cincinnati Gazette*, Aug. 17, 1876; "Maj. M'Kinley Nominated For Congress" and "17th District Congressional Convention," *Repository* (Canton, OH), Aug. 18, 1876; and "McKinley for Congress," *Repository* (Canton, OH), Aug. 25, 1876.

29 "The Reunion of the Twenty-third Ohio Regiment," *Cincinnati Gazette*, Sept. 15, 1876.

30 "The Seventeenth District," *Cleveland Leader*, Sept. 25, 1876, and "Mass Meeting At Salineville," *Cleveland Leader*, Oct. 2, 1876.

31 "Maj. McKinley at Youngstown," *Repository* (Canton, OH), Sept. 22, 1876.

32 "Forming Alliances," *Repository* (Canton, OH), Sept. 1, 1876.

33 "Mass Meeting At Salineville," *Cleveland Leader*, Oct. 2, 1876.

34 "From Alliance," *Plain Dealer* (Cleveland, OH), Sept. 26, 1876; Levi Leslie Lamborn, *American Carnation Culture* (Alliance, OH: Lo Ra L. Lamborn, 1901); and Olcott, *McKinley*, I, 81–82. Olcott wrongly calls McKinley's opponent Sanborn.

35 "In Deadlocked Race, Neither Side Has Ground Game Advantage," Pew Research Center, Oct. 31, 2012. Accessed 2015, http://www.people-press.org/2012/10/31/in-deadlocked-race -neither-side-has-ground-game-advantage/. Obama contacted 32 percent, Romney 31 percent.

36 "Prospects in the 17th and 19th Districts," *Repository* (Canton, OH), Sept. 29, 1876; "Political Signs," *Cleveland Leader*, Sept. 28, 1876; Olcott, *McKinley*, I, 81–82; Morgan, *McKinley and His America*, 42; "Blaine's Welcome" and "The Welcome To Blaine" in *The Times* (Philadelphia), Oct. 16, 1876; and Russell, *Lives*, 147–48.

37 "The Silver Currency Question," *New York Times*, April 1, 1876 and Senator Francis M. Cockrell, "Restoration of Silver To Equal Monetary Functions With Gold," Speech to U.S. Senate, October 9–11, 1893, accessed 1/5/15, http://fraser.stlouisfed.org/docs/publications/mq53c/mq53c-vlsen -0017.pdf.

38 William Vincent Byars, *American Commoner—The Life and Times of Richard Parks Bland, a Study of the Last Quarter of the 19th Century* (Columbia, MO: E. W. Stephens Publishing, 1900), 35–37.

39 "Finance And Commerce," *Inter-Ocean* (Chicago, OH), June 14, 1876; "House of Representatives," *New-York Tribune*, May 4, 1876; "From Our Regular Correspondent," *New York Herald*, July 22, 1876; "Washington," *Cincinnati Gazette*, July 26, 1876; "Unlimited Silver," *New-York Tribune*, July 26, 1876; "Washington," *New York Herald*, July 26, 1876; "Payment of Bonds in Silver," *New-York Tribune*, July 27, 1876; "Washington" and "XLIVth Congress" in *New-York Tribune*, Aug. 3, 1876; "Washington," *New-York Tribune*, Aug. 5, 1876; "Washington," *New York Times*, Aug. 5, 1876; "The Congressional Financial Inquiry," *New-York Tribune*, Aug. 22, 1876; *Chicago Tribune*, Dec. 13, 1876; "House of Representatives" and "Forty-Fourth Congress" in *New York Times*, Dec. 13, 1876; "The Joint Rules," *Chicago Tribune*, Dec. 13, 1876; "Washington," *New York Times*, Dec. 14, 1876; Byars, *American Commoner*, 107–8; and Weinstein, *Prelude*, 192–93.

40 "Silver," *Chicago Tribune*, March 3, 1877, and "Silver Money," *New-York Tribune*, March 3, 1877.

41 The vote was 163 to 34 with 66 Republicans and 97 Democrats ayes with 24 Republicans and 10 Democrats nays. "The Silver Party" and "The Congress-Extra Session" in *New-York Tribune*, Oct. 30, 1877; "Volley of New Bills," *New-York Tribune*, Oct. 31, 1877; "A Fraud Upon The House," "Inflation In The House," and "Mr. Bland As A Smuggler" in *New-York Tribune*, Nov. 6, 1877; "The Bland Silver Bill Receives a Large Majority in the House," *Chicago Tribune*, Nov. 6, 1877; Weinstein, *Prelude*, 238–39 and 306; and Ari Hoogenboom, *The Presidency of Rutherford B. Hayes* (Lawrence: University Press of Kansas, 1988), 55–56.

42 Hoogenboom, *Presidency of Hayes*, 94.

43 "Washington," *Chicago Tribune*, Nov. 21, 1877; "The Silver Bill," *New York Times*, Nov. 21, 1877; "Silver Remonetization," *New York Times*, Nov. 22, 1877; "The Battle Over Silver" in *New-York*

Tribune, Feb. 16, 1878; "The Silver Dollar" and "The Debate" in *Chicago Tribune*, Feb. 16, 1878; "The Senate On Silver," *Washington Post*, Feb. 16, 1878; "Struggle Over The Silver Bill," *New York Times*, Feb. 16, 1878; "Washington," *Chicago Tribune*, Feb. 17, 1878; Weinstein, *Prelude*, 304–6, 323, and 332–33; Unger, *Greenback Era*, 361–62; and Leland L. Sage, *William Boyd Allison: A Study in Practical Politics* (Des Moines: State Historical Society of Iowa, 1956), 152.

44   "204 to 72," *Chicago Tribune*, Feb. 22, 1878; "House Of Representatives," *New York Times*, Feb. 22, 1878; and "Regular Proceedings," *Washington Post*, Feb. 22, 1878; and H. J. Eckenrode, *Rutherford B. Hayes: Statesman of Reunion* (New York: Dodd, Mead, 1930), 294.

45   "The Veto," *Chicago Tribune*, March 1, 1878; "A Black Eye For Hayes," *Washington Post*, March 1, 1878; Weinstein, *Prelude*, 344–45; Hoogenboom, *Presidency of Hayes*, 96–97; and Eckenrode, *Hayes*, 358–60.

46   "A Veto Vetoed," *Chicago Tribune*, March 1, 1878; "In The House" and "Scenes In The House" in *Washington Post*, March 1, 1878; "The End" and "The Silver Bill A Law" in *New-York Tribune*, March 1, 1878; "Forty-Fifth Congress," *New York Times*, March 1, 1878; and Entry for Feb. 28, 1878, Garfield diary in Garfield papers.

47   John Sherman, *Recollections of Forty Years in the House, Senate, and Cabinet*, Vol. II (Chicago: Werner, 1895), 30–32.

CHAPTER 4: RISE AND FALL

1   "Eighty Years Of Lodging," *Washington Post*, October 30, 1872; James M. Goode, *Capital Losses: A Cultural History of Washington's Destroyed Buildings* (Washington D.C.: Smithsonian Institute Press, 1979), 178–80; Leech, *Days*, 20; Russell, *Lives*, 153; and Porter, *Life*, 128–30. The National Press Club now occupies the site of the Ebbitt Hotel.

2   Leech, *Days*, 21, 24; Russell, *Lives*, 152–53; "Explore Capitol Hill," Architect of the Capitol, http://www.aoc.gov/capitol-buildings/house-office-buildings, accessed 3/27/15. Most congressmen had no official office until the Longworth Building opened in 1908.

3   Leech, *Days*, 23; Beer, *Hanna*, 110; and Porter, *Life*, 152–53.

4   "The Sixteenth District," *Repository* (Canton, OH), Sept. 25, 1878; Russell, *Lives*, 147 and 152; Porter, *Life*, 152–55, and Leech, *Days*, 23.

5   Henry Watterson, quoted by Tarbell, *Tariff in Our Times*, 83.

6   Leech, *Days*, 24, and Olcott, *McKinley*, I, 110–11 and 130.

7   "The Proposed Tariff," *New-York Tribune*, Jan. 31, 1878; "Tariff Revision," *Chicago Tribune*, Jan. 31, 1878; "Fernando Wood's Tariff Bill," *New York Times*, Jan. 31, 1878; "Miscellaneous Comment on the Subject of the New Tariff Bill," *Chicago Tribune*, Feb. 1, 1878; and "The Proposed Tariff Bill" and "Practical Tariff Reform" in *New York Times*, Feb. 1, 1878.

8   McKinley did not speak during the 45th Congress's 1st session (which ran from Oct. 15 to Dec. 3, 1877) and while he presented 27 petitions and pension requests in the 45th Congress's 2nd session (Dec. 8, 1877, to June 20, 1878), his April 15 speech was his first address. See *Congressional Record*, 45th Congress, 1st Session, Vol. VI, 131 and *Congressional Record*, 45th Congress, 2nd Session, Vol. VII, 412–13.

9   Joseph P. Smith, ed., *Speeches and Addresses of William McKinley, From His Election To Congress to the Present Time* (New York: D. Appleton, 1893), 1–23, and Olcott, *McKinley*, I, 128 and 131–34.

10   *Congressional Record*, 45th Congress, 2nd Session, 2542–62 and 4154-55; "Killed," *Chicago Tribune*, June 6, 1878; "The Last Of The Tariff Bill" and "A Dead Monster" in *New-York Tribune*, June 6, 1878; Tarbell, *Tariff In Our Times*, 87–90; Edward Stanwood, *American Tariff Controversies in the Nineteenth Century*, Vol. 2 (Boston: Houghton Mifflin, 1904), 197–99; Olcott, *McKinley*, I, 114–88; Russell, *Lives*, 148–51; and James G. Blaine, *Twenty Years of Congress 1861–1881*, Vol. 2 (Philadelphia: Henry Bill, 1886), 602.

11   Olcott, *McKinley*, I, 83–84.

12   "The Ohio Democratic Fraud," *Repository* (Canton, OH), May 18, 1878; "The Ohio Vote," *Cincinnati Gazette*, Oct. 17, 1878; [Untitled], *Repository* (Canton, OH), Oct. 16, 1878; "Correct," *Repository* (Canton, OH), Nov. 1, 1878; and Hayes to James M. Comley, Oct. 29, 1878, in Hayes papers.

13   *Congressional Record*, 46th Congress, 1st Session, April 18, 1879, 548ff; Russell, *Lives*, 158–58; Fallows, *Life of William McKinley*, 93–97; and Smith, *History of the Republican Party I*, 399, 407–8.

14   "Thoman's Little Trick," *Repository* (Canton, OH), Sept. 20, 1880; "McKinley At Salem," *Repository* (Canton, OH), Sept. 10, 1880; "A Protection Pole," *Repository* (Canton, OH), Sept. 8, 1880;

"Buckeye Booms," *Cleveland Leader*, Sept. 18, 1880; "Major McKinley In The Wigwam," *Repository* (Canton, OH), Oct. 12, 1880; and "Glorious Republican Triumph" and "Ohio, Indiana and Everything" in *Repository* (Canton, OH), Oct. 13, 1880.

15 "By Telegraph," *Daily Press* (Portland, ME.), Aug. 17, 1880; Stanwood, *American Tariff Controversies*, II, 199–201; Justus D. Doenecke, *The Presidencies of James A. Garfield and Chester A. Arthur* (Lawrence: University Press of Kansas, 1981), 24–30; Allan Peskin, *Garfield* (Kent, OH: The Kent State University Press, 1978), 491–95 and 510–13; H. Wayne Morgan, *From Hayes to McKinley: National Party Politics 1877–1896* (Syracuse: Syracuse University Press, 1969), 116–21; and McKinley to J. C. Parton, Dec. 30, 1889, quoted by Beer, *Hanna*, 105.

16 Olcott, *McKinley*, I, 135–36, and Russell, *Lives*, 157.

17 Tarbell, *Tariff In Our Times*, 94–97; Peskin, *Garfield*, 314–17; Candice Millard, *Destiny of the Republic: A Tale of Madness, Medicine, and the Murder of a President* (New York: Doubleday, 2011), 127–32 and 227–32; and Morgan, *McKinley and His America*, 56.

18 "The President's Message," *New York Times*, Dec. 7, 1881.

19 Smith (ed.), *Speeches*, 70–105.

20 "Washington," *Chicago Tribune*, May 6, 1882; "The Tariff Debate Ended," *New York Times*, May 6, 1882; "Passage Of The Tariff Commission Bill," *Chicago Tribune*, May 7, 1882; "The Tariff Commission," *New York Times*, May 7, 1882; George Frederich Howe, *Chester A. Arthur: A Quarter Century of Machine Politics* (New York: Dodd, Mead, 1934), 220–21; and Stanwood, *Tariff Controversies*, II, 199–201 and 203–6.

21 "The Tariff Commission" and "Tariff Report" in *Chicago Tribune*, Dec. 5, 1882; "Tariff Reform–A Strong Report," *New-York Tribune*, Dec. 5, 1882; "Report Of The Commission," *New York Times*, Dec. 5, 1882; "The Tariff Commission," *Washington Post*, Dec. 5, 1882; "What The Tariff Commission Did Not Report," *Chicago Tribune*, Dec. 6, 1882; "The Tariff Commission's Report," *New York Times*, Dec. 6, 1882; "The Revenue Tariff Bill," *New-York Tribune*, March 3, 1883; "The Record," *Chicago Tribune*, March 4, 1883; "The Tariff Bill Passed" and "The New Tariff" in *New York Times*, March 4, 1883; "The Defeated Obstructionists," *Washington Post*, March 7, 1883; Tarbell, *Tariff In Our Times*, 100–108 and 127–30; Stanwood, *Tariff Controversies*, II, 203–20; and Olcott, *McKinley*, I, 140–42.

22 "The Coming Tariff Fight," *New York Tribune*, April 15, 1884; "A Soporific Tariff Debate," *Puck*, Vol. 14–16, April 23, 1884; "The Debate" and "The Day At The Capital" in *Chicago Tribune*, April 16, 1884; "The Tariff Debate Begun," *New York Times*, April 16, 1884; Tarbell, *Tariff In Our Times*, 127–30 and 137–38; and Stanwood, *Tariff Controversies*, II, 207–20.

23 Smith (ed.), "The Morrison Tariff Bill," *Speeches*, 131–59, and "Major McKinley's Tariff Speech," *Repository* (Canton, OH), April 24, 1884. Smith places the speech on April 30, a mistake repeated by Olcott, *McKinley*, I, 143.

24 "Tobacco And Fruit Brandy," *Washington Post*, July 3, 1884; "At Washington," *Chicago Tribune*, May 1, 1884; "Crippling The Morrison Bill," *Chicago Tribune*, May 2, 1884; "Tariff Reform," *Chicago Tribune*, May 4, 1884; and "To Close On Tuesday," *Washington Post*, May 2, 1884.

25 Olcott, *McKinley*, I, 145.

26 "Eighteenth District," *Repository* (Canton, OH), Aug. 9, 1882; William McKinley to Abner McKinley on March 12, 1882 in McKinley papers; [Untitled], *Plain Dealer* (Cleveland, OH), Aug. 22, 1882; "In The Field Of Politics," *Cincinnati Gazette*, Sept. 9, 1882; "In The Field Of Politics," *Cincinnati Gazette*, Sept. 11, 1882 and "Meeting at Malvern, Carroll County," *Plain Dealer* (Cleveland, OH), Sept. 16, 1882; [Untitled], *Repository* (Canton, OH), Sept. 22, 1882; [Untitled], *Repository* (Canton, OH), Sept. 29, 1882; "Massillon," *Repository* (Canton, OH), Sept. 30, 1882; "Foster and McKinley in Leetonia," *Cleveland Leader*, Oct. 7, 1882; and "A Lively Night at Canton," *Cleveland Leader*, Oct. 12, 1882.

27 Morgan, *From Hayes to McKinley*, 159–61; "Whiskey Did It," *Repository* (Canton, OH), Oct. 13, 1882; "Returns Of The Election," *Cincinnati Gazette*, Oct. 14, 1882; [Untitled], *Cincinnati Commercial Tribune*, October 14, 1882; "The Result," *Repository* (Canton, OH), Oct. 14, 1882; and Smith, *History of the Republican Party I*, 399–402.

28 "Barely Elected to be Bounced," *Plain Dealer* (Cleveland, OH), Oct. 14, 1882; "To Be Contested," *Repository* (Canton, OH), Oct. 16, 1882; "Wallace Will Contest McKinley's Seat," *Cleveland Leader*, Nov. 14, 1882; and "McKinley The Man," *Repository* (Canton, OH), Dec. 6, 1882.

29 "McKinley to be Ousted," *Plain Dealer* (Cleveland, OH), May 12, 1884; "Wallace vs. McKinley," *Repository* (Canton, OH), May 13, 1884; "Wallace vs. McKinley," *Repository* (Canton, OH),

May 15, 1884, and "The Wallace-M'Kinley Case," *Chicago Tribune*, May 17, 1884; "Wallace Vs. M'Kinley," *Cleveland Leader*, May 27, 1884; and "At Washington," *Chicago Tribune*, May 27, 1884.

30 "M'Kinley Unseated," *Cleveland Leader*, May 28, 1884; "Exit M'Kinley—Enter Wallace," *Washington Post*, May 28, 1884; and "M'Kinley Unseated," *Chicago Tribune*, May 28, 1884.

31 Olcott, *McKinley*, I, 244.

32 "Ohio. A Blaine-Sherman Slate" and "The Ohio Convention" in *Chicago Tribune*, April 25, 1884; "Sherman Gets Three," *Washington Post*, April 25, 1884; "Canton's Congressman," *Repository* (Canton, OH), May 1, 1884; Russell, *Lives*, 173–75; Porter, *Life of McKinley*, 134–37; and Morgan, *McKinley and His America*, 76–77.

33 Joseph B. Foraker, *Notes of a Busy Life* (Cincinnati: Stewart & Kidd, 1916), 83–86; "Ohio Republicans" and "Clamoring For Sherman" in *New-York Tribune*, June 6, 1883; "In Convention" and "The Sherman Boom" in *Cleveland Leader*, June 6, 1883; "The Political Field," *Washington Post*, June 7, 1883; and Everett Walters, *Joseph Benson Foraker: An Uncompromising Republican* (Ohio: Ohio History Press, 1948), 21–23.

34 Foraker, *Busy Life*, 118–19, 126, and 131–34, and Walters, *Foraker*, 23–25.

35 Hanna to McKinley, April 28 and May 2, 1884, in McKinley papers, L.C.

36 Mark W. Summers, *Rum, Romanism and Rebellion: The Making of a President, 1884* (Chapel Hill, NC: The University of North Carolina Press, 2000), 124–32.

37 "Negro In The Chair," *Washington Post*, June 4, 1884, and "Convention Pictures," *New-York Tribune*, June 4, 1884.

38 "The First Trial Of Strength" and "The Ohio Delegation Excited" in *New-York Tribune*, June 4, 1884, and "Blaine Leads," *Cleveland Leader*, June 4, 1884.

39 Republican National Convention, Chicago, 1884, *Official Proceedings of the Eighth Republican National Convention Held at Chicago, IL, June 3, 4, 5, and 6, 1884* (Rand, McNally and Company, 1884), 3–22; "Blaine Leads" and "A Recapitulation" in *Cleveland Leader*, June 4, 1884; "A Series Of Curious Scenes" and "Arthur And Blaine Men Discouraged" in *Washington Post*, June 4, 1884; "Blaine Leads," *Cleveland Leader*, June 4, 1884, and "The Chicago Convention," *New-York Tribune*, June 4, 1884; "Blaine Still Ahead" and "Selecting A Temporary Chairman" in *New-York Tribune*, June 4, 1884; and "Committee On Platform," *Chicago Tribune*, June 3, 1884.

40 "The Routine Work Completed," *New York Times*, June 6, 1884; "Major McKinley Presides Over The Convention," *Repository* (Canton, OH), June 6, 1884; "Disposing Of Committee Reports," *New-York Tribune*, June 6, 1884; and *Eighth Republican National Convention*, 91–94.

41. *Eighth Republican National Convention*, 97–120; "In Line," *Cleveland Leader*, June 6, 1884; and "Placed In Nomination" and "The Question Of A Ballot" in *New-York Tribune*, June 6, 1884.

42 *Eighth Republican National Convention*, 120–28 and, "In Line," *Cleveland Leader*, June 6, 1884.

43 *Eighth Republican National Convention*, 128–35, and "Placed In Nomination" and "The Question Of A Ballot" in *New-York Tribune*, June 6, 1884.

44 Foraker, *Busy Life*, 163.

45 *Eighth Republican National Convention*, 151–55; "The Convention's Closing Work," *New York Times*, June 7, 1884; "Details Of The Contest," *Washington Post*, June 7, 1884; and Summers, *Rum, Romanism and Rebellion*, 141.

46 *Eighth Republican National Convention*, 155–64, and "How The Result Was Reached," *Washington Post*, June 7, 1884.

47 Sherman to Foraker, June 9, 1884, in Foraker papers, quoted by Foraker, *Busy Life*, 160.

48 Hanna to Shuckens, July 8, 1884, Hanna to McKinley, July 11, 1884 (two), July 19, 1884, and August 5, 1884, in McKinley papers, LoC.

49 "On Ohio Soil," *Cleveland Leader*, Oct. 8, 1884; "Greeting To Blaine," *Repository* (Canton, OH), Oct. 8, 1884; " 'Rah' For Blaine" and "Memories Of Massillon" in *Repository* (Canton, OH), Oct. 9, 1884; Hanna to McKinley Sept. 27 and Oct. 7, 1884, in McKinley papers; and Foraker, *Busy Life*, 173.

50 "McKinley's Majority 1500 Or More," *Repository* (Canton, OH), Oct. 16, 1884; Olcott, *McKinley*, I, insert between 82 and 83 and Smith, *History of the Republican Party I*, 490.

51 "Latest Efforts Of The Tricksters," *Repository* (Canton, OH), Oct. 12, 1886; "At Carrollton," *Repository* (Canton, OH), Oct. 22, 1886; "Congressman McKinley," *Repository* (Canton, OH), Nov. 2, 1886; and Smith, *History of the Republican Party I*, 527.

52 "The Ticket," *Cleveland Leader*, June 12, 1885; "Major McKinley Won't Accept," *Cincinnati Gazette*, June 5, 1885; "Ohio Republicans," *Repository* (Canton, OH), June 12, 1885; "The Republicans Of Ohio," *New-York Tribune*, June 12, 1885; and Foraker, *Busy Life*, 186–91.

53 Walters, *Foraker*, 33–35; Foraker, *Busy Life*, 192–210; and Croly, *Hanna*, 125.
54 Croly, *Hanna*, 128–29; Foraker, *Busy Life*, 321–23; Walters, *Foraker*, 321; and William T. Horner, *Ohio's Kingmaker: Mark Hanna, Man and Myth*, (Athens, OH: Ohio University Press, 2010), 66–68. Croly mistakenly says Foraker appointed McKinley's man, but the Major was advocating former state senator Edwin Hartshorn, whose brother Orville was president of Mt. Union College. Hanna's candidate was William M. Bayne, whom Hanna had run unsuccessfully for Cleveland mayor. Hartshorn was eventually given a deputy inspector's job.
55 Croly, *Hanna*, 129–31.
56 "Eloquence At A Dinner," *Chicago Tribune*, Feb. 13, 1887; "Republican Words of *Hope*," *New-York Tribune*, Feb. 13, 1887; "Ready for the Row," *Plain Dealer* (Cleveland, OH), July 27, 1887; Hanna to Foraker, April 22, 1887 in Foraker papers; Smith, *History of the Republican Party I*, 541; and Foraker, *Busy Life*, 248–56, 268–71, and 315.
57 "Foraker's Sad Fate," *Plain Dealer* (Cleveland, OH), June 28, 1887; Foraker, *Busy Life*, 257; Walters, *Foraker*, 315–18; and Morgan, *McKinley and His America*, 78.
58 Hanna to Foraker, Nov. 28, 1887, Foraker to Hanna, Nov. 30, 1887, and Hanna to Foraker, Dec. 3, 1887, in Foraker papers, LoC.; Foraker, *Busy Life*, 321–22; Croly, *Hanna*, 125 and 128–29; and Horner, *Ohio's Kingmaker*, 66–68.

CHAPTER 5: THREE STEPS CLOSER, ONE STEP BACK

1 Friedman and Schwartz, *Monetary History*, 93.
2 Irwin, Douglas, "Higher Tariffs, Lower Revenues? Analyzing the Fiscal Aspects of the Great Tariff Debate of 1888," *The Journal of Economic History*, Vol. 58, No. 1, March 1998, XX.
3 "The Tariff Reduction," *Chicago Tribune*, April 12, 1886; "The Hybrid Tariff Bill," *New-York Tribune*, April 12, 1886; "The Tariff Reform Bill," *New York Times*, April 12, 1886; "Wool," *Chicago Tribune*, April 17, 1886; "Morrison Is Defeated," *Chicago Tribune*, June 18, 1886; "The Vote On The Tariff," *Washington Post*, June 18, 1886; "Morrison's Tariff Bill," *Chicago Tribune*, June 20, 1886; and "A Free-Trade Defeat," *New-York Tribune*, June 18, 1886.
4 "The Message," *Los Angeles Times*, Dec. 7, 1887.
5 "The Home Market Club," *Sun* (Baltimore), Feb. 10, 1888; "Hon. William McKinley," *Boston Daily Advertiser*, Feb. 10, 1888; and "Begins At Home," *Boston Herald*, Feb. 10, 1888.
6 "Views Of The Minority," from Smith (ed.), *Speeches and Addresses*, 290–335; "Mr. M'Kinley Report," *Chicago Tribune*, April 3, 1888; and "Riddling The Mills Bill," *New York Times*, April 3, 1888.
7 Morgan, *From Hayes to McKinley*, 281.
8 "A Bad Day For Mills," *Chicago Tribune*, May 19, 1888; "A Day Of Great Oratory," *Washington Post*, May 19, 1888; "Free Trade On Trial," *New-York Tribune*, May 19, 1888; "A Fatal Big Suit," *New-York Tribune*, May 21, 1888; and "The Mills Tariff Bill," from Smith (ed.), *Speeches and Addresses*, 290–335.
9 "The Senate Tariff Bill," *New York Times*, Aug. 5, 1888; Morgan, *From Hayes to McKinley*, 208–35; Summers, *Rum, Romanism & Rebellion*, 299–301; and 303–15 and Allan Nevins, *Grover Cleveland: A Study in Courage*, Vol. I (New York: Dodd, Mead, 1932), 373–82 and 169–75.
10 "Will Run No Risks," *Plain Dealer* (Cleveland, OH), May 24, 1888, and "John Is The Jonah," *Plain Dealer* (Cleveland, OH), May 30, 1888.
11 Croly, *Hanna*, 132–34; Foraker, *Busy Life*, 336–39, and Foraker to Hanna, May 10, 1888, in Foraker papers. Foraker vigorously disputes Croly's characterization of his actions, but to little effect.
12 Morgan, *From Hayes to McKinley*, 282–84.
13 "Jay Hubbell's Views," *Daily Inter Ocean* (Chicago, IL), June 15, 1888; "In The Clouds," *Plain Dealer* (Cleveland, OH), June 18, 1888; Sage, *Allison*, 216–17; and Morgan, *McKinley and His America*, 89.
14 "The Deluge Of Badges," *Chicago Tribune*, June 23, 1888.
15 "Convention Picture" and "Doings In Committee" in *Chicago Tribune*, June 20, 1888; "The First Day," *Plain Dealer* (Cleveland, OH), June 20, 1888; "Platform Workers," *Los Angeles Times*, June 20, 1888; and Republican National Convention, Chicago, 1888, *Official Proceedings of the Ninth Republican National Convention Held at Chicago, IL, June 19, 20, 21, 22, 23, and 25, 1888*, reported by Gustavus P. English (The Blakely Printing Co., 1888), 7–35.
16 *Ninth Republican National Convention*, 62–64, and "Two Styles Of Oratory," *Chicago Tribune*, June 21, 1888.

17 *Ninth Republican National Convention,* 108–13; "The Republican Platform" and "In the Convention Hall" in *Chicago Tribune,* June 22, 1888; "The Platform Read," *Repository* (Canton, OH), June 21, 1888; and "Sugar And The Tariff," *Brooklyn Daily Eagle,* July 8, 1888.

18 *Ninth Republican National Convention,* 113–24 and Morgan, *From Hayes to McKinley,* 286–89 and 291.

19 Morgan, *From Hayes to McKinley,* 286–87.

20 *Ninth Republican National Convention,* 141–43, 147–51, and 152–60; Morgan, *McKinley and His America,* 90, and "Convention Incidents," *New-York Tribune,* June 24, 1888; "Can Allison Make It," *Washington Post,* June 23, 1888; and "Work Of The Day" and "Three Ballots in Chicago" in *New-York Tribune,* June 23, 1888.

21. "A Combination On McKinley," *New-York Tribune,* June 23, 1888; "M'Kinley As A Dark Horse," *Washington Post,* June 23, 1888; Russell, *Lives,* 206–7; and Beer, *Hanna,* 110.

22 Marcus A. Hanna and Joe M. Chapple, *Mark Hanna: His Book* (Boston: The Chapple, Ltd., 1904), 48–50.

23 "Another Snub to Foraker," *Repository* (Canton, OH), June 23, 1888; "He Told McKinley to Sit Down," *Repository* (Canton, OH), July 5, 1888; and *Ninth Republican National Convention,* 173–74.

24 Hanna, *His Book,* 50.

25 *Ninth Republican National Convention,* 172–84.

26 Foraker, *Busy Life,* 366–67; Walters, *Foraker,* 72–74; and Morgan, *McKinley and His America,* 91.

27 Charles Foster to Thomas Beer, Nov. 15, 1901, quoted in Beer, *Hanna,* 110.

28 Hanna to Sherman, June 23, 1888; Murat Halstead to Sherman, June 23, 1888; and Sherman to Hanna, June 23, 1888, in Sherman papers, LoC.

29 "Blaine Or McKinley," "Mr. Sherman In The Fight To The End" and "Strongly Favoring McKinley" in *New-York Tribune,* June 25, 1888; John Little to Robert P. Porter, Dec. 6, 1895 quoted in Porter, *Life,* 143–48; and "Another Speech," *Repository* (Canton, OH), July 12, 1888.

30 "A Blaine Conference," *Chicago Tribune,* June 25, 1888; "Blaine Out Of The Race," *Washington Post,* June 25, 1888; Morgan, *McKinley and His America,* 93; Morgan, *From Hayes to McKinley,* 298; and Foraker, *Busy Life,* 368.

31 *Ninth Republican National Convention,* 185–242; "Harrison And Morton," *Washington Post,* June 26, 1888; Morgan, *From Hayes to McKinley,* 298–99; Foraker, *Busy Life,* 363–66; Foraker to Murat Halstead, July 2, 1888, in Halstead papers; and Croly, *Hanna,* 136–37 and 140–42.

32 Hayes to McKinley, June 27, 1888, in Hayes papers.

33 "The Ohio Governorship," *New-York Tribune,* June 26, 1889.

34 Charles W. Calhoun, *Minority Victory: Gilded Age Politics and the Front Porch Campaign of 1888* (Lawrence, KS: University Press of Kansas, 2008), 151–54 and 178–80, and Reitano, *Tariff Question,* 112–13.

35 Calhoun, *Minority Victory,* 139–141 and 144–151, and Reitano, *Tariff Question,* 114.

36 Calhoun, *Minority Victory,* 149–51, and Croly, *Hanna,* 149.

37 Morgan, *From Hayes to McKinley,* 317, and Calhoun, *Minority Victory,* 180.

38 "State Convention," *Repository* (Canton, OH), June 25, 1889; [Untitled], *Repository* (Canton, OH), June 26, 1889; and Smith, *History of the Republican Party I,* 576.

39 "Left The Hall," *Repository* (Canton, OH), June 24, 1889; "Foraker's Fourth Time," *Washington Post,* June 27, 1889; "Vim, Vigor and Victory," *Repository* (Canton, OH), June 26, 1888; "For U.S. Senator," *Repository* (Canton, OH), June 27, 1889; and [Untitled], *Plain Dealer* (Cleveland, OH), June 29, 1889.

40 "Mr. Campbell's Bill," *Cincinnati Commercial Tribune,* Oct. 2, 1889; "Publicly Branded As A Liar," *Washington Post,* Oct. 4, 1889; "Campbell's Silence," *Cincinnati Commercial Tribune,* Oct. 8, 1889; and "Ballot Box Trust," *Summit County Beacon* (Akron, OH), Oct. 9, 1889.

41 "The Ballot Box Boomerang," *Plain Dealer* (Cleveland, OH), Oct. 11, 1889; "Campaign Incidents In Ohio," *New York Times,* Oct. 12, 1889; "Halstead Taken In," *Chicago Tribune,* Oct. 12, 1889; "Why Campbell Waited," *Plain Dealer* (Cleveland, OH), Oct. 13, 1889; and "Mr. Halstead Backs Down," *New York Times,* Oct. 20, 1889.

42 Smith, *History of the Republican Party I,* 578.

43 James Grant, *Mr. Speaker!: The Life and Times of Thomas B. Reed—The Man Who Broke the Filibuster* (New York: Simon & Schuster, 2012), 214–15.

44 Croly, *Hanna,* 150, and Morgan, *McKinley and His America,* 96.

45   Arthur W. Dunn, *From Harrison to Harding: A Personal Narrative, Covering a Third of a Century, 1888–1921* (New York: G. P. Putnam's Sons, 1922), 20 and 22, and William A. Robinson, *Thomas B. Reed: Parliamentarian*, (New York: Dodd, Mead, 1930), 197.

46   "Reed Is The Winner," *Chicago Tribune*, Dec. 1, 1889, and "Reed To Be Speaker," *Washington Post*, Dec. 1, 1889.

47   Dunn, *From Harrison to Harding*, 20, and Horner, *Ohio's Kingmaker*, 82.

48   Grant, *Mr. Speaker!*, 229 and 250–51.

49   "Ready For Work," *Chicago Tribune*, Dec. 3, 1889; "Remarks About The Speaker-Elect," *Washington Post*, Dec. 2, 1889; Grant, *Mr. Speaker!*, 259–67; Robinson, *Parliamentarian*, 207–16; and A. W. Dunn, *From Harrison to Harding*, 26–30 and 31–33.

50   Porter, *Life*, 280, and Stanwood, *Tariff Controversies*, II, 258–59.

51   Stanwood, *Tariff Controversies*, II, 259–60.

52   Tarbell, *Tariff in Our Times*, 201–2; Sage, *Allison*, 222–23; and Morgan, *McKinley and His America*, 336.

53   Porter, *Life*, 283–85; Stanwood, *Tariff Controversies*, II, 270–74 and 266–67; and Tarbell, *Tariff in Our Times*, 187–88.

54   Ida McKinley to Hayes, Jan. 18, 1890, in Hayes papers.

55   "Big Debate Begun," *Los Angeles Times*, May 8, 1890; "Major M'Kinley's Day," *Chicago Tribune*, May 8, 1890; "M'Kinley Is Happy," *Chicago Tribune*, May 22, 1890; "Only A Pair Of Bolters," *Washington Post*, May 22, 1890; "Tariff Bill Reported," *Washington Post*, June 19, 1890; and Stanwood, *Tariff Controversies*, I, 263.

56   "More Silver Debate," *Los Angeles Times*, May 16, 1890; "Too Hot To Talk Tariff," *Chicago Tribune*, July 8, 1890; "The Silver Compromise," *New York Times*, July 10, 1986; "Senate Proceedings," *Los Angeles Herald*, July 11, 1890; Homer E. Socolofsky and Allan B. Spetter, *The Presidency of Benjamin Harrison* (Lawrence: The University Press of Kansas, 1987), 59; Morgan, *McKinley and His America*, 108–9; Elmer Ellis, *Henry Moore Teller: Defender of the West* (Caldwell, ID: The Caxton Printers, Ltd., 1941), 190–96; and Morgan, *Hayes to McKinley*, 343–45.

57   "Will Wreck The Party," *Chicago Tribune*, June 21, 1890; "Something Like A Bomb," *Chicago Tribune*, June 22, 1890; "Work Of Congress," *Los Angeles Times*, July 27, 1890; "Hurried Into Conference," *New York Times*, Sep. 16, 1890; Russell, *Lives*, 227–28; Harry J. Sievers, *Benjamin Harrison, Vol. 3: Hoosier President* (Indianapolis: The Bobbs-Merrill, Inc., 1968), 164–65; Edward P. Crapol, *James G. Blaine: Architect of Empire* (Lanham, MD: Rowman & Littlefield, 1999), 121–23; and Morgan, *Hayes to McKinley*, 338.

58   "M'Kinley On His Tariff Bill," *New York Herald*, July 11, 1890; "Patching Up The Tariff" and "Tariff Bill Finished" in *Chicago Tribune*, Sep. 20, 1890; "The Completed Tariff," *New York Times*, Oct. 2, 1890; "Approval Of The Tariff," *Washington Post*, Oct. 2, 1890; and Sievers, *Hoosier President*, 171–72.

59   Russell, *Lives*, 216–20.

60   Stanwood, *Tariff Controversies*, I, 292; Olcott, *McKinley*, I, 182, 185, and 190–91; and Tarbell, *Tariff in Our Times*, 211.

61   Russell, *Lives*, 230; Porter, *McKinley*, 165–66; and "Maj. M'Kinley's Fight," *Washington Post*, June 27, 1890.

62   "Carlisle Will Be There," *Plain Dealer* (Cleveland, OH), Sept. 21, 1890; Russell, *Lives*, 234; Porter, *McKinley*, 286; Olcott, *McKinley*, I, 180; Morgan, *McKinley and His America*, 114–15; and Sievers, *Hoosier President*, 175–76.

63   "Maj. McKinley at Home," *Plain Dealer* (Cleveland, OH), Oct. 4, 1896; "The First Onslaught," *Cleveland Leader*, Oct. 6. 1890; "President In Canton," *Repository* (Canton, OH), Oct. 11, 1890; "McKinley In Michigan," *Cincinnati Commercial Tribune*, Oct. 14, 1896; "A Boost By Benjamin," *Plain Dealer* (Cleveland, OH); Oct. 14, 1896, and "McKinley's Campaign," *Cincinnati Commercial Tribune*, Nov. 4, 1890.

64   "M'Kinley, Reed and Alger," *Plain Dealer* (Cleveland, OH), Oct. 18, 1896; "Speaker Reed in Chicago," *Cincinnati Commercial Tribune*, Oct. 26, 1890; and Sievers, *Hoosier President*, 179.

65   Russell, *Lives*, 234; Olcott, *McKinley*, I, 266; and Smith, *History of the Republican Party I*, 598.

66   "Hard Blow At The Republican Party," *Chicago Tribune*, June 2, 1890; Stanwood, *Tariff Controversies*, I, 293–94; Sage, *Allison*, 243; Morgan, *Hayes to McKinley*, 353–55; and Robinson, *Parliamentarian*, 241.

67 Socolofsky and Spetter, *Presidency of Harrison*, 89–91; Morgan, *Hayes to McKinley*, 331–32 and 354–56; and Grant, *Mr. Speaker!*, 288.

68 Russell, *Lives*, 235–40; Olcott, *McKinley*, I, 190; and "History Repeats Itself," *Repository* (Canton, OH), Nov. 8, 1890.

69 Leech, *Days Of McKinley*, 48–49.

CHAPTER 6: RESURRECTION

1   Smith, *History of Republican Party*, 592–93 and 598.

2   Walters, *Foraker*, 99, and Foraker, *Notes*, 443–44.

3   Walters, *Foraker*, 98.

4   "The State Convention," "The Fight On," and "M'Kinley's Reception" in *Cleveland Leader*, June 17, 1891; "M'Kinley Named" and "Major M'Kinley's" in *Repository* (Canton, OH), June 18, 1891; and Walters, *Foraker*, 99.

5   "The Republican Party Greater Than Any Individual Member Thereof," *Cincinnati Commercial Gazette*, July 19, 1891, and Walters, *Foraker*, 100.

6   Smith, *History of the Republican Party I*, 603–4; "A Handsome Reception," "The Parade" and "Canton's Contingent" in *Repository* (Canton, OH), Aug. 22, 1891; and Russell, *Lives*, 245.

7   "The Key-Note," *Cincinnati Post*, Aug. 22, 1891, and Russell, *Lives*, 246–48.

8   "Piqua 'Tin Plate," *Plain Dealer* (Cleveland, OH), Oct. 4, 1891; "Honest Coin Hoodoo," *Plain Dealer* (Cleveland, OH), Oct. 16, 1891; [Untitled], *Repository* (Canton, OH), Oct. 22, 1891; "Addresses in 84 Counties," *Boston Journal*, Oct. 31, 1891; Russell, *Lives*, 248; and Porter, *Life*, 174.

9   "Fire Alarm Foraker," *Plain Dealer* (Cleveland, OH), Oct. 11, 1891; "Can't Last Ten Days," *Plain Dealer* (Cleveland, OH), Oct. 26, 1891; "At Cincinnati," *Repository*, (Canton, OH), Nov. 2, 1891; "The Finish," *Repository*, (Canton, OH), Nov. 3, 1891; Walters, *Foraker*, 100–101; and Olcott, *Life of McKinley*, I, 272.

10 "A Bar'l Of Boodle," *Plain Dealer* (Cleveland, OH), Oct. 26, 1891; "Mark Is The Man," *Plain Dealer* (Cleveland, OH), Oct. 27, 1891; Olcott, *Life of McKinley*, I, 272; Leech, *Days of McKinley*, 51; and Croly, *Hanna*, 159–62.

11 Walters, *Foraker*, 102–3, and Sherman to Hanna, Jan. 9, 1892, quoted by Croly, *Hanna*, 162.

12 Morgan, *From Hayes to McKinley*, 329–31; Dunn, *From Harrison to Harding*, 92; Sievers, *Hoosier President*, 174 and 205–6; and Olcott, *McKinley*, II, 343–44.

13 "All Ohio In Harmony," *Chicago Tribune*, April 29, 1892; "Students In Politics," *Chicago Tribune*, May 18, 1892; "College Men Organize," *Illinois State Journal* (Springfield, IL), May 18, 1892; and "Keep It Up, Boys," *Daily Inter Ocean* (Chicago, IL), May 18, 1892.

14 Morgan, *From Hayes to McKinley*, 425–26, and Leech, *Days of McKinley*, 56.

15 Louis J. Lang, *The Autobiography of Thomas Collier Platt* (New York: B. W. Dodge, 1910), 210–12 and 246, and James A. Kehl, *Boss Rule in the Gilded Age: Matt Quay of Pennsylvania* (Pittsburgh: University of Pittsburgh Press, 1981), 162–68.

16 "All Ohio In Harmony" and "They Are Perplexed" in *Chicago Tribune*, April 29, 1892; Smith, *History of the Republican Party I*, 615; Foraker, *Notes*, 448; and Walters, *Foraker*, 104–5.

17 Sievers, *Hoosier President*, 216.

18 "Blaine Resigns," *Chicago Tribune*, June 5, 1892; "Blaine Gives His Reasons," *Chicago Tribune*, June 5, 1892; and "Mr. and Mrs. Blaine Talk" and "Strained Relations" in *Washington Post*, June 5, 1892.

19 "Only To Ratify," *Chicago Tribune*, June 5, 1892; "Secretary Blaine Resigns" and "Two Camps Were Startled," *New-York Tribune*, June 5, 1892; "Foraker Serenely Confident" and "Among The Western Delegates" in *New York Times* June 5, 1892; and "All Doubt Removed" and "Blaine!" in *Washington Post*, June 5, 1892.

20 Croly, *Hanna*, 165.

21 Leech, *Days of McKinley*, 56; Foraker, *Notes*, 448; and Walters, *Foraker*, 105.

22 Croly, *Hanna*, 166; "Harrison Holds His Own," *New York Times*, June 6, 1892; "Alger Is For Blaine" and "The Crisis Still On" in *Washington Post*, June 6, 1892; "On The Convention's Eve," *Los Angeles Times*, June 7, 1892; "In A Losing Fight" and "Blaine Men In Wisconsin" in *Chicago Tribune*, June 7, 1892; "Statement of Senator Charles Dick of Akron, OH, made in Washington, D.C., Feb. 10, 1906," in Maria Loretta Petit, ed., *Senator Charles Dick Manuscript*, (N.p.: N.p., 1948), 2; and Sievers, *Hoosier President*, 230.

23 "M'Kinley For Chairman," *Chicago Tribune*, June 8, 1892; "M'Kinley Firm For Harrison," *New-York Tribune*, June 7, 1892; and Sievers, *Hoosier President*, 215.

24 "McKinley Looms Up," *Washington Post*, June 7, 1892.

25 "The Convention At Work," *New-York Tribune*, June 8, 1892; "Lines Of Battle Drawn," "Permanently Organized," and "The Work At Minneapolis," *New-York Tribune*, June 9, 1892; "The Second Day's Work," *New York Times*, June 9, 1892; "It Is A Waiting Game," *Washington Post*, June 9, 1892; and Republican National Convention, Minneapolis, 1892, *Official Proceedings of the Tenth Republican National Convention Held at Minneapolis, MN, June 7, 8, 9, and 10, 1892*, reported by Theodore C. Rose and James F. Burke (Harrison & Smith, 1892), 27–29.

26 "The Fight Over Seats," *New-York Tribune*, June 10, 1892; "Minneapolis," *Los Angeles Times* June 10, 1892; "Story Of The Session," *Chicago Tribune*, June 10, 1892; and *Tenth Republican National Convention*, 36–89.

27 "William McKinley Jr.," *Los Angeles Times*, June 10, 1892; "A Review Of The Situation," *New-York Tribune*, June 10, 1892; Croly, *Hanna*, 124; and *Tenth Republican National Convention*, 132.

28 *Tenth Republican National Convention*, 89–142 and 142–52; Smith, *History of the Republican Party I*, 616–17; and Russell, *Lives*, 254. McKinley's alternate was Robert M. Nevin, a stout, mustachioed Dayton lawyer and former county prosecutor. Another delegate, former Congressman William C. Cooper, had thrown McKinley off by voting for Harrison, but switched to the Major during the canvass.

29 Leech, *Days of McKinley*, 57.

CHAPTER 7: THE MAJOR'S WAR PLAN

1 Hanna, *His Book*, 50–51.
2 "Statement of Sen. Charles Dick, Feb. 10, 1906," 14.
3 Russell, *Lives*, 295–96.
4 "Canvassing A State," *Inter Ocean* (Chicago, IL), Oct. 25, 1892; "In Old Missouri," *Inter Ocean* (Chicago, IL), Oct. 26, 1892; "Cheered By Thirty Thousand," *Chicago Tribune*, Oct. 28, 1892; "Heard By Thousands," *Inter Ocean* (Chicago, IL), Oct. 29, 1892; "Statement of Sen. Charles Dick, Feb. 10, 1906," 4; and Morgan, *McKinley and His America*, 129.
5 "It Benefits All," *Inter Ocean* (Chicago, IL), Aug. 3, 1892; "M'Kinley In Nebraska," *New York Herald*, Aug. 3, 1892; and Morgan, *McKinley and His America*, 129.
6 "Ohio Campaign On," *Chicago Tribune*, Sep. 11, 1892; "Ohio Republicans," *Los Angeles Times*, Sep. 11, 1892; "Gov. M'Kinley To Philadelphians," *Chicago Tribune*, Sep. 24, 1892; "M'Kinley At Clermont Rink," *Chicago Tribune*, Nov. 1, 1892; and "Crowds All The Way," *Inter Ocean* (Chicago, IL), Nov. 3, 1892.
7 Charles Bawsel to Almina Downes, Nov. 17, 1892, quoted by Morgan, *McKinley and His America*, 129.
8 "Surprising Failure," *Cleveland Leader*, Feb. 18, 1893; "Surprising Failure," *Repository* (Canton OH), Feb. 18, 1893; Russell, *Lives*, 269; Olcott, *McKinley*, I, 288–89; Leech, *Days of McKinley*, 58–59; Anthony, *Ida McKinley*, 58; and Morgan, *McKinley and His America*, 129–33.
9 "Misfortunate Befalls Gov. M'Kinley," *New-York Tribune*, Feb. 18, 1893; "M'Kinley Is Caught," *Chicago Tribune*, Feb. 18, 1893; and Thomas B. Mott, *Myron T. Herrick, A Friend of France; An Autobiographical Biography* (Garden City, NY: Doubleday, Doran, 1929), 49.
10 "Hotel Sketches," *Plain Dealer* (Cleveland, OH), Feb. 19, 1893; Mott, *Herrick*, 48; and H. H. Kohlsaat, *From McKinley to Harding Personal Recollections of Our Presidents* (New York & London: Charles Scribner's Sons, 1923), 10–11. Kohlsaat erroneously says he read of McKinley's troubles on February 22, but that was the following Tuesday.
11 Olcott, *McKinley*, I, 289–90.
12 Russell, *Lives*, 290; Olcott, *McKinley*, I, 290–91; and Kohlsaat, *From McKinley to Harding*, 13.
13 "About $90,000" and "He Denies It" in *Repository* (Canton, OH), Feb. 21, 1893; "Gov. M'Kinley In Adversity," *New-York Tribune*, Feb. 22, 1893; "M'Kinley To Surrender Everything," *Chicago Tribune*, Feb. 22, 1893; and Olcott, *McKinley*, I, 291.
14 "Bankrupt!," *Plain Dealer* (Cleveland, OH), Feb. 23, 1893; "The Fund For Gov. M'Kinley," *New York Times*, March 14, 1893; Russell, *Lives*, 270; Kohlsaat, *From McKinley to Harding*, 15; John Taliaferro, *All the Great Prizes: The Life of John Hay, From Lincoln to Roosevelt* (New York: Simon & Schuster, 2013), 282; Olcott, *McKinley*, I, 290–92; Leech, *Days of McKinley*, 59; and George W. Hazlett to McKinley, Feb. 23, 1893, in McKinley papers.
15 Mott, *Herrick*, 51–54, and Kohlsaat, *From McKinley to Harding*, 15–16.
16 "Words Of Praise," *Cleveland Leader*, Feb. 25, 1893; "Gov. M'Kinley's Misfortune," *Washington Post*, Feb. 20, 1893; and "Mr. M'Kinley's Misfortune" and "Town Talk" in *Repository* (Canton, OH), Feb. 23, 1893.

17 Mott, *Herrick*, 48; "Foraker," *Cincinnati Post*, June 7, 1893; "Discord," *Plain Dealer* (Cleveland, OH), June 7, 1893; "In Session," *Cleveland Leader*, June 8, 1893; and "M'Kinley Renominated," *Cleveland Leader*, June 9, 1893.

18 Wiebe, *Search For Order*, 11 and 22; Friedman and Schwartz, *Monetary History*, 104–13; Brands, *American Colossus*, 447 and 459–61; J. Rogers Hollingsworth, *The Whirligig of Politics: The Democracy of Cleveland and Bryan* (Chicago: University of Chicago Press, 1963), 10–15; and Sievers, *Hoosier President*, 128.

19 R. Hal Williams, *Realigning America: McKinley, Bryan, and the Remarkable Election of 1896* (Lawrence, KS: University Press of Kansas, 2010), 27–28, and Paul W. Glad, *McKinley, Bryan and the People* (Philadelphia: J. B. Lippincott, 1964), 71.

20 "Denver Fears A Riot," *Chicago Tribune*, July 28, 1893; "Giving Relief," *Los Angeles Times*, July 29, 1893; and Williams, *Realigning America*, 28.

21 "Missouri's Law," *Los Angeles Times*, July 29, 1893; "Idle Men Pouring In," *Chicago Tribune*, July 31, 1893; Brands, *American Colossus*, 460–61; and Williams, *Realigning America*, 28.

22 "Twenty-five Thousand Unemployed," *Washington Post*, Aug. 6, 1893; "Danger of Great Riots," *Washington Post*, Aug. 9, 1893; "Thousands Suffering," *Chicago Tribune*, Dec. 3, 1893; and "Great Suffering In Chicago," *New York Times*, Dec. 7, 1893.

23 Russell, *Lives*, 271–72.

24 "Issues Named," *Cleveland Leader*, Sept. 13, 1893; and "The Keynote Sounded," *Repository* (Canton, OH), Sept. 12, 1893.

25 Donald L. Kinzer, *An Episode in Anti-Catholicism: The American Protective Association* (Seattle: University of Washington Press, 1964), 3–32 and 37.

26 Kinzer, *Episode in Anti-Catholicism*, 41.

27 Porter, *Life*, 284–97; Kohlsaat, *From McKinley to Harding*, 18–20; Leech, *Days of McKinley*, 76–78; and Smith, *History of the Republican Party I*, 644.

28 "M'Kinley Renominated," *Cleveland Leader*, June 9, 1893.

29 "The Dawn Of '96," *Cleveland Leader*, Nov. 18, 1893.

30 Porter, *Life*, 220–27. Porter writes that McKinley traveled 12,000 miles, visited 16 states and 300 communities and delivered 371 speeches, but began his analysis with McKinley's Sept. 25 Indiana trip, ignoring his earlier travels to New England. Others who relied on Porter's summary included Morgan, *McKinley and His America*, 218.

31 [Untitled], *Plain Dealer* (Cleveland, OH), Sept. 4, 1894; "Defended His Bill," *Boston Herald*, Sept. 9, 1894; Porter, *Life*, 401–4; and Olcott, *McKinley, I*, 298.

32 "M'Kinley Goes South," *Chicago Tribune*, Oct. 20, 1894; "Great Speech By Gov. M'Kinley," *Chicago Tribune*, Oct. 21, 1894; "M'Kinley Down South," *Washington Post*, Oct. 21, 1894; "McKinley's Great Oration," *New Orleans Item*, Oct. 21, 1894; and Porter, *Life*, 230–42.

33 "Thirteen Speeches in One Day," *Daily Citizen* (Jackson, MI), Oct. 9, 1894; "McKinley's Day," *Daily Intelligencer* (Wheeling, WV), Oct. 24, 1894; "Stirred Up By M'Kinley," *New York Herald-Tribune*, Oct. 27, 1894; "A Million And A Quarter People," *Repository* (Canton, OH), Nov. 5, 1894; and Olcott, *McKinley, I*, 298.

34 "Immense Gathering," *Los Angeles Times*, Oct. 4, 1896; "Cheers For M'Kinley," *Chicago Tribune*, Oct. 9, 1894; "Cheers In His Path," *Chicago Tribune*, Oct. 20, 1894; "Grow Wild With Joy," *Chicago Tribune*, Oct. 25, 1894; "Stirred Up By M'Kinley," *New York Herald-Tribune*, Oct. 27, 1894; and Porter, *Life*, 242–45.

35 "He Tried A New Role," *Kansas City Tribune*, Oct. 3, 1894; "Shrine of M'Kinleyism," *World-Herald* (Omaha, NE), Oct. 5, 1894; "Stirs Up The People," *Chicago Tribune*, Oct. 11, 1894; "M'Kinley On The Warpath," *Chicago Tribune*, Oct. 13, 1894; "In Old Ohio," *Cleveland Leader*, Oct. 31, 1894; and Russell, *Lives*, 242–43.

36 "McKinley," *Hutchison News* (Hutchison, KS), Oct. 3, 1894; "With M'Kinley In Iowa," *Washington Post*, Oct. 6, 1894; "McKinley!" *Daily Telegram* (Adrian, MI), Oct. 11, 1894; "Stirred Up By M'Kinley," *New York Herald-Tribune*, Oct. 27, 1894; and "Cannon Explodes," *San Jose Evening News*, Oct. 30, 1894.

37 "M'Kinley's Greeting At Madison," *Chicago Tribune*, Oct. 10, 1894; "Wild Over M'Kinley," *New York Herald-Tribune*, Oct. 26, 1894; and "His March A Triumph," *Inter Ocean* (Chicago, IL), Oct. 30, 1894.

38 "Speaks To A Great Crowd," *Kansas City Star*, Oct. 2, 1894; "Shouts for M'Kinley," *St. Paul Daily Globe*, Oct. 7, 1894; "New Yell For Him," *Grand Rapids Press*, Oct. 10, 1894; and "M'Kinley Was Here," *State Register* (Springfield, IL), Oct. 11, 1894.

39   "The A.P.A. Snubbed," *Kansas City Star*, Oct. 3, 1894, and "For Protection And Prosperity,"
     Philadelphia Inquirer, Oct. 28, 1894.
40   Dawes, entry for March 10, 1895, in *Journal*, 51; John E. Pixton Jr., "Charles G. Dawes and
     McKinley Campaign," *Journal of the Illinois Historical Society* 48 (Autumn 1955); and Kohlsaat,
     From McKinley to Harding, 21.
41   Paul R. Leach, *That Man Dawes: The Story of a Man Who Has Placed His Name High Among the
     Great of the World in This Generation Because He Ruled His Life by Common Sense* (Chicago: Reilly
     & Britton, 1930), 39.
42. Dawes to Joseph P. Smith, October 22, 1894, in Dawes papers.
43. "Last Words," *Cleveland Leader*, Nov. 6, 1894, and "His Vote," *Repository* (Canton, OH), Nov. 6,
     1894.

CHAPTER 8: AUDACIOUS FIRST STRIKE

1   Richard C. Bain and Judith H. Parris, *Convention Decisions and Voting Records* (Washington,
     D.C.: Brookings Institution, 1974), 104, 115, 125, and 140.
2   "Let Them Come," *Daily Times-Enterprise* (Thomasville, GA), March 14, 1895; Stanley L. Jones,
     The Presidential Election of 1896 (Madison: University of Wisconsin Press, 1964), 129; and Croly,
     Hanna, 176.
3   Vincent P. De Santis, *Republicans Face the Southern Question—The New Departure Years, 1877–
     1897* (Baltimore: John Hopkins Press, 1959), 188 and 254.
4   "McKinley on Wrecks," *Atlanta Constitution*, March 13, 1895. Evans was in the House from
     1889 to 1891.
5   "Gone to Meet Gov. McKinley," *Daily Times-Enterprise* (Thomasville, GA), March 12, 1895;
     "Gov. M'Kinley Dined At Atlanta," *Chicago Daily Ocean*, March 13, 1895; "McKinley in
     Georgia," *Columbus Daily Enquirer*, March 13, 1895; "M'Kinley's Tour in the South," *Chicago
     Tribune*, March 13, 1895; "M'Kinley of Ohio," *Atlanta Constitution*, March 12, 1895; and Olive
     Hall Shadgett, *The Republican Party in Georgia: From Reconstruction Through 1900* (Athens, GA:
     University of Georgia Press, 1964), 189. Buck invited McKinley to be his guest in Atlanta in a
     January 26 letter, pumping J. F. Hanson, a prominent and wealthy Democratic businessman
     who was in the process of becoming a Republican because of the protection issue. McKinley to
     A. E. Buck, February 1, 1895, in McKinley papers.
6   "Local Happenings," *Daily Times-Enterprise* (Thomasville, GA), March 17, 1895; "At the
     Mitchell: An Occasion Long to Be Remembered," *Daily Times-Enterprise* (Thomasville, GA),
     March 21, 1895; and "At the Mitchell: An Occasion Long to Be Remembered," *Weekly Times-
     Enterprise* (Thomasville, GA), March 23, 1895.
7   Kohlsaat, *From McKinley to Harding*, 23, and Croly, *Hanna*, 175–76.
8   Horace Baker to William B. Allison, April 30, 1895, in Allison Papers; "A United States Senator
     Here," *Daily Times-Enterprise* (Thomasville, GA), March 15, 1895; "M'Kinley Visit A Mystery,"
     Savannah Morning News, March 22, 1895; "M'Kinley Has Mild Grip," *The World* (New York),
     March 23, 1895; M'Kinley Highly Honored," *Savannah Morning News*, March 21, 1895; "Still
     at Thomasville," *Macon Weekly Telegram*, March 25, 1895; McKinley to J. C. Pritchard, April 13,
     1895, in McKinley Papers; and Joseph L. Bristow, *Fraud and Politics and the Turn of the Century:
     McKinley and His Administration As Seen by His Principle Patronage Dispenser and Investigator*
     (New York: Exposition Press, 1952), 73. The "Toothpick State" was a reference to the practice of
     early Arkansas settlers to carry large knives. The murder in 1837 of one state legislator by another
     using his "toothpick" saddled the state with the nickname until the twentieth century.
9   Dorothy Sterling, *Captain of the Planter: The Story of Robert Smalls* (New York: Doubleday, 1957),
     75–88 and 230–34.
10   "Thomasville Topics," *Savannah Tribune*, March 30, 1895, and "Deveaux Calls On McKinley,"
     Thomasville Times-Enterprise (Thomasville, GA), March 30, 1895. Georgia State Industrial Col-
     lege is now Savannah State University.
11   "It Confronted McKinley at Jacksonville, Fla.," *Boston Daily Journal*, March 29, 1895, and "Flor-
     ida 'Boom,'" *Boston Daily Journal*, March 25, 1895.
12   "It Confronted McKinley at Jacksonville, Fla.," *Boston Journal*, March 29, 1895, and McKinley
     to Hanna, Feb. 25, 1895, McKinley papers.
13   *Savannah Tribune*, March 30, 1895.
14   Lang, *Autobiography*, 331.
15   Hamilton Disston to Quay, April 1, 1895 in Quay papers.

16   "Gov. M'Kinley To Visit Hartford," *New York Times*, April 4, 1895; "Gov. William M'Kinley In
      The City," *New York Times*, April 9, 1895; "Gov. M'Kinley Talks," *Scranton Tribune,* April 10,
      1895; "Harps on Tariff," *St. Paul Daily Globe,* April 10, 1895; and "Gov. M'Kinley At Hartford,"
      New York Times, April 10, 1895. While this Platt was no relation to New York's Easy Boss, when
      he spoke to the dinner, he "refrained from making personal mention of Mr. McKinley," accord-
      ing to the *Times.*
17   "M'Kinley's Boom," *Evening Star* (Washington, D.C.), April 11, 1895.
18   Diary entry for Jan. 23, 1895, in Dawes, *Journal,* 49–50; Bascom N. Timmons, *Portrait of an
      American: Charles G. Dawes* (New York: Henry Holt, 1953), 37; and Leach, *That Man Dawes,* 50.
19   Diary entry for Jan. 23, 1895, in Dawes, *Journal,* 50; Timmons, *Portrait,* 35; and Leach, *That
      Man Dawes,* 51.
20   Hanna to Dawes on January 11, 1895, in Dawes Papers; Dawes, *Journal,* 51; diary entries for
      March 10 and March 24, 1895, in Dawes, *Journal,* 51; Hanna to Dawes, February 20; and
      Hanna to Dawes, April 20, 1895, in Dawes papers.
21   Diary entry for March 10, 1895, in Dawes, *Journal,* 51.
22   Henry L. Fowkes (ed.), *Historical Encyclopedia of Illinois, I* (Christian County, IL: Munsell, 1918),
      518; "The Patronage of Senators," *New York Times,* October 16, 1883; "Senator Cullom," *Chicago
      Tribune,* October 14, 1883; and James W. Neilson, *Shelby M. Cullom, Prairie State Republican*
      (Champaign, IL: University of Illinois Press, 1962), 68–69, 140, and 160–62.
23   Joel Arthur Tarr, *A Study in Boss Politics: William Lorimer of Chicago* (Champaign: University of
      Illinois, 1971), 5 and 8–10, and Neilson, *Cullom,* 239.
24   Tarr, *Study in Boss Politics,* 5 and 9–10, and Neilson, *Cullom,* 240.
25   Tarr, *Study in Boss Politics,* 10–15 and 22–23, and Neilson, *Cullom,* 240.
26   Dawes to Hanna, March 8, 1895 in Dawes Papers.
27   John McNulta, "Biographical Directory of the United States Congress," at http://bioguide.congress
      .gov/scripts/biodisplay.pl?index=M000587; John M. Lansden, *A History of the City of Cairo, Illinois*
      (Carbondale, IL: Southern Illinois University Press, 1976), 156; "Trainmen To Meet," *Chicago
      Tribune,* May 19, 1895; and "W. G. Eden's Chances For Secretary," *New York Times,* June 21, 1895.
28   Diary entries for March 29, April 3, 1895, May 10 and May 11, 1895, in Dawes, *Journal,* 51–52
      and 54, and Hanna to Dawes, April 5 and April 20, 1895, in Dawes papers.
29   "Crucial War Is On," *Chicago Tribune,* Jan. 7, 1895.
30   Tarr, *Study in Boss Politics,* 43–45.
31   Diary entry for February 4, 1896, in Dawes, *Journal,* 67–68.
32   Hanna to John Hay, Dec. 21, 1895, in Hay Papers; Taliaferro, *All the Great Prizes,* especially
      188–89, 252–55, 264–70, 276–77; and Patricia O'Toole, *The Five of Hearts: An Intimate Portrait
      of Henry Adams and His Friends, 1800–1981* (New York: Clarkson Potter, 1990), 217–20, 227,
      229.
33   Mott, *Herrick,* 57.
34   Foraker, *Notes,* I, 453.
35   Foraker, *Notes,* I, 452–56; Winfield S. Kerr, *John Sherman: His Life and Public Services,* II (White-
      fish, MT: Kessinger Publishing, 2010), 349–50; and Walters, *Foraker,* 107–9.
36   "Lining Up For Battle," *Washington Post,* May 28, 1895; "Foraker Beats M'Kinley," *New York
      Times,* May 29, 1895; "Ready For The Race," *Chicago Tribune,* May 30, 1895, "Foraker Has Tri-
      umphed," *New York Times,* May 30, 1895; "To Private Life," *Cincinnati Enquirer,* May 30, 1895;
      "McKinley Was Hit Hard," *Detroit Free Press,* May 30, 1895; "Foraker Beats M'Kinley," *New
      York Times,* May 29, 1895; "Mr. Allison's Good Fortune," *Washington Post,* June 4, 1895; "The
      Foraker-McKinley Feud," *Washington Post,* June 1, 1895; "M'Kinley and Ohio," *Boston Morning
      Journal,* June 4, 1895; "Ohio Republicans," *News Herald* (Hillsboro, Ohio), June 6, 1895; Mor-
      row, *Interview with Charles Dick,* February 10, 1904, 8–10; and Croly, *Hanna,* 176–77. Croly
      depicts Zanesville as "a discouraging set-back."
37   Clarkson to Allison, June 17, 1895, in Allison Papers; "Congressman Grosvenor 'Explains,' " *New
      York Times,* June 24, 1895; "McKinleyism Out Of Date," *New York Times,* June 16, 1895; and
      "Too Much Of McKinleyism," *New York Times,* June 19, 1895.
38   "Ohio Republicans," *Perrysburg Journal* (Ohio), June 1, 1895; "Ohio Republicans," *News Herald*
      (Hillsboro, Ohio), June 6, 1895; and "Farmers Were 'Not In It,' *Ohio Farmer,* June 6, 1895.
39   "M'Kinley Is All Right," *Aberdeen Daily News,* June 3, 1895.
40   "Farmers Were Not In It," Ohio Farmer, June 6, 1895, and "The Week," *The Nation,* June 6,
      1895.

CHAPTER 9: THE PEOPLE AGAINST THE BOSSES

1   Harold Gosnell, *Boss Platt and His New York Machine* (Chicago: University of Chicago Press, 1924), 26–37, and Morgan, *From Hayes to McKinley*, 129–37.

2   Kehl, *Boss Rule in The Gilded Age*, 13–16, 46–58, and 65–83.

3   "Matt Quay's Grim Fight," *New York Times*, Aug. 26, 1895; "Comment of the Press," *Scranton Tribune*, Aug. 2, 1895; "Pennsylvania Republicans," *Los Angeles Herald*, Aug. 27, 1895; and Kehl, *Boss Rule*, 191.

4   "The Situation," *Scranton Tribune*, Aug. 26, 1895, and Kehl, *Boss Rule*, 190–92.

5   "The Pennsylvania Pot and Kettle," *New York Times*, Aug. 21, 1895; "Quay As A Reformer," *Scranton Tribune*, Aug. 31, 1895; "Hon. Matthew Stanley Quay," *Middleburgh Post* (Middleburgh, PA), Aug. 1, 1895; and Kehl, *Boss Rule*, 192–93.

6   "Threatening the Judges Again," *Scranton Tribune*, Aug. 8, 1895; "Blood May Be Spilled," *New York Times*, Aug. 25, 1895; "Quay Enforced Harmony," *New York Times*, Aug. 29, 1895; "Are All Quay Men Now," *Washington Post*, Aug. 30, 1895; and Kehl, *Boss Rule*, 193–94.

7   Kehl, *Boss Rule*, 196–97.

8   Harrison to DeAlva S. Alexander, June 14, 1895, in Harrison Papers.

9   Robinson, *Parliamentarian*, 321.

10 Thomas Settle to Reed, Sep. 3, 1894, in Reed Papers, quoted in Grant, *Mr. Speaker!*, 333.

11 Robinson, *Parliamentarian*, 322.

12 Marcus, *Grand Old Party*, 37, 104, and 180.

13 Robinson, *Parliamentarian*, 331.

14 Roosevelt to Anna Roosevelt, June 8, 1895, in *Letters to Anna Roosevelt Cowles*, 156–57.

15 Theodore Roosevelt, "The Issues of 1896: A Republican View," *Century Magazine*, November 1895, 68–72, and Theodore Roosevelt, "Thomas Brackett Reed And The Fifty-First Congress," *Forum*, December 1895, 414, 416–417.

16 Roosevelt to Lodge, June 5, 1895, in *Selections from the Correspondence of Theodore Roosevelt and Henry Cabot Lodge: 1884–1918, I* (New York & London: Charles Scribner's Sons, 1923), 146–47.

17 Roosevelt to Lodge, July 30, 1895 in *Correspondence, I*, 155–56.

18 "The Week," *The Nation*, June 6, 1895.

19 Matthew S. Quay to Platt, April 19, 1895, in Platt papers.

20 Sage, *Allison*, 239–40 and 260–63.

21 Neilson, *Cullom*, 116–17, 145–46 and 159–64.

22 Oscar D. Lambert, *Stephen Benton Elkins: American Foursquare* (Pittsburgh: University of Pittsburgh Press, 1955), 192–93.

23 Lambert, *Elkins*, 193.

24 "Minnesota's Candidate," *Evening Star* (Washington, D.C.), April 12, 1895.

25 "Two Famous Guests," *Atlanta Constitution*, Sep. 22, 1895.

26 "Comrades Now," *Atlanta Constitution*, Sep. 22, 1895.

27 "A Notable Dinner," *Atlanta Constitution*, Sep. 22, 1895, and "Suggested By Statesmen," *Atlanta Constitution*, Sep. 24, 1895.

28 "Morton's Call On Ohio," *The World* (New York), Dec. 15, 1895.

29 Russell A. Alger to Matthew Quay, May 8 and June 8, 1895, in Quay Papers.

30 "An Excellent Dinner," *New York Times*, May 31, 1896; "Dr. Depew's Big Pow-Wow," *New York Times*, May 29, 1896; and "To Dine With Depew," *Chicago Tribune*, May 29, 1896.

31 "Dr. Depew's Hospitality," *New York Times*, May 30, 1896.

32 Russell A. Alger to Quay, June 8, 1895, in Quay Papers, and Mott, *Herrick*, 59–60. If Herrick's memory was correct, Hanna's meeting took place after May, since Herrick took a four-month vacation early that year to Hawaii and California. He returned no earlier than May 1 and probably later. Alger letter's suggests the earliest Hanna could have met with "The Combine" was mid-to-late June and maybe even July.

33 Mott, *Herrick*, 60.

34 Kohlsaat, *McKinley to Harding*, 30–31. Platt may have thought Harrison undependable on New York patronage matters, but Empire State reformers like Theodore Roosevelt thought "Platt seems to have a ring in the President's nose as regards New York." Roosevelt to Henry Cabot Lodge, March 30, 1889, *Letters*, 155–56.

35 Mott, *Herrick*, 60–62.

36 Kohlsaat, *McKinley to Harding*, 30–31.

37 Mott, *Herrick*, 61.

38   Leech, *Days*, 64.

39   "A Big Crowd," *Cleveland Plain Dealer*, Nov. 3, 1895.

40   Smith, *History of the Republican Party I*, 665–67.

41   Foraker, *Busy Life*, 456.

42   Walters, Foraker, 127, and McKinley to Foraker, Jan. 29, 1896, in Foraker Papers.

43   "Ohio Has A New Ruler," *Chicago Tribune*, Jan. 14, 1896, and "He Is Out," *Plain Dealer* (Cleveland, OH), Jan. 14, 1896.

44   McKinley to Whitelaw Reid, Jan. 22, 1896, in McKinley Papers.

CHAPTER 10: DEMOCRATS FALL APART

1   "A New Administration Begun," *New York Times*, March 5, 1893.

2   Friedman and Schwartz, *Monetary History*, 130. This number is the silver and Treasury Notes of 1890 held outside the Treasury.

3   Nevins, *Study in Courage*, 523–26; Morgan, *From Hayes to McKinley*, 446–50; Friedman and Schwartz, *Monetary History*, 106–13; and Williams, *Realigning America*, 27.

4   Nevins, *Study in Courage*, 523–28, and James A. Barnes, *John G. Carlisle: Financial Statesman* (New York: Dodd, Mead, 1931), 254–60.

5   "Congress to Meet Aug. 7," *New York Times*, July 1, 1893; "It Is Repeal," *Los Angeles Times*, Aug. 9, 1893; Richard E. Welch Jr., *The Presidencies of Grover Cleveland* (Lawrence: University Press of Kansas, 1988), 117–19; and Morgan, *From Hayes to McKinley*, 451–52.

6   "Free Coinage," *Los Angles Times*, June 29, 1893; "Opinion of Two Silver Kings," *Chicago Tribune*, July 1, 1893; "Sound Fight Money Power," *Washington Post*, July 12, 1893; and "Blood to the Horses' Bridles," *New York Times*, July 12, 1893.

7   *Bradstreet's Weekly*, Vol. 21, Aug. 12, 1893, 511; Welch, *Presidencies of Cleveland*, 116; and Williams, *Realigning America*, 28.

8   "To Keep It Intact," *Chicago Tribune*, Aug. 14, 1893; "Mr. Bryan's Fine Speech," *Washington Post*, Aug. 17, 1893; and "With Silver As The Text," *New York Times*, Aug. 17, 1893.

9   Morgan, *From Hayes to McKinley*, 453–55, and Welch, *Presidencies of Cleveland*, 122.

10   "Union Pacific Succumbs," *New York Times*, Oct. 14, 1893; Joseph G. Pyle, *The Life of James J. Hill*, Vol. I (New York: Doubleday Page, 1917), 486–87; Nevins, *Study in Courage*, 545–48; Morgan, *From Hayes to McKinley*, 455–58; and Williams, *Realigning America*, 35.

11   "Silver Is Fallen, " *Chicago Tribune*, Oct. 31, 1893; "Repeal A Fixed Fact," *Washington Post*, Nov. 2, 1893; Welch, *Presidencies of Cleveland*, 122–24; Barnes, *Carlisle*, 250–86; and Williams, *Realigning America*, 35.

12   "Atchison Goes Under," *New-York Tribune*, Dec. 24, 1893; Glad, *McKinley, Bryan and the People*, 72; and Williams, *Realigning America*, 28 and 36.

13   "Text Of The Message," *New-York Tribune*, March 30, 1894; "Cleveland Vetoes Bland's Bill," *Chicago Tribune*, March 30, 1894; *Congressional Record*, 53rd Cong., 2nd Session, 1176; Glad, *McKinley, Bryan and the People*, 84; Nevins, *Study in Courage*, 595–99 and 600–603; and Welch, *Presidencies of Cleveland*, 124–26.

14   "Opinions On The Veto," *Washington Post*, March 30, 1894; "Views Of The Congressmen," *New York Times*, March 30, 1894; "Ready To Cut Loose," *Chicago Tribune*, March 30, 1894; and Morgan, *From Hayes to McKinley*, 458–59.

15   Quoted by Williams, *Realigning America*, 67–68.

16   "Hustled from the Capitol When He Tried to Speak," *New York Times*, May 2, 1894; Morgan, *From Hayes to McKinley*, 465–68; H. W. Brands, *The Reckless Decade: America in the 1890s* (Chicago: University of Chicago Press, 2002), 162–76; and Benjamin F. Alexander, *Coxey's Army: Popular Protest in the Gilded Age* (Baltimore: John Hopkins University Press, 2015), 97–102.

17   "Talk Of Civil War," *Washington Post*, July 5, 1894; "Wild Trip On A Rock Island Train," *Chicago Tribune*, July 6, 1894; Nevins, *Study in Courage*, 611–28; Welch, *Presidencies of Cleveland*, 141–47; and Morgan, *From Hayes to McKinley*, 468–70.

18   "Gov. Altgeld Makes Complaint," *New York Times*, July 6, 1894, and Harry Barnard, *Eagle Forgotten: The Life of John Peter Altgeld* (Secaucus, NJ: Lyle Stuart, Inc., 1938), 295–98.

19   "Gov. Altgeld Makes Complaint," *New York Times*, July 6, 1894; "President Cleveland Replies," *Los Angeles Times*, July 6, 1894; and Barnard, *Eagle Forgotten*, 303.

20   "Breaks Loose Again," *Chicago Tribune*, July 7, 1894, and Barnard, *Eagle Forgotten*, 304–7.

21   Lawrence Goodwyn, *The Populist Moment: A Short History of the Agrarian Revolt in America* (Oxford: Oxford University Press, 1978), 245–46; Hollingsworth, *Whirligig of Politics*, 33–34; and

Gretchen Ritter, *Goldbugs and Greenbacks: The Antimonopoly Tradition and the Politics of Finance in America* (Cambridge: Cambridge University Press, 1999), 1 and 20–21.

22   Tarbell, *Tariff In Our Times*, 217–36; Stanwood, *Tariff Controversies*, II, 321–59; "Gorman's Triumph," *Harper's Weekly*, Vol. 38, No. 1968, Sept. 8, 1894; Nevins, *Study in Courage*, 564–87; Welch, *Presidencies of Cleveland*, 131–39; Morgan, *From Hayes to McKinley*, 460–65 and 473–76; and James F. Rhodes, *History of the United States from the Compromise of 1850 to the McKinley-Bryan Campaign of 1896*, XIII (New York & London: Macmillan, 1920), 418–24. Welch says Wilson-Gorman duties averaged 7 percent less than those in the McKinley Tariff.

23   "Another Fight Over Sugar," *New York Times*, Aug. 15, 1894, and Morgan, *From Hayes to McKinley*, 475–76.

24   Morgan, *From Hayes to McKinley*, 477–78.

25   Louis W. Koenig, *A Political Biography of William Jennings Bryan* (New York: Putnam, 1971), 147–48.

26   "It's A Gold Message," *The World* (New York), Jan. 29, 1895; "The Gold Exodus," *Los Angeles Times*, Jan. 29, 1895; "The Gold Outflow Ceases," *New-York Tribune*, Feb. 2, 1895; "Bond Issue Hangs Fire," *Washington Post*, Feb. 3, 1895; "Reception Of The Message," *New York Times*, Jan. 29, 1895; "Only A Bubble," *Atlanta Constitution*, Jan. 30, 1895; "Killed In The House," *Washington Post*, Feb. 8, 1895; "How The Votes Were Finally Taken," *Chicago Tribune*, Feb. 8, 1895; and "The Administration's Defeat," *New-York Tribune*, Feb. 8, 1895.

27   "Makes A Quiet Deal," *Chicago Tribune*, Feb. 3, 1895; "Work On Bonds Stops," *Washington Post*, Feb. 6, 1895; "Belmont And Morgan," *The World* (New York), Feb. 8, 1895; "Belmont And Morgan Visit Grover," *Chicago Tribune*, Feb. 8, 1895; Barnes, *Carlisle*, 363–68; Welch, *Presidencies of Cleveland*, 126; and Nevins, *Study in Courage*, 658–62. Belmont built the horse track that bears his name.

28   "The President's Action," *New York Times*, Feb. 9, 1895; "Sold To A Syndicate," *Washington Post*, Feb. 9, 1895; "Applauded By Banks," *Chicago Tribune*, Feb. 10, 1895; Welch, *Presidencies of Cleveland*, 126; "Belmont And Bonds," *The World* (New York), Feb. 12, 1895; and Nevins, *Study in Courage*, 662–65.

29   "Rage At The Bonds," *Chicago Tribune*, Feb. 9, 1895; "Mr. Carlisle Explains," *New-York Tribune*, Feb. 13, 1895; "Option On All Bonds," *Washington Post*, Feb. 14, 1895; "Relief Is Refused," *The World* (New York), Feb. 15, 1895; "May Not Say Gold," *Chicago Tribune*, Feb. 15, 1895; "Cleveland Snubbed Again," *New-York Tribune*, Feb. 15, 1895; "Hot Talk By Senators," *Washington Post*, Feb. 17, 1895; "The President Defended," *New York Times*, Feb. 17, 1895; "Buncoed Out Of Millions and Millions," *The World* (New York), Feb. 21, 1895; "Object To Bond Bids," *Chicago Tribune*, Feb. 22, 1895; "A More Than Princely Gift," *New-York Tribune*, Feb. 22, 1895; "To Be Allotted Today," *New-York Tribune*, Feb. 23, 1895; "The Price Of Success," *New York Times*, Feb. 23, 1895; "May Not Keep Gold," *Chicago Tribune*, Feb. 24, 1895; "Bonds Parceled Out," *New-York Tribune*, Feb. 24, 1895; Barnes, *Carlisle*, 390; and Nevins, *Study in Courage*, 663–66.

30   "Silver Men To Confer," *Evening Star* (Washington, D.C.), Feb. 27, 1895; "For A Silver Party," *Chicago Tribune*, March 6, 1895; "The New Party," *Los Angeles Times*, March 6, 1895; and "Bimetallic Infant Born," *New York Times*, March 6, 1895.

31   "Forming A New Silver Party," *Washington Post*, Feb. 27, 1895; "Schemes Of Silver Democrats," *Chicago Tribune*, Feb. 27, 1895; "Mr. Bryan's Plan Fails," *New York Times*, March 2, 1895; "To Organize For Silver," *Washington Post*, March 2, 1895; "A Poor Lot Of Leaders," *New York Times*, March 7, 1895, and "Bryan's Free Silver Democracy," *Chicago Tribune*, March 9, 1895; and William J. Bryan, *The First Battle: A Story of the Campaign of 1896* (Hammond, IN: W. B. Conkey, 1896), 155–58.

32   John Peter Altgeld, *Live Questions: Including our Penal Machinery and its Victims* (Chicago: Donohue & Henneberry, 1890), 467–69.

33   "Silver As The Issue," *Inter-Ocean* (Chicago, IL), April 5, 1895; "Free Silver Or Ruin," *Chicago Tribune*, April 6, 1895; "Governor Altgeld's Opinion," *Illinois State Journal* (Springfield, IL), April 6, 1895; and "Hot Times In Sight," *Chicago Tribune*, April 13, 1895.

34   "Cannot Go To Chicago," *Washington Post*, April 13, 1895; "For Aggressive Work," *New York Times*, April 13, 1895; "Hits Fiat Men Hard," *Chicago Tribune*, April 16, 1895; "Its Weakness Excites Pity" and "Facts For Cleveland" in *Inter-Ocean* (Chicago, IL), April 16, 1895; "He Answers The President," *World-Herald* (Omaha, NE), April 16, 1895; "It Rends The Party," *Chicago Tribune*, April 19, 1895; "Will Make A Vigorous Fight," *New York Times*, April 20, 1895; "Cheap Dollar Gang In Disrepute," *Chicago Tribune*, April 25, 1895; F. H. Jones to Henry T. Thurber,

April 19, 1895, in Cleveland papers; and Allan Nevins, *Letters of Grover Cleveland: 1850–1908* (Boston & New York: Houghton, 1933), 384–86.

35 "Tomorrow's Convention," *Illinois State Register* (Springfield, IL), June 4, 1895.

36 "Bryan In The Crowd," *Chicago Tribune*, June 5, 1895; "16 to 1," *Illinois State Register* (Springfield, IL), June 5, 1895; "Silver Babe Is Born" and "Listen To A Speech By Bryan" in *Chicago Tribune*, June 6, 1895; Bryan, *First Battle*, 160–61; Koenig, *Bryan*, 158–59; and William H. Hinrichsen to Bryan, April 15, 1895, in Bryan papers. Koenig says Hinrichsen was Bryan's classmate at Illinois College, but this is incorrect. Hinrichsen attended what became the University of Illinois-Champaign. See "Hinrichsen, William Henry," Biographical Directory of the United States Congress, http://bioguide.congress.gov/scripts/biodisplay.pl?index=H000637. Hinrichsen was a deputy in Jacksonville, Illinois, while Bryan was in college there. Altgeld allies later suggested Bryan crashed the gathering, showing up uninvited and begging the convention's chairman, Samuel P. McConnell, to speak. Judge McConnell supposedly responded, "Of course, the convention will need entertainment." See Barnard, *Eagle Forgotten*, 367 and McConnell, MS, "The Silver Campaign of 1895–96." This is untrue. Bryan was a friend of Hinrichsen, who organized the convention, invited the speakers and announced eleven days before the convention that Bryan would speak. See "Hinrichsen Expects A Big Crowd," *Chicago Tribune*, May 25, 1895, and "Hinrichsen Cock Of The Walk," *Inter Ocean* (Chicago, IL), May 15, 1895.

37 "Silver Babe Is Born" and "Then Came The Governor's Turn" in *Chicago Tribune*, June 6, 1895.

38 "16 to 1," *Illinois State Register* (Springfield, IL), June 5, 1895; "Silver Babe Is Born," *Chicago Tribune*, June 6, 1895; "Silver In The Saddle," *Inter Ocean* (Chicago, IL), June 6, 1895; "Leaders Were Absent," *Washington Post*, July 3, 1895; "The Democrats Staid Away," *New York Times*, July 3, 1895; "Hoisted The Flag," *Denver Post*, July 3, 1895; "The Ohio Campaign," *New-York Tribune*, Aug. 29, 1895; "Utah Democrats Meet," *World-Herald* (Omaha, NE), Sept. 6, 1895; and "Solution at Shreveport," *The Daily Picayune* (New Orleans), Dec. 19, 1895.

39 "Getting Ready To Howl," *New York Times*, Aug. 6, 1895; "Preparing For Silver Meeting," *Chicago Tribune*, Aug. 6, 1895; "Bland's Disciples Speak," *New York Times*, Aug. 7, 1895; "Silver Their Cry," *Arkansas Gazette* (Little Rock), Aug. 7, 1895; "Convention Organizes," "Getting Down to Business" and "It's Labor Finished," *Kansas City Times*, Aug. 7, 1895; "They Will Discuss," *Los Angeles Times*, July 16, 1895; and Byars, *American Commoner*, 230–33.

40 "They Crowd Into Memphis," *World-Herald* (Omaha, NE), June 11, 1895; "Bimetallists Are Plenty," *World-Herald* (Omaha, NE), June 12, 1895; and "Senator Turpie Is Made Chairman" and "All Are For 16 to 1" in *Chicago Tribune*, June 13, 1895.

41 "A Great Day" and "The Proceedings" in *Los Angeles Times*, June 13, 1895; "The Second Day," *Los Angeles Times*, June 14, 1895; "Sibleyism Not Popular," *New York Times*, June 14, 1895; "In Silver's Cause," *The Sun* (Baltimore), June 15, 1895; and Francis B. Simkins, *Pitchfork Ben Tillman: South Carolinian* (Gloucester, MA: Peter Smith, 1964), 315.

42 "Have Adopted A Platform," *World-Herald* (Omaha, NE), June 14, 1895; "The Resolutions," *New York Times*, June 14, 1895; "A Great Day," *Los Angeles Times*, June 13, 1895; "The Silver Convention," *Times-Picayune* (New Orleans), June 11, 1895; and "Sibleyism Not Popular," *New York Times*, June 14, 1895.

43 "Harris on the New League," *Trenton Evening Times* (NJ), June 16, 1895; "A Free-Coinage Powwow," *New York Times*, June 26, 1895; "To Confer In Washington," *Washington Post*, June 15, 1895; "Plan of the Bimetallic League," *Commercial Appeal* (Memphis), June 15, 1895; and "Silver Conference Ends," *New York Times*, Aug. 16, 1895.

44 "Silver Theorists And Soreheads," *New York Times*, Aug. 14, 1895, and "Another Silver Fiasco," *New York Times*, Aug. 15, 1895.

CHAPTER 11: MANEUVERING

1 "Mr. Manley Talks Little," *New-York Tribune*, November 18, 1895; "Manley Favors San Francisco," *New York Times*, October 31, 1895; and "Reed Headquarters in Chicago," *New York Times*, November 17, 1895.

2 Diary entries for Nov. 16, 17, 20, 21 and 22, 1895 in Dawes, *Journal*, 59–61.

3 "With An Eye On Reed," *Washington Post*, Dec. 6, 1895; "The McKinley Boomers," *New York Times*, Dec. 6, 1895; "It Is An Exciting Fight," *New York Times*, Dec. 9, 1895; and "McKinley Is Satisfied," *New York Times*, Dec. 11, 1895. The other team members were former Ohio Representative A.C. Thompson, state Attorney General John K. Richards, and Ohio Secretary of State Samuel M. Taylor.

4   "St. Louis, June 16" and "After The Battle" in *Washington Post*, Dec. 11, 1896, and "Mr. Platt On New-York's Committee," *New York Times*, Dec. 11, 1895.

5   McKinley to R. C. Kerens, Dec. 4, 1895, and McKinley to F. B. Brownell, Dec. 18, 1895 in McKinley Papers.

6   Jones, *Election of 1896*, 141. Platt even threatened Morton that failure to appoint Platt's man as Inspector of Gas Meters would affect the Easy Boss's ability to deliver national convention delegates. See Platt to Morton, Dec. 11, 1895, in Morton Papers.

7   "Gov. Morton in the Field," *New York Times*, Jan. 1, 1896; "Governor Morton Is Now In The Race, *Chicago Tribune*, Jan. 1, 1896; "Gov. Morton Has Consented," *Washington Post*, Jan. 2, 1896; and "Morton Takes A Plunge," *New York Times*, Jan. 2, 1896.

8   "To Head Off M'Kinley," *Washington Post*, Jan. 3, 1896; "Gov. Morton's Candidacy," *Chicago Tribune*, Jan. 4, 1896; and "Morton Is Platt's Tool," *Chicago Tribune*, Jan. 6, 1896. Roberts was popular in western New York, hailing from Buffalo.

9   Leaflet, "Some Important Political Facts," Jan. 27, 1896, in Dawes Papers.

10 Morton to William Youngblood, Jan. 9, 1896, and Youngblood to Morton, Feb. 28, 1896, in Morton papers.

11 Hanna to Hay, Jan. 6, 1896, in John Hay papers.

12 "Off for St. Louis," *New-York Tribune*, Jan. 8, 1896, and Croly, *Hanna*, 178–79.

13 "Setback for McKinley," *Chicago Tribune*, Jan. 8, 1896; "Quay and Platt Confer," *The Evening Times* (Washington), Jan. 9, 1896; and "Platt and Quay Confer," *The Sun* (New York), Jan. 9, 1896.

14 "Platt and Quay Confer," *The Sun* (New York), Jan. 9, 1896, and Clarkson to Allison, Feb. 10, 1896, in Allison papers.

15 "Quay and Platt Confer," *The Evening Times* (Washington), Jan. 9, 1896.

16 "Is Quay for Morton," *New-York Tribune*, Jan. 10, 1896.

17 "Quay and Platt Confer," *The Evening Times* (Washington), Jan. 9, 1896, and Osborne to McKinley, Jan. 16, 1896, in McKinley papers.

18 Morgan, *McKinley and His America*, 140, and Leech, *Days*, 64–65.

19 Harrison to Wanamaker, Nov. 12, 1894, quoted by Sievers, *Hoosier President*, 259; "Benny Bolts," *Los Angles Times*, Feb. 4, 1896; and Harrison to Stephen B. Elkins, Feb. 3, 1896, in Harrison papers.

20 "Pleased M'Kinley Leaders," *St. Paul Daily Globe*, Feb. 4, 1896; "Believe Gen. Harrison Is Sincere," *Chicago Tribune*, Feb. 4, 1896; "Not A Decisive Letter," *New York Times*, Feb. 4, 1896; and "Must Tie To A New Son," *Chicago Tribune*, Feb. 6, 1896.

21 Croly, *Hanna*, 181; "Statement of Sen. Charles Dick, Feb. 10, 1906," 5–8; and E. H. Nebeker to Dunlap, Feb. 8, 1896, Morton Papers, quoted in Jones, *Election of 1896*, 118.

22 Harrison to Elkins, April 28, 1896, in Harrison papers and Jones, *Election of 1896*.

23 Sage, *Allison*, 262, and "Invitation to Marquette Club Tenth Annual Banquet," undated, in Dawes Papers.

24 "McKinley Men Are Seated," *San Francisco Chronicle*, June 13, 1896, and "Marquette Club Guests," undated, in Dawes Papers. This ten-page handwritten document lists 148 guests from 30 states, two territories, and the District of Columbia in alphabetical order by state. It is a partial listing, starting with Alabama and ending with New York. Before July 2013, it was accidentally filed with Dawes' business, not political, papers.

25 Diary entry for Feb. 12, 1896, in Dawes, *Journal*, 69, and "Lincoln's Day Politics," *New York Times*, Feb. 13, 1896.

26 "Round The Board," *Chicago Tribune*, Feb. 12, 1896.

27 "Lincoln His Theme," *Chicago Tribune*, Feb. 13, 1896, and diary entry for Feb. 5, 1896, in Dawes, *Journal*, 68.

28 "Lincoln His Theme" and "Honor To Two Men," *Chicago Tribune*, Feb. 13, 1896.

29 "Honor To Two Men," *Chicago Tribune*, Feb. 13, 1896.

30 "Has Not McKinley Given The Required Pledge?" *New York Times*, Feb. 14, 1896; "Major M'Kinley's Address," *Chicago Tribune*, Feb. 13, 1896; "Where The Applause Came In," *Chicago Tribune*, Feb. 14, 1896; "A Splendid Tribute" and "M'Kinley At Chicago" in *Los Angeles Times*, Feb. 13, 1896; "Ovation to M'Kinley," *Washington Post*, Feb. 13, 1896; Harrison G. Otis, "Great Themes" in *Los Angeles Times*, Feb. 13, 1896; and Harrison G. Otis, "Snow and Politics," *Los Angeles Times*, Feb. 19, 1896.

31 "Two More In The Lists," *Chicago Tribune*, Feb. 8, 1896; "State Republican Committee," *Omaha Daily Bee*, Feb. 14, 1896; "Names Are Not Spoken" and "McKinley Supporters Suspicious,"

Chicago Tribune, Feb. 15, 1896; [Untitled], *Lincoln Courier*, Feb. 15, 1896; and "General Manderson's Candidacy," *Omaha Daily Bee*, Feb. 16, 1896.

32 Poster, "The Nebraska McKinley Club And Their Friends" from the Dawes papers.

33 "Picking A President" and "No Favorite Son For Nebraska," in *Chicago Tribune*, Feb. 17, 1896; and Diary entry for Feb. 17, 1896, in Dawes, *Journal*, 69–70.

34 "Two More In The Lists," *Chicago Tribune*, Feb. 8, 1896; James M. Blythe to Grenville Dodge, Feb. 24, 1896, in Dodge Papers; and Clarkson to Allison, Feb. 25, 1896, in Allison papers.

35 "Almost All For Quay," *Titusville Morning Herald*, Feb. 22, 1896; "Mr. Quay's Candidacy," *Washington Post*, Feb. 21, 1896; "The Quay Presidential Boom," *New York Times*, Feb. 17, 1896; Andrew James to Quay, Feb. 18, 1896; and Felix W. Newman to Quay, Feb. 25, 1896, in Quay Papers and Kehl, *Boss Rule*, 200.

36 Swank to Hanna, Feb. 28, 1896, in McKinley papers.

37 Hanna to McKinley, Feb. 28, 1896, and Hanna to Philander C. Knox, Feb. 28, 1896, in McKinley Papers.

38 "Under The Dome," *Washington Post*, Feb. 23, 1896.

39 Roosevelt to Anna Roosevelt Cowles, March 21, 1896, *Letters to Anna Roosevelt Cowles*, 178; Lodge to Roosevelt, Feb. 27, 1896, in Lodge Papers; Roosevelt to Lodge, Jan. 19, Feb. 16, and Feb. 25, 1896, *Correspondence*, I, 210–16; and Grant, *Mr. Speaker!*, 340.

40 "Col. Clarkson's Trip," *Evening Star* (Washington, D.C.), March 13, 1896; Clarkson to William B. Allison, Feb. 25, 1896, in Allison Papers; and Clarkson to Grenville Dodge, March 6, 1896, in Dodge Papers.

41 "McKinley Should Repudiate Them," *Chicago Tribune*, March 16, 1896; "The Boodle Candidate," *New York Times*, March 17, 1896; and "Chandler is Persistent," *New York Times*, March 24, 1896.

42 "Grosvenor on Senator Chandler," *Chicago Tribune*, March 17, 1896; Holt, *By One Vote*, 182, 189–94, and 255; and Roy Morris Jr., *Fraud of the Century: Rutherford B. Hayes, Samuel Tilden, and the Stolen Election of 1876* (New York: Simon & Schuster, 2003), 175–76.

43 "A New Reformer," *Houston Daily Post*, March 27, 1896; "The Fighting Factions," *The Anaconda Standard*, March 27, 1896; "Chandler is Persistent," *New York Times*, March 24, 1896; and Leon B. Richardson, *William E. Chandler, Republican* (New York: Dodd, Mead, 1940), 335–36.

44 "The Ohio Mans Boodle," *New York Times*, March 18, 1896; [No Title] *Anaconda Standard*, March 27, 1896; and "Very Perplexing Enigma," *Austin Weekly Statesman*, March 26, 1896.

45 "Chandler's Vilification of M'Kinley," *Austin Daily Statesman*, March 26, 1896, and "Senator Chandler," *The Record Union* (Sacramento, CA), March 23, 1896. Chandler's biographer points to Swank as the source of Chandler's information. Swank had received a letter from Hanna asking his help raising money to "counteract the efforts" being made by other candidates in the South. But Swank's complaint was sent to Quay eight days after Chandler made his charge. See James M. Swank to Quay, March 24, 1896, in Quay papers and Richardson, *Chandler*, 512–15.

CHAPTER 12: THE BATTLES BEGIN

1 Foraker to McKinley, Jan. 28, 1896, in Foraker papers; "Convention," Marietta Daily Leader, March 12, 1896; "Foraker's Keynote Speech," *Plain Dealer* (Cleveland, OH), March 12, 1896; and Walters, *Foraker*, 128.

2 "A Shrill Keynote," *Plain Dealer* (Cleveland, OH), March 11, 1896; "Foraker's Keynote Speech," *Plain Dealer* (Cleveland, OH), March 12, 1896; "A Love Feast of Party Leaders," *Ohio State Journal*, March 11, 1896; "Strictly Busin'ss," *Ohio State Journal*, March 12, 1896; "For M'Kinley," *Los Angeles Times*, March 11, 1896; "Foraker's Humiliation," *Plain Dealer* (Cleveland, OH), March 12, 1896; and McKinley to Foraker, March 9, 1896, in Foraker papers. Either McKinley misdated his letter or he had read a draft of Foraker's keynote.

3 Horace Baker to Allison, August 12, 1895, and Clarkson to Allison, June 17, 1895, in Allison papers; "Are All For M'Kinley," *Washington Post*, March 4, 1896; "Arkansas Instructs for M'Kinley," *Chicago Tribune*, March 4, 1896; "Arkansas For McKinley," *New York Times*, Jan. 19, 1896; "Kansas Republican Convention," *Chicago Tribune*, March 11, 1896; "Wisconsin for M'Kinley," *Chicago Tribune*, March 19, 1896; "Situation In South Dakota," *Washington Post*, March 25, 1896; "Off His Perch," *Los Angeles Times*, March 26, 1896; and "Votes for Sound Money," *Chicago Tribune*, March 26, 1896.

4 "M'Kinley Forces In Louisiana," *Washington Post*, Dec. 20, 1895; "Reed Men Charge 'Boodling,'" *New York Times*, Dec. 21, 1895; "Early Work In Louisiana," *New York Times*, Dec. 23, 1895; "Hard

At Work Louisiana," *New York Times*, Dec. 30, 1895; McKinley to Henry C. Warmoth, Dec. 30, 1895; and McKinley to William McKinley Osborne, Dec. 30, 1895, in McKinley papers.

5   "Republican Troubles in Louisiana," *Washington Post*, Jan. 22, 1896; "Two Each for Reed and M'Kinley," *Chicago Tribune*, Jan. 31, 1896; and Appleton, *Annual Cyclopaedia and Register of Important Events of the Year 1896* (New York: D. Appleton, 1897), 424.

6   "Yielded to M'Kinley," *Washington Post*, March 29, 1896; "All Shouted for McKinley," *The Minneapolis Tribune,* March 15, 1896; "Senator Davis Retires," *New York Times*, March 25, 1896; and Cushman K. Davis to Henry A. Castle, March 12 and April 6 and 19, 1896, Castle papers quoted by Jones, *Election of 1896*, 115.

7   Reed to Platt, March 26, 1896 and March 28, 1896, in Platt papers.

8   Sage, *Allison,* 262–63; "The Iowa Republicans," *Los Angeles Times*, March 12, 1896; Appleton, *Annual Cyclopaedia* (1897), 362; and Clarkson to Platt, March 11, 1896, in Platt Papers.

9   "Political Prattle," *The Record Union* (Sacramento, CA), March 23, 1896.

10   "Stands By Its Governor," *Chicago Tribune*, March 25, 1896; "Not All Morton Men," *Evening Transcript* (Boston), March 24, 1896; and Appleton, *Annual Cyclopaedia* (1897), 526.

11   "The Republicans! The Territorial Convention a Grand, Glorious Success," *Albuquerque Weekly Citizen*, March 28, 1896; "New Mexico Republicans," *Washington Post*, March 24, 1896; and "Machine-Made Delegates," *Guthrie Daily Leader*, March 29, 1896.

12   "Ten Reed Men Victorious," *Austin Statesman*, March 29, 1896; Appleton, *Annual Cyclopaedia* (1897), 620; McKinley to Dawes, March 27, 1896, in Dawes Papers; "Bay State for T. B. Reed," *New York Times*, March 27, 1896; "Every Man For Reed," *Washington Post*, March 28, 1896; and [Untitled], *Baltimore American*. March 26, 1896.

13   Alger to Platt, March 28, 1896, in Platt Papers.

14   "A Split In Mississippi," *New York Times,* March 5, 1896; "Lynch Heads One Delegation," *Washington Post*, March 5, 1896; Clarkson to Grenville Dodge, March 6, 1896, in Dodge Papers; Clarkson to Allison, April 9 and May 18, 1896, in Allison papers; Daugherty to Elkins, May 18, 1896, in Elkins papers; "M'Kinley In The Lead," *New York Times,* March 5, 1896; "Uninstructed, But For M'Kinley," *Chicago Tribune*, March 6, 1896; and Appleton, *Annual Cyclopaedia* (1897), 290. Hanna dispatched J. Stahl to observe the convention while New York Tax Commissioner Charles S. Wilbur attended for Morton and Pennsylvania GOP state executive chairman Frank A. Leach was there for Quay.

15   "The Delegates Arriving," *Austin Statesman*, March 23, 1896.

16   "The Delegates Arriving" and "The M'Kinley Managers" in *Austin Statesman*, March 23, 1896, and "Scene Of Bedlam," *Galveston News*, March 27, 1896.

17   "Cuney Will Make A Fight," *Austin Statesman*, March 24, 1896; "Combine Against McKinley," *Washington Post*, March 24, 1896; and Alwyn Barr, *Reconstruction to Reform: Texas Politics, 1876–1906* (Dallas: Southern Methodist University Press, 2000), 186. Barr says E.H.R. Green, the millionaire playboy son of eccentric Wall Street investor Mrs. Hetty Green, was a Reed co-chairman with McDonald.

18   Maud C. Hare, *Norris Wright Cuney: A Tribune of the Black People* (New York: The Crisis, 1913), 16, 27–28, 57, and 178–80.

19   *Austin Statesman*, March 26, 1896; "Cuney Won His Fight," *Austin Statesman*, March 25, 1896; "The State Republican Convention," *Austin Statesman*, March 28, 1896; and "Inclined to Concessions," *Austin Statesman*, March 24, 1896.

20   "Cuney Won His Fight," *Austin Statesman*, March 25, 1896.

21   "Combine Against McKinley," *Washington Post*, March 25, 1896; "Texas Is For Reed" and "Dickering in Texas" in *Los Angeles Times*, March 26, 1896; "It Was A Howling Mob," *Austin Statesman*, March 27, 1896; "Cuney Credentials," *Galveston News*, March 27, 1896; "Texas Republican Convention," *New York Times*, March 25, 1896; and Grenville Dodge to William B. Allison, March 26, 1896, in Allison papers.

22   "The Republican Meeting: A Hungry Set," *Austin Statesman*, March 26, 1896; "It Was A Howling Mob," *Austin Statesman*, March 27, 1896; and "Scene Of Bedlam," *Galveston News*, March 27, 1896.

23   "It Was A Howling Mob," *Austin Statesman*, March 27, 1896.

24   "Scene Of Bedlam," *Galveston News*, March 27, 1896; "It Was A Howling Mob," *Austin Statesman*, March 27, 1896; "Texas Not For McKinley," *Chicago Daily News,* March 27, 1896; "Scrap in Texas," *Detroit Free Press*, March 27, 1896; "A Split in The Texas Convention," *San Francisco Chronicle*, March 27, 1896; and "Texas Row and Split," *Washington Post*, March 27, 1896.

25 "It Was A Howling Mob," *Austin Statesman*, March 27, 1896; "Scene Of Bedlam," *Galveston News*, March 27, 1896; and "A Split In Texas," *New York Times*, March 27, 1896.

26 "It Was A Howling Mob," *Austin Statesman*, March 27, 1896; "Scene Of Bedlam," *Galveston News*, March 27, 1896; "The M'Kinley Convention," *Galveston News*, March 27, 1896; "A Split In Texas," *New York Times*, March 27, 1896; and "McDonald Charges Corruption–Head Charges Grant With Rebellion," *Galveston News*, March 27, 1896.

27 Paul Douglas Casdorph, "Norris Wright Cuney and Texas Republican Politics, 1883–1896," *Southwestern Historical Quarterly*, LXVII, April 65, Number 4, 462–63, and "The Convention Aftermath," *Austin Statesman*, March 28, 1896.

28 "That Republican Split," *Austin Statesman*, March 29, 1896; "Cuney Won His Fight," *Austin Statesman*, March 24, 1896; Bristow, *Politics and Fraud*, 94–95; and Hanna to McKinley, Feb. 28, 1896, in McKinley Papers. Hanna reports Grant "was 'breathlessly' awaiting a remittance so I gave him a contribution."

CHAPTER 13: MCKINLEY GAINS TRACTION

1 "The First Gun," *Concord Evening Monitor*, March 31, 1896, and "Chandler at the Helm," *Chicago Tribune*, April 1, 1896.

2 "The First Gun," *Concord Evening Monitor*, March 31, 1896, and "Reed and McKinley," *Evening Star* (Washington, D.C.), March 31, 1896.

3 "New Hampshire Convention," *Los Angeles Times*, April 1, 1896; "Mr. Reed Loses A State," *New York Times*, April 1, 1896; "Split Even With Reed," *Washington Post*, April 1, 1896; and Richardson, *Chandler*, 516.

4 "Reed Men Are Whistling" *New York Times*, April 2, 1896.

5 "Putney Does Some Explaining," *Boston Daily Globe*, April 3, 1896, and Hanna to McKinley, April 8, 1896, in McKinley papers.

6 Kinzer, *Episode in Anti-Catholicism*, 120, and Jensen, *Winning the Midwest*, 218–27.

7 "Plans of the A.P.A." *Evening Star* (Washington, D.C.), March 23, 1896; "Looking Over Candidates," *Evening Star* (Washington, D.C.), March 26, 1896; "The Presidential Canvass," *New York Evening Post*, April 8, 1896; "Will M'Kinley Be Nominated," *St. Louis Post-Dispatch*, April 13, 1896; "Position of the A.P.A.," *St. Louis Post-Dispatch*, April 16, 1896; "A.P.A. Advisory Board," *Evening Star* (Washington, D.C.), April 17, 1896; "Cullom's Forces In Great Straits," *St. Louis Post-Dispatch*, April 17, 1896; and Kinzer, *An Episode in Anti-Catholicism*, 214–15.

8 Joseph P. Smith to Dawes, April 16 and April 21, 1896, in Dawes Papers, and Morrow, interview with Charles Dick, February 10, 1905, 9.

9 "Will Ignore Them," *Plain Dealer* (Cleveland, OH), April 15, 1896; "Denies A.P.A. Reports," *Chicago Tribune*, April 16, 1896; "The A.P.A. And The Candidates," *New York Tribune*, April 18, 1896; George Hester to McKinley, December 18, 1896, in McKinley papers; and Hanna to McKinley, April 21, 1896, in McKinley papers.

10 McKinley to William McKinley Osborne, April 17, 1896, in McKinley papers, and Diary entry for April 17, 1896, in Dawes, *Journal*, 76.

11 (Name blanked out) to General McNulta, April 14, 1896, in Dawes Papers; H. Clay Wilson to Dawes, April 15, 1896; A.P. Yates to Dawes, April (undated), 1896; and Andrew J. Lester to Dawes, April 18, 1896, in Dawes Papers and Joseph P. Smith to Dawes, April 21, 1896, in Dawes papers.

12 Clarkson to Platt, March 9, 1896, in Platt papers.

13 Clarkson to Platt, March 9 and March 12, 1896, in Platt papers

14 Francis E. Warren to Hanna, April 8, 1896 and April 24, 1896, in Warren papers, quoted by Lewis L. Gould, *Wyoming: A Political History, 1868–1896* (New Haven, CT: Yale University Press, 1968), 240, 242, and Gould, *Wyoming*, 238–39 and 244. Van Devanter was appointed an appellate judge by President Theodore Roosevelt and a Supreme Court Justice by President William Howard Taft.

15 Clarkson to Platt, March 29, 1896, in Thomas Collier Platt papers.

16 Clarkson to William B. Allison, April 9, 1896, in Allison Papers, State Historical Society of Iowa, Des Moines.

17 "Quay Any Way," *Los Angles Times*, April 23, 1896; "Quay's Boom Launched," *New York Times*, April 24, 1896; and Appleton, *Annual Cyclopaedia* (1897), 630–31.

18 Quay telegram to 64 delegates dated May 9, 1896, in Quay papers.

19 "Rhodes Island for Reed," *Washington Post*, April 11, 1896; "Mr. Reed's Home State," *Boston Morning Journal*, April 18, 1896; "Way Back In Maine," *Los Angeles Times*, April 16, 1896; and Appleton, *Annual Cyclopaedia* (1897), 446 and 685.

20 "Is Quay for Morton," *New York Tribune*, January 10, 1896; "State Conventions," *Daily Capitol Journal* (Salem, OR), April 9, 1896; "State Conventions," *Daily Capitol Journal* (Salem, OR), April 10, 1896; "Oregon for M'Kinley and Silver," *Chicago Tribune*, April 11, 1896; "Oregon for McKinley," *The Hartford Courant*, April 11, 1896; "Free Silver Turned Down," *Washington Post*, April 16, 1896; "Conventions: Republicans Getting Up Steam Again," *Los Angles Times*, April 23, 1896; "Virginia Instructs for M'Kinley," *Chicago Tribune*, April 24, 1896; "The Ohio Man Wins," *Richmond Dispatch*, April 24, 1896; Clarkson to Allison, Feb. 10, 1896, in Allison papers; and Appleton, *Annual Cyclopaedia* (1897), 539, 627, 728, and 812.

21 B.G. Dawes to Charles G. Dawes, March 30, 1896, in Dawes papers; "Makes War On Thurston," *Chicago Tribune*, April 16, 1896; and Appleton, *Annual Cyclopaedia* (1897), 505.

22 "M'Kinley Forces Carry The Day," *Atlanta Journal*, April 29, 1896, and "Republican Clans Are Gathering," *Atlanta Constitution*, April 28, 1896.

23 "Looks Like A Bolt In Georgia," *Chicago Tribune*, April 29, 1896; "Bars Doors Against Reed Men," Chicago *Tribune*, April 30, 1896; Appleton, *Annual Cyclopaedia* (1897), 312; and "Republican Fight is On," *Atlanta Constitution*, April 29, 1896.

24 "Republicans Badly Split," and "Call for McKinley," in the *Atlanta Journal*, April 30, 1896; "M'Kinley's Hosts Are Happy Now," *Atlanta Constitution*, May 1, 1896; "Tis A Bad Split In Georgia's GOP," *Atlanta Journal*, May 1, 1896; "Republican State Convention," *Savannah Tribune*, May 2, 1896; and McKinley to A.E. Buck, May 20, 1896, in McKinley papers.

25 "In Bradley's Stronghold," *Los Angeles Times*, April 16, 1896; Jones, *Election of 1896*, 135; Joseph P. Smith to Dawes, April 7, 1896, in Dawes papers; and Appleton, *Annual Cyclopaedia* (1897), 377.

26 Appleton, *Annual Cyclopaedia* (1897), 519.

27 "Victory for McKinley," *New York Times*, April 22, 1896; "Maryland Does Not Instruct," *Boston Daily Globe*, April 23, 1896; and Appleton, *Annual Cyclopaedia* (1897), 224 and 454–55.

CHAPTER 14: HIGH STAKES IN SPRINGFIELD

1 "Statement by Sen. Charles Dick, Feb. 10, 1906," 12.

2 Diary entries for Jan. 27 and 28, 1896, in Dawes, *Journal*, 65–66, and Neilson, *Cullom*, 165–66.

3 "Speakers At The Feast," *Chicago Tribune*, Jan. 29, 1896; diary entry for Jan. 29, 1896, in Dawes, *Journal*, 66; and Tarr, *Study of Boss Politics*, 54.

4 Diary entries for Feb. 2 and Feb. 3, 1896 in Dawes, *Journal*, 66–67.

5 "The Snap County Conventions, *Chicago Tribune*, Feb. 3, 1896; "Will Meet Feb. 15," *Chicago Tribune*, Feb. 4, 1896; diary entries for Feb. 2 and Feb. 3, 1896, in Dawes, *Journal*, 66–67; Clarkson to William B. Allison, Feb. 10 and 25, 1896, in Allison Papers; and Tarr, *Study in Boss Politics*, 55–56.

6 Diary entries for Feb. 4 and Feb. 5, 1896, in Dawes, *Journal*, 67–68.

7 "Few But Enthusiastic," *Chicago Tribune*, Feb. 10, 1896, and Neilson, *Cullom*, 159.

8 Joseph P. Smith to Dawes, March 3, 1896, and Charles D. Clark to A. C. Kenneburg, March 9, 1896, in Dawes Papers; diary entry for March 4, 1896, in Dawes, *Journal*, 71; Neilson, *Cullom*, 166; and Paul R. Leach, *That Man Dawes*, 61.

9 "McKinley's Canvass," *New York Times*, March 9, 1896; "A Troublesome Boom," *New York Times*, March 11, 1896; and "Cullom Repudiated in His Own District," *St. Louis Globe Democrat*, March 23, 1896.

10 Diary entry for March 14, 1896, in Dawes, *Journal*, 72–73.

11 "Illinois Republicans," *St. Louis Daily Globe-Democrat*, March 23, 1896; "McKinley Delegates Chosen," *San Francisco Chronicle*, March 27, 1896; "Believed To Favor M'Kinley," *Austin Daily Statesman*, March 27, 1896; "Major On The Wane," *Chicago Tribune*, March 30, 1896; W. F. Calhoun to Dawes, March 21, 1896, H. O. Hilton to Dawes, March 23, 1896, William McKinley Osborne to Dawes, March 23, 1896, in Dawes papers; and Charles Chamberlain to Dawes, March 27, 1896, Charles Chamberlain to Dawes, March 28, 1896, and W. F. Calhoun to Dawes, March and March 28, 1896, and diary entries for March 21 and 23, 1896, in Dawes, *Journal*, 73.

12 Diary entries for March 29 and April 10, 1896, in Dawes, *Journal*, 74-75, and Charles W. Raymond to McKinley, March 30, 1896, in Dawes papers.

13 Joseph P. Smith to Dawes, April 3, 1896, in Dawes papers.

14   Diary entries for April 12, 15, 18 and 19 in Dawes, *Journal,* 75–76.
15   Charles W. Raymond to Dawes, April 14, 1896, Charles L. Chamberlin to Dawes, April 18, 1896, and Joseph P. Smith to Dawes, April 16, 1896, in Dawes papers.
16   Diary entry for April 17, 1896, in Dawes, *Journal*, 76.
17   Diary entry for April 20, 1896, in Dawes, *Journal*, 76; Neilson, *Cullom*, 168; and Tarr, *Study in Boss Politics*, 56–57.
18   Diary entry for April 21, 1896, in Dawes, *Journal*, 76, and Herman Kohlsaat to Hanna and Andrew J. Lester to William McKinley, April 22, 1896, in Dawes papers.
19   Diary entries for April 14, 1896, in Dawes, *Journal*, 76.
20   Diary entry for April 24, 1896, in Dawes, *Journal*, 76–77.
21   Diary entry for April 26, 1896, in Dawes, *Journal*, 77–78, and Tarr, *Study in Boss Politics*, 57.
22   "Fix Plan of Peace" and "Machine Caucus For To-Day," in the *Chicago Tribune*, April 28, 1896.
23   "Calhoun Put In Charge," *Chicago Tribune*, April 29, 1896.
24   "Cullom To Hold On," "Machine To Yield," "Senator Cullom Is Hopeful," and "Glad Hand For Cullom," in *Chicago Tribune*, April 28, 1896; Neilson, *Cullom*, 168–69; and Diary entry for April 27, 1896, in Dawes, *Journal*, 78.
25   "He Hits At Madden," *Chicago Tribune*, Oct. 16, 1895; "The Suit Against Ald. Madden," *Chicago Tribune*, Oct. 17, 1895; "Madden For The Chair," *Chicago Tribune*, April 27, 1896; and "Madden For The Senate," *Chicago Tribune*, May 2, 1896.
26   "Fix Plan of Peace," *Chicago Tribune*, April 28, 1896; "They Fall In Line," "Agree On A Truce," and "Chance for Orators," in *Chicago Times-Herald*, April 29, 1896; "A Truce Arranged," *Illinois State Register*, April 29, 1896; "Small Fry Subside," *Illinois State Journal*, April 29, 1896; and diary entry for April 28, 1896, in Dawes, *Journal*, 78–79.
27   "Changed Their Slate" and "A Truce Arranged" in *Illinois State Register*, April 29, 1896, and "They Fall In Line," and "Calhoun Put In Charge," in *Chicago Tribune*, April 29, 1896.
28   "Convention Hall Arrangements," *Chicago Tribune*, April 28, 1896, and "View Of The Big Hall," *Chicago Tribune*, April 30, 1896.
29   "Fight Is Put Off," *Chicago Times-Herald*, April 30, 1896.
30   "New Triumph: Vermont Gets Into Line for McKinley," *New York Times,* April 30, 1896. The *Times* mistakenly identified Stewart as "John D. Stuart of Middleberry," mangling his name and hometown.
31   "McKinley Captures Vermont," *New York Times*, April 30, 1896; "As Goes Vermont So Goes the Country," *Burlington Free Press and Times*, April 30, 1896; "A McKinley Wave," *The Vermont Phoenix*, May 1, 1896; and "William McKinley," *The Vermonter*, Vol. VI, October 1901, No. 3, 325–26.
32   "Machine Victory," *Illinois State Register*, April 30, 1896, and "Fight Is Put Off," *Chicago Times-Herald*, April 30, 1896.
33   "Will Wage The Big Fight Today" and "Routine Proceedings" in the *Chicago Tribune*, April 30, 1896.
34   "Vermont Is In Line" and "Story Of The Fight," in *Chicago Times-Herald*, May 1, 1896; "M'Kinley Away On Top," *Washington Post*, May 1, 1896; "Men In High Place" and "How Fights Were Won" in *Chicago Tribune*, May 1, 1896; "Illinois Instructs for M'Kinley," *Illinois State Journal*, May 1, 1896; and "Machine Beaten," *Illinois State Register*, May 1, 1896.
35   "Story Of The Fight," *Chicago Times-Herald*, May 1, 1896, and "Illinois Instructs for M'Kinley," *Illinois State Journal*, May 1, 1896.
36   "Illinois Speaks for McKinley," *Chicago Tribune*, May 1, 1896, and "Story Of The Fight," *Chicago Times-Herald*, May 1, 1896.
37   "Story Of The Fight," *Chicago Times-Herald*, May 1, 1896; "Illinois Speaks for McKinley" and "How Fights Were Won," in *Chicago Tribune*, May 1, 1896; and Neilson, *Cullom*, 169. The *Illinois State Register* reports the vote as 505 to 830 in "Machine Beaten," *Illinois State Register*, May 1, 1896.
38   "Gov. Oglesby Arraigned," *New York Times*, May 21, 1888; "Big Four Selected," *Chicago Times-Herald*, May 1, 1896; "How Fights Were Won," *Chicago Tribune*, May 1, 1896; and "Illinois For McKinley," *New York Times*, May 1, 1896.
39   "Cullom Quite Cool," *Chicago Times-Herald*, May 1, 1896; "It Was A Fair Fight," *Chicago Tribune*, May 2, 1896; and Tarr, *Study in Boss Politics*, 58–59.
40   "Story Of The Fight," *Chicago Times-Herald*, May 1, 1896; "Swept All Before Him" and "What Is Said In Washington" in *New-York Tribune*, May 1, 1896; "Illinois For McKinley," *New York*

Times, May 1, 1896; "Illinois Has Decided The Nomination," *Chicago Tribune*, May 2, 1896; "M'Kinley A Sure Winner," *New-York Tribune*, May 2, 1896; and George H. Lyman to Lodge, April 30, 1896, in Lodge papers.

41 Robert Marcus, *Grand Old Party: Political Structure in the Gilded Age, 1880–1896* (Oxford: Oxford University Press, 1964), 221.

42 McNulta to McKinley, April 10, 1896, in McKinley papers.

43 Diary entry for April 30, 1896, in Dawes, *Journal*, 78; Joseph P. Smith to Dawes, April 30, 1896, in Dawes papers; and diary entry for May 21, 1896, in Dawes, *Journal*, 83.

44 William McKinley to Dawes, April 30, 1896, in Dawes papers.

CHAPTER 15: LAST-MINUTE ATTACKS BEFORE ST. LOUIS

1   Benjamin F. Tracy to Harrison, May 1, 1896, in Harrison papers. Tracy was then representing New York police commissioner Andrew Parker against a lawsuit for negligence filed by his fellow commissioner, Theodore Roosevelt. See Edmund Morris, *The Rise of Theodore Roosevelt* (New York: Coward, McCann, & Geoghegan, 1979), 526–36.

2   John H. Gear to Harrison, May 4, 1896, and Harrison to Gear, May 8, 1896, in Harrison papers.

3   L. T. Michener to E. Frank Tibbott, May 8, 1896, in Harrison papers.

4   "In The Convention Hall," *Los Angeles Times*, May 8, 1896; "Indiana Wants M'Kinley," *New York Times*, May 8, 1896; "That Ought to Settle It," *San Francisco Chronicle*, May 8, 1896; and Appleton, *Annual Cyclopaedia* (1897), 358. Appleton says the delegates were instructed for McKinley only if Harrison didn't run, but the platform was unconditional, saying the national delegates "are directed to cast their vote for William McKinley as frequently and continuously as there is any hope of his nomination."

5   "California Republicans," *Washington Post*, May 6, 1896; "Up in Michigan," *Los Angeles Times*, May 9, 1896; McKinley to Elkins, April 7, 1896, McKinley Papers; Lambert, *Elkins*, 201; Appleton, *Annual Cyclopaedia* (1897), 92–93 and 486; Marcus, *Grand Old Party*, 206; and Jones, *Election of 1896*, 133–34. Jones erroneously claims White was Governor in 1896. Instead, White was elected in 1900. The taboo against running mates from adjoining states was not broken until 1992, when Bill Clinton of Arkansas picked Al Gore Jr. of Tennessee as his running mate.

6   "Both Will Be For McKinley," *Washington Post*, April 7, 1896; "M'Kinley Not Endorsed," *Washington Post*, April 15, 1896; "Alabama Republicans Fall Out," *Chicago Tribune*, April 29, 1896; "McKinley Men Lose and Bolt," *New York Times*, May 1, 1896; "They Prefer M'Kinley," *Washington Post*, April 30, 1896; McKinley to Whitelaw Reid, December 30, 1895 in McKinley papers; Samuel D. Smith, *The Negro in Congress: 1870–1901* (Chapel Hill: University of North Carolina Press, 1940), 135; and Appleton, *Annual Cyclopaedia* (1897), 10 and 705. The Major's Arizona forces were led by Myron H. McCord, who served with McKinley in the House from 1889 to 1891. After being defeated in 1890 and again in 1892 and then declaring bankruptcy, he had lit out for the Arizona territory. President McKinley appointed McCord territorial governor in 1897.

7   "Quay and Platt Confer," *The Evening Times* (Washington, D.C.), Jan. 9, 1896; "Platt and Quay Confer," *The Sun* (New York), Jan.9, 1896; James M. Blythe to Grenville Dodge, Feb. 24, 1896, in Dodge papers; McKinley to Filley, April 24, 1896, in McKinley papers; and Bristow, *Politics and Fraud*, 92.

8   "Riot at St. Joseph," *Detroit Free Press*, May 13, 1896; "Filley and Kerens Row," *Chicago Tribune*, May 13, 1896; "Filley At The Head In Missouri," *Chicago Tribune*, May 14, 1896; "Mr. Kerens Defeated," *The Sun* (Baltimore), May 14, 1896; Appleton, *Annual Cyclopaedia* (1897), 495; and Bristow, *Politics and Fraud*, 92–93.

9   "A Split in Delaware," *New York Times*, May 13, 1896; "A Stormy Session," *Los Angles Times*, May 13, 1896; "Higgins Friends Bolted," *Washington Post*, May 13, 1896; "Addicks and Higgins," *New York Times*, May 14, 1896; and Appleton, *Annual Cyclopaedia* (1897), 240.

10 "The Passing Throng," *Atlanta Constitution*, April 4, 1896; "Nevada Idea in National Politics," *Chicago Tribune*, May 10, 1896; "Montana Republicans for Silver," *Chicago Tribune*, May 12, 1896; "Declared For Free Silver," *St. Louis Post-Dispatch*, May 12, 1896; "The Colorado Delegates," *Los Angeles Times*, May 15, 1896; "Senator Dubois Indorsed," *Washington Post*, May 17, 1896; Diary entry for May 9, 1896, in Dawes, *Journal*, 82; "Colorado And Silver," *National Bimetallist*, I, May 20, 1896, 492; Appleton, *Annual Cyclopaedia* (1897), 135–136, 346, 498, and 511; and Ellis, *Teller*, 253–54.

11 "Sound As To Money," *Chicago Tribune*, April 28, 1896, and "M'Kinley's Bimetallism," *The National Bimetallist*, I, May 6, 1896, 455.

12 "Will Pass Two Bills," *Washington Post*, Dec. 24, 1895; "Tariff Bill Near Ready," *New York Times*, Dec. 25, 1895; "Day's Proceedings In The House," *Chicago Tribune*, Dec. 27, 1895; "Passed The Bond Bill," *Washington Post*, Dec. 29, 1895; "Quay's Views," *Los Angeles Times*, Jan. 9, 1896; "Silver Rules the Senate," *New York Times*, Feb. 1, 1896; "Silver In the Snow," *Chicago Tribune*, Feb. 14, 1896; "Allen Makes a Bold Proposition," *Chicago Tribune*, Feb. 27, 1896; and Ellis, *Teller*, 244–49.

13 Ellis, *Teller*, 246.

14 "Silver Stock is Rising," *Evening Transcript* (Boston), March 24, 1896.

15 "M'Kinley On Silver," *Chicago Tribune*, March 15, 1896; "Speak Out, Man," *Sun* (Baltimore, MD), March 16, 1896; "McKinley and Silver," *New York Times*, March 17, 1896; "Is M'Kinley For Free Silver?" *Chicago Tribune*, April 2, 1896; "M'Kinley On Finance," *Washington Post*, April 2, 1896; and "Maj. M'Kinley's Sound-Money Record," *Los Angeles Times*, April 21, 1896.

16 William M. Stewart to McKinley, April 3 and April 28, 1896, in McKinley papers. Sherman made the comments in a letter to the Young Men's Republican Club of Brooklyn.

17 "Kansas Republican Convention," *Chicago Tribune*, March 11, 1896; "Off His Perch," *Los Angeles Times*, March 26, 1896; "In The Convention Hall," *Los Angeles Times*, May 8, 1896; "Indiana Wants McKinley," *New York Times*, May 8, 1896; "Up In Michigan," *Los Angeles Times*, May 9, 1896; "Instructed: Washington's Delegates Are for McKinley," *Los Angeles Times*, May 15, 1896; "More Votes For McKinley," *New York Times*, May 15, 1896; "North Carolina Republicans," *Washington Post*, May 17, 1896; and Appleton, *Annual Cyclopaedia* (1897), 373.

18 "M'Kinley's Answer," *The World* (New York), May 18, 1896; "M'Kinley Dodges," *The World* (New York), May 17, 1896; "McKinley and Finance," *The Evening Star* (Washington, D.C.), May 13, 1896; and "His Position Is Clear," *Chicago Daily News*, May 20, 1896.

19 "Parallel for A Reply," *Chicago Tribune*, May 12, 1896.

20 "Why He Opposes McKinley," *New York Times*, May 11, 1896.

21 "Platt Continues On The Warpath," *Chicago Tribune*, May 14, 1896.

22 "Straddle Bug" and "Two Candidates Who Have Spoken" in *The Sun* (New York), May 15, 1896.

23 "The Week," *The Nation*, May 7, 1896.

24 Louis T. Michener to E. Frank Tibbott, May 19, 1896, in Harrison Papers.

25 "The Week," *The Nation*, May 21, 1896; Glad, *McKinley, Bryan, and the People*, 107; and R. Hal Williams; *Years of Decision*, 101.

26 "Says It Will Be Reed," *Chicago Tribune*, May 20, 1896; "M'Kinley Sent for Quay," *The Sun* (New York), May 22, 1896; and "Mr. Quay Has Gone," *Evening Star* (Washington, D.C.), May 22, 1896.

27 Clarkson to Platt, May 21, 1896, in Platt papers. McKinley was code-named "Gallery," Quay "Gable," Platt "Gaff," and Hanna "Grasp."

28 "Quay's Knock Answered" and "Why Brown Went," in *Morning Times* (Washington, D.C.), May 23, 1896; "Quay Visits M'Kinley," *New-York Tribune*, May 23, 1896; and "Quay Meets M'Kinley," *The Sun* (New York), May 23, 1896.

29 "Mr. Quay Has Gone," *Evening Star* (Washington, D.C.), May 22, 1896; "Platt And Quay," *Atlanta Constitution*, May 22, 1896; Marcus, *Grand Old Party,* 209; and Kehl, *Boss Rule*, 202.

30 J. Sloat Fassett to Platt, May 30, 1896, in Platt papers.

31 "Ex-Senator Platt Here," *Washington Post*, May 31, 1896; "Mr. Platt's Flying Trip," *New York Times*, June 1, 1896; "Lauterbach Gives Up," *New-York Tribune*, June 2, 1896; and "Quay Concedes McKinley's Nomination," *Los Angeles Times*, June 2, 1896.

32 Lodge, *Selections*, 222.

33 Roosevelt to Anna Roosevelt Cowles, June 14, 1896, *Letters to Anna Roosevelt Cowles*, 182.

CHAPTER 16: BATTLE FOR AN IDEA

1 "Bonds Subscribed Five Times Over," *New York Times*, Feb. 6, 1896; Barnes, *Carlisle*, 412–22; and Nevins, *Study in Courage*, 684–88

2 "More Bonds," *World-Herald* (Omaha, NE), Jan. 7, 1896; "Criticized Cleveland," *Washington Post*, Jan. 16, 1896; "Washington News," *Chicago Tribune*, Jan. 30, 1896; "Cockrell's Criticism," *Washington Post*, March 14, 1896; and Welch, *Presidencies of Cleveland*, 126.

3 "Silver Rules The Senate," *New-York Tribune*, Feb. 2, 1896; "The Silver Protection Fight," *New York Times*, Feb. 15, 1896; and Nevins, *Study in Courage*, 689.

4 "In Chicago, July 7," *Chicago Tribune*, Jan. 17, 1896; "Chicago Wins The Fight," *New-York Tribune*, Jan. 18, 1896; "Silver Men Are Beaten," *New York Times*, Jan. 18, 1896; and Nevins, *Study in Courage*, 689.

5   "Butler Is Ineligible," *New York Times*, Jan. 13, 1896; "Populists Talk Of Party Policy," *Chicago Tribune*, Jan. 18, 1896; and Williams, *Realigning America*, 111–12.

6   "Trumball For President," *New York Times*, Jan. 13, 1896; "Could Win On Silver," *Washington Post*, Jan. 18, 1896; Williams, *Years of Decision*, 111–13; and George P. Kinney to Bryan, Jan. 2, 1896, James B. Weaver to Bryan, Jan. 3, 1896, and Senator Marion Butler to Bryan, Jan. 8, 1896, in Bryan papers. Kinney was the American Bimetallic League's West Coast organizer.

7   "Could Win On Silver," *Washington Post*, Jan. 18, 1896; "People's Party People," *Los Angeles Times*, Jan. 18, 1896; "Have Settled On St. Louis," *Omaha Daily Bee*, Jan. 19, 1896; "Populists Select St. Louis," *New-York Tribune*, Jan. 19, 1896; "They Stand By Taubeneck," *Washington Post*, Jan. 19, 1896; and Williams, *Realigning America*, 113.

8   Diary entry for Feb. 16, 1896, in Festus P. Summers (ed.), *The Cabinet Diary of William L. Wilson, 1896–1897* (Chapel Hill, NC: University of North Carolina Press, 1957), 27–28.

9   "A Fight For Sound Money," *New York Times*, March 1, 1896; "Fighting For Silver," *Washington Evening Star*, March 4, 1896; "Georgians To Debate," *Washington Post*, March 20, 1896; "Mr. Crisp Replies," *Atlanta Constitution*, April 3, 1896; "Crisp Cancels All His Dates," *Washington Post*, April 14, 1896; diary entries for March 8 and March 24, 1896; Summers, *Cabinet Diary*, 41 and 51; Nevins, *Study in Courage*, 693; Dewey W. Grantham, *Hoke Smith and the Politics of the New South* (Baton Rouge: Louisiana State University Press, 1958), 100–101 and 105–6. Crisp's health deteriorated and he died Oct. 23, depriving the Georgia Silver Democrats of their choice to succeed Senator John B. Gordon.

10 "Carlisle's Sound Money Address to the Workingman," *Chicago Tribune*, April 16, 1896; "He Stands By Gold," *Chicago Tribune*, April 16, 1896; "Carlisle Talks on Currency," *Los Angeles Times*, April 16, 1896; and Champ Clark, *My Quarter Century Of American Politics, I* (Whitefish, MT: Kessinger, 2007), 236, quoted by Barnes, *Carlisle*, 449.

11 "Laboring Men Hear Carlisle," *The Courier-Journal* (Louisville, KY), April 17, 1896; "The Effort Will Prove Futile," *Atlanta Constitution*, April 17, 1896; "Carlisle On Labor," *World-Herald* (Omaha, NE), April 18, 1896; and "Carlisle's Great Chicago Speech," *The Courier-Journal* (Louisville, KY), April 18, 1896.

12 Diary entry for April 17, 1896, in Summers, *Cabinet Diary*, 67.

13 "Acts of Democrats," *Dalles Daily Chronicle* (The Dalles, OR), April 10, 1896; "State Conventions," *Daily Capitol Journal* (Salem, OR), April 10, 1896; "A Lost Opportunity," *Dalles Daily Chronicle* (The Dalles, OR), April 11, 1896; "Senator Tillman Airs Himself and Then the Convention Meets," *Los Angeles Times*, April 16, 1896; "Colorado Threatens A Bolt," *Washington Post*, April 16, 1896; and "Mississippi Pledged For Free Silver," *Washington Post*, April 30, 1896.

14 "Must Have All Or Nothing," *St. Louis Post-Dispatch*, March 14, 1896; "Silver Was Supreme," *Washington Post*, April 16, 1896; "Missouri Democrats For Silver," *Chicago Tribune*, April 16, 1896; "In Full Control," *New York Times*, June 1, 1896; and Appleton, *Annual Cyclopaedia* (1897), 494–95.

15 "Silver Wins In Alabama," *Atlanta Constitution*, April 23, 1896, and diary entry for April 16, 1896, in Summers, *Cabinet Diary*, 66.

16 "Sound Money Wins In Nebraska," *Chicago Tribune*, April 27, 1896; "Was All Over In An Hour," *World-Herald* (Omaha, NE), April 30, 1896; "Nebraska Gold Democrats," *Chicago Tribune*, April 29, 1896; "Nebraska Not Silver Mad," *New York Times*, April 30, 1896; "Gold Faction Denounces Silver," *Chicago Tribune*, April 30, 1896; and Koenig, *Bryan*, 168.

17 "Michigan For Sound Money," *New York Times*, April 30, 1896; "Silver Men Defeated," *Washington Post*, April 30, 1896; "It's Sound," *Detroit Free Press*, April 30, 1896; and "Indorse The Administration," *World-Herald* (Omaha), April 30, 1896.

18 "Free Silver In The Lead," *Washington Post*, April 29, 1896; "The Week," *The Nation*, May 7, 1896; "Silver Democrats Lose The Day," *Chicago Tribune*, April 30, 1896; "Michigan For Sound Money," *New York Times*, April 30, 1896; "State Democrats Disappointed," *New-York Tribune*, May 1, 1896; and diary entry for April 29, 1896, in Summers, *Cabinet Diary*, 73.

19 Cleveland to Dickinson, March 25, 1896, and Dickinson to Cleveland March 31, 1896, and Nevins, *Letters*, 432–33 and 435.

20 "A Blow To Sound Money," *New York Times*, June 1, 1896; "All The Silver Men's Way," *Wichita Daily Eagle*, (Wichita, KS), June 3, 1896; "Hiss At The President," *Chicago Tribune*, June 4, 1896; "Hissed The Gold Men," *Washington Post*, June 4, 1896; "Blackburn Urged Unseating Carroll," *Courier Journal* (Louisville), June 6, 1896; Emmett Orr to William Campbell Preston Breckinridge, April 20, 1896, in Breckinridge papers, quoted by Barnes, *Carlisle*, 449; Williams, *Years of*

Decision, 109; and Appleton, *Annual Cyclopaedia* (1897), 377. Breckinridge lost his House seat in 1894 in part because a former mistress sued him for breach of promise.

21   Champ Clark, *My Quarter Century Of American Politics, I,* 237.

22   "But 31 Were for Gold," *Washington Post,* June 26, 1896; "Silver Wins in Iowa," *Chicago Tribune,* May 21, 1896; "With Tillman at Its Head," *Washington Post,* May 20, 1896; and "The Palmetto State Solid," *Atlanta Constitution,* May 21, 1896.

23   "Virginia's Silver Men," *Washington Post,* June 4, 1896; "Virginia For Free Silver," *New York Times,* June 5, 1896; "A Daniel Among Democrats," *Los Angeles Times,* June 5, 1896; and Appleton, *Annual Cyclopaedia* (1897), 539 and 812–13.

24   Simpkins, *Pitchfork Ben Tillman,* 315–17.

25   "Silver Is Weakening," *New York Times,* June 1, 1896, and Appleton, *Annual Cyclopaedia* (1897), 516.

26   "The Farmers for Gold," *New York Times,* June 12, 1896; "Gold Democrats Won," *Washington Post,* June 12, 1896; "Minnesota Democrats For Gold," *Chicago Tribune,* June 12, 1896; Bain, *Convention Decisions,* 365; and Appleton, *Annual Cyclopaedia* (1897), 490.

27   Michael Doran to W. W. Thurber, June 12, 1896, in Cleveland Papers; diary entry for June 10, 1896 from Summers, *Cabinet Diary,* 99; and Nevins, *Study in Courage,* 208.

28   Diary entries for May 23, 26, 27, and 28, 1896, in Summers, *Cabinet Diary,* 90–92.

29   Cleveland to Don M. Dickinson, June 10, 1896, in Nevins, *Letters,* 439.

30   "Mr. Whitney Going To Chicago," *New York Times,* June 18, 1896; Mark D. Hirsch, *William C. Whitney: Modern Warwick* (New York: Dodd, Mead, 1948), 488–89; and Cleveland to Don M. Dickinson, June 17, 1896, in Nevins, *Letters,* 441–42.

31   Diary entry for June 20, 1896, in Summers, *Cabinet Diary,* 105; Hirsch, *Whitney,* 489–90; and Jones, *Election of 1896,* 200–201.

32   Hirsch, *Whitney,* 489.

33   "Mr. Cleveland Speaks For Sound And Honest Money," *New York Herald,* June 17, 1896, and Nevins, *Letters,* 440–41.

34   "Mr. Cleveland's Letter," *Minneapolis Journal,* June 17, 1896; "Mr. Cleveland's Call For Looters," *World-Herald* (Omaha, NE), June 18, 1896; and "That Last Letter," *Atlanta Constitution,* June 18, 1896.

35   The *St. Louis Post-Dispatch* was tracking the delegate count, including district conventions in states yet to hold their state gatherings, and reported there were 391 silver delegates to 241 gold, but this appears to ignore the impact of the unit rule, which bound some Gold delegates because they were part of a delegation that was majority Silver. "Now For Chicago," *St. Louis Post-Dispatch,* June 19, 1896.

CHAPTER 17: CREDENTIALS AND CURRENCY FIGHTS

1   "M'Kinley Men Anxious," *New York Times,* June 6, 1896; "Listen to Hanna While He Talks" and "McKinley in Great Peril" in *St. Louis Post-Dispatch,* June 7, 1896; "Visited the Major," *Cleveland Plain Dealer,* June 7, 1896; "Mr. Kerens Called to Canton," *St. Louis Globe-Democrat,* June 7, 1896; "Filley Nearly Caused a Panic," *St. Louis Post-Dispatch,* June 8, 1896; "Called to Canton," *Cleveland Plan Dealer,* June 8, 1896; and diary entry for June 6, 1896, in Dawes, *Journal,* 84.

2   "The National Committee," *St. Louis Globe-Democrat,* June 11, 1896, and Jones, *Election of 1896,* 163–64.

3   "Hanna and His Suite Arrive," *New York Times,* June 11, 1896; "The Worlds of McKinley," *St. Louis Globe-Democrat,* June 11, 1896; "All Hail to Mr. Hanna," *Chicago Tribune,* June 11, 1896; and Diary entry for June 6, 1896, in Dawes, *Journal,* 84.

4   "The Contest for Seats," *New-York Tribune,* June 10, 1896; "Mr. Platt's Early Start," *New York Times,* June 10, 1896; "Many Seats in Doubt," *Washington Post,* June 10, 1896; "Platt and His Friends En Route," *Chicago Tribune,* June 11, 1896; "The National Committee," *St. Louis Globe-Democrat,* June 11, 1896; and "Slight Chance Against McKinley," *New York Times,* June 12, 1896.

5   "Are With McKinley," *Chicago Tribune,* June 11, 1896, and "The National Committee," *St. Louis Globe-Democrat,* June 11, 1896.

6   "Manley Gives It Up," *New York Times,* June 11, 1896.

7   "McKinley on the First Ballot," *Chicago Tribune,* June 11, 1896; "Manley Gives It Up," *New York Times,* June 11, 1896; and "Reed's Manager Gives Up the Fight," *New York Tribune,* June 11, 1896.

8   "Maine's Pot of Sorrow Boils Over," *Chicago Tribune*, June 11, 1896; "Betrayed by Manley,"
    Washington Post, June 12, 1896; "Reed Still in the Fight," *New York Times*, June 12, 1896;
    "Speaker Reed's Forlorn Hope," *New York Tribune*, June 12, 1896; "Now He's Sorry He Said It,"
    St. Louis Post-Dispatch, June 12, 1896; "Contempt for Manley," *New York Times*, June 13, 1896;
    "Conventional Phrases," *New York Times*, June 14, 1896; Frank G. Carpenter, "Snap Shots of the
    St. Louis Convention by Two Veterans," *San Francisco Chronicle*, June 18, 1896; Reed to Lodge,
    June 10, 1896, in Lodge Papers; and Manley to Reed, December 12, 1896, in McCall, *Life of
    Reed*, 224.

9   "McKinley Men Get Seats," *Chicago Tribune*, June 12, 1896; "Seating McKinley Delegates," *New
    York Times*, June 12, 1896; "It Is the Field Against McKinley," *Atlanta Constitution*, June 12,
    1896; and "Deciding on the Delegates," *Los Angeles Herald*, June 12, 1896.

10 "McKinley Men Get Seats," *Chicago Tribune*, June 12, 1896; "Seating McKinley Delegates," *New
    York Times*, June 12, 1896; "It Is the Field Against McKinley," *Atlanta Constitution*, June 12,
    1896; and "Deciding on the Delegates," *Los Angeles Herald*, June 12, 1896.

11 "M'Kinley Men Anxious," *New York Times*, June 6, 1896; "Listen to Hanna While He Talks"
    and "McKinley in Great Peril" in *St. Louis Post-Dispatch*, June 7, 1896; "Visited the Major,"
    Cleveland Plain Dealer, June 7, 1896; "Mr. Kerens Called to Canton," *St. Louis Globe-Democrat*,
    June 7, 1896; "Filley Nearly Caused A Panic," *St. Louis Post-Dispatch*, June 8, 1896; "Called
    to Canton," *Cleveland Plan Dealer*, June 8, 1896; "Filley Gets A Hard Knock," *St. Louis
    Post-Dispatch*, June 12, 1896; "M'Kinley and Hobart" and "The Committee on Credentials" in
    Washington Post, June 12, 1896; "McKinley Men Get Seats," *Chicago Tribune*, June 12, 1896;
    "Seating McKinley Delegates," *New York Times*, June 12, 1896; "It Is the Field Against McKin-
    ley," *Atlanta Constitution*, June 12, 1896; "Speaker Reed's Forlorn Hope" and "Filley Against
    Kerens" in *New York Tribune*, June 12, 1896; and "Deciding on the Delegates," *Los Angeles Her-
    ald*, June 12, 1896.

12 "Work of the Committee" and "M'Kinley Men Are Seated" in *San Francisco Chronicle*, June 13,
    1896, and "Doings of the National Committee," *Chicago Tribune*, June 13, 1896.

13 Frank G. Carpenter, "Thomas Platt," *Indianapolis Journal*, June 13, 1896; "Platt Full of Fight,"
    New York Times, June 12, 1896; and "Platt's Course Welcomed," *New York Times*, June 13, 1896.

14 "Platt's Course Welcomed," *New York Times*, June 13, 1896, and "Platt to Make A Fight," *Chi-
    cago Tribune*, June 13, 1896.

15 "The Louisiana Fight," *St. Louis Post-Dispatch*, June 13, 1896; "Doings of the National Com-
    mittee," *Chicago Tribune*, June 13, 1896; "Busy With Contests," *New York Times*, June 13, 1896;
    "Work of the Committee," *San Francisco Chronicle*, June 13, 1896; "Quay and Platt Join Forces,"
    Atlanta Constitution, June 13, 1896; "It Is Waxing Hot," *Hartford Courant*, June 13, 1896; and
    "Quay and Platt Join Forces," *Atlanta Constitution*, June 13, 1896.

16 "It Is Waxing Hot," *Hartford Courant*, June 13, 1896; "Busy With Contests" and "Length of
    the Convention" in New *York Times*, June 13, 1896; "The Committee Getting Tired," *St. Louis
    Post-Dispatch*, June 13, 1896; and "Quay and Platt Join Forces," *Atlanta Constitution*, June 13,
    1896.

17 "More Contests Decided," *New York Times*, June 14, 1896; "Blindfolded by M'Kinley," *St. Louis
    Post-Dispatch*, June 14, 1896; "All Night on Contests," *Chicago Tribune,* June 14, 1896; "Hard
    Work of the Committee," *San Francisco Chronicle*, June 14, 1896; and Paul Douglas Casdorph,
    "Norris Wright Cuney and Texas Republican Politics, 1883–1896," *Southwestern Historical
    Quarterly* 67, no. 4 (April 1965): 463.

18 "All Night on Contests," *Chicago Tribune,* June 14, 1896; "More Contests Decided," *New York
    Times*, June 14, 1896; "Hard Work of the Committee," *San Francisco Chronicle*, June 14, 1896;
    "Blindfolded by M'Kinley," *St. Louis Post-Dispatch*, June 14, 1896; and Casdorph, "Norris
    Wright Cuney and Texas Republican Politics, 1883–1896." The Texas McKinley congressional
    districts were the 1st, 2nd, 3rd, 4th, 6th, 8th, and 9th, and the Reed districts the 7th and 10th.

19 "Grosvenor Not Afraid of Platt," *New York Times*, June 14, 1896, and "Platt Haters Seated," *New
    York Times*, June 15, 1896.

20 "Mr. Bliss Is Left Out," *New York Times*, June 14, 1896; "Blindfolded by M'Kinley," *St. Louis
    Post-Dispatch*, June 14, 1896; "Platt and Anti-Platt" and "New York Cases Are Taken" in *Chicago
    Tribune*, June 14, 1896; "It Was A Red-Hot Fight," *The Sun* (New York), June 15, 1896; "Hard
    Work of the Committee," *San Francisco Chronicle*, June 14, 1896; and "Very Well-Rounded Re-
    publican: the Several Lives of John S. Wise," *Virginia Magazine of History and Biography*, Vol. 71,
    No. 4 (October, 1963), 462–78.

21   "Hard Work of the Committee," *San Francisco Chronicle*, June 14, 1896; "Platt and Anti-Platt," *Chicago Tribune*, June 14, 1896; "It Was A Red-Hot Fight," *The Sun* (New York), June 15, 1896; "Blindfolded by M'Kinley," *St. Louis Post-Dispatch*, June 14, 1896; and "Platt Is Thrown Down," *Chicago Tribune*, June 15, 1896.

22   "Platt Will Not Bolt," *Washington Post*, June 15, 1896, and "Off-Hand Decision of Contests" and "Platt Talks of His Treatment" in *New York Times*, June 15, 1896.

23   "The McKinley Convention," *The Sun* (New York), March 12, 1896.

24   "Silver Men At Sea," *The World* (New York), June 14, 1896; "Statement of Sen. Charles Dick, Feb. 10, 1906," 13–14; and Mott, *Herrick*, 68.

25   "Sound As to Money," *Chicago Tribune*, June 13, 1896; "Great Day for Gold," *Chicago Tribune*, June 17, 1896; and "How They Stand," *St. Louis Post-Dispatch*, June 9, 1896.

26   "Protection the Great Issue, Says Perry Heath" and "Gen. Grosvenor's Belief" in *Courier Journal* (Louisville, Kentucky), June 6, 1896, and "Clever, Say M'Kinley," *The World* (New York), June 14, 1896.

27   "Teller Will Bolt," *New York Times*, June 14, 1896.

28   "Single Gold Standard," *Courier Journal* (Louisville), June 10, 1896; Foraker, *Notes, I*, 467–70; Whitelaw Reid to McKinley and Reid to Hanna, June 13, 1896, in McKinley papers; and James F. Rhodes, the *McKinley and Roosevelt Administrations, 1897–1909* (New York & London: Macmillan, 1922), 15. Whitelaw Reid ran the campaign's draft plank by J. P. Morgan and mailed Morgan's reactions to McKinley, including a paragraph drafted by Morgan supporting the issuance of more gold bonds as Cleveland had done. Reid mailed his memo after the campaign had settled on its position.

29   "All Talk Is of Money" *New York Times*, June 11, 1896; "Mr. Platt's Cool Reception," *Washington Post*, June 12, 1896; "Platt Comes to Fight," *Chicago Tribune*, June 12, 1896; "Mr. Platt Arrives," *Los Angeles Times*, June 12, 1896; and "The Republicans At St. Louis," *New York Times*, June 12, 1896.

30   "May Have Second Place," *New York Times*, June 11, 1896; "Quay Is There" and "Platt's Course Welcomed" in *New York Times*, June 13, 1896; "Platt to Make A Fight" and "For A Gold Basis" in *Chicago Tribune*, June 13, 1896; and Frank G. Carpenter, "Thomas Platt," *Indianapolis Journal*, June 13, 1896.

31   "Cranks Worry Hanna," *Chicago Tribune*, June 13, 1896.

32   "A Day of Inertia," *New York Times*, June 13, 1896; Frank G. Carpenter, "Thomas Platt," *Indianapolis Journal*, June 13, 1896; Frank G. Carpenter, "Snap Shots of the St. Louis Convention by Two Veterans," *San Francisco Chronicle*, June 18, 1896; Kohlsaat, *From McKinley to Harding*, 34; diary entry for June 15, 1896, in Dawes, *Journal*, 85; and Croly, *Hanna*, 196–97. Dawes is hazy about the meeting's date, thinking it was Friday or Saturday, June 12 or 13. Croly puts the meeting on Friday morning or afternoon.

33   "Platt Not the Leader," *New-York Tribune*, June 18, 1896; "Campaign Work," *The Evening Star* (Washington, D.C.), June 22, 1896; Stone from *Fifty Years a Journalist*, quoted by Kohlsaat, *From McKinley to Harding*, 43; Kohlsaat, *From McKinley to Harding*, 35–39; and Jones, *Election of 1896*, 167, esp. a very compelling footnote at 378–79. Kohlsaat says he was asked to go to Hanna's room, when the Clevelander supposedly told him, "You probably have noticed I have dropped you entirely for a couple of months. Well, I want to tell you I am just as strong a gold-man as you are, but if I had been as outspoken as you we would not have gotten the votes for McKinley, but I want you to know I love you just as much as ever." Kohlsaat, *From McKinley to Harding*, 35–36. The egotistical publisher also later slyly suggested he was the prime mover behind the decision by writing "I had nothing whatever to do with writing the plank, except to put the word 'gold' between the words 'existing' and 'standard.' " Which was the essence of the decision. He was to expend much energy to solidify his claim to be the plank's author.

34   James Creelman, "An Inglorious Convention," *The World* (New York), June 14, 1896.

35   "Free Silver Programme," *St. Louis Post-Dispatch*, June 9, 1896; "Ingalls on the Financial Issue," *St. Louis Post Dispatch*, June 15, 1896; "Silver States Are Very Shy," *St. Louis Post-Dispatch*, June 16, 1896; "Silver Men Hesitate," "Fighting for A Declaration for Gold," "Gold Men of the Middle West," and "Teller Against A 'Straddle' " in *New York Times*, June 15, 1896; "Silver Contingent," *Detroit Free Press*, June 15, 1896; "The Silver States," *The Sun* (Baltimore), June 15, 1896; and "The Silver Republicans Say," *Boston Globe*, June 16, 1896. On Monday, Colorado, Idaho, Montana, and Nevada refused to submit names for their representative on the Notification Committee that would deliver the official word on his nomination to the party's candidate.

36 "Ultimatum to Hanna," *The Sun* (New York), June 15, 1896.
37 "Ultimatum to Hanna," *The Sun* (New York), June 15, 1896; "Bold Stand by Gold Men," *New York Times*, June 15, 1896; Lodge to Henry Croly, July 27, 1910, in Lodge Papers; Thomas Collier Platt, *The Autobiography of Thomas Collier Platt* (New York: B.W. Dodge, 1910), 323–24; John A. Garraty, *Henry Cabot Lodge: A Biography* (New York: Alfred A. Knopf, 1965), 169–70; and Kohlsaat, *From McKinley to Harding*, 37. Garraty erroneously has this meeting on Sunday, June 15, but Sunday was the 14th. Kohlsaat offered a colorful account of the meeting that Lodge forever denied. In the Chicago publisher's telling, the meeting went "Mr. Lodge said: 'Mr. Hanna, I insist on a positive declaration for a gold-standard plank in the platform.' Hanna looked up and said: 'Who the hell are you?' Lodge answered: 'Senator Henry Cabot Lodge, of Massachusetts.' 'Well, Senator Henry Cabot Lodge, of Massachusetts. You can go plumb to hell. You have nothing to say about it,' replied Mr. Hanna. Lodge said: 'All right, sir, I will make my fight on the floor of the convention.' 'I don't care a damn where you make your fight,' Mr. Hanna replied." Lodge is more credible on this.
38 "Ultimatum to Hanna," *The Sun* (New York), June 15, 1896; Platt, *Autobiography*, 324; and Garraty, *Lodge*, 170.
39 "For A Gold Plank," *Chicago Tribune*, June 16, 1896; "Lodge Says It Will Be for Gold," *Chicago Tribune*, June 16, 1896; "Lodge Says Gold Has Won," *New York Times*, June 16, 1896; "Struggle Over the Platform," *St. Louis Post-Dispatch*, June 16, 1896; Lodge to E.S. Draper, January 12, 1900 in Lodge Papers; Platt, *Autobiography*, 324–25; and Garraty, *Lodge*, 170. Again, Garraty has his dates wrong. He places this as Tuesday morning but the platform subcommittee drafted the Gold plank Monday, June 15.
40 "Will Declare for Gold," *Chicago Tribune*, June 16, 1896; "Big Gains for Gold," *New York Times*, June 16, 1896; "The Convention Meets," *New-York Tribune*, June 17, 1896; Lodge to Royal Cortissoz, May 23, 1921, in the Lodge Papers; Foraker, *Notes*, I, 477–79; Platt, *Autobiography*, 326; Williams, *Years of Decision*, 102; and Garraty, *Lodge*, 170. A *Chicago Tribune* survey of the Resolutions committee showed twenty-four Gold men, eleven Silver bugs, and sixteen unknown or straddlers. The Gold men on the subcommittee were Lodge, Fessenden, Merriam, Patterson of the *Chicago Tribune*, Louisiana's former Gov. Henry C. Warmoth, and A. F. Burleigh of Washington State, a railroad lawyer.
41 Frank G. Carpenter, "Snap Shots of the St. Louis Convention by Two Veterans," *San Francisco Chronicle*, June 18, 1896; Olcott, *Life of McKinley, I,* 310; and Mott, *Herrick*, 68. Arizona, California, Colorado, Idaho, Montana, Nevada, New Mexico, North Carolina, Oklahoma, and Utah voting no.
42 "The Platt Victories," *New-York Tribune*, June 17, 1896.
43 "Mr. Platt At St. Louis," *New York Times*, June 19, 1896; Walter H. Moler and George R. Sheldon to Platt, June 15, 1896; Frank J. Sprague, Erasmus Sterling, James A. Burden, Eugene Kelly, and Listers Agricultural Chemical Works to Platt, June 16, 1896; Henry Clews to Platt, June 17, 1896; M. D. Wheeler to Platt, June 20, 1896; New York Assemblyman Horace White to Platt, June 25, 1896, in Platt Papers; and Lang, *Autobiography*, 310. Wheeler was the Chief Post Office Inspector in D.C. and a Democrat patronage appointee.

CHAPTER 18: GOP CONVENTION

1 "Whiling Away the Time," *Chicago Tribune*, June 13, 1896.
2 "Gay Flags in the Great Hall," *Chicago Tribune*, June 13, 1896; James Creelman, "Not A Cheer for M'Kinley," *The World* (New York), June 17, 1896; and Republican National Convention, St. Louis, 1896, *Official Proceedings of the Eleventh Republican National Convention Held in St. Louis, MO, June 16, 17, and 18, 1896* (N.p: n.p., 1896), 22–23. *Eleventh Republican National Convention* has the building 180' by 260'.
3 "Gay Flags in the Great Hall," *Chicago Tribune*, June 13, 1896, and "Business Is Begun," *Chicago Tribune*, June 17, 1896.
4 1896 Republican National Convention Admission Tickets and Envelope, Susan H. Douglas Political Americana Collection, Rare and Manuscript Collections, Cornell University Library, http://www.flickr.com/photos/cornelluniversitylibrary/4359517575/; and McFeely, *Grant*, 59–60.
5 *Eleventh Republican National Convention*, 25.
6 Frank G. Carpenter, "Snap Shots of the St. Louis Convention by Two Veterans," *San Francisco Chronicle*, June 18, 1896; "Hanna Takes Charge," *New York Times*, June 18, 1896; "Puts in Good Day," *Chicago Tribune*, June 18, 1896; and *Eleventh Republican National Convention*, 43–45.

7   *Eleventh Republican National Convention,* 49–50.
8   "Business Is Begun," *Chicago Tribune,* June 17, 1896; "First Roll Call," *New York Times,* June 18, 1896; "McKinley's Solid Phalanx," *New-York Tribune,* June 18, 1896; James Creelman, "Hanna's Iron Hand," *The World* (New York), June 18, 1896; and *Eleventh Republican National Convention,* 50–51.
9   "Will Mean Gold But Avoid the Word," *New York Times,* June 14, 1896; "Platt Men Angry With Morton," *New York Times,* June 15, 1896; "Gov. Morton's Declination," *The Sun* (New York), June 15, 1896; "Morton Would Accept It," *New-York Tribune,* June 18, 1896.
10 "New York Breach Growing Wide," *Chicago Tribune,* June 17, 1896; "Morton for Second Place," *St. Louis Post-Dispatch,* June 17, 1896; B. F. Tracy to Morton, June 15 and June 16, 1896; and B. F. Tracy to Platt, June 17, 1896, in Platt Papers.
11 "The Bug Convention at St. Louis," *New York Times,* June 16, 1896, and "Teller Mad Enough to Talk," *St. Louis Post-Dispatch,* June 16, 1896.
12 "Five Out of Ranks," *Chicago Tribune,* June 18, 1896.
13 "Name A Good Ticket," *Chicago Tribune,* June 19, 1896; James Creelman, "Wild for M'Kinley," *The World* (New York), June 19, 1896; and *Eleventh Republican National Convention,* 81–83.
14 *Eleventh Republican National Convention,* 85–86.
15 "Taking the Vote," *St. Louis Post-Dispatch,* June 18, 1896; "Name A Good Ticket," *Chicago Daily News,* June 19, 1896; James Creelman, "Wild for McKinley," *The World* (New York), June 19, 1896; and *Eleventh Republican National Convention,* 86–96.
16 James Creelman, "Wild for McKinley," *The World* (New York), June 19, 1896; White, *Autobiography,* 140–42; and *Eleventh Republican National Convention,* 98–101.
17 "Silver Men Have Bolted," *St. Louis Post-Dispatch,* June 18, 1896; "The Walk-Out," *St. Louis Post-Dispatch,* June 19, 1896; "Its Duty Is Done," *Chicago Tribune,* June 19, 1896; and James Creelman, "Wild for McKinley," *The World* (New York), June 19, 1896.
18 "Cannon Boom in Colorado," *St. Louis Post-Dispatch,* June 19, 1896, and James Creelman, "Wild for McKinley," *The World* (New York), June 19, 1896.
19 "Silver Men Will Confer," *St. Louis Post-Dispatch,* June 18, 1896.
20 "Honored by His Townsmen," *New York Tribune,* June 18, 1896; "McKinley's Plans," *The World* (New York), June 19, 1896; and Leech, *Days of McKinley,* 81.
21 James Creelman, "Wild for McKinley," *The World* (New York), June 19, 1896; "Name A Good Ticket," *Chicago Tribune,* June 19, 1986; Sage, *Allison,* 265; and *Eleventh Republican National Convention,* 106–9.
22 "Dr. Depew Starts West," *New York Times,* June 12 1896; James Creelman, "Wild for McKinley," *The World* (New York), June 19, 1896; "Name A Good Ticket," *Chicago Tribune,* June 19, 1896; and *Eleventh Republican National Convention,* 113–16.
23 James Creelman, "Wild for McKinley," *The World* (New York), June 19, 1896.
24 *Eleventh Republican National Convention,* 117–88.
25 "Name A Good Ticket," *Chicago Tribune,* June 19, 1896; "Wild Over McKinley," *New York Times,* June 19, 1896; and Olcott, *McKinley,* I, 314–15.
26 "McKinley's Plans," *The World* (New York), June 19, 1896; Leech, *Days of McKinley,* 82 and Foraker, *Notes,* I, 487.
27 "Honored by His Townsmen," *New-York Tribune,* June 18, 1896; "Name A Good Ticket," *Chicago Tribune,* June 19, 1896; and Tarr, *Boss Politics,* 59.
28 "Reed's Boom Revives," *New York Times,* June 15, 1896, and "Honored by His Townsmen," *New-York Tribune,* June 18, 1896.
29 "Mrs. M'Kinley Cried," *The World* (New York), June 19, 1896; Foraker, *Notes, I,* 488; and Williams, *Realigning America,* 64.
30 James Creelman, "Wild for McKinley," *The World* (New York), June 19, 1896; "Its Duty Is Done" and "Name A Good Ticket" in *Chicago Tribune,* June 19, 1896; and *Eleventh Republican National Convention,* 128–29.
31 *Eleventh Republican National Convention,* 130–31.
32 "Sizing Up the 'Bar'ls,'" *New York Times,* June 12, 1896; "Fight for Second Place," *New-York Tribune,* June 18, 1896; "Morton's Ultimatum," *St. Louis Post-Dispatch,* June 18, 1896; and "No Surprise to Gov. Morton," *New-York Tribune,* June 19, 1896.
33 "Hobart in the Race," *New York Times,* June 16, 1896; "Turn Down for Platt," *Chicago Tribune,* June 18, 1896; "Hobart's Prospects Bright," *New-York Tribune,* June 18, 1896; diary entry for June 16, 1896, in Dawes, *Journal,* 86; and Jones, *Election of 1896,* 176.

34 "Working for Bulkeley," *New York Times*, June 16, 1896; "Fight for Second Place," *New-York Tribune*, June 18, 1896; "Southern Delegates Talk Evans," *Chicago Tribune*, June 18, 1896; "Its Duty Is Done," *Chicago Tribune*, June 19, 1896; and *Eleventh Republican National Convention*, 132–39.

35 "How Hobart Heard of It," *Chicago Tribune*, June 18, 1896.

36 "Congratulate the Boss," *New York Times*, June 19, 1896, and Mott, *Herrick*, 61–62.

37 "M'Kinley and Hobart Named," *New-York Tribune*, June 19, 1896.

38 J. H. Gallinger to Charles Marseilles, May 30, 1896, in Gallinger papers, and Croly, *Hanna*, 184.

39 "Canton Preparing to Celebrate," *New-York Tribune*, June 17, 1896; "Honored by His Townsmen," *New-York Tribune*, June 18, 1896; "McKinley's Plans," *The World* (New York), June 19, 1896; and "Canton Was Happy," *St. Louis Post-Dispatch*, June 19, 1896.

40 "Honored by His Townsmen," *New-York Tribune*, June 19, 1896, and Smith, *McKinley, the People's Choice*, 13.

41 Diary entry for June 18, 1896, in Summers, *Cabinet Diary*, 104.

42 "Silver Men Walk Out," *New York Times*, June 19, 1896.

43 "Mark Hanna in Full Sway," *St. Louis Post-Dispatch*, June 19, 1896; "Hanna At the Helm," *Chicago Tribune*, June 20, 1896; "Going Home in Disgust" and "New Boss Hanna Slept Late" in *St. Louis Post-Dispatch*, June 19, 1896; "Mike DeYoung Shot," *New York Times*, Nov. 20, 1884; and "Spreckels [née de Bretteville], Alma Emma," Christopher Craig, *Encyclopedia of San Francisco*, http://www.sfhistoryencyclopedia.com/articles/biography/spreckelsAlma.html.

44 "Hanna At the Helm," *Chicago Tribune*, June 20, 1896.

45 "Hanna on His Journey Homeward," *Chicago Tribune*, June 20, 1896; "Campaign Work," *Evening Star* (Washington, D.C.), June 22, 1896; and Rhodes, *McKinley and Roosevelt Administrations*, 17.

CHAPTER 19: REPUBLICANS' SHAKY START

1 "M'Kinley Meets Hanna," *Los Angeles Times*, June 23, 1896, and "Mr. Hanna Visits Canton," *New-York Tribune*, June 23, 1896.

2 "Women Greet McKinley," *New-York Tribune*, June 27, 1896; "The Women," *Los Angeles Times*, June 27, 1896; and "Woman's Day At Canton" and ""McKinley Talks on Live Topics" in *Chicago Tribune*, June 27, 1896.

3 Hanna to Matthew Quay, July 2, 3, and 6, 1896, and McKinley to Matthew Quay, July 7, 1896, in Quay papers.

4 Diary entries for June 26 and July 7, 1896, Dawes, *Journal*, 87–88.

5 "Hanna At the Helm," *Chicago Tribune*, June 20, 1896; "Arrangements for the Notification," *New-York Tribune*, June 25, 1896; and "Mr. Hanna Visits Canton," *New-York Tribune*, June 23, 1896.

6 "Hanna A Great Hero," *The World* (New York), June 22, 1896; "Mr. Hanna Visits Canton," *New-York Tribune*, June 23, 1896; "Hanna Meets M'Kinley," *New York Times*, June 23, 1896; and "The Week," *The Nation*, July 2, 1896.

7 "First Mention of Money," *Austin Daily Statesman*, June 23, 1896; "A New Focus," *Los Angeles Times*, June 23, 1896; Frederick W. Holls to Hanna, June 27, 1896, in Holls papers; and Glad, *McKinley, Bryan and the People*, 183.

8 Olcott, *Life of McKinley*, 1, 321.

9 "Bryan on the Issue," *St. Louis Post-Dispatch*, June 19, 1896; "Altgeld on the St. Louis Racket," *Chicago News*, June 20, 1896; and "Altgeld on the Convention," *Boston Evening Transcript*, June 20, 1896.

10 "Teller for President," *New York Times*, June 19, 1896, and "The Silver Men's Address," "Teller Finds His People True," and "Silver Men Have Bolted" in *St. Louis Post-Dispatch*, June 19, 1896.

11 "Silver Must Have A Chance," *World-Herald* (Omaha, NE), June 20, 1896; "The Silver Men's Address," *St. Louis Post-Dispatch*, June 18, 1896; "One Democrat for Teller" and "Smith of Alabama" *St. Louis Post-Dispatch*, June 19, 1896; "A Rich Man's Ticket," *The Denver Times*, June 19, 1896; and "A Political Crisis," *Fort Worth Gazette*, June 20, 1896.

12 "Teller Wanted by Populists," "Claims Made for Teller," and "Populist View of H. M. Teller" in *St. Louis Post-Dispatch*, June 20, 1896; "Wail of the Populists," *New York Times*, June 22, 1896; and "Union Ticket," *Evening Star* (Washington, D.C.), June 22, 1896.

13 "Silver's Chance," *St. Louis Post-Dispatch*, June 20, 1896.

14 "To Transform Major M'Kinley," *New-York Tribune*, June 28, 1896.

15 "Where M'Kinley Stands," *New-York Tribune*, June 30, 1896; "A Party Call," *Los Angeles Times*, June 30, 1896; and "Runs Up His Flag," *Chicago Tribune*, June 30, 1896.

16 "A Party Call," *Los Angeles Times*, June 30, 1896.

17 "Side by Side," "Hobart Visits M'Kinley," and "Mr. M'Kinley May Be There" in *New-York Tribune*, July 2, 1896; "Side by Side" and "His Busy Day" in *Los Angeles Times*, July 2, 1896; "Mr. Hobart Home Again," *New York Tribune*, July 3, 1896; "Hobart Visits M'Kinley," *Chicago Tribune*, July 2, 1896; and R. Graham Ford to R. C. Kerens, June 30, 1896, in McKinley papers.

18 "M'Kinley Seeks A Rest," *Chicago Tribune*, July 1, 1896.

19 "A Revolt in Minnesota," *New York Times*, July 3, 1896; "Here Is Another Bad Leak," *World-Herald* (Omaha, NE), July 3, 1896; and "Silver Or Slavery," *Duluth News-Tribune*, July 3, 1896.

20 "Agree on a Committee," *Chicago Tribune*, July 3, 1896.

21 "Kansas May Be Lost," *New York Times*, July 2, 1896, and William Allen White, *Masks in a Pageant* (New York: Macmillan, 1928), 288.

22 "Chief Arthur Praises M'Kinley," *New-York Tribune*, July 3, 1896; "M'Kinley to Workingmen," *New-York Tribune*, July 4, 1896; "Tariff Talk At Canton," *New York Times*, July 4, 1896; "Chairman Hanna," *Los Angeles Times*, July 4, 1896; "His Friends," *Los Angeles Times*, July 4, 1896; Hanna to Matthew Quay, July 3, 1896, in Quay papers; and Rhodes, *McKinley and Roosevelt Administrations*, 17.

23 *New-York Tribune*, July 21, 1896; "Harrison's Message to Hanna on the Money Question," *St. Louis Republic*, July 27, 1896; McKinley to Foraker, July 6, 1896, in McKinley papers; Hanna to Harrison, July 8, 1896, and Harrison to Hanna, July 10, 1896, in Harrison papers; and Rhodes, *McKinley and Roosevelt Administrations*, 17.

24 "Agree on A Committee," *Chicago Tribune*, July 3, 1896; "Hanna's Executive Committee," *Chicago Tribune*, July 8, 1896; "To Call on Mr. Hobart," *New-York Tribune*, July 7, 1896; "Will Switch Off and Pitch In," *Los Angeles Times*, July 8, 1896; "Mr. Hobart Informed," *New-York Tribune*, July 8, 1896; and "To Map Out the Campaign," *New-York Tribune*, July 9, 1896.

25 "Chat About Prominent Men," *New-York Tribune*, July 6, 1896.

CHAPTER 20: THE SILVER EDGE

1 "Ohio Stands by McLean," *Chicago Tribune*, June 25, 1896; "The Democratic Platform," *The Daily Democrat*, June 29, 1896

2 Josephus Daniels, *Editor in Politics* (Westport, CT: Praeger Publishing, 1974), 157.

3 "Great Enthusiasm for Bland," *Washington Post*, June 18, 1896; "Arkansas Democratic Ticket," *Chicago Tribune*, June 18, 1896; and "Arkansas Democrats for Silver," *Chicago Tribune*, June 20, 1896.

4 "Sweep for Silver," *The World* (New York), June 23, 1896.

5 "Mr. Whitney's Statement," *New York Times*, June 22, 1896, and "Mr. Whitney and His Party" and "Mr. Whitney's Appeal" in *New-York Tribune*, June 23, 1896;

6 "Mr. Whitney's Manifesto to Democrats," *Chicago Tribune*, June 23, 1896, and "Mr. Whitney's Statement," *Washington Post*, June 23, 1896.

7 "Mr. Whitney's Statement," *New York Times*, June 22, 1896.

8 "New York's Keynote," *The World* (New York), June 25, 1896, and Hirsch, *Whitney*, 492–494.

9 "Tillman Talks to Gotham," *Austin Statesman*, June 26, 1896; "Free Silver Their Cry," *New York Times*, June 26, 1896; and "Tillman in New York," *Washington Post*, June 26, 1986.

10 "A Unique Convention," *Los Angeles Times*, June 23, 1896; "Machine Grabs It All," *Chicago Tribune*, June 23, 1896; "Free Silver Furies," *The World* (New York), June 24, 1896; "Rant, Cant, and Rubbish," *New York Times*, June 24, 1896; "Democrats Divided," *Baltimore Sun*, June 24, 1896; 'For Anarchy," *Los Angeles Times*, June 24, 1896; and Barnard, *Forgotten Eagle*, 375.

11 "To the Field of Battle," *The World* (New York), July 2, 1896, and "Sound Money Men Start West," *New York Times*, July 3, 1896.

12 [Untitled], *New York Times*, July 29, 1895; " 'Dick' Bland Here," *St. Louis Republic*, Oct. 21, 1895; "One to Hear Mr. Bland," *The Sun* (Baltimore), Nov. 29, 1895; [Untitled], *Columbus Daily Enquirer* (Columbus, GA), Dec. 8, 1895; "Altgeld's Illinois Machine Wants An Extreme Silver Man" and "Silver Men for Boies" in *New York Times*, June 8, 1896; "Indorsed 'Silver Dick' Bland," *Washington Post*, June 17, 1896; "The Bland Boom," *Evening Star* (Washington, D.C.), June 20, 1896; and "Mississippi Not for Teller," *New York Times*, July 1, 1896.

13   "Bland Makes the Issue Clear," *The World* (New York), July 1, 1896.

14   "Silver Men for Boies," *New York Times*, June 8, 1896; "Alabama Democrats Would Name the Free-Silver Bankers," *New York Times*, June 8, 1896; "Boies's Geographical Position Will Make Him a Favorite," *New York Times*, June 8, 1896; and "Stevenson or Boies," *New York Times*, June 8, 1896.

15   "Skirmishing Has Commenced," *Atlanta Constitution*, July 2, 1896, and Simkins, *Pitchfork Ben Tillman*, 332–33.

16   "M'Lean for President," *Washington Post*, June 25, 1896; "Silver Was the Keynote," *Austin Statesman*, June 25, 1896; and Bryan, *First Battle*, 162–63.

17   "Gag Law for Hoosiers," *Chicago Tribune*," June 25, 1896; "Mr. Bynum Protests," *Washington Post*, June 25, 1896; "Convention Proceedings," *Austin Statesman*, June 25, 1896; "The Proceedings," *Los Angeles Times*, June 25, 1896; and Appleton, *Annual Cyclopaedia* (1897), 353.

18   Altgeld Holds the Key," *Chicago Record*, June 23, 1896; "Altgeld on Top in Illinois," *New-York Tribune*, June 23, 1896; "A Talk With Teller" and "Silver Forces Are on Hand" in *Atlanta Constitution*, July 1, 1896; "Silver Men on Hand Early," *World-Herald* (Omaha, NE), July 1, 1896; "A Bland-Altgeld Alliance," *New York Times*, July 1, 1896; "Taubeneck Has A Word," *World-Herald* (Omaha, NE), July 2, 1896; "Populists Not for Bland," *New York Times*, July 2, 1896; "No Silver Man Can Win," *Chicago Tribune*, July 2, 1896; "Senator Teller's Merit Fully Recognized" and "The Day At Greeley" in *Denver Post*, July 2, 1896; "He Is Treated Like A King," *World-Herald* (Omaha, NE), July 2, 1896; and Ellis, *Teller*, 263–64 and 268–71.

19   Robert W. Cherny, A *Righteous Cause: The Life of William Jennings Bryan* (Norman, OK: Oklahoma City Press, 1994), 49, and Paulo E. Coletta, *William Jennings Bryan: Political Evangelist, 1860–1908* (Lincoln, NE: University of Nebraska Press, 1964), 100–101.

20   *World-Herald* (Omaha, NE), April 26, 1895; "Ingalls and Bryan on Silver," *Washington Post*, May 4, 1895; "Bryan Replies to Carlisle," *Chicago Tribune*, May 25, 1895; "Bryan At Jackson," *Los Angeles Times*, May 26, 1895; "Bryan in Missouri," *World-Herald* (Omaha, NE), May 29, 1895; "Favors Bland for President," *Inter Ocean* (Chicago), May 17, 1895; Koenig, *Bryan*, 156; and Coletta, *Political Evangelist*, 104.

21   "Bryan Must Have Been a Bolter," *Chicago Daily Tribune*, July 18, 1896, and Coletta, *Political Evangelist*, 105.

22   "Bryan at Fort Worth," *Arkansas Gazette* (Little Rock), June 29, 1895; "The Silver Speech," *Dallas Morning News*, June 30, 1895; and Rosser, *Crusading Commoner*, 11–15.

23   "Bryan's Illinois Dates," *World-Herald* (Omaha, NE), Oct. 13, 1895; "Hot Campaign Opened," *World-Herald* (Omaha, NE), Oct. 22, 1895; "Eloquent," *Fort Worth* Gazette, Nov. 2, 1896; "Free Silver Day," *Galveston Daily News,* Nov. 2, 1896; "Pointer to All Democrats," *World-Herald* (Omaha, NE), Nov. 5, 1895; "Bryan Talks for Silver," *Kansas City Times*, Nov. 10, 1895; "Invited to Omaha," *World-Herald* (Omaha, NE), Nov. 23, 1895; Koenig, *Bryan*, 166–67; and Charles M. Rosser, *The Crusading Commoner: A Close-Up of William Jennings Bryan and His Times* (Dallas: Mathis, Van Nort & co., 1937), 19–22 and 24–25.

24   "Arkansas Is for Free Silver," *St. Louis Post-Dispatch*, April 19, 1896; Mary Bryan to Bryan, March 19, 1896, in Bryan Papers; Jones, *Election of 1896*, 188; and Rosser, *Crusading Commoner*, 24.

25   W. J. Bryan, "The Philosophy of Bolting," *World-Herald* (Omaha, NE), Feb 24, 1896; B. Lundy Kent to Bryan, Feb. 29, 1896; Charles S. Thomas to Bryan, April 13, 1896; Josephus Daniels to Bryan, April 30, 1896; E. W. Carmack to Bryan, May 4, 1896; M.A. Miller to Bryan, April 20, 1896; H. H. Seldomridge to Bryan, April 18, 1896; and J. J. Hallett to Bryan, April 20, 1896 (Colorado) in Bryan Papers. Also Koenig, *Bryan*, 166–67; Coletta, *Political Evangelist*, 113; and Cherny, *Righteous Cause*, 55.

26   Bryan to M. A. Miller, April 23, 1896; T. O. Towles to Bryan, April 9, 1896; and Josephus Daniels to Bryan, April 30, May 6, and May 9, 1896, in Bryan papers.

27   "Bryan of the Nineties," *Harper's Weekly*, Oct. 11, 1913, 6–7; C. P. Thomas to Bryan, April 18, 1896, in Bryan Papers; and Bryan to Charles S. Thomas, April 16, 1896, in Bryan papers.

28   "Boom of Mr. Bland" and "Some Here, Some Absent" in *Chicago Tribune*, July 1, 1896.

29   "Some Here, Some Absent" in *Chicago Tribune*, July 1, 1896; "Boies Is Happy," *World-Herald* (Omaha, NE), July 4, 1896; "Boies Comes Today," "Views of Leading Democrats," and "Bland Asked to Come" in *Chicago Tribune*, July 4, 1896.

30   "Some Here, Some Absent," *Chicago Tribune*, July 1, 1896; "New Thing in Booms," "Big Political Guns Reach Town," and "Views of Leading Democrats" in *Chicago Tribune*, July 2, 1896; and "Permanent Silver Caucus," *World-Herald* (Omaha, NE), July 2, 1896.

31 "How Booms Wax, Wane, Wither," *Chicago Tribune*, July 1, 1896; Koenig, *Bryan*, 169–70; and Barnard, *Forgotten Eagle*, 368.

32 Willis J. Abbot, *Watching the World Roll By* (New York: Little, Brown, 1933), 157–59, and Barnard, *Forgotten Eagle*, 368.

33 "Altgeld Is in Command" in *Chicago Tribune*, July 2, 1896; "Skirmishing Has Commenced," *Atlanta Constitution*, July 2, 1896; "Gold Men Defiant" and "First Clash of Gold and Silver" in *The World* (New York), July 2, 1896; and "Silver to Bow Or Bolt," "A Precedent From Iowa," and "Views of Leading Democrats" in *Chicago Tribune*, July 2, 1896.

34 "Fix It in Advance," *Chicago Tribune*, July 2, 1896, and "A Deadlock Likely Unless," *The World* (New York), July 2, 1896.

35 "Some Here, Some Absent," *Chicago Tribune*, July 1, 1896; "There Was No Enthusiasm" and "Arrival of the Left" in *Atlanta Constitution*, July 4, 1896; "Whitney's Crowd Arrives," *World-Herald* (Omaha, NE), July 4, 1896; and Hirsch, *Whitney*, 497.

36 "Gold Men At Chicago," *New York Times*, July 4, 1896; Nevins, *Study in Courage*, 699–700; and Hirsch, *Whitney*, 497–99.

37 "Gold Men Will Bolt," *Chicago Tribune*, July 4, 1896; "Gold Fight Begun," *The World* (New York), July 4, 1896; "Gold Men At Chicago," *New York Times*, July 4, 1896; "Gold Men Caucus," *Atlanta Constitution*, July 4, 1896; and Hirsch, *Whitney*, 498.

38 "Illinois Is for Bland," *Chicago Tribune*, July 5, 1896, and "Scramble for Office," *New York Times*, July 5, 1896.

39 "Tammany Hall's Great Day," *World-Herald* (Omaha, NE), July 5, 1896; "Cleveland's Friend Speaks," *The World* (New York), July 5, 1896; and "Democratic National Convention: Events of Yesterday," *Chicago Tribune*, July 5, 1896.

40 "Gold Men's Policy," *The World* (New York), July 5, 1896; "Hope of the Gold Men," *Chicago Tribune*, July 5, 1896; and Hirsch, *Whitney*, 500–501.

41 "A Party Led by Fools," *New York Times*, July 5, 1896.

42 "Big Rally for Gold," *Chicago Tribune*, July 5, 1896; "A Sound Money Rally," *New York Times*, July 5, 1896; "Gold Bugs Talk It All Over" and "Suggest No Remedy" in *World-Herald* (Omaha, NE), July 5, 1896; and Hirsch, *Whitney*, 495.

43 "Harrity Faces A Crisis," *Chicago Tribune*, July 6, 1896, and "Regular Hurdle Race," *Los Angeles Times*, July 6, 1896.

44 "Gold Men in Conference," *New York Times*, July 6, 1896, and "Hill for the Chair," *Washington Post*, July 6, 1896.

45 "Is for Senator Daniel," *Chicago Tribune*, July 6, 1896; "Wild and Woolly Western Men" and "A High Fence for 'Em" in *Los Angeles Times*, July 6, 1896; and "Silver Men At War," *The World* (New York), July 6, 1896.

46 "Great Joint Debate At Crete Chautauqua," *World-Herald* (Omaha, NE), July 2, 1896; "At the Crete Chautauqua," *World-Herald* (Omaha, NE), July 5, 1896; "Nebraskans to Boom Bryan," *New York Times*, July 6, 1896; "He Had Long Contemplated It," *Los Angeles Times*, July 11, 1896; William J. Bryan and Mary Baird Bryan, *Memoirs of William Jennings Bryan, by Himself and His Wife* (Chicago, IL: United Publishers of America, 1925), 103–4, and 107; and *Congressional Record*, 53rd Congress, 3rd Sessions, Appendix (Dec., 22, 1894), 153.

CHAPTER 21: THE LOGIC OF THE SITUATION

1 "Round-Up of the Clans," *Chicago Tribune*, July 7, 1896.

2 "Jewbaiter Is for Bryan," *The Sun* (New York), September 16, 1896.

3 "Hill Wins Over Daniel," *Chicago Tribune*, July 7, 1896; "An Exciting Meeting," *New York Times*, July 7, 1896; "Hill by 4 Majority," *The World* (New York), July 7, 1896; "A Delegate Secedes," *Los Angeles Times*, July 7, 1896; Clark Howell, "How Matters Stand," *Atlanta Constitution*, July 7, 1896; and Democratic Party National Convention, Chicago, 1896, *Official Proceedings of the Democratic National Convention Held in Chicago, IL, July 7, 8, 9, 10, and 11, 1896* (Logansport, IN, 1896), 68a–68b.

4 "Hill Wins Over Daniel," *Chicago Tribune*, July 7, 1896; Clark Howell, "How Matters Stand," *Atlanta Constitution*, July 7, 1896; "National Committee Did As Expected," *Atlanta Constitution*, July 7, 1896; "Seats the Bolters," *World-Herald* (Omaha, NE), July 7, 1896; and *Official Proceedings of the DNC*, 68b.

5   "Hill by 4 Majority," *The World* (New York), July 7, 1896; "Selection of Hill Causing Trouble," *Atlanta Constitution*, July 7, 1896; "Hill Wins Over Daniel," *Chicago Tribune*, July 7, 1896; and *Official Proceedings of the DNC*, 68c.

6   "Silver Men Are Agreed," *Chicago Tribune*, July 7, 1896.

7   Clark Howell, "How Matters Stand," *Atlanta Constitution*, July 7, 1896; "Strength of Leaders," *New York Times*, July 7, 1896; "On the Eve of the Battle," *Los Angeles Times*, July 7, 1896; "Booms, Big and Little," *The World* (New York), July 7, 1896; and "Groping," *Courier Journal* (Louisville, KY), July 7, 1896.

8   Daniels, *Editor in Politics*, 160–61.

9   "A Look Over the Ground," *Atlanta Constitution*, July 7, 1896.

10 "Another Account" and "Democratic Ghost Dance" in *Los Angeles Times*, July 8, 1896; "Field Day From Silver in Chicago Yesterday" and "Selection of Hill Causing Trouble" in *Atlanta Constitution*, July 7, 1896; "Proceedings in Detail," *Washington Post*, July 8, 1896; "Hill Turned Down," *The World* (New York), July 8, 1896; and *Official Proceedings of the DNC*, 70–72.

11 "Marston Tells of A Mistake," *Chicago Tribune*, July 8, 1896; "Daniel Was Elected," *Washington Post*, July 8, 1896; "Story Told in Detail," *Atlanta Constitution*, July 8, 1896; "Silver Men Display Their Power" and "The Issue Joined" in *New York Times*, July 8, 1896; John D. Merrill, "First Fight of Convention," *Boston Globe*, July 8, 1896; "Hill Turned Down," *The World* (New York), July 8, 1896; and *Official Proceedings of the DNC*, 80–90. The *Post, Constitution*, and *Globe* mistakenly identified Marston as "Marsden."

12 *Official Proceedings of the DNC*, 93–98. Hill refused to vote for himself.

13 "Story Told in Detail, *Atlanta Constitution*, July 8, 1896; "Proceedings in Detail" and "Daniel Was Elected" in *Washington Post*, July 8, 1896; and "What They Think of It," *Chicago Tribune*, July 6, 1896.

14 "Democratic Ghost Dance," *Los Angeles Times*, July 8, 1896, and *Official Proceedings of the DNC*, 98–108.

15 "Daniel's Effort," *Los Angeles Times*, July 8, 1896, and *Official Proceedings of the DNC*, 108–12.

16 "Silver At 16 to 1," *Chicago Tribune*, July 8, 1896; "Making A Platform," *New York Times*, July 8, 1896; Robert Adamson, "Georgia Is in the Push," *Atlanta Constitution*, July 8, 1896; "Building of A Platform," *Chicago Tribune*, July 9, 1896; and Bryan, *Memoirs*, 108–9.

17 "Convention Proceedings," *St. Louis-Post Dispatch*, July 8, 1896; "A Stolen Triumph," *The World* (New York), July 9, 1896; "A Semblance of Business" and "A Session Devoted to Talk" in *New York Times*, July 9, 1896; "Listened to Oratory," *Washington Post*, July 9, 1896; Bryan, *Memoirs*, 107 and 110; Bryan, *First Battle*, 615; and *Official Proceedings of the DNC*, 113–24.

18 "A Stolen Triumph," *The World* (New York), July 9, 1896; "Altgeld Suggests Hill Be Heard," *Chicago Tribune*, July 9, 1896; "A Semblance of Business," *New York Times*, July 9, 1896; "Listened to Oratory," *Washington Post*, July 9, 1896; Bryan, *Memoirs*, 107 and 110; Bryan, *First Battle*, 615; and *Official Proceedings of the DNC*, 124. White's comment does not appear in the *Official Proceedings of the DNC*. The *Post* has White saying, "Why will you insist on a man who is not here?"

19 "Silver Rides to Win" and "Cream of the Day" in *Chicago Tribune*, July 9, 1896; "Silver Men Seated," *Washington Post*, July 9, 1896; "Altgeld Suggests Hill Be Heard," *Chicago Tribune*, July 9, 1896; and *Official Proceedings of the DNC*, 124–25.

20 "A Stolen Triumph," *The World* (New York), July 9, 1896; "Cream of the Day" in *Chicago Tribune*, July 9, 1896; *Official Proceedings of the DNC*, 127–31; Clarence Darrow, *The Story of My Life* (New York: Da Capo Press, 1996), 90; Altgeld, *Live Questions*, 585–90; and Barnard, *Forgotten Eagle*, 370–71.

21 "A Stolen Triumph" and "Unseated 44 Gold Men" in *The World* (New York), July 9, 1896; "No Quarter Was Given Them," "Contested Seats," and "Weary Waste of Words" in *Los Angeles Times*, July 9, 1896; "Silver Men Seated," *Washington Post*, July 9, 1896; "The First Sensation" and "A Session Devoted to Talk" in *New York Times*, July 9, 1896; "Bryan" and "Cream of the Day" in *Chicago Tribune*, July 9, 1896; Clark Howell, "The Michigan Fraud," *Atlanta Constitution*, July 9, 1896; "Convention Proceedings," *St. Louis-Post Dispatch*, July 8, 1896; and *Official Proceedings of the DNC*, 131–35. Darrow later wrote Bryan "carried the contest to the convention and took the platform to present his claim. In a few moments he had the attention of the great audience of twenty or twenty-five thousand that crowded the hall." Darrow's memory was faulty: Bryan did not address the convention on the Nebraska challenge. See Darrow, *Story of My Life*, 90–91.

22 "Text of the Platform," *The World* (New York), July 8, 1896; "Building of A Platform," "Democratic Planks Adopted by Resolutions Committee," and "An Income Tax Demanded" in *Chicago Tribune*, July 9, 1896; "Congealed Thoughts Here," *Los Angeles Times*, July 9, 1896; "Here's the Platform," *Atlanta Constitution*, July 9, 1896; "The Fight on Resolutions" and "Silver Men's Platform" in *New York Times*, July 9, 1896; "Making the Platform," *The World* (New York), July 9, 1896; and *Official Proceedings of the DNC*, 192–96.

23 Bryan, *Memoirs*, 109–10, and Bryan, *First Battle*, 206.

24 "Senator Tillman Will Talk," *New York Times*, July 9, 1896; Bryan, *Memoirs*, 110–11; and Koenig, *Bryan*, 190.

25 "Credentials," *Los Angeles Times*, July 8, 1896; "How Silver Will Get Two-Thirds," *The World* (New York), July 8, 1896; "Unseated 44 Gold Men," *The World* (New York), July 9, 1896; "Contested Seats," *Los Angeles Times*, July 9, 1896; "Committee on Credentials," *Washington Post*, July 9, 1896; *Official Proceedings of the DNC*, 136–38; and Rosser, *Crusading Commoner*, 19.

26 "A Stolen Triumph" and "Unseated 44 Gold Men," *The World* (New York), July 9, 1896; "No Quarter Was Given Them," "Contested Seats," and "Weary Waste of Words" in *Los Angeles Times*, July 9, 1896; "Silver Men Seated," *Washington Post*, July 9, 1896; and *Official Proceedings of the DNC*, 131–35.

27 "Making A Two-Thirds Majority," *New York Times*, July 9, 1896, and *Official Proceedings of the DNC*, 139–49.

28 *Official Proceedings of the DNC*, 149–57.

29 *Official Proceedings of the DNC*, 162–67.

30 "Silver Rides to Win," *Chicago Tribune*, July 9, 1896; "No Quarter Was Given" and L. E. Mosher, "Night Howls" in *Los Angeles Times*, July 9, 1896; "A Stolen Triumph," *The World* (New York), July 9, 1896; "Silver Men Seated," *Washington Post*, July 9, 1896; Clark Howell, "The Michigan Fraud," *Atlanta Constitution*, July 9, 1896; and *Official Proceedings of the DNC*, 162–67.

31 "Silver Men Seated," *Washington Post*, July 9, 1896.

32 "Bland Leads the Race" and "Office Will Seek Bland" in *The World* (New York), July 9, 1896; "Bland" and "Boies" in *Chicago Tribune*, July 9, 1896; Robert Adamson, "Georgia for Silver Dick," *Atlanta Constitution*, July 9, 1896; and *Official Proceedings of the DNC*, 167–73.

33 Bryan, *Memoirs*, 105–6. Coletta places this incident three days earlier, on July 5, but Bryan writes "I am not sure whether North Carolina had acted then or later in the evening," which would place the meeting with Patterson, Towne, and Hartman sometime in the afternoon or evening of July 8. Coletta, *Political Evangelist*, 124.

34 Rosser, *Crusading Commoner*, 37–38.

CHAPTER 22: CROSS OF GOLD

1 Francis E. Leupp, "Dark Horse Convention," *The Outlook*, 101, 297–302. The men next to Leupp were Henry George and journalist John Russell Young. Young was minister to China under Arthur. McKinley appointed him Librarian of Congress.

2 "Reading of the Platform," *St. Louis Post-Dispatch*, July 9, 1896; "Debate on Platform" and "Bryan in the Field" in *Washington Post*, July 10, 1896; Bryan, *Memoirs*, 112; *Official Proceedings of the DNC*, 192; and Koenig, *Bryan*, 193.

3 "Reading of the Platform," *St. Louis Post-Dispatch*, July 9, 1896; "The Detail Proceedings," *Atlanta Constitution*, July 10, 1896; "Bryan Struck the Chord," *New-York Tribune*, July 10, 1986; "The Debate in Full," *Los Angeles Times*, July 10, 1896; "Bryan Made A Lion," *Chicago Tribune*, July 10, 1896; "Silver Rules," *The Sun* (New York), July 10, 1896; "Tillman Opens the Debate," *New York Times*, July 10, 1896; "Debate on Platform," *Washington Post*, July 10, 1896; "The Convention," *New Orleans Times-Picayune*, July 10, 1896; and *Official Proceedings of the DNC*, 198–209.

4 Robert Adamson, "The Note Sent to Bryan Before He Spoke," *Atlanta Constitution*, July 11, 1896; Bryan, *Memoirs*, 111–12; and Coletta, *Political Evangelist*, 135–36.

5 "Debate on Platform," *Washington Post*, July 10, 1896; "Bryan Made A Lion," *Chicago Tribune*, July 10, 1896; and *Official Proceedings of the DNC*, 209–10.

6 *Official Proceedings of the DNC*, 210–14.

7 "Bryan in the Field," *Washington Post*, July 10, 1896; "Bryan Made A Lion," *Chicago Tribune*, July 10, 1896; "Bryan Struck the Chord," *New-York Tribune*, July 10, 1986; and *Official Proceedings of the DNC*, 214–19.

8 Bryan, *Memoirs*, 112–13, and Koenig, *Bryan*, 194.

9 "Debate on Platform," *Washington Post*, July 10, 1896; "Bryan Made A Lion," *Chicago Tribune*, July 10, 1896; "William Eustis Russell," *New York Times*, July 17, 1896; Daniels, *Editor in Politics*, 163; and *Official Proceedings of the DNC*, 224–26.

10 "The Debate in Full," *Los Angeles Times*, July 10, 1896; "Bryan Made A Lion" and " 'Boy Orator' Scores A Big Hit" in *Chicago Tribune*, July 10, 1896; "Bryan's Bid for First Place," *New York Times*, July 10, 1896; Koenig, *Bryan*, 195; "Bryan Struck the Chord," *New-York Tribune*, July 10, 1986; and *Official Proceedings of the DNC*, 226.

11 Francis E. Leupp, "Dark Horse Convention," *The Outlook*, 101, June 8, 1912, 297–302; *Official Proceedings of the DNC*, 226–27 and Daniels, *Editor in Politics*, 163–64.

12 "Silver Rules," *The Sun* (New York), July 10, 1896; "Bryan's Bid for First Place," *New York Times*, July 10, 1896; Robert Adamson, "Never to Be Forgotten" and Edward W. Barnett, "Bryan Receives An Ovation," in *Atlanta Constitution*, July 10, 1896; Bryan, *Memoirs*, 115; and Koenig, *Bryan*, 196. Koenig mistakenly identifies James as a Congressman, but he was not elected from Kentucky's 1st District until 1902.

13 *Official Proceedings of the DNC*, 227–28.

14 " 'Boy Orator' Scores A Big Hit" and "Bryan Made A Lion" in *Chicago Tribune*, July 10, 1896; Rosser, *Crusading Commoner*, 48–49; and *Official Proceedings of the DNC*, 228–29.

15 " 'Boy Orator' Scores A Big Hit," *Chicago Tribune*, July 10, 1896; "Debate on Platform," *Washington Post*, July 10, 1896; and *Official Proceedings of the DNC*, 229–31.

16 "Bryan Made A Lion," *Chicago Tribune*, July 10, 1896; "Debate on Platform," *Washington Post*, July 10, 1896; and *Official Proceedings of the DNC*, 231–32.

17 *Official Proceedings of the DNC*, 232–33.

18 *Official Proceedings of the DNC*, 233–34.

19 Francis E. Leupp, "Dark Horse Convention," *The Outlook*, 101, June 8, 1912, 297–302; "The Platform Adopted," *New-York Tribune*, July 10, 1896; "Words That Thrilled," *Atlanta Constitution*, July 11, 1896; and *Official Proceedings of the DNC*, 234.

20 "The Debate in Full" and "Democracy Is Ruptured" in *Los Angeles Times*, July 10, 1896; L. E. Mosher, "Put the Party on Record," *Los Angeles Times*, July 10, 1896; and Daniels, *Editor in Politics*, 164.

21 "Bryan Struck the Chord," *New-York Tribune*, July 10, 1986; "The Detail Proceedings," *Atlanta Constitution*, July 10, 1896; "Bryan Made A Lion," *Chicago Tribune*, July 10, 1896; "The Debate in Full" and "Put the Party on Record" in *Los Angeles Times*, July 10, 1896; Robert Adamson, "Never to Be Forgotten," *Atlanta Constitution*, July 10, 1896; Edward W. Barnett, "Bryan Receives An Ovation," *Atlanta Constitution*, July 10, 1896; and "The Great Platform Fight," *The Sun* (New York), July 10, 1896. Barnett says the first standard to appear was North Carolina's. Others say it was Tennessee's, but most reports say Texas.

22 "Bryan the Silver Idol," *New Orleans Times-Picayune*, July 10, 1896; "Put the Party on Record" and "Democracy Is Ruptured" in *Los Angeles Times*, July 10, 1896; " 'Boy Orator' Scores A Big Hit" and "Bryan Made A Lion" in *Chicago Tribune*, July 10, 1896; "The Noisy Georgians," *Atlanta Constitution*, July 10, 1896; James Creelman, "A Bryan Cyclone!," *The World* (New York), July 10, 1896; and "The Convention," *New Orleans Times Picayune*, July 10, 1896.

23 Darrow, *Story of My Life*, 91, and Koenig, *Bryan*, 199.

24 Bryan, *Memoirs*, 113–14.

25 Williams, *Realigning America*, 102; William D. Harpine, *From the Front Porch to Front Page: McKinley and Bryan in the 1896 Presidential Election* (College Station, TX: Texas A&M University Press, 2006), 56–68; and Harpine, "Bryan's 'A Cross of Gold': The Rhetoric of Polarization at the 1896 Democratic Convention," *Quarterly Journal of Speech 87* (August 2001), 296–98.

26 Edward W. Barnett, "Bryan Receives An Ovation," *Atlanta Constitution*, July 10, 1896; Robert Adamson, "The Georgians Led the Van," *Atlanta Constitution*, July 10, 1896; "Lebanon Gets A Chill," *Chicago Tribune*, July 10, 1896; and "No Nomination Made," *Washington Post*, July 10, 1896.

27 "Bryan Awaits His Fate," *Chicago Tribune*, July 11, 1896.

28 "The Detail Proceedings," *Atlanta Constitution*, July 10, 1896; "Bryan Made A Lion," *Chicago Tribune*, July 10, 1896; and *Official Proceedings of the DNC*, 235–41. The Gold states were Connecticut, Minnesota, New Hampshire, New Jersey, New York, Pennsylvania, Rhode Island, South Dakota, Vermont, Wisconsin, and Alaska with most of Delaware, Maine, Maryland, and Massachusetts.

29   "Named for the Contest," *Chicago Tribune*, July 10, 1896; "Naming the Big Runners" and "The Uproar" in *Los Angeles Times*, July 10, 1896; "Convention At Work on Ticket" and "Crush At the Night Session" in *New York Times*, July 10, 1896; "Ready to Vote," *The Sun* (New York), July 10, 1896; "The Night Session," *New Orleans Times Picayune*, July 10, 1896; and *Official Proceedings of the DNC*, 241–50.

30   "No Nomination Made," *Washington Post*, July 10, 1896; "The Night Session," *Atlanta Constitution*, July 10, 1896; "The Uproar," *Los Angeles Times*, July 10, 1896; "Named for the Contest," *Chicago Tribune*, July 10, 1896; "Convention At Work on Ticket" and "The Standard Bearer Not Yet Named" in *New York Times*, July 10, 1896; "Ready to Vote," *The Sun* (New York), July 10, 1896; "The Night Session," *New Orleans Times Picayune*, July 10, 1896; and *Official Proceedings of the DNC*, 257–65.

31   *Official Proceedings of the DNC*, 265–266; "The Night Session," *Atlanta Constitution*, July 10, 1896; Robert Adamson, "Bryan Nominated by Hon. Hal Lewis" and "The Georgians Led the Van" in *Atlanta Constitution*, July 10, 1896; "Bryan Takes It Easily" and "The First Word for Bryan" in *New York Times*, July 10, 1896; "Named for the Contest," *Chicago Tribune*, July 10, 1896; and "The Night Session," *New Orleans Times Picayune*, July 10, 1896.

32   "The Night Session," *Atlanta Constitution*, July 10, 1896; "No Nomination Made," *Washington Post*, July 10, 1896; "Turpie Names Matthews," *New York Times*, July 10, 1896; and *Official Proceedings of the DNC*, 266–83.

33   "The Night Session" and "Naming Men for the Race," *Atlanta Constitution*, July 10, 1896; "No Nomination Made," *Washington Post*, July 10, 1896; "Ex-Gov. Boies of Iowa" and "The Uproar" in *Los Angeles Times*, July 10, 1896; and "Boies's Turn Next," *New York Times*, July 10, 1896.

34   "Bryan for One Term Only," *The Sun* (New York), July 11, 1896.

35   "A Speech for Blackburn," *New York Times*, July 10, 1896; "Ex-Gov. Boies of Iowa," *Los Angeles Times*, July 10, 1896; "Ready to Vote," *The Sun* (New York), July 10, 1896; and *Official Proceedings of the DNC*, 283–87 and 289–95.

36   "Named for the Contest," *Chicago Tribune*, July 10, 1896; and *Official Proceedings of the DNC*, 187–289 and 295–96. The *Proceedings* sanitized Edward S. Bragg's statement to read "Wisconsin cannot participate in nominating a Democrat to stand upon the platform" and shortened his other comments to reduce the sarcasm.

37   "Mr. Bland's Busy Day," *The World* (New York), July 10, 1896; "He Claims It for Bland," *Chicago Tribune*, July 10, 1896; and Byars, *American Commoner*, 296.

38   "Bryan Takes It Easily," *Chicago Tribune*, July 10, 1896; Daniels, *Editor in Politics*, 165; Barr, *Reconstruction to Reform*, 165; and Koenig, *Bryan*, 200.

39   "The Nomination of Mr. Bryan," *New York Times*, July 11, 1896; "Call on Presidential Nomination" and "Rise of Bryan's Sun" in *Chicago Tribune*, July 11, 1896; and "Convention Live Topics," *The Sun* (New York), July 11, 1896.

40   *Official Proceedings of the DNC*, 298–99.

41   "Wild At Bryant Home," *Chicago Tribune*, July 11, 1896.

42   "Bryan Nominated" and "The Fizzle of Tillman" in *The Sun* (New York), July 11, 1896; "Call on Presidential Nomination," *Chicago Tribune*, July 11, 1896; "Captured by Bryan," *Washington Post*, July 11, 1896; "Missouri Did It," *The World* (New York), July 11, 1896; and *Official Proceedings of the DNC*, 299–303 and 312–16.

43   "Bryan Is the Nominee," *World-Herald* (Omaha, NE), July 10, 1896; "The Third Ballot," *New York Times*, July 11, 1896; "Lebanon At Last Aroused," *St. Louis Post-Dispatch*, July 10, 1896; and *Official Proceedings of the DNC*, 318–19.

44   Robert Adamson, "The Georgians Led the Van," *Atlanta Constitution*, July 10, 1896; "Bryan Is the Nominee," *World-Herald* (Omaha, NE), July 10, 1896; "Rise of Bryan's Sun" and "Bland Happy in Defeat" in *Chicago Tribune*, July 11, 1896; "Sudden Rise to Fame," *Washington Post*, July 11, 1896; E. W. Barrett, "A Good Man Chosen," *Atlanta Constitution*, July 10, 1896; *Official Proceedings of the DNC*, 320–21; and Koenig, *Bryan*, 202.

45   "Bryan Nominated," *The Sun* (New York), July 11, 1896; "Fifth and Deciding Ballot," "Bryan Wins," and "Rise of Bryan's Sun" in *Chicago Tribune*, July 11, 1896; "Bryan Is the Nominee," *World-Herald* (Omaha, NE), July 10, 1896; L. E. Mosher, "Buncoed by Billy Bryan," *Los Angeles Times*, July 11, 1896; and *Official Proceedings of the DNC*, 322–24.

46   "Bryan Nominated," *The Sun* (New York), July 11, 1896; "Captured by Bryan," *Chicago Tribune*, July 11, 1896; "Mr. Bland's Withdrawal" *Washington Post*, July 11, 1896; and *Official Proceedings of the DNC*, 323–24.

47 Robert Adamson, "The Georgians Led the Van," *Atlanta Constitution*, July 11, 1896; "Captured by Bryan," *Washington Post*, July 11, 1896; and "Howls for Nebraskans," *Chicago Tribune*, July 11, 1896.

48 "Sudden Rise to Fame," *Washington Post*, July 11, 1896; "Bryan Is Duly Modest," *New York Times*, July 11, 1896; "Bryan for One Term Only," *The Sun* (New York), July 11, 1896; "Bryan Awaits His Fate," *Chicago Tribune*, July 11, 1896; and "Sketch of the Proceedings," *Los Angeles Times*, July 11, 1896.

CHAPTER 23: CHANGE COURSE OR FAIL

1 "Bryan Will Be An Easy Victim," *Chicago Tribune*, July 11, 1896; "M'Kinley Gets the News," *The Sun* (New York), July 11, 1896; and "M'Kinley is Pleased," *Chicago Times-Herald*, July 11, 1896.

2 "M'Kinley's Rallying Cry," *New-York Tribune*, July 12, 1896.

3 "Hanna Satisfied," *Plain Dealer* (Cleveland, OH), July 12, 1896.

4 "Hanna's Own Aids," *The World* (New York), June 25, 1896, and "Named by Chairman Hanna," *New-York Tribune*, July 14, 1896.

5 "It Turns to Chicago," *Chicago Tribune*, July 15, 1896

6 "In New-York and Chicago," *New-York Tribune*, July 16, 1896; "To Work From Chicago," *Chicago Tribune*, July 16, 1896; "New-York and Chicago," *New York Times*, July 16, 1896; and "To Begin Work At Once," *Chicago Tribune*, July 17, 1896.

7 "To Work From Chicago," *Chicago Tribune*, July 16, 1896; Morrow, Interview with Charles Dick, February 10, 1904, 15–16; and Dawes, *Journal*, insert between 88 and 89. Charles Dick, named secretary of the Chicago office, later claimed to have been in charge of the Chicago headquarters, saying, "The details of the organization at the Chicago headquarters were upon me." This is inaccurate. He admits he did not arrive in the city until August 11, twenty-two days after Dawes began work and well after the headquarters was staffed up and operating. And in the official photo of the Chicago staff, Hanna is the center and Dawes occupies a higher slot than does Dick.

8 Dawes to Hanna, July 23, 24, and 25, 1896, McKinley to Dawes, July 30, 1896, and Diary entries for July 16–18, 19–20 and 23, 1896, in Dawes, *Journal*, 89–91.

9 Dawes to Osborne, Aug. 1, 1896, and Dawes to McKinley, Aug. 1, 1896, in Dawes papers.

10 "College Men for M'Kinley Line," *New-York Tribune*, July 26, 1896; "College Men in Line," *Chicago Tribune*, July 27, 1896; "Get Ready for Hanna," *Chicago Tribune*, July 29, 1896; Dawes to Hanna, July 23, 1896; and American College Republican League to Dawes, undated, in Dawes papers.

11 Dawes to McKinley, Aug. 1, 1896, in Dawes papers.

12 W. S. Lloyd, "Why Not Coxey," *Plain Dealer* (Cleveland, OH), July 11, 1896; M'Kinley to Set A Pace," *Chicago Tribune*, July 28, 1896; and Rhodes, *McKinley and Roosevelt Administrations*, 26–27.

13 "M'Kinley Gets the News," *The Sun* (New York), July 11, 1896; "M'Kinley Will Visit Kansas," *Washington Post*, July 18, 1896; "M'Kinley to Stay Home," *Washington Post*, July 22, 1896; "Mr. McKinley to Speak Only in Ohio," *New York Times*, July 26, 1896; "The Campaign," *Los Angeles Times*, July 28, 1896; "M'Kinley Talks of Bryan," *The World* (New York), July 22, 1896; Mott, *Herrick*, 64; and Timmons, *Portrait of an American*, 56.

14 "Women Praise M'Kinley," *New-York Tribune*, July 16, 1896; "Comrades," *Los Angeles Times*, July 16, 1896; "To His Old Comrades," *New-York Tribune*, July 17, 1896; and "Call to Old Soldiers," *Washington Post*, July 17, 1896.

15 "Toilers Visit Canton," *Washington Post*, July 26, 1896, and "Call From Chicago," *Chicago Tribune*, July 30, 1896. Ickes was the father of Harold L. Ickes Jr., President Bill Clinton's Deputy Chief of Staff.

16 "Tariff to the Fore," *Chicago Tribune*, July 31, 1896, and "The Debt to the Veterans," *New-York Tribune*, Aug. 1, 1896.

17 "In Praise of Education," *Chicago Tribune*, July 24, 1896; "M'Kinley to Workingmen," *New-York Tribune*, July 24, 1896.

18 "Will Stick to Canton," *New York Times*, July 29, 1896.

19 Eugene Hale to William E. Chandler, July 16, 1896, in Chandler papers.

20 "M'Kinley to Set A Pace," *Chicago Tribune*, July 28, 1896; A. E. Woodward to Dawes, July 15, 1896, C. A. Atkinson to Dawes, July 12, 1896, Frank R. Stewart to Dawes, Aug. 19, 1896, and H. G. McMillan to A. B. Cummins, Aug. 20, 1896, in Dawes papers; and Williams, *Realigning America*, 139.

21   Rhodes, *McKinley and Roosevelt Administrations*, 18–19.
22   "To Confer in New York," *Chicago Tribune*, July 25, 1896; "Maj. M'Kinley in Cleveland," *Washington Post*, July 28, 1896; and "Talked of New-York Matters," *New-York Tribune*, July 28, 1896.
23   "No Dodging," *Los Angeles Times*, July 29, 1896; "Chairman Hanna Here," *New-York Tribune*, July 29, 1896; and "Mr. Hanna Is With Us," *The World* (New York), July 29, 1896.
24   "No Dodging," *Los Angeles Times*, July 29, 1896; "Mr. Hanna in This City," *New York Times*, July 29, 1896; and "Hanna in the Field," *Chicago Tribune*, July 29, 1896.
25   "Chairman Hanna Here," *New-York Tribune*, July 29, 1896.
26   "Mr. Hanna in This City," *New York Times*, July 29, 1896; Roosevelt to Lodge, July 29, 1896, *Correspondence I*, 225–26; and Roosevelt to Platt, July 29, 1896, in Platt papers.
27   "Hanna Summons Platt," *The Sun* (New York), Aug. 1, 1896, and "Are to Meet At Last," *New York Times*, Aug. 1, 1896.
28   "Hanna and Platt Meet," *New York Times*, Aug. 2, 1896; "Work of Chairman Hanna," *New-York Tribune*, Aug. 2, 1896; "Hanna and Platt Confer," *World-Herald* (Omaha, NE), Aug. 2, 1896; and "Good News, *Los Angeles Times*, Aug. 3, 1896
29   Platt to Morton, Aug. 4, 1896, in Morton Papers and Gosnell, *Boss Platt*, 53.
30   "Hanna Sleeps At Ophir," *The Sun* (New York), July 31, 1896; Dawes to Hanna, July 30, 1896, in Dawes Papers; and Osborne to McKinley, Aug. 11, 1896, in McKinley Papers.
31   "Mr. Hanna Goes Home," *Washington Post*, Aug. 7, 1896; "Mr. Hanna Goes West" and "A Consultation in Philadelphia" in *New-York Tribune*, Aug. 7, 1896; "Doing Good Work," *Los Angeles Times*, Aug. 8, 1896; and Dawes to Hanna, Aug. 6, 1896, in Dawes papers.
32   "Hanna Not Talking About Platt," *New-York Tribune*, Aug. 8, 1896.
33   "The Bolting Senators," *Chicago Tribune*, July 14, 1896; "Teller Out for Bryan," *Chicago Tribune*, July 21, 1896; and "Bryan Is Their Choice," *Washington Post*, July 21, 1896. Senators Teller (CO), Fred T. Dubois (ID), and Lee Mantle (MT) and Congressmen Charles S. Hartman (MT), Edgar Wilson (ID), and John Shafroth (CO) signed the statement, as well as Archie M. Stevenson, a Colorado GOP national convention delegate and Silver bolter. Senators Richard F. Pettigrew (SD) and Frank J. Cannon (UT) were in agreement, but did not sign.
34   "A Campaign of Education," *New York Times*, July 26, 1896, and Sage, *Allison*, 267.
35   "Think Bryan Is Weaker," *Chicago Tribune*, July 26, 1896; "Populists Nominate Bryan," *Chicago Tribune*, July 26, 1896; and Sage, *Allison*, 267.
36   "Hanna Not Obeyed," *New York Times*, July 28, 1896; "Maj. M'Kinley in Cleveland," *Washington Post*, July 28, 1896; "Both Are Earnest," *World-Herald* (Omaha, NE), July 28, 1896; "Talked of New-York Matters," *New-York Tribune*, July 28, 1896; McKinley to Elkins, July 30, 1896, in McKinley papers; and Roosevelt to Anna Roosevelt Cowles, July 26, 1896, *Letters*, 550.
37   McKinley to Wilbur F. Wakeman, Aug. 7, 1896, in McKinley papers.

CHAPTER 24: THREE REVOLTS

 1   "Bryan Is Opposed to M'Lean," *Washington Post*, July 11, 1896; "Wrangle in the Silver Camp," *New-York Tribune*, July 12, 1896; and Daniels, *Editor in Politics*, 166–68.
 2   "Convention's Last Day," *New-York Tribune*, July 12, 1896; "Running Story of the Session," *Chicago Tribune*, July 12, 1896; "East on the Ticket," *Washington Post*, July 12, 1896; "Sewall Hears News," *Chicago Tribune*, July 12, 1896; "Arthur Sewall's Life" and "The Ticket, Bryan and Sewall" in *The World* (New York), July, 12, 1896; "Convention's Last Day," *New-York Tribune*, July 12, 1896; *Official Proceedings of the DNC*, 335–50, 355–61, and 372; and Byars, *American Commoner*, 297.
 3   "Mr. Sewall Chats," *Los Angeles Times*, July 12, 1896; "Running Story of the Session," "Sewall Hears News," and "They Hear the News in Maine" in *Chicago Tribune*, July 12, 1896; and "Sewall Hears the News," *New-York Tribune*, July 12, 1896.
 4   "To Go Right Into the Enemy's Camp," *Atlanta Constitution*, July 13, 1896.
 5   "From the Democratic Nominee," *The World* (New York), July 13, 1896; "Bryan Bows At A Tomb," *Chicago Tribune*, July 13, 1896; and "Declined A Special Train." *St. Louis Republic*, July 15, 1896.
 6   "Mr. Bryan's Illinois Tour," *Kansas City Star*, July 14, 1896; "William J. Bryan Has Arrived At the Place of His Birth" *St. Louis Republic*, July 14, 1896; and Bryan, *First Battle*, 233.
 7   "Bland Greets Bryan," *Washington Post*, July 17, 1896; "Is One Continued Ovation," *World-Herald* (Omaha, NE), July 17, 1896; "Mr. Bryan's Trip Across Missouri to Kansas City," *St. Louis Republic*, July 17, 1896; "Bryan Talks Glibly On," *New-York Tribune*, July 17, 1896;

"Bland Greets Bryan," *Washington Post*, July 17, 1896; "Mr. Bryan in Missouri," *Kansas City Star*, July 16, 1896; "Many Grasp His Hand," *World-Herald* (Omaha, NE), July 16, 1896; and Bryan, *First Battle*, 235–36.

8   "His Largest Crowd" and "The Hurrah Boys Campaign" in *Los Angeles Times*, July 17, 1896; "Bryan Beards the Lion," *Chicago Tribune*, July 17, 1896; "Bland Greets Bryan," *Washington Post*, July 17, 1896; "Kansas City Gave to William J. Bryan A Royal Welcome," *St. Louis Republic*, July 17, 1896; "Mr. Bryan Nearing Home," *Kansas City Star*, July 17, 1896; "Bryan Lands At Home," *Chicago Tribune*, July 18, 1896; and Bryan, *First Battle*, 236–37.

9   "Germans Cannot Stand Bryan," *The Sun* (New York), July 11, 1896.

10   "A Party of Repudiation and Revolution," *New York Times*, July 10, 1896, and *The Sun* (New York) as quoted in the *Literary Digest, Vol. XIII.*, (New York: Funk & Wagnalls Co., 1896) p. 387, accessed 8/7/15, http://bit.ly/1MTHtiV. The *Staat-Zeitung*'s publisher was Washington Hesing, a Cleveland appointee as Chicago's postmaster.

11   "Amounts to Nothing," *Atlanta Constitution*, July 11, 1896; "Bolt Bryan and Silver," *Chicago Tribune*, July 12, 1896; "Irish-American Rejects Bryan" and "La Crosse Chronicle Scorns the Ticket" in *New York Times*, July 12, 1896; "More Papers in Revolt," *Chicago Tribune*, July 14, 1896; and "The Revolt," *Los Angeles Times*, July 24, 1896.

12   "Gold Men Deliberation," *New York Times*, July 15, 1896.

13   "Chicago Ticket Not Indorsed," *New-York Tribune*, July 12, 1896; "Administration in Doubt," *New-York Tribune*, July 14, 1896; and "Indorse Sound Money Democrats," *Chicago Tribune*, July 16, 1896.

14   "Kentucky Pops Ask for Teller," *Chicago Tribune*, July 14, 1896; "A Victory for Bryan," *New York Times*, July 24, 1896; "Calls Him A Bloated Capitalist," *Chicago Tribune*, July 18, 1896; "Ante-Convention Gossip," *New-York Tribune*, July 21, 1896; and "James Harvey Davis," *New Handbook of Texas*, II, 530–31.

15   J. Swan, et al, to Bryan, July 20, 1896, in Bryan Papers.

16   "Expected to Have A Big Row," *New York Times*, July 19, 1896; "Opposition to Mr. Bryan," *New York Times*, July 18, 1896; "Middle-Of-The-Road Men Still Guessing About Candidates," *St. Louis Republic*, July 21, 1896; "Engineering A Compromise" and "Ignatius Donnelly's Opinion" in *Los Angeles Times*, July 21, 1896; "Looks Like Bryan," *Atlanta Constitution*, July 21, 1896; and "Ante-Convention Gossip," *New-York Tribune*, July 21, 1896.

17   "The Bryan Delegates" and "Boss Bryan" in *Los Angeles Times*, July 21, 1896; "Steering Committee Chosen" and "Course Is Undecided" in *Washington Post*, July 21, 1896; "Compromise Plans Fail to Dissipate Shadows of A Bolt," *St. Louis Republic*, July 21, 1896; and "Loud Threats of Bolting," *New-York Tribune*, July 21, 1896.

18   "Butler Chosen to Preside," *Washington Post*, July 22, 1896; "The Pop's Pot," *Los Angeles Times*, July 22, 1896; "Morning Session," *St. Louis Republic*, July 24, 1896; "Allen Is Chairman," *World-Herald* (Omaha, NE), July 24, 1896; "The Populists' First Test Vote," *St. Louis Post-Dispatch*, July 24, 1896; and "A Victory for Bryan," *New York Times*, July 24, 1896.

19   "The Convention Adopts Rules," *New York Times*, July 25, 1896; "Populists Reject Sewall" and "Usual Order Reversed" in *New-York Tribune*, July 25, 1896; "Majority Report Adopted," *Atlanta Constitution*, July 25, 1896; "War of Words and Plan," *The World* (New York), July 25, 1896; and P. J. Moran, "Bryan Demanded," *Atlanta Constitution*, July 26, 1896.

20   "Watson Is Selected," *New York Times*, July 25, 1896.

21   "Nominations for Second Place," *New York Times*, July 25, 1896; "Bad for the Popocrats," *Chicago Tribune*, July 25, 1896; "Long-Winded Populists," *New-York Tribune*, July 25, 1896; and Woodward, *Watson,* 1–6 and 12–45.

22   "Long-Winded Populists," *New-York Tribune*, July 25, 1896; "Watson Named," *Atlanta Constitution*, July 25, 1896; "Senator Stewart Was Howled Down," *St. Louis Republic*, July 25, 1896; "Bryan's Ear At A 'Phone,'" *Chicago Tribune*, July 25, 1896; "Watson Is Selected," *New York Times*, July 25, 1896; and P. J. Moran, "Bryan Demanded," *Atlanta Constitution*, July 26, 1896.

23   "Bryan Stands by Sewall," *The World* (New York), July 25, 1896; "Bryan Stands by Sewall," *New-York Tribune*, July 25, 1896; and "Bryan Has Not Reconsidered," *St. Louis Post-Dispatch*, July 25, 1896.

24   "Bryan Stands by Sewall," *The World* (New York), July 25, 1896; "Bryan Refuses," *Atlanta Constitution*, July 26, 1896; "Populists Rally to Bryan," *World-Herald* (Omaha, NE), July 25, 1896; "Bryan Agreed," *Los Angeles Times*, July 26, 1896; and "Bryan Their Candidate," *New-York Tribune*, July 26, 1896.

25 "Wild Scenes in the Hall" and "Iowa for Bryan" in *St. Louis Post-Dispatch*, July 25, 1896, and "Populists End Their Work," *New-York Tribune*, July 26, 1896.

26 "Bryan Their Candidate," *New-York Tribune*, July 26, 1896; "Populists Rally to Bryan," *World-Herald* (Omaha, NE), July 25, 1896; "Nominates Bryan and Adjourns," *New York Times*, July 26, 1896; and C. Vann Woodward, *Tom Watson: Agrarian Rebel* (New York: Oxford University Press, 1938), 301.

27 "Wild Scenes in the Hall," *St. Louis Post-Dispatch*, July 25, 1896; "A Wild and Weird Spectacle," *New York Times*, July 26, 1896; "Populists End Their Work," *New-York Tribune*, July 25, 1896; and "Billy Boy Bryan," *Los Angeles Times*, July 26, 1896.

28 "Message That Wasn't Read," *Washington Post*, July 26, 1896; "Allen Had No Curiosity," *St. Louis Post-Dispatch*, July 26, 1896; "Bryan the Candidate," *The World* (New York), July 26, 1896; "The Last Day" and "Billy Boy Bryan" in *Los Angeles Times*, July 26, 1896; and Goodwyn, *Populist Moment*, 259–60.

29 P. J. Moran, "Bryan Demanded," *Atlanta Constitution*, July 26, 1896; "Bryan's Relatives See Sights," *Chicago Tribune,* July 26, 1896; "Tricky Populist Leaders," *New-York Tribune*, July 27, 1896; "Populists End Their Work," *New-York Tribune*, July 25, 1896; "A Wild and Weird Spectacle," *New York Times*, July 26, 1896; and "Bryan Their Candidate," *New-York Tribune*, July 26, 1896.

30 "Populist Committee Selected Butler National Chairman," *St. Louis Republic*, July 26, 1896; "The Populists Have Organized," *St. Louis Post-Dispatch*, July 26, 1896; "Butler Elected Chairman," *Washington Post*, July 26, 1896; and "The Mongrel Alliance," *New-York Tribune*, July 28, 1896.

31 "Bryan Men Control," *The World* (New York), July 24, 1896; "Bryan Sticks to Sewall," *Chicago Tribune*, July 24, 1896; and "Bryan Stands by Mr. Sewall," *St. Louis Post-Dispatch*, July 23, 1896.

32 "What Sewall Says About It," *The World* (New York), July 26, 1896; "Watson Defines His Position," *Chicago Tribune*, July 26, 1896; "Watson Will Accept," *New York Times*, July 26, 1896; "Watson Perfectly Willing," *New-York Tribune*, July 26, 1896; "Talks With the Hon. Thomas E. Watson," *Atlanta Constitution*, July 26, 1896; "Poked Fun At Bryan," *Washington Post*, July 26, 1896; and "That Mixture," *Los Angeles Times*, July 27, 1896.

33 "Talks With the Hon. Thomas E. Watson," *Atlanta Constitution*, July 26, 1896; "Watson Will Not Withdraw," *Washington Post*, July 27, 1896; "Watson's Quiet Sunday," *The World* (New York), July 27, 1896; and "Watson Says He Will Not Withdraw," *Chicago Tribune*, July 27, 1896.

34 "Tokens of Luck," *St. Louis Post-Dispatch*, July 28, 1896; "Watson Before and After," *New-York Tribune*, July 30, 1896; "Billy Boy's Caudal Affixes," *Los Angeles Times*, July 31, 1896; [Untitled], *People's Party Paper*, July 31, 1896; and Arthur Sewall to Bryan, July 25, 1896, in Bryan papers.

35 "Jones Confers With Bryan," *New-York Tribune*, July 27, 1896; "Bryan's Two-In-Hand," *Chicago Tribune*, July 27, 1896; "In Conference With Bryan," *Washington Post*, July 27, 1896; "Jones and Stone Deliberate," *Los Angeles Times*, July 28, 1896; "Bryan Under Cover," *New-York Tribune*, July 28, 1896; and "Bryan's Plea for Harmony," *New York Times*, July 28, 1896.

36 "Will Not Notify Him," *Washington Post*, July 27, 1896; "Tricky Populist Leaders," *New-York Tribune*, July 27, 1896; "Will Bryan Withdraw," *Washington Post*, July 28, 1896; "Populists Will Stick to Bryan," *New York Times*, July 29, 1896; and "Need Not Notify," *Atlanta Constitution*, July 29, 1896.

37 "Kansas Populists," *St. Louis Post-Dispatch*, Aug. 5, 1896, and "In Kansas and Nebraska," *Washington Post,* Aug. 7, 1896.

38 Bryan, *First Battle*, 300, and Koenig, *Bryan*, 223.

39 "Mr. Bryan At Chicago," *Washington Post*, Aug. 9, 1896; "Free Talk Along the Road," *New-York Tribune*, Aug. 11, 1896; "Bryan One Day Nearer," *The Sun* (New York, NY), Aug. 11, 1896; Bryan, *First Battle*, 300–306; "Bryan Meets Iowans" and "An Ovation in Des Moines" in *Carroll Sentinel* (Carroll, IA), Aug. 8, 1896.

40 "Mr. Bryan At Chicago," *Washington Post*, Aug. 9, 1896, and "Free Talk Along the Road," *New-York Tribune*, Aug. 11, 1896.

41 "Well, Bryan Spoke," *The Sun* (New York), Aug. 12, 1896, and "Gathering of the Clans," *New-York Tribune*, Aug. 13, 1896.

42 "Well, Bryan Spoke," *The Sun* (New York), Aug. 12, 1896; "Candidates Notified," *Washington Post*, Aug. 13, 1896; and "Bryan's Notification," *The World* (New York), Aug. 13, 1896.

43 Rhodes, *McKinley and Roosevelt Administrations*, 20, and "Mr. Bryan Feels Sore," *Chicago Tribune*, Aug. 14, 1896.

44 "Where Stand the Eastern Wage Earners?," *Review of Reviews*, XIV (September, 1896), 261–262; Williams, *Years of Decision*, 116; and Bryan, *First Battle*, 299.

45 "Bryan in A Quiet Spot," *New York Times*, Aug. 18, 1896.

46 "Bourke Cockran for M'Kinley" and "The Effect of A Third Ticket" in *New York Times*, Aug. 3, 1896; Ralph Guy Martin, *Jennie: The Life of Lady Randolph Churchill, the Romantic Years, 1854–1895* (London: Littlehampton Book Services, 1969), 309–19, 331–34, and 343–54; and Martin Gilbert, *Churchill and America* (New York: Simon & Schuster, 2008), 17, 58–59. Churchill had stayed with Cockran in New York the previous year while en route to Cuba, where the young Englishman was to observe the Spanish military as a war correspondent.

47 "W. Bourke Cockran Arrives," *New-York Tribune*, Aug. 2, 1896; "Mr. Cockran on the Issues," *New-York Tribune*, Aug. 3, 1896; "Bourke Cockran for M'Kinley," *New York Times*, Aug. 3, 1896; "He Prefers M'Kinley," *Washington Post*, Aug. 3, 1896; "A Cockran to the Rescue," *Washington Post*, Aug. 4, 1896; Cockran to C. E. Sanford, Aug. 7, 1896, in Cockran papers and James McGurrin, *Bourke Cockran: A Free Lance in American Politics* (New York: Charles Scribner's Sons, 1948), 149–51.

48 "Rally of Gold Men," *Washington Post*, Aug. 19, 1896; "Thousands Hear W. Bourke Cockran," *New York Times*, Aug. 19, 1896; "Hit Shot for Bryan," *Chicago Tribune*, Aug. 19, 1896; "Cockran to Bryan," *The World*, Aug. 19, 1896; "Bryanism Riddled," *The Sun* (New York), Aug. 19, 1896; and "Speech of Hon. W. Bourke Cockran in Reply to Hon. William J. Bryan," Democratic Honest Money League, in Cockran papers.

49 McGurrin, *Cockran*, 159–60.

CHAPTER 25: THE FRONT-PORCH CAMPAIGN

1 "Bryan Takes the Stump," *New York Times*, Aug. 23, 1896; "Talked to A Small Crowd," *Los Angeles Times*, Aug. 23, 1896; and "Is Again on the Stump," *Chicago Tribune*, Aug. 23, 1896.

2 "Bryan Speaks At Buffalo," *New York Times*, Aug. 28, 1896; "At Cleveland's Home," *Washington Post*, Aug. 28, 1896; and Bryan, *First Battle*, 353.

3 "Mr. Bryan's Day," *Syracuse Daily Standard*, August 26, 1896; "Bryan Talks All Day," *Chicago Tribune*, August 27, 1896; "Bryan Talks His Way West," "His Voice Gives Out Again," and "From Utica To Buffalo" in *New-York Tribune*, August 27, 1896; "One Crowd Of 10,000 Disappointed" and "Bryan Talks To 40,000" in *New York Times*, August 27, 1896; "Bryan At Rochester," *Washington Post*, August 27, 1896; "Bryan Talks To Farmers," *New York Times*, August 29, 1896; and "Long Talk At Rural Picnic," *Chicago Tribune*, August 29, 1896.

4 "Bryan Talks At A Fair," *The World* (New York), Aug. 30, 1896; "Crowd Fears A Panic," *Chicago Tribune*, Aug. 30, 1896; and "Good-Bye to New York," *Chicago Tribune*, Aug. 31, 1896.

5 "Only Mr. Bryan Will Speak," *New York Times*, Aug. 24, 1896; "Invited to Visit Hill," *Washington Post*, Aug. 24, 1896; and "Bryan Dines With Senator Hill," *Chicago Tribune*, Aug. 26, 1896.

6 "McKinley Will Not Stump," *New York Times*, Aug. 18, 1896.

7 Harrison to Reid, Oct. 9, 1888, in Reid Papers; Morgan, *From Hayes to McKinley*, 306; Calhoun, *Minority Victory*, 133; and Sievers, *Hoosier Statesman*, 371–73.

8 "In M'Kinley's Home Town," *New-York Tribune*, June 28, 1896, and "Cheer for Good Times," *Chicago Tribune*, June 28, 1896.

9 Morrow, Interview with Charles Dick, February 10, 1904, 16–18, and Williams, *Realigning America*, 130–34.

10 Morgan, *McKinley and His America*, 177, and Williams, *Realigning America*, 171.

11 White, *Autobiography*, 144–48.

12 "Silver Forces Unite," *Washington Post*, Aug. 5, 1896; H. G. McMillan to Clarkson, Sept. 5, 1896, in Clarkson papers; and Appleton, *Annual Cyclopaedia* (1897), 136.

13 "Hanna Says Talk Money," *New York Times*, July 21, 1896; "M'Kinley Will Not Stump," *New-York Tribune*, Aug. 18, 1896; Roosevelt to Anna Roosevelt Cowles, Aug. 15, 1896, in *Letters*, 557; and Adelbert Bower Sageser, *Joseph L. Bristow: Kansas Progressive* (Lawrence: University Press of Kansas, 1968), 28.

14 Hay to Henry Adams, Sept. 8, 1896, in Henry Adams papers, Massachusetts Historical Society.

15 Dawes to Hanna, Aug. 29, 1896, in Dawes papers; Lodge to Roosevelt, Sept. 16, 1896, in Lodge Papers; Williams, *Realigning America*, 137; and Ron Chernow, *The House of Morgan: An American Banking Dynasty and the Rise of Modern Finance* (New York: Grove Press, 2001), 77.

16 "M'Kinley's Letter of Acceptance," *Chicago Tribune*, Aug. 27, 1896; "Gold Standard Must Be Maintained," *Chicago Tribune*, Aug. 28, 1896; "His Letter in Demand," *Chicago Tribune*, Aug.

30, 1896; Diary entry for Aug. 23, 1896, in Dawes, *Journal*, 95; and Joseph P. Smith, *McKinley's Speeches in August* (Canton, OH: The Repository Press, 1896), 115–27.

17 "General Harrison Is Here," *New-York Tribune*, Aug. 27, 1896; "Harrison Squarely for Sound Money" and "Gen. Harrison's Speech" in *The World* (New York), Aug. 28, 1896; and "Gen. Harrison Heard." *New York Times*, Aug. 28, 1896.

18 "Gen. Harrison's Speech" in *The World* (New York), Aug. 28, 1896; "Harrison's Strong Appeal," *New-York Tribune* (New York), Aug. 28, 1896; and "Honor Above Booty," *The Sun* (New York), Aug. 28, 1896.

19 "It Has Votes to Spare" and "The Vermont Election" in *Chicago Tribune*, Sept. 1, 1896.

20 "E.J. Phelps on the Issue," *New-York Tribune*, Aug. 25, 1896; "39,000" and "Country Will Follow Vermont" in *Chicago Tribune*, Sept. 2, 1896; "Interest in the Returns," *Washington Post*, Sept. 2, 1896; "Vermont and Wall Street," "Pleased With the Results," "An Important Victory," and "The Voice of Vermont" in *New York Times*, Sept. 3, 1896; and "Portends A Tidal Wave," *Chicago Tribune*, Sept. 3, 1896.

21 "Mr. Quay Is in Control," *New York Times*, Sept. 2, 1896.

22 "Col. Jon. S. Mosby on the Presidential Candidate and Money Question" in Special Collections, University of Virginia Library.

23 "Gold Men Divided," *Atlanta Constitution*, Aug. 7, 1896; "Goldbugs Meet in Conference," *St. Louis Post-Dispatch*, Aug. 7, 1896; "To Name A New Ticket," *Washington Post*, Aug. 8, 1896; "New Party Formed," *The World* (New York), Aug. 8, 1896; "Wanted," *Los Angeles Times*, Sept. 1, 1896; "Bragg Is in the Lead," *New York Times*, Sept. 2, 1896; "Talk of the Convention," *Indianapolis News*, Sept. 2, 1896; and "Many Men to Choose From," *New York Times*, Sept. 3, 1896.

24 "Ex-Gov. Flowers' Speech," *Los Angeles Times*, Sept. 3, 1896; and "Bragg Has A Boom," *Logansport Pharos-Tribune* (Logansport, IN), Sept. 2, 1896.

25 "Frowns for Cleveland's Boom," *Logansport Pharos-Tribune* (Logansport, IN), Sept. 2, 1896; "Palmer and Buckner," *New York Times*, Sept. 3, 1896; and "Senator Palmer Will Work," *New York Times*, Sept. 4, 1896.

26 "Guided by Principle," *New York Times*, Sept. 4, 1896.

27 "Warrior and Statesman," *New York Times*, Sept. 4, 1896.

28 "Many Distinguished Democrats," *New York Times*, Sept. 3, 1896; "Plans for the Campaign," *New York Times*, Sept. 4, 1896; Nevins, *Study in Courage*, 707; and Daniels, *Editor in Politics*, 180.

29 "New Ticket Is Costly to Bryan," *Chicago Tribune*, Sept. 5, 1896; and "Hanna on the Third Ticket," *Washington Post*, Sept. 5, 1896.

30 "From Jamestown to Cleveland," *Titusville Herald* (Titusville, PA), Sept. 1, 1896; "Other Politics," *Los Angeles Times*, Sept. 1, 1896; Bryan, *First Battle*, 357–59.

31 "Bryan Receives A Great Ovation," *Plain Dealer* (Cleveland, OH), Sept. 1, 1896; "Bryan in Indiana," *Fort Wayne Gazette*, Sept. 4, 1896; "Indiana Greets Bryan," *Washington Post*, Sept. 4, 1896; "Railroad Men Ridiculed," *New York Times*, Sept. 4, 1896; and Bryan, *First Battle*, 362–65.

32 "Bryan At Columbus," *Daily Herald* (Delphos, OH), Sept. 2, 1896; "Mr. Bryan At Springfield" and "Bryan Visits Toledo" in *Washington Post*, Sept. 3, 1896; "Sea of Humanity," *Fort Wayne Sentinel*, Sept. 4, 1896; and Bryan, *First Battle*, 359–62.

33 Diary entries for Sept. 4, 1896, and Sept. 5, 1896, in Dawes, *Journal*, 96.

CHAPTER 26: MESSAGE FOR THE WORKINGMAN

1 "M'Kinley to the Workingmen," *Chicago Tribune*, Sept. 7, 1896; "Won't Stump," *Plain Dealer* (Cleveland, OH), Sept. 6, 1896; "McKinley to Stay in Canton," *New York Times*, Sept. 6, 1896; and Joseph P. Smith, *McKinley's Speeches in September* (Canton OH: The Repository Press, 1896), 161–68.

2 "Bryan to Laboring Men," *The World* (New York), Sept. 8, 1896; "Labor Unions All Right," *New York Times*, Sept. 8, 1896; "Parade on Labor Day," "Address of William J. Bryan," and "W. J. Bryan on Toil" in *Chicago Tribune*, Sept. 8, 1896; and Bryan, *First Battle*, 375–83.

3 "Bryan Again Notified," *The World* (New York), Sept. 9, 1896; "Lincoln Welcomes Bryan," *Sioux City Journal*, Sept. 9, 1896; and "Bryan Hears His Fate," *New-York Tribune*, Sept. 9, 1896.

4 "Watson's Speech," *Dallas Morning News*, Sept. 8, 1896; "Watson Lashes Sewall," *New-York Tribune*, Sept. 8, 1896; "Sewall Is A Wart," *Chicago Tribune*, Sept. 8, 1896; and "Sewall Must Get Off," *Washington Post*, Sept. 8, 1896.

5 "Watson Making Trouble," *Kansas City Star*, Sept. 10, 1896; "Tom Watson Denounces Sewall," *Omaha Daily Bee*, Sept. 17, 1896; "Watson Pleases Populists," *Omaha Daily Bee*, Sept. 17, 1896;

"Tom Watson in Denver," *Rocky Mountain Sun* (Denver, CO), Sept. 19, 1896; and Harrison to William J. Steele, September 18, 1896, in Harrison papers.

6   "Directors Allege Coercion and Urge All Railroad Employees to Support Bryan," *The World* (New York), Sept. 11, 1896.

7   "Groans for Powderly," *The Sun* (New York), Sept. 11, 1896; "No Bryanism for Him," *Chicago Tribune*, Sept. 11, 1896; "Powderly Is Hissed," *The World* (New York), Sept. 11, 1896; and "Wager-Earners Aroused," *New-York Tribune*, Sept. 11, 1896.

8   "Powderly for the Gold Standard," *Chicago Tribune*, Sept. 12, 1896, and "No Bryanism for Him," *Chicago Tribune*, Sept. 11, 1896.

9   "Against A Sliced Dollar" and "Theodore Roosevelt's Speech" in *New York Times*, Sept. 12, 1896; Roosevelt, *Campaign and Controversies*, 363; and Roosevelt to Lodge, Sept. 14, 1896, *Correspondence, I*, 232.

10 "McKinley to Stay at Canton," *New York Times*, Sept. 12, 1896; Roosevelt to Lodge, Sept. 14, 1896, *Correspondence I*, 232–34; Fred S. Wood, ed., *Roosevelt as We Knew Him: Personal Recollections of 150 Friends* (Philadelphia: John C. Winston Company, 1927), 41; and Morris, *Rise of Theodore Roosevelt*, 549. T.R. appears to be in Chicago Sept. 7 or 8 on his way home from hunting in North Dakota.

11 Thomas B. Reed to Cockran, August 14, 1886, and "Black Eye to Silver," *Chicago Tribune*, Sept. 16, 1896.

12 "Honesty is the Issue," *Chicago Tribune*, Sept. 23, 1896, and Smith, *McKinley's Speeches in Sept.*, 237–47, 253–60, and 266–70.

13 "William McKinley," *The Vermonter*, Vol. VI, October 1901, No. 3, 325–26; and Smith, *McKinley Speeches in Sept.*, 172–82, 253–60, and 266–70.

14 "McKinley to Steel Workers," *New York Times*, Sept. 13, 1896; "McKinley on Free Wool," *Chicago Tribune*, Sept. 15, 1896; and Smith, *McKinley Speeches in Sept.*, 183–87 and 197–208.

15 "Big Day At Canton," *Chicago Tribune*, August 30, 1896; "Fest Undtreu," *Los Angeles Times*, August 30, 1896; and Smith, *McKinley Speeches in Sept.*, 203–20.

16 "Talks to First Voters," *Chicago Tribune*, Sept. 24, 1896, and Smith, *McKinley's Speeches in Sept.*, 239–53.

17 "William McKinley," *The Vermonter*, Vol. VI, October 1901, No. 3, 325–26.

18 "On a Trip to Canton," *Chicago Tribune*, Sept. 12, 1896, and Smith, *McKinley Speeches in Sept.*, 187–97 and 203–20.

19 Smith, *McKinley Speeches in Sept.*, 203–20.

20 Smith, *McKinley Speeches in Sept.*, 220–36, and "Great Day of All," *Chicago Tribune*, Sept. 19, 1896.

21 "M'Kinley Favorite in the Betting," *Chicago Tribune*, Sept. 27, 1896, and Reed to Platt, Sept. 20, 1896, in Platt Papers.

22 "Bryan's Day," *The Courier* (Lincoln, NE), Sept. 12, 1896; "Bryan Takes the Road," *Chicago Tribune*, Sept. 12, 1896; "Bryan on His Second Tour," *Omaha Daily Bee*, Sept. 12, 1896; and "Bryan Travels East," *Washington Post*, Sept. 12, 1896.

23 "Passing Through Illinois," *Morning World-Herald* (Omaha, NE), Sept. 15, 1896; "An Ovation At the Altar Steps," *St. Louis Post-Dispatch*, Sept. 14, 1896; "Bryan Cheered As An Anarchist," *The Sun* (New York), Sept. 16, 1896; and Bryan, *First Battle*, 443–48.

24 "Bryan," *Evening Bulletin* (Marysville, KY), Sept. 16, 1896; "In North Carolina," *Wilmington Morning Star* (Wilmington, NC), Sept. 16, 1896; "Says Bryan Is Being Betrayed," *Chicago Tribune*, Sept. 17, 1896; "Incidents of Wm. J. Bryan's Visit," *Wilmington Messenger* (Wilmington, NC), Sept. 19, 1896; Daniels, *Editor in Politics*, 189–92; and Bryan, *First Battle*, 443–51.

25 "Bryan and His Cause," *Washington Post*, Sept. 20, 1896; "Visits the Capital," *Sunday World-Herald* (Omaha, NE), Sept. 20, 1896; and Bryan, *First Battle*, 459–64.

26 "A Farmer's Letter to the Silver Question," Pamphlet F and Dawes to C. H. Bosworth, Sept. 17, 1896, in Dawes papers.

27 "Silver Arguments Simply Answered," Pamphlet A, and "American Farmers Were Protected by the McKinley Tariff Law," in Dawes Papers.

28 Mark W. Summers, *Party Games: Getting, Keeping, and Using Power in Gilded Age Politics* (Chapel Hill, NC: The University of North Carolina Press, 2004), 56, 59, 64, and 216; Calhoun, *From Bloody Shirt to Full Dinner Pail*, 4; Glenn C. Altschuler and Stuart M. Blumin, *Rude Republic: Americans and their Politics in the Nineteenth Century* (Princeton: Princeton University Press, 2000), 178; and Desantis, "Republican Party Revisited, 1877–1897," *Gilded Age*, 93.

29 "Veterans for M'Kinley," *New York Times*, July 31, 1896, and Calhoun, *From Bloody Shirt to Full Dinner Pail*, 30–31.

30 "Veterans' Protest Against Bryan," *Chicago Tribune*, Sept. 21, 1896, and "Gen. Sickles Sounds His War Cry" and "Line up for Battle" in *Chicago Tribune*, Sept. 22, 1896.

31 "Gen. Stewart Speaks As Private," *Chicago Tribune*, Sept. 22, 1896.

32 "Party of Generals Reaches Kansas City," *Kansas City Daily Journal*, October 4, 1896; "The Generals' Sunday," *Kansas City Daily Journal*, October 5, 1896; "Where They Go," *Kansas City Daily Journal*, October 6, 1896; "Vets on A Dashing Tour," *Chicago Tribune*, October 7, 1896; Mary R. Dearing, *Veterans in Politics: The Story of the G.A.R.* (Westport, CT: Greenwood Press, 1974), 454–66.

33 Butler to James K. Jones, Sept. 21, 1896, in Butler papers, and B. F. Keith to Butler, Sept. 19, 1896, quoted by Jones, *Election of 1896*, 311–12.

34 "Bryan Confers With Managers," *Chicago Tribune*, Sept. 21, 1896, and "Bryan in Delaware," *New York Times*, Sept. 22, 1896.

35 "Bryan Quotes M'Kinley," *Chicago Tribune*, Sept. 22, 1896; "Bismarck's Letter Was Garbled," *The World* (New York), Sept. 26, 1896; "Bryan in Delaware," *Washington Post*, Sept. 22, 1896; Daniels, *Editor in Politics*, 193; and Bryan, *First Battle*, 464–75.

36 "Bryan Talks to Thousands" and "Crowds Welcome Bryan" in *Philadelphia Times*, Sept. 23, 1896.

37 "Bryan Night in Brooklyn," *Brooklyn Daily Eagle*, Sept. 24, 1896; "His First Insult" and "At the Capitol" in *Boston Daily Globe*, Sept. 25, 1896; "Great Crowd At New Haven," *Morning World-Herald* (Omaha, NE), Sept. 25, 1896; Daniels, *Editor in Politics*, 194–95; and Bryan, *First Battle*, 479–89.

38 "Great Crowd At New Haven," *Morning World-Herald* (Omaha, NE), Sept. 25, 1896; "Yale Hooted Bryan" and "Great Crowds Greet Bryan" in *The World*, (New York), Sept. 25, 1896; and Bryan, *First Battle*, 484–88.

39 "Bryan Visits the Hub," *Washington Post*, Sept. 26, 1896; "Boston Goes Wild," *Morning World-Herald* (Omaha, NE), Sept. 26, 1896; "Bryan's Huge Audience," *New York Times*, Sept. 26, 1896; and Daniels, *Editor in Politics*, 196.

40 "Bryan Tammany's Guest," "Mr. Bryan's Address," and "The Wigwam Crowded" in *New York Times*, Sept. 30, 1896; and Bryan, *First Battle*, 507–11.

41 "Ticket At Buffalo," *Washington Post*, Sept. 15, 1896; "The Slate May Be Broken," *New-York Tribune*, Sept. 16, 1896; "Thacher Will Accept," *The Sun* (New York), Sept. 17, 1896; and "Hill's Hand Apparent," *Washington Post*, Sept. 16, 1896.

42 "Mr. Danforth Disappointed," *New York Times*, Sept. 22, 1896; "Thacher Will Not Run," *Chicago Tribune*, Sept. 27, 1896; "Mr. Bryan Is At Bath," *Chicago Tribune*, Sept. 27, 1896; "Mr. Bryan Will Not Talk of New York," *Washington Post*, Sept. 27, 1896; "Bryan Tammany's Guest," *New York Times*, Sept. 30, 1896; Daniels, *Editor in Politics*, 194; and Koenig, *Bryan*, 234.

43 "Palmer Speakers for Gold," *The World* (New York), Sept. 23, 1896; "7,000 Cheer Palmer," *New York Times*, Sept. 23, 1896; "Palmer in New York," *Chicago Tribune*, Sept. 23, 1896; "Palmer and Buckner Here," *New-York Tribune*, Sept. 22, 1896; "Bourke Cockran's Great Speech for Gold," *The Sun* (Baltimore), Sept. 28, 1896; "Bourke Cockran Cheered," *New-York Tribune*, Sept. 28, 1896; Thurlow Weed Barnes to Cockran, Sept. 5, 1896; Cockran to Barnes, Sept. 9, 1896; and "Speech of Hon. W. Bourke Cockran," Honest Money League of Maryland, in Cockran papers.

44 Hay to Whitelaw Reid, Sept. 23, 1896, in Whitelaw Reid Papers; Dawes to Sam J. Roberts and Dawes to Judge William L. Day, Sept. 26, 1896, Hanna to Dawes, Sept. 28, 1896, and J. N. Huston to Dawes, Sept. 29, 1896, in Dawes papers.

45 Lodge to Roosevelt, September 16, 1896, in Lodge Papers, and Dawes to Hanna, Sept. 26, 1896, in Dawes papers.

CHAPTER 27: CLOSING ARGUMENTS

1 "Talks to Many Farmers," *Chicago Tribune*, Oct. 1, 1896.

2 "Big Week for McKinley," *Chicago Tribune*, Oct. 5, 1896; "M'Kinley on Hard Times," *New York Times*, Oct. 7, 1896; "M'Kinley on the Issues," *Chicago Tribune*, Oct. 7, 1896; and Joseph P. Smith, *McKinley's Speeches in October* (Canton, OH: The Repository Press, 1896), 350–56.

3 "President Garland for McKinley," *New-York Tribune*, Oct. 7, 1896; "McKinley's Day of Talk" and "Mr. McKinley's Remarks" in *New York Times*, Oct. 4, 1896; and Smith, *McKinley's Speeches in Oct.*, 313–38.

4 Smith, *McKinley's Speeches in Oct.*, 370–73.

5   Abram P. Funkhouser to McKinley, Oct. 6, 1896, in McKinley papers, and Smith, *McKinley's Speeches in Oct.*, 370–79.

6   "River of Gold Men," "Day Is A Big Surprise," "Vignettes of the March," and "Sent to Distant Ears," in *Chicago Tribune*, Oct. 10, 1896; "Sound Money Legions," *New-York Tribune*, Oct. 10, 1896; "The Cheers Echoed in Canton," *New York Times*, Oct. 10, 1896; and G.W. Steevens, *Land of the Dollar (An Englishman's Impressions of America)* (New York: Dodd, Mead, 1897), 192–94.

7   "Quay and Hanna At Odds?," *New York Times*, Oct. 2, 1896; "To Make An Effort South," *New York Times*, Oct. 4, 1896; and Shadgett, *Republican Party in Georgia*, 135. Florida, Tennessee, and Virginia were the other Southern states to receive significant help.

8   "Hanna Has a New Plan," *Chicago Tribune*, Oct. 6, 1986; "Centre of the Contest," *New York Times*, Oct. 7, 1896; and "Mark Hanna Comes West to Stay," *Chicago Tribune*, Oct. 7, 1896.

9   Jones, *Election of 1896*, 335.

10   "Outlook in West Virginia," *New York Times*, Oct. 2, 1896; "Bryan Wants Congress," *New York Times*, Oct. 6, 1896; and Bryan, *First Battle*, 525.

11   "Bryan in West Virginia," *New York Times*, Oct. 1, 1896; "Mr. Bryan Goes West," *Washington Post*, Oct. 1, 1896; "Crowds Greet Bryan" and "Mr. Bryan At Clarksburg" in *Washington Post*, Oct. 2, 1896; "Will Keep on Till Election" and "Bryan Quotes McKinley" in *New York Times*, Oct. 2, 1896; "At Burlington," *Cedar Rapids Evening Gazette*, Oct. 8, 1896; "Quotes His Opponent," *Washington Post*, Oct. 9, 1896; "Bryan to the Iowans," *Chicago Tribune*, Oct. 9, 1896; and Bryan, *First Battle*, 512–16.

12   "Bryan At Indianapolis," *Chicago Tribune*, Oct. 7, 1896; "Big Crowds Greet Bryan," *New York Times*, Oct. 7, 1896; "A Day With Bryan," *Logansport Reporter* (Logansport, IN), Oct. 7, 1896; and Bryan, *First Battle*, 526–32.

13   "Big Crowd At Wheeling," *New York Times*, Oct. 2, 1896, and "Vast Crowds Cheer," *Morning World-Herald* (Omaha, NE), Oct. 2, 1896.

14   "Bryan Has a Busy Day," *Chicago Tribune*, Oct. 4, 1896.

15   Bryan, *First Battle*, 534.

16   "To Close His Campaign in Illinois," *New-York Tribune*, Oct. 9, 1896, and "Bryan in Illinois Eight Days," *Chicago Tribune*, Oct. 9, 1896.

17   "Bryan's Partner for McKinley," *Omaha Daily Bee*, Oct. 9, 1896, and "Bad News for W.J.," *Burlington Hawk Eye* (Burlington, IA), Oct. 9, 1896.

18   "Bryan At Fargo," *Eau Claire Leader*, Oct. 11, 1896; "Through the Dakota," *Los Angeles Times*, Oct. 11, 1896; "The Long Trip to St. Paul," *New York Times*, Oct. 11, 1896; "Bryan's Oratory Fires His Friends," *St. Paul Globe*, Oct. 11, 1896; and Bryan, *First Battle*, 536–37.

19   "Bryan At Minneapolis," *Austin Daily Herald* (Austin, MN), Oct. 13, 1896; "Mr. Bryan in Michigan," *Detroit Free Press*, Oct. 15, 1896; "Bryan Reaches Grand Rapids," *Marshall Daily Chronicle* (Marshall, MI), Oct. 16, 1896; "Touring the State" and "Big Turnout at Traverse City" in *Detroit Free Press*, Oct. 16, 1896; "A Mistake," *Benton Harbor Evening News*, Oct. 16, 1896; and Bryan, *First Battle*, 538–54.

20   "Thirty Thousand Silver Rooters," *St. Paul Globe*, Oct. 13, 1896; "To Men and Women," *Washington Post*, Oct. 13, 1896; "Bryan in Minneapolis," *New-York Tribune*, Oct. 13, 1896; "Up in Towne's District," *Chicago Tribune*, Oct. 15, 1896; "Silver Wave Is Checked," *Chicago Tribune*, Oct. 12, 1896; and Bryan, *First Battle*, 538–54.

21   "Bryan Urges Fusion," *New-York Tribune*, Oct. 7, 1896, and "Straight Tickets in Demand," *New York Times*, Oct. 2, 1896.

22   "Threatened to Mob 'Coin,'" *New York Times*, Oct. 7, 1896; "Vets on A Dashing Tour" and "Union Veterans Make Many Talks" in *Chicago Tribune*, Oct. 7, 1896; "Tour of the Generals," *Chicago Tribune*, Oct. 9, 1896; and "Trip in Illinois Ends," *Chicago Tribune*, Oct. 11, 1896.

23   Lodge to Roosevelt, August 1, 1896, in Lodge Papers, and Roosevelt to Lodge, August 8, 1896, in *Correspondence I*, 229.

24   Maria Longworth Storer, "How Theodore Roosevelt Was Appointed Assistant Secretary of the Navy," *Harper's Weekly*, 56, no. 2893 (July 1, 1912); Morris, *Rise of Theodore Roosevelt*, 540; and Nathan Miller, *Theodore Roosevelt: A Life* (New York: William Morrow, Inc., 1992), 240. Mrs. Storer places the visit in July 1896, but letters and diaries place it as Aug. 1 and 2.

25   Roosevelt to Bellamy Storer, Aug. 10, 1896, and Roosevelt to Maria Longworth Storer, Aug. 10, 1896, in *Letters*, 556.

26   "A Rally in Oneida County," *New-York Tribune*, Sept. 30, 1896, and "Truths by the Roots," *Buffalo Evening News*, Oct. 1, 1896.

27   "Lodge and Roosevelt," *Evening Journal* (Jamestown, NY), Oct. 1, 1896, and "Two Great Speeches," *Evening Journal* (Jamestown, NY), Oct. 2, 1896.

28   Hay to Henry Adams, Oct. 4, 1896, in the Hay Papers.

29   "Confidence Is His Text," *Chicago Tribune*, Oct. 3, 1896; "Callers on Maj. M'Kinley," *Washington Post*, Oct. 3, 1896; "Good Cheer for M'Kinley," *The Sun* (New York), Oct. 3, 1896; and Roosevelt to Anna Roosevelt Cowles, Oct. 4, 1896, in *Letters to Anna Roosevelt Cowles*, 194–95.

30   "Teddy Hits the Pops," *Chicago Tribune*, Oct. 16, 1896, and Roosevelt, "The Menace of the Demagogue," *Campaigns and Controversies*, 258–74.

31   "The Republican Campaign," *Jackson Citizen* (Jackson, MI), Oct. 17, 1896, and "Theodore Roosevelt," *Jackson Citizen* (Jackson, MI), Oct. 18, 1896.

32   "Logical!," *Detroit Free Press*, Oct. 18, 1896, and Roosevelt, "Jack Cade," *Campaigns and Controversies*, 275–79.

33   "Michigan Tour Over," *Washington Post*, Oct. 18, 1896, and Bryan, *First Battle*, 562–65.

34   "Monroe Captured by Roosevelt," *Detroit Free Press*, Oct. 18, 1896, and "Rattling Gold Speech Made by Roosevelt at Ypsilanti," *Detroit Free Press*, Oct. 20, 1896.

35   "Letter to the Archbishop" and "Bury It Out of Sight" in *St. Paul Globe*, Oct. 12, 1896, and "He Hoists A Signal," *Chicago Tribune*, Oct. 12, 1896.

36   "Now the Final Battle," *Chicago Tribune*, Oct. 13, 1896.

37   "A Moving Picture of M'Kinley," *New-York Tribune*, Oct. 13, 1896.

38   "A Busy Day for M'Kinley," *New York Times*, Oct. 11, 1896; "Canton Is A Mecca," *Chicago Tribune*, Oct. 11, 1896; and Smith, *McKinley's Speeches in Oct.*, 377–402.

39   "Mr. McKinley on Trusts," *New York Times*, Oct. 17, 1896, and Smith, *McKinley's Speeches in Oct.*, 405–28.

40   "Greatest of all Days," *Chicago Tribune*, Oct. 18, 1896, and Smith, *McKinley's Speeches in Oct.*, 442-43.

41   "At the M'Kinley Home," *Chicago Tribune*, Oct. 19, 1896; "One Umbrella for Three," *New York Times*, Oct. 19, 1896; and Bryan, *First Battle*, 565.

42   "Sound Money Their Text," *New York Times*, Oct. 19, 1896, and Daniels, *Editor in Politics*, 198.

CHAPTER 28: COERCION AND FARM PRICES

 1   "McKinley's Six Speeches," *New York Times*, Oct. 23, 1896; and Smith, *McKinley's Speeches in Oct.*, 512–17 and 531–37.

 2   "Bryan's Reply to Hanna," *Chicago Tribune*, Oct. 20, 1896; " 'Flag Day' Hits Popocrats," *Chicago Tribune*, Oct. 21, 1896; "Again Invades Ohio," *Ohio Democrat* (Logan, OH), Oct. 20, 1896; and Bryan, *First Battle*, 566–67.

 3   "Governor Stone Reiterates His Coercion Charges," *St. Louis Republic,* September 29, 1896; "Discharged Employees," *St. Louis Republic,* Oct. 13, 1896; "Typos Object to Coercion," *St. Louis Republic,* Oct. 14, 1896; Richard J. Jensen, *Winning of the Midwest: Social and Political Conflict, 1888–1896* (Chicago: University of Chicago Press, 1971), 49; and Robert F. Durden, *The Climax of Populism: The Election of 1896* (Lexington, KY: University of Kentucky Press, 1966), 140.

 4   "National Committee Strikes A Warning Note," *Atlanta Constitution*, Oct. 20, 1896; "Gives Out A Manifesto," *Chicago Tribune*, Oct. 20, 1896; "Jones Appeal," *Boston Daily Globe*, Oct. 20, 1896; "An Appeal and a Warning," *New York Times*, Oct. 20, 1896; "Hanna on Coercion Cry," *Chicago Tribune*, Oct. 21, 1896; and "Mr. Hanna and Coercion," *New York Times*, Oct. 22, 1896.

 5   "M'Kinley Sees Old Friends," *New York Times*, Oct. 22, 1896; "The Like Was Never Seen," *Los Angeles Herald,* Oct. 25, 1896; and "How M'Kinley Feels," *New York Times*, Oct. 25, 1896.

 6   "Plot to Anger Workers," *Chicago Tribune*, Oct. 23, 1896; "Leaders Bandy Hot Talk," *Chicago Tribune*, Oct. 24, 1896; and "Hanna Answers Coercion Charges," *San Francisco Chronicle*, Oct. 22, 1896.

 7   "Railroad Men Against Bryan," *The Sun* (New York), Oct. 28, 1896, and "Bryan's Final Effort," *New-York Tribune*, Oct. 28, 1896.

 8   "Harrison's Tour Begins," *New York Times*, Oct. 21, 1896, and "To Whom Did He Allude?," *New York Times*, Oct. 26, 1896.

 9   "Reply by Carl Schurz," *Chicago Tribune*, Oct. 25, 1896; "It Is Sacrilege," *Los Angeles Times*, Oct. 25, 1896; and "Gen. Schurz Cuts Up Altgeld and Defends Lincoln" and "Schurz's Reply to Altgeld" in *Chicago Tribune*, Oct. 26, 1896.

10   "Wheat Breaking Record," *New York Times,* Oct. 20, 1896; "Bryan in Minnesota," *Chicago Tribune*, Oct. 21, 1896; Gilbert C. Fite, "Republican Strategy and the Farm Vote in the Presidential

Campaign of 1896," *American Historical Review* (LXV, 4) July 1960, 797; Gilbert C. Fite, "William Jennings Bryan and the Campaign of 1896: Some Views and Problems," *Nebraska History* (Volume 47, Number 3), September 1966, 263; and Williams, *Realigning America*, 142.

11 "Liars May Figure But Figures Won't Lie" and "Why Wheat Rises While Silver Falls," *Upper Des Moines* (Algona, IA), Oct. 21, 1896; and *Orange Judd Farmer*, Oct. 26, 1896, quoted by Gilbert C. Fite, "Republican Strategy and the Farm Vote in the Presidential Election of 1896," *American Historical Reviews*, 65, No. 4 (July 1960).

12 "Wheat, Silver and Elections," *Journal of Commerce and Commercial Bulletin* (New York), Oct. 15, 1896; "Call It A Goldbug Trick," *Morning Times* (Washington), Oct. 20, 1896; "Wheat Mounting Higher," *New-York Tribune*, Oct. 20, 1896; "Nails It As A Fake," *St. Paul Globe*, Oct. 21, 1896; and "High Gold, Low Wheat," *Stark County Democrat* (Canton, OH), Oct. 22, 1896.

13 "The Effect on Bryan," *New York Times*, Oct. 21, 1896, and "The Rise in Wheat," *Evening Star* (Washington), Oct. 20, 1896.

14 "Due to Wheat Rise," *Chicago Tribune*, Oct. 19, 1896, and "Free Coinage Rejected by Farmers," *Chicago Tribune*, Oct. 30, 1896.

15 Walter D. Burnham, *Presidential Ballots: 1836–1892* (Baltimore: John Hopkins Press, 1955), 370–71.

16 Hawthorne, Julian, "Bryan's Campaigning," *Washington Post*, October 29, 1896.

17 "To Greet Mr. Bryan," *Chicago Tribune*, October 27, 1896; "Bryan Busy in Chicago," *New York Times*, October 28, 1896; and "Chicago Extends Wild Welcome," *St. Louis Post-Dispatch*, October 28, 1896.

18 "Talks under a Canopy of Canvas" in *Chicago Tribune*, October 28, 1896, and "Twelve Talks by Bryan," *Chicago Tribune*, October 30, 1896.

19 "Addresses Women at Battery D" and "Late At the People's Institute" in *Chicago Tribune*, October 29, 1896, and "Great Sport At the Big Tent" in *Chicago Tribune*, October 30, 1896.

20 "Toilers Listen in Novotny's Hall," "Polish Women Hear the Orator," and "Charges 25 Cents to Hear Bryan" in *Chicago Tribune*, October 29, 1896.

21 "Bryan Talks to Business-men," *Chicago Daily News*, October 29, 1896, and "Bryan's Second Day in Chicago," *Atlanta Constitution*, October 29, 1896.

22 "Bryan Making Votes," *Washington Post*, October 29, 1896; "Bryan Talks to Business-men," *Chicago Daily News*, October 29, 1896; and "Bryan's Second Day in Chicago," *Atlanta Constitution*, October 29, 1896.

23 "Bryan Welcomed At Battery 'D'," *Chicago Tribune*, Oct. 28, 1896; "Tuesday Night's Speeches," *St. Louis Post-Dispatch*, Oct. 28, 1896; and Bryan, *First Battle*, 580–82.

24 "Bryan in the City," *Chicago Tribune*, October 28, 1896; "Gaining Votes," *St. Louis Post-Dispatch*, October 29, 1896; W. A. Edwards, "Bryan Leaves Chicago," *St. Louis Post-Dispatch*, October 30, 1896; "Fears of Bryan's Collapse," *New York Times*, October 30, 1896; and James Creelman, "Bryan's Hurricane Chicago Campaign," *The World* (New York), October 30, 1896.

25 "All Canton Visited Him" and "Tariff Will Be Visible" in *New York Times*, Oct. 29, 1896, and Smith, *McKinley's Speeches in Oct.*, 528–29.

26 "Big Odds are Given," "Four to One Against Altgeld," and "$300,000 to $100,000 Bet" in *New York Times*, Oct. 31, 1896.

27 "Like Penance to Reed" and "Injustice to Mr. Reed" in *Washington Post,* Oct. 27, 1896; "Rallying to Reed," *Oakland Tribune* (Oakland, CA), November 2, 1896; "Tom Reed Closes the Campaign," *Oakland Tribune* (Oakland, CA), November 3, 1896; Grant, *Mr. Speaker!*, 13–16; and Robinson, *Parliamentarian*, 17–19.

28 "Flag Day in Other Places, *New-York Tribune*, November 1, 1896, and "Flags Flaunted" and "Biggest Parade of Worcester" in *Boston Daily Globe*, November 1, 1896.

29 "Like a Dozen Fourths of July in Philadelphia" and "The Parades in Pittsburgh," in *The Sun* (New York), November 1, 1896; "Claims Are Even in Michigan," *Omaha Daily Bee*, November 1, 1896; and "An Enthusiastic Rally in Atlanta," *New-York Tribune*, November 1, 1896.

30 "Flag Day in Ohio," *St. Paul Globe*, November 1, 1896, and "Along the Line," *Logansport Pharos-Tribune* (Logansport, IN), November 1, 1896.

31 "Honor the Flag Today," *Chicago Tribune*, Oct. 31, 1896; "Flag Day Duly Honored," *Chicago Tribune*, November 1, 1896; and "Flag Day in Chicago," *The Sun* (New York), November 1, 1896. Williams says there were "a hundred thousand marchers" in Chicago, but there was no Flag Day parade in the Windy City, given the earlier parade in September. See Williams, *Realigning America*, 143.

32   "Rally 'Round the Flag," *New-York Tribune*, October 28, 1896.

33   "To-Day's Great Parade," *New-York Tribune*, Oct. 31, 1896.

34   Smith, *McKinley's Speeches in Oct.*, 555; "Flag Day's Spirit Voiced," *New-York Tribune*, November 1, 1896; "The Flag and McKinley," *New York Times*, November 1, 1896; "Closing At Canton," *Xenia Daily Gazette* (Xenia, OH), November 2, 1896; "M'Kinley Halts A Panic," *The World* (New York), November 1, 1896; and Williams, *Realigning America*, 143 and 145.

35   "The Republican Leader," *Los Angeles Times*, November 2, 1896; "Sunday Delegation At Canton," *Washington Post*, November 2, 1896; and "Lads of Detroit," *Steubenville Herald* (Steubenville, OH), November 2, 1896.

36   James Creelman, "His Last Day," *The World* (New York), November 2, 1896; "Bryan Spends One Day At Home," *Chicago Tribune*, November 2, 1896; "Bryan At Home," *Los Angeles Times*, November 2, 1896.

37   Diary entry for November 1, 1896, in Dawes, *Journal*, 104.

38   "Bryan Flies to Rescue" and "Hot Fight in Nebraska" in *Chicago Tribune*, Oct. 30, 1896, and "Size Up of Nebraska," *Chicago Tribune*, November 2, 1896.

39   "His Last Day," *The World* (New York), November 2, 1896; "Made Seven Speeches," *Kearney Daily Hub* (Kearney, NE), November 3, 1896; "Bryan's Last Speech Made," *Omaha Daily Bee*, November 3, 1896; "Ovation At Boyd's," *World-Herald* (Omaha, NE), November 3, 1896; Bryan, *First Battle*, 602–4; Calhoun, *From Bloody Shirt to Full Dinner Pail*, 163; Cherny, *Righteous Cause*, 66; Jones, *Election of 1896*, 315–16; and Williams, *Realigning America*, 99. Jones mistakenly says Bryan stopped at "Grand Rapids," but there is no Nebraska town by that name.

40   "Confidence in Canton," *Washington Post*, November 3, 1896; "The Next President," *Los Angeles Times*, November 3, 1896; and "Major McKinley Confident," *New York Times*, November 3, 1896.

41   "Mr. Bryan's Vote," *New-York Tribune*, November 4, 1896; "Whom Did He Vote For?" *Los Angeles Times*, November 4, 1896; and "William M'Kinley Is President," *Atlanta Constitution*, November 4, 1896.

42   "Whom Did He Vote For?," *Los Angeles Times*, November 4, 1896; "Bryan Swears in His Vote," *New York Times*, November 4; James Creelman, "Bryan Silent Under Defeat," *The World* (New York), November 4, 1896; and Bryan, *First Battle*, 602–604.

43   "Major Voted Early," *Salem Daily News* (Salem, OH), November 3, 1896, and "Major M'Kinley," *Canton Repository*, November 4, 1896.

44   "An Imposing Spectacle," *New York Times*, November 4, 1896.

CHAPTER 29: MCKINLEY'S TRIUMPH

1   "Steady Gains in the State," *St. Louis Post-Dispatch*, Nov. 4, 1896

2   Jensen, *Winning of the Midwest*, 292–98; Jones, *Election of 1896*, 346; and Kleppner, *Cross of Culture*, 288, 296, 324, and 351.

3   Jones, *Election of 1896*, 346.

4   James Creelman, "Bryan Silent Under Defeat," *The World* (New York), Nov. 4, 1896; "Refuses to Talk Or Be Seen," *Chicago Tribune*, Nov. 4, 1896; and Bryan, *First Battle*, 605.

5   "M'Kinley Retires At 4 a.m.," *Washington Post*, Nov. 4, 1896, and "Excitement in Canton," *St. Louis Post-Dispatch*, Nov. 4, 1896.

6   Jones, *Election of 1896*, 345; Williams, *Realigning America*, 152; and McSeveney, *Political Behavior in the Northeast*, 178–79.

7   Nathan B. Scott in *Hanna, Memorial Addresses*, 39–40.

8   Kohlsaat, *From McKinley to Harding*, 96.

9   Storer, "How Theodore Roosevelt Was Appointed Assistant Secretary of the Navy," and Morris, *Rise of Theodore Roosevelt*, 672 and 686.

10 Morgan, *McKinley and His America*, 177, and Jensen, *Winning of the Midwest*, 287. Jensen says the railroads reported carrying 756,000 excursion passengers to Canton.

11 Jensen, *Winning of the Midwest*, 291.

12 Morgan, *From Hayes to McKinley*, 509; Morgan, *McKinley and His America*, 173; and Jensen, *Winning the Midwest*, 288.

13 Morgan, *McKinley and His America*, 173; Jones, *Election of 1896*, 283; Croly, *Hanna*, 220; and Dawes to Hanna, Nov. 22, 1896, in Dawes papers.

14 Jones, *Election of 1896*, 346.

BIBLIOGRAPHY

Abbott, Richard H. *The Republican Party and the South, 1855–1877: The First Southern Strategy.* Chapel Hill: University of North Carolina Press, 1986.

Abbot, Willis J. *Watching the World Go By.* New York: Little, Brown, 1933.

Adams, Henry. *The Education of Henry Adams.* New York: Library of America, 2009.

Alexander, Benjamin F. *Coxey's Army: Popular Protest in the Gilded Age.* Baltimore: John Hopkins University Press, 2015.

Altgeld, John P. *Live Questions: Including Our Penal Machinery and Its Victims.* Chicago: Donohue & Henneberry, 1890.

Altschuler, Glenn C., and Stuart M. Blumin. *Rude Republic: Americans and Their Politics in the Nineteenth Century.* Princeton, NJ: Princeton University Press, 2000.

Anthony, Carl Sferrazza. *Ida McKinley: The Turn-of-the-Century First Lady Through War, Assassination, and Secret Disability.* Kent, OH: Kent State University Press, 2013.

———. *Ida Saxton: The Early Life of Mrs. McKinley.* Canton, OH: National First Ladies Library, 2007.

Appleton. *Annual Cyclopaedia and Register of Important Events of the Year 1896.* New York: D. Appleton and Company, 1897.

Argersinger, Peter H. *The Limits of Agrarian Radicalism: Western Populism and American Politics.* Lawrence: University Press of Kansas, 1995.

Armstrong, William H. *Major McKinley: William McKinley & the Civil War.* Kent, OH: Kent State University Press, 2000.

Bain, Richard C., and Judith H. Parris. *Convention Decisions and Voting Records.* Washington, D.C.: Brookings Institution, 1974.

Baker, Jean H. *Affairs of Party: The Political Culture of Northern Democrats in the Mid-Nineteenth Century.* Bronx, NY: Fordham University Press, 1998.

Barnard, Harry. *Eagle Forgotten: The Life of John Peter Altgeld.* Secaucus, NJ: Lyle Stuart, 1938.

Barnes, James A. *John G. Carlisle: Financial Statesman.* New York: Dodd, Mead, 1931.

Barr, Alwyn. *Reconstruction to Reform: Texas Politics, 1876–1906.* Dallas: Southern Methodist University Press, 2000.

Barrett, Don C. *The Greenbacks and Resumption of Specie Payments, 1862–1879.* Cambridge, MA: Harvard University Press, 1931.

Baxter, Maurice. *Henry Clay and the American System.* Lexington: University Press of Kentucky, 2004.

Beer, Thomas. *Hanna.* New York: Knopf, 1929.

———. *The Mauve Decade: 1880–1890.* Garden City, NY: Garden City, 1926.

Belden, Henry S., III. *Grand Tour of Ida Saxton McKinley and Sister Mary Saxton Barber, 1869.* Canton, OH: Reserve, 1985.

Bensel, Richard F. *Passion and Preferences: William Jennings Bryan and the 1896 Democratic National Convention.* Cambridge: Cambridge University Press, 2008.

———. *The Political Economy of American Industrialization, 1877–1900.* Cambridge: Cambridge University Press, 2000.

Blaine, James G. *Twenty Years of Congress 1861–1881.* Vol. 2. Philadelphia: Henry Bill, 1886.

Boorstin, Daniel J. *The Americans: The Democratic Experience.* New York: Vintage Books, 1973.

Boyd, Thomas B. *The Blaine and Logan Campaign of 1884*. Chicago: J. L. Regan, 1884.

Brands, H. W. *American Colossus: The Triumph of Capitalism 1865–1900*. New York: Doubleday, 2010.

———. *Man Who Saved the Union: Ulysses Grant in War and Peace*. New York: Anchor, 2013.

———. *The Reckless Decade: America in the 1890s*. Chicago: University of Chicago Press, 2002.

Bristow, Joseph L. *Fraud and Politics and the Turn of the Century: McKinley and His Administration As Seen by His Principal Patronage Dispenser and Investigator*. New York: Exposition Press, 1952.

Bryan, William J. *The First Battle: A Story of the Campaign of 1896*. Hammond, IN: W. B. Conkey, 1896.

Bryan, William J., and Mary Baird Bryan. *Memoirs of William Jennings Bryan, by Himself and His Wife*. Chicago: United Publishers of America, 1925.

Budiansky, Stephen. *The Bloody Shirt: Terror After the Civil War*. New York: Penguin, 2008.

Burnham, Walter D. *Critical Elections and the Mainsprings of American Politics*. New York: Norton, 1971.

———. *Presidential Ballots: 1836–1892*. Baltimore: John Hopkins University Press, 1955.

Burnham, Walter D., Thomas Ferguson, and Louis Ferleger. *Voting in American Elections*. Palo Alto, CA: Academica Press, 2009.

Butterworth, Alex. *The World That Never Was: A True Story of Dreamers, Schemers, Anarchists and Secret Agents*. New York: Pantheon Books, 2010.

Byars, William V. *An American Commoner: The Life and Times of Richard Parks Bland, a Study of the Last Quarter of the 19th Century*. Columbia, MO: E. W. Stephens, 1900.

Calhoun, Charles W. *Benjamin Harrison: The American Presidents Series: The 23rd President, 1889–1893*. Edited by Arthur M. Schlesinger. New York: Times Books, 2005.

———. *From Bloody Shirt to Full Dinner Pail: The Transformation of Politics and Governance in the Gilded Age*. New York: Hill & Wang, 2010.

———, ed. *The Gilded Age: Perspectives on the Origins of Modern America*. Lanham, MD: Rowman & Littlefield, 2006.

———. *Minority Victory: Gilded Age Politics and the Front Porch Campaign of 1888*. Lawrence: University Press of Kansas, 2008.

———. *Conceiving a New Republic: The Republican Party and the Southern Question, 1869–1900*. Lawrence: University Press of Kansas, 2006.

Cashman, Sean D. *America in the Gilded Age: From the Death of Lincoln to the Rise of Theodore Roosevelt*. New York: New York University Press, 1988.

Chernow, Ron. *The House of Morgan: An American Banking Dynasty and the Rise of Modern Finance*. New York: Grove Press, 2001.

Cherny, Robert W. *American Politics in the Gilded Age, 1868–1900*. Wheeling, IL: Harlan Davidson, 2009.

———. *A Righteous Cause: The Life of William Jennings Bryan*. Norman: University of Oklahoma Press, 1994.

Clark, Champ. *My Quarter Century of American Politics*. Vol. 1. Whitefish, MT: Kessinger, 2007.

Coletta, Paolo E. *William Jennings Bryan: Political Evangelist, 1860–1908*. Lincoln: University of Nebraska Press, 1964.

Cowles, Anna R., comp. *Letters from Theodore Roosevelt to Anna Roosevelt Cowles, 1870–1918*. New York: Charles Scribner's Sons, 1924.

Craig, Lee A. *Josephus Daniels: His Life & Times*. Chapel Hill: University of North Carolina Press, 2013.

Crapol, Edward P. *James G. Blaine: Architect of Empire*. Lanham, MD: Rowman & Littlefield, 1999.

Crichton, Judy. *America 1900: The Sweeping Story of a Pivotal Year in the Life of the Nation*. New York: Henry Holt, 2000.

Croly, Herbert D. *Marcus Alonzo Hanna: His Life and Work*. New York: Macmillan, 1912.

Cullom, Shelby M. *Fifty Years of Public Service*. Gloucester, UK: Dodo Press, 2009.

Current, Richard N. *Those Terrible Carpetbaggers: A Reinterpretation*. Oxford: Oxford University Press, 1988.

Cushman, Charles R. *Memorial Addresses: Abraham Lincoln, James Garfield, William McKinley*. Washington, D.C.: U.S. Government Printing Office, 1903.

Dalton, Kathleen. *Theodore Roosevelt: A Strenuous Life*. New York: Knopf, 2002.

Daniels, Josephus. *Editor in Politics*. Westport, CT: Praeger, 1974.

Darrow, Clarence. *The Story of My Life*. New York: Da Capo Press, 1996.

Dawes, Charles G. *A Journal of the McKinley Years*. Chicago: Lakeside Press, 1950.

Dawson, George F. *The Republican Campaign Text-Book for 1888*. New York: Brentano's, 1888, accessed June 11, 2013. http://archive.org/stream/republicancampa00usgoog#page/n4/mode/2up.

———. *The Republican Campaign Text-Book for 1892*. New York: Republican National Committee, 1892, accessed June 11, 2013. http://archive.org/stream/republicancampa01usgoog#page/n4/mode/2up.

———. *The Republican Campaign Text-Book for 1896*. Washington, D.C.: Hartman & Cadick, 1896.

Davenport, Homer. *Cartoons*. St. Paul: De Witt, 1899.

Dearing, Mary R. *Veterans in Politics: The Story of the G.A.R.* Westport, CT: Greenwood Press, 1974.

Degler, Carl N. *Age of the Economic Revolution, 1876–1900*. Glenview, IL: Scott, Foresman, 1967.

Democratic National Committee. *Campaign Text Book of the Democratic Party for the Presidential Election of 1892*. New York: M. B. Brown, 1892. Accessed June 11, 2013. http://archive.org/stream/campaigntextboo00goog#page/n6/mode/2up.

———. *Campaign Text Book of the National Democratic Party 1896*. 2nd ed. Chicago and New York: n.p., 1896.

Democratic Party National Convention, Chicago, 1896. *Official Proceedings of the Democratic National Convention Held in Chicago, Ill., July 7th, 8th, 9th, 10th and 11th, 1896*. Reported by Edward B. Dickinson. Logansport, IN: Wilson, Humphreys, 1896.

De Santis, Vincent P. *Republicans Face the Southern Question—The New Departure Years, 1877–1897*. Baltimore: John Hopkins University Press, 1959.

———. *The Shaping of Modern America: 1877–1920, 3rd Edition*. Boston: Allyn and Bacon, 1973.

Doenecke, Justus D. *The Presidencies of James A. Garfield and Chester A. Arthur*. Lawrence: University Press of Kansas, 1981.

Dray, Philip. *Capitol Men: The Epic Story of Reconstruction Through the Lives of the First Black Congressmen*. Boston: Houghton Mifflin, 2008.

Dunn, Arthur W. *From Harrison to Harding: A Personal Narrative, Covering a Third of a Century 1888–1921*. New York: G. P. Putnam's Sons, 1922.

Durden, Robert F. *The Climax of Populism: The Election of 1896*. Lexington: University of Kentucky Press, 1966.

Eckenrode, H. J. *Rutherford B. Hayes: Statesman of Reunion*. New York: Dodd, Mead, 1930.

Edwards, Rebecca. *New Spirits: Americans in the Gilded Age, 1865–1905*. Oxford: Oxford University Press, 2006.

Egerton, Douglas R. *The Wars of Reconstruction: The Brief, Violent History of America's Most Progressive Era*. New York: Bloomsbury Press, 2014.

Ellis, Elmer. *Henry Moore Teller: Defender of the West*. Caldwell, ID: Caxton, 1941.

Engs, Robert F., and Randall M. Miller, eds. *The Birth of the Grand Old Party: The Republicans' First Generation*. Philadelphia: University of Pennsylvania Press, 2002.

Everett, Marshall. *Complete Life of William McKinley and Story of His Assassination: An Authentic and Official Memorial Edition Containing Every Incident in the Career of the Immortal Statesman Soldier Orator and Patriot, Memorial Edition*. N.p.: n.p., 1901.

Fallows, Samuel, ed. *Life of William McKinley: Our Martyred President*. Chicago: Regan, 1901.

Fifty-Sixth United States Congress. *Memorial Addresses on the Life and Character of Richard P. Bland Delivered in the House of Representatives and Senate*. Washington, D.C.: U.S. Government Printing Office, 1900.

Foner, Eric. *Free Soil, Free Labor, Free Men: The Ideology of the Republicans Party Before the Civil War*. New York: Oxford University Press, 1970.

———. *Reconstruction: America's Unfinished Revolution: 1863–1877*. New York: Harper & Row, 1988.

Foote, Shelby. *Civil War: A Narrative: Volume One: Fort Sumter to Perryville*. New York: Vintage Books, 1986.

———. *Civil War: A Narrative: Volume Three: Red River to Appomattox*. New York: Random House, 1974.

Foraker, Joseph B. *Notes of a Busy Life*. Cincinnati: Stewart & Kidd, 1916.

Foraker, Julia B. *I Would Live It Again*. New York and London: Harper & Brothers, 1932.

Fowkes, Henry L. *Historical Encyclopedia of Illinois*. Vol. 1. Christian County, IL: Munsell, 1918.

Franklin John Hope. *Reconstruction After the Civil War*. 2nd ed. Chicago: University of Chicago Press, 1991.

Friedman, Milton and Anna Jacobson Schwartz. *A Monetary History of the United States, 1867–1960*. Princeton, NJ: Princeton University Press, 1971.

Garraty, John A. *Henry Cabot Lodge: A Biography*. New York: Knopf, 1965.

————. *The New Commonwealth: 1877–1890*. New York: Harper & Row, 1968.

Gilbert, Martin. *Churchill and America*. New York: Simon & Schuster, 2007.

Glad, Paul W. *McKinley, Bryan, and the People*. Philadelphia: J. B. Lippincott, 1964.

————. *The Trumpet Soundeth: William Jennings Bryan and His Democracy, 1896–1912*. Lincoln: University of Nebraska Press, 1966.

Golway, Terry. *Machine Made: Tammany Hall and the Creation of Modern American Politics*. New York: Liveright, 2014.

Goode, James M. *Capital Losses: A Cultural History of Washington's Destroyed Buildings*. Washington, D.C.: Smithsonian Institution Press, 1979.

Goodwyn, Lawrence. *The Populist Movement: A Short History of the Agrarian Revolt in America*. Oxford: Oxford University Press, 1978.

Gordon, John S. *An Empire of Wealth: The Epic History of American Economic Power*. New York: Harper Perennial, 2004.

Gosnell, Harold S. *Boss Platt and His New York Machine: A Study of the Political Leadership of Thomas C. Platt, Theodore Roosevelt and Others*. Chicago: University of Chicago Press, 1924.

Gould, Lewis L. *Grand Old Party: A History of the Republicans*. New York: Random House, 2003.

————. *The Modern American Presidency*. Lawrence: University Press of Kansas, 2003.

————. *The Presidency of William McKinley*. Lawrence: University Press of Kansas, 1981.

————. *Wyoming: A Political History, 1868–1896*. New Haven, CT: Yale University Press, 1968.

Gould, Lewis L., and Craig H. Roell. *William McKinley: A Bibliography*. London: Meckler, 1988.

Graff, Henry F. *Grover Cleveland*. New York: Times Books, 2002.

Grant, James. *Mr. Speaker! The Life and Times of Thomas B. Reed—The Man Who Broke the Filibuster*. New York: Simon & Schuster, 2012.

Grantham, Dewey W. *Hoke Smith and the Politics of the New South*. Baton Rouge: Louisiana State University Press, 1958.

Halstead, Murat. *The Illustrious Life of William McKinley, Our Martyred President*. N.p.: n.p., 1901.

————. *Life and Distinguished Services of William McKinley, Our Martyred President*. N.p.: n.p., 1901.

Hanna, Marcus A., and Joe M. Chapple. *Mark Hanna: His Book*. Boston: Chapple, 1904.

Hare, Maud C. *Norris Wright Cuney: A Tribune of the Black People*. New York: The Crisis, 1913.

Harpine, William D. *From the Front Porch to the Front Page: McKinley and Bryan in the 1896 Presidential Campaign*. College Station: Texas A&M University Press, 2006.

Harvey, William H. *Coin's Financial School*. Edited by Richard Hofstadter. Cambridge, MA: Harvard University Press, 1963.

Hartzell, Josiah. *Sketch of the Life of Mrs. William McKinley*. Washington, D.C.: Home Magazine Press, 1896.

Haugen, Nils P. *Pioneer and Political Reminiscences*. Evansville, WI: Antes Press, n.d.

Hay, John. *Letters of John Hay and Extracts from Diary*. Vol. 3. Washington, D.C.: n.p., 1808.

————. *William McKinley, Memorial Address*. New York: Thomas Y. Crowell, 1902.

Hays, Samuel P. *The Response to Industrialism: 1885–1914*. Chicago: University of Chicago Press, 1957.

Hepburn, A. Barton. *History of Coinage and Currency in the United States and the Perennial Contest for Sound Money*. New York: Macmillan, 1903. Accessed June 11, 2013. http://archive.org/stream /cu31924021526037#page/n5/mode/2up.

Hirsch, Mark D. *William C. Whitney: Modern Warwick*. New York: Dodd, Mead, 1948.

Hirshson, Stanley. *Farewell to the Bloody Shirt: Northern Republicans and the Southern Negro, 1877–1893*. Bloomington: Indiana University Press, 1962.

Hoar, George Frisbie. *Autobiography of Seventy Years*. Vol. 1. New York: Charles Scribner's Sons, 1905.

Hofstadter, Richard. *The Age of Reform*. New York: Vintage Books, 1955.

————. *The Paranoid Style in American Politics*. New York: Vintage Books, 2008.

Hollingsworth, J. Rogers. *The Whirligig of Politics: The Democracy of Cleveland and Bryan*. Chicago: University of Chicago Press, 1963.

Holt, Michael F. *By One Vote: The Disputed Presidential Election of 1876*. Lawrence: University Press of Kansas, 2011.

Hoogenboom, Ari. *The Presidency of Rutherford B. Hayes*. Lawrence: University Press of Kansas, 1988.

————. *Rutherford B. Hayes, Warrior & President*. Lawrence: University Press of Kansas, 1995.

Horner, William T. *Ohio's Kingmaker: Mark Hanna, Man and Myth*. Athens: Ohio University Press, 2010.

Howe, George F. *Chester A. Arthur: A Quarter Century of Machine Politics*. New York: Dodd, Mead, 1934.

Hunt, James L. *Marion Butler and American Populism*. Chapel Hill: University of North Carolina Press, 2003.

Jacker, Corinne. *The Black Flag of Anarchy: Antistatism in the United States*. New York and London: Charles Scribner's Sons, 1968.

Jensen, Richard J. *The Winning of the Midwest: Social and Political Conflict, 1888–1896*. Chicago: University of Chicago Press, 1971.

Johns, A. Wesley. *The Man Who Shot McKinley: A New View of the Assassination of the President*. New York: A. S. Barnes, 1970.

Johnson, Donald B., and Kirk H. Porter. *National Party Platforms, 1840–1972*. Champaign: University of Illinois Press, 1973.

Johnson, Robert U. *Remembered Yesterdays*. Whitefish, MT: Kessinger, 2004.

Jonas, Frank H., ed. *Politics in the American West*. Salt Lake City: University of Utah Press, 1969.

Jones, Stanley L. *The Presidential Election of 1896*. Madison: University of Wisconsin Press, 1964.

Jordan, David M. *Winfield Scott Hancock: A Soldier's Life*. Bloomington: Indiana University Press, 1996.

Jordan, Philip D. *Ohio Comes of Age, 1873–1900*. Columbus, OH: Ohio Archaeological and Historical Society, 1943.

Josephson, Matthew. *The Politicos, 1865–1896*. San Diego: Harcourt Brace & World, 1938.

———. *The Robber Barons: The Classic Account of the Influential Capitalists Who Transformed America's Future*. New York: Harcourt, 1932.

Kazin, Michael. *A Godly Hero: The Life of William Jennings Bryan*. New York: Anchor, 2007.

———. *The Populist Persuasion: An American History*. New York: Basic Books, 1995.

Kehl, James A. *Boss Rule in the Gilded Age: Matt Quay of Pennsylvania*. Pittsburgh: University of Pittsburgh Press, 1981.

Keller, Morton. *Affairs of State: Public Life in Late Nineteenth Century America*. Cambridge, MA: Belknap Press of Harvard University Press, 1977.

Kenney, Christopher. *The McKinley Monument: A Tribute to a Fallen President*. Charleston, SC: History Press, 2006.

Kenney, Kimberly A. *Canton, OH: A Journey Through Time*. Mount Pleasant, SC: Arcadia, 2003.

Kerr, Winfield S. *John Sherman* Vol. II: *His Life and Public Services*. Whitefish, MT: Kessinger, 2010.

Kinzer, Donald L. *An Episode in Anti-Catholicism: The American Protective Association*. Seattle: University of Washington Press, 1964.

Kirkland, Edward C. *Industry Comes of Age, Business, Labor, and Public Policy 1860–1897*. Chicago: Quadrangle Books, 1967.

Kleppner, Paul. *Continuity and Change in Electoral Politics, 1893–1928*. Westport, CT: Greenwood Press, 1987.

———. *The Cross of Culture: A Social Analysis of Midwestern Politics, 1850–1900*. New York: Free Press, 1970.

———. *Third Electoral System, 1853–1892: Parties, Voters, and Political Cultures*. Chapel Hill: University of North Carolina Press, 1979.

———. *Who Voted? The Dynamics of Electoral Turnout, 1870–1980*. Westport, CT: Praeger, 1982.

Knight, Lucian Lamar. *Georgia's Landmarks, Memorials, and Legends, Part 1*. Gretna, LA: Pelican, 2006.

Koenig, Louis W. *Bryan: A Political Biography of William Jennings Bryan*. New York: Putnam, 1971.

Kohlsaat, H. H. *From McKinley to Harding: Personal Recollections of Our Presidents*. New York and London: Charles Scribner's Sons, 1923.

Kohn, Edward P. *Heir to the Empire City: New York and the Making of Theodore Roosevelt*. New York: Basic Books, 2014.

———. *Hot Time in the Old Town: The Great Heat Wave of 1896 and the Making of Theodore Roosevelt*. New York: Basic Books, 2010.

Kousser, J. Morgan. *The Shaping of Southern Politics: Suffrage Restriction and the Establishment of the One-Party South, 1880–1910*. New Haven, CT: Yale University Press, 1974.

Lachman, Charles. *The Last Lincolns: The Rise and Fall of a Great American Family*. New York City: Union Square Press, 2008.

La Follette, Belle C., and Fola La Follette. *Robert M. La Follette: June 14, 1855–June 18, 1925*. Vol. 1. New York: Macmillan, 1953.

Lambert, Oscar D. *Stephen Benton Elkins: American Foursquare*. Pittsburgh: University of Pittsburgh Press, 1955.

Lamborn, Levi L. *American Carnation Culture*. Alliance, OH: Lo Ra L. Lamborn, 1901.

Lang, Louis J., ed. *The Autobiography of Thomas Collier Platt*. New York: B. W. Dodge, 1910.

Lansden, John M. *A History of the City of Cairo, Illinois*. Carbondale: Southern Illinois University Press, 1976.

Larson, Laurence M. *The Log Book of a Young Immigrant*. Northfield, MN: Norwegian-American Historical Association, 1939. Accessed June 11, 2013. http://archive.org/stream/logbookofyoungim00 lars#page/n5/mode/2up.

Leach, Paul R. *That Man Dawes: The Story of a Man Who Has Placed His Name High Among the Great of the World in This Generation Because He Ruled His Life by Common Sense*. Chicago: Reilly & Britton, 1930.

Leech, Margaret. *In the Days of McKinley*. New York: Harper & Brothers, 1959.

Lemann, Nicholas. *Redemption: The Last Battle of the Civil War*. New York: Farrar, Straus & Giroux, 2006.

Lloyd, Caro. *Henry Demarest Lloyd*. Vol. 1. Charleston, SC: Bibliolife, 2009.

Luebke, Frederick C. *Immigrants and Politics: The Germans of Nebraska, 1880–1900*. Lincoln: University of Nebraska Press, 1969.

Magliocca, Gerard N. *The Tragedy of William Jennings Bryan*. New Haven and London: Yale University Press, 2014.

Marcus, Robert. *Grand Old Party: Political Structure in the Gilded Age, 1880–1896*. Oxford: Oxford University Press, 1971.

Martin, Ralph G. *Jennie: The Life of Lady Randolph Churchill, the Romantic Years, 1854–1895*. London: Littlehampton Book Services, 1969.

Mayer, George. *The Republican Party, 1854–1964*. Oxford: Oxford University Press, 1964.

Mayhew, David R. *Electoral Realignments: A Critique of an American Genre*. New Haven, CT: Yale University Press, 2002.

McCall, Samuel W. *The Life of Thomas Brackett Reed*. Boston and New York: Houghton Mifflin, 1914.

McClure, Alexander K., and Charles Morris. *The Authentic Life of William McKinley, Our Third Martyr President*. Toronto: W. E. Skull, 1901.

McCormick, Richard L. *The Party Period and Public Policy: American Politics from the Age of Jackson to the Progressive Era*. Oxford: Oxford University Press, 1986.

McCullough, David. *Mornings on Horseback*. New York: Simon & Schuster, 1981.

McDonald, Forrest. *E Pluribus Unum: The Formation of the American Republic, 1776–1790*. Indianapolis, IN: Liberty Fund, 1979.

McElroy, Richard L. *William McKinley and Our America: A Pictorial History*. Canton, OH: Stark County Historical Society, 1996.

McFeely, William S. *Grant: A Biography*. New York: Norton, 1982.

McGerr, Michael E. *The Decline of Popular Politics: The American North, 1865–1928*. Oxford: Oxford University Press, 1988.

———. *A Fierce Discontent: The Rise and Fall of the Progressive Movement in America, 1870–1920*. New York: Free Press, 2003.

McGurrin, James. *Bourke Cockran: A Free Lance in American Politics*. New York: Charles Scribner's Sons, 1948.

McKinley, William. *McKinley, the People's Choice. The Congratulations of the Country, the Calls of Delegations at Canton, the Addresses by Them. His Eloquent and Effective Responses. Full Text of Each Speech or Address Made by Him from June 18 to August 1, 1896*. Compiled by Joseph P. Smith. Canton, OH: Repository Press, 1896.

———. *McKinley Speeches in August*. Compiled by Joseph P. Smith. Canton, OH: Repository Press, 1896.

———. *McKinley Speeches in September*. Compiled by Joseph P. Smith. Canton, OH: Repository Press, 1896.

———. *McKinley Speeches in October*. Compiled by Joseph P. Smith. Canton, OH: Repository Press, 1896.

———. *Speeches and Addresses of William McKinley, From His Election to Congress to the Present Time*. Compiled by Joseph P. Smith. New York: D. Appleton, 1893.

McMillin, Benton. *Democratic Party National Committee and Democratic Congressional Committee. Democratic Campaign Book Presidential Election of 1896*. Washington, D.C.: Hartman & Cadick, 1896.

McSeveney, Samuel T. *Politics of Depression: Political Behavior in the Northeast: 1893–1896*. Oxford: Oxford University Press, 1972.

Merrill, Horace S. *Bourbon Democracy of the Middle West, 1865–1896*. Seattle: University of Washington Press, 1967.

———. *Bourbon Leader: Grover Cleveland and the Democratic Party*. New York: Little, Brown, 1957.

Millard, Candice. *Destiny of the Republic: A Tale of Madness, Medicine, and the Murder of a President*. New York: Doubleday, 2011.

Miller, Nathan. *Theodore Roosevelt: A Life*. New York: William Morrow, 1992.

Miller, Scott. *The President and the Assassin: McKinley, Terror, and Empire at the Dawn of the American Century*. New York: Random House, 2011.

Moos, Malcolm. *The Republicans*. New York: Random House, 1956.

Morgan, H. Wayne. *From Hayes to McKinley: National Party Politics, 1877–1896*. Syracuse, NY: Syracuse University Press, 1969.

———, ed. *The Gilded Age: A Reappraisal*. Syracuse, NY: Syracuse University Press, 1970.

———. *William McKinley and His America*. Kent, OH: The Kent State University Press, 2003.

Morison, Elting E. *The Letters of Theodore Roosevelt*. Vol. 1, *The Years of Preparation: 1868–1898*. Cambridge, MA: Harvard University Press, 1951.

Morris, Charles R. *The Dawn of Innovation: The First American Industrial Revolution*. New York: Public Affairs, 2012.

Morris, Edmund. *The Rise of Theodore Roosevelt*. New York: Coward, McCann & Geoghegan, 1979.

Morris, Roy, Jr. *Fraud of the Century: Rutherford B. Hayes, Samuel Tilden, and the Stolen Election of 1876*. New York: Simon & Schuster, 2003.

Morrison, Joseph L. *Josephus Daniels: The Small-d Democrat*. Chapel Hill: University of North Carolina Press, 1966.

Mott, Thomas B. *Myron T. Herrick, Friend of France; An Autobiographical Biography*. Garden City, NY: Doubleday, Doran, 1929.

Myers, Gustavus. *The History of Tammany Hall*. 2nd ed. New York: Boni & Liveright, Inc., 1917.

Nasaw, David. *The Chief: The Life of William Randolph Hearst*. New York: Houghton Mifflin, 2000.

Neilson, James W. *Shelby M. Cullom, Prairie State Republican*. Champaign: University of Illinois Press, 1962.

Nevins, Allan. *Grover Cleveland: A Study in Courage*. Vol. 1. New York: Dodd, Mead, 1932.

———. *Grover Cleveland: A Study in Courage*. Vol. 2. New York: Dodd, Mead, 1932.

———. *Letters of Grover Cleveland: 1850–1908*. Boston & New York: Houghton, 1933.

Nichols, Jeannette P., and James G. Randall. *Democracy in the Middle West, 1840–1940*. New York: D. Appleton-Century, 1941.

Olcott, Charles S. *The Life of William McKinley*. Vols. 1 and 2. Boston and New York: Houghton Mifflin, 1916.

Olcott, William D. *Burrows of Michigan and the Republican Party*. Vol. 1. New York: Longmans, Green, 1917. Accessed June 11, 2013. http://archive.org/stream/burrowsofmichiga01orcu#page/n7/mode/2up.

Ostler, Jeffrey. *Prairie Populism: The Fate of Agrarian Radicalism in Kansas, Nebraska, and Iowa, 1880–1892*. Lawrence: University Press of Kansas, 1992.

O'Toole, Patricia. *The Five of Hearts: An Intimate Portrait of Henry Adams and His Friends: 1880–1981*. New York: Clarkson Potter, 1990.

Painter, Nell Irvin. *Standing at Armageddon: A Grassroots History of the Progressive Era*. New York: Norton, 2008.

Palmer, Bruce. *"Man Over Money": The Southern Populist Critique of American Capitalism*. Chapel Hill: University of North Carolina Press, 1980.

Paschen, Stephen H., and Leonard Schlup, eds. *Presidential Campaign Letters and Speeches of James A. Garfield (1880), Benjamin Harrison (1896), and William Howard Taft (1908)*. Lewiston, NY: Edwin Mellen Press, 2010.

Perman, Michael. *The Road to Redemption: Southern Politics, 1869–1879*. Chapel Hill: University of North Carolina Press, 1984.

———. *Struggle for Mastery: Disfranchisement in the South 1888–1908*. Chapel Hill: University of North Carolina Press, 2001.

Perret, Geoffrey. *Ulysses S. Grant: Soldier and President*. New York: Modern Library, 1998.

Perry, James. M. *Touched with Fire: Five Presidents and the Civil War Battles That Made Them*. New York: Public Affairs, 2003.

Peskin, Allan. *Garfield*. Kent: Kent State University Press, 1978.

Peterson, Merrill D. *Olive Branch and Sword: The Compromise of 1833*. Baton Rouge: Louisiana State University Press, 1982.

Phillips, Kevin. *William McKinley: The American Presidents Series: The 25th President, 1897–1901.* Edited by Arthur M. Schlesinger. New York: Times Books, 2003.

Porter, Robert P. *Life of William McKinley: Soldier, Lawyer, Statesman.* Cleveland: N. G. Hamilton, 1906.

Powers, Samuel L. *Portraits of a Half Century.* Boston: Little, Brown, 1925.

Pringle, Henry F. *Theodore Roosevelt: A Biography.* New York: Cornwall Press, 1931.

Pyle, Joseph G. *The Life of James J. Hill.* Vol. 1. New York: Doubleday Page, 1917.

Ratner, Sidney, James H. Soltow, et al. *The Evolution of the American Economy: Growth, Welfare, and Decision Making.* 2nd ed. New York: Macmillan, 1993.

Rauchway, Eric. *Murdering McKinley: The Making of Theodore Roosevelt's America.* New York: Hill & Wang, 2003.

Rehnquist, William H. *Centennial Crisis: The Disputed Election of 1876.* New York: Vintage Books, 2004.

Reichley, James A. *The Life of the Parties: A History of American Political Parties.* Lanham, MD: Rowman & Littlefield, 2000.

Reitano, Joanne. *The Tariff Question and the Gilded Age: The Great Debate of 1888.* University Park: Pennsylvania State University Press, 1994.

Remini, Robert V. *Henry Clay: Statesman for the Union.* New York: Norton, 1993.

Republican National Convention, Chicago, 1884. *Official Proceedings of the Eighth Republican National Convention Held at Chicago, IL, June 3, 4, 5, and 6, 1884.* Rand, McNally and Company, 1884.

Republican National Convention, Chicago, 1888. *Official Proceedings of the Ninth Republican National Convention Held at Chicago, IL, June 19, 20, 21, 22, 23, and 25, 1888.* Reported by Gustavus P. English. The Blakely Printing Co., 1888.

Republican National Convention, Minneapolis, 1892. *Official Proceedings of the Tenth Republican National Convention Held at Minneapolis, MN, June 7, 8, 9, and 10, 1892.* Reported by Theodore C. Rose and James F. Burke. Harrison & Smith, 1892.

Republican National Convention, St. Louis, 1896. *Official Proceedings of the Eleventh Republican National Convention Held at St. Louis, MO, June 16, 17, and 18, 1896.* Reported by James Francis Burke. N.p.: n.p., 1896.

Rhodes, James F. *History of the United States from the Compromise of 1850 to the McKinley-Bryan Campaign of 1896.* New York and London: Macmillan, 1920.

———. *The McKinley and Roosevelt Administrations, 1897–1909.* New York and London: Macmillan, 1922.

Richardson, Heather C. *The Death of Reconstruction: Race, Labor, and Politics in the Post–Civil War North, 1865–1901.* Cambridge, MA: Harvard University Press, 2001.

———. *The Greatest Nation of the Earth: Republican Economic Policies During the Civil War.* Cambridge, MA: Harvard University Press, 1997.

Richardson, Leon B. *William E. Chandler, Republican.* New York: Dodd, Mead, 1940.

Ridge, Martin. *Ignatius Donnelly: The Portrait of a Politician.* St. Paul: Minnesota Historical Society Press, 1991.

Ritter, Gretchen. *Goldbugs and Greenbacks: The Antimonopoly Tradition and the Politics of Finance in America.* Cambridge, MA: Cambridge University Press, 1999.

Rixey, Presley M. *Medical and Surgical Report of the Case of the Late President of the United States: Extracted from the Report of the Surgeon General, U.S. Navy.* Washington, D.C.: U.S. Government Printing Office, 1901.

Robinson, William A. *Thomas B. Reed: Parliamentarian.* New York: Dodd, Mead, 1930.

Roe, Edward T. *The Life Work of William McKinley.* Chicago: Laird & Lee, 1901.

Roosevelt, Theodore. *Campaigns and Controversies.* Vol. 14 of *The Works of Theodore Roosevelt.* New York: Charles Scribner's Sons, 1926.

Roosevelt, Theodore, and Henry C. Lodge. *Selections from the Correspondence of Theodore Roosevelt and Henry Cabot Lodge: 1884–1918.* Vol. 1. New York and London: Charles Scribner's Sons, 1923.

Roseboom, Eugene H. *A History of Presidential Elections.* New York: Macmillan, 1957.

Rosser, Charles M., and Josephus Daniels. *The Crusading Commoner: A Close-Up of William Jennings Bryan and His Times.* Dallas, TX: Mathias, Van Nort & Co., 1937.

Russell, Henry B. *The Lives of William McKinley and Garret A. Hobart, Republican Presidential Candidates of 1896.* Hartford, CT: A. D. Worthington, 1896.

Sage, Leland L. *William Boyd Allison: A Study in Practical Politics.* Des Moines: State Historical Society of Iowa, 1956.

Sageser, Adelbert B. *Joseph L. Bristow: Kansas Progressive*. Lawrence: University Press of Kansas, 1968.

Seibert, Jeffrey W. *I Done My Duty: The Complete Story of the Assassination of President McKinley*. Berwyn Heights, MD: Heritage Books, 2002.

Shadgett, Olive H. *The Republican Party in Georgia: From Reconstruction Through 1900*. Athens: University of Georgia Press, 1964.

Sheldon, William DuBose. *Populism in the Old Dominion: Virginia Farm Politics, 1885–1900*. Gloucester, MA: Peter Smith, 1935.

Sherman, John. *Recollections of Forty Years in the House, Senate, and Cabinet*. Vol. 2. Chicago: Werner, 1895. Accessed June 11, 2013. http://archive.org/stream/johnshermanrecoll02sherrich#page/n7/mode/2up.

Siepel, Kevin H. *Rebel: The Life and Times of John Singleton Mosby*. New York: St. Martin's Press, 1983.

Sievers, Harry J. *Benjamin Harrison*. Vol. 1, *Hoosier Warrior*. New York: University Publishers, 1952.

———. *Benjamin Harrison*. Vol. 2, *Hoosier Statesman*. New York: University Publishers, 1959.

———. *Benjamin Harrison*. Vol. 3, *Hoosier President*. Indianapolis: Bobbs-Merrill, 1968.

Simkins, Francis B. *Pitchfork Ben Tillman: South Carolinian*. Gloucester, MA: Peter Smith, 1964.

Simpson, Brooks D. *The Reconstruction Presidents*. Lawrence: University Press of Kansas, 1998.

Smith, Jean E. *Grant*. New York: Simon & Schuster, 2001.

Smith, Joseph P. *The History of the Republican Party in Ohio*. Vol. 1. Gale, Sabin Americana, 2012.

Smith, Samuel D. *The Negro in Congress: 1870–1901*. Chapel Hill: University of North Carolina Press, 1940.

Socolofsky, Homer E., and Allan B. Spetter. *The Presidency of Benjamin Harrison*, Lawrence: University Press of Kansas, 1987.

Spielman, William C. *William McKinley, Stalwart Republican: A Biographical Study*. Hicksville, NY: Exposition Press, 1954.

Stampp, Kenneth M. *The Era of Reconstruction, 1865–1877*. New York: Vintage Books, 1965.

Stanwood, Edward. *American Tariff Controversies of the Nineteenth Century*. Boston: Houghton Mifflin, 1903.

Steevens, G. W. *The Land of the Dollar (An Englishman's Impressions of America)*. New York: Dodd, Mead, 1897.

Sterling, Dorothy. *Captain of the Planter: The Story of Robert Smalls*. New York: Doubleday, 1957.

Stern, Clarence A. *Golden Republicanism: The Crusade for Hard Money*. Ann Arbor, MI: Edward Brothers, 1970.

———. *Republican Heyday: Republicanism Through the McKinley Years*. Ann Arbor, MI: Edward Brothers, 1962.

———. *Resurgent Republicanism: The Handiwork of Hanna*. Ann Arbor, MI: Edward Brothers, 1968.

Stoddard, Henry L. *As I Knew Them: Presidents and Politics from Grant to Coolidge*. New York: Harper & Brothers, 1927.

Summers, Mark W. *The Era of Good Stealings*. Oxford: Oxford University Press, 1993.

———. *Party Games: Getting, Keeping, and Using Power in Gilded Age Politics*. Chapel Hill: University of North Carolina Press, 2004.

———. *The Press Gang: Newspapers and Politics, 1865–1878*. Chapel Hill: University of North Carolina Press, 1994.

———. *Rum, Romanism & Rebellion: The Making of a President, 1884*. Chapel Hill: University of North Carolina Press, 2000.

Sundquist, James L. *Dynamics of the Party System: Alignment and Realignment of Political Parties in the United States*. Washington, D.C.: Brookings Institution Press, 1983.

Taliaferro, John. *All the Great Prizes: The Life of John Hay, from Lincoln to Roosevelt*. New York: Simon & Schuster, 2013.

Tarbell, Ida M. *The Tariff in Our Times*. New York: Macmillan, 1911.

Tarr, Joel A. *A Study in Boss Politics: William Lorimer of Chicago*. Champaign: University of Illinois Press, 1971.

Taussig, F.W. *The Tariff History of the United States*. New York: G. P. Putnam's Sons, 1910.

Taylor, William A. *Hundred-year Book and Official Register of the State of Ohio*. Columbus, OH: Westbote, 1891.

Thayer, William R. *The Life and Letters of John Hay*. Vol. 2. Boston and New York: Houghton Mifflin, 1915.

Thelen, David P. *The New Citizenship: Origins of Progressivism in Wisconsin, 1885–1900*. Columbia: University of Missouri Press, 1972.

Thornbrough, Emma Lou. *Indiana in the Civil War Era: 1850–1880*. Vol. 3. Indianapolis: Indiana Historical Society, 1989.

Timberlake, Richard H. *Monetary Policy in the United States: An Intellectual and Institutional History*. Chicago: University of Chicago Press, 1993.

Timmons, Bascom N. *Portrait of an American: Charles G. Dawes*. New York: Henry Holt, 1953.

Tindall, George B. *South Carolina Negroes: 1877–1900*. Columbia: University of South Carolina Press, 1953.

Townsend, Colonel G. W. *Memorial Life of William McKinley: Our Martyred President*. Philadelphia and Chicago: Memorial, 1901.

Trachtenberg, Alan. *The Incorporation of America: Culture and Society in the Gilded Age*. New York: Hill & Wang, 1982.

Traxel, David. *1898: The Birth of the American Century*. New York: Knopf, 1998.

Tugwell, Rexford G. *Grover Cleveland*. New York: Macmillan, 1969.

Unger, Irwin. *The Greenback Era: A Social and Political History of American Finance, 1865–1879*. Princeton, NJ: Princeton University Press, 1964.

Walters, Everett. *Joseph Benson Foraker: An Uncompromising Republican*. Columbus: Ohio History Press, 1948.

Watson, Thomas E. *The Life and Speeches of Thomas E. Watson*. Charlottesville: University of Virginia Press, 1908.

Weeks, Philip. *Buckeye Presidents: Ohioans in the White House*. Kent, OH: The Kent State University Press, 2003.

Weinstein, Allen. *Prelude to Populism: Origins of the Silver Issue, 1867–1878*. New Haven, CT: Yale University Press, 1970.

Welch, Richard E., Jr. *The Presidencies of Grover Cleveland*. Lawrence: University Press of Kansas, 1988.

White, Leonard D. *The Republican Era: A Study in Administrative History, 1869–1901*. New York: Macmillan, 1958.

White, William Allen. *The Autobiography of William Allen White*. Lawrence: University Press of Kansas, 1990.

———. *Masks in a Pageant*. New York: Macmillan, 1928.

Whyte, Kenneth. *The Uncrowned King: The Sensational Rise of William Randolph Hearst*. New York: Random House Digital, 2009. Accessed June 4, 2013. http://books.google.com/books?id=U3h _7BDZL_QC&dq=hanna+cartoon+dollar+sign+cufflinks&source=gbs_navlinks_s.

Wiebe, Robert. *The Search for Order, 1877–1920*. New York: Hill & Wang, 1966.

Williams, R. Hal. *The Democratic Party and California Politics 1880–1896*. Stanford, CA: Stanford University Press, 1973.

———. *Realigning America: McKinley, Bryan, and the Remarkable Election of 1896*. Lawrence: University Press of Kansas, 2010.

———. *Years of Decision: American Politics in the 1890s*. Long Grove, IL: Waveland Press, 1993.

Wilson, William L. *The Cabinet Diary of William L. Wilson, 1896–1897*. Edited by F. Paul Summers. Chapel Hill: University of North Carolina Press, 1957.

Wister, Owen. *Roosevelt: The Story of a Friendship, 1880–1919*. New York: Macmillan, 1930.

Witcover, Jules. *Party of the People: A History of the Democrats*. New York: Random House, 2003.

Woodward, C. Vann. *Origins of the New South, 1877–1913*. Baton Rouge: University of Louisiana State University, 1951.

———. *Tom Watson: Agrarian Rebel*. New York: Oxford University Press, 1938.

Workers of the Writers' Program of the Works Progress Administration in the State of Georgia, comp. *Georgia, A Guide to Its Towns and Countryside*. Athens: University of Georgia Press, 1940.

Young, Art. *Art Young: His Life and Times*. Young Press, 2007.

INDEX

Dawes, Charles G.
  and APA attack on McKinley, 176
  Bryan and, 106, 320
  and delegates to Republican 1896 National
    Convention, 179
  elections of 1894 and, 106
  and Flag Day, 356
  Hanna and, 106, 116, 200, 241
  and Illinois Republican 1896 State
    Convention, 183–94
  Kohlsaat and, 184, 193
  Lorimer and, 184, 185
  and McKinley 1896 presidential campaign,
    241, 287, 288, 289, 292, 311, 314, 315,
    320, 328, 333, 338, 355, 356, 360, 374–75,
    376
  and McKinley 1896 presidential nomination,
    236
  and McKinley acceptance of 1896 presidential
    nomination, 244
  McKinley first meeting with, 106
  and McKinley Marquette Club speech,
    156–57, 158
  McKinley presidential primary campaign and,
    116, 118, 119, 156–57, 158, 159
  McKinley relationship with, 187, 194, 376,
    377
  and McKinley strategy for 1896 nomination,
    106
  move to Illinois by, 116
  Nobel Prize for, 376
  professional career of, 106, 116, 376
  and Republican 1896 National Convention,
    235
  talents of, 118
  Tanner and, 184
  views about elections of 1896 of, 360
Day, William R., 99, 242, 313
de Young, Michael, 238, 243
Debs, Eugene V., 323
debts
  and Bryan campaign, 352, 354
  Cleveland and, 205
  currency issues and, 16, 17, 205, 207, 239,
    246, 267, 285, 352
  and reasons for McKinley 1896 victory, 366
Delaware
  Bryan campaign in, 320, 331
  currency issues in, 211
  Democratic 1896 State Convention in, 211
  election returns for 1896 in, 369
  elections of 1872 in, 369
  and reasons for McKinley 1896 victory, 369
  and Republican 1896 National Convention,
    219, 229
  Republican 1896 State Convention in, 197
Democratic Congressional Campaign
  Committee, 352

Democratic National Committee (DNC)
  Bryan campaign and, 320, 330, 339
  Cleveland control of, 149, 257
  and coercion of employees, 249
  and Democratic 1896 National Convention,
    257, 259–60, 261, 262, 264, 272
  and divisions within Democratic Party,
    149–50
  funds of, 369
  Jones election as chairman of, 296
  See also Bimetallic Democratic National
    Committee
Democratic National Convention (Chicago,
    1896)
  Bryan speech at, 272–80
  campaigning at, 256
  chairmanship of, 257, 259–60, 262–63, 264,
    265, 266
  Cleveland and, 257, 259, 260, 267, 284, 285
  credentials for, 209, 214, 257, 259, 260, 261,
    262, 263, 266, 267, 268
  currency issues and, 147, 150, 206, 207, 208,
    213, 214, 256–60, 261–69, 270–80
  and divisions within Democratic Party, 147,
    150, 277, 284
  DNC and, 257, 259–60, 261, 262, 264, 272
  Free Silver and, 243, 257, 259, 260, 261, 267,
    269, 273–74, 275, 276, 277
  "Lady in White" at, 279–80
  presidential nominees and, 206, 251–55,
    262–69, 277–83
  and protectionism, 266, 275
  Republican views about, 246–47
  silver Republicans at, 243
  speakers at, 266–69, 270–80
  and taxes, 267, 271, 274
Democratic Party
  and Democrats as McKinley supporters,
    298–99, 307, 366
  divisions within, 138–50, 205–14, 242,
    248–60, 270–80, 284, 293, 332, 340, 370
  favorite sons of, 208, 209, 212, 252, 280, 296
  McKinley views about, 11, 327
  revolt in, 277
  See also Democratic Congressional
    Committee; Democratic National
    Committee (DNC); Democratic National
    Convention (Chicago, 1896); Democratic
    State Conventions (1896); National
    Democrats; specific person or topic
Democratic State Conventions (1896), 206–14,
    248–55. See also specific state
demographics: and reasons for McKinley 1896
  victory, 367
Depew, Chauncey M., 71, 133, 153, 231, 233
Detroit Free Press, 345
Deveaux, John H., 113, 114, 180
Dewalt, Christiana, 22, 26, 27

PHOTO CREDITS

ABOUT THE AUTHOR

KARL ROVE served as Senior Advisor to President George W. Bush from 2000 to 2007 and Deputy Chief of Staff from 2004 to 2007. He now writes a weekly op-ed for *The Wall Street Journal* and is a Fox News contributor. Before he became known as "The Architect" of President Bush's 2000 and 2004 campaigns, Rove was president of Karl Rove + Company, an Austin-based public affairs firm that was involved in more than seventy-five campaigns for Republican candidates for president, governor, and senator, as well as handling nonpartisan causes and nonprofit groups.